Tomahawks & Treaties

Tomahawks & Treaties
Micajah Callaway and the Struggle for the Ohio River Valley

Rex Callaway

American History Press
Franklin Tennessee

Copyright © 2010 Rex Callaway

All rights reserved. No part of this book may be transmitted in any form by any means electronic, mechanical or otherwise using devices now existing or yet to be invented without prior written permission from the publisher and copyright holder.

American History Press
Franklin, Tennessee
(888) 521-1789

Visit us on the Internet at
www.Americanhistorypress.com

ISBN 13: 978-0-9842256-9-9
ISBN 10: 0-9842256-9-2
Library of Congress Control Number 2010935482

First Edition September 2010

Images of the three paintings by John Buxton found in this book are used with the written permission of the artist.

Additional paintings may be seen on his website: www.Buxtonart.com

Layout and typography by Gordon Bond

Printed in the United States of America on acid-free paper
This book meets all ANSI standards for archival quality.

Dedication

This book is dedicated to my father and mother, Elmer Earl and Mary Steele Callaway, my brother Steve Callaway, my wife Rebecca Lee Oliver Callaway, my son Brian Andrew Callaway, and all of my Callaway cousins. I owe a special debt of gratitude to cousin Roy Callaway, the keeper of Micajah's memory for many years.

In addition, this book is dedicated to the past and present members of the resilient Shawnee Nation. It has been many, many years since the tomahawk was buried and the bones of our fallen warriors were covered with soil. May the chain of friendship between our peoples remain bright and the road of peace between us open and free forever!

Table of Contents

List of Maps i
List of Illustrations iii
Preface v
Acknowledgments xiii
A Note to the Reader xv

1 - Introduction 1
2 - Lord Dunmore's War 17
3 - The Wilderness Road 37
4 - Revolution 53
5 - Kentucky and Fort Boonesborough 68
6 - Captured 87
7 - The Bluegrass War 109
8 - Micajah Callaway, White Shawanese 163
9 - The War's End 195
10 - The False Peace 212
11 - The Federal Treaties of Conquest 217
12 - War in the Wabash Country 236
13 - Col. Benjamin Logan's Expedition 249
14 - Prisoner Exchange at Limestone (1787) . 253
15 - The Northwest Ordinance and Ensuing Indian War 262
16 - Battle of Fallen Timbers (1793-1794) ... 276
17 - The Pioneer Expatriates 316
18 - The Indiana Territory 328
19 - The War of 1812 347
20 - White Wampum 362

Epilogue 372
List of Principal Characters 375
Appendix A - The Case for Chief Black Beard/Nenessica
　as the Adoptive Shawanese Father of Micajah Callaway 383
Endnotes 387
Bibliography 431
Index 441
About the Author 453

List of Maps

List of Maps Created by the Author

Map 1	The Major Indian Nations of Eastern North America in the 1600s	3
Map 2	Shawanese Towns in Ohio River Valley in 1735-1755	5
Map 3	Shawanese Towns of Ohio in 1758-1774	12
Map 4	The Western Frontier in Lord Dunmore's War (1774)	25
Map 5	The Battle of Point Pleasant	31
Map 6	Bedford County and the the Callaway Brothers in the 1750s	39
Map 7	The Wilderness Road (1775)	45
Map 8	Shawanese Towns of Ohio in 1776	47
Map 9	Kentucky Bluegrass Region in 1777	81
Map 10	Little Chalaakaatha in 1778	99
Map 11	Kentucky Bluegrass Region in 1779-1780	147
Map 12	The Battle of Piqua (1780)	154
Map 13	Shawanese Towns of Ohio in 1780-1782	159
Map 14	Shawanese Towns of Ohio in 1782-1786	191
Map 15	Kentucky Bluegrass Region in 1783	209
Map 16	Micajah and James Callaway Jr. Land Grants in 1783	210
Map 17	Boundaries of Treaty at the Mouth of the Greater Miami River (January, 1786)	234
Map 18	General George Rogers Clark's Campaign of 1786	244
Map 19	Shawanese Towns of Ohio in 1787-1791	260
Map 20	General Arthur St. Clair's Defeat (1791)	273
Map 21	Shawanese Towns of Ohio: The Grand Glaize in 1792	277
Map 22	General Anthony Wayne's Campaign of 1794	296
Map 23	The Battle of Fallen Timbers: August 20, 1794	302
Map 24	Boundaries of the Treaty of Greenville (1795)	311
Map 25	The Migration to Missouri (1799)	317
Map 26	Micajah's Missouri Homestead (1799)	321
Map 27	The Indiana Territory and Indian Treaty Boundaries (1804-1809)	330
Map 28	Callaway Fort-1810	337
Map 29	The Blue River and Muscatatuck River Country (1810-1813)	343
Map 30	The War of 1812 in Ohio and Upper Canada	348

List of Illustrations

1. Elmer E. Callaway and sons Rex and Steve c. 1955
   [author's personal collection] vi

2. *Muted by the Vista* [© John Buxton] 71

3. *George Rogers Clark* [© John Buxton] 123

4. *The Battle of Piqua* [© John Buxton] 152

5. Treaty at the Mouth of the Greater Miami (1786)
   [Courtesy of the Library of Congress] 232

6. Photograph of James A. Callaway, grandson of Micajah Callaway, son of Noble Callaway, and great-grandfather of the author
   [author's personal collection] 365

7. Micajah Callaway's tombstone in Peugh Cemetery near Salem, Indiana
   [author's personal collection] 372

Preface

THE LIFE AND TIMES OF MY GREAT-GREAT-GREAT grandfather Micajah Callaway, who lived a fascinating life of adventure and intrigue on the outer boundaries of the North American frontier, are the focal point of this book.

I can trace its inspiration to a specific hike taken with my father Elmer and younger brother Steve in a hardwood forest near my maternal grandfather Earl Steele's farm at the foot of the bluffs of the Wabash River near Huntington, Indiana. I was five years old, and Steve was four.

We left the farmhouse and hiked up a small gulch into the wooded bluffs above it. Father found a level place in the bottom of the gulch where he cleared away the dried leaves on the forest floor in a circular area about five feet in diameter. After digging a small pit in the center of this space, he laid stones in a ring around its outside edge and then constructed a small pile of dried twigs and grass at the bottom of it. Then he started a fire while Steve and I watched in round-eyed fascination. The photograph on the next page was taken by my mother during this event.

Father explained that this was the kind of fire that Daniel Boone built when he was camping in the forest long, long ago. The pit served the dual function of protecting the fire from the wind and hiding the flame from the Indians. To our surprise, he also said that our own Callaway ancestors were at Daniel Boone's side when he settled in Kentucky and fought the Indians, and they had camped together around many fires just like this one.

My imagination was set afire with exotic visions of rugged buckskin-clad heroes battling their painted Indian enemies in the primitive forest. My

Elmer E. Callaway and sons Rex and Steve c. 1955

family had taken part in a great adventure long ago! In grade school, I now read all of the books about Daniel Boone that I could find and became an avid fan of James Fenimore Cooper while reading all of *The Leatherstocking Tales*.

As I grew older, I was struck by the fact that I had never met an American Indian who lived in Illinois, Indiana, Ohio, or Kentucky and that it did not appear that there were any federally recognized reservations in those states. It became clear, in my youth, that some cataclysmic event or series of events must have taken place to virtually eradicate them from the middle and lower Ohio River Valley. What had happened to the Indians? Why were they gone and where did they go? Was my family involved in their disappearance?

Evidence of the former presence of the Indians could be found almost everywhere. I was born in the small town of Onarga, Illinois, in Iroquois County. Onarga was reputedly named after an Iroquois "princess" who had found refuge there. The name "Indiana" refers to the Indians who were once populous in the territory. My mother's family farm in Huntington, Indiana, was located on the site of an important Miami Indian village at a historic Wabash River portage, and we used to find Miami arrowheads in the fields there in my childhood. Finally, there was the Callaway family connection to Daniel Boone and the Shawnee Indians.

Preface

In 1997, I set out on a genealogical and historical quest to find the answers to my questions and try to separate fact from fiction. I quickly confirmed that my direct ancestor Micajah Callaway was among the earliest non-native pioneers in Kentucky, Missouri, and Indiana, and that he was indeed a companion of Daniel Boone and related to him through his brother's marriage to Boone's daughter.

The basic outline of the events of his life was relatively easy to establish. Micajah was born in the back country of Virginia during the French and Indian War. He was captured and adopted by warriors of the Shawnee Nation during the American War for Independence. He later returned to his native state and served as a soldier, scout, spy, and interpreter. He also worked for the new United States government during the extended Indian Wars that continued in the middle and lower Ohio River Valley into the final decade of the eighteenth century. His associates included Daniel Boone, General George Rogers Clark, General "Mad Anthony" Wayne, General Richard Butler, Simon Kenton, and the leading Shawnee chiefs of his time.

New questions entered my mind as I reviewed my initial information. What chain of events had brought him into the center of such a violent conflict between two cultures? How well did he really know Daniel Boone? Who were his adoptive Shawnee father and mother? Did he have a Shawnee wife and children? Where did his loyalties lie? Did he willingly join the British and Shawnee to fight against the Virginians and his Callaway family as a Tory renegade during the war? Was he forced to fight against them under duress? Did the Shawnee believe that he had betrayed them when he returned to Kentucky after the war and later served as a scout and interpreter for Virginia and the United States? Was he a double agent? How did he cope with such a stressful life? Was he emotionally scarred by some of his harrowing experiences? I felt compelled to dig deeper and learn more.

Initially, I reviewed genealogical and historical information provided by the Callaway Family Association. That information in turn led me to the microfilmed manuscripts of the famous nineteenth century historian Lyman C. Draper in the genealogy collection of the Carlsbad, California public library. I "hit the jackpot" with what I discovered in those manuscripts: Mr. Draper had collected many documents concerning different episodes in Micajah's life and had made notes of interviews with three of his sons!

Answers to some of my specific questions began to emerge from the mists of the past. I was hopelessly captivated and my curiosity drove me onward.

Subsequently, I spent thousands of hours over the course of six years delving into old manuscripts and the musty texts of nineteenth century books and periodicals. I traveled to Salem, Indiana, and Louisville, Kentucky, to research the local records and delved into the extensive collections of historical records at the University of California, Los Angeles, San Diego State University, and Indiana University.

I traced down primary sources of information whenever possible. I read and analyzed hundreds of such documents, including: Indian treaties, military records and journals, and British Indian Department records; colonial records from Virginia, Pennsylvania, Maryland, New York, North Carolina, and South Carolina; correspondence, original maps, obituaries, petitions, and interview notes; deeds, surveys, depositions, declarations, pension applications, and wills. I also read and studied secondary sources such as textbooks, treatises, and biographies.

My research efforts were richly rewarded as I found more and more relevant information. A more detailed story of Micajah Callaway's life and an objective history of Kentucky and the Old Northwest Territory began to emerge from the scattered records as I pieced the information together. I established a chronological outline of the information on my personal computer and that outline evolved into a draft book manuscript.

I am not a historian by trade. However, I know that ascertaining the truth about human events and experiences is highly affected by the personal perceptions and biases of witnesses, since no two witnesses experience and perceive the same event in the same way. The interpretations and deductions of those who come later further influence fact-finding. There is always some level of uncertainty in our efforts to ascertain the facts and determine the truth.

I incorporated a fact, event, or perception into the main text and storyline of the book if it seemed that the weight of the available direct and circumstantial evidence and inferences based upon it tended to establish that something was more likely to have occurred than not. I added emotional depth by coloring the story with Micajah's likely perceptions, feelings, and interactions with other people during certain key events in his life. I identify

Preface

and discuss the uncertainties concerning my conclusions about some of the more important facts in either the text or the chapter endnotes of the book.

The most difficult challenge that I faced during my research and writing was to identify the Shawnee chief/warrior and his wife who adopted Micajah into the Shawnee Nation after he was captured with Daniel Boone and his salt-boiler soldiers in 1778. I have addressed my conclusion and the basis for it in Appendix A.

One of my goals in writing this book was to infuse Micajah's life story and the history of his times with vision and energy. I prepared a series of maps to address that issue, and to illustrate the events covered in the text. The maps depict early Shawnee towns and pathways, buffalo paths, early pioneer settlements, and military campaigns and battles, along with several Callaway family settlements and homesteads.

Contemporaneous perspectives of individuals on both sides of the wars and treaty negotiations were purposely included in the book. For example, the perspective of the British Indian Department and Shawnee Indians is juxtaposed with the Kentucky militia viewpoint on the same military campaigns and battles.

I incorporated a great deal of information about the customs and lifestyles of the Shawnee and earliest frontier settlers into the manuscript. Dwellings, fortifications, towns, foods, clothing, and personal items are described. Shawnee religion and ceremonies are addressed. Hunting techniques for buffalo, elk, deer, and black bear are covered and battle tactics explained.

A number of fascinating Shawnee individuals, some of whom have not been described before in the literature, emerged from the bits of data that I uncovered. Shawnee Queen Lamatumque is a notable example. She was a strikingly beautiful young leader and a courageous, selfless, and passionate advocate for peace between the two warring peoples.

A comprehensive political and military history of the British-American conquest and settlement of Kentucky and the Old Northwest Territory unfolds in the recounting of Micajah's life. The book chronicles the entire history of the wars between Virginia and the Shawnee Nation, and documents the astounding transformation of Kentucky and the American Midwestern heartland from a sparsely populated wilderness into a settled land.

The Shawnee Nation and the colony/state of Virginia were the principal protagonists in the extended Ohio River Valley Indian Wars of the mid- to-late eighteenth century, which played such a pivotal role in the birth and growth of the United States. Those wars were primarily waged for possession of the middle and lower Ohio River Valley.

The brilliant and energetic "Long Knives" (as the Shawnee referred to the Virginians) were the vanguard of the ambitious westward expansion of Great Britain's North American colonies. Their goal was to conquer and remove the Indian nations westward and establish an American empire stretching from the Atlantic Ocean to the Pacific. The familiar names of George Washington, Thomas Jefferson, Patrick Henry, James Madison, brothers William and George Rogers Clark, Meriwether Lewis, and William Henry Harrison still resonate today, and all were Virginians.

The Shawnee Nation found itself directly in the path of the Virginians' ambitious plans. Fierce and proud Shawnee warriors joined together with their allies to stand their ground against the invasion in defense of their homeland. The Virginians had to remove this obstacle in order to achieve their far-reaching goals.

The indomitable Shawnee chiefs proved themselves to be military and diplomatic geniuses of the highest order. They organized military alliances of disparate Indian nations that stretched from the crest of the Appalachian Mountains to the Mississippi River and from Canada to Florida. A few hundred Indian soldiers held many thousands of Virginians and their allies at bay, and time after time inflicted resounding defeats upon their more numerous and better-equipped enemy. The determination of these courageous people as they fought to preserve their homeland and cultural integrity is an inspiration for all men and women who cherish freedom.

Micajah Callaway was caught up in the central events of the wars and had friends and enemies on both sides. A noted historian has described Micajah as a "cultural intermediary" between the Shawnee Nation and Virginia. That description, while accurate, grossly understates the jarring reality of his action-filled life. He survived many close brushes with a violent death as he alternated his roles of soldier, scout, interpreter, diplomat, and intelligence operative.

Ultimately, the Shawnee and their allies were worn down by the sheer

Preface

weight of superior numbers. The victorious Americans removed the Indian survivors to reservations west of the Mississippi River in the 1830s. Only Shawnee bones, placenames, artifacts, and a handful of descendants were left behind in the middle and lower Ohio River Valley.

By the end of Micajah's long life, the Ohio River Valley had been conquered by the United States of America, and was subsequently surveyed and parceled out. The virgin forests of Kentucky and the Old Northwest Territory had been cut down and converted to farmland. The buffalo, elk, and wolves had been exterminated, and the Shawnee Indians and their allies had been removed from the land. After cities and towns had been founded and were prospering, they were followed by the establishment of state, county, and town governments. The face of the earth itself was being transformed by the unfolding Industrial Revolution.

It is my hope that the reader will enjoy reading this book and glean new insights into American history and the nature of human conflict. Micajah's life and experiences at the cross-roads of two cultures illuminates the conclusion that both sides of the Ohio River Valley Indian wars were equally human, with all of the noble traits and tragic flaws that mark our species. Compassion competed with cruelty, and victory and the spoils of war simply went to the strongest and most numerous people.

I conclude my work with a sense of empathy, admiration, and gratitude for Micajah Callaway. He was a living witness to the birth and growth of the American nation. He personally knew both those who founded it and those who were destroyed by its creation. Micajah found himself at the point where the "hammer hit the anvil" in the forge of human history, on the front lines of a violent clash between two civilizations. He survived by some miracle to raise a family late in his life and die in old age. If he had not survived, I would not be here today to tell his story.

Acknowledgments

I WAS ASSISTED BY SEVERAL INDIVIDUALS AND organizations during my investigation of Micajah Callaway's life and times.

First and foremost, I acknowledge the support and assistance of Roy Callaway, a fellow descendant of Micajah, who studied and maintained a record of Micajah's life for many years. Roy unselfishly provided me with copies of all of the information that he had collected and helped me conduct additional research into the local Washington County, Indiana records. He served as a critical sounding board as I developed and explored hypotheses regarding my research.

I also thank the Callaway Family Association, whose annual publication, *The Callaway Journal*, provided the foundation and starting point for further research for several key parts of the book. In particular, the late Bobbie Callaway and her sister Mary Callaway DuBois supplied a great deal of useful information concerning Micajah's life in Missouri and Kentucky.

My appreciation also goes to Barbara Lehmann, President of the Simon Kenton Historic Corridor and Tribal Historian and Member of the Elders Council of the Piqua Shawnee Tribe. She provided valuable feedback and input when I was in the later stages of writing the book.

I would also like to express my gratitude to authors Allan W. Eckert, Daniel Mack Faragher, and Richard Pangburn, all of whom encouraged me along the way. Their own books about Daniel Boone and the Shawnee Indians were very helpful as sources of leads for further research.

Finally, I must acknowledge my special debt to my wife Becky and son Brian, who have endured the thousands of hours that I have spent in libraries and archives and at my desk and computer intently focused on my goal. I could not have completed the book without their patience and support.

Rex Callaway
Poway, California
September, 2010

A Note to the Reader

THE SHAWNEE PEOPLE HISTORICALLY CALLED THEMSELVES THE "Shaawanwa" people.[1] The colonial French called them "Ontouagannha" or "Chaouanons."[2] They came to be known as the "Shawanese" or "Shawanoe" Indians in the northern British colonies and the "Savannah" Indians in the southern colonies. The name "Shawanese" will be used for the remainder of the book as it was most commonly used name in the primary British colonial and early American records of the time. Similarly, I decided against the use of the term "Native American" in favor of the more contemporaneous British and early American term "Indian."

One | Introduction

The Ohio River

THE OHIO RIVER IS A RELATIVELY YOUNG river from the perspective of geological time. It was formed during the Pleistocene Epoch by the westward drainage of melt waters along the southern margin of the Wisconsin Age continental glaciers.[1] The ancestors of Indian peoples arrived in this area during the period of its formation and found woolly mammoth and other Ice Age megafauna living on the lands to the south of the nascent river. They hunted them until they became extinct. The climate moderated as the ice sheets retreated, and Indian civilizations rose and fell along the river as the centuries passed, leaving behind their mysterious mounds, bones, and artifacts.

The Ohio River flowed through a vast and fertile drainage basin of temperate lands with balanced rainfall and moderate climate at the time of Micajah Callaway's birth near Lynchburg, Virginia, in 1760.[2] The land in the Ohio River Valley had attained a nearly mythical status as an earthly paradise in colonial Virginia. It shone in the distance as a beacon of hope, opportunity, and ambition for a bright and happy future for thousands of Virginians from all walks of life who wanted to acquire land and live there.

The Ohio River cast a similar spell over other nations. The word "Ohio" means "beautiful river" in the Iroquoian language. The French named the Ohio River "La Belle Rivière" and coveted the river and its valley.[3]

The Shawanese Nation[4] and the Virginia "Long Knives" were destined to engage in a bitter conflict for possession of the Ohio River Valley for many years. Micajah Callaway and his family would find themselves caught up in that struggle for three generations. It was in many respects a righteous holy war for possession of a sacred land. In order to understand the escalation of that conflict in the late 1760s and into the subsequent four decades, it is important to review the political, historical, and cultural context and events in the seventeenth through mid-eighteenth centuries that set the stage.

The Shawanese Nation and Virginia

THE SHAWANESE NATION OCCUPIED THE LAND TO the southwest of the western end of Lake Erie into the middle and lower Ohio River Valley at the time of their first contact with Europeans. French explorer Robert Cavelier, Sieur de la Salle, discovered them in possession of and living in the middle Ohio River Valley above the Falls of the Ohio River (Louisville, Kentucky) during his explorations in 1668.[5]

The Shawanese Nation was one of the smaller Eastern Woodland Algonquin Indian nations at the time of their first contact with Europeans. The peak of their nation's population is estimated at no more than three or four thousand individuals, and was comprised of five divisions or sub-nations: Chalaakaatha ("Chillicothe"), Makujay ("Mequache" or "Mekoche"), Thawikila, Kispoko ("Kispokogi"), and Piqua ("Pekowi" or "Pekowith"). These divisions probably originated from clans related by blood ties.

The Shawanese people believed that Moneto (the Great Spirit) himself had given the Ohio River lands to them. They were entitled to possess and live upon them as long as He found them to be worthy and favored them.

The first major setback in the long struggle of the Shawanese Nation to retain possession of their traditional Ohio River Valley homeland was the displacement of much of their population from the valley during a long series of wars between the Eastern Woodland Indian nations in the second half of the seventeenth century. These wars have been called the "Beaver Wars" as they were caused by competition for the lucrative North American fur trade between the new European colonies and their respective Indian nation allies.

France allied itself with the powerful Huron (Wyandot) Nation dur-

Introduction

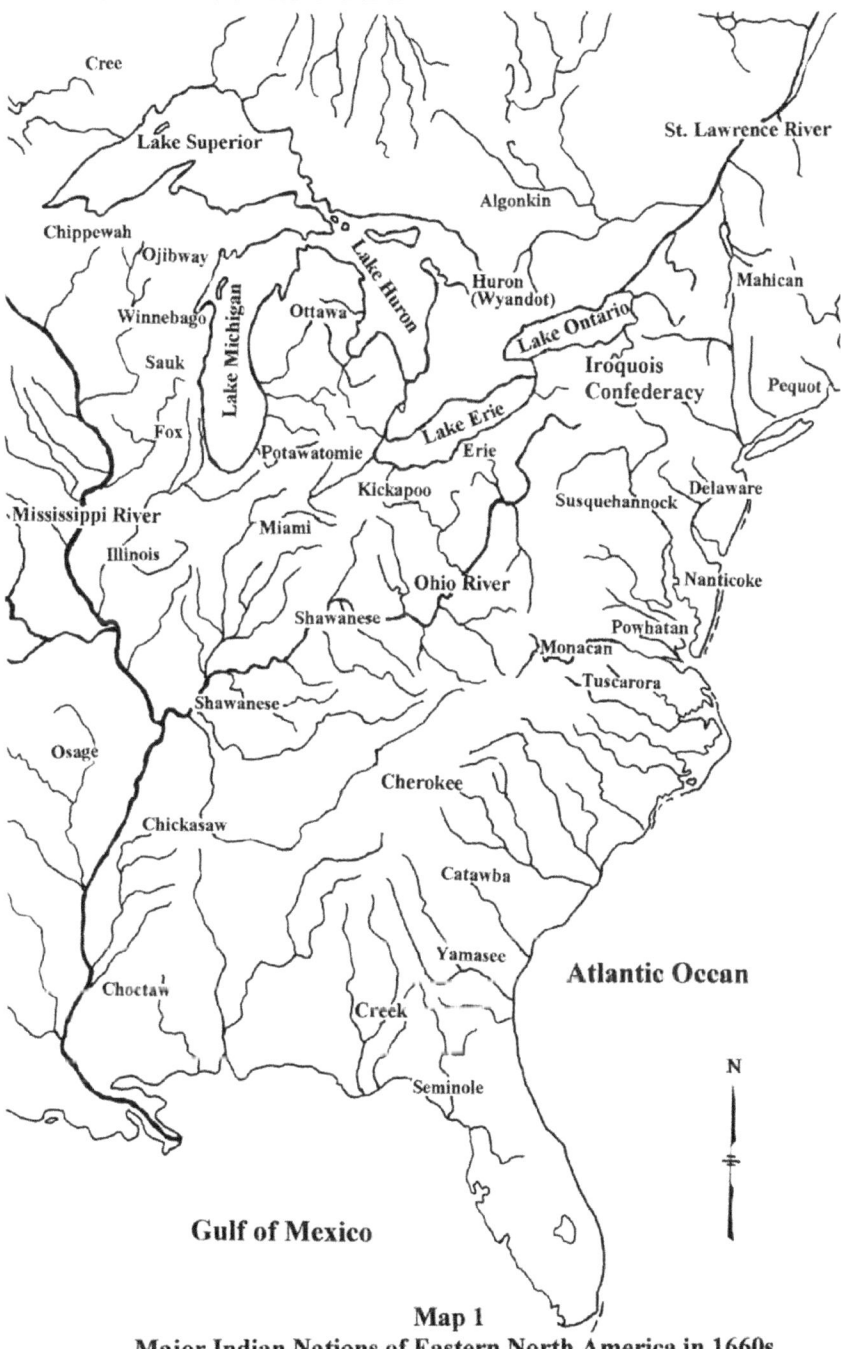

Map 1
Major Indian Nations of Eastern North America in 1660s

ing the Beaver Wars. The British colony of New York allied itself with the powerful Five Nations of the Iroquois Confederacy comprised of the Mohawk, Oneida, Onandaga, Cayuga, and Seneca Nations.

The Iroquois Confederacy became known as the "Six Nations" with the addition of the Tuscarora Nation in 1722. The alliance between New York and the Iroquois Confederacy was called the "Covenant Chain" alliance. The Seneca Nation led the Iroquois invasion of the Ohio River Valley. They conclusively defeated the Shawanese in a disastrous battle on Big Sandy Island just below the Falls of the Ohio River in 1672.[6]

The first documented contact between Virginians and the Shawanese occurred soon after this defeat, when the Shawanese captured a young Virginian named Gabriel Arthur during a skirmish with Cherokee warriors. They returned him to Virginia in 1674.[7]

The Shawanese Nation barely avoided complete annihilation and dispersed to several scattered locations in eastern North America. These included the villages of the Creek Nation in the Chattahoochee River valley in Alabama, the Savannah River valley on the border of South Carolina and Georgia, and the French Fort St. Louis on the Illinois River. Some remained in Kentucky, between the Kentucky River and Cumberland River.

The Shawanese began to reassemble in New York and Pennsylvania in the 1690s with the encouragement of their Delaware allies. The Delaware were considered to be the Algonquin "Grandfathers" of the Shawanese and were shown great respect and deference in intertribal diplomatic exchanges and council meetings.[8] Such masculine familial designations reflected a "seniority ranking" or "pecking-order" in diplomatic relationships among the Eastern Woodland Indians.

A large contingent of Makujay Shawanese from Kentucky moved to New York and joined the Covenant Chain alliance in 1694. Another large contingent of Makujay and Piqua Shawanese settled near Conestoga, Pennsylvania. Pennsylvania Proprietor William Penn met with Shawanese King Opessah and other leaders on February 23, 1701, and entered into a peace treaty. They pledged to treat each other as equals and "as true friends and brothers."[9]

The Shawanese and their Delaware allies became disenchanted with life in New York and Pennsylvania and began a westward migration back to

Introduction

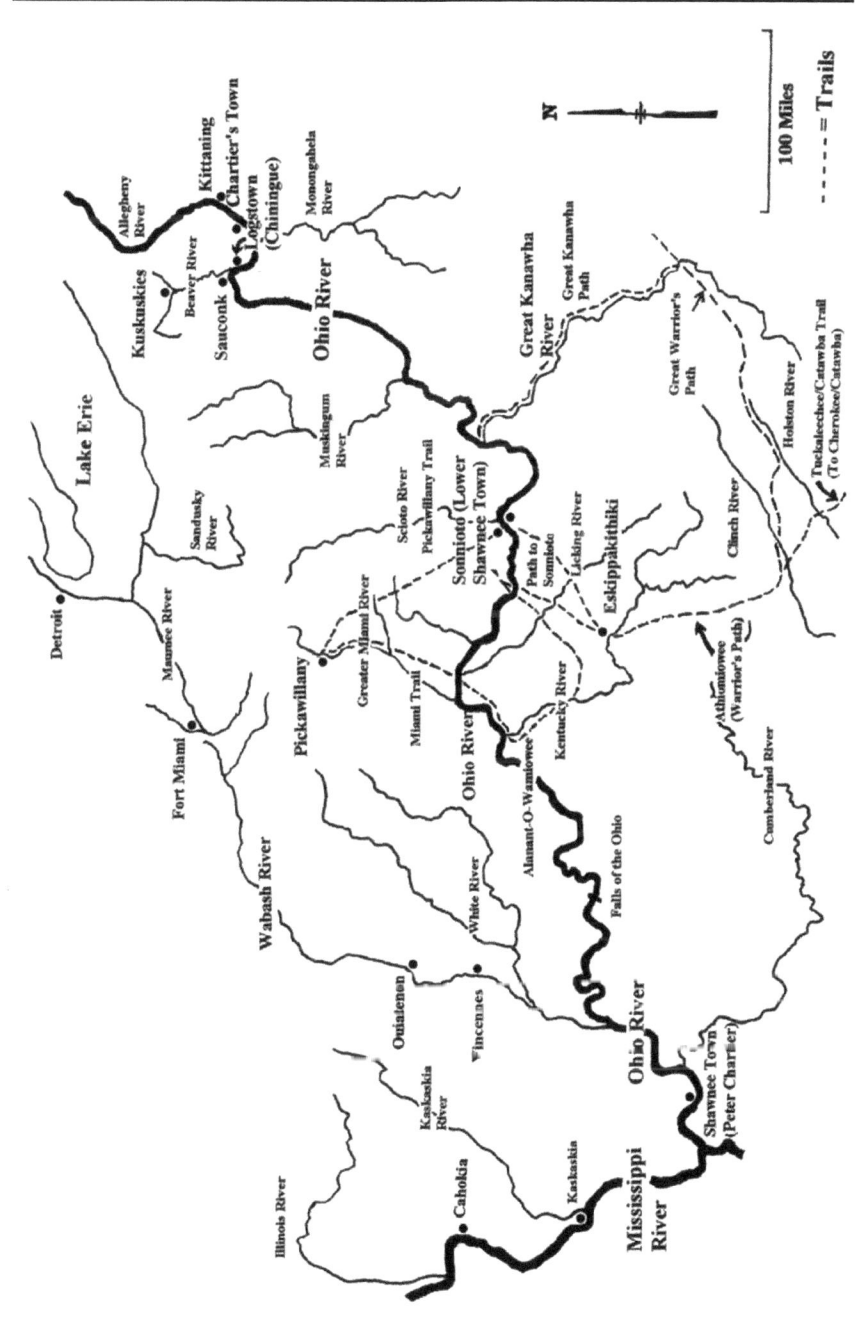

Map 2
Shawanese Towns in Ohio River Valley in 1735-1755.

their ancestral Ohio River Valley homeland in the 1720s through 1740s. They attributed their decision to harassment by Pennsylvania traders selling rum, interference from Virginia slave owners invading their towns to recover runaway slaves, land cessions to the colony of Pennsylvania by the Six Nations, and the ceaseless depredations of Catawba war parties from the south.

The Shawanese fervently believed that Moneto had given them a second chance to earn the right to live in their ancestral homeland. They established six major new towns in the Allegheny and Ohio River valleys: Chartier's Town, Logstown, Sauconk, Upper Shawanese Town (on the south side of the Ohio River just above the mouth of the Great Kanawha River), Lower Shawanese Town (Sonnioto) at the mouth of the Scioto River, and Eskippakithiki in Kentucky.

While the Shawanese continued the woodland lifestyle of their ancestors upon their return to the Ohio River Valley, they had also adopted a number of European customs. Many of their dwellings in their new Ohio River valley towns were rugged Swedish-style log cabins instead of traditional Shawanese elm bark wegiwas.

Most of the major new Shawanese towns included one or more British or French trading posts. Shawanese men favored calico shirts, muskets and rifles, steel tomahawks, and steel knives over buckskins, bows and arrows, war clubs, and flint knives. Some of them rode horses. Shawanese women decorated themselves with silver jewelry and cooked in brass pots and pans provided by the traders in exchange for furs and skins.

Eskippakithiki had grown into a sizable town with a population estimated at between eight hundred and one thousand individuals by 1736. The famous Shawanese Chiefs Catehecassa (Black Hoof) and Nenessica (Black Beard) lived there as children.[10]

A well-traveled Shawanese warpath connected Eskippakithiki to Sonnioto at the mouth of the Scioto River. A larger warpath, called the Warriors' Path by the Virginians, the Catawba Trail by the Pennsylvanians, and Athiamiowee ("path of the armed ones") by the Shawanese, also passed through Eskippakithiki.[11] It was the key north-south route west of the Allegheny Mountains taken by war parties during the extended warfare between the northern Indian nations and southern Cherokee and Catawba Nations in the first half of the eighteenth century.[12]

The Shawanese found buffalo, deer, elk, beaver, and otter living in abundance upon their return to Kentucky. They thanked Moneto for allowing them to return to a place that so perfectly suited their lives. The residents of Eskippakithiki welcomed and hosted visiting Shawanese hunting parties from the other Shawanese towns that joined them in the annual winter hunts.

Mineral springs (salt licks) and canebrakes were found throughout Kentucky. The salt licks contained salts and other minerals that attracted deer and herds of buffalo and elk. The canebrakes of Kentucky consisted of tracts of moist bottomlands covered by dense thickets of an American species of bamboo called canebrake or *Arundinaria gigantea*. The canes of bamboo grew very close together and reached a height of up to twenty-five feet under ideal conditions. The tender cane shoots began to sprout in the late winter and provided the large herbivores with a critical late winter food source.

Large herds of buffalo wintered in the Kentucky canebrakes in the Kentucky River and Licking River watersheds and concentrated at several large and small salt licks in the area, including Big Bone Lick, Drennon's Lick, and the Upper and Lower Blue Licks. These buffalo were a critical source of food for the Shawanese during the hard months of winter.

The buffalo herds created a network of deeply worn buffalo paths (traces) in Kentucky and forded the Ohio River every spring to spend the summers in the grassy prairies interspersed among the woodlands of Ohio and Illinois. The buffalo reassembled into large herds and retraced their pathways to the canebrakes and salt licks of Kentucky each autumn.[13]

The Falls of the Ohio River was the only natural barrier to navigation on the river's entire length. It consisted of long and relatively shallow rapids across the only place where the hard Devonian limestone bedrock was exposed on the bed of the river.[14] It served as one of the major buffalo crossing points on the river, since buffalo could cross it without swimming.

THE KINGS OF FRANCE AND GREAT BRITAIN both claimed the Ohio River Valley among their North American lands, and their competition for its possession and development escalated in the early part of the eighteenth century. France fortified the waterways by constructing Forts Detroit, Miami, Ouiatenon, and Vincennes in 1701 and 1702, thus providing critical communication and trade connections between their French Canada and Louisiana colonies.

Great Britain established new county governments and settlements of armed Scotch-Irish immigrants to occupy and defend the "Valley of Virginia" to the west of the Blue Ridge Mountains in the 1730s and 1740s. The "Valley of Virginia" included lands located on the so-called "Western Waters"—tributaries of the Ohio River claimed by France—including the New River and Holston River. The valleys of the Western Waters reached far to the west and southwest from the original Virginia settlements in the Virginia Tidewater and Piedmont.

France actively encouraged the Shawanese to abandon their Covenant Chain alliance with Great Britain and join with France in the struggle for possession of the Ohio River Valley. A large band of Shawanese commanded by a half-Frenchman named Peter Chartier moved to Eskippakithiki in Kentucky and allied themselves to France in King George's War in 1744.[15] The other Shawanese bands generally remained either neutral or loyal to Great Britain.

The neutral Shawanese formed an alliance in 1747 called the "Ohio Confederacy" with their Delaware Grandfathers and Iroquois immigrants into the Ohio River Valley, commonly called "Mingo." The term "Mingo" was derived from the Delaware word for Iroquois—"Mengwe."[16] The Ohio Confederacy Indians were sometimes referred to collectively as the "Ohio Indians."

France was defeated in King George's War and withdrew their traders from the Ohio River Valley. Pennsylvania traders and Virginia land development companies, such as the Ohio Company and Loyal Land Company, quickly surged deep into the valley to fill the vacuum. George Washington's older brother Lawrence was a principal of the Ohio Company,[17] and Thomas Jefferson's father Peter Jefferson was a principal of the Loyal Land Company.[18]

The actions of the Pennsylvania traders and Virginia land development companies in turn forced France to take drastic measures, so France fortified and garrisoned the upper Ohio River Valley in 1753.[19] A Virginia militia company commanded by young Major George Washington attacked a French company in western Pennsylvania near Uniontown and precipitated the French and Indian War in 1754.[20]

Great Britain met with a series of setbacks at the outset of the war. British General Braddock and his army were crushed by a combined French and Indian army in a failed effort to capture French Fort Duquesne (today the site of downtown Pittsburg) at the Forks of the Ohio River on July 9, 1755. Colonel George Washington commanded the Virginia Regiment in the battle, which is now commonly referred to as Braddock's Defeat.

The only good news for the British in the first year of the war came from New York in September of 1755. Colonel William Johnson and his Mohawk allies crushed a French army commanded by Baron von Dieskau in a brilliant victory at Lake George. The Crown rewarded Johnson with a baronetcy and appointment as the superintendent of a new Northern Indian Department. Sir William's organization evolved into the British Indian Department, which would serve as an important military liaison between Great Britain and its Indian allies well into the nineteenth century.[21]

Although the Shawanese were generally neutral at the start of the war and do not appear to have been significant participants in General Braddock's defeat, many of them rallied to the French side after the battle. Other Shawanese continued to maintain their neutrality, including Makujay Principal Chief Paxinosa.

A large contingent of Chalaakaatha and Piqua Shawanese commanded by Captain John Peter (Owistogah)[22] joined with Delaware Chiefs King Shingas and Beaver and French Captain Jacques Duperon Bâby in attacking Pennsylvania and Virginia frontier settlements in a series of bloody raids in 1755[23] and 1756.[24] A war party of sixty Shawanese warriors struck in the upper James River area on July 25, 1757. Several settlers were killed and a total of sixty-eight people were taken prisoners,[25] Robert Rennick was killed during the attack, and his wife and five children (including son Joshua) were captured.[26]

The Shawanese abandoned Eskippakithiki between 1754 and 1755, and the residents of the town moved north of the Ohio River and joined their tribesmen living in the Scioto River valley. Shawanese Chief Black Hoof said that Eskippakithiki was abandoned because of Catawba raids.[27] Shawanese hunters continued to cross the Ohio River into Kentucky each year for their winter hunts.

British General John Forbes assembled an army of six thousand regular British soldiers and American colonial militia in 1758. They were joined by warriors from the Cherokee and Catawba Nations, and the combined force marched west and defeated the French and their Indian allies and captured Fort Duquesne on November 25, 1758.[28] Afterwards, Shawanese Captain John Peter and his band of warriors made peace with the British.

Chief Paxinosa was a mortal enemy of the Catawba Nation and could not tolerate an alliance with them. He decided to abandon neutrality and belatedly joined the French coalition in May of 1758.[29] Makujay War Chief Cornstalk and his sister Nonhelema led several raids into western Virginia and killed and captured many settlers over the course of the next two years.[30] Some scholars believe that Cornstalk was Paxinosa's son.[31] Others believe that he was a grandson of Paxinosa. The author believes that Paxinosa was Cornstalk's father because of their comparative ages.[32]

At the Treaty of Paris on February 10, 1763, France ceded Canada to Great Britain and the Louisiana territory to Spain to conclude the French and Indian War. Delaware Chiefs King Shingas and Beaver demanded three times that the British withdraw their soldiers and settlers to the east behind the crest of the Allegheny Mountains. The British gave bland assurances but remained in the valley and strengthened their fortifications.

Mingo Seneca Chief Guyasuta took the first steps to organize a military response to the continuing British occupation in 1761. He circulated a black wampum war belt among the northwestern Indian nations and called for the formation of a great Indian Confederacy to drive the British back east behind the Allegheny divide.[33]

Wampum belts and strings were used to send messages between the Eastern Woodland Indian nations over long distances and for dramatic presentation during speeches and negotiations to emphasize and record important points. The wampum belts and strings of "wampum diplomacy" were initially made from pieces of shell crafted into beads but were later made from colorful glass European trade beads.[34]

The Wyandot, Ottawa, Pottawatomie, Ojibwa, Miami, Shawanese, Delaware, and several other Indian nations responded to Guyasuta's wampum belt and formed the Wyandot Confederacy in a Grand Council at a village near Detroit on October 5, 1761. The Grand Council Fire of the new confederacy was kept there and entrusted to the Wyandot Nation as its Keeper.[35]

Ottawa War Chief Pontiac commanded the warriors of the Wyandot

Introduction

Confederacy. Their military objective was to drive the British out of the Ohio River Valley and back to the eastern side of the mountains. The warriors of the confederacy simultaneously struck several forts and settlements in a broadly coordinated attack and set the frontiers of Virginia and Pennsylvania aflame. Shawanese war parties led by Cornstalk and Nonhelema once again attacked the western Virginia settlements.[36]

King George III of Great Britain addressed the grievances of the northwestern Indians in his Proclamation of 1763, which established a boundary line along the crest of the Allegheny Mountains between the British settlements and the Indian nations. No British settlement was allowed to the west of the line unless it was on land acquired by the Crown by purchase from the Indian nations. The Proclamation also provided for large land grants to compensate the American veterans of the war as payment for their military service. However, they could not receive their grants until the Crown had first purchased land from the Indian nations.

Pontiac's War continued until Colonel Henry Bouquet and his army consisting of regular British soldiers, Royal Americans, and Virginia militia was dispatched to subdue the Indians. Colonel Bouquet marched into the Ohio River Valley and persuaded the Shawanese and their allies to give up the fight in November of 1764. A peace treaty was signed with the Shawanese in May 10, 1765.[37] However, a deep hatred and mistrust lingered between many Shawanese and Virginians when the fighting ended.

THE SHAWANESE NATION HAD MANAGED TO PRESERVE and maintain a population of approximately three thousand individuals into the early to middle 1770s despite many years of warfare, displacement, and disease.[38] Most of them had moved to the valleys of the middle and upper Scioto River and the Muskingum River by the end of Pontiac's War. The Shawanese towns in the Scioto River valley were called the "Lower Shawanese Towns." The towns in the Muskingum River valley were called the "Upper Shawanese Towns" and were largely settled by the Shawanese that had formerly lived in the "Upper Shawanese Town" on the south side of the Ohio River just above the mouth of the Great Kanawha River from 1751 to 1758.[39]

A rift developed between the chiefs of the Makujay Shawanese and the

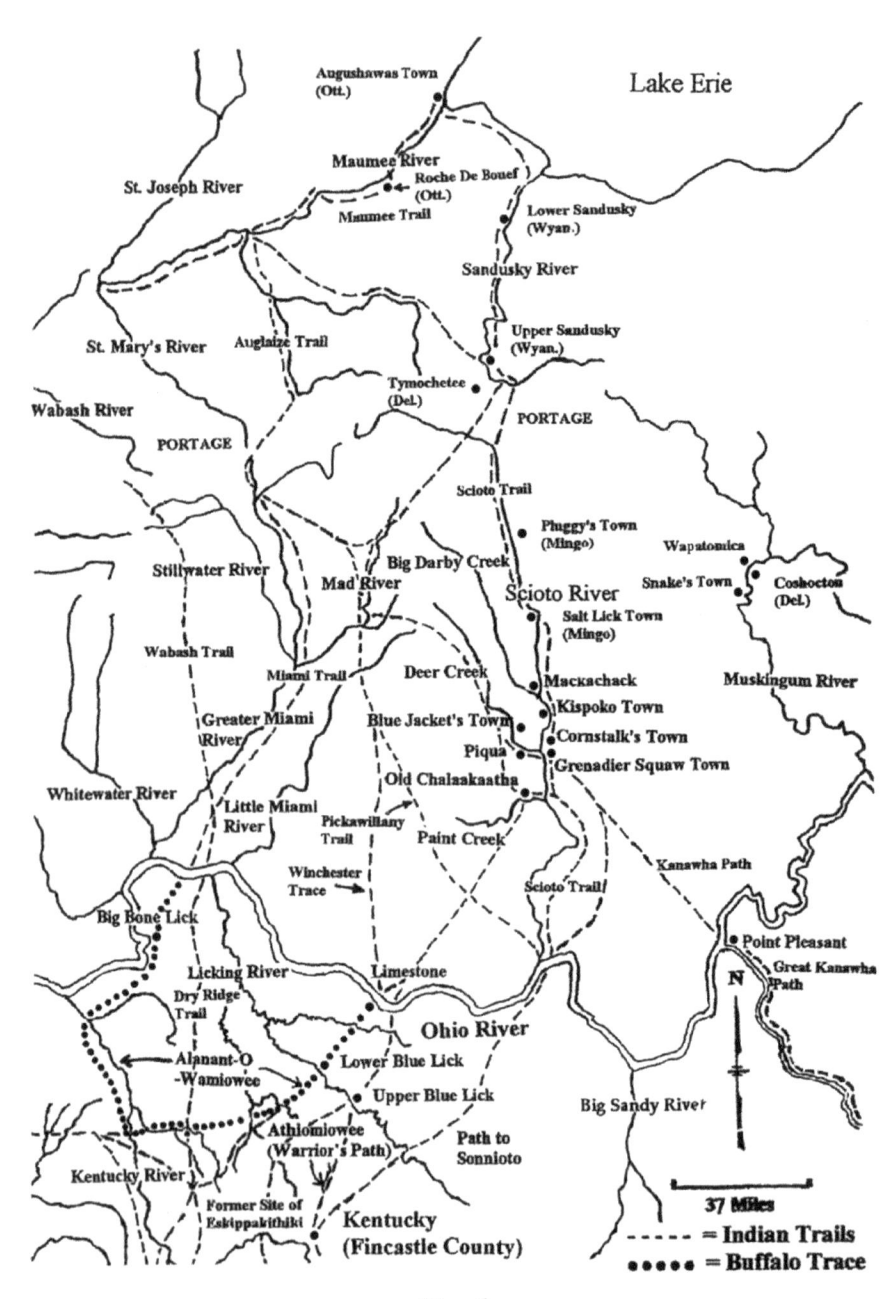

Map 3
Shawnese Towns of Ohio in 1758-1774

chiefs and warriors of the Chalaakaatha, Piqua, and Kispoko Shawanese in the late 1760s and early 1770s. The chiefs of all the divisions shared the same grievances about British incursion into their Kentucky hunting grounds, but they disagreed about how to respond.

The Makujay chiefs believed that they were outmanned and outgunned by the Virginians and preferred to negotiate for diplomatic solutions. Their leaders were the most eloquent advocates for a humane and just resolution.

The Chalaakaatha, Piqua, and Kispoko war chiefs and warriors rejected the politics of conciliation and believed that war was the only way to preserve their territory and way of life. The war faction appears to have been headed by Chalaakaatha Chiefs Yellow Hawk and Black Fish, Piqua Chief White Bark, and Kispoko War Chiefs Pucksinwah and Captain Snake. These war chiefs saw the "Long Knives" of Virginia (referred to as the "Shemanese" in the Shawanese language) as their principal enemies.[40]

Makujay Principal Chief Kishenosity ("Hard Man" or "Erection"), Chief Cornstalk, Cornstalk's sisters Coitcheleh and Nonhelema, and Cornstalk's younger brothers Nimwha and Silver Heels formed the core of the Makujay Shawanese leadership and peace faction. Kishenosity had succeeded Paxinosa as the Makujay Principal Chief in the late 1760s. He was the son of Paxinosa's predecessor, the late Chief Kakowatchecky.[41] Piqua War Chief Wryneck appears to have supported the Makujay peace faction.

Cornstalk was the Principal War Chief of the Shawanese Nation during this period.[42] He was a tall and powerfully built man in his early fifties with a noble appearance and charismatic bearing. Although Kishenosity was the overall Principal Chief of the nation, he often deferred to Cornstalk's leadership by allowing him to serve not only as their war leader but also as their chief spokesman in negotiations and diplomacy, since Cornstalk was renowned for his oratorical skills.

Cornstalk's brother Nimwha (Munseka) was a senior civil chief of the Makujay division. He was an eloquent speaker and frequently represented the nation at councils and treaty negotiations.[43] Cornstalk's sister Coitcheleh was the Headwoman of the Shawanese Nation. She attended the important councils and was her nation's chief female spokesperson and advocate for peace, families, women, and children.[44] Cornstalk's sister Nonhelema was the village chief of Grenadier Squaw Town on Scippo Creek. She had been baptized and given the Christian name Catherine ("Kate"). Nonhelema was the mother of a daughter, Fanny, and a son, Morgan.[45]

Virginia veterans and land development companies led by George Washington and other former senior officers of the Virginia militia during the French and Indian War put constant pressure on the British Royal Government to acquire land in the Ohio River Valley from the Indians to grant to the veterans. Their efforts succeeded and culminated in the First Treaty of Fort Stanwix in 1768, pursuant to which Great Britain purchased from the Six Nations all of the land to the south of the Ohio River down to the mouth of the Tennessee River.[46]

The Six Nations maintained that they had the authority to sell the land because the Shawanese and other Indian nations in the Ohio River Valley had either been conquered by them during the Beaver Wars or had joined the Covenant Chain alliance governed by the Six Nations. They were supported by Sir William Johnson and the British Indian Department.

The Ohio Indian nations were outraged by the terms of the treaty. The militant Shawanese living in the Lower Shawanese Towns protested that their winter hunting grounds in Kentucky had been "given away" without their consent. Many of their hunters had lived in Eskippakithiki in their youth and were passionately attached to the Kentucky plains as an integral component of the ancestral Shawanese home territory.

The resilient and defiant Shawanese Nation now found itself at the epicenter of the political turbulence on the edges of the western frontier, where the cultures of the Eastern Woodland Indians and Europe met and mingled. The physical buffer zone of distance that had protected the Shawanese since their return to the Ohio River Valley was fast disappearing as the increasingly powerful and bellicose Virginia "Long Knives" surged west. Many Shawanese warriors vowed to make a stand to face the invaders rather than retreat once again.

The leadership of the Shawanese Nation knew that it was critical to acquire allies to stop the invading Virginians if they were to remain in their Ohio River Valley homeland. They initiated efforts to form a new military Indian Confederacy less than six months after the signature of the Treaty of Fort Stanwix.

Shawanese warriors told Deputy Indian Agent Alexander McKee on

September 18, 1769, that they were determined to resist the advancing settlements, and " . . . they may as well die like men as be kicked about like dogs . . ."[47] McKee further reported in a letter dated the same day that the Shawanese and Delaware had built a large council house on the Scioto River and invited several nations to meet there in June or July of 1770 to discuss the formation of a new confederacy.[48]

Sir William Johnson and the British Indian Department thwarted their efforts. The Shawanese made a second attempt in 1771 and were thwarted again.

Settlements in southwestern Virginia and northwestern North Carolina rapidly expanded to the southwest along the valleys of the Western Waters as hundreds of emigrating families made their way down the Valley of Virginia. The white settlements along the Holston River in southwestern Virginia expanded across the North Carolina boundary line in 1769.

The rapidly growing settlements crowded close to the towns of the Overhill Cherokee on the Holston River and Tellico River and caused renewed tensions with that nation. The Cherokee and Ohio Indian nations feared that these new settlements would form the springboards for the next wave of westward migration deep into Kentucky and beyond.

Shawanese hunters returning to their Ohio towns from hunting trips into Kentucky in 1769 reported more and more signs of the incursion of white "Long Hunters" from the new western settlements seeking furs and skins for the fur trade. The Shawanese war chiefs resolved to drive the hunters back east of the Allegheny divide.

OLD PENNSYLVANIA TRADER JOHN FINDLEY SPENT THE winter of 1768 with his long-time friend Daniel Boone at Boone's family cabin on the Yadkin River in North Carolina. They had served together as wagon drivers during Braddock's Campaign.

Findley had lived and worked in Eskippakithiki in the early 1750s. His glowing stories of the beautiful and fertile Kentucky plains stirred Daniel Boone's imagination. Boone, his brother Squire, his brother-in-law John Stewart, and Findley agreed to form a "Long Hunter" enterprise to explore Kentucky and harvest furs.

Daniel Boone and his contemporaries used a muzzle-loading flintlock gun of advanced design called the "Pennsylvania (and later Kentucky) long rifle." The design of the long rifle was derived from a German hunting rifle called a *Jaegar*. The Pennsylvania Dutch had extended the length of the barrel by several inches. The barrels were typically forty-two inches or more in length.

The long rifle had six to eight rifling grooves cut into the inside of the barrel that spun the rifle ball and gave it a high degree of accuracy. It was very lightweight compared to muskets and earlier rifle designs, and was amazingly accurate from one hundred fifty yards up to three hundred yards.

Daniel Boone and his Long Hunters set out for Kentucky on May 1, 1769. They had several encounters and skirmishes with hostile Shawanese hunters and warriors during their hunts there, including Captain Will and his band. The Boone party did not return to the settlements until 1771. Their reports of the beauty, wealth, and fertility of the Kentucky plains spread rapidly through the frontier communities of North Carolina and Virginia, a portent of things to come.

Two | *Lord Dunmore's War*

The Invasion of Kentucky

JOHN MURRAY, THE FOURTH EARL OF DUNMORE, Viscount Fincastle, and Baron of Blair, Monlin and Tillimet, replaced Baron de Botetourt as the Royal Governor of Virginia in 1772. Lord Dunmore had served in the House of Lords in London for ten years before serving as the Royal Governor of New York from 1770 to 1772.[1]

The number and intensity of grievances of the Virginia colonists against King George III mounted as Lord Dunmore began his term. The Virginia veterans of the French and Indian War pressed hard for western land grants under the Royal Proclamation of 1763. Lord Dunmore opted to walk a fine line between the Indian and western land policy direction coming to him from London and the demands of the Virginians. He approved a distribution of bounty lands to George Washington and his former Virginia Regiment soldiers on November 6, 1772, including a 20,147-acre parcel for Washington. Dunmore also claimed 100,000 acres along the Ohio River for himself and his family.[2]

Dunmore and the Virginia General Assembly formed Fincastle County on December 2, 1772, in the far west of the territory that they claimed under the Virginia Royal Charter. Kentucky was included within the boundaries of the new county. The aggressive policy of Lord Dunmore toward westward expansion confirmed the worst fears of the Shawanese, and the Shawanese war faction began to gain influence within their nation.

Captain Pipe of the Munsee Delaware told Pennsylvania authorities that "this difference between the Governor of Virginia and the Shawnees gives us all great uneasiness."[3]

The first wave of Virginia surveyors and settlers bound for Kentucky began early in 1773.[4] Virginia's official survey party was comprised of a company of thirty-five men commanded by Captain Thomas Bullit.

Robert McAfee and his Scotch-Irish family and friends from Botetourt County, Virginia, joined the Bullitt party at the mouth of the Great Kanawha River.[5] The combined party set forth in April of 1773 on an expedition to the Falls of the Ohio and Kentucky.[6] Captain Bullitt visited Chalaakaatha and presented a speech to the Shawanese and Delaware in the Grand Council House on June 9 using Pennsylvania trader Richard Butler as his interpreter.

Richard Butler and his younger brother William had lived for several years at their trading post in Kispoko Town,[7] and were accepted by the Shawanese as friends and neighbors. Richard fathered two children by a Shawanese Kispoko woman—a daughter named Polly Butler and a son who grew up to become Shawanese chief and warrior Tamenatha, also known as "Captain Butler" to the Americans.[8]

Captain Bullitt explained the purposes of his expedition and assured the Shawanese that their hunters would be able to hunt on the settlers' lands without objection. Shawanese Chief Cornstalk expressed satisfaction that the Shawanese would be allowed to hunt in Kentucky after settlement and his hope that the young men on both sides would obey their leaders' directions to preserve the peace.

The McAfees went up the Kentucky River while Captain Bullitt and his men continued on down the Ohio River to the Falls of the Ohio.[9] The McAfees confirmed the already-legendary abundance of wild game in Kentucky as they explored and surveyed their way up the Kentucky River Valley. Buffalo, elk, deer, beaver, and wolves were plentiful, and they hunted them. They shot at a large herd of buffalo at Drennon's Lick and recklessly caused a stampede.

The McAfees returned to the Virginia settlements through the Powell Mountains and arrived at the home of Captain William Russell II on the Clinch River on August 14.[10] Captain Russell was in the process of moving to Kentucky with his family and had hired Daniel Boone to serve as his scout and guide for the expedition. The Boones had closed out their affairs in North Carolina and passed the McAfee party as the McAfees were leaving Captain Russell's homestead.[11]

The Russell/Boone expeditionary party left Castle's Wood on September 25, 1773, bound for the Cumberland Gap and Kentucky. There were forty men, women, and children in the party. Captain Russell and his family, including sons Henry and fifteen-year-old William Russell III, and Daniel Boone and his family, were among them.

Alexander McKee reported to Sir William Johnson that Chief Cornstalk had voiced a speech on September 25, 1773, warning Indian traders to stay away from the Shawanese Towns for their own safety because the militants were still angry about Captain Bullitt's expedition.[12] Cornstalk's warning did not reach the Russell/Boone expedition in time.

They were attacked near the Cumberland Gap on October 9 by a war party of Shawanese, Cherokee, and Delaware warriors reportedly commanded by a Shawanese warrior known as "Big Jim." Daniel Boone's oldest son, James, and Henry Russell were captured, brutally tortured, and put to death as a stern warning against any further attempts to settle in Kentucky.[13] The heartbroken Russell and Boone families retreated to Moore's Fort.

The shocking news of the deaths of James Boone and Henry Russell caused consternation and anger throughout the western British settlements. The news of their attempt at settlement also spread like a shock wave through the Ohio Indian nations. The invasion of Kentucky was underway, and blood had been spilled.

The Virginians were undeterred. Colonel Preston published a notice in the *Virginia Gazette* on February 24, 1774, stating that veterans who claimed grants under the Royal Proclamation of 1763 should assemble at the confluence of the Ohio River and Great Kanawha River to begin the survey of Fincastle County lands below the mouth of the Great Kanawha River. Lord Dunmore issued certificates to the veterans entitling them to the amounts of land specified in the old Proclamation.[14]

Lord Dunmore appointed Dr. John Connolly as his personal representative and directed that he take possession of Fort Pitt and garrison it with Virginia militia forces. Connolly arrived at the village of Pittsburgh on January 6, 1774, and boldly occupied the abandoned Fort Pitt, renaming it "Fort

Dunmore." He quickly suppressed attempts by the colony of Pennsylvania to regain possession of the fort.[15]

A surveying party headed by Captain John Floyd set off down the Ohio River from Wheeling on April 22, 1774, to survey land on behalf of Dr. Connolly and George Washington, Patrick Henry, and other influential Virginia veterans. Michael Cresap and George Rogers Clark led another surveying party that met at the mouth of the Little Kanawha River in early April of 1774.

A letter from Dr. Connolly was delivered to Cresap on April 24, 1774, which said that the Shawanese were "ill-disposed towards white men" and that the people should be ready "to repel any insults that might be offered." The letter was interpreted as a declaration of war against the Shawanese people.[16]

Cresap's party killed a friendly Shawanese man and Cherokee man that Pennsylvania trader William Butler sent down the Ohio River to pick up his furs. They also attacked a party of fourteen Shawanese and killed a Shawanese chief on the following day.[17]

The celebrated Mingo chief and orator "Logan" (Taghahjute) was the leader of the friendly Mingo settlement "Logan's Camp" on the north shore of the Ohio River at the mouth of Yellow Creek (near present-day Steubenville, Ohio). His sister, who was the consort of Pennsylvania trader John Gibson, lived there with him, and was pregnant with Gibson's child.[18]

Daniel and Jacob Greathouse, Joshua Baker Sr., and a group of drunken Virginia rowdies murdered thirteen residents of Logan's Camp on May 3, 1774.[19] Chief Logan was not present, and his family was annihilated. Jacob Greathouse strung Logan's pregnant sister up between two trees, disemboweled her with a tomahawk, and then scalped her fetus and impaled it on a stake. Lord Dunmore, Thomas Jefferson, and George Rogers Clark all spoke out against the barbarous actions of Greathouse and his drunken thugs.

Alexander McKee dispatched Delaware Chief Captain White Eyes to Wakatomica on May 6, 1774, to counsel and calm the Shawanese. Shawanese Principal Chief Kishenosity told him that "... the Shawanese are all warriors, and will not listen to us until they have satisfaction of us for what injuries they have received from the Virginians..."[20]

Chief Logan and his vengeful Mingo warriors set off on the warpath to obtain their revenge. A handful of Upper Shawanese Town warriors accompanied the Mingo war party. Richard and William Butler were selected as the first targets for retribution.

Cornstalk learned of Logan's plan and dispatched five Shawanese warriors commanded by his younger brother Silverheels to warn and escort the Butler brothers back to Pittsburgh. He entrusted Silverheels to deliver a letter to the Butlers with a request that they in turn deliver it to Alexander McKee at Fort Pitt. In his letter, Cornstalk protested the Virginians' attacks on his people and promised that he would prevent the "foolish People" among the Shawanese from doing any more harm until they knew the intentions of the Long Knives.[21]

Silverheels and his warriors rescued the Butler brothers at Hockhocking Creek and safely escorted them to Pittsburgh on June 16, 1774. Richard Butler requested that Dr. Connolly provide protection for Silverheels and his band of warriors on their return journey to their towns. Dr. Connolly snarled his refusal and dispatched a party of forty militiamen to arrest the Shawanese.

Richard Butler secretly escorted his Shawanese friends back across the river, gave them a monetary reward for their good faith and friendship, and wished them well. The Butler brothers chose to remain in Pittsburgh and not return to their trading post in Kispoko Town because of the growing danger.

Dr. Connolly sent two armed parties in pursuit of the Shawanese when he learned of their escape.[22] One of them caught up with the Shawanese and opened fire, and Silverheels was severely wounded.[23]

The Shawanese escaped and returned to their towns. Shocked by the treachery of the Virginians, the episode was never forgotten or forgiven by them. Captain Arthur St. Clair of the Pennsylvania militia wrote at the time, "What may be the consequence God knows."[24]

Chief Logan's Mingo warriors turned their wrath upon the frontier settlements and brutally slaughtered thirteen innocent Virginia and Pennsylvania settlers. Logan seemed to be satisfied with a one-for-one retribution for the Yellow Creek massacre after the death of the thirteenth settler. He said that he "... will sit still until he hears what the Long Knife ... will say."[25]

Lord Dunmore issued a circular letter to the County Lieutenants of Virginia claiming that no peace was possible with the Shawanese and Mingo and directed them to muster the frontier county militia.[26] Some of the

Virginia legislators in the House of Burgesses openly questioned whether the situation was as grave as portrayed.[27]

The Shawanese leadership met in council to determine a course of action after the treacherous attack on Silverheels. Cornstalk gave his people a final warning of the dangerous consequences of a general war with the Long Knives. The council ignored his advice and declared for war.

Chief Cornstalk and the war chiefs "placed their old men, women, and children at their backs" and took charge of their nation. Shawanese diplomats and messengers were dispatched to deliver black wampum belts to the other northwestern Indian nations in a desperate search for allies. The belts were rejected by all nations that received them. Not even their traditional Delaware allies were willing to help. The Shawanese would face the Long Knives with only a handful of their most loyal Mingo Seneca and northern Cherokee friends at their side. The red tomahawk was circulated through the Shawanese towns to summon all of the nation's warriors to Chalaakaatha.

THE RELATIONSHIP BETWEEN GREAT BRITAIN AND ITS American colonies continued to deteriorate as the Virginians and Shawanese prepared for war. The Boston Tea Party had taken place in Boston Harbor on December 16, 1773. Great Britain responded to this rebellious act by enacting the punitive Boston Port Act which effectively closed Boston Harbor on June 1, 1774.

The Virginia House of Burgesses reaffirmed their sympathy for their Massachusetts compatriots by passing a resolution designating June 1, 1774, "as a day of fasting, humiliation, and prayer, imploring the divine interposition to avert the heavy calamity that threatened destruction to their civil rights, and the evils of a civil war."[28] Lord Dunmore dissolved the House of Burgesses to suppress any further seditious statements or actions.

The Parliament of Great Britain enacted the Quebec Act on June 22, 1774. The Act expanded the boundaries of the Province of Quebec to include all of the northwestern territories to the north of the Ohio River and east of the Mississippi River.[29] This created yet another conflict with the land claims of Virginia and the other colonies under their long-standing Royal Charters. Furthermore, the provincial government established by the Act was to be appointed in London and did not include an elected representative legislative body.

The enactment of this new law raised the political stakes for Lord Dunmore, as he was already well along in executing Virginia's ambitious plans for the settlement and development of the lower Ohio River valley. He challenged the Quebec Act and, thereby, the king's authority by continuing to assert Virginia's rights to possess and grant lands "on the Scioto, the Wabash and the Illinois" under prior Royal Charter.[30]

Lord Dunmore left the Governor's Mansion on July 10, 1774, and rode off with his entourage, bound for Lord Fairfax's Greenway Court estate southeast of Winchester on the western flanks of the Blue Ridge Mountains. There he established his headquarters for a Shawanese campaign.

The Battle of Point Pleasant

SIR WILLIAM JOHNSON DIED AT JOHNSON'S HALL on July 7, 1774, while working with the assembled leadership of the Six Nations to address the crisis with the Shawanese.[31] His nephew Colonel Guy Johnson assumed his duties as Superintendent of the Northern Indian Department and his son Sir John Johnson inherited his title and estate at Johnson's Hall. Mohawk Joseph Brant was appointed as Guy Johnson's secretary in the Indian Department.[32]

Lord Dunmore's western adventure was the first problem faced by the new leadership of the British Indian Department. The Department and Grand Council of the Six Nations dispatched Mingo Vice Regent Guyasuta on a final mission to persuade the Shawanese and Mingo to make peace with Virginia. Guyasuta was unable to persuade them to bury the tomahawk.

Lord Dunmore issued his campaign plans in a letter to Colonel Andrew Lewis dated July 24, 1774. The Royal Governor would assemble and take personal command of a northern division of militia volunteers at Lord Fairfax's Greenway Court estate to march to Fort Dunmore and from there down the Ohio River to attack the Lower Shawanese towns. He directed Colonel Lewis to assemble and take command of a southern division in his quarter.[33] The two divisions would rendezvous at the mouth of the Hockhocking River and proceed from there into the Shawanese homeland.[34]

Among the many who volunteered to serve under Lord Dunmore were George Rogers Clark, Simon Kenton, and Simon Girty.[35] Simon Girty and his brothers, James and George, had been captured by Delaware warriors during the attack on Fort Granville in Pennsylvania on August 1, 1756. Simon was adopted by the Seneca Nation, George was adopted by the Delaware Nation, and James was adopted by the Shawanese Nation.[36] They were among prisoners released at Fort Pitt at the conclusion of Bouquet's Treaty in 1765.

Colonel Lewis directed the troops of the western Virginia counties to rendezvous at a location on the Greenbrier River named Union Camp (the current location of Lewisburg, West Virginia). They would march from there down the Greenbrier River and across the mountain divide to the Great Kanawha River and on down that river to its mouth at the Ohio River.

Colonel William Fleming of Botetourt County was directed to recruit a company of militia to join Colonel Lewis' southern division from the surrounding counties. Fleming lived on a plantation named "Belmont" some twenty miles to the southwest of Great Lick (Roanoke).

Micajah Callaway's twenty-year old brother, Dudley Callaway, volunteered to serve in Captain Henry Pauling's company in Colonel Fleming's Botetourt County regiment.[37] He joined the volunteers at Colonel Fleming's Belmont estate.

Pennsylvania Governor John Penn sent a final letter of warning to the Shawanese leadership on August 6, 1774, expressing his concern over the deteriorating relationship between the Shawanese and the Virginians:

> " . . . Brethren: If you continue to act in this manner the People of Virginia must do the same Thing by you, and then there will be nothing but War between you. Consider, Brethren, that the People of Virginia are like the Leaves upon the Trees, very numerous, and you are but a few, and although you should kill ten of their People for one that they kill of yours, they will at last wear you out and destroy you . . ."[38]

Colonel William Fleming arrived at Union Camp with four hundred Botetourt County troops under his command on about September 2 and

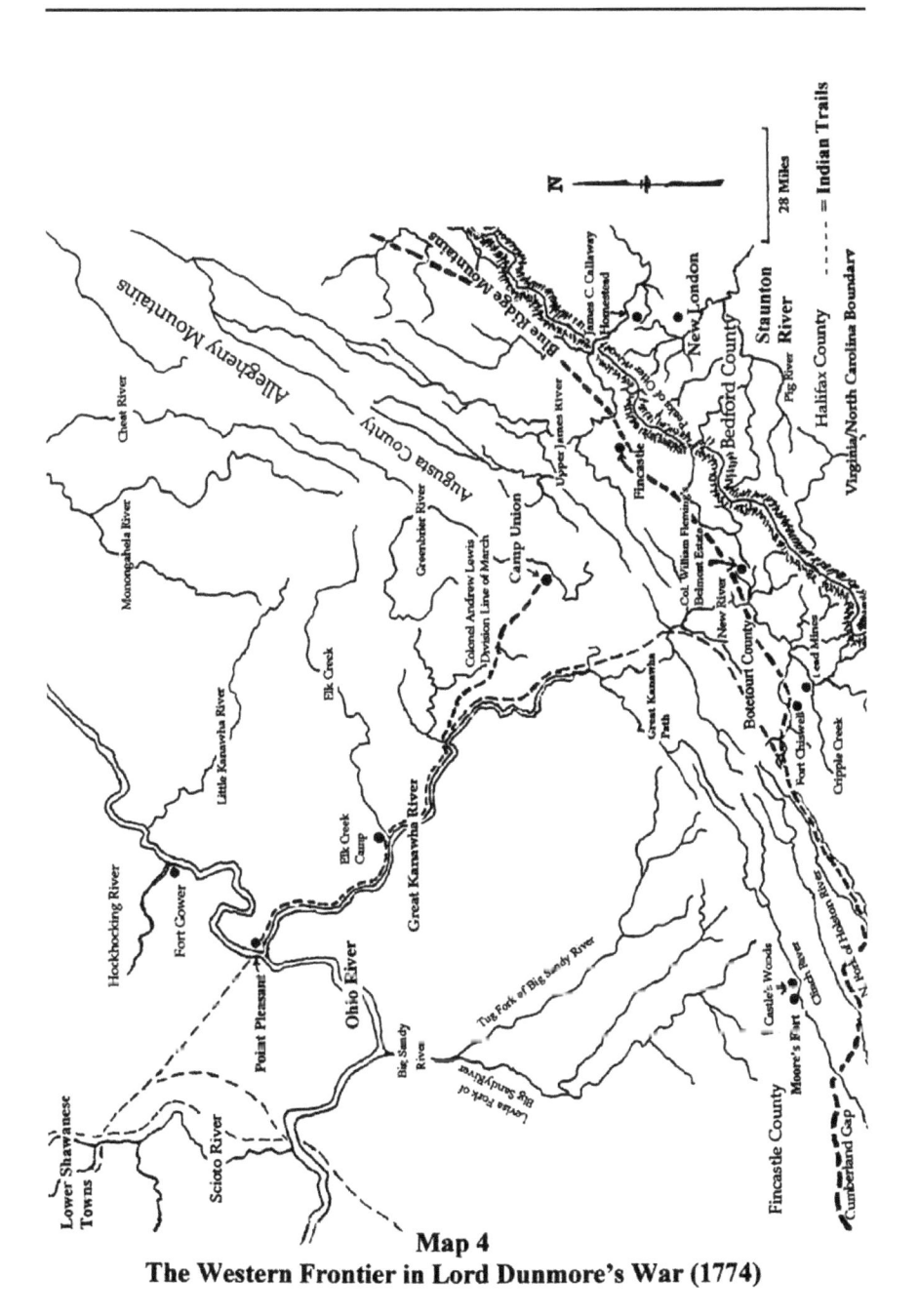

Map 4
The Western Frontier in Lord Dunmore's War (1774)

joined the other troops assembling there. The total number of southern division men assembled there reached 1,490 by September 4, 1774.

Colonel Lewis and the southern division left Union Camp on September 7 and reached the mouth of Elk Creek (the present location of Charleston, West Virginia) on September 21.[39] They paused there to build a sturdy storehouse, and also constructed eighteen large dugout canoes from tree trunks in order to speed and ease the transport of the huge quantity of provisions down the river.[40]

Dudley Callaway was one of four "canoemen" selected by Captain Pauling to lead the construction and loading and pilot the canoes.[41] The four canoemen were placed under the command of Sergeant Obadiah H. Trent.[42]

James Mooney and other Virginia scouts detected signs of several Indian scouting parties in the area as the division was camped at Elk Creek. The guard was strengthened and Virginia scouts were dispatched down the river to gather intelligence.[43]

The balance of the southern division continued to march down the forested river path while the canoemen and their crews ferried the provisions down the river. The nights were growing cool and the trees were displaying their autumn colors as they approached the mouth of the Great Kanawha River.

LORD DUNMORE MARCHED OUT OF GREENWAY COURT and down Braddock's Road at the head of the northern division on August 27, 1774. They arrived at Fort Dunmore at the Forks of the Ohio River by the end of the month. The sturdy Scottish Lord earned the admiration of his frontier soldiers as he marched on foot with them and carried his own knapsack.[44]

He met with Captain McKee, Delaware Chiefs Custaloga and Captain White Eyes, and Mingo Mohawk Chief Pluggy at Fort Dunmore and explained Virginia's grievances against the Shawanese Nation. He convinced Mingo Chiefs Pluggy and Big Apple Tree to cooperate with Wyandot and Delaware chiefs in an intensive last-ditch effort to broker a peace between the Shawanese and Long Knives.[45]

Lord Dunmore sent a message to the Shawanese inviting them to meet with him farther down the Ohio River in order to negotiate a treaty. He left Fort Dunmore with his northern division on September 17 in a flotilla of one hundred canoes and rendezvoused with Colonel William Crawford and his soldiers at Fort Gower at the mouth of the Hockhocking River.[46]

Shawanese scouts had observed the two Long Knife armies from the very beginning of their formation and had tracked their progress towards the Shawanese Towns. It was apparent to Cornstalk and Pucksinwah that the two armies would eventually combine into a single force that would outmatch the Shawanese in numbers and firepower. The Shawanese tightened their surveillance, looking for a mistake that would give them an advantage.

Colonel Lewis's southern division reached the triangular point of land at the confluence of the Great Kanawha River and the Ohio River known as "Point Pleasant" on October 6, 1774. Point Pleasant and the confluence had been an important strategic location for the northwestern Indian nations for many generations. The Great Kanawha Indian Path had long been a corridor for war parties passing between the northern and southern Indian nations and was still used by Shawanese raiders to reach the Virginia and North Carolina backcountry. Virginia settlers and surveyors were now relying on it themselves to support their migration into the Ohio River Valley.

Point Pleasant consisted of a relatively flat triangle of floodplain of about half a mile in width along the Ohio River side and three-quarters of a mile wide along the Great Kanawha River side. A substantial wooded hill loomed above the Point. The hill was quite steep, with 350 feet of vertical rise within less than a half-mile of horizontal distance. It was covered by trees dressed in their full autumn splendor. The floodplain was also heavily forested.

A small stream named Crooked Creek flowed along the base of the hill parallel to the Ohio River before discharging into the Great Kanawha River just over a half-mile above the confluence. A slight rise lay to the immediate west of Crooked Creek between the creek and the Ohio River.

Colonel Lewis ordered his division to encamp near the end of the point on October 7, 1774. The men set up their tents and constructed a light breastwork stretching from one bank to the other. Colonel Fleming ordered the canoemen and their crews to unload their vessels.

Shawanese scouts detected the arrival and encampment of Colonel Lewis's army at Point Pleasant. They noted that Colonel Lewis's division was not going to rendezvous with Lord Dunmore's division in the immediate future. Colonel Lewis and his troops were isolated and vulnerable. This was the opportunity that they had been looking for, and the scouts raced back to the Lower Shawanese Towns and reported their observations to the war chiefs.

All of the chiefs and warriors of the Shawanese Nation were summoned and assembled at the council house in Cornstalk's Town for a Grand Council. Cornstalk spoke first and again admonished his people about the grave dangers and likely adverse consequences of a general war with the Long Knives. He recommended that they accept Lord Dunmore's request for a council. The other Shawanese chiefs and counselors resoundingly disagreed and argued for war.

Cornstalk abided by the decision of his people. If the Shawanese Nation was for war, so be it! He would lead them into battle himself. He ended his speech dramatically by plunging his tomahawk into the painted war pole. The council house erupted with war whoops and a great war dance ensued to the throbbing pulse of war drums. A thousand fiercely painted warriors danced in the fire-light, and the great war chiefs punctuated the dance with inspiring speeches. The throb of war drums and dancing continued through the night until early dawn.

Cornstalk and the war chiefs conferred and devised a brilliant but risky military strategy. They would march to the Ohio River to attack Colonel Lewis and his division at Point Pleasant before his division could join forces with Lord Dunmore's division. They would surround Colonel Lewis on the point and conduct a surprise attack at dawn. The Shawanese would then move on to attack Lord Dunmore's division after defeating Colonel Lewis.

The army of Shawanese warriors marched to war early the next morning. Cornstalk led them stealthily down the Kanawha Path toward the Ohio River, and they arrived undetected at the mouth of Campaign Creek on the northwest shore of the Ohio River about two miles above Point Pleasant on the night of October 9.

Cornstalk and his warriors discretely constructed seventy rafts and slipped silently across the river. They set up a concealed camp just off the southeastern shore of the Ohio about two miles upstream of Colonel Lewis's encampment at the former location of their "Upper Shawanese Town" abandoned in 1758.[47] They would attack the Long Knives at dawn. The warriors fasted that night to prepare themselves for battle in accordance with their custom.

Simon Kenton and Simon Girty arrived at Point Pleasant on October 9 with renewed orders from Lord Dunmore directing Colonel Lewis to join him at the mouth of the Hockhocking River. Lewis refused to do so before his men were rested and the remainder of his soldiers had joined him. Kenton and Girty returned up river that night and somehow missed the Shawanese army as they passed by their camp.[48]

The Shawanese awoke well before dawn in the cool autumn morning darkness of October 10. The warriors stripped off all of their clothing except for their mocassins and breechcloths, and painted their faces black and red. They tucked their tomahawks and scalping knives into their breechcloth belts and slung the straps of their powder horns and shot bags over their shoulders. They refreshed and double-checked the powder and priming of their muskets and rifles. Detachments of warriors were dispatched and posted across the Ohio River and Great Kanawaha River from Point Pleasant with orders to shoot any Long Knives who tried to swim to safety.

Scouts Joseph Hughey and James Mooney from Captain William Russell II's company arose before dawn on October 10 and paddled up the Ohio River in a canoe in search of game.[49] Mooney had accompanied Daniel Boone on his Kentucky long hunt in 1769.

The two scouts stumbled across the awakened Indian encampment and instantly turned away, fleeing for their lives. Shawanese sentries fired at both soldiers. Hughey was killed but Mooney managed to reach Colonel Lewis's camp to warn the Long Knives. Sergeant James Robertson and Valentine Sevier from Captain Evan Shelby's company reported the discovery of a party of thirty warriors at about the same time.[50]

The war chiefs quickly formed their warriors for the attack. Cornstalk ordered a large body of warriors to drive across the neck of Point Pleasant to the banks of the Great Kanawha River and cut the Long Knife army off from any means of escape. A Shawanese battle line was soon in place stretching for over a mile, from the banks of the Ohio River to the banks of the Great Kanawha River between the Long Knife breastworks and Crooked Creek. The Long Knives were trapped and would have to fight for their lives. One thousand Shawanese warriors faced twelve hundred Virginians on the field of battle.

Colonel Andrew Lewis was awakened by Mooney's warning shouts and calmly took command. Dudley Callaway rubbed his eyes and scrambled for his weapons after being rudely awakened by a kick in the ribs, and reported for duty to Captain Pauling within minutes.

Colonel Lewis ordered his troops into battle array as he coolly lit his pipe in the grey dawn light. The Scotch-Irish warlords of the Virginia frontier were prepared to show their mettle against the elite warriors of the Shawanese Nation. They had learned much from their mistakes in the failed Shawnee Expedition of 1756 and other early failures and had evolved into a well-supplied and formidable corps of disciplined riflemen.

Colonel Lewis ordered Colonel Fleming to lead a column of 150 Botetourt County troops to his left flank to probe for the enemy along the Ohio River where they had been sighted by Mooney. He ordered his brother, Colonel Charles Lewis, and 150 Augusta County troops to form a column and attempt to turn the Shawanese left flank.[51]

The battle was joined in the dawn light of October 10, 1774, as Colonel Charles Lewis's Augusta County forces made their first contact with Cornstalk's left flank about three quarters of a mile from the Long Knife camp.[52] The Long Knives charged and the warriors fell back slightly, but Shawanese resistance stiffened and a furious counterattack soon followed. The warriors fired and reloaded as they ran toward their enemy. The Long Knife column was driven back but kept up a steady fire and maintained their discipline as they retreated toward their main camp. Colonel Charles Lewis was mortally wounded.

The Shawanese engaged Colonel Fleming's column on the Long Knife left flank and drove them back about two hundred yards. Fleming was struck twice in the left arm and took a musket ball in the chest just below his left nipple. The ball pushed still-inflated lung tissue out of the exit wound in his back.

Colonel Fleming's medical training saved his life. He managed to walk back to the camp where a young soldier followed his instructions and pushed the lung tissue back into his body, and he amazingly survived his terrible wound.

Colonel Andrew Lewis ordered Colonel John Field and his men to move forward to bolster and hold the Long Knife line. Captain Pauling's company was ordered to reinforce Colonel Charles Lewis's beleaguered forces on the right flank. The Long Knife soldiers surged forward through a hail of musket balls and arrows to engage the enemy.

Lord Dunmore's War

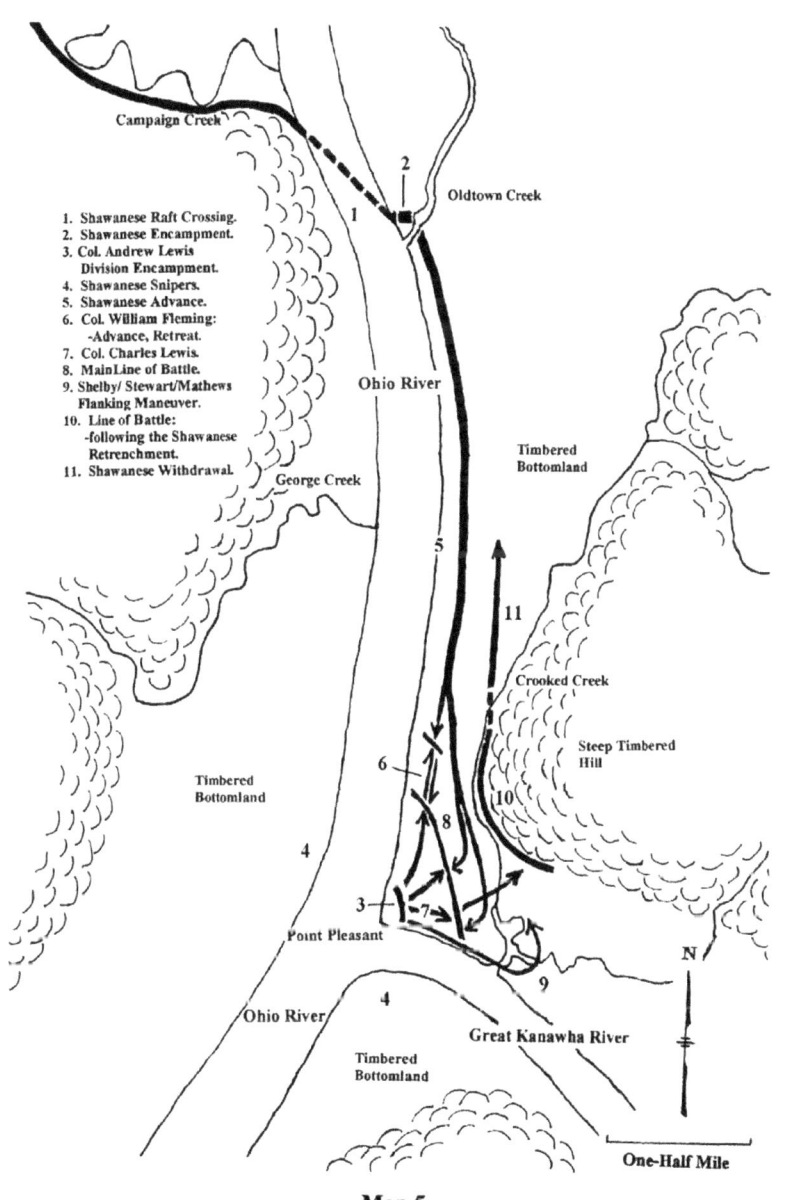

1. Shawanese Raft Crossing.
2. Shawanese Encampment.
3. Col. Andrew Lewis Division Encampment.
4. Shawanese Snipers.
5. Shawanese Advance.
6. Col. William Fleming: -Advance, Retreat.
7. Col. Charles Lewis.
8. Main Line of Battle.
9. Shelby/ Stewart/Mathews Flanking Maneuver.
10. Line of Battle: -following the Shawanese Retrenchment.
11. Shawanese Withdrawal.

**Map 5
The Battle of Point Pleasant**

The Shawanese attacked with great determination and held the rise to the immediate west of Crooked Creek. The reinforced Virginians resolutely stood their ground. All combatants fought as if possessed by demons, pouring gunfire into each other's ranks. The battle lines were never more than twenty yards apart and sometimes less than six, with hand-to-hand combat up and down the line.

The battle continued in this manner throughout the morning. The Shawanese cursed the Virginians in English as "White Sons of Bitches!" and tauntingly asked why they didn't play their fifes? The Shawanese would teach them how to shoot![53]

Dudley Callaway and the rest of Captain Pauling's Botetourt County soldiers were in the thick of the battle on the right flank. Musket balls whizzed past Dudley's head as he popped out from behind his cover to fire his long rifle and duck back. Dudley was an excellent marksman and made his shots count, fighting on as his comrades fell, wounded or dead, around him. The gunsmoke was so heavy in the air that it was like a thick fog.

The Shawanese war chiefs calmly walked behind their lines, encouraging their warriors to "lie close," "shoot well," and "fight and be strong." Dudley could hear the booming voice of Cornstalk exhorting his warriors in the Shawanese language above the din of battle. The smell of gunpowder, blood, and death filled the air. The warriors took the scalps of those that they killed, and the Virginians did the same.

Chief Pucksinwah was suddenly hit in the chest by a Virginia rifle ball and spun to the ground, mortally wounded. The dying Pucksinwah urged his oldest son, Chiksika, to swear an oath that he would never make peace with the Long Knives and never stop fighting for their homeland and their people. Chiksika promised that he would honor his wish and that he would ask his younger brother, Tecumseh, to make the same oath. Pucksinwah died on the battlefield. Tecumseh later honored his father and made the oath.

The Shawanese attempted to turn the right flank of the Virginians and gain the advantage around noon. Captain Pauling and his company found themselves at the center of the attack. They called for reinforcements and gave ground grudgingly. Dudley made every precious shot count. Shawanese and Virginian corpses littered the field.

The Virginians counterattacked. Colonel Lewis ordered young

Lieutenant Isaac Shelby and Captains James Stewart and George Mathews and their companies to sneak down the banks of the Great Kanawha River around the Long Knives' far right flank and along the Crooked Creek watercourse to attack the rear of the Shawanese.

The Long Knife plan was executed perfectly. The Shawanese gave way and abandoned the rise to the west of Crooked Creek as their left flank was caught in a cross-fire. They were forced to leave a number of their fallen warriors on the field of battle, but quickly retrenched at the base of the forested hill looming over the Point. The Long Knife commanders ordered their troops to move forward to consolidate their gain.[54]

The battle lines reformed and stalemated as sharpshooters on both sides continued to snipe at their enemies until darkness fell. The Shawanese warriors taunted the soldiers, calling out "That they had two thousand men for them tomorrow and that they had 1100 men now as well as they."[55]

Chief Cornstalk knew that the Lower Shawanese Towns were in great danger of a flanking maneuver by Lord Dunmore's division. He had hoped for a quick and decisive victory at Point Pleasant, but victory had eluded him. He ordered his warriors to pull out of the fight, and the Shawanese army quietly slipped away from the battlefield under the cover of night. They returned to their encampment and crossed back over the river on the rafts that they had used the previous night, speeding toward their endangered towns.

The Shawanese had bravely fought the Long Knives at Point Pleasant, but only to a draw. Seventy-five Virginians had been killed and 140 wounded. Thirty warriors were killed (twenty-seven Shawanese and three Seneca) and eighteen wounded. Piqua Chief White Bark was among the wounded Shawanese. The Virginians considered the battle a major victory, despite the relatively few casualties inflicted on the Shawanese. They collected twenty scalps, eighty blankets, forty guns, and numerous tomahawks from the battlefield.

Lord Dunmore seized the opportunity to capture the Lower Shawanese Towns while they were unprotected. He mobilized his northern division and departed on a rapid march for the towns on October 11. News of the Shawanese withdrawal from Point Pleasant reached Dunmore while he was on the march. He quickened the pace to ensure that his division would reach their destination before the Shawanese army could return.[56]

As Cornstalk led his army back to the Lower Shawanese Towns, scouts informed him that Lord Dunmore's division was rapidly approaching. Cornstalk's worst fears had been realized. He led his warriors in a wide circle around Dunmore's forces and slipped into Grenadier Squaw Town. Cornstalk assembled his war chiefs and warriors for a hastily convened council in his sister's council house. He tried to rally his demoralized warriors to fight on but they would not.

Cornstalk had warned them of the great risk of failure in a war with the Long Knives and had urged them not to attack. They had not heeded his warning. He was now frustrated by their lack of commitment to fight on. Cornstalk angrily struck his tomahawk into the war pole and left it there. "I will go and make peace!" he said and stormed out of the council house.[57]

Trader Matthew Elliot rode out from the Shawanese Towns to meet Lord Dunmore under a flag of truce. Dunmore chose Captain John Gibson to serve as his interpreter. Elliot told Lord Dunmore of Cornstalk's request for peace negotiations. Lord Dunmore marched on and set up a fortified encampment about four miles to the northeast of Cornstalk Town and Grenadier Squaw Town on Scippo Creek. He named the encampment "Camp Charlotte."

Cornstalk and Nonhelema rode together on their horses to meet Lord Dunmore at Camp Charlotte and sued for peace. Lord Dunmore received their overture graciously.[58]

An express messenger arrived at Point Pleasant on October 13 with a message from Lord Dunmore urging Colonel Lewis to join him at Camp Charlotte. Lewis and most of his forces departed on October 17. Lord Dunmore himself intercepted Colonel Lewis on the banks of Scippo Creek. He congratulated the colonel on his victory and persuaded him to return to Point Pleasant. Colonel Lewis accepted the compliment and willingly obeyed the governor's order.[59]

Sergeant Obadiah Trent and his canoemen, including Dudley Callaway, were ordered to go up the Great Kanawha River to the mouth of Elk Creek to pick up a large quantity of flour at the supply depot there and bring it back to Point Pleasant. Captain Buford's company and the balance of Captain Pauling's company were ordered to begin the construction of a substantial fortification at Point Pleasant.[60]

Lord Dunmore's War ended on October 27, 1774, with the interim Treaty of Camp Charlotte between the Shawanese and Virginians. The terms of the treaty included Shawanese commitments that they would return stolen slaves and property and would no longer hunt or visit the south side of the Ohio River or molest boat traffic. Virginia committed that whites would not hunt on the north side of the river. Both parties agreed to meet in Pittsburgh the following spring to negotiate a final treaty.[61] Four Shawanese hostages were given to the Virginians to secure the peace: Cornstalk's son Biaseka (the Wolf), Chenusaw (the Judge), Cuttenwa (Cuttemwha), and Newa (Newau).

Many of the Mingo and the Shawanese chiefs and warriors of the Chalaakaatha, Piqua, and Kispoko divisions did not support the relinquishment of their Kentucky hunting grounds in the treaty. Kispoko War Chief Captain Snake, Chalaakaatha War Chief Black Fish, Chief White Bark of the Piqua division, and Mingo Chief Logan were foremost among the leaders of the dissenters.

Lord Dunmore summoned Chief Logan to the encampment in an effort to bring the Mingo Nation into the Camp Charlotte Treaty negotiations. They met under a large elm tree. Chief Logan replied as follows:

> I appeal to any white man to say if ever he entered Logan's cabin hungry and he gave him not meat; if ever he came cold and naked and he clothed him not? During the course of the last long and bloody war, Logan remained idle in his camp, an advocate for peace. Such was my love for the whites that my countrymen pointed as I passed and said, 'Logan is the friend of the white man.' I had even thought to have lived with you, but for the injuries of one man . . . , the last spring, in cold blood and unprovoked, murdered all of the relations of Logan, not even sparing my women and children. There runs not a drop of my blood in the veins of any living creature. This called on me for revenge. I have sought it. I have killed many. I have fully glutted my vengeance. For my country I rejoice at the beams of peace; but don't harbor a thought that mine is the joy of fear. Logan never felt fear. He will not turn on his heel to save his life. Who is there to mourn for Logan? Not one![62]

Colonel William Crawford was dispatched with 250 soldiers to attack Mingo Chief Pluggy's Town. Crawford's forces killed five Mingo, captured fourteen, and burned the town. Chief Pluggy had been an ally of the British up to this point and had supported Lord Dunmore in the council at Fort Pitt in September. The governor's betrayal filled him with hatred and drove him into the arms of the militants.[63]

Colonel Lewis and his forces returned to Point Pleasant where they paused to complete the construction of the fortification there. They named it Fort Blair, and it was later renamed Fort Randolph. Captain Russell was placed in command of the garrison stationed at the fort.[64]

The gritty, hunting shirt-clad Virginia frontiersmen had undergone a fundamental transformation during the Battle of Point Pleasant. They had fought the battle-tested warriors of the Shawanese Nation to a standstill and had demonstrated that they were now a military force to be reckoned with. The news of Long Knife soldiers on the march would ever after spread terror through the Ohio Indian nations.

Lord Dunmore had also proven his mettle in the American wilderness. The Freeholders of Fincastle County presented him with an address on April 8, 1775, that expressed their heartfelt gratitude.[65] The Royal Government and the colonies of Pennsylvania and New York were less enchanted with Lord Dunmore's actions and severely chastised him.

Larger events would soon overtake the escalating conflicts among the northwestern Indian nations and Virginia on the western frontier. The political decisions made over the next three years would weigh heavily on the ultimate fates of the Shawanese Nation and the Virginians.

Three
The Wilderness Road

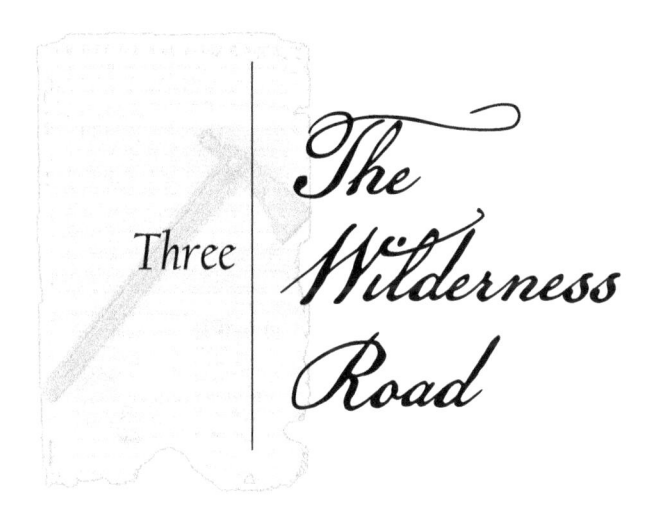

Kentucky and the Transylvania Company Venture

FOURTEEN-YEAR OLD MICAJAH CALLAWAY EAGERLY PREPARED TO go deer hunting with his twenty-six-year-old brother Flanders in rural Bedford County, Virginia, on a cold and wintry day in late January of 1775.[1] Flanders had been exceptionally busy lately, and several months had passed since their last hunting trip together.

Micajah hastily pulled on his oznaburg hunting breeches and leggings in the family cabin as Flanders waited outside.[2] He thrust his arms through the sleeves of his brown fringed hunting shirt, tied a sash around his waist, and jammed his tomahawk and hunting knife into the sash. He pulled a buckskin overcoat over the shirt, put on his round-brimmed farmer's hat, picked up his late father's long rifle, and ran out the door to join Flanders.[3]

Micajah and Flanders set off into the forest. After they had trekked for a couple of miles along the base of Fleming Mountain, they paused for a brief rest.

Flanders addressed Micajah by his nickname "Cagey."[4] After some small talk about the weather and the game sign along the trail, Flanders told Micajah that their Uncle Richard had learned about an opportunity to obtain land and settle in Kentucky. Flanders had decided to move there with his uncle and was in the process of selling his nearby Ivy Creek property.

Micajah was caught by surprise and paused as a wave of conflicting thoughts and emotions passed through him. He choked back his feelings and asked if he could go with Flanders, but Flanders declined. Micajah was too young, and their mother still needed his help at home. Micajah was deeply disappointed.

JAMES C. CALLAWAY, THE LATE FATHER OF FLANDERS and Micajah, was the youngest of six brothers who had settled and helped found Bedford County and Halifax County, Virginia, on the eastern flanks of the Blue Ridge Mountains in the early 1740s. Thomas, William, Francis, John, Richard, and James were sons of English immigrant Joseph Callaway, Jr.[5]

Five of the brothers had served in the Virginia militia during the French and Indian War. Colonel William Callaway served as the County Lieutenant for Bedford County in the late 1750s, had founded the frontier trading community of New London in Bedford County and represented the county in the Virginia House of Burgesses.[6] William's younger brother Richard Callaway was commissioned as a field colonel in command of the Bedford County militia.[7] Francis Callaway served as a lieutenant, and Micajah's father James served as a private.

Oldest brother Thomas Callaway had served as captain of the Halifax County militia company based at Fort Trial during the French and Indian War. He was acclaimed for his courageous and dogged pursuit of the French, Shawanese, and Miami war party led by French Captains Francois-Marie Picot de Belestre and Jacques Duperon Bâby that attacked and destroyed Fort Vause in June of 1756.[8]

James had married Sarah Bramlett Callaway sometime before 1748.[9] He purchased a two-hundred-acre parcel of land in May of 1751 along Ivy Creek near the foot of Fleming Mountain, not far from present-day Lynchburg, Virginia, and developed the property into a modest tobacco plantation.[10] There James and Sarah raised a family of ten children in their humble log cabin: Flanders, Dudley, Elizabeth, John, Chesley, James Jr., Micajah, Edmund, William, and Mary (Polly).[11]

James died suddenly from a "fever" in 1767 and his surviving family was reduced to poverty.[12] Sarah fought to retain possession of and manage the family plantation while raising the ten children on her own. James's older brother Richard lived nearby and helped her in her struggle. Richard mentored her oldest son Flanders on matters of business, finance, and law.[13]

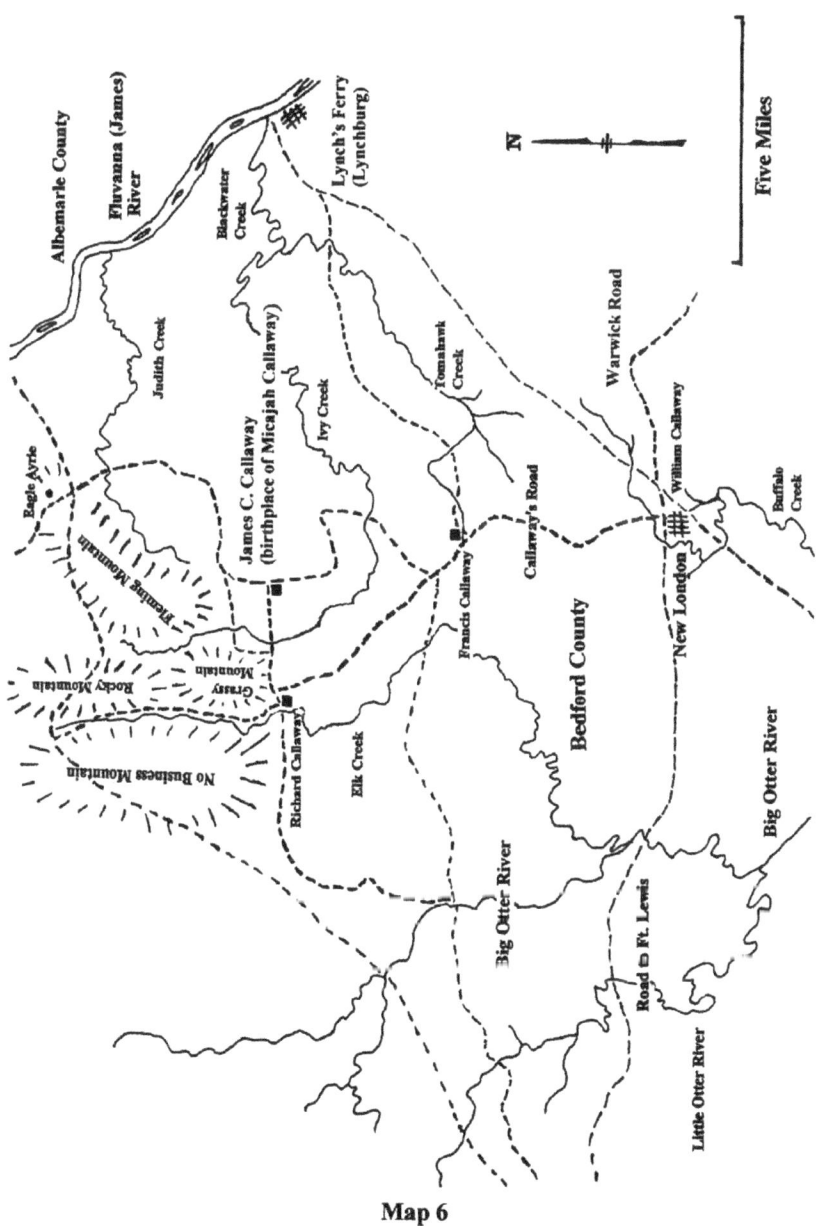

Map 6
Bedford County and the Callaway Brothers in the 1750s

Flanders Callaway was a master woodsman, marksman, and hunter. He was described in later years by his father-in-law Daniel Boone: "Colonel Boone used to say that Flanders Callaway was the best shot he ever knew in an excitement, or in an Indian fight—he was so cool & collected. He was under medium size, swarthy, & had a singularly black keen eye. He was a tall, spare, thin-visaged, and swarthy man."[14]

Flanders had taken young Micajah under his wing when their father died and was a father figure to Micajah as well as a brother. He began to take Micajah on hunting trips when he was a child and instructed him in the use and care of the long rifle, and young Micajah had shown an uncanny gift for tracking, stalking, and marksmanship.[15]

A severe recession gripped the economies of Great Britain's North American colonies in the early 1770s as a consequence of the boycotts, embargoes, and blockades in the escalating conflict between the American colonists and the Royal Government. The Scottish creditors of sixty-two-year-old Thomas Callaway and fifty-seven-year-old Richard Callaway pressed the brothers for accelerated repayment of loans that they had secured with their properties. The creditors threatened to foreclose on the loans.[16]

Thomas Callaway stoically faced the daunting prospect of finding a new means to support himself and his family at a late stage of his life. He sold his real estate investments in Halifax County and Pittsylvania County, Virginia to pay off his creditors, and used his remaining funds to purchase a tract of land in North Carolina on a branch of the Yadkin River not far from Daniel Boone's former home. He moved his family to a new homestead there in May of 1774.[17]

As Thomas settled into his new home, he learned that Judge Richard Henderson and other North Carolina investors had pooled their resources to form a real estate investment and development corporation named the Transylvania Company. They planned to establish a new proprietary colony in Kentucky to be named "Transylvania."[18]

The Cherokee Nation claimed the Kentucky lands lying south of the Kentucky River. Judge Henderson and the Transylvania Company planned to negotiate with the Cherokee Nation for conveyance of a vast tract of Kentucky land south of the river. The final negotiations were to be conducted at Sycamore Shoals, on the Watauga River in northwestern North Carolina.[19]

Richard Callaway's financial troubles had also mounted throughout

The Wilderness Road

1774 and had come to a crisis in November when his Scottish creditors demanded the discharge of his debts. He was forced to sell all off his personal property and much of his real property in order to satisfy a Deed of Trust that he had granted to James Donald & Co. in June of 1773.[20] Richard teetered on the brink of financial ruin.[21]

Thomas Callaway learned of a Transylvania Company effort to procure cattle to feed the negotiators at Sycamore Shoals through his North Carolina and Cherokee trading contacts. He told Richard about the opportunity. Richard seized it and entered into a contract to supply the cattle.[22]

Flanders had listened to his Uncle Richard's description of the Transylvania Company venture with great interest. He could not resist the lure of adventure and opportunity in Kentucky and put his Ivy Creek property up for sale so he could accompany Richard. Richard's son-in-law Charles Gwatkin purchased it from him on February 3, 1775.[23]

Richard and Flanders Callaway delivered the cattle to Sycamore Shoals on the Watauga River in early March.[24] Judge Henderson invited them to participate in the company's planning meetings soon after their arrival.

The company planned to purchase the title to an extensive tract of land lying between the Kentucky River and the Cumberland River from the Cherokee Nation.[25] They also planned to build an improved road from Long Island on the Holstein River to Daniel Boone's recommended site for a fortified settlement on the south shore of the Kentucky River.

Judge Henderson hired Daniel Boone to lead and command the first Transylvania expeditionary party into Kentucky. He had known the Boone family for many years and knew that Daniel Boone was a natural leader. Boone was familiar with the Kentucky landscape as a result of his long hunting expeditions there over the prior decade.

Richard and Flanders Callaway were among the thirty men that Daniel Boone handpicked to form the expeditionary road-building party.[26] Daniel Boone's brother Squire was also among those chosen.

The company promised to give Boone a bounty of two thousand acres for his efforts. Each of the other thirty men was paid ten pounds, ten shillings, and was also promised substantial tracts of land. The trailblazers departed for Kentucky on March 10 as the negotiations with the Cherokee neared completion.

Judge Henderson continued to negotiate with the Cherokee chiefs after Boone's party departed for Kentucky. He promised to give the chiefs the keys to a house full of trade goods if they would sign the deeds that the company had drafted.

Young War Chief Dragging Canoe (Chincanacina) became upset during the negotiations, stormed out of the conference, and did not return. Some said that he was angered by the company's refusal to request conveyance of lands to the north of the Kentucky River because of Virginia's claims. Others said that Dragging Canoe was angered because the white men were requesting too large a portion of the Cherokee hunting grounds.[27]

The Cherokee chiefs signed deeds on March 17, 1775, for the conveyance of two hundred thousand acres of land located between the Kentucky River and Cumberland River to the Transylvania Company.[28]

After their departure, Daniel Boone and the trail-blazers proceeded from Sycamore Shoals to Long Island on the Holston River and began work on an improved road. It became known as the Wilderness Road to most of those who followed in their footsteps.

They first undertook to improve a local trace from Long Island north to Mocassin Gap, the gateway to the mountains of southwest Virginia.[29] The trailblazers progressed across southwest Virginia into the Powell River Valley in the Cumberland Mountains, where they picked up additional provisions at Martin's Station. They worked their way west from there through the Cumberland Gap to the Cumberland River, crossed the river and proceeded onward for eight more miles to Big Flat Lick.

Big Flat Lick was a dangerous place, since it was the traditional campsite of the warriors who traveled the Shawanese Athiawiomee ("path of the armed ones").[30] Passing war parties had carved and painted striking totems and symbols on the trees there.

The road crew had followed well-established Indian and buffalo traces up to this point. There were only the faintest of traces for much of the remaining distance. They cut their way on to the Hazel Patch following the course of a faint old buffalo trace used by the Long Hunters and Indian hunters. The trace divided there.[31]

Daniel Boone and his crew took the northern branch, which later became known as Boone's Trace. They proceeded north from the Hazel Patch to the gap at Big Hill which had an expansive view of the rolling plains of Kentucky to the north. They then continued along a faint buffalo trace down through canebrakes and meadows toward the banks of the Kentucky River.

Daniel Boone had selected a bench of meadowland in the floodplain on the south shore of the river as the ideal location for the settlement. It was located approximately twelve miles downstream of the mouth of the Red River and fifteen miles to the southwest of the former site of the Shawanese town Eskippakithiki on the Athiamiowee path.

The party of woodsmen arrived at their destination on the south bank of the Kentucky River on April 1, 1775. They startled a herd of two or three hundred buffalo in the meadows as they descended the final hill down to the river bank.[32] There they established a temporary camp on a level clearing not far to the southwest of a freshwater spring in Sycamore Hollow called Lick Spring.[33]

Judge Henderson decided to construct the permanent fort at a site on the eastern end of an elevated bench of open meadowland between the Kentucky River and the Sycamore Hollow on the south side of river. The site was about a mile and a quarter downstream from the mouth of Otter Creek, and the towering cliffs of the Kentucky River Gorge loomed above it on the northern shore of the river.

The stockade was to be constructed of heavy timbers set deep into the ground and would be 240 feet long and 180 feet wide. The main gate would be on the south side of the fort facing away from the river. Two-story blockhouses would be erected on the four corners and cabins would face inward along the walls. The new fortified community was named Fort Boonesborough in honor of the leader of the expedition. Construction of the fort began immediately.[34]

Richard Callaway's rivalry with Daniel Boone for the leadership of Fort Boonesborough began when Judge Henderson arrived at the fort and treated Richard as one of the leaders of the new community.[35] Judge Henderson surveyed nineteen town lots with the assistance of "Captain Boone and Colonel Callaway" four days following his arrival. They agreed that a large cabin would be constructed in the central courtyard of the fort facing the gate for Richard and his family, and that Squire Boone's smithy would be located next to it.[36]

Richard was selected to serve as a delegate to the first Transylvania

Company convention on May 20, 1775, along with Boone, Henderson, Moore, and Cocke. The first organic laws of the new proprietary colony were proposed and enacted on May 23, 1775.[37]

Richard Callaway returned to the eastern Virginia settlements and rode triumphantly into Bedford County with a small party in early July of 1775.[38] He was delighted to learn that his wife Elizabeth had given birth to another son during his absence. The baby boy was named John and nicknamed "Jacky."[39]

Richard paid a brief visit to Flanders's mother Sarah and reassured her that Flanders was in good health. He went on to describe the beautiful Kentucky Country. Cornfields had been cleared and planted by the newly arrived pioneers, and the fertility of the land astounded them as the corn grew rapidly in the muggy summer heat.

Buffalo and other wild game abounded at the nearby salt licks and canebrakes. Simon Kenton had counted over 1100 buffalo walking in single file toward the Lower Blue Licks to the northeast.[40]

There were other forts and stations that had been established in 1775, and more were planned.[41] Harrodsburg was re-occupied by James Harrod and several other men and their families in March of 1775. Another little settlement was established at Boiling Springs, about six miles southeast of Harrodsburg. Saint Asaph was founded along Skagg's Trace near the Dick's River by Captain John Floyd on May 1, 1775. A militia captain from the Holston River settlements named Benjamin Logan assumed the leadership role at Saint Asaph, and it came to be known as Logan's Fort.[42] John Hinkston and his family and friends built a blockhouse on the north shore of the South Fork of the Licking River that summer. Their settlement was known as Hinkston's Station.[43] John McClelland and his family and friends from Westmoreland County, Pennsylvania, founded McClelland's Station in October of '75, and built their settlement at the Royal Springs near where the Alanant-O-Wamiowee and Dry Ridge Trail intersected on the North Branch of the Elkhorn River.[44]

Richard Callaway was full of optimism about the future of Kentucky and had decided to move his family there. They would be among the first families to settle in Kentucky. He persuaded other Bedford County families to join them in the move west.

The Wilderness Road

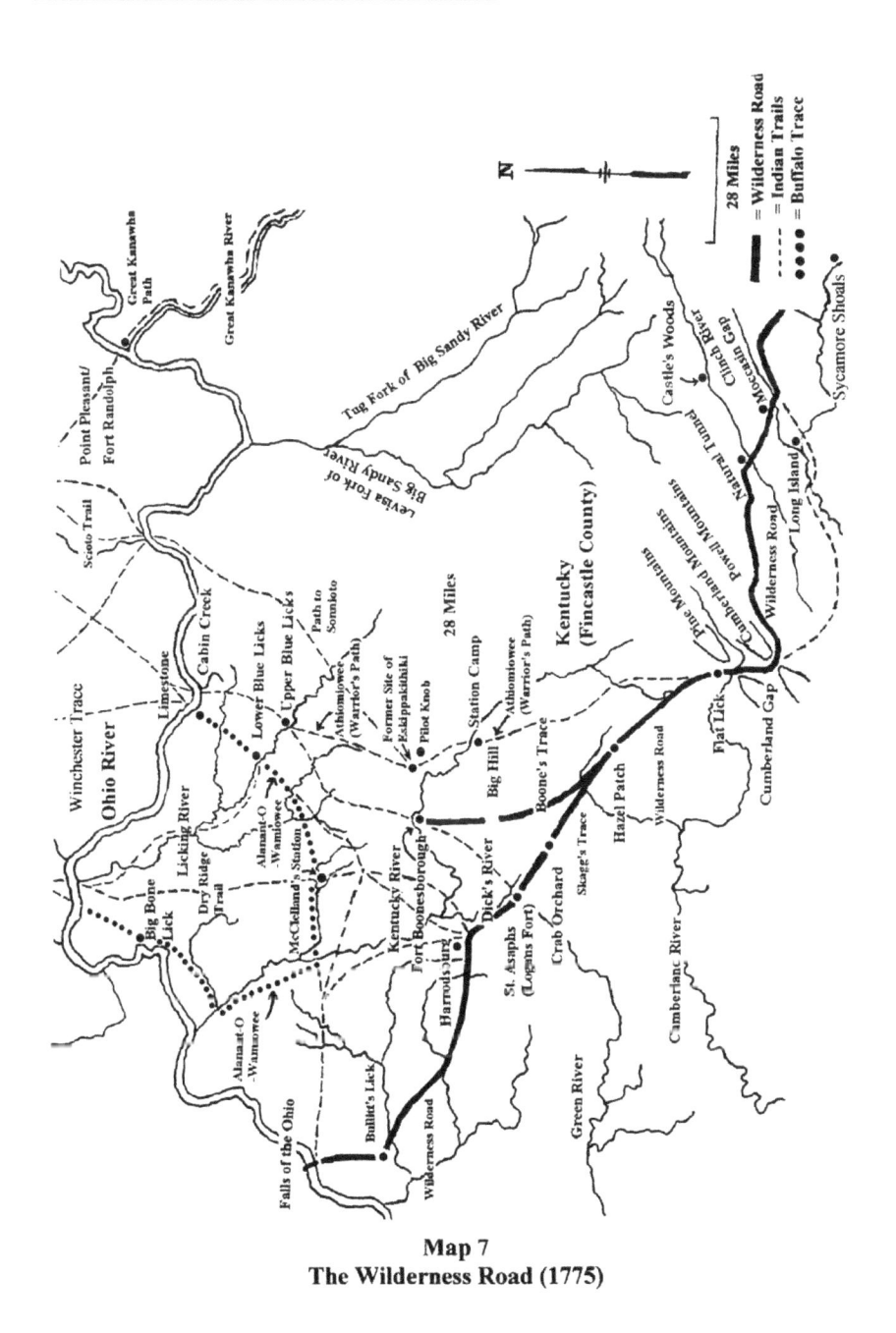

Map 7
The Wilderness Road (1775)

After closing out his affairs in Bedford County, he and his family departed for Kentucky. They transported all of their earthly possessions on their horses and wagons, and were accompanied by the Pogues and several other families. Along the way they encountered a small hunting party of Cherokee warriors and shared a peaceful venison dinner with them.[45]

Flanders greeted Richard on Boone's Trace one day's journey from the fort and escorted him for the final stage of their trek. They arrived safely at Fort Boonesborough on September 25, 1775, and some forty or fifty sorely needed new settlers were thus added to the struggling community. A half-dozen cabins were completed and two sides of the fort were constructed by the time of their arrival. Work had also begun on Richard's large cabin in the central courtyard.[46]

"A Bad Wind has Blown Up!"

THE POLITICAL RELATIONSHIP BETWEEN GREAT BRITAIN AND its American colonies deteriorated as the Kentucky pioneers established their new settlements in the wilderness. New England militia forces engaged British regular troops in the Battles of Lexington and Concord on April 18, 1775. The New England revolutionaries pressed for help from their American brothers and sisters in Virginia.

The Shawanese Nation was at a critical point in their own history after their bitter defeat in Lord Dunmore's War. They abandoned their settlements in the Muskingum River valley and temporarily concentrated their population in the Scioto River valley in 1775 following their defeat.

Over the course of the period from 1775 through 1777 they began to relocate from there to new town sites farther west and closer to their treasured hunting grounds in Kentucky. The new Shawanese towns were located on the tributaries of the Greater Miami River and Little Miami River just to the southwest of the Wyandot villages of central Ohio.[47]

The capital town of the Shawanese Nation was relocated to the Mad River, a tributary of the Greater Miami River, in 1777.[48] It was called "Wakatomica" and "Upper Shawneetown" by the British but was also known by the name "Wapatomica."[49] The new Kispoko Town, later called

The Wilderness Road

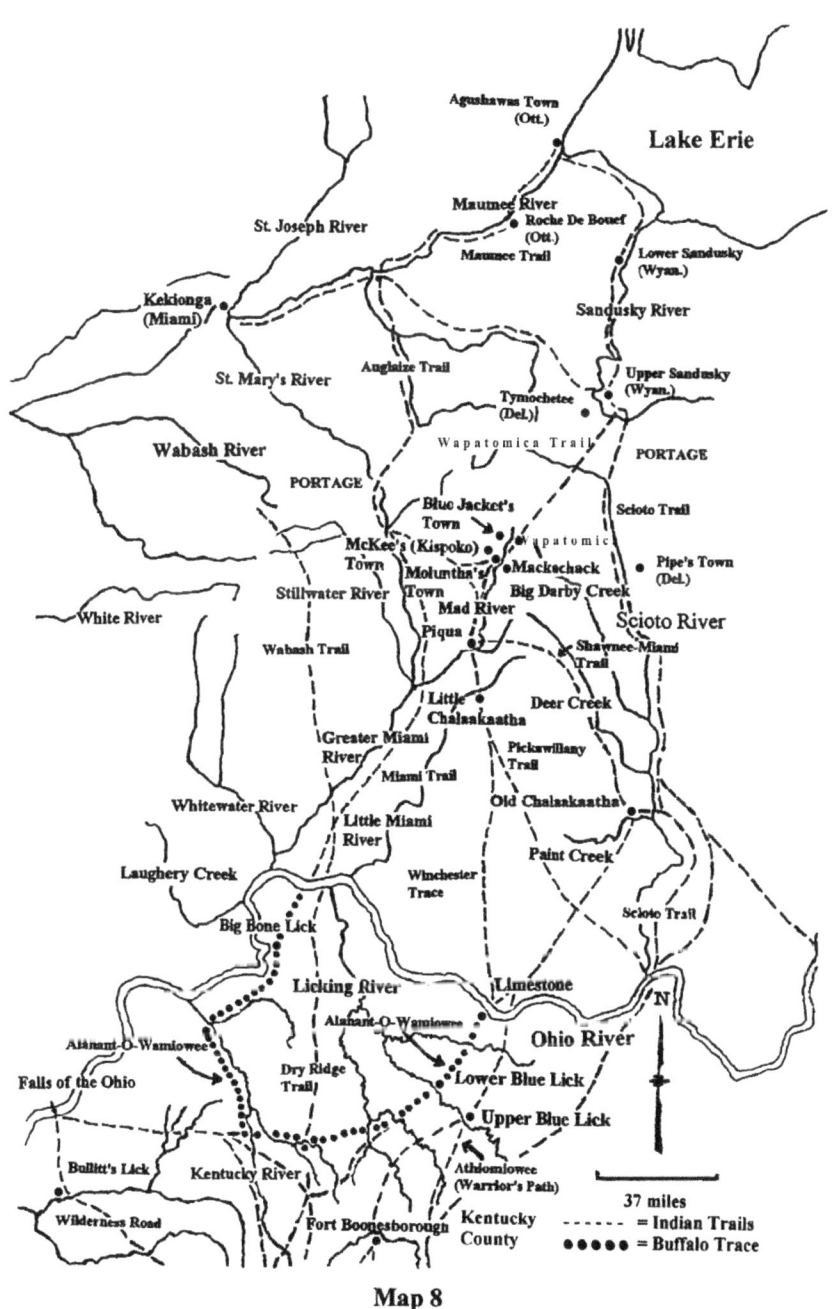

Map 8
Shawanese Towns of Ohio in 1776

McKee's Town, was relocated about two miles to the north and four miles to the west of Wapatomica.[50] Blue Jacket's Town was relocated to a site two and a half miles northeast of the new Kispoko Town.[51]

Chalaakaatha was relocated to a site at the juncture of Massie's Creek and the Little Miami River and was often distinguished from its former location on Paint Creek by calling it "Little Chalaakaatha."[52] French trader Pierre-Louis de Lorimier ("Louis Lorimier") established a branch trading post there. His main post, "Loramie's Store," was located on Loramie Creek near old Pickawillany on the portage between the Maumee and Great Miami Rivers.[53]

Piqua was relocated to a site on the Mad River twelve miles to the northeast of Little Chalaakaatha and several miles downstream from Wapatomica.[54] Captain Will established a small town named Willstown five or six miles to the northwest of Little Chalaakaatha.[55]

Chief Cornstalk made a concerted effort to comply with the Treaty at Camp Charlotte and "brighten the chain of friendship" with the Long Knives. He visited Captain Russell at Fort Randolph on June 4, 1775, and told him that he had heard of the battles of Concord and Lexington, and asked for an explanation of the significance of those events.

BRITISH GENERAL GAGE ESTABLISHED INTERIOR BRITISH POSTS under the command of Sir Guy Carleton in March of 1775. He issued orders to Sir Carleton and Indian Superintendent Guy Johnson to collaborate in courting the Indian nations as potential military allies. A band of Mohawk warriors arrived at Johnson's Guy Park estate in early May and called upon their allies in the Six Nations to join them there.[56]

The American revolutionaries did not have the financial resources to match a concerted British effort to foster military alliances with the Indian nations, so they moved quickly to obtain commitments to neutrality before the British could exert their full influence.

The Virginia House of Burgesses passed a resolution on June 24, 1775, appointing six commissioners for the upcoming treaty negotiations with the northwestern nations in Fort Dunmore. The Virginia revolutionaries planned to substitute themselves for the administration of Lord Dunmore that had initially called for those negotiations. This resolution was the last act of the old colonial House of Burgesses before its final dissolution.

The revolutionary government of Virginia dispatched a company of one hundred soldiers to take possession of Fort Dunmore. They restored the fort's old name, "Fort Pitt."[57]

Captain James Wood Jr. was appointed to serve as Virginia's emissary to the northwestern Indian nations. He visited nearly every Indian town to invite its leaders to the impending treaty conference at Fort Pitt.

Captain Wood met with Shawanese Chiefs Kishenosity, Shade, Snake, Milkman, and Shawanese Ben on August 2, 1775. The chiefs complained about the new Kentucky settlements and the encroachments of white hunters to the north of the Ohio River.[58]

Wood learned that British Captain Lernault and Msr. Jacques Duperon Bâby had warned the Wyandot and Delaware to be on guard against attacks by Virginians. Msr. Bâby reportedly presented them with a belt and string of black wampum and told them that the French king was willing to help King George III protect their land from the Long Knife encroachers.[59] He advised them not to attend the treaty negotiations at Fort Pitt and to avoid alliances with the doomed American rebels.

Captain Wood returned to Fort Dunmore on August 11. He reported to the Second Continental Congress that he had discovered that the British had been conniving to turn the northwestern Indian nations against the Americans.

The First Treaty of Fort Pitt (1775)

THE CONTINENTAL CONGRESS CREATED THREE INDIAN DEPARTMENTS on July 12, 1775. A Middle Department was established at Fort Pitt and given jurisdiction over the lands to the west of the Appalachian Mountains. Richard Butler, the former Pennsylvania Indian trader, was appointed to serve as the American Indian agent for the Middle Department.

Richard Butler began his new duties as Indian agent on August 22, 1775, and set out on his own journey to visit every important town and influential chief in the Ohio country on behalf of the Continental Congress. He covered much of the same ground as Captain Wood, although Butler represented the Continental Congress while Wood represented Virginia.[60]

Butler met with two Mingo scouts in Pluggy's Town who had spoken with Long Knife hunters in Kentucky. The Long Knives had told them that three strong new forts had been built in Kentucky and would soon be fully garrisoned. The hunters also told the Mingo that the Long Knives planned to cross the Ohio River to settle in the Ohio Country after they had first fortified and settled Kentucky.

The reports from the Mingo scouts were widely disseminated among the northwestern Indian nations and created widespread panic. Butler did his best to reassure them that the Long Knives had no intention to settle north of the Ohio.

Butler rode on to the Shawanese towns and arrived late in the day on September 9. The Makujay Shawanese leadership assembled and met with him in council on the following day. Senior Makujay women attended the council. The Makujay valued the wisdom of their women in diplomatic matters because "Some women were wiser than some men."[61] Butler repeated the American invitation to attend the treaty negotiations at Fort Pitt, and the chiefs promised to attend the conference.

Butler received a message from a head woman of the Makujay division on the morning of September 12 inviting him to visit her alone in her house. It is very likely that this was Cornstalk's sister Coitcheleh, who was generally sympathetic to the Americans.[62] She warned Butler that the Chalaakaatha and Piqua Shawanese divisions had been heavily influenced by anti-American Wyandot and Mingo leaders, and advised that they could not be trusted.[63]

The Makujay Shawanese delegates began to arrive at Fort Pitt on September 26. Representatives of the Six Nations (including the Mingo faction) and the Shawanese, Wyandot, Delaware, and Ottawa Nations had arrived by October 7.

Many speeches were made by the Indians and the Americans. Cornstalk impressed a Virginia officer with his presence and eloquence:

> When he arose he ... spoke in a distinct and audible voice without stammering or repetition and with peculiar emphasis. His looks ... were truly grand and

majestic; yet graceful and attractive. I have heard the first orators in Virginia, Patrick Henry and Richard Henry Lee, but never have I heard one whose powers of delivery surpassed those of Cornstalk.[64]

Cornstalk pleaded for peace and understanding, with these words:

> Brothers, I imagined all Matters were settled last fall and that we were as one People. I now find that there is a bad Wind Blown up. I know not from whence it has Arisen but I desire the White People will search into it. I hope they will not let that Interrupt the Good work that we are now about. If we are Strong and finish the good work we have begun our Children now Growing up will live in peace but if we regard what wicked and foolish People do it may be an impediment to our living in friendship.[65]

The Americans presented the Shawanese with a road belt showing the open road of peace between them and a large friendship belt showing the Shawanese council fire and the thirteen council fires (the Thirteen Fires) of the United Colonies together.[66]

The Treaty of Fort Pitt of 1775 was concluded on October 19, 1775.[67] It reaffirmed the Ohio River as the boundary between Virginia and the Indian country as provided in the 1768 Treaty of Fort Stanwix. The Shawanese leaders promised to remain neutral in the war between the American Continental Congress and Great Britain.

Richard Butler had done his job well. The Americans had successfully co-opted and completed the negotiations begun by Lord Dunmore and achieved a result favorable to their revolutionary cause. The British faced the daunting challenge of reversing the Americans' clever diplomatic success at Fort Pitt.

Unfortunately, the Treaty at Fort Pitt of 1775 did not bring peace to Kentucky. Mingo warriors commanded by Chiefs Conneodico, Stone, and Pluggy unleashed a series of murderous raids in Kentucky with the support of militant Chalaakaatha and Piqua Shawanese warriors.

The Kentucky settlements were deeply shaken by the raids. Simon Kenton abandoned his camp near the Limestone Crossing of the Ohio River and took refuge at Hinkston's Station. John Hinkston in turn abandoned Hinkston Station, and Kenton joined John McClelland at McClelland's Station.[68] The Makujay Shawanese continued to strive for peace with the Americans. Cornstalk blamed the Kentucky raids on the Mingo and a few foolish young Shawanese warriors.

Four | *Revolution*

Lieutenant Governor Henry Hamilton and Detroit

COLONEL HENRY HAMILTON, THE NEW LIEUTENANT GOVERNOR of the British Province of Quebec, arrived at the British military post at Fort Detroit on November 9, 1775.[1] Hamilton had been directed to upgrade and strengthen the fort in anticipation of expansion of the war with the American colonies.

Fort Detroit had been established by the French in 1701 at a strategic position on the Detroit River which connected Lake Huron and Lake Erie. The community that had grown up around the fort was now a prosperous settlement of fifteen hundred residents and stretched some thirteen miles along the Detroit River.

Upon his arrival, Colonel Hamilton immediately set about rebuilding the fortifications, bolstering the lines of supply, and increasing the size of the garrison. The restored fort was defended by eighty cannon and a moat eighteen feet wide and twelve feet deep.

Superintendent Guy Johnson had relocated the British Northern Indian Department from Fort Pitt to Detroit when the Americans assumed control of Fort Pitt in June of 1775. Lieutenant Governor Hamilton was directed to work closely with the British Indian Department.

The British at Fort Niagara sent a letter to Alexander McKee at Fort Pitt in February of 1776, inviting him to attend an important council at Fort Niagara. The British requested that McKee brief them there on what he knew about the "rebels." Richard Butler and the Americans at Fort Pitt learned about the invitation from a spy. The West Augusta Committee of Safety gathered at McKee's house and demanded that he post parole in the form of a promise not to flee to Canada.[2]

George Morgan and the Shawanese Peace Faction

RICHARD BUTLER RESIGNED HIS COMMISSION AS INDIAN Agent for the Middle Department on April 10, 1776, and was replaced by George Morgan. Morgan was a former Pennsylvania Indian trader and had served as the secretary and agent for the Indiana Company for several years. He was particularly beloved by the Makujay Shawanese, who gave him the name Weepemachukthe ("White Deer").[3]

Morgan began his term while a major British treaty conference with the northwestern Indian nations was underway in Niagara. There was increasing concern among them about the ominous new Kentucky settlements, and British trade goods were seducing them to the British interest. Morgan concluded that the Americans were rapidly losing ground to the British in the courtship of the northwestern Indian nations.

George Morgan sent a message to the Shawanese leadership on May 31, 1776, inviting them to another treaty conference at Fort Pitt to reaffirm the 1775 treaty. He met in council with the senior Shawanese, Delaware, and Mingo leadership of the Ohio Confederacy in Kispoko Town beginning on June 19. With Chief Cornstalk's help, Morgan succeeded in obtaining commitments from the leading Shawanese, Delaware, and Mingo chiefs of the Ohio Confederacy to attend his treaty conference.

Cornstalk also offered to help persuade the powerful Wyandot Nation and their confederacy to join with them:

> "But Brothers as you have ask'd our advice & assistance in this good work & as we are sincere in it we recommend you to keep your Eye on our Elder Brothers the Wyandots who are in strict Friendship with fourteen different Western Nations, and have more influence

Revolution

> than we have ... Therefore we will accompany your Messengers & deliver all your Wampum to them & will join our interests with theirs to promote the good work you have desired your peace Belt shall pass through all Nations—Our Grandfathers the [Lenape] Delawares who have come with you & our Brothers of the Six Nations settled among us, promise to be strong & join us in promoting this good Friendship."[4]

The Shawanese War Faction

CORNSTALK'S EFFORTS TO PRESERVE SHAWANESE NEUTRALITY WERE undermined by members of his own nation. A delegation of militant "northern Indians" comprised of fifteen individuals representing the Mingo, Shawanese, Ottawa, Nanticoke, and Delaware Nations arrived at the Overhill Cherokee capital of Chote in mid-June of 1776. The delegation requested permission to present a grand "talk" to the assembled Cherokee council.[5]

The northern delegation was reportedly headed by a Mohawk man, most likely Mingo Chief Pluggy. Pluggy was conspicuously absent from George Morgan's conference with the Mingo chiefs in Kispoko Town earlier in June. The timing of the northern delegation's arrival in Chote is consistent with Mingo Chief Logan's warning to George Morgan on June 20: "I must tell you three or four foolish people are gone off privately to the Big (Ohio) River, we suppose on bad intentions."[6]

The Cherokee council was held in Chote in late June or early July of 1776. The northern Indians directed their "talk" to the militant young Cherokee War Chief Dragging Canoe (Chincanacina). Deputy Superintendent Henry Stuart of the British Southern Indian Department described the senior Shawanese spokesperson in the northern delegation as a "noted French partisan."[7] The Shawanese spokesman

> ... produced a War Belt about 9 feet long and six inches wide of purple Whampum strewed over with vermilion. He began with pathetically enumerating the dis-

tresses of his own and other Nations. He complained particularly of the Virginians who after having taken away all their Lands and cruelly and treacherously treated some of their people, had unjustly brought war upon their Nation and destroyed many of their people; that in a very few years their Nation from being a great people were now reduced to a handful; that their Nation possessed Lands almost to the Sea Shore and that the red people who were once Masters of the whole Country hardly possessed ground enough to stand on; that the Lands where but lately they hunted close to their Nations were thickly inhabited and covered with Forts & armed men; that wherever a Fort appeared in their neighbourhood, they might depend there would soon be Towns and Settlements; that it was plain, there was an intention to extirpate them, and that he thought it better to die like men than to diminish away by inches; That their Fathers the French who seemed long dead were now alive again; that they had supplied them plentifully with ammunition, arms and provisions and that they promised to assist them against the Virginians; that their cause was just and that they hoped the Great Being who governs everything would favour their cause; ... The Belt was received by Chincanacina ... [8]

A number of Cherokee warriors accompanied the northern Indians on their departure from Chote a few days before July 8. Jarett Williams reported in a deposition " . . . that they all planned to strike the settlers in Kentucky."[9] It appears that neither George Morgan nor Henry Stuart sent timely warnings to Fort Boonesborough.

Daniel Boone to the Rescue

DANIEL BOONE'S DAUGHTER JEMIMA AND RICHARD CALLAWAY'S daughters Fanny and Betsy had grown tired of their confinement in Fort

Boonesborough. The restless teenage girls decided to take a canoe ride and pick wildflowers along the Kentucky River on the afternoon of Sunday, July 7, 1776. As the girls slowly drifted and paddled down the river, they approached the opposite shore. An Indian warrior suddenly leaped from the bank with a blood-curdling war whoop and grabbed the front of the canoe. The girls screamed. Four other warriors joined the first, dragged the canoe to shore, and captured the three girls.

The war party consisted of two Cherokee and three Shawanese warriors on the return journey from the "talk" in Chote.[10] One of the Cherokee warriors was Hanging Maw, who knew Daniel and Jemima from North Carolina.[11] One of the Shawanese warriors was the son of War Chief Black Fish (Chiungalla).

Richard Callaway's young son Caleb was outside the fort. After hearing the girls scream, he ran toward the fort calling for help. He found Nathaniel Reed and Captain John Floyd standing under the "Divine Elm" tree used as a public meeting place near the southern gates of the fort. They all ran together into the fort and discovered Richard already loading and priming his rifle. A pursuit party quickly formed and crossed over the river to pick up the trail of the Indians and girls.

The pursuit party included Richard and Flanders Callaway, Daniel Boone, John Floyd, John Holder, Samuel Henderson, Nathaniel Reed, Richard Wade, Jesse Hodges, William Buchanan, Thomas Brooks, and Nathaniel Bullock.[12] They met at the top of the banks on the north shore of the river to plan the pursuit.

Daniel Boone directed that the men divide into two parties so that they would be more certain to pick up the trail quickly. He believed that the war party would eventually head for the Athiawiomee and the Ohio towns. Daniel would lead a party on foot to directly pursue the warriors and intercept them before they reached the Athiawiomee. Flanders, who had fallen in love with Jemima, joined Daniel Boone's party. A second party of horsemen under Richard Callaway's command would ride to intercept the Indians farther up the Athiawiomee in case Boone's party could not catch up with them.

The girls left a deliberate trail as they were carried along by their captors, twisting their heels in the mud, leaving bits of cloth, and breaking twigs. Daniel circled the canebrake into which the Indians had first disappeared and picked up their trail. His party pursued the warriors and their prisoners for two days. They raced up the Hunter's Trace past Grassy Lick and across both the Stoner Fork and the Hinkston Fork of the Licking River. Then they left the main trace and cut through the forest toward the Upper Blue Lick and the Athiawiomee.

The pursuers caught up with the war party near Bald Eagle Creek, midway between the Hinkston Fork and the Upper Blue Licks. Daniel knew that they were getting close to the warriors because of the muddy water at the Bald Eagle Creek crossing. The rescuers checked and primed their rifles and crept forward silently from that point onward.

The Indian party was spotted through the trees in a small clearing near a canebrake several yards ahead. The warriors were eating and napping around a campfire. The girls were sitting together, huddled on a log. The two younger girls were crying with their heads cradled in Betsy's lap.

Daniel motioned to Flanders to stay calm, fearing that the young lover would do something rash to rescue his sweetheart. Daniel crept forward on his belly with his rifle cradled in his arms. Jemima saw him and their eyes locked. Daniel motioned for her to be quiet. She later said that he looked like a snake crawling on his belly.

One of the other men prematurely fired the first shot. At the sound of the report, Jemima shrieked with joy, "That's Daddy's gun!"

The rest of the men fired in a barrage. Flanders shot at Chief Black Fish's son as he squatted by the fire. He fell backward and crawled into the canebrake. Fanny later said that she saw blood burst from his chest before she heard the sound of the shot.

Daniel yelled to the girls to lie down so that they would not be hit by the gunfire. Jemima and Fanny did so, but Betsy was hysterical and remained standing. She was nearly brained when a warrior swung his war club at her head as he ran past her toward the canebrake, but he missed.

The surviving warriors disappeared into the canebrake without firing a single shot themselves. The son of Chief Black Fish was dead.

The rescuers could see that that the girls had not been seriously harmed. They continued on toward the Athiawiomee and met up with Richard Callaway's party there. Never had there been a more joyous reunion. Richard threw his arms around his precious Betsy and Fanny and said, "Now, let's all sit down and have a good cry for joy!"

All three girls later married men from their rescue party. Samuel Henderson married Betsy Callaway and Captain John Holder married Fanny Callaway in the late summer of 1776. Flanders Callaway asked Daniel Boone for Jemima's hand in marriage, and he approved. Their wedding was planned for the following summer.[13]

The Cherokee Expedition

THE WARDENS OF THE ANGLICAN CHURCH IN Bedford County worked through the Bedford County Court to "bind out" impoverished Sarah Callaway's younger male children to serve as trade apprentices through legally binding court orders. The surviving children of a deceased father ("orphans") were bound out under this system until the age of twenty-one years and their guardian was obligated to provide food and clothing, teach them a trade, and teach the orphan how to read and write.[14]

Dudley Callaway was the first of Sarah's sons to be bound out, on July 26, 1770. John was bound out on July 29, 1772. Chesley was bound out to his older cousin Zachariah ("Zack") Callaway on November 28, 1774, to learn the gunsmith trade. Zack was the oldest son of Richard Callaway.

Micajah was also bound out to Zack, as an armourer's apprentice, on July 22, 1776.[15] His mother had not had time to teach him to read and write after his father died, and this was his opportunity to learn.[16]

Micajah packed his few belongings into bundles on the following day and loaded them onto two packhorses. He kissed his mother goodbye and waved to his brothers and sisters as he road off to Zack's residence. He was greeted there by Zack, Chesley, and Zack's wife Susannah.

DRAGGING CANOE LEFT THE CHEROKEE SETTLEMENTS WITH 350 Cherokee warriors and marched to attack the Long Island settlement on the Holston River. A force of 175 militia soldiers marched out from Long Island to intercept them, and battle was joined on July 20, 1776. The militia flanked the Cherokee force and drove them from the battlefield. Thirteen Cherokee dead were found on the ground, and

Dragging Canoe was wounded. The militia suffered four wounded and no deaths.[17]

Governor Patrick Henry ordered the muster of 1500 Virginia militiamen to take the offensive and march on the Overhill Cherokee Towns. The Virginia Committee of Safety directed that six companies of rangers be mustered from Fincastle, Augusta, and Botetourt County on June 23, 1776. They also directed that Micajah's cousin Captain James Callaway supply lead for the six companies from the Fort Chiswell lead mines.[18]

Zack and Chesley Callaway joined Captain Buford's company in Colonel William Christian's Botetourt County regiment just a few days after Micajah moved in with them. Zack volunteered to serve as the regimental armourer with Chesley as his assistant.[19]

As Zack and Chesley frantically packed provisions, gunsmithing tools, arms, and similar items for the expedition, Micajah asked Zack what he should do in his absence. Zack was quite distracted at the time and offhandedly suggested that Micajah help his slaves in the fields and work on the backlog of gun repair orders. He promised to begin Micajah's training when he returned.

Colonel Christian's Botetourt County regiment marched for North Carolina on July 24, 1776. Captain James Callaway was ordered on July 26, 1776, to supply the Virginia militia with two tons of lead from the Chiswell mines and deliver any remaining inventory to the North Carolina Council of Safety.[20]

Colonel Christian and his troops arrived at Fort Patrick Henry on Long Island on September 21, 1776, and joined the other Virginia and North Carolina militia forces gathering there. Sixteen hundred Long Knife soldiers set off on the 115-mile march from Fort Patrick Henry to the Overhill Cherokee Towns on October 1. They called the campaign "the Cherokee Expedition."

The Long Knife army found three thousand painted Cherokee warriors assembled to fight them on the shores of the Tellico River just above Chote. The Long Knives primed their rifles and muskets and prepared for battle. As they began their advance, the Cherokee warriors inexplicably fell back and fled into the mountains without a fight. Their towns, homes, women, and children were abandoned and left to the mercy of the Long Knives. Colonel Christian ensured that the Long Knives did not harm the women and children.

Colonel Christian met with a few of the Cherokee chiefs and obtained a preliminary peace agreement, although he was unable to assemble the Cherokee principal chiefs to negotiate a formal peace treaty. Dragging Canoe withdrew far to the southwest to establish his own new town near the mouth of the Chickamauga River on the Tennessee River.

Zack and Chesley did not return to Zack's plantation until late December, 1776, when the Cherokee Expedition was concluded.

Grand Council in Detroit

THE MAKUJAY SHAWANESE CHIEFS DUTIFULLY FOLLOWED THROUGH with their promises to George Morgan and invited the Wyandot and their confederacy to attend the treaty conference at Fort Pitt. The Wyandot convened a Grand Council in Detroit to publicly review the American invitation in the presence of their British Fathers. The Americans were summoned to Detroit to present their invitation, and Chief Cornstalk accompanied them.

Lieutenant Governor Hamilton described his response to the American invitation at the Grand Council in a September 2, 1776, letter to the Earl of Dartmouth. He explained that the spokesmen for the Americans

> ... had the insolence to bring a letter, a string, and a Belt, from the Agent for the Virginian Congress, soliciting the Confederacy of Western Indians to go to a Council in Pittsburgh. I tore their letters, and cut their Belt in presence of all the Indians and sent them off ... They had a *Pennsylvania Gazette* of the 25th of July containing a declaration of Colonies, by which they entirely throw off all Dependence on the Mother Country.[21]

The chiefs of the Six Nations and the Wyandot Confederacy nations told Hamilton at the Grand Council that they were prepared to fight on the side of their Great Father, King George III of Great Britain. Hamilton provided the king's new Indian allies with a large wampum Belt of Alliance. He promised to come to their aid if American forces ever threatened their towns and villages.

Hamilton planned to launch a military campaign against the Virginians with Great Britain's new Indian allies in the spring of 1777. The Ohio Confederacy nations were internally divided over which side to take in the imminent war. The Miami (Wabash) Confederacy remained noncommittal for the time being.

The Second Treaty of Fort Pitt (1776)

INDIANS FROM THROUGHOUT THE OHIO RIVER BASIN gathered and headed to Fort Pitt for George Morgan's treaty conference. Shawanese Makujay Chiefs Kishenosity, White Fish (Koketha), Cornstalk, Johnny, and Nimwha led a delegation of over one hundred Makujay Shawanese. The Piqua, Chalaakaatha, and Kispoko Shawanese divisions were ominously unrepresented.[22]

The treaty conference began on October 26, 1776. Six hundred forty-four Indians from the Six Nations and the Delaware, Shawanese, Munsee, and Mohican Nations attended. The Wyandot, Lake Indians (the "Three Fires" Confederacy of the Ottawa, Pottawatomie, and Chippewa nations), and most of the Mingo boycotted the conference.

Shawanese Chief Cornstalk complained to the Continental Congress about the Kentucky settlements on November 7, 1776, and pleaded for justice for his people:

> When God created this World he gave this Island to the red people & placed your younger Brethren the Shawnees here in the Center—Now we & they see your people seated on our Lands which all Nations esteem as their & our heart—all our Lands are covered by the white people, & we are jealous that you still intend to make larger strides—We never sold you our Lands which you now possess on the Ohio between the Great Kanawha and Cherokee, & which you are settling without ever asking our leave, or obtaining our consent—Foolish people have desired you to do so & you have taken their advice—We live

by Hunting & cannot subsist in any other way—That was our hunting Country & you have taken it from us. This is what sits heavy upon our Hearts & on the Hearts of all Nations, and it is impossible for us to think as we ought to do whilst we are thus oppress'd with your [blank]. Now I stretch my Arm to you my wise Brethren of the United States met in Council in Philadelphia—I open my hand & pour into your heart the cause of our discontent in hopes that you will take pity on your younger Brethren, and send us a favorable Answer, that we may be convinced of the sincerity of your profession.[23]

The second Treaty at Fort Pitt was concluded between the Americans and the northwestern nations and signed in early November, 1776. The treaty restated the terms of the treaty from the prior year.

The second Treaty of Fort Pitt no doubt helped delay a large-scale, general Indian war in the northwestern frontier. However, the leaders of the American Revolution began to accept that they had only bought time before the inevitable occurred. They anticipated that a general war with the northwestern Indian nations would begin the following spring.

Kentucky County, Virginia

A GROUP OF HARRODSBURG SETTLERS THAT HAD settled in Kentucky independently from the Transylvania Company enterprise formed a revolutionary Committee of Safety called the "Committee of West Fincastle." They drafted and signed a petition to the Virginia Convention dated June 20, 1776, that pleaded for Virginia to assert its authority over the new Transylvania settlements.[24]

George Rogers Clark and John Gabriel Jones rode to Williamsburg to deliver the petition and to make a request for gunpowder, lead, and a body of soldiers to protect the Kentucky settlements.[25] Governor Henry and the Executive Council promised on August 23, 1776, to provide five hundred pounds of gunpowder and sufficient lead and the assistance of the Virginia militia if Clark and Jones could convince the Virginia Convention to void the Transylvania Company deeds and create a new Kentucky County for Virginia.

The Virginia Convention debated the future of the Transylvania Company and Kentucky as the remaining months of 1776 passed. The legislators convened hearings to investigate and took depositions. Richard Callaway was deposed twice.[26]

The Virginia Convention voided the Transylania Company transactions at the conclusion of their deliberations and created Kentucky County from the western portion of Fincastle County on December 17, 1776. The Transylvania Company had little recourse against the actions of the Virginia Convention and offered no resistance. Daniel Boone and Richard Callaway managed to preserve their roles at Fort Boonesborough under the new Virginia regime.[27]

The West Fincastle Committee of Safety had fulfilled their part of the bargain with Governor Henry and the Virginia Executive Council. The council honored their commitments and arranged to provide the provisions and military assistance that they had promised.

George Rogers Clark and John Gabriel Jones immediately departed from Williamsburg for Fort Pitt to collect five hundred pounds of gunpowder and lead for transport by boat down the Ohio River to Kentucky.[28] Governor Henry commissioned John Bowman as "Colonel of the Militia of Kentucky County" on December 21, 1776, and directed him to assemble a militia force to march to the aid of the Kentucky settlements.

George Rogers Clark and John Gabriel Jones set off down the Ohio River with five other men in a large dugout pirogue loaded with the gunpowder and lead on December 25, 1776. Simon Kenton served as Clark's scout. Clark made an impressive figure leading the party. He was tall with ramrod straight posture, flaming red hair, piercing hazel eyes, and unusually translucent white skin.

The party of Virginians was discovered by Mingo Chief Pluggy's band of Mingo and Shawanese warriors near the Limestone Crossing.[29] Pluggy and his warriors jumped into five canoes and paddled after them. Clark and his men fled from the larger force in a desperate race down the river and were forced to land and temporarily hide the gunpowder and lead on the lowest and largest of the Three Islands in the Ohio River, near Limestone (present day Maysville).

Clark and his men fled down the Big Buffalo Road past the Lower Blue Licks and the abandoned Hinkston's Station and on to McClelland's Station. They discovered that McClelland's Station did not have enough fighting men to withstand attack by the large force pursuing them. Clark and Kenton continued on to Harrodsburg to seek reinforcements while Jones and the others remained behind to help defend McClelland's Station.

John Todd and eight other men arrived at McClelland's Station before Clark and Kenton returned. Gabriel Jones decided that they had enough men to retrieve the hidden gunpowder and left with Todd and his men to do so. They were attacked by Pluggy and forty warriors near the Lower Blue Licks. Jones and William Graden were killed and two other men were captured.

Chief Pluggy and his warriors attacked McClelland's Station on December 29, 1776, and Pluggy and John McClelland were killed in the ensuing battle. Pluggy's surviving warriors gave up the attack and retreated back toward the Ohio River.

Simon Kenton and Bates Collins recovered the hidden cache of gunpowder from the Three Islands. James Harrod and his Harrodsburg men helped them distribute it among the Kentucky settlements.

McClelland's Station was abandoned in February of 1777. This reduced the number of surviving settlements in Kentucky to three: Fort Boonesborough, Logan's Fort, and Harrodsburg. The remaining settlers would need every grain of their hard-won gunpowder.

Micajah's Choice

MICAJAH SPENT THE MONTHS AFTER ZACK AND Chesley Callaway departed on the Cherokee Expedition living and working on Zack's plantation. He helped Zack's slaves cut tobacco suckers in the tobacco fields and worked on the backlog of smaller gun repair projects, as Zack had requested.

Young Micajah was depressed, feeling that he had been abandoned. No one was teaching him the gunsmithing trade or how to read or write as had been promised.[30]

Micajah's brother James Callaway Jr. was two years older than Micajah and frequently visited him. The boys hunted together and divided the game that they killed between Sarah's and Zack's families. They talked for hours about the adventure and opportunity of life in Kentucky and resolved to run away to Kentucky at the first opportunity.

Zack and Chesley Callaway returned to Bedford County from their service in the Cherokee Expedition in late December of 1776. They learned that Colonel Bowman would soon be calling for volunteers to join a militia force to be sent to the aid of Fort Boonesborough and the other Kentucky settlements.

The militia commanders planned to muster and send an initial company of Botetourt County militia for the immediate reinforcement of the Kentucky settlements under the command of Captain Henry Pauling, Dudley's former commander during Lord Dunmore's War. After Captain Pauling returned to Botetourt County, two additional companies led by Colonel Bowman himself would depart for Kentucky. Captain Pauling and Captain Gwatkins would command the two additional companies.

James Jr. and Micajah honed their plan in February and early March of 1777. Micajah repaired and trued the aim of their two old long rifles until they were as good as new. They bartered for second-hand powder horns, shot-pouches, small iron ladles for melting and pouring lead, bullet molds, and patches. They collected and packed clothing, canteens, and other gear into their oznaburg knapsacks.

Micajah was physically ready for the challenge ahead. Although he was still only a sixteen-year-old adolescent, he was physically mature for his age. He was approaching his adult height of six feet two inches tall and weight of two hundred pounds.[31] His body was heavily muscled from hard work in the fields. He wore his long dark hair pulled back and tied into a queue, and his dark eyes were keen and penetrating.[32]

James Jr. was a stocky young man and stood six feet in height. He had dark eyes like his brother. He was rather stubborn and single-minded, as well as brave and resolute.[33]

The official call for volunteers for the defense of Kentucky came in the first week of April. Able-bodied men were directed to muster with Captain Henry Pauling on the morning of the appointed day in mid-April at the arsenal at Colonel William Fleming's Belmont estate in Botetourt County.

The volunteers were directed to arrive at Belmont mounted on horseback, fully provisioned, and prepared for an immediate march to Kentucky.

Each volunteer was to bring his own biscuit, dried beef, and parched corn meal. Colonel Fleming in turn would provide muskets and bayonets from the arsenal magazine for those who had none. Each man would receive two pounds of powder and four pounds of lead. No uniforms were provided.

James Jr. spent a final night with Micajah at Zack's plantation so they could prepare together. They gathered the required provisions and finished packing their knapsacks. The two young men arose long before dawn and dressed. They each wore round-brimmed felt "farmer's hats," their best fringed linsey-woolsey hunting shirts, buckskin breeches and leggings, and Indian moccasins.

The boys finished packing their horses and tucked their tomahawks and knives into their sashes. They slung the shoulder straps of their rifles, shot pouches, and powder horns over their shoulders, mounted their horses, and road off toward the family homestead at a fast trot, arriving there just before dawn.

Sarah had been awake for awhile, engaged in her morning chores. The two young men rode their horses up to where she was standing, dismounted, and told her about their plans. Sarah pleaded with them to change their minds. She urged Micajah not to run away and violate his binding order, but she did not persuade them.

Sarah stood there for a moment, regaining her composure. She wiped away her tears with her apron and silently went into the cabin. She emerged and gave each of her boys a neatly wrapped packet of jerked venison and pie.

The two young men kissed and hugged their mother and said goodbyes to their siblings. They mounted their horses, wheeled, and galloped off down the trail.

Micajah turned one last time to look back at the little cabin and his family. His mother was waving, a tiny figure set against the vast backdrop of the wilderness of the Blue Ridge Mountains. He waved, turned, and set his spurs into the side of his horse, his mind racing with thoughts and visions of the great adventures and opportunities to come.

Five

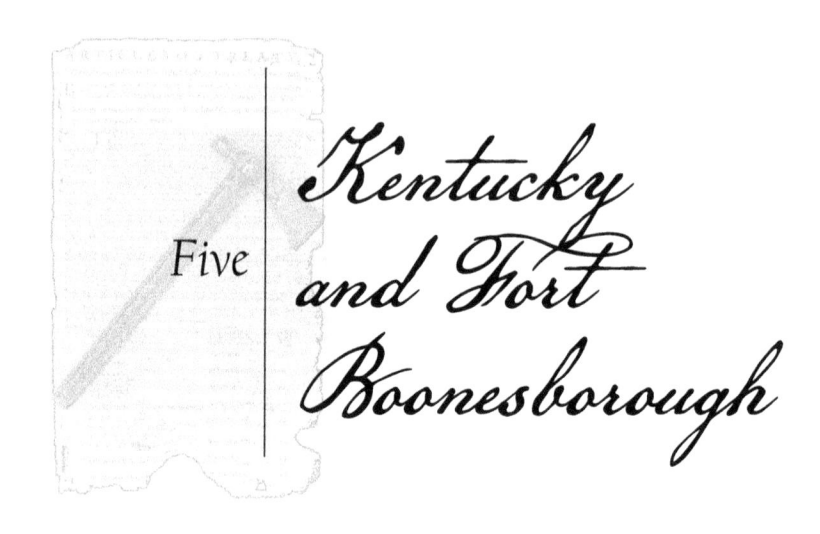

Kentucky and Fort Boonesborough

"A Diversion on the Frontiers of Virginia"

KING GEORGE III APPOINTED LORD GEORGE GERMAIN to serve as his American Secretary in overall command of the war effort in North America.[1] Lord Germain sent a letter to Quebec Governor General Sir Guy Carleton on March 26, 1777, communicating His Majesty's approval of Lieutenant Governor Henry Hamilton's proposed strategy:

> ... as it is His Majesty's resolution that the most vigorous Efforts should be made, and every means employed that Providence has put into His Majesty's Hands, for crushing the Rebellion & restoring the Constitution it is the King's Command that you should direct Lieutenant Governor Hamilton to assemble as many of the Indians of his District as he conveniently can, and placing proper persons at their Head, ... employ them in making a Diversion and exciting an alarm upon the frontiers of Virginia and Pennsylvania ...[2]

Lieutenant Governor Hamilton immediately implemented the king's decision by informing the war chiefs of the Indian Confederacy nations that the warpath was now free and clear. British officers formally assumed com-

Kentucky and Fort Boonesborough 69

mand of the combined military operations of the British and Indian alliance. Fifteen war parties averaging nineteen Indian warriors and two white men each were dispatched to Kentucky.[3]

Long Knife Soldiers

CAPTAIN HENRY PAULING'S BOTETOURT COUNTY, VIRGINIA, COMPANY of fifty mounted volunteers was sworn into service and immediately departed for Kentucky in mid-April of 1777. Lieutenant Dawson Wade served as second-in-command to Captain Pauling.[4] A couple of dozen packhorses carried their provisions and munitions.

The company rode hard down the Valley Pike to Fort Chiswell as Captain Pauling pressed his company to reach Fort Boonesborough as quickly as possible. They encamped for a brief rest at Fort Chiswell and restocked their provisions at James McGavock's Ordinary.[5]

The company of volunteers rode on down the wagon road from Fort Chiswell to Long Island on the Holston River. They restocked their provisions at Fort Patrick Henry and continued up the Wilderness Road through the Clinch and Powell River valleys to Martin's Station. After a brief rest there they pushed on into the Cumberland Mountains.

The captain reflected back on the events of the past few months as they rode along the Wilderness Road through a heavy rain shower, nearing the Cumberland Gap. There had been a long delay in their departure since the Virginia Executive Council decided in December to send reinforcements to Kentucky. There were so many conflicts with the British at so many locations in Virginia that provisioning any single expedition was increasingly difficult.[6]

Chalaakaatha Shawanese War Chief Black Fish had emerged as the leader of the militant factions of the Chalaakaatha, Piqua, and Kispoko divisions. He assumed the leadership of the growing Ohio Confederacy Indian army upon the death of Mingo Chief Pluggy. Black Fish's implacable hatred of the Long Knives was fueled by his desire for revenge for the death of his son when Daniel Boone and Flanders rescued Jemima and the Callaway girls.[7]

The Mingo and Shawanese attacks in Kentucky had resumed in late

February.[8] The besieged settlements were severely undermanned and their casualties were mounting. Reinforcements were urgently needed.

Captain Pauling's company pressed on through the Cumberland Gap and rode on to the Big Flat Lick where the Warriors' Path (Athiawiomee) crossed over the Wilderness Road. They cautiously rode through the crossroads with a sharp lookout for the enemy and continued heading northwest along the Wilderness Road to the forks at the Hazel Patch.

They turned due north at the Hazel Patch and up Boone's Trace toward Fort Boonesborough. They paused briefly to enjoy the view of the rolling Kentucky plains to the north from the heights of Big Hill and rode on toward Fort Boonesborough.

The residents of the fort had been alerted to their approach. Men and women and children stood on the stockade ramparts and just outside the gate, and as the soldiers approached, they clapped and cheered. A surge of pride flushed the faces of young James Jr. and Micajah and their companions as they rode toward the station.

Micajah began to pick out details of the people, the fort, and its surroundings as they drew closer. The cornfields were small and close to the fort. The peoples' clothing was ragged and dirty, and they were gaunt. Construction of the fort had been suspended short of completion.[9] Micajah could see that several of the men were freshly bandaged and obviously in pain.

The crowd parted as they entered the gate into the courtyard. A few trees had been left standing inside the enclosure. Small cabins ringed the four walls of the fort. The outer walls of the cabins served as portions of the stockade wall and had no windows in them. Vertical timbers were placed between the ends of the cabins to complete a continuous stockade wall. The only light and ventilation for the cabins was through the door and small windows facing the courtyard. There was still a gap in one wall where construction had not been completed, and two out of the four corner blockhouses were also incomplete.

Richard Callaway's large cabin was in the center of the courtyard next to Squire Boone's smithy, and faced the gate.[10] The residents of the fort called Uncle Richard "Colonel Callaway," a term that he insisted upon based upon his prior rank in the Bedford County militia.

Emaciated cattle and hogs crowded into small pens within the fort, and chickens ran around loose, scattering and squawking this way and that as peo-

Kentucky and Fort Boonesborough 71

Muted by the Vista [© John Buxton]

ple and horses moved around within its confines. Latrines were built within the confines of the compound for safety reasons. Micajah had grown up on the farm and was accustomed to animal smells but this was far more intense.

Captain Daniel Boone was standing in the doorway of his cabin. His leg was bound in a cast of slippery elm bark and he was leaning on homemade crutches. Daniel was about five feet ten inches tall. His body was solid and muscular. His hair was a sandy reddish color and his skin was fair. He had a high forehead and deep-set, hollow-looking eyes, and his nose was somewhat long and slightly hooked. His mouth was wide and firm with a set of solid, healthy white teeth. The net effect of his appearance was very pleasant. He was polite, good-natured, and well-mannered.[11]

Captain Pauling rode up to Daniel, stopped, saluted, and explained his mission. Daniel returned the salute and invited Pauling into his cabin. James Jr. and Micajah hitched their horses to a post. They spotted Flanders and worked their way through the milling group of soldiers and residents of the fort toward him, although he had not seen them yet. They snuck up behind him and surprised him. Flanders turned and did a double-take, and then glanced at their frontier military gear and shook his head. He stepped forward to greet them both with a warm handshake and hug.

James Jr. and Micajah took a close look at Flanders. He was thinner than ever and looked haggard. However, the steely strength of his will and resolve shone through his dark eyes like two hot embers.

Flanders led them over to Daniel Boone's cabin and went inside. He returned with Jemima and introduced her to James Jr. and Micajah. She was a trim, attractive young woman with bright, intelligent eyes, whose head of long dark hair nearly reached to the floor. After introductions and some small talk, Flanders led James Jr. and Micajah to his own small cabin.

Flanders had furnished his cabin with a sturdy puncheon table, benches, and stools that he had made himself. They all took their seats on the stools.

The conversation began with many questions from Flanders. James Jr. and Micajah filled him in on the latest news from Bedford County. In the course of the discussion Flanders supported their decision to enlist.

Flanders vividly remembered the little dark-eyed child that Micajah had once been and could hardly believe what a large and powerful young man he had become. Nonetheless, Micajah was only sixteen years old and the experienced Shawanese and Mingo warriors that they were fighting were formidable. Flanders would have to look out for his younger brothers.

Flanders briefed his brothers on what he knew of the general state of affairs between the Kentucky settlements and the Mingo and Shawanese. January and early February 1777 had been relatively quiet in Kentucky in the aftermath of the battle with Chief Pluggy and his warriors at McClelland's

Kentucky and Fort Boonesborough

Station in December, 1776. The Mingo and Shawanese warriors were engaged in hunting for meat for their families for the winter hunting season.

During this period of relative calm, George Rogers Clark was chosen by the Kentucky settlers to serve as major in command of all of the Kentucky County militia while awaiting military assistance from eastern Virginia. Daniel Boone, John Todd, James Harrod, and Benjamin Logan were selected as captains.

The Mingo and Shawanese attacks on Kentucky resumed in February of 1777. Several settlers were killed. There were only 140 fighting Long Knife men in all of Kentucky County, and they were concentrated in the three remaining fortified communities of Fort Boonesborough, Harrodsburg, and Logan's Fort. It was very risky for individuals or small parties to venture outside of the forts alone, so the surviving settlers were forced to tend their crops and hunt in groups at night.[12]

The Long Knife hunters found the best hunting grounds to the north of the Kentucky River in the canebrakes and forests of the Licking River basin, where buffalo, elk, black bear, deer, and turkeys abounded. This had also been the favorite hunting ground of the Shawanese since the days when they had lived in old Eskippakithiki just a few miles to the northeast of Fort Boonesborough. Ironically, the more the Shawanese and Mingo warriors isolated the Long Knife forts, the more the Long Knives were forced to hunt deep into the ancestral Shawanese hunting grounds to feed their families and survive.

The night hunters would travel to the place that they planned to hunt on the following day. They chose well-hidden campsites, dug small pits, and made small fires from smokeless white oak bark in the pits. The hunters lay next to the fire to stay warm and sleep until morning. They would discretely hunt on the following day and dress their game, then return to the fort on the following night.

Flanders continued. A large war party of Shawanese and Mingo warriors commanded by Chief Black Fish swept through Kentucky in early March. Logan's Fort sustained the initial attack. The warriors moved on from there and attacked Harrodsburg. Black Fish sent his scouts ahead to Fort Boonesborough to probe for any weakness in their defenses.

Simon Kenton, Flanders Callaway, and Daniel Boone slipped out of Fort Boonesborough at night to scout the nearby countryside and found traces of the Indian scouts. The fort was placed on alert. The general attack on Boonesborough came on March 7, 1777, but the settlers held their ground and beat the attackers back. The war party returned to Harrodsburg and attacked it once again.

Chief Black Fish and his main force surreptitiously returned to Fort Boonesborough during the night of April 23, 1777, and positioned themselves for an ambush. A couple of men from Fort Boonesborough ventured outside the fort to gather firewood on the following day.[13] Simon Kenton and two other armed men were posted at the gate to provide protective cover.

On a signal from Chief Black Fish, several warriors suddenly fired at the wood gatherers and charged toward them. One of the two men was shot, tomahawked, and scalped as the other fled back toward the fort. Kenton and the other two men posted at the gate charged the advancing warriors. The gate to the fort opened up and ten more men, led by Daniel Boone, surged forward and fired a salvo from their long rifles. Eight riflemen, including Flanders Callaway, remained in the fort.[14]

Chief Black Fish sprang his trap. The main body of his warriors rushed from their hiding places in the forest to cut the exposed Long Knives off from the fort. Daniel Boone, Simon Kenton, and the others realized that they had run into a trap, halted their charge, fired again, and sprinted for the gate. A barrage of gunfire poured upon them.

Daniel shouted, "Boys, we have to fight! Sell your lives as dear as possible!"[15] Kenton and Boone reloaded and fired their guns.

Daniel's ankle was shattered by a musket ball, and he went down. A warrior ran up to him and raised his tomahawk for the kill. Simon Kenton fired his long rifle and the warrior dropped dead. Kenton scooped Boone up onto his shoulder like a small child and sprinted through the gate. The other survivors were close behind. The gate was closed and barred.[16]

A siege followed and lasted for three days before the war party withdrew and attacked Harrodsburg again. The siege had lifted just a few days before the arrival of Captain Pauling's company at Fort Boonesborough. Captain Boone and several others who survived the battle were just beginning to recover from their wounds.

Flanders continued briefing his brothers. Richard Callaway's fortunes were improving as Fort Boonesborough came under Virginia's protection. He

Kentucky and Fort Boonesborough

had just been selected to serve as one of the first two Kentucky County representatives to the Virginia General Assembly and would be leaving soon for Williamsburg.[17] Captain John Todd was the other Kentucky County representative. Richard's political connections in Williamsburg would be invaluable to the Kentucky settlements.

CAPTAINS PAULING AND BOONE MUSTERED THEIR TROOPS in the inner grounds of the fort on the following morning after the boys' meeting with Flanders. They divided the reinforcements into three groups to be assigned to the three settlements: Fort Boonesborough, Harrodsburg, and Fort Logan. The soldiers would temporarily serve under the commanding officers of the militia at the forts. Micajah and James Jr. were both assigned to Fort Boonesborough.

Captain Pauling went into conference with Major Clark, and Captains Pauling, Boone, Harrod, Todd, and Logan, to discuss the dire situation. Captain Todd was asked to deliver an urgent letter to Williamsburg requesting immediate assistance. Richard Callaway and John Todd departed for Williamsburg on May 23, 1777.

It appears that Richard Callaway did not welcome Micajah at Fort Boonesborough. There are reports that Richard beat him upon his arrival.[18] It is likely there is some truth to the account of the beating because it is consistent with Richard Callaway's stern "law and order" approach to life and helps explain Micajah's future behavior.

Micajah had run away from home in violation of a Bedford County court order that had bound him to Richard's son Zack as an apprentice. The order had been issued by a court that Richard had helped found and had served on for many years as a justice of the peace. Richard would take the violation of the order very seriously and very personally.

Micajah was a sensitive young man of strong likes and dislikes. He was very loyal to his friends and family. However, if he was insulted or believed he had been wronged, he was very slow to forgive those who had offended him and would avoid ever having anything to do with them again.[19] He had been beaten by his uncle and humiliated in front of his comrades in arms, and this would be difficult to forgive.

The newly arrived recruits did not have long to wait for a fight. Painted

Shawanese and Mingo warriors arrived at the fort late on the same day that Richard Callaway and John Todd left for Williamsburg.

The soldiers were helping tend the corn in the fields near Fort Boonesborough when a guard spotted a musket barrel glinting in the sun and sounded the alarm. The settlers and soldiers had only a brief opportunity to organize and prepare their defense before the Shawanese and Mingo warriors attacked.[20]

Micajah and James Jr. raced to their assigned posts in the corner blockhouse at the sound of the alarm and faced the advancing war party. The warriors attacked with a deafening chorus of war whoops and crash of musket fire. The boys exchanged glances, tended to their firearms, took aim, and fired their first volley together. Micajah's heart pounded with adrenalin. He rammed another patched round into the muzzle of his long rifle, primed, cocked, and fired again. A warrior dropped. James Jr. fired and reloaded as he shouted curses and taunts at the warriors.

The defenders stalled the Indian attack, and a hot exchange of gunfire continued until eleven o'clock at night when the Indians finally withdrew. Micajah and James Jr. lay awake late into that night, their minds racing and replaying the scenes of their first battle. They talked very little.

The warriors attacked again at dawn. Micajah and James Jr. resumed their posts in the blockhouse and continued the fight. The warriors made several attempts to set the fort on fire with torches to burn the settlers out. Micajah and James Jr. joined the desperate settlers as they successfully snuffed out the flames. The battle lasted through the entire second day until midnight when the warriors again withdrew. Three Virginians had been wounded but none fatally. The enemy reportedly suffered considerable casualties.

The warriors moved on to Logan's Fort and placed it under siege beginning on May 30. The Virginians successfully defended their fort, losing one man with two wounded before the raiders appeared to withdraw. The warriors then ambushed and killed seven settlers who ventured outside the fort to procure water.

Richard Callaway returned to Fort Boonesborough in June. He had lobbied in Williamsburg for more troops, gunpowder, and lead for Kentucky County and had briefed his fellow legislators on the status of the Kentucky frontier.

Richard was appointed a justice of the peace and was commissioned as a field colonel in the Kentucky County militia later that month.[21] He now outranked Captain Boone in the Kentucky County militia hierarchy and was second-in-command to Colonel Bowman.

Flanders and Jemima were married in the fort in late June in a simple civil ceremony. Colonel Richard Callaway presided and administered the oath of marriage.[22] Flanders was dressed in his nicest hunting shirt, oznaburg knee breeches, and moccasins. Jemima was radiant in a new calico dress. Daniel Boone gave Jemima away. Richard and Micajah purposely avoided each other during the ceremony and reception.

Shawanese and Mingo warriors attacked Fort Boonesbourough again on July 4. Micajah and his brothers fought in the action, and the settlers held the attackers at bay once again. The warriors returned to their Ohio towns after destroying most of the settlement's corn crop and killing the livestock that could not be kept in the fort.[23]

Flanders left Fort Boonesborough one evening to scout for the enemy. He heard some stones scuffling and voices as he was returning to the fort and hid under a ledge of rocks. A party of Shawanese warriors passed very close by him but did not see him. He remained in hiding until they passed and then returned to the fort. The following day, he returned to his hiding place with a party from Fort Boonesborough. They found that the warriors had camped in a sinkhole very close by. Flanders was lucky to have survived.[24]

Buffalo Hunting in Contested Ground

AS THE REMAINDER OF JULY AND AUGUST came and went, sentries were posted at all times and the soldiers maintained readiness to respond quickly to an attack. Most of the corn crop and livestock at Fort Boonesborough had been destroyed. Micajah, James Jr., and the other soldiers helped salvage and harvest the small amount of corn that survived from the raids. Corn was rationed to one pint per person per day.[25] The surviving livestock was moved to pens just outside the fort walls.

The Long Knife settlers were now almost completely dependent upon hunting and gathering in the forests for their food. Paw-paws and wild grapes were harvested in the fall. Large quantities of walnuts and hickory nuts were collected and laid out in the sun to dry for storage and consumption in the winter.

The eastern woodland buffalo was the preferred wild game of the Long Knife hunters. Although the buffalo in the immediate vicinity of Fort Boonesborough had already been driven away by increased hunting pressure, they were still numerous in the canebrakes and salt licks to the north of the Kentucky River, in the area known today as the Bluegrass Region of Kentucky. This was the sacred ancestral hunting ground of the Shawanese Nation.

Daniel Boone's leg had healed sufficiently for him to walk and ride horses by mid-summer. He resumed his hunting and scouting trips with Flanders. They took young Micajah and James Jr. with them.

The Long Knife hunters armed themselves to the teeth with long rifles, powder and ball, scalping knives and tomahawks and crossed the river to hunt. Their rifles were loaded, primed, and cocked with their fingers on the trigger as their eyes keenly penetrated every suspicious cover. The hunters dressed in hunting shirts and breechcloths for comfort. The breechcloths were identical to those worn by the Indian hunters and warriors.[26] Their hunting dogs helped them track game and also served as watch dogs at camp.

The Shawanese saw the signs of the increased activities of the efficient Long Knife hunters everywhere in the Bluegrass Region. Colonel Richard Callaway, Daniel Boone, Flanders Callaway, and John Martin were among the most active. The Long Knife hunters were a direct threat to the Shawanese food supply, and this hardened the resolve of the Shawanese to drive the Long Knives out of Kentucky.

The eastern woodland buffalo was a very large and dangerously unpredictable animal. Mature bulls could weigh over a ton and a half and could run at speeds of up to forty miles an hour. It was difficult to predict when they would run away or when they would charge.

A charging buffalo could easily kill a hunter. The beasts would gore their pursuers with their horns, toss them in the air, and then trample them. It was best to have an escape route planned before firing and to keep an extra couple of rifle balls in the mouth in case it was necessary to quickly reload while on the run.

The buffalo had powerful herding instincts. When a herd was located,

Kentucky and Fort Boonesborough

the hunters would careful observe it from cover and try to determine which of the buffalo was the leader of the herd, usually an older female. If they could kill the leader, the other buffalo would become easy targets, since they would stay near the body.

Daniel and Flanders explained to the boys to shoot the buffalo behind their shoulder in order to bring them down in one clean shot through the heart. A rifle ball fired into the forehead of a buffalo would just flatten and bounce off the thick skull.

Daniel was a master at dressing game and passed on his technique to Micajah and James Jr. The hunters would cut open the carcass, remove the stomach and intestines, and lay the carcass on its belly in order to protect the meat from taint. The meat of the buffalo's shoulder hump and tongue was considered a particular delicacy. The hunters dug a shallow pit for a fire and ringed it with stones so that flames would not be as visible to any passing Indian scouts. Strips of buffalo hump were skewered on thin green sticks and roasted over the fire. Wet hickory shag-bark was placed in the fire and the thick cloud of aromatic smoke gave the meat a savory hickory flavor. When the meat was done cooking, they ate it right off the sticks. It was a feast fit for royalty.

Buffalo tongues were first laid in the fire to singe off the skin. When ready, they were retrieved from the fire, skewered on a sturdy stick of green spice-bush, and propped over the coals to cook slowly through the night. The spice-bush added a mild mint flavor to the delicacy.

A NETWORK OF BUFFALO PATHS AND TRACES crisscrossed the Kentucky River and Licking River basins to the north of Fort Boonesborough. The Alanant-O-Wamiowee (the buffalo trace) was the most important buffalo path for the Shawanese hunters in the area. They crossed the Ohio River between the mouths of the Little Miami and Greater Miami Rivers at the northern trailhead of the Alanant-O-Wamiowee.[27]

The Alanant-O-Wamiowee headed south and west from there through the Big Bone Lick and on to cross the Kentucky River to Drennon's Lick. Then it passed south along the western bank of the Kentucky River before turning east to cross the river again at the Great Buffalo Crossing near present-day Frankfort.

The Alanant-O-Wamiowee continued east, passing near McClelland's Station (present-day Georgetown) and the Lower Blue Licks on the Licking River, and from there to the Limestone Crossing of the Ohio River.[28] The path continued north on the Ohio side of the Limestone Crossing to the Shawanese town of Little Chalaakaatha on the Little Miami River. The Ohio portion was later called the Winchester Trace.[29]

The southern and eastern portion of the Alanant-O-Wamiowee was joined by another major buffalo path which began several miles to the northwest of Fort Boonesborough near the future site of Lexington and headed to the northeast along the Houston Fork of the Licking River. It crossed the Stoner Fork of the Licking River before merging with the Alanant-O-Wamiowee just before the latter crossed the Hinkston Fork of the Licking River. The Kentucky settlers named this buffalo path and the Alanant-O-Wamiowee from this juncture to the Limestone Crossing "Big Buffalo Road."[30]

There were several hunters' paths or traces that headed north from Fort Boonesborough into the Bluegrass hunting grounds. The most important of these was called the Salt Lick Trace. This trace connected Fort Boonesborough and the Lower Blue Licks on the Middle Fork of the Licking River. It was marked by tomahawk blazes on the trunks of trees along its course.

The Salt Lick Trace proceeded north from the ford across the Kentucky River at the mouth of Lower Howard Creek, through a forest of sycamore trees in the bottomlands called the "Sycamore Forest." It proceeded from there uphill to the crest of the divide with the Licking River basin and the headwaters of Strode Creek. The trace then generally followed the meandering course of Strode Creek downstream to the north, crossing it many times. After crossing Strode Creek a final time at Rocky Ford, it crossed the Stoner Fork of the Licking River to Harrod's Lick at the mouth of Harrod's Creek. This salt lick was a popular hunting ground of the Fort Boonesborough hunters.

The Salt Lick Trace continued on from Harrod's Lick up Harrod's Creek to the northwest and beyond to another salt lick called Flat Lick. Flat Lick lay on the south bank of the Hinkston Fork of the Licking River about a mile upstream of its confluence with the Brushy Fork. Herds of buffalo were concentrated at Flat Lick and along Hinkston Fork, so it was the favorite hunting location for both the Fort Boonesborough hunters and the Shawanese. The Salt

Kentucky and Fort Boonesborough

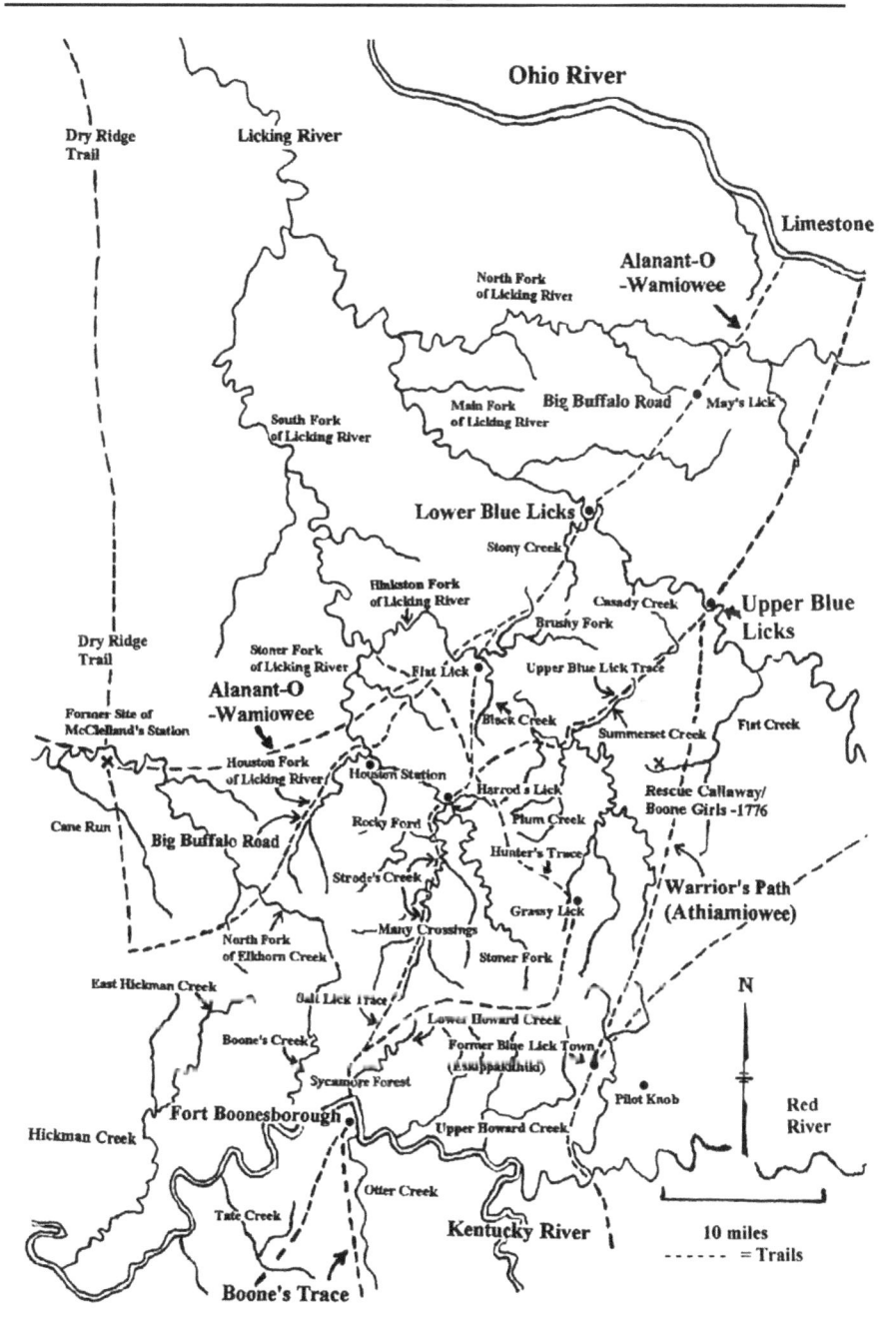

Map 9
Kentucky Bluegrass Region in 1777

Lick Trace then crossed the Hinkston Fork and the Brushy Fork and intersected with and joined the heavily trodden Big Buffalo Road.[31]

Flanders, Micajah, and James Jr. went on a hunting expedition of their own to the head of the Houston Fork of the Licking River toward the end of summer. The lower reaches of the Big Buffalo Road passed through this area and followed the Houston Fork down to its confluence with the Stoner Fork. The headwaters of the Houston Fork sprung from uplands that also served as the source area for Green Creek, Hancock Creek, and a branch of North Elkhorn Creek. The Callaway brothers found abundant buffalo, elk, black bear, and deer there. The land there was well-watered and well-drained. It would be an excellent place to settle.[32]

COLONEL JOHN BOWMAN ARRIVED AT FORT BOONESBOROUGH in early August with two additional companies of volunteers commanded by Captain Pauling and Captain Gwatkins. Colonel Bowman was a very large man, standing six feet four inches tall and weighing almost three hundred pounds. He was forty-three years old.[33] The militia commanders assigned approximately one-third of the reinforcements to each of the three remaining forts. Micajah and James Jr. remained posted at Fort Boonesborough.

Micajah's brother Chesley had joined the new company commanded by Captain Pauling, so there were now four of Sarah Callaway's boys in Fort Boonesborough. They celebrated both Chesley's arrival and Micajah's seventeenth birthday.[34]

Major George Rogers Clark formally relinquished his temporary command of the Kentucky County militia to Colonel Bowman in August. The ambitious Clark was already devoting much of his attention to the Illinois Country to the north of the Ohio River.

The first court session ever held in Kentucky took place on September 2, 1777. Richard Callaway was one of the five justices of the peace presiding over the sessions along with John Todd, John Floyd, Benjamin Logan, and Colonel Bowman.[35]

The settlers in Fort Boonesborough were cheered in early November by the news that American forces led by Generals Horatio Gates and Daniel Morgan had scored a major victory over British forces led by General John

Burgoyne at Saratoga, New York, on October 11, 1777. Micajah's brother Dudley and several other Bedford County riflemen fought with distinction in General Morgan's sharpshooting rifle corps.[36]

The settlers celebrated around a large bonfire of dry cane. The door of every cabin in the fort was open and candle and fire light glowed from within. The fort gates remained barred and sentries stood guard as the festivities continued well into the night.[37]

General Burgoyne had surrendered several thousand troops and a large supply of critically needed artillery, ordnance, and provisions. The credibility of the American revolutionaries was vastly enhanced by this victory, and France now entered into serious negotiations for a military alliance with the American rebels. News of the British defeat caused great uneasiness among their northwestern Indian allies.

IT WAS ESSENTIAL TO THE SURVIVAL OF the Fort Boonesborough settlement to lay away as much food as possible in anticipation of winter and further sieges by the Indians. Large hunting parties went on extended hunts up the Salt Lick Trace to Harrod's Lick and Flat Lick throughout the autumn of 1777. The hunting parties included Colonel Richard Callaway, Flanders Callaway, James Henderson, John Martin, and several other men from Fort Boonesborough.[38]

Although the hunters were able to kill sufficient quantities of game to feed the fort, the meat could not be eaten quickly enough before much of it spoiled. They had to take additional measures to preserve and store it for the lean times ahead. The only workable solution was to preserve the meat with salt, but there was not enough of it available for their needs. The other two fortified Kentucky County settlements faced the same situation.

The citizens of Fort Boonesborough sent a petition to the Virginia General Assembly on November 25, 1777, requesting that a law be enacted requiring every person owning salt springs to produce salt and distribute it or, alternatively, to authorize the government to do so. The petition was signed by a number of the citizens of Fort Boonesborough including Captain Boone, Richard Callaway, James Callaway Jr., and Chesley Callaway.[39] Flanders and Micajah were apparently out hunting at the time and did not sign. The Virginia General Assembly rejected the petition.

Red Tomahawk

THE SHAWANESE MAKUJAY LEADERS FOUND THEMSELVES LOSING any remaining influence that they had within the Shawanese Nation by the summer of 1777. Nonhelema carried a warning to the American garrison at Fort Randolph that her nation had joined the British alliance.[40]

The son of Shawanese Chief Red Hawk and a one-eyed warrior named Old Yie, arrived at Fort Randolph at Point Pleasant on September 19, 1777. They delivered a white and a black wampum string to the fort commander, Captain Matthew Arbuckle.

They explained that they had heard that General Edward Hand was about to invade their country. The Shawanese Nation had taken up arms to repel the invasion. The son of Red Hawk and Yie begged that the Makujay division be spared from any attack, but Captain Arbuckle detained the two Shawanese as spies and locked them in the fort's brig.

Cornstalk was also jailed when he arrived. Captain Arbuckle sent a message to General Edward Hand asking what he should do with his prisoners, "as I am well satisfied that the Shawanese are our enemies." Cornstalk's son Elinipsico visited the fort to check on the well-being of his father on November 9, and he was also jailed.[41]

Cornstalk and Captain Arbuckle conferred on November 10. The dejected Cornstalk admitted that the Makujay were going to have to "run with the stream" as all of the other Indian nations had decided to ally with the British with the exception of the dwindling pro-American Delaware faction under the leadership of Captains White Eyes and Killbuck.

Later in the day, a mob of local men broke into the brig where Cornstalk and the other Shawanese prisoners were confined. Captain Arbuckle tried to stop them but failed, and Cornstalk and the other prisoners were murdered in cold blood.[42]

The leadership of the American Revolution was shocked and saddened by the news of Cornstalk's murder. The governors of Virginia and Pennsylvania sent urgent messages of regret to the Shawanese and offered to pay reparations. Their futile gestures were too little, too late, and were refused. As General Hand recognized, "If we had anything to expect from that Nation it is now Vanished."⁴³ Governor Patrick Henry blamed the murder on a Tory conspiracy.⁴⁴

Cornstalk's murderers were never brought to justice or punished, and this enraged the entire Shawanese Nation. Most of the Makujay Shawanese warriors that had remained neutral with Cornstalk finally accepted the red tomahawk.⁴⁵

The dwindling contingent of Makujay chiefs who chose to continue to support neutrality to the bitter end moved to the Delaware capital of Coshocton to live with Captain White Eyes and the other Delaware that continued to align themselves with the Americans. Old Kishenosity and a small Makujay band were living there in April of 1778. Chief Moluntha and the remaining Makujay relocated Mackachack to the banks of the Mad River not far to the south of the new Wapatomica town site.⁴⁶

Nonhelema abandoned her people and moved to Fort Randolph with her herd of cattle. She pledged her loyalty to the Americans and subsequently acted as an interpreter and messenger for them through the remainder of the Revolutionary War, and for this she was disowned and exiled by the Shawanese Nation.

Chief Black Fish was chosen to succeed Cornstalk as the Principal War Chief of the Shawanese Nation, and the Ohio Shawanese united behind his leadership. Black Fish and his supporters recognized a great opportunity for their nation in the war between Great Britain and the American rebels. They believed that Great Britain and France were going to join forces to suppress the rebellion. An American victory seemed implausible against those odds.

The British hinted broadly that they would reconsider the Kentucky cession in the first Treaty of Fort Stanwix if the Shawanese would join them. They would not hold the Shawanese to the cessions of Kentucky to the United Colonies in the two treaties of Fort Pitt. Shawanese hope for repossession of their beloved Kentucky hunting grounds was rekindled and fueled the will of their nation to fight and stake their future on the outcome of the war. It was a desperate gamble, but there was no hope of recouping Kentucky through any other means.

British arms and supplies began to flow in volume from Detroit to the Shawanese and their Ohio Indian allies. Chief Black Fish began preparations for a major military expedition into Kentucky immediately after Cornstalk's death. Cornstalk's brother Nimwha (Munseka) and other Makujay chiefs and warriors joined Black Fish's Chalaakaatha, Piqua, and Kispoko war party to seek revenge for the murder of Cornstalk. Lieutenant Governor Hamilton established a bounty equivalent to fifty dollars for each American scalp and one hundred dollars for each American prisoner delivered by the king's Indian allies.[47]

Six | *Captured*

Chief Black Fish and the Saltboilers

WHEN THEY LEARNED THAT THE VIRGINIA GENERAL Assembly had rejected their November 25, 1777, salt-making petition, the leaders of the three remaining Kentucky settlements decided to send a company of militia led by Captain Daniel Boone to the Lower Blue Licks on the Licking River to manufacture a large quantity of salt.[1] The Lower Blue Licks was selected for the best location for this because of the high quality and large quantity of salt that could be produced from the salty mineral waters found there.[2] The finished product was to be distributed equally between Fort Boonesborough, Harrodsburg, and Logan's Fort.

Micajah and James Jr. enlisted in Captain Boone's company in December after the expiration of their enlistment with Colonel Bowman and Captain Pauling.[3] Boone and his company departed from Fort Boonesborough early on the frigid morning of New Years Day, 1778, and headed north up the Salt Lick Trace. Boone rode at the head of the single-file column of thirty mounted soldiers and packhorses.[4] Flanders Callaway and Thomas Brooks accompanied the soldiers as civilian scouts and hunters.

The column moved at a fast walk. James Jr. and Micajah rode in the middle of the column, with James Jr. directly ahead of Micajah. Micajah wore homespun woolens that his mother and sister had made for him under his hunting shirt and leggings. He wrapped a woolen blanket more tightly around his shoulders to keep out the winter chill.

The company's packhorses were at the back of the column, followed by two soldiers serving as rear guard. The packhorses were burdened with provisions for the soldiers as well as the large black iron and brass kettles to be used for boiling the mineral waters from the salt springs.[5]

The column of soldiers crossed the Kentucky River at the ford at the mouth of Lower Howard Creek. They followed the Salt Lick Trace from there to the north through the Sycamore Forest and through the Many Crossings and Rocky Ford of Strode's Creek. They proceeded from there across the Stoner Fork, past Harrod's Lick and Flat Lick, and across the Hinkston Fork. The hunters took note of the abundant buffalo sign there. The column continued on across Brushy Fork to the juncture with the Big Buffalo Road, which they followed the remainder of the distance to the Lower Blue Licks.[6]

The long, cold journey took about four days. The company set up a semi-permanent camp upon their arrival at their destination. Some of the men built a small cabin for storage and security.[7] Since they had no tents, the men slept on the frozen winter ground in their bedrolls, using their knapsacks for pillows. They collected firewood and kept their campfires burning throughout the days and nights in an effort to stay warm.

The day after their arrival, the soldiers began preparations for producing salt. A dozen pits were dug through the frozen ground to the depth of six feet, and fires were kindled in them. Trenches were dug in the muddy springs to ease the collection of the salty mineral water.[8] The kettles were filled with the water and placed over the fires.

The men worked very hard over many long days. A constant supply of firewood was required and crews were continuously dispatched to cut and bring a sufficient supply for the fires. As the salt water boiled away, more water was hauled from the springs to the fires. The saltboilers soon deduced that boiling down a dozen kettles of water yielded about a gallon of salt. The heavy labor continued daily. By February 7, 1778, nearly three hundred bushels of salt had been produced.

The dawn of February 8 was bitterly cold. As the soldiers awoke, they discovered that snow had fallen and covered them as they slept.[9] They shook and brushed the snow off of themselves as they stirred.

There were twenty-seven soldiers in the salt camp that morning, including Captain Boone. The others, including Flanders Callaway, were either hunting or making an early delivery of salt to Fort Boonesborough so the settlers could begin salting meat.[10] Snow continued to fall throughout the day.

Daniel Boone left the camp early in the morning to hunt for fresh meat for his men. He rode back down the Big Buffalo Road and Salt Lick Trace to the Hinkston Fork near Flat Lick.

It was easy to track game in the fresh snow. Daniel found the track of a buffalo, followed it, and killed it. He skinned and butchered the buffalo, bundled the meat in the hide, and packed the bundle on his horse in preparation for returning to the salt camp.

Chief Black Fish had crossed the Ohio River into Kentucky with 120 Shawanese and Mingo warriors seeking revenge for the death of Cornstalk at about the same time that Captain Boone and his company left Fort Boonesborough. The war party included Chalaakaatha War Chief Black Fish; Cornstalk's brother Nimwha (Munseka),[11] a chief named Pappiqua;[12] Piqua Chief Blue Jacket; Captain Will; Nenessica ("Black Beard");[13] black (African-American) Shawanese Caesar and Pompey; and French traders Louis Lorimier and Charles Beaubien.[14] The faces of the chiefs and warriors were painted black and red for war.

The group established a base camp on the Hinkston Fork at a small salt lick near the river and sent out several scouting parties, one of which was lead by Blue Jacket. He is described in an account from adopted captive O.M. Spencer:

> This chief was the most noble in appearance of any Indian I ever saw. His person, about six feet high, was finely proportioned, stout, and muscular; his eyes large, bright and piercing; his forehead high and broad; his nose aquiline; his mouth rather wide, and his countenance open and intelligent, expressive of firmness and decision.[15]

Blue Jacket and his party came across the fresh tracks of a solitary man and horse as they scouted along the Hinkston Fork.[16] The warriors dismounted and stealthily followed the tracks with their muskets loaded, primed, and cocked. They soon located the man leading a horse fully loaded with buffalo meat. Boone spotted them. With a fierce war whoop, Blue Jacket and his warriors fired their muskets and charged.

As musket balls whizzed around him, Daniel Boone desperately tried to cut the buffalo meat loose from his horse so he could escape on horseback unencumbered. His knife was frozen in the scabbard and his hands were too greasy from butchering the buffalo to get a grip on it, so he abandoned his horse and ran for his life. The warriors drew closer. Musket balls flew by, snapping twigs and branches next to him.

Blue Jacket stopped, aimed, and fired his musket. The musket ball cut the straps of Daniel's powder horn, and it fell away. Daniel quickly ducked behind a tree with his heart pounding while gasping for breath. He could run no farther and could no longer defend himself. After a pause, he reached around the tree and leaned his long rifle against it in full view of the warriors, stepped out from behind the tree, and offered his surrender.[17]

Blue Jacket and his men realized that their captive was none other than Daniel Boone, whom they had long admired as a hunter and warrior. Blue Jacket bound him and escorted his valuable prize back to the main camp.[18]

The warriors in the main camp surrounded Daniel as he stood calmly before them. Daniel recognized Captain Will among the warriors. He had captured Boone many years ago in Kentucky and warned him to stay away from Kentucky. Daniel stepped forward and grabbed Captain Will's hand and shook it, asking, "How d'you do?" Captain Will was puzzled at first but remembered Daniel after a few moments and vigorously pumped his hand.

Pompey stepped forward to interpret. He told Daniel that another Shawanese scouting party had discovered the saltboiler camp. Chief Black Fish was preparing to surprise and kill all of the soldiers there. The Shawanese planned to march on to Fort Boonesborough after they were finished with that bloody business and kill all of its occupants.

Daniel persuaded Black Fish that the Shawanese could less afford to fight and lose warriors than the numerous Long Knives. Only women and children were left at Fort Boonesborough because the soldiers were out on patrol, and it was now too cold for the women and children to travel to the Shawanese towns. The Shawanese could return to Fort Boonesborough in the spring. Boone would then surrender the fort, and the Shawanese could take the women and children back to their towns as prisoners.

Black Fish agreed to accept the bloodless surrender of Boone's soldiers in exchange for the promise that they would not be mistreated or killed. He specifically promised not to force them to run the dangerous gauntlet.

The soldiers at the salt lick were sitting next to their campfires and relaxing around noon on the following day. Salt production had stopped because high water in the river had temporarily flooded the licks. The snow had continued through the night, and the temperature was dropping. The men were quietly talking among themselves, and a few were napping in the cabin.

As Micajah and James Jr. warmed their hands by the fire and rested with half-closed eyes, they heard a distant voice shouting, "Halloo! Halloo!" The men turned to face the crest of the hill on the opposite side of the Licking River. They could see the distant figure of Daniel Boone waving at them, a white kerchief in his hand. Standing around him were massed a large group of fully armed and painted Shawanese and Mingo warriors. The men ran for their guns and cursed as they primed their rifles.

Boone and the warriors moved down the hill closer to the camp. Boone shouted to his men that they should put down their guns and surrender peacefully. The Shawanese had promised him that they would not be killed or mistreated.

A vigorous discussion ensued among the soldiers. Several of the men were for fighting and took up positions in the cabin. Micajah and James Jr. argued that Boone could be trusted and that they should obey his orders. They were heavily outnumbered and would soon be surrounded. Battle would be futile. The men agreed to surrender and laid down their weapons.

Daniel Boone and the warriors crossed the river. The warriors encircled the camp. They ordered the soldiers to form a circle and stack their guns in the center. The Shawanese and Mingos then formed two circles: one circle of warriors within and one outside of the circle of prisoners, and then ordered the prisoners to sit down.[19]

This was Micajah's first opportunity to see Shawanese warriors up close. They were generally a handsome people—lean, muscular, and, on average, somewhat small in stature. The warriors' heads were shaved with the exception of an area about four or five inches across on the top, from which a long scalp lock hung. Silver nose rings were common. The lower portions of the rims of their ears were cut away from the main body of the ear and stretched to hang loose. They decorated their pendulous ear rims with silver ornaments and feathers.

Most of the warriors wore long calico shirts with ruffled bottoms, belted just above the waist, almost appearing as short dresses. Silver brooches were liberally used for decorative effect. The chiefs and more influential warriors hung silver gorgets over their chests.

Each warrior wore a breechcloth and hung it over a belt to cover and protect his private parts, front and back. Leggings were hung from the belt by buckskin cords to protect his legs, and they were commonly made of buckskin or wolf skin and were decorated with fringe, brightly died pompoms, and decorative knee bands. They wore beautiful beaded moccasins with buffalo hide soles to protect the bottoms of their feet.

The warriors wore a variety of headdresses. Turbans of black silk, wolf skin, and otter skin were popular. The turbans were left open at the top so that the scalp lock could hang down.

Blue Jacket favored an ominous raven-skin cap. Black Hoof (Catehecassa) wore a buffalo headdress with buffalo horns mounted on the sides. A few of the warriors wore wolf skin hats with red "ears" of dyed deer hair. Some warriors simply fastened a single eagle or swan feather or a silver trinket to dangle from the base of their scalp lock.

The faces of the warriors were painted red and black. Some even painted their entire faces black. Others painted the main part of their faces black and painted their eye sockets red. Others painted their faces red with black eye sockets. The overall effect was frightening.

The warriors wore fringed buckskin overshirts and wrapped themselves in wool trade blankets for their winter battle dress. A tomahawk, or war club, and a scalping knife were tucked in their belts. Shot pouches, powder horns, and muskets completed their armaments.

The Shawanese warriors held a council that afternoon to confirm the fate of the prisoners. Such important decisions were made by consensus according to their customs. When all of the Shawanese had finished speaking, Daniel Boone was allowed to make a closing statement:

> Brothers! What I have promised you, I can much better fulfill in the spring than now. Then the weather will be warm, and the women and children can travel from Boonesborough to the Indian towns, and all live with you as one people. You have got all the young men; to kill them, as has been suggested, would displease the Great Spirit, and you could not then expect future success in hunting nor war; & if you spare them, they will make you fine warriors, and excellent hunters to kill game for your squaws and children. These young men have done you no harm; they unresistingly surrendered upon my assurance that such a step was the only safe one; I consented to their capitulation on the express condition that they should be made prisoners of war and treated well. Spare them, and the Great Spirit will smile on you.[20]

Micajah, James Jr., and the other young soldiers listened to Daniel Boone's speech and only then appreciated how tenuous their situation was. They hung on every word that Daniel said. When his speech was completed, the Shawanese chiefs and warriors voted. Sixty-one voted for sparing the prisoners and fifty-nine voted to execute them. Their lives were saved by a small margin.

After the vote, Daniel noticed that some of the Shawanese were clearing a large area in the snow. He reminded Black Fish of his promise that his men would not run the gauntlet. Black Fish replied that he had only promised that Boone's men would not have to run the gauntlet and had made no promise that Boone would not have to do so. Daniel ran the gauntlet that afternoon. The warriors restrained themselves and did not cause any serious injuries.

The Shawanese warriors tossed the salt that had been collected onto the snow and plundered the material goods of the soldiers, taking several of the brass kettles and anything else of value. The prisoners were then prepared for the long march back to the Shawanese town of Little Chalaakaatha on the Little Miami River, the home of Black Fish and many of his warriors.[21]

The prisoners were loaded up with burdens of booty. Micajah was assigned to carry several kettles.[22] James Jr. resisted the Shawanese instructions from the beginning and refused to carry more than his own gear and a couple of extra blankets. The party set off up the Big Buffalo Road toward the Limestone Crossing with warriors in front, behind, and to the sides of the prisoners.

After walking for several miles along the road, a warrior who had been carrying a kettle asked James Jr. to carry it for him. He refused to do so. The Indian continued to insist and James Jr. stubbornly continued to refuse. The exasperated warrior finally drew his tomahawk and raised it to strike.

James Jr. removed his hat, bent his head forward to receive the blow, and patted the top of his head with his hand, saying, "Here, strike! I would as lief lie here as go along—I won't tote your kettle!"[23] The warrior turned away with a dry smile, tucked his tomahawk back into his belt, and carried the kettle himself.

The Shawanese war party and their prisoners camped along the Big Buffalo Road on the first night of their captivity. The prisoners were still in a state of shock and dejection at their sudden misfortune. As evening fell, their arms were tightly bound behind their backs using buffalo hide tugs (cords). They were each assigned to warriors who were charged with their custody and care. Bells were tied to the prisoners so they would make noise if they tried to escape in the night.[24]

Daniel interceded with Black Fish on behalf of Micajah and James Jr. to ensure that they were not mistreated. He explained that the two young men were part of his extended family and should be properly cared for.

It appears that the boys were placed in the custody of Shawanese Chief Nenessica (Black Beard).[25] Nenessica was a senior member of the Makujay Shawanese division but lived with the Chalaakaatha division in their town of Little Chalaakaatha. He probably was in his fifties at the time of their capture. There are fragmentary descriptions of him in the historical record indicating that he was a tall and rangy man. One would expect from his name that he also wore a black beard. He was a very intelligent man and was both a war leader and diplomat for his nation. The British described him as "a very confidential man."[26]

Nenessica cleared a place in the snow and motioned for Micajah and James Jr. to sit down. Their hands were still tied behind their backs. When they were seated, Nenessica took two sturdy, forked saplings that he had cut, motioned for Micajah to place his legs together, and Micajah complied. Nenessica placed the fork of the sapling over his legs and pounded it into the ground to a depth of two feet.[27] Micajah was tightly secured. Nenessica did the same to James Jr., and left the two men in the cold and dark.

The brothers could hear the Shawanese warriors talking and arguing around their campfires not far away. James Jr. sat up and looked in the direction of the fires. The warriors had driven short forked stakes into the ground around the fire and had laid long cross-poles across them against which they leaned and slept. Their weapons were at their sides. It was their custom to sleep on such "laying poles" while on the warpath, in order to be ready for an instant response to a surprise attack.

James Jr. told Micajah what he had observed, but Micajah was depressed and not interested in looking. Micajah later learned that the subject of discussion among the warriors that night was whether the rims of the prisoners' ears should be slit in the Shawanese style.[28]

The two brothers lay back on their sides because of their bound hands. They were given no gloves or blankets. Micajah lay on the ground shaking as the deepening cold of the night drained the warmth from his body. He looked up into the dark overcast sky and watched the snowflakes fall into the circles of light from the campfires. He had heard horrible things about the tortures that the Shawanese sometimes subjected their prisoners to, and also knew that sometimes they adopted captives to replace sons and daughters that they had lost. He shuddered at the thought of the fate that might await him.

Micajah's thoughts returned to Bedford County. He thought of the warm little family cabin in the Blue Ridge Mountains, seemingly so far away. His family would be sleeping now. It was good to think about home. It made him feel almost warm as the cold and exhaustion carried him to sleep.

Micajah awoke with a sharp pain in his side. He turned his head to see Nenessica aiming another kick at him. James Jr. was receiving the same treatment. The chief stopped when he saw that he was awake. Nenessica said something unintelligible and motioned for them both to sit up.

The morning temperature was near zero degrees Fahrenheit. Six more inches of snow had fallen overnight. There was now over two and a half feet of snow on the ground.[29]

Nenessica brushed the snow off their legs and with considerable effort pulled the forked stakes from the frozen ground. Micajah couldn't feel his legs. James Jr. was having similar problems and began flexing and slapping them. Micajah tried to do the same, but his inanimate legs felt like they belonged to someone else.

Nenessica cut James Jr.'s bonds and made clear the penalty for any attempts at escape with a threatening gesture across his throat. James Jr. rubbed his legs with his hands and was soon able to stand up and stomp around to improve the circulation. He then vigorously massaged Micajah's legs. Micajah began to feel them and was on his feet stomping around after several minutes. His toes tingled as the feeling returned and then began to throb painfully. Nenessica commanded, "Wetemeloh (come with me)!"[30] He motioned for Micajah and James Jr. to follow him.

The other prisoners were also moving about and warming their limbs. Their captors organized and loaded them with their burdens of plunder and set out on the trail for another day's march. The snow stopped falling during the day.

The war party reached the mouth of Johnson's Fork near the Limestone Crossing late in the day, after marching the entire day with wet feet through the deep snow. The Shawanese had hidden a boat there made from four buffalo hides sewn together and stretched over a crude wooden framework. The boat could carry about twenty persons across the ice-cold Ohio River.[31] It took a few hours for the entire party to shuttle across the river. They camped a short distance into the Ohio Country on the second night along the Winchester Trace.[32]

The prisoners were bound again for the second night in the same fashion as the first. This night was even more inhospitable. It was just as cold, but there was no snowfall to insulate them. Micajah could not feel his feet as he walked the following day and had to be very careful not to stumble over the smallest of obstacles.

The Shawanese retrieved the first cache of the stored bear meat that evening. There was not enough to share among the 150 hungry warriors and captives. Small portions of their parched corn rations were allocated to the prisoners. All received some food but no one got enough.

The third day was similar to the previous two. The effects of the severe cold and increasing hunger took their toll. It was clear now that Micajah's feet had been severely frostbitten. Although he could force himself to march on with considerable pain, it was tearing up his feet. Micajah would tell his sons when he was an old man that if the young soldiers had possessed their guns three days after their surrender, they would have fought with desperation to regain their liberty.[33]

Micajah showed his feet to Nenessica. His toes, which were blistered and icy to the touch, were obviously frozen and were beginning to turn black. Nenessica took pity on young Micajah and sought the help of the Shawanese shaman who had accompanied the war party.

The shaman had been prepared for cold weather problems such as this and gave Nenessica a poultice made from white walnut bark.[34] Nenessica applied it to the frozen part of Micajah's feet to remove the "mequamah" (ice).[35] It seemed to help. Some of the warriors with split ear rims had suffered frostbite on their ears, and they were also treated with the poultice.

They finally approached Little Chalaakaatha on the fourteenth day of their hellish journey.[36] Two large "war poles" about fifteen feet in height had been set into the ground along the trace just outside of the town. One was painted red for war and the other was painted black to indicate that the town's warriors had captured prisoners.[37]

Little Chalaakaatha was the primary town of the Chalaakaatha division of the Shawanese Nation. Several hundred individuals lived there. Chief Yellow Hawk (Othaawaapeelethee) was the village chief and Black Fish was their war chief.[38]

The town was located on a small rise to the south of the Little Miami River, just below its confluence with Massies Creek. Several small springs flowed from the base of the rise. Cornfields covered several hundred acres in the floodplain to the west, between the town and the river, and in the highlands to the south of the town. To the east, a forest bordered the edge of town.

A large council house was located to the north of the center of the town. Broad avenues radiated from the site of the council house and hundreds of dwellings lined the avenues. They were a mixture of log cabins and traditional Shawanese bark wegiwas. A branch trading post of French trader Louis Lorimier was located adjacent to and facing the council house.[39] There was an open field next to the council house which was used for ritual football games.[40]

The council house was a large and impressive log structure. It was 120 feet long and 40 feet wide. The peaked roof reached a height of 20 feet and was shingled with elm bark and covered with sod. Smoke-holes had been cut through the peak of the roof at the tops of the end walls.

A row of five large beech tree trunks ran down the centerline of the interior from one end of the house to the other, serving as supporting columns beneath heavy crossbeams. Animal motifs and religious symbols were carved and painted on them.[41] Snakes, turtles, and distorted human faces were among the carvings, and twists of tobacco were hung over each of them.[42]

There were doorways at each end of the building and they were hung with buffalo hide doors. Small portholes had been cut into the walls and covered in scraped, greased rabbit skins to let in natural light during the day.[43]

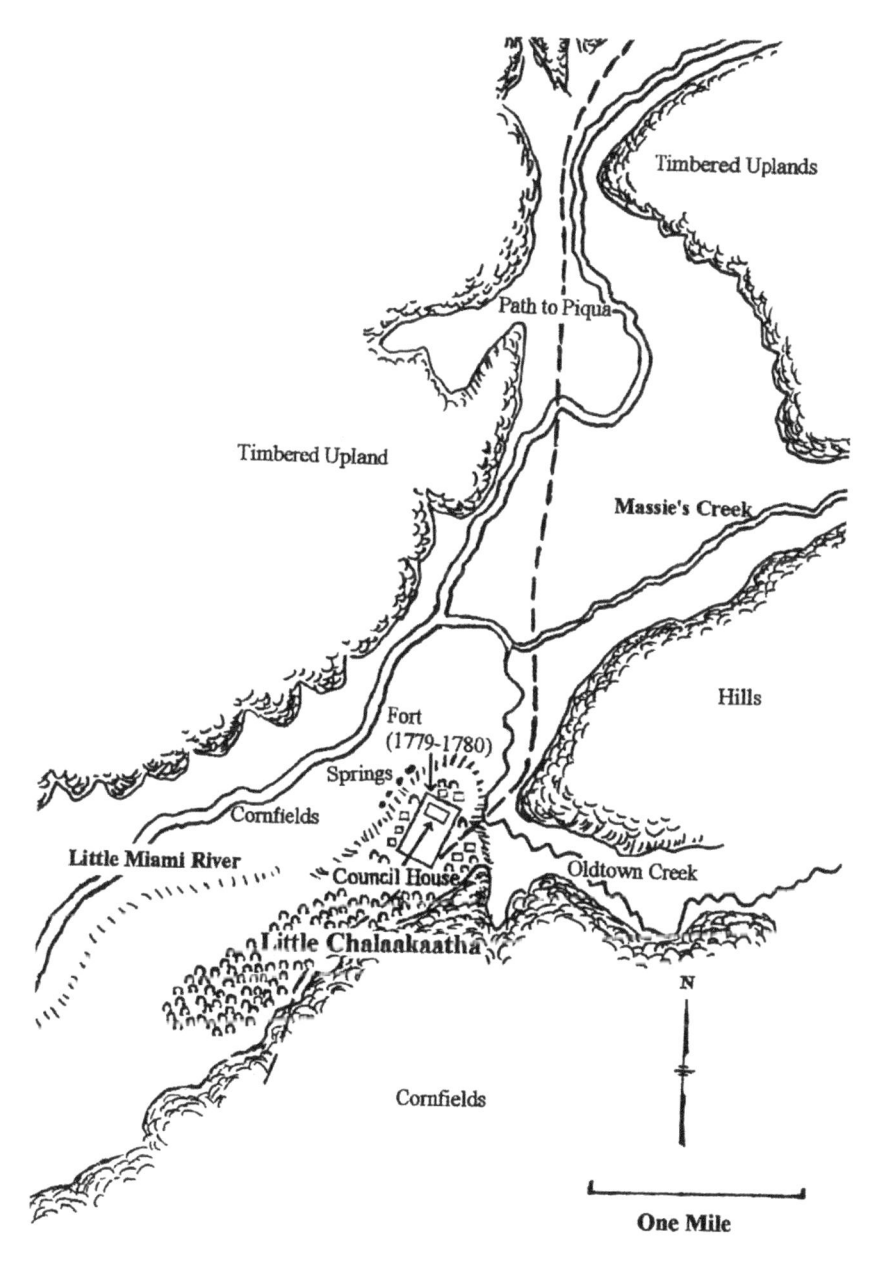

**Map 10
Little Chalaakaatha in 1780**

Chief Black Fish directed his warriors to paint the faces of the prisoners with red paint as they prepared to enter the town. Black paint would have marked them for torture and death. The prisoners were given rattles and ordered to shake them and sing a Shawanese prisoner song to alert the residents to the war party's return.[44]

As the warriors marched on with their captives, they raised the war whoop and fired their guns into the air. The prisoners sang and shook their rattles. A large swarm of women and children emerged from the town and came down the path toward the prisoners, and they were waving sticks and clubs in the air as they approached.

Several older women raced toward them and seemed to compete to see who would touch them first with their hands. Black Fish stepped out to bar their way and engaged in a heated discussion with them. The women backed down and joined the general mob. Micajah later learned that the racing women were a head woman and four old women from a Shawanese cannibal society. According to Shawanese custom, their lives would be spared if the head woman touched them first. They would have been executed and eaten if the cannibal society women had done so.[45]

The path into the town led to a crude bridge that had been constructed across a muddy area. The whooping and shrieking crowd beat the prisoners with their sticks and clubs as they stepped off of the end of the bridge. Daniel Boone became angry after a few blows and knocked one of his tormentors into the mud. The warriors laughed and patted him on the back.[46] James Jr. pushed back, too, and Micajah dodged and darted as best as he could with his crippled feet.

The prisoners were escorted through the wild mob and into the council house. Two to three hundred chiefs and warriors had assembled there as well as several prestigious head women and their children. A large council fire blazed in a ring of stones at the center of the building. The temperature in the council house was cool but well above freezing. The prisoners were stripped of their clothing, bound, and staked to the ground in a closely packed group to one side of the council fire. Micajah did not yet understand the Shawanese language but was later able to reconstruct a rough approximation of what transpired in the council house.

A war pole was set in place in a posthole next to the council fire and dirt was packed around its base. It was painted black with a diagonal red stripe spiraling around it. A cluster of scalps was tied to the top.

A chief entered the council house carrying a water drum under one arm. He began to beat the drum and sing a war song.[47] Several chiefs and principal warriors began to sing along with him.[48] James Jr. and Micajah exchanged worried glances.

Captain Snake walked into the council house with great ceremony as the singing and drumming continued.[49] He was the brother of Cornstalk's widow, Wasekakotha, and was among the leaders of those who sought revenge for Cornstalk's murder.[50] He carried the sacred war bundle of the Kispoko division in his arms.

The water drum pulsed and the war song continued as the war chiefs and warriors prepared themselves for the war dance. Captain Snake carried the sacred war bundle into a screened-off corner of the council house where no one could see and opened it. Micajah later learned that there were several sacred relics kept inside of it. Captain Snake removed four plumed headdresses and a sacred "mesquaway teckhawk" (red tomahawk).[51]

Chiefs Black Fish, Nenessica, and Black Hoof joined Captain Snake and stripped down to their breechcloths. They painted their faces red and black and donned the four sacred headdresses.

The other chiefs and warriors in the council house also stripped down and painted themselves. Micajah picked out Blue Jacket among them, and later learned that Chiaxi (Captain Tommy) of the Chalaakaatha division, young Buffalo and Wabapusito of the Piqua division, and Chiefs Nimwha and Moluntha of the Makujay division took part in the dance.

The water drum and war songs continued as the chiefs and warriors positioned themselves in a large circle around the council fire, about an arm's length apart from one another. Each was armed with a tomahawk in his right hand and a scalping knife in the left.

Captain Snake suddenly brandished the red tomahawk and his scalping knife above his head, screamed a fiercely piercing war whoop, and began to dance. The other dancers immediately responded with a chorus of war-whoops and joined him. The chiefs and warriors twisted and writhed with fierce expressions and contortions as they mimicked the acts of scalping, tomahawking, and shooting their enemies. Each dancer danced with his own variation of rhythmic, rapid alternations of toe and heal stepping, jingling the bells on his moccasins in unison with the pulsing rhythm of the water drum and war songs.

 The exaggerated shadows of the chiefs and warriors capered and gyrated on the council house walls as the mesmerizing cadence of the drums and singing droned on. They looked like plumed birds of prey from hell rather than human beings. Micajah spotted a British officer standing by a doorway in his scarlet uniform, the firelight glinting off the shiny buttons on his jacket. Micajah felt completely helpless.

 Captain Snake began to sing a mournful war song. The other chiefs and warriors joined in the song as they danced. A chief or warrior would occasionally swoop low and circle out in front and return to his place. Captain Snake's war song lasted for about fifteen minutes. Then the dancers all gave a great war whoop together, sat down, and hung their heads.

 Black Fish picked up the red tomahawk, stepped in front of the drummer, and began to speak in a booming voice. He gestured wildly with the tomahawk and his scalping knife as he re-enacted the triumph in Kentucky. He dramatically struck the sacred red tomahawk into the war pole at the conclusion of his oration. All of the warriors whooped wildly, stood up, and resumed the war dance. Black Fish sat down and Blue Jacket stood up to take his place.

 Blue Jacket retrieved the red tomahawk from the war pole and led the war song. His dramatic raven's skin headdress enhanced his ferocious appearance. He ended the song with a war whoop and proceeded to describe and re-enact his capture of Daniel Boone. His dramatic story caused great excitement in the council house as he emphasized his daring achievement with a final sharp tomahawk strike into the war pole. The dancers all jumped up at once and whooped and writhed around the war pole to the conclusion of the war dance late that night.

 The prisoners were unstaked and untied and were allowed to dress when the war dance ended. They were escorted into a holding area of several wegiwas and were rebound and staked to the ground. Warm buffalo hides were provided for them to sleep under. Their Shawanese keepers told them that there would be a council on the following day to discuss their fates once again.

The chiefs and warriors who had been on the warpath remained in the council house for a purification ceremony that lasted for four days. They ate little and drank potions made from medicinal plants. Sexual contact between men and women was forbidden.[52]

The prisoners were awakened at dawn on the following morning and fed a small amount of parched corn and venison jerky. A group of warriors grabbed James Jr. by his arms and dragged him to a large snowy field at the edge of the town, where he was forced to run the gauntlet.[53] He knocked two Shawanese down a snowy slope during his run, and the rest of the crowd howled with laughter.

Daniel Boone learned that James Jr. had been made to run the gauntlet and promptly complained to Chief Black Fish that his promise had been broken. Other prisoners including Ansel Goodman and William Hancock had endured the same fate. Black Fish investigated and reprimanded the warriors involved.

The Shawanese chiefs and principal warriors held a council at the conclusion of their purification period in order to decide the fate of prisoners.[54] The council decided to divide them into two groups. The first group would remain at Little Chalaakaatha for the time being and be evaluated for potential adoption into the tribe. Those who were not adopted could either be retained as slaves or later sold to the British in Detroit. The group of potential adoptees included Daniel Boone, Micajah Callaway, Joseph Jackson, William Hancock, John Dunn, George Hendricks, Benjamin Kelly, John Holley, and Ansel Goodman.[55]

The second group was comprised of prisoners who were perceived to be less cooperative and posing a greater risk of escape. They would be delivered and sold to the British in Detroit. This troublesome group was in turn subdivided into two smaller subgroups, one to leave immediately and the other to leave after helping the Shawanese with their spring planting. The first subgroup of ten included James Callaway Jr., William Tracy, Daniel

Asbury, Jesse Copher, William Brooks, Samuel Brooks, and Nathaniel Bullock. Daniel Boone would accompany the Shawanese and the first subgroup to Detroit in order to meet with Lieutenant Governor Hamilton and then return to Little Chalaakaatha. The second subgroup included John Brown and Richard Wade.[56]

Black Fish instructed Daniel Boone to explain the council decisions to his men. Daniel advised Micajah how to behave to minimize the risk of reprisals from the Shawanese while he was gone. He emphasized that any attempt at escape would have to be very well planned. They would almost certainly be put to death by the tomahawk, or worse, by the burning stake, if they attempted to escape and failed.

Micajah hobbled out to say goodbye to the north-bound prisoners as they prepared to leave. Black Fish and his escort of warriors were accompanied by Louis Lorimier and Charles Beaubien.[57] As James Jr. walked off with the group headed to Detroit, he looked back at Micajah, smiled, waved, and turned to face his future.[58]

Black Fish took Daniel Boone to meet Lieutenant Governor Hamilton upon their arrival at Detroit several days later. Hamilton treated Daniel with respect and promised to honor the promises made to Boone by the Shawanese to treat the prisoners well.

Daniel Boone repeated his promise to arrange the peaceful surrender of Fort Boonesborough. Hamilton gave Daniel the gift of a horse and saddle.[59] Black Fish and the Shawanese delegation sold the obstinate James Callaway Jr., Samuel Brooks, William Brooks, and Nathaniel Bullock to the British and returned to Little Chalaakaatha with Daniel.[60]

Little Chalaakaatha

THE PRISONERS WHO STAYED IN LITTLE CHALAAKAATHA were divided up and allotted to individual chiefs and warriors. Micajah continued in the custody of Nenessica and his wife.

Nenessica was a war chief of the Makujay division but lived among the Chalaakaatha division and served as one of Black Fish's senior war captains. He was related to Louis Lorimier's half-French wife Charlotte ("Pemanpieh")

Bougainville.[61] Nenessica's wife was a good-natured, heavy-set woman and was among the leading women of Little Chalaakaatha.

Nenessica was a respected and courageous war leader and an excellent hunter. As a senior Makujay Shawanese chief, he was also closely allied to the Shawanese Makujay leadership in Kishenosity's and Cornstalk's families and played a key role in diplomatic affairs and intelligence operations. He may have chosen to take custody of Micajah because he knew of Micajah's connection to the influential Boone and Callaway Long Knife families. That connection might prove useful in future conflicts and negotiations.

Nenessica and his wife lived in a sturdy one-room log cabin not far from the council house. Micajah was kept in a wegiwa behind their cabin.

The couple were demanding wardens but were not brutal. Nenessica's wife nursed his damaged toes and feet until they had healed, although they were heavily scarred and a source of chronic pain for the remainder of his life. She gave him a soft and supple pair of Shawanese "mockeethena" (mocassins) to wear.

Micajah was initially escorted by Nenessica or his wife when he went out into the village. He was later allowed limited freedom of movement within the town during the day, but was bound at night.

As his weeks of his captivity turned into months, Micajah began to observe the many religious ceremonies, dances, and games that enriched Shawanese life. He was surprised at their depth and complexity. There was much to learn. Language was the key to understanding his captors, and Micajah resolved to learn their language as quickly as possible.

Nenessica and his wife began to teach him the Shawanese language as they taught him the duties and limitations of a prisoner. Micajah also taught Nenessica to speak and understand some English.

Black Shawanese interpreter Caesar had established a smithy in Little Chalaakaatha where he engaged in both blacksmith and gunsmith work.[62] Caesar was born in Africa and had first joined the Shawanese in their southern towns in the Creek territory of Alabama before moving to their northern towns in Ohio.[63] Nenessica first met Caesar in the Creek towns and had known him for many years. He was a gifted linguist and spoke French, Spanish, English, and several African and Indian languages. He may have helped Micajah learn the Shawanese language.

Kishenosity and Nimwha were the senior civil chiefs of their nation but they were very old and their health was declining. Chief Moluntha was also aged but he was healthy and full of vitality. At eighty-five, he had a vast reservoir of life experience and was skilled in the art of negotiations. Moluntha's influence grew as Kishenosity and Nimwha weakened.

The passage of time had not dimmed Moluntha's passion for the pleasures of marital union, and this was a subject of much amusement among his tribesmen. He was married to Cornstalk's niece Lamatumque—an exquisitely beautiful and refined young lady of about twenty years of age.[64] Moluntha and his family lived in a small village named Moluntha's Town, located on the summit of a compact hill rising above the floodplain of the Mad River, directly across the river a short distance from Mackachack.[65]

Daniel Boone cultivated a friendship with Black Fish after their return to Little Chalaakaatha from Detroit. Black Fish adopted him into his family as a son and gave him the Shawanese name of "Shel-tow-ey" (Big Turtle). Daniel replaced Black Fish's biological son, who had been killed during the rescue of the Callaway girls and Jemima Boone.[66]

William Hancock was adopted into Captain Will's family.[67] Joseph Jackson, one of the other saltboiler prisoners from Bedford County, was adopted by Louis Lorimier's wife Pemanpieh. She was a relative of Nenessica.[68] They gave Jackson the name "Fish." Micajah was adopted by Nenessica and his wife. Jack Dunn, George Hendrick, Benjamin Kelly, John Holley, and Ansel Goodman were also adopted.[69]

Micajah was adopted in a typical Shawanese adoption ceremony. Shawanese women shaved his head except for a scalp-lock on the very top of his head. He was made to run a gentle form of the gauntlet which amounted to little more than hazing with switches. He was stripped naked and his body was painted. He was then taken to the Little Miami River where he was washed clean by the women, to "wash away the white blood." He was given an Indian name and dressed in Shawanese clothing.[70]

There were many other white people living among the Shawanese in Little Chalaakaatha and the other Shawanese towns. Most were prisoners, adoptees, or traders, but many of them chose to live with the Shawanese as a matter of preference because the less regimented lifestyle appealed to them.

Piqua War Chief Wryneck (Joshua Rennick) lived in the town of Piqua, on the Mad River to the north of Little Chalaakaatha. He had been captured in Virginia and adopted into the Shawanese Nation during the French and Indian War. White Wolf (John Ward) and Shawnute (Richard Sparks) were also adopted into the nation during the same time period.[71]

Daniel Boone truly enjoyed the Shawanese way of life after his adoption by Chief Black Fish. He grew fond of Black Fish and his wife and became quite attached to their little twin daughters, Pommepesy and Pimmepesy.[72] He earned sufficient trust that he was allowed to hunt alone, although he was limited to a ration of two bullets on each hunting trip to discourage him from running away. Despite appearances, Daniel still planned to return to his white family and developed a plan to escape with Micajah.[73]

Andrew Johnson was the first of the saltboilers to escape from Little Chalaakaatha just a few weeks after his capture. He made his way back to Fort Boonesborough and brought with him a disturbing story of Daniel Boone's defection to the British.[74]

Daniel Boone learned in early June that Chief Black Fish and the British planned to send an army of four hundred Shawanese warriors accompanied by a company of French Canadian militia to Fort Boonesborough. The Shawanese and British would offer to accept the fort's surrender as Boone had promised them. If the occupants of the fort would not surrender, the combined force would attack and destroy them. Daniel had to act quickly to escape and warn his family and friends of the impending offensive.

Black Fish and a group of Shawanese warriors went to the salt lick near Old Chalaakaatha on Paint Creek near the Scioto River to hunt bear and turkey and make salt before the Shawanese army departed for Kentucky. The Paint Creek area still abounded with bear and other wild game. Boone accompanied them, and Black Fish's wife and a few other women also went along to help.

Daniel had secretly saved three or four extra rifle balls and gunpowder and hid them in his hunting shirt. He repaired a rifle stock for an adopted white Shawanese warrior named Jimmy Rogers while they camped near Paint Creek. He was paid with an old gun barrel and lock.

Black Fish's party headed back to Little Chalaakaatha after making enough salt. The warriors decided to hunt and kill some bear on the return trip so their families would have enough meat while the warriors were gone to Kentucky. As they prepared for the hunt, they heard turkeys gobbling in the forest and spontaneously took off after them.

Daniel was left alone with the women. He saw his opportunity to escape and seized it. The horse that Daniel was riding had a couple of salt-boiling kettles fastened on behind the saddle. He cut the cords holding the kettles fast, and they tumbled to the ground with a crash. Daniel shouted to Black Fish's wife and the other women that he wanted to go home to Kentucky to see his wife and children.

The women cried out for their warriors. Daniel made off at full speed, and the warriors pursued him. He had a good headstart and rode hard until his horse gave out. Daniel abandoned the exhausted horse in the forest and ran on, frequently breaking his course by running upon fallen trees across his path. He increased the distance of his lead over his pursuers as they struggled to track his trail. He finally outstripped them so much that they gave up the chase.[75]

William Hancock was the next prisoner to escape from Captain Will, not long after Daniel Boone's escape. Like Andrew Johnson, he accused Boone of being a Tory and betraying his country and the people of Fort Boonesborough.[76]

Black Fish and Captain Will were both heartbroken and furious over the escapes of their adopted sons. Black Fish redoubled security measures for the remaining prisoners, and Micajah's limited freedoms were severely restricted.

Seven | The Bluegrass War

The Gathering Storm (1778)
The British and Indian Alliance

ALTHOUGH MICAJAH WAS STILL BOUND AND STAKED to the ground at night, Nenessica allowed him to have greater freedom of movement during daylight as the summer of 1778 passed. Micajah accompanied him on several hunting trips. To Micajah's great delight, Nenessica had saved his long rifle and his knife at the time of his capture, and he returned them both to him.

Nenessica soon came to appreciate Micajah's uncanny skill in tracking and silently stalking prey. Micajah could pass through the woods like a silent woodland spirit. If your back was turned, he could come up behind you without detection.[1]

When the hunters spotted a feeding white-tailed deer, Micajah would remove some distance downwind so that the deer would not catch his scent. He waited to begin his stalking advance until the deer put its head down to browse. The deer's tail would always twitch before it raised its head, and Micajah would stop his advance and stand motionless, resuming his advance only when the deer put its head down again. In this manner, Micajah could draw close enough to the deer to make an easy shot.[2] He helped Nenessica dress deer and packed the meat back to town on his back.

Micajah used his daytime freedom to become acquainted with several of the other prisoners. He became good friends with Fish Jackson and made the acquaintance of Lewis Wetzel and other non-saltboiler prisoners.

One day a group of the saltboiler prisoners were talking under a tree near the council house. One of them asked Micajah how he felt about the beating his Uncle Richard had administered to him in Fort Boonesborough. Micajah vented some of his angry, pent-up feelings about that incident, saying that he would get even with his uncle some day if he had the opportunity.[3]

ALEXANDER MCKEE, MATTHEW ELLIOT, AND SIMON GIRTY left Fort Pitt to defect to the British side on March 28, 1778. Lieutenant Governor Hamilton welcomed McKee upon his arrival in Detroit and immediately appointed him to serve as Deputy British Indian Agent in the British Indian Department. He was also commissioned as a captain in the Royal Army. Matthew Elliot had worked with McKee at Fort Pitt on Indian affairs after leaving Piqua with his Shawanese wife.[4] Elliot swore his loyalty to the king and went to work with McKee in Detroit.

Simon Girty was short and stocky with black hair.[5] His heavy brows shaded piercing deep-set grey eyes above a flat nose. He wore a red silk bandana around his head and wore Indian clothing without ornamentation.[6] Simon was retained to serve as an interpreter for the Indian Department for $2.00 per day, and was joined by his brothers George and James.[7]

The British held another Grand Council with the northwestern Indian nations in Detroit from June 14 to June 20, 1778. One thousand six hundred eighty-three Indians attended, including the Shawanese leaders. The British delivered presents to all of the Indians in attendance.[8]

Lieutenant Governor Hamilton introduced Captain Alexander McKee to the Indian nations in his new capacity as the Deputy Indian Agent at Detroit. The leaders of the nations had known and respected McKee for many years and were delighted that he had joined their fight against the Long Knives. Hamilton also introduced Simon Girty and explained that he would serve the British as an interpreter.

McKee and his men set about improving the network of communications between and among the Indian nations and towns after the council concluded. They instituted a system of express riders and increased the volume and distribution of trade goods and munitions. Many French Canadians worked with McKee in the Indian Department.[9]

The Shawanese and Wyandot Nations were the most active fighters in the Indian Confederacy. The Wyandot concentrated on the upper Ohio River valley around Wheeling and Fort Pitt, and the Shawanese focused on Kentucky. They were supported by their Mingo friends and militants from the Delaware Nation.

Captain McKee, Matthew Eliott, and Simon and George Girty frequently visited the Shawanese towns. The Shawanese chiefs and Alexander McKee agreed that their most important military objective was the capture and destruction of Fort Boonesborough.

Micajah and the remaining saltboiler prisoners developed an escape plan. A Shawanese woman who understood English overhead them discussing the plan and told Black Fish and Simon Girty what she had heard.[10] Two husky warriors escorted Micajah to the edge of the town, warned him to give up his escape plans, and beat him until he was nearly senseless. He was forced to run the gauntlet and was bound for several weeks following the incident.

The Siege of Fort Boonesborough

COLONEL RICHARD CALLAWAY WAS THE SECOND-RANKING OFFICER in the Kentucky County militia behind Colonel John Bowman and was technically the commanding officer at Fort Boonesborough. However, his authority was clouded by the presence of Major William Bailey Smith from Colonel George Rogers Clark's Illinois Regiment. Smith claimed higher authority over the county militia via Clark's direct commission from the Virginia General Assembly.[11] Colonel Callaway and Major Smith shared the command by consensus in order to avoid a paralyzing dispute and stalemate over who was in charge.

Flanders's brother John Callaway arrived at Fort Boonesborough and joined Captain John Holder's militia company in the spring of 1778. He reported that news of the tragedy of the saltboilers had traveled back to Bedford County, and that their mother Sarah was very upset. Younger brothers Edmund and William were also beginning to talk about moving to Kentucky.

Daniel Boone returned to Fort Boonesborough on June 20, 1778, after his daring escape. He had traveled the astounding distance of 160 miles on foot in four days. Daniel was disappointed to find that his wife Rebecca and younger children had returned to Virginia and only his loyal daughter Jemima remained at Fort Boonesborough with her husband Flanders.

Colonel Richard Callaway bluntly accused Daniel of treason. Several of the men at the fort agreed with him. Daniel reassured his accusers that the surrender of the saltboilers and promise to give up the fort were ruses intended to fool the Shawanese and minimize the loss of life. Colonel Callaway reluctantly set aside his accusations for the time being in the interests of preparing for the common defense.

The Long Knives rushed to prepare the fort for the coming engagement. The last gap in the stockade wall was closed and the last two corner bastions completed. Rotting timbers in the stockade were replaced. Arms and ammunition were issued to all able-bodied men, including African-American slaves.[12] They were able to muster about sixty fighters. African-American Monk Estil manufactured gunpowder in preparation for the battle.[13]

LIEUTENANT FONTENOY DE QUINDRE FROM THE BRITISH INDIAN Department in Detroit was placed in command of a combined Shawanese and French Canadian army tasked to capture and reduce Fort Boonesborugh.[14] Chief Black Fish assembled four hundred Shawanese warriors for the campaign, and McKee and Simon Girty arranged for the participation of forty French Canadian militiamen to augment the Shawanese force.[15] Louis Lorimier and interpreter Pierre Drouillard accompanied them.[16] The British and Indian commanders decided not to bring cannon with them based on the assumption that Daniel Boone would surrender as he had promised.

Nenessica joined the war party and left instructions for his wife to watch Micajah closely to prevent an escape attempt while he was gone. The warriors painted their faces red and black and held a large war dance. Their shamans augured the future and predicted success. The little army departed from Little Chalaakaatha and marched single-file to the south, down the path to the mouth of the Licking River on the Ohio River. They sang inspirational war songs as they marched.

The Bluegrass War

DANIEL BOONE RECOMMENDED A BRIEF OFFENSIVE EXPEDITION against the Shawanese in late August. The objective was the small Shawanese community still living in the remnants of the town of Old Chalaakaatha on the Paint Creek tributary of the Scioto River. Boone had been there with Black Fish's family immediately before his escape and had fresh intelligence on the number and disposition of the Shawanese living there. Colonel Callaway objected because the expedition would leave the fort too lightly defended. His objections were to no avail.[17]

Daniel Boone assembled a raiding party of eighteen men for the Paint Creek expedition. Captain John Holder and Micajah's brother John Callaway were among the raiders, and[18] Simon Kenton served as the advance scout. They marched off to the north and crossed the Ohio River.

Daniel Boone and his men engaged a Makujay war party in a brief but intense firefight and drove the warriors from the field of battle. One of Chief Moluntha's sons was killed in the engagement. Boone and his men returned to the fort just before the main body of the Shawanese and French Canadian invasion force arrived.[19]

The Shawanese and British army crossed the Kentucky River a mile and a half upstream from Fort Boonesborough and marched into view in single file along the crest of the ridge to the south of the fort at 10:00 a.m. on September 8, 1778. Chief Wryneck, Nenessica, and Chief Black Hoof served as Black Fish's war captains.[20]

Old Chief Moluntha accompanied them to avenge the death of his son on Paint Creek. He had tracked Boone's raiding party from Old Chalaakaatha back to the fort.[21] The combined Shawanese and British army contained nearly eight times as many fighters as the Long Knife fighters in the fort.

The Shawanese army struck their flag south of the Fort Boonesborough gate just out of rifle shot range from the fort and halted. They built a temporary shelter there for their chiefs. As soon as their encampment was secured, Pompey approached the fort and climbed up on a stump. He shouted that Chief Black Fish had come to accept the surrender of the fort as Daniel Boone had promised at the Lower Blue Licks and Detroit. He had letters from Lieutenant Governor Hamilton promising safe conduct to Detroit.[22]

Chief Black Fish called out in the Shawanese language for Daniel Boone to come out of the fort and meet with him. Daniel shouted back that he was no longer in charge of the fort and would have to consult with those who were.

Daniel obtained the consent of the fort commanders to parley with Chief Black Fish and walked over to meet with him in his shelter.[23] They greeted each other warmly and sat down to parley. Chief Black Fish openly wept as he asked Daniel why he had run away. Daniel replied that he did so because he wanted to see his family and children. The occupants of the fort were very disturbed by the obvious affection that they showed for each other.

Chief Moluntha angrily asked Daniel why his son had been killed. Daniel denied any knowledge of the incident. Moluntha said that he had tracked Boone back to the fort himself and called him a liar.

Chief Black Fish handed the letter from Lieutenant Governor Hamilton to Daniel and presented him with a wampum belt with rows of red, white, and black wampum beads. The red represented the warpath, the white was the path of peace that they could take together to Detroit, and the black symbolized their death if they did not surrender.[24]

Daniel returned to the fort with the wampum belt and held a council with the other settlers. They debated their options until Colonel Richard Callaway had heard enough. He issued an ultimatum. There would be no surrender and, furthermore, he would personally shoot any man who tried to do so.[25]

There was no further serious discussion of surrender. The settlers decided to stall and negotiate with the Shawanese as they prepared for a siege. They were soon hard at work preparing for the worst.

Chief Black Fish and the other Indians asked Daniel to introduce them to his daughter Jemima. Daniel had often described her to them in Little Chalaakaatha. He agreed that they could meet her. Colonel Callaway escorted Jemima to the gate and partially opened it. He carried a loaded and primed long rifle in his arms. Other riflemen covered them from the bastions.

Jemima stepped into the open gateway and greeted the Shawanese. They asked her to undo her beautiful long dark hair so that they could see it. She obligingly untied it and shook it loose. Several warriors ran up to Richard and Jemima and asked to touch her hair and shake her hand. Colonel Callaway cocked and aimed his rifle and told them to step back. If they touched her, he would blow a hole through them. Richard pressed Jemima into the fort, backed his way through the gate, and barred it.[26]

The Long Knives told Pompey to tell Chief Black Fish that evening that they would never surrender to the Shawanese. Black Fish was shocked. He had not expected them to refuse and apparently did not have an alternative plan. It would be very difficult to overcome the sturdy fort without cannon to knock down the walls. He decided to negotiate and asked for a parley. His decision in turn surprised the Long Knives.

The Long Knife leaders debated among themselves and agreed to accept the invitation.[27] Colonel Richard Callaway, Major William Bailey Smith, Captain Daniel Boone, Flanders Callaway, Squire Boone, William Hancock, Stephen Hancock, and William Buchanan were selected to serve as Treaty Commissioners.[28]

They agreed to meet under the great "Divine Elm" tree in front of the fort gate on September 9. Colonel Callaway asked the women in the fort to dress in men's hats and hunting shirts so that it would look like they had more soldiers when the Indians drew nearer to the fort, and the women complied. Jemima tucked her long hair under a hat and took her place on the ramparts.[29] Sharpshooters were posted in the bastions to cover the commissioners.

The Long Knife and Shawanese representatives cautiously moved forward from their secured positions and met under the elm tree. Daniel Boone and Colonel Callaway spoke for the Long Knives and Black Fish spoke for the Shawanese chiefs. The discussions lasted for hours. They finally appeared to reach a peaceful resolution that preserved the safety of the fort and its occupants and gave assurances to the Shawanese that they would not be driven off their lands. The Shawanese chiefs asked to shake their hands to consummate their agreements.

Two Shawanese chiefs stepped up to each Long Knife commissioner to shake both of their hands. Richard Callaway sensed a trap and jerked himself away. A scuffle ensued and the sharpshooters posted in the bastions opened fire. The entire Shawanese and French Canadian army responded with a deafening chorus of war whoops and a huge barrage of musket fire and arrows.

Richard Callaway, Daniel Boone, Flanders Callaway, and the other commissioners ran for their lives toward the fort gate.[30] Daniel ducked between the legs of a warrior who blocked his path to the gate and stood up to flip him over his back. The warrior slammed a tomahawk between his shoulder blades. Fortunately the blade was turned flat and only caused a severe bruise.[31]

Flanders lost the tip of the little finger on his left hand to a musket ball. Squire Boone was shot in his heel as he ran through the gate, and Richard Callaway received a bloody but superficial wound in the neck.[32] The gate was closed and barred as the last of the commissioners ran inside.

The Shawanese attacked in force and a siege ensued. Women and children took refuge in Colonel Callaway's sturdy cabin in the center of the compound.[33] Everyone in the fort helped in the defense, including the women, and there were many instances of heroism.

Colonel Richard Callaway projected strength, confidence, and optimism. He knew that this battle would decide the future of the Long Knives and the Shawanese. This was his moment in history. He loosened his long black- and grey-streaked hair, removed his shirt, tucked his tomahawk into his belt, took up his long rifle, and fought bare-chested from the bastions.[34] His calm and determined demeanor encouraged and preserved the morale of the outnumbered defenders. He was later described by admiring participants as "laboring like a Titan" throughout the siege.[35]

The Long Knives and Shawanese shouted insults at each other. "Yellow sons of bitches!" the Long Knives cursed. "Come out and fight like men!" the Shawanese retorted. Several of the participants later said that they heard the most creative swearing of their entire lives during the siege.[36]

Daniel Boone's and Flanders Callaway's deadly marksmanship made every rifle ball that they fired count. A tall warrior taunted the Long Knives by stepping out from behind a tree to show himself and then ducked back behind the tree before they could hit him. Daniel, Flanders, and a few other men elevated their gunsights to different levels and fired simultaneously at Daniel's signal when the warrior showed himself again. The warrior dropped dead on the ground.[37]

Jemima molded lead rifle balls, cradled them in her skirt, and ran them out to the men while they were still too hot to handle with her hands. She was struck in her buttock by a spent musket ball. The ball pushed her clothing into her flesh without tearing the cloth, and popped right out when she tugged the cloth. She continued her heroic efforts despite the painful wound.[38]

The Shawanese tried to set the fort on fire every night. They slung burning bundles of flax and hickory shag-bark onto the cabin roofs with ropes. Jemima helped the men pull the burning bundles off the cabin roofs and extinguish them.[39] It was their good fortune that it rained nearly every night, which helped to douse the fires.[40]

Captain Holder dashed out through the fort gate to put out a fire started against an exterior door to the fort. He shouted curses as Indian musket balls struck all around him. Colonel Callaway's wife Elizabeth chided him for cursing when he should be praying. Holder heatedly responded that he did not have time to pray.[41]

Squire Boone fabricated a wooden cannon. It fired successfully once and then exploded on the second attempt. The Shawanese hooted derisively.

The Shawanese and French militiamen began to dig a tunnel from the river-bank to undermine the stockade walls beginning on about September 12. The defenders of the fort heard suspicious sounds coming from the river-bank and built a tall watch-tower on top of Judge Henderson's cabin. They confirmed their suspicions when they observed dirt being thrown from the river-bank into the river.[42]

Daniel Boone directed the defenders to dig a trench on the inside wall of the stockade to intercept the tunnel and gain the element of surprise through ambush. Pompey was killed by William Collins when he poked his head up from the tunnel entrance to look toward the fort.[43] On September 16, the Shawanese tunnel collapsed from the effects of the rainfall before it reached the fort.

The Shawanese unleashed a ferocious final assault on the night of September 17. A large swarm of whooping, painted warriors with torches left their protective cover and rushed the fort from all sides. The balance of the Shawanese force provided a fierce cover of musket fire for their attacking comrades.

There were more attacking warriors than could be gunned down before they reached the fort, and they succeeded in starting several fires. The glow of the torches, fires, and exploding gunpowder lit up the night sky and was visible for miles around. The exhausted defenders desperately fought the flames and battled for their lives as musket fire and arrows poured into the fort.

The Long Knives' accurate return fire killed and wounded many warriors. Their desperate efforts succeeded, and they barely prevented the enemy from breaching their defenses. A late rain put out the remaining fires, and the fighting tapered off into the night.

The discouraged Shawanese and French Canadians withdrew from the field of battle on September 18.[44] Thirty-seven Shawanese warriors had been killed during the siege,[45] but only two of the fort occupants were lost. The decision not to bring artillery to breach the fort walls had proven to be a critical strategic error by the Shawanese.

The Long Knives at Fort Boonesborough had survived and preserved their tenuous foothold in Kentucky. They had proven that families as well as soldiers could live there. The Shawanese had made their very best effort to dislodge them, but at a high cost in human life. It had not been enough. This was a pivotal point in American history.

The alienation of Colonel Richard Callaway and Captain Daniel Boone was complete and irreconcilable after the siege ended. Colonel Callaway and Captain Benjamin Logan filed formal charges of treason against Daniel Boone. They alleged that he had conspired with the British and Shawanese against the Americans at Fort Boonesborough. Colonel Callaway "insisted he was a Tory (in) favour of the British and he ought to be broak of his commission."

A court-martial trial ensued. Colonel John Bowman served as the prosecutor and Colonel Daniel Trabue served as the judge. Daniel Boone testified on his own behalf. He explained his elaborate, crafty, and ultimately successful strategy of deception. He emphasized that he had preserved the lives of the saltboilers, had delivered a timely warning of the invasion, and successfully supported the defense of Fort Boonesborough with minimal loss of life. He was exonerated at the conclusion of the humiliating trial.[46]

Logan's Fort was besieged again by Shawanese and Mingo war parties not long after the conclusion of the court-martial proceeding. Captain Logan sent an express rider to Colonel William Fleming urgently requesting additional military assistance from Botetourt County.

Colonel Fleming called together a Botetourt County council of war. The council directed Colonel Bowman and Captain Pauling to return to Kentucky with two hundred additional soldiers for the immediate relief of Logan's Fort. They were directed to remain in Kentucky until the following spring and then attack Little Chalaakaatha.

The council of war issued a call for volunteers. One hundred sixty men

Little Chalaakaatha

MICAJAH LEARNED THE OUTCOME OF THE SIEGE of Fort Boonesborough after the warriors returned to Little Chalaakaatha in the fall of 1778. Nenessica was in a dark mood. Micajah was careful to show no emotion at hearing the news. He put thoughts of an immediate escape out of his mind for the time being.

He had been on his best behavior since his aborted escape attempt and his captors once again allowed him to move about the town during the day with relative freedom as time passed. Micajah continued to learn the Shawanese language and had many teachers. He may have helped Caesar at the smithy and assisted the women in the cornfields. He helped the women harvest pumpkins, cut them into strips, and dry them in the sun. He accompanied Nenessica on hunting trips when he returned from the war.

Nenessica introduced Micajah to Shawanese hunting etiquette and techniques. When two men hunted together, the first game killed by each was offered to the other. It was always graciously accepted with thanks. The Shawanese also engaged in ritualistic "medicine hunting." Four painted medicine sticks were used to tap out an intricate rhythm and accompany magical songs that drew game near their hunting camps for an easy kill. Game was hung from trees as it was killed and was then collected at the end of the hunt. There was no theft. The women and children skinned the game, prepared the furs and hides for use or trade, and cut the meat into strips for drying.[48]

Micajah accompanied Nenessica's wife on a trip to collect firewood one day not long after the siege of Fort Boonesborough. As they were passing by a group of Shawanese women gathered near Louis Lorimier's branch post, he heard peels of clear, ringing female laughter as he walked by.

The source of the laughter was an unusually beautiful young woman. Her doeskin shift was artfully decorated with bead and quillwork and was highlighted with hundreds of pieces of sparkling silver jewelry.[49] A dot of red paint had been applied to the middle of each of her cheeks. The young woman was animatedly talking to an older woman who was also very well dressed. They were looking at a piece of silver jewelry.

The young woman smiled at him as he passed by. Micajah quickly looked down, but tugged at Nenessica's wife's sleeve after they had passed them and subtly motioned back to the young lady. She smiled and said, "She is Lamatumque, wife of Moluntha. She carries his unborn child. The older woman is her mother, our Headwoman Coitcheleh, sister of Cornstalk."[50]

COLONEL JOHN BOWMAN SENT SIMON KENTON, ALEXANDER Montgomery, and George Clark (not to be confused with George Rogers Clark) to spy on Little Chalaakaatha in September of 1778. The three scouts stole seven horses from the Shawanese, but the horses balked at crossing the Ohio River. This gave their Shawanese pursuers enough time to catch up with them on September 13. Montgomery was killed and Kenton was captured by a warrior named Bonah following a brief skirmish. Clark eluded capture and carried his intelligence back to Colonel Bowman.

Bonah gave Kenton a lesson in Shawanese morality and followed it with a beating:

> "Young man, didn't you know it was wrong to steal Indians' horses?"
>
> "No, I did not, for you come and steal our horses."
>
> "Don't you know the Great Spirit don't love people that steal?"
>
> "No—did you ever know it?"
>
> "Yes, 20 years ago. Indians have got no cattle about their doors like white people—the buffalo are our cattle, but you come here and kill them; you have no business to kill Indians' cattle: Did you know that?"
>
> "No, I did not."[51]

Kenton was forced to run the gauntlet as they approached Little Chalaakaatha.[52] Since Micajah lived there he may have witnessed the event.

Caesar advised Kenton to break through the lines and run for the council house for safety. Kenton attempted to do so but was trapped and severely injured.[53]

The Shawanese council sentenced Simon Kenton to die by burning at the stake. His life was ultimately saved after running several more gauntlets when Pierre Drouillard, the British Indian Department interpreter for the Wyandot Nation, took him to Detroit for interrogation.[54]

Colonel George Rogers Clark and the Illinois Country

GOVERNOR PATRICK HENRY OF VIRGINIA DIRECTED COLONEL George Rogers Clark to form a regiment comprised of seven companies of fifty men each in January of 1778. The regiment was named the Illinois Regiment.[55] Governor Henry ordered Colonel Clark to secretly proceed from Fort Pitt down the Ohio River and then overland to attack and capture the British Post at Kaskaskia in the Illinois Country along the Mississippi River.

Most of the white European population living in the northwestern frontier was French. The old French towns of Kaskaskia, Cahokia, Vincennes, Ouiatenon, and Detroit and the outlying French trading posts continued as viable communities. Kaskaskia was the largest and oldest of the French towns with a population of 3,500 residents.[56]

The Frenchmen on the frontier found themselves facing a difficult choice. The recent Quebec Act had restored their rights and dignity.[57] Many Frenchmen such as Captain Jacques Duperon Bâby and trader Louis Lorimier elected to remain loyal to King George III.[58] They were instrumental in convincing the northwestern Indian nations to ally themselves with the British.[59]

Other Frenchmen on the frontier never lost their antipathy toward Great Britain after the French and Indian War. These anti-British Frenchmen were potentially valuable allies for the Virginians in the northwestern theater of war.[60]

Governor Henry told Colonel Clark that he could expect little help from Virginia or Congress on his mission and would have to be self-sufficient. Despite these limitations, Clark was able to muster two hundred men for the Illinois Regiment. The little army departed down the Ohio River on its mission on May 12, 1778.

Colonel Clark encamped with his regiment on a small island on the Ohio River at the Falls of the Ohio and established a base of operations for his campaign. They constructed a small stockade, planted a crop of corn on the island, and named it "Corn Island." They completed their preparations and continued on the campaign.

Clark's mission was helped tremendously when France and the United States entered into a treaty of alliance on February 2, 1778, following the American victory at Saratoga. The treaty was ratified by the Continental Congress on May 4, 1778.

Colonel Clark and his men left Corn Island on a small fleet of boats and disembarked at the old abandoned French Fort Massac on the north shore of the Ohio River between the mouths of the Cumberland and Tennessee Rivers. They trekked across the southern Illinois Country and arrived at Kaskaskia on July 4, 1778.

Jesuit Father Pierre Gibault unlocked the gates of the town and met with Colonel Clark to discuss the purpose of his visit. He advised the citizens of Kaskaskia to welcome Clark and his men and support the new French-American alliance.[61]

Clark's bloodless victory at Kaskaskia was followed immediately by successful sorties to the nearby town of Cahokia, to the north, as well as the other French posts on the Mississippi River. The Frenchmen welcomed the Virginians as friends and allies.[62] Father Gibault advised Colonel Clark that the real key to possession of the northwestern frontier was not Kaskaskia. It was the strategically located old French town of Vincennes and its British Fort Sackville on the Wabash River.

Clark seized Vincennes and its fort with Gibault's full endorsement.[63] He placed Captain Leonard Helm in command of a small garrison there and returned west to Cahokia.

Colonel Clark next turned his attention to pacifying as many of the northwestern Indian allies of Great Britain as possible in August and September of 1778. He called for a council of the northwestern Indian nations to assemble and parley at Cahokia. Most of the nations attended his council.

The Indian nations had already learned of the new American alliance with France. They were also impressed by Clark's feats and the force of his personality. Ten or twelve of the nations attending the Cahokia council signed treaties with Clark and became allies of the United Colonies and France in the war with Great Britain. The signatory nations included the powerful Chippewa, Ottawa, Pottawatomie, Winnebago, Sauk, Fox, and Osage Nations. The Kickapoo and Piankashaw Nations in the Wabash country also joined the alliance in response to letters from Clark.[64]

The Shawanese sent Chief Wryneck to the Cahokia council as an observer. Wryneck was greatly impressed by Colonel Clark, and Clark asked him to return to the Shawanese to counsel with his nation and pass along Clark's request that they also sign a treaty of peace. Chief Wryneck depart-

George Rogers Clark [© John Buxton]

ed from Cahokia and promised Clark to return within twenty days with the chiefs of the Shawanese Nation to treat for peace.[65]

The Shawanese chiefs were troubled by Chief Wryneck's report and passed Wryneck's intelligence on to their British allies. Clark was clearly a very capable and forceful man. The Americans now had Indian allies in the west. The British northwestern strategy had been at least partially frustrated. Nonetheless, the Shawanese chiefs made the fateful decision not to attend Clark's council.

The Long Knives Strike Back (1779)
Colonel Clark's Revenge

LIEUTENANT GOVERNOR HAMILTON PLANNED A BRITISH COUNTERSTROKE as the Americans celebrated their victories. He would personally lead a military expedition from Detroit to Vincennes with the goal of recapturing Fort Sackville.

Micajah's brother James Callaway Jr., Samuel Brooks, and Josiah Dickson had been held in a British prison in Detroit since their capture with Daniel Boone. They learned of Hamilton's planned expedition from informants and redoubled their efforts to escape so that they could warn their people of the British plans.

The three prisoners overpowered their Indian guards while they were sleeping and stole their guns, killing two or three of the guards in the process. The young men completed their escape before dawn, stole a canoe, and paddled down the Detroit River through an early morning fog.[66]

The fog cleared off as the morning sun intensified. Unfortunately, the escapees found themselves in the midst of an Indian town along the banks of the stream when the fog cleared. They were recaptured and made to run the gauntlet. They were then returned to confinement in Detroit where they were overheard planning yet another attempt to escape. The British placed the troublesome prisoners in irons and removed them to Quebec.[67]

Lieutenant Governor Hamilton marched from Detroit in the autumn of 1778 at the head of a small army of British regulars, Canadian militia, and

Indian allies, to attack the American garrison at Fort Sackville. A contingent of Shawanese warriors accompanied Hamilton under the leadership of Alexander McKee. Captain Helm and his small American garrison at Fort Sackville surrendered to the British and Indians on the wintry day of December 17, 1778.[68]

The British and their allies did not enjoy their victory at Vincennes for long. Colonel Clark learned of the British reoccupation of Fort Sackville from French militiamen who had slipped away from Vincennes as the British and Indian force arrived. He resolved to recapture it without loss of time.

Clark and his hardy Illinois Regiment set off from Kaskaskia on February 5, 1779, on a desperate long-distance mission to recapture Fort Sackville. They were accompanied by two companies of Frenchmen mustered from Father Gibault's congregation at Kaskaskia.[69]

Clark and his little army rapidly marched many miles through floods, ice, and snow.[70] After an epic journey of eighteen days and many hardships, they arrived at Vincennes on February 23.[71] They once again gained the element of surprise over the enemy, assisted, no doubt, by the fact that many of the local Indians were in Detroit for a British-led council rather than patrolling the frontier.

The Virginians and Kaskaskia Frenchmen attacked and laid siege to Fort Sackville. Lieutenant Governor Hamilton surrendered on February 24, 1779, and was taken prisoner.[72]

Colonel Richard Callaway and a military escort took custody of Hamilton at the Hazel Patch on the Wilderness Road in Kentucky and escorted him to Williamsburg. Hamilton contemptuously referred to Richard as "our disciplinarian" in his journal of the trip.[73] Hamilton was imprisoned in Williamsburg in a dreary dungeon for the remainder of the war.[74]

The Illinois Regiment's victories in the Illinois Country and the successful defense of Fort Boonesborough cheered beleaguered American patriots throughout the thirteen American colonies. British intelligence reports indicated that the Indians allies of Great Britain were discouraged and increasingly concerned about the reliability and effectiveness of their British ally.[75]

A renewed flood of settlers poured into Kentucky through the Cumberland Gap and down the Ohio River. The new settlers included many able-bodied fighters that would augment the Long Knife militia forces.

Colonel George Rogers Clark was commissioned in May of 1779 as commander-in-chief of all Virginia forces in the northwestern country, including Kentucky and Illinois Counties. Clark remained posted in Vincennes until September of 1779 when he removed his headquarters to the Falls of the Ohio near the new settlement of Louisville, Kentucky. He built a new fort there on the south shore of the Ohio River to replace the small stockade on Corn Island. The new fort was called "Fort-on-Shore."[76]

Major Arent De Peyster was appointed as the new Commandant of the British post at Detroit to replace Lieutenant Governor Hamilton on July 3, 1779. He faced a tremendous challenge. The British and Indians would have to treat Colonel Clark and the increasingly powerful Long Knives with the utmost respect in their war planning.[77]

Little Chalaakaatha: January - May, 1779

THE SHAWANESE NATION HELD A COUNCIL IN late March of 1779 to address the recent Long Knife victories. Representatives of a large percentage of the Thawekila, Piqua, and Kispoko divisions announced their decision to leave the Ohio Country and join their Shawanese kinsmen living in the Creek Towns in Alabama.[78] They had grown weary of fighting the Long Knives and were discouraged by the course of the war. The emigrants were led by Chiefs Black Stump, Yellow Hawk, and Kishkalwa.[79] They departed and took four hundred warriors with them.[80]

Most of the Chalaakaatha and Makujay Shawanese divisions and remnants of the other three divisions elected to remain in the Ohio Country to fight on. The greatly weakened Ohio Shawanese would now face the Long Knives with a total of only about five hundred warriors.[81] Their survival in the Ohio Country would depend more than ever on the resolve and support of their allies.

Old Chief Kishenosity had died in the summer of 1778. Cornstalk's brother Nimwha (Munseka) succeeded Kishenosity as the Principal Civil Chief of the Shawanese Nation for a brief term before he died in late 1779. Moluntha succeeded Nimwha as the Principal Civil Chief or "King" of the Shawanese Nation.[82]

Micajah's acculturation to the Shawanese way of life continued as the seasons passed. He adopted the Shawanese way of dressing. His scalp lock was now shoulder length, greased with bear grease, and braided. His comprehension of the Shawanese language continued to improve, and he was now able to engage in halting, basic conversation. He began to make the beginnings of friendships with members of the Shawanese Nation. His commitment to escape dimmed as he found the Shawanese to be far more welcoming than his Uncle Richard had been.

Micajah became friends with several of the women and children who stayed in town when their warriors were off to war. The women told Micajah about their fears for the future of their nation and their children. Many chiefs and young warriors had already died in the war and funerals were a constant activity. The women feared that they might lose other family members.

The women said that they firmly believed that the Long Knives were determined to take away their lands by either killing them or driving them off. There were many accounts of brutal atrocities committed by the Long Knives against Shawanese women and children, and they were afraid of them. Micajah assured them that not all Long Knives were cruel and greedy, yet they remained skeptical.

The Shawanese in general were noted for their sense of humor and frequent laughter.[83] Micajah befriended a young Chalaakaatha warrior of about his own age named Chiaxi, who was a wiry, athletic young man of medium height and an excellent warrior. He had light skin for an Indian and said that he was "one third white" with French blood.[84] He had an excellent sense of humor and enjoyed life, sometimes drinking too much alcohol. Micajah joined him on more than one raucous occasion of drinking and rough-housing.

Micajah learned the basic tenets of Shawanese religion from his captors. The universe and all of its people are governed by Moneto, the Great Spirit, and Grandmother Kokomthena. The *idea* of creation came from Moneto and the *act* of creation was accomplished by Kokomthena. Moneto created Kokomthena who in turn created the earth, water, people, and animals.

Kokomthena lived in a spacious bark wegiwa in Heaven from which she observed her earthly grandchildren through her window in the sky. Heaven is located in the farthest reaches of the far west. The Thunderbirds are the guardians of the gates of Heaven. Lightning is the flashing of their eyes, and thunder is the flapping of their great wings. They are the patrons of war.[85]

Moneto created a great island for the Shawanese people to live upon. The island rests upon the back of a great turtle that Moneto made the grandfather of the Shawanese. Kindly Grandfather Turtle listens to his Shawanese grandchildrens' complaints and treats them with kindness.

The great evil spirit in the world is named Meearleetheena. He is far less powerful than Moneto but causes much evil among men.[86] There are other deities such as Kokomthena's Silly Boys and Cyclone Person. Cyclone Person was created by Kokomthena and lives with her. Her whirling hair tears down trees during tornadoes and hurricanes.[87]

The sacred fire of the Shawanese Nation was kept by two custodians, one from the Kispoko division and the other from the Chalaakaatha division. The identity and welfare of the Shawanese Nation depended upon its preservation and security. The mystical fire was contained in a bound hide bundle hanging by a tether from the roof of its own special dwelling.[88]

Each of the five Shawanese divisions kept its own sacred bundle. The bundles contained relics of great religious and magical significance. The welfare of the Shawanese Nation also depended upon their preservation.

Tobacco was the principal Truth Bearer of the Shawanese. A palm full of tobacco was thrown into a consecrated sacred fire as an offering during all of the important religious ceremonies. A pinch was thrown into a fire whenever a prayer was offered to Moneto or Kokomthena. The tobacco smoke carried their prayers to Heaven.[89]

Micajah learned from his new friends that the men of the Shawanese Nation were primarily responsible for hunting and defense of their towns. They rarely helped the women with house and field work and spent their time in the towns socializing and resting. The women were generally responsible for planting and harvesting plant foods. They were the primary child care providers, although the men were loving and supportive fathers. The women were also responsible for cooking and maintenance of the home.

Nenessica and his band of warriors came and went on war parties through the late winter and spring. He took Micajah along on hunting trips when he was home from the war, and Micajah dressed and packed the meat at the end of their hunts.

Nenessica taught Micajah the Shawanese technique for hunting black bear in late winter. The bears were awakening from their hibernation at that time of year and left their dens every two to three days to get a drink of water. They always stepped in the same places and left deep impressions in the spongy thawing earth. It was easy to track them back to their dens. The hunters tossed smoky torches into their dens to smoke the occupants out into the open, and the bear were killed as they emerged.[90]

Nenessica told Micajah stories about his birth and early life in Eskippakithiki and Kentucky as they sat around their nightly campfires. His family had lived with Peter Chartier and his Makujay warriors before they fled to the Creek towns in Alabama to avoid Catawba raiders during the French and Indian War. Nenessica had returned to Kentucky for annual winter hunts ever since then and was determined that his people never lose their hunting grounds there. This was the cause for which he fought with such passion.

Micajah helped the women with their work in the corn and vegetable fields during Nenessica's long absences on military excursions. Although the women were very good farmers, Micajah had learned a great deal about farming during his youth in Bedford County, and the women came to respect his knowledge.

He helped the women render bear oil and grease following a successful bear hunt. The bear oil was stored in bags made from raccoon hides. The renderings had many uses.[91] Dried venison and dried pumpkin were delicious when cooked in bear oil, and bear grease was used to dress hair and cover the body for warmth in the winter.

Micajah participated in the annual Spring Bread Dance for the first time that year. It was presided over by the Piqua division who were generally charged with governing the religious affairs of their nation. The Shawanese held the ceremony in the spring to herald the arrival of new life in the new year. The women would plant no crops until they had completed the ritual.

It was more important to the Shawanese people than ever to maintain the rhythm of their ceremonial life despite the difficulties of doing so in the current troubled times. If they did not do so, they would fall out of grace with Moneto and Kokomthena. The Shawanese women in particular strove to maintain some semblance of normalcy, sheltering their precious children as much as possible from the ravaging winds of war.

The Spring Bread Dance was preceded by a game of football between the men and women. The game was dedicated to Kokomthena and the Thunderbirds and was believed to help ensure the arrival of the spring rains. Over a hundred individuals were on each side. The losers were required to clean and prepare the ground for the ceremonial dance.

The men and women made a prayer hoop in preparation for the game. The hoop was made of a flexible band of white oak bent and tied into a circle. The festival cooks decorated one half of the hoop with small fur packets of corn, squash, pumpkin, cucumber, and watermelon seeds. The festival hunters decorated the other half with four small fur packets containing skunk fur, deer hair, raccoon hair, and a turkey feather. The hoop represented the world and was a prayer to the Great Spirit for abundance in the coming year. The blessed seeds were saved and planted after the ceremony.

The object of the football game was to put the buckskin football through the goal of the opponent. The goals were formed by two stakes driven into the ground about six feet apart at opposite ends of a grassy clearing. A chief tossed the ball into the air in the center of the grounds with an invocation to the deities. The game began with a rush to the center and a general melee to chase down the ball.

The men had to move the ball with their feet and were forbidden to touch the ball with their hands on penalty of forfeiting the game. The women were allowed to use their hands and throw it as often as they liked. When a woman had the ball, the men were allowed to catch her and shake her as long as they did not touch the ball with their hands.[92] The football game was great fun, and there was much laughter. The men lost, as usual, and were put to work cleaning and preparing the ceremonial grounds.

Twelve festival hunters pursued bear and deer for the ceremonial feast in the next phase of the ceremony. The hunters rested in their cabins and wegiwas upon their return while twelve women prepared a feast of fresh cooked bear meat, dried deer tongue, cornbread, hominy, and delicious "blue bread" made from cornmeal, hominy grits, and the ashes of black-eyed pea hulls.

The singing and dancing began to the rhythm of a single water drum and two rattles. A line of female dancers filed onto the dance ground, led by the twelve cooks and danced counterclockwise around the food, dancing toe/heel (the Straight Dance). The women thanked the singers as they passed them. Twelve men then repeated the same dance. The women and girls then performed the Dove or Shuffle Dance, followed by the men and women performing the Straight Dance together.

Chief White Bark of the Piqua division then prayed to Kokomthena and thanked Her for the abundance of food and the good things in life. He pleaded for a bountiful harvest to come and tossed a palmful of tobacco into the fire to carry their prayers to Heaven. The feasting followed the prayer. Each Shawanese individual ate with their own personalized spoon carved from wood or buffalo horn.[93]

Colonel Bowman's Campaign of 1779

COLONEL JOHN BOWMAN MUSTERED A MILITIA REGIMENT comprised of 264 volunteers at Harrodsburg in late May. Their military objective was to attack and destroy Little Chilaakaatha. He organized the regiment into seven companies commanded by Captains Benjamin Logan, Richard May, Levi Todd, John Holder, Isaac Ruddell, James Harrod, and David Gass. Captain Todd was the grandfather of President Abraham Lincoln's wife, Mary Todd Lincoln.[94]

Captain Holder commanded the Fort Boonesborough volunteers, including Micajah's brother John Callaway and former saltboiler prisoner William Hancock.[95] Captain Harrod's company comprised about seventy men who had come to the Falls of the Ohio from the Monongahela River valley to locate new lands in Kentucky.[96] George Clark and his brother-in-law William Whitley served as scouts for the expedition.[97]

Colonel Bowman's regiment assembled at the mouth of the Licking River (where Cincinnati, Ohio, and Covington, Kentucky, are now located) and crossed the Ohio River in two keel boats and three canoes. They left thirty-two men at the river to guard the boats and rendezvous with the main body of troops at the mouth of the Little Miami River for the return trip to Kentucky.[98]

The regiment marched up the Miami Trail to its juncture with a trail that followed along the course of the Little Miami River.[99] As it approached Little Chalaakaatha on the Little Miami River path just after midnight on Sunday morning, a full moon bathed the land in moonlight. There were scattered pockets of fog in low places.[100]

The Long Knives reconnoitered and conferred in a clearing near the town. The regiment was divided into three divisions. Captain Logan commanded the left division, Captain Holder the central division, and Captain Harrod the right division. Captain Logan's division would encircle the town to the left around the west side and Captain Harrod's division would encircle the town to the right around the east side until their forces connected on the north side of town. Captain Logan's position lay between the town and the Little Miami River.[101]

Captain Holder and his division would surreptitiously approach the town and then lie in ambush a short distance outside its south side. This would leave an apparent gap in the encirclement of the town, tempting the warriors to leave the protection of their cabins and council house to slip through the gap into the ambush.[102]

John Callaway crouched as he crept up on the edge of the settlement from the cornfields in the floodplain and onto the bench of land upon which the town lay. He knew his brother Micajah was held here and hoped for the chance to rescue him.

The Long Knife soldiers fanned out in the moonlight and took up their positions. They had surrounded the town by dawn, and the Shawanese had not detected their enemies.

John and several other soldiers spotted a warrior walking out of the town in the darkness with his musket, apparently setting off on a dawn hunt. A shot rang out. Bill Ross had fired prematurely. The wounded warrior fell down, weakly shouted the alarm, and dragged himself back toward the cabins.[103]

Two Indian drummers beat the alarm and warriors poured out of their cabins and wegiwas screaming the war whoop. Shawanese women cried out in terror, "Kentuck! Kentuck!"

Chief Black Fish assembled a group of warriors and ran to investigate the cause of the shooting. He quickly understood the situation and exhorted his warriors to be strong and whip the Kentucky squaws. His warriors cried out affirmatively, "Ye-aw, ye-aw, ye-aw!" and returned fire.[104]

Black Fish was almost immediately wounded in his right knee as he crouched. The rifle ball traveled up his thigh to his hip joint and shattering the hip bone. He maintained his composure and fought on despite his agonizing pain. He ordered his people to run to the council house to make a stand. Chiefs Black Hoof and Nenessica (Black Beard) took command of the warriors and battled on as Black Fish weakened.[105]

The Long Knives and the Shawanese warriors continued to exchange a hot fire as the fighting continued. John Callaway hid behind a log with some other soldiers and kept his head down except when he fired. Tom Smith was not so careful or lucky. A musket ball struck him in the forehead as he peered over the log and hesitated.

Hugh McGary shouted at Josiah Collins and Rob Kirkham to hold their fire as some of the figures seen scrambling from the cabins appeared to be white prisoners.[106] John shouted out to remind them that he had a brother among the captives. He called out to Micajah but doubted that the sound of his voice had carried over the roar of the battle.

The desperate struggle continued as the dawn came and the morning wore on. The Long Knives fought their way up to the cabins on the northeastern edge of town. The Shawanese warriors fell back and abandoned the outer cabins. Half the town was burning and had been plundered by ten o'clock in the morning, including Louis Lorimier's branch post.[107]

The Long Knives did not realize that Little Chalaakaatha was lightly defended by only one hundred warriors at the time of their attack, since many Chalaakaatha warriors had recently followed Yellow Hawk in his exodus to the Creek towns. Many of the remaining Chalaakaatha warriors were attending a large council meeting with the British and other Indian nations.[108]

Sixty warriors broke through the encirclement during the first exchange of gunfire and fled into the surrounding countryside with the precious sacred fire, sacred bundle, and wampum belts of their people. There were only forty armed fighters left behind to defend the town, including several young boys who took up guns for the first time.

Micajah was sound asleep when the first gunshot rang out when the battle began. He sat straight up at the sound as if scalded by hot water. The fog of sleep quickly cleared from his mind, and he realized what was happening: The town was under attack.

Micajah flipped aside the buffalo hide bedding that covered him and yelled for Nenessica's wife to come and cut his bonds. He shouted that he couldn't move and might be accidentally killed. The bark wegiwa that he was in would not stop the ball from a Kentucky long rifle. An agitated young warrior then spun through the door with his tomahawk drawn, freed him from his bonds, and motioned for Micajah to follow him.

The warrior shoved Micajah along as they ran toward the council house. The Long Knife gunfire paused for a moment. Micajah could have sworn he heard his name called out as they ran.

They reached the council house and ran through one of the doors. Over two hundred women and children had taken refuge there. Seven or eight warriors blocked the door, tore out the greased rabbit skin window coverings, and fired from the windows.[109] Micajah and the other prisoners were bound to the support columns. Other warriors barricaded themselves inside the cabins immediately surrounding the council house and fought from there. An old shaman named Assetakoma called out encouragement to the Shawanese warriors as the battle continued.

The Shawanese sent an old African-American woman carrying a white flag to deliver a message to the Long Knives after the battle had raged for some four hours.[110] She told Colonel Bowman and his officers that a runner had been sent to Piqua to summon Simon Girty and several hundred warriors staying there. She said that they were expected to arrive soon and reinforce the Shawanese in Little Chalaakaatha.

Colonel Bowman had expected a quick victory and had not anticipated the fierce resistance by the tenacious Shawanese defenders. He had decided that he did not need to bring artillery with him to smash through the log walls of the council house and cabins.[111] That decision was proving to be a mistake.

Colonel Bowman's regiment was bogging down in a stalemate with the barricaded warriors, and he had to consider the possibility that Shawanese reinforcements were in fact on their way. He ordered his men to retreat.

Captain Harrod's and Captain Logan's wings retreated as Captain Holder's men kept up a covering fire from their central position. Holder's men were pinned down by Shawanese gunfire and dug in behind the large log. Several were killed or wounded before they fell back.[112]

John Callaway looked for Micajah throughout the battle and checked the bodies of the fallen soldiers and warriors as the Long Knives withdrew. As he left the town, he called out to Micajah to keep his spirits up because he had not been forgotten by his family.

The Shawanese had bluffed and duped the Long Knives. Simon Girty was actually in Detroit rather than Piqua at the time of Colonel Bowman's attack. Piqua was only able to provide several dozen warriors to reinforce Little Chalaakaatha rather than several hundred.[113]

The Shawanese began to emerge from their places of refuge in Little Chalaakaatha as the Long Knife regiment marched away. Micajah and the other prisoners were untied and stepped out of the council house. They were sobered by the scene of destruction that greeted them.

The warriors collected their dead and wounded. Forty Shawanese had been killed or mortally wounded including men, women, and children.[114] Black Fish was among the mortally wounded. Louis Lorimier's branch post had been looted and burned to the ground, and over three hundred horses had been taken. The sound of weeping women and children provided a sad background dirge to the scene.

A group of about seventy warriors from Piqua rode into town as evening approached. A war party was quickly organized and set off down the warpath after the Long Knives. Micajah could hear their cries for revenge as they galloped away.

The Shawanese remaining at Little Chalaakaatha found eight bodies of Long Knives that had been left behind. The bodies of the dead soldiers were scalped and mutilated by angry Shawanese women.

The Shawanese pursuit party caught up with the Long Knives on the following day. Both sides lost one man and collected one scalp in their final encounter. The Long Knives then marched home to Kentucky.[115]

Little Chalaakaatha; June – December, 1779

THERE WERE MANY FUNERALS IN THE FAMILIES of Little Chalaakaatha in the days following the Long Knife attack. Black Fish lingered for about six weeks before dying of gangrene poisoning.[116] The Shawanese sorrowfully buried their great war chief in a grave lined with puncheon logs. The war had come home to the beleaguered Shawanese Nation.

Kispoko War Chief Captain Snake was chosen as the new Principal War Chief. Nenessica was selected to take Black Fish's place as the senior Chalaakaatha war chief.

The white prisoners at Little Chalaakaatha helped clear the debris of battle and rebuild the town. It would take several months for life to return to some semblance of normalcy in Little Chalaakaatha although a palpable feeling of insecurity would always remain.

The British took steps to reassure their anxious allies. It was obvious that some changes needed to be made in the conduct of the war now that the Long Knives had demonstrated an ability to defend themselves and mount sizable offensive operations into the Shawanese homeland.

In August of 1779, Captain McKee, Matthew Elliot, and the Girty brothers established a forward Indian Department command post at the Shawanese capital of Wapatomica on the Mad River.[117] McKee and Captain Bird traveled to Little Chalaakaatha and a council of war was held there.

The British advisers counseled the Shawanese to adopt stronger defensive measures to protect their vulnerable towns. More sentries and improved intelligence were required to warn of approaching invaders. The British helped construct stockade fortifications for the Shawanese at both Little Chalaakaatha and Piqua,[118] and they built a blockhouse at Wapatomica.[119]

Micajah helped construct the stockade at Little Chalaakaatha. The Shawanese mounted a large carved and painted figurehead of a fierce Shawanese warrior above the entrance gate and celebrated with a war dance when the fort was completed.[120]

The Shawanese also established a system of regular scouting patrols along the Ohio River so they would have early warning of future invasion forces. The British encouraged them to capture prisoners during raids into Kentucky as a means of gathering intelligence regarding the enemy's future plans. They discouraged the execution of prisoners before intelligence had been extracted from them.

Lieutenant Colonel John Butler of the British Army had established a "Corps of Rangers" to fight alongside Great Britain's Indian allies in the war against the American rebels on September 15, 1777. His corps was recruited from tough American Tory woodsmen.[121]

Lieutenant William Caldwell and a company of green-coated Butler's Rangers were deployed to Detroit in 1779 to provide additional military assistance to the northwestern Indian nations. Caldwell met with the chiefs of Little Chalaakaatha on December 26, 1779, and assured them that Butler's Rangers would fight at their sides.[122]

Kentucky: June - December, 1779

THE FLOOD OF NEW SETTLERS CONTINUED TO pour into Kentucky as 1779 drew to a close. That year, the Virginia General Assembly had enacted a law establishing a new Virginia Land Commission to replace the old Colonial Land Office that had ceased operation at the onset of the War for Independence. The commission was created for the purpose of providing a means to establish clear title to land in Kentucky for the benefit of all settlers and also protect the just claims of settlers who had moved into Kentucky in the early days and suffered during the war.[123]

Bryant's (aka Bryan's) Station was founded in 1779 by William Bryant on the south bank of the North Fork of the Elkhorn River about five miles northeast of Lexington. The station initially consisted of twelve to fourteen cabins arranged in a hollow square connected by log pickets. It was located on a ridge next to the Big Buffalo Road as it headed to the northwest toward the Houston Fork of the Licking River.[124]

The Virginia Land Commission met at Bryant's Station in October of 1779. Micajah and James Callaway Jr. were eligible for the land grants because they had assisted the Fort Boonesborough settlers with the 1777 corn harvest.

Flanders Callaway was kind enough to file land claims there on October 14, 1779, on behalf of Micajah and James Jr. Their claims were for adjacent four-hundred-acre parcels of land in the Bluegrass Region at the head of the Houston Fork of Licking River where Flanders, James Jr., and Micajah had hunted in the autumn of 1777. Captain John Holder kindly paid the filing fees for each of the parcels.

Each of the two claims was complemented with a pre-emption right for an additional one thousand adjacent acres:

> *"Cert iss'd for 1400 by order of Court at Bryants fees &c pd D.D. to Capt. Holder"*
>
> Micajah Callaway this day by Flanders Callaway claimed a settlement and preemption to a tract of land in the district of Kentucky lying on the Waters of the South fork of licking Creek known by the name of Hustons fork adjoining James Callaway land on the East side by settling in the Country in the year 1777 & residing ever since satisfactory proof being made to the Court they are of Opinion that the said Callaway has a right to a settlement of 400 Acres of land including the above location & the preemption of 1000 Acres adjoining Cert. Not issue until the further order of this Court[125]

Colonel Richard Callaway emerged as the dominant leader of Fort Boonesborough and the Bluegrass Region of Kentucky following the siege of Fort Boonesborough and Daniel Boone's court-martial trial. Callaway and James Harrod served as the two Kentucky County representatives for the October 1779 session of the Virginia General Assembly in Williamsburg.

The General Assembly passed an act on October 3, 1779, providing for the construction of an improved wagon road over the Cumberland Mountains into Kentucky. Richard Callaway and Evan Shelby were authorized to survey and construct the new road and obtain the assistance of a militia guard to protect them from hostile Indians.

The General Assembly passed another act on October 4, 1779, specifically awarding Richard Callaway a license to establish and operate a ferry crossing from Boonesborough to the land on the opposite side of the Kentucky River. Richard envisioned his ferry as the gateway for settlers migrating north of the Kentucky River from the Wilderness Road into the Bluegrass Region.[126]

Upon the conclusion of the General Assembly session, Colonel Callaway organized a pack train of forty packhorses loaded with gunpowder and lead from the Chiswell Mines.[127] He led the pack train into Boonesborough in a triumphal return in December of 1779.[128]

The older settlements were strengthened and many new settlements were established in Kentucky as 1779 drew to a close. The new town of Louisville and the "Beargrass Stations" were founded near the Falls of the Ohio River. Floyd's Station, Linn's Station, Brashear's Station, and Sullivan's Station were among the better-known of the Beargrass Stations. Daniel Boone's brother Squire Boone founded the Painted Stone Station on Clear Creek near the present location of Shelbyville, Kentucky.

Daniel Boone moved out of Boonesborough to avoid Colonel Richard Callaway's enmity and established the new community of Boone's Station on December 26, 1779. It was located about six miles to the northwest of Fort Boonesborough in the Bluegrass Region, on Boofman's Fork of Boone's Creek. Flanders and Jemima Callaway moved to Flanders's new grant on East Hickman Creek not far from Boone's Station.

Colonel Richard Callaway, Captain Daniel Boone, Flanders Callaway, Cyrus Boone, Joseph Drake, Ephriam Drake, Samuel Henderson, William Hancock, Thomas Foote, and other hunters from Fort Boonesborough went on a long hunt into the Bluegrass Region in 1779. They traveled up the Salt Lick Trace to the Big Buffalo Road and followed it to the Lower Blue Licks where they hunted deep into the Shawanese hunting grounds. They returned via the Big Buffalo Road to the Bryant's Station area.[129]

The buffalo population was hit hard by the unrelenting and increasing hunting pressure from the Long Knives, and fell into a precipitous decline. The new Bluegrass settlements partially encircled the buffalo wintering grounds in the Bluegrass Region and disrupted their seasonal migration routes. The buffalo migration route from Kentucky across the Ohio River into the Illinois Country was blocked by the settlement of Louisville and the Beargrass Stations at the Falls of the Ohio. The surviving animals retreated farther back into the remaining forests and rough terrain.

The desperation of the Shawanese increased as their scouts reported the expansion of the Long Knife settlements and the continuing degradation of their Kentucky hunting grounds. They were forced to take the fight back to the Long Knife settlements if they were to restore their ancestral hunting grounds and preserve their way of life.

Colonel Richard Callaway's energetic role in the Long Knife invasion of Kentucky had not gone unnoticed by the British and Shawanese. The sixty-three-year-old colonel led his people with the energy of a man half his age. He seemed to be everywhere at once. The Shawanese had directly observed him help lead the defense of Fort Boonesborough. Their scouts had observed him at the head of Long Knife hunting parties into the Bluegrass Region. He was known as a leader in the establishment of government, transportation systems, and real estate development in Kentucky.

The Shawanese and British knew that Micajah Callaway was Colonel Richard Callaway's nephew and was a valuable prize of war. They had hoped to use his capture as negotiating leverage at a future date. However, time had run out for negotiated solutions to the question of who would possess Kentucky.

Richard Callaway was a marked man. Fort Boonesborough was kept under close surveillance as Shawanese scouts looked for an opportunity to strike.

Stroke and Counter-stroke (1780)
The Death of Colonel Richard Callaway

A SMALL SHAWANESE RAIDING PARTY RETURNED TO Little Chalaakaatha from Kentucky in late March and rode into town whooping and waving scalps in the air. Word quickly spread that they had killed and scalped a great Long Knife colonel. A crowd quickly formed around them.

Fish Jackson and Micajah moved to the fringe of the crowd. They could see that one of the scalps had come from a man with long, graying hair.[130] The crowd quieted as the warrior who held the grey-haired scalp described how he had obtained it.

The warriors in the raiding party had observed a party of men with axes set out to walk along the south shore of the Kentucky River below the fort. They were led by the Long Knife colonel. The work party stopped on Canoe Ridge on the colonel's orders and began cutting down trees while he sat on a log and directed their work.

One of the warriors crept close through the underbrush and shot the colonel in the head. He was blown over backwards off of the log into oblivion.[131]

The warriors ran up to the fallen colonel and shot him again to make sure that he was dead. They scalped him, stripped off his clothes, disemboweled him, broke all of the major bones in his body, and rolled his mangled remains in the mud of the riverbank. They had killed a great warrior and breaking his bones would ensure that his powerful spirit would not follow them on the trail back to their towns.

Micajah looked closely at the scalp. There could be no doubt that it was his Uncle Richard's scalp. Micajah later learned that Richard was supervising the cutting of the trees for timbers to construct the ferry when he was killed. Captain John Holder and his men carried Richard's mutilated body back to the fort and buried him next to Fort Boonesborough.[132]

A surge of conflicting thoughts and emotions welled up inside Micajah. He grieved for the loss of a family member who had been an important part of his life for as long as he could remember, yet he was still angry at Richard for beating him.[133] He was angry at the Shawanese for killing Richard and their cruelty toward their prisoners, but was also angry at the Long Knives for attacking women and children in the Shawanese towns. Why did these two peoples have to treat each other in such a despicable way?

How could he survive in this hellish situation? Would the hard-line Shawanese warriors expect him to celebrate Richard's death to show his loyalty to his new nation and new family? Would they kill him if he did not? Would the whites in Kentucky or his own family consider him a traitorous conspirator in Richard's death? Would he face a court-martial and, possibly, execution? What if he found himself face-to-face with Flanders in a desperate battle?

Micajah left the crowd in confusion and ran into the forest to find a quiet place. He sat down on a log and wept bitterly. Micajah rued the day that he had left Bedford County for Kentucky. His life thus far had turned into a disaster.

The town warriors celebrated their victory with a war dance and purified themselves in the council house for four days after their return. Nenessica and his wife knew of Micajah's relationship to Richard and deflected inquiries to protect his privacy.

The Kentucky settlements reeled at the news of Colonel Callaway's death. Captain David Gass wrote a desperate letter to Colonel Bowman on March 10, 1780, proposing that they immediately organize an expedition commanded by George Rogers Clark to attack the Shawanese towns in retaliation.[134]

Richard Callaway had been an iron-willed and inspirational leader in the establishment and defense of Fort Boonesborough and was spearheading the Long Knife migration into the Bluegrass Region when he died. Kentucky had lost a great leader. Callaway County, Kentucky, was named in his honor in 1820.[135]

Captain Henry Bird's Campaign (May - July, 1780)

IN MAY OF 1780, CAPTAIN HENRY BIRD of the King's Eighth Regiment was ordered to take command of a British and Indian expeditionary force for the invasion of Kentucky. The force was comprised of one hundred British regular soldiers from the King's Eighth Regiment and Aubrey's 47th Regiment of Foot, seventy French Canadian militia volunteers, and about one hundred Lake Indians assembled in Detroit.

Captain Jacques Duperon Bâby was among the French Canadian officers.[136] Simon, George, and James Girty also took part. The little army was supported by a three-pound and six-pound cannon intended to knock down the stockade walls of the Kentucky forts.

Captain Bird's army departed on their journey and traveled by boat from the Detroit River up the Maumee River and then up its Auglaize River tributary. They portaged from the Auglaize River to Louis Lorimier's store on the Loramie Creek tributary of the Greater Miami River and encamped there on May 21, 1780. Captain Bird and his soldiers set about constructing additional pirogues (small, flat-bottomed boats usually pointed at both ends) while they awaited word from the Wyandots as to whether they would join the army.

Shawanese Principal War Chief Captain Snake directed the final Shawanese preparations for the expedition. He was middle-aged and portly but, despite his appearance, he was an ardent Indian patriot and an excellent battlefield commander.[137] He commanded the front lines during battle and led the younger warriors by example. Nenessica would serve as one of his senior war captains. Nenessica directed Micajah to accompany him on Captain Bird's expedition in order to help carry booty.[138]

The Bluegrass War

Shawanese women prepared parched cornmeal for the carrying pouches of their warrior mates. Each warrior checked and cleaned his musket, inspected his shot, powder, and flints, and sharpened his tomahawk and scalping knife. The Shawanese warriors painted their faces black and red.

A Kispoko shaman conjured the future and predicted a great victory for the Indian Confederacy. He prepared a medicine bag for Captain Snake to carry into battle. It possessed supernatural powers and contained various talismans. The warrior who acquired the greatest distinction in the campaign could carry the medicine bag on the return journey.

Captain Snake began the war dance early in the afternoon around a fire and war pole set up outside the council house. The dance continued through the night and well into the following day accompanied by the unrelenting throb of the water drum.

Captain Snake was the final speaker during the war dance and gave an inspirational speech which whipped his warriors into a frenzy of war whoops and menacing dance. He explained the order of march and plan of attack for the campaign. With a final flourish, he plunged his tomahawk into the war pole, wrenched it free, snatched up his musket, and set off down the warpath with a dancing stomp-trot as he sang a war song.

Captain Snake's warriors joined in with the song in a stirring antiphonal chorus, grabbed their own weapons, and fell in behind him in single-file. The warriors sang and stomp-trotted down the path to the rendezvous point at the forks of the Greater Miami River and Mad River.

As the Shawanese war party departed Little Chalaakaatha, they were joined at the end of their line by Alexander McKee, Micajah, and a handful of other white men from the Indian Department on horseback. Micajah noted the unusual clarity of the afternoon sky and a few traces of remaining dogwood blooms in the spring-green forest as they left Little Chalaakaatha.

THE SHAWANESE WAR PARTY RENDEZVOUSED WITH CAPTAIN Bird's expedition at the forks on May 31, 1780. A total force of six hundred Indians from the Lake, Six Nations, and Ohio Confederacy nations had assembled there.[139]

Captain Bird and Captain McKee received intelligence that Colonel Clark and a contingent of two hundred troops from Vincennes and the Falls of the Ohio had departed for the mouth of the Ohio River. They planned to complete the construction and garrisoning of Fort Jefferson there and defend Cahokia from the impending attack by a British force commanded by Emanuel Hesse.

Clark's departure left the fort at the Falls of the Ohio defended only by Colonel George Slaughter and his regiment of 150 regular soldiers of the Virginia Line.[140] The Kentucky County militia was reportedly weakened by a lack of provisions and an epidemic of dysentery.

The Indians met in council for two days in a concealed encampment just to the north of the Ohio River and debated their options. Captains McKee and Bird urged the Indians to take advantage of Colonel Clark's absence and attack the undermanned fort at the Falls.

The chiefs refused and decided to continue to march up the Licking River valley into the Bluegrass Region. It was more important to them to drive the Long Knife settlements out of the Shawanese hunting grounds.[141] The British officers relented and agreed to support their Indian allies.[142]

The army departed from the mouth of the Greater Miami River and went up the Ohio River to the mouth of the Licking River. They marched overland from there to the North and South Forks of the Licking River. They paused there temporarily to build a blockhouse and stockade (near present-day Falmouth) and then marched on to the south along the South Fork into their beloved and endangered Bluegrass hunting grounds.[143]

Ruddle's Station on the South Fork of the Licking River was the closest Bluegrass fort to the Shawanese homeland and was selected as the first target for attack. The warriors encamped at a hidden location near Ruddle's Station on the night of June 23.[144]

The warriors awakened before dawn on June 24, 1780. They stripped down to their breechcloths and mocassins and painted themselves. The remainder of their clothing, kettles, and provisions were hidden in the forest. Captain Snake opened the medicine bag and distributed various charms and talismans to the warriors for their protection. As his warriors made their final preparations, he exhorted them to be strong and fight hard for their people. He detailed the plan of attack and led his warriors into battle.

A violent thunderstorm and torrential rain greeted them as they took up their positions around the fort just before dawn. Micajah stayed to the rear of the warriors. They opened the attack on Ruddle's Station with small arms fire.[145] The occupants of the fort returned the fire and put up a stiff resistance. Simon Girty was slightly wounded in the hand.[146] Captain Bird demanded that Captain Ruddle surrender and Ruddle refused.

An artillery battery was constructed of logs and earth, and the British opened fire. Realizing that their situation was hopeless, Captain Ruddle and the occupants of the fort surrendered under a white flag. They agreed to the following terms: 1) they would surrender and be permitted to retain their wearing apparel, 2) the women and children would be conducted to the nearest station and freed, and 3) the men would be conducted safely to a settlement near Detroit.[147] The goods and provisions within the fort would be forfeited to the British and Indians as spoils of war.

Micajah moved forward from the rear of the fighting to prepare to pick up a load of plunder for Nenessica when the fort gates opened up. A group of warriors from the Lake Indian nations shocked both sides with a sudden savage assault on the occupants.[148]

Micajah stood at the fort gate, backed up against the wall, and watched in disbelief as the warriors slaughtered twenty unarmed men, women, and children with their tomahawks amid screams of horror and agony. One warrior grabbed the infant child of Captain Ruddle and bashed its brains out against the fort wall. All of the cattle in the fort were slaughtered.

Captain Bird shouted in fury at his Indian allies and demanded that they stop the killing. He said that if they did not stop, the invasion would be terminated. The war chiefs of the Lake nations agreed to restrain their warriors from further slaughter.

As the bodies of the slain settlers were scalped and removed from the ruined fort, Nenessica and Micajah walked into the fort to pick up a load of plunder. The smell of blood and fear hung in the air around them. Micajah loaded as much onto his back as he could carry. As the surviving occupants were led from the ruins of the fort, Micajah overheard one of them say, "Hey! Isn't that Cagey Callaway?"[149] Micajah put his head down and continued his task. He felt numb inside.

The British and Indian forces encamped next to the fort that night. The stench of rotting human and cattle carcasses was overwhelming in the summer heat the following day.

Captain Bird's troops besieged Martin's Station on June 26, 1780, seven miles further up the South Fork of the Licking River. The occupants surrendered on the same terms as agreed to at Ruddle's Station.[150] Once again, the Lake Indians breached the terms of surrender and slaughtered several settlers and all of the cattle before the British could intervene. After burning Martin's Station, Captain Bird and his expedition moved on to burn the abandoned Houston Station.

A party of sixty warriors was dispatched down the Big Buffalo Road along the Houston Fork of the Licking River to attack Grant's Station. Two men named Stucker and a woman named Mitchell were killed there and the station was burned to the ground. A small raiding party stole horses from Strode's Station.

The British and Indians decided not to march any deeper into the Bluegrass Region. They had partially succeeded in liberating the Shawanese hunting grounds by pushing the whites back to the south and west. A total of four hundred men, women, and children had been captured at Ruddle's Station and Martin's Station.[151]

The British/Indian army met with an Indian scouting party returning from the Falls of the Ohio when they passed the ruins of Ruddle's Station on their return journey. The spies reported that Colonel Clark was expected to return to the fort at the Falls very soon. He was then to depart on July 10 with a large volunteer militia force to engage the assembled Indians in battle.

Captains Bird and McKee were unable to persuade the Indians to remain together to hold their hard-won ground in Kentucky. The Indians feared that Clark might attack their unguarded and vulnerable towns to the north. They precipitously withdrew across the Ohio River and began the long return trip to the Ohio towns and Detroit.[152]

Captain McKee returned to Little Chalaakaatha with the Shawanese. He sent Shawanese scouting parties back down to the Ohio River and toward the Falls to spy in case the Long Knives should follow.[153]

Captain Bird and his remaining force arrived at the portage on the Greater Miami River on July 24 after a fourteen-day journey up the rivers. Most of the surviving prisoners were taken to Detroit where they were imprisoned.[154]

The Bluegrass War

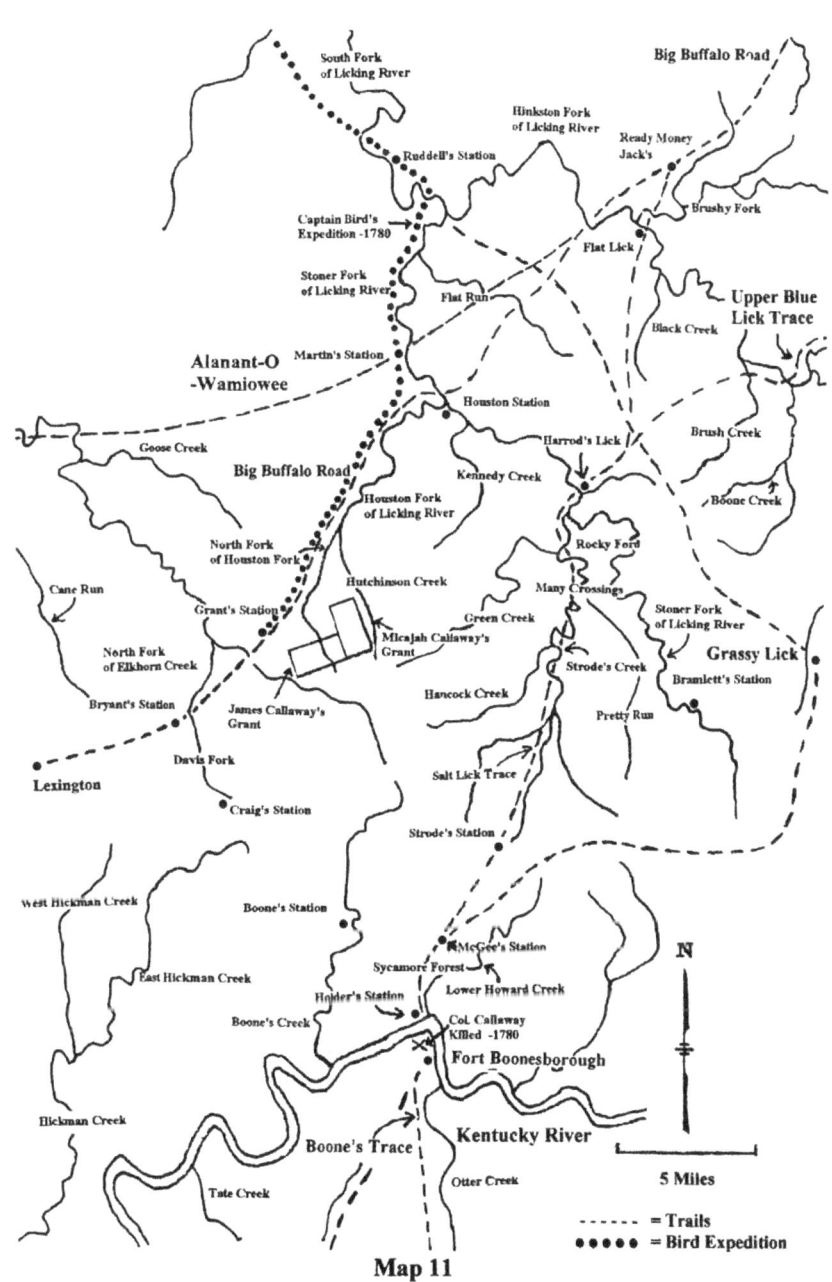

Map 11
Kentucky Bluegrass Region in 1779-1780

Colonel Clark's 1780 Campaign and the Battle of Piqua (August 1780)

COLONEL CLARK RETURNED TO KENTUCKY AS RAPIDLY as possible to engage with Captain Bird after successfully helping Spanish Governor de Leyba defend Post St. Louis against British attack. He placed guards to block any attempts by potential militiamen to flee from Kentucky over the Wilderness Road and summoned the leadership of the Kentucky County militia.

The Long Knife leadership met in a council of war. They directed that an expeditionary force be assembled and placed under the overall command of Colonel Clark to attack and destroy Little Chalaakaatha and Piqua in direct retaliation for the British and Indian attack.

Colonel Clark would assemble a division comprised of Clark's Illinois Regiment and Kentucky County militiamen from the Falls of the Ohio, the Beargrass settlements, and the Harrodsburgh area. Captain Squire Boone and fourteen men from the Painted Stone Station would also join them. Clark's division would assemble at the Falls and then travel upriver by boat toward the Ohio Country.

Colonel Benjamin Logan had replaced the late Colonel Richard Callaway as the second-in-command of the Kentucky County militia. He would assemble a second division from the Bluegrass settlements at Bryant's Station and then march to a rendezvous with Clark's division on the north bank of the Ohio River, opposite the mouth of the Licking River. The two divisions would march from their rendezvous to the Shawanese towns under the overall command of Colonel Clark.[155]

Clark's division was transported in skiffs built at Louisville under the direction of Colonel Slaughter and his regular soldiers. They hugged the shore in their little boats as they moved up the Ohio River. The Long Knives had learned to expect Shawanese fortifications and brought along a six-pound cannon that Colonel Clark had captured at Fort Sackville.

A party commanded by Hugh McGary landed on the north shore between the mouths of the Kentucky River and Licking River to hunt. They were attacked by a Shawanese war party as they were reboarding their boats. Nine soldiers were killed and several were wounded in the skirmish.[156]

Daniel Boone, Simon Kenton, and young Abraham Thomas served as advance scouts for Colonel Logan's forces along the Kentucky side of the Ohio River. When the main forces arrived at the rendezvous location, Colonel Logan and his men constructed a stockade there for a small garrison and the storage of provisions for their return march.[157] This was the first Long Knife fort on the north shore of the Ohio River.

The Long Knife army consisting of 970 men marched up the Miami Trail into the Ohio Country on August 2, 1780. Colonel Clark's division was in the vanguard, followed by the cannon and baggage in the middle of the force. Colonel Logan's division marched in the rear. The foot soldiers were deployed in four columns forty yards apart with a line of flankers to each side. There was a small advance party and rear guard.

John Clary slipped out of Bryant's Station before Logan's division marched north and rode off to warn the British and Indians of the American plans. Micajah was returning from helping Nenessica's wife cultivate the corn in her fields when Clary arrived with his warning. Louis Lorimier was dispatched to escort Clary to Detroit, and they reached their destination on August 5, 1780.[158]

THE LITTLE CHALAAKAATHA CHIEFS CONVENED AN EMERGENCY council. The chiefs knew that they were outnumbered and outgunned. They decided that it was best to retreat to Piqua which was located twelve miles to the north on the Mad River. There were additional warriors there, and they could make a stand together.

The chiefs ordered the execution of all white male prisoners that they believed posed a risk of desertion or spying for the Long Knives. The doomed prisoners were taken from the town into the woods and dispatched by tomahawk. Micajah was spared.[159]

The sacred bundle, sacred fire, and wampum belts were secured and carried to Wapatomica by their custodians under armed guard. Dwellings were set on fire so that the Long Knives could not use or plunder them. Two cabins full of furs and the council house were spared in the hope that they could return later and salvage them.

Micajah helped Nenessica and his wife pack their food and belongings. They set fire to their cabin and wegiwa when they were finished packing and headed north on the well-trodden road to Piqua. Micajah did not look back.

Piqua was located in a beautiful setting. The town was nestled on the western side of the Mad River on the edge of a large prairie of rich bottomland. It was at the base of forested bluffs rising over one hundred feet above the town. The prairie was about three miles long and one mile wide and was covered by fields of corn, wildflowers, and tall weeds. A rail fence separated the town from the fields. The road from Little Chalaakaatha crossed the river directly across from the town.

Piqua was built parallel to the river with the cabins and wegiwas extending to the north. Kispoko Shawanese had settled close to the river and provided a buffer to the Piqua Shawanese living up close to the hills. A triangular stockade fort enclosing about one-half acre was located just outside the southwestern end of the town.[160]

A limestone cliff of some twenty-five to thirty feet in height edged the bluffs on the northwestern side of the river beginning about a mile to the north of the town. The bottomland between the cliffs and the river was timbered.[161]

The Little Chalaakaatha refugees arrived in Piqua after a few hours' march. The women, children, and prisoners and a small guard of warriors were immediately removed to a hidden camp set up among the boulders at the base of the limestone cliffs. It was situated a couple of miles to the north of Piqua where a gap in the cliffs provided an escape route.[162]

The Shawanese chiefs and warriors from Little Chalaakaatha and Piqua held a council of war. It is likely that Chiefs White Bark, Wryneck, Nenessica, and Black Hoof led the council. Simon, James, and George Girty attended.[163] Chiaxi and The Buffalo were probably among the young warriors.

The war chiefs dispatched scouts back to Little Chalaakaatha to observe the approaching Long Knife army. Runners were sent to the other

Shawanese villages as well as to Detroit to plead for assistance. Simon Girty and his Mingo warriors left for Mackachack to ready a stand if Clark's army advanced beyond Piqua. The chiefs and warriors painted themselves red and black and prepared to receive their enemy.

THE LONG KNIFE ARMY APPROACHED LITTLE CHALAAKAATHA at about two o'clock in the afternoon of August 6, 1780, on the trail along the Little Miami River. They could see a large column of smoke rising above the trees as they drew closer.

The town was bordered on the south and east by large cornfields. Colonel Clark set up his six-pound cannon on a hill to the south and east of town and fired it over the cornfields toward the town as a precautionary measure, in case the warriors were waiting in ambush in the cornfields, but they were empty.[164]

The Long Knives discovered that the fort and most of the cabins and wegiwas in the town had been abandoned and were in flames as they entered the town. The soldiers tore down the warrior figurehead over the gate of the fort, chopped it to pieces with their tomahawks, and fed it to the flames. They found the two cabins full of stored furs and the council house still intact. There were seven horses in the council house. They took the horses and left the cabins and council house standing.[165]

The army camped near the town that night. The corn in the fields was ripe for roasting and eating, so the soldiers picked it and enjoyed a feast. They destroyed several hundred remaining acres of corn the next day.

Colonel Clark and his army left the smoking ruins of Little Chalaakaatha late in the afternoon of August 7, 1780, and marched north on the road to Piqua. They were no more than a mile from Little Chalaakaatha when a very heavy thunderstorm overtook them with thunder, lightning, drenching rain, and heavy winds. They had no tents or shelter so the men and their equipment were soon completely drenched.

Clark ordered his troops to prepare to camp on the spot. He ordered the soldiers to form a square with the baggage, horses, military stores, and artillery in the center. He then directed that one company at a time fire their guns and reload with dry powder. They then settled in for the night.

THE SHAWANESE SCOUTS REPORTED BACK TO THE war chiefs in Piqua that the sacred Thunderbirds had come to the aid of the Shawanese. They had raised a great storm that had forced the Long Knives to stop their march. However, the Long Knives were well organized, vigilant, and showed no fear. As the sacred Thunderbirds flashed their eyes, beat their wings, and rained down on the Long Knife encampment, the Long Knives had boldly answered back with volleys of crashing gunfire.

The Shawanese shamans shuddered at the thought of an enemy so fearless and determined that they would challenge the power of the Thunderbirds. The shamans augured that their people should use caution and not risk all in a battle with these Long Knives. The war chiefs held another council of war that night and recalled their scouts to await the arrival of the Long Knives.

THE LONG KNIVES AROSE BEFORE SUNRISE ON the following morning and set off rapidly down the wide, well-traveled path to Piqua. The army arrived at the

The Battle of Piqua [© John Buxton]

prairie bottomlands across the Mad River from the town at eight o'clock in the morning of August 8, and crossed the river about a half-mile below the town.

Colonel Clark directed Colonel Logan and his division to the eastern flank to circle around and cut off any Shawanese escape attempt to the east and north through gaps in the limestone cliffs. Colonels William Linn, James Harrod, and John Floyd were directed to the western flank to encircle the town from the south and west. General Clark would lead a frontal assault with Colonel Slaughter's infantry and artillery.[166] Colonel Logan's division encountered swampy and rocky terrain as it swung to the east and north, and bogged down.[167]

The Shawanese sharply counterattacked against the Long Knives' extending western flank. There was a large cornfield in the prairie bottomlands there that was fenced off from the river bank by a long pole fence. The cornfield ended in open prairie woodlands at the base of the river bluffs and hills to the southwest. The counterattacking warriors ran through the cornfield along the pole fence, firing as they ran, keeping pace with the Long Knife flanking movement.

The Long Knives returned their fire and continued to drive to the southwest in their effort to turn the Shawanese flank. A large body of warriors concealed in the prairie woodlands opened fire as the Long Knives drew near.

The warriors in the cornfield dropped back to circle behind the prairie woodlands to the top of a large wooded hill among the river bluffs about two hundred yards beyond. The combatants in the prairie woodlands stood their ground to fire their muskets and then fell back to join the others on the high ground. The determined Long Knives continued to drive their left flank for nearly a mile to the south before turning west up into the bluffs to the south of the Shawanese force. They then turned back to the north and fought to drive the Shawanese warriors back toward the town.

The fighting to the southwest continued for several hours through the long day as the Shawanese slowly fell back from ridgetop to ridgetop. As the Long Knives reached the top of one ridge, the Shawanese warriors were soon climbing another. This continued until the warriors had fallen back to the large hill immediately above their town. There they formed a line of battle to make a stand. They constructed an impromptu breastwork by piling poles and chunks of wood on two fallen oak trees. The fighting was heavy along the battleline well into the afternoon.[168]

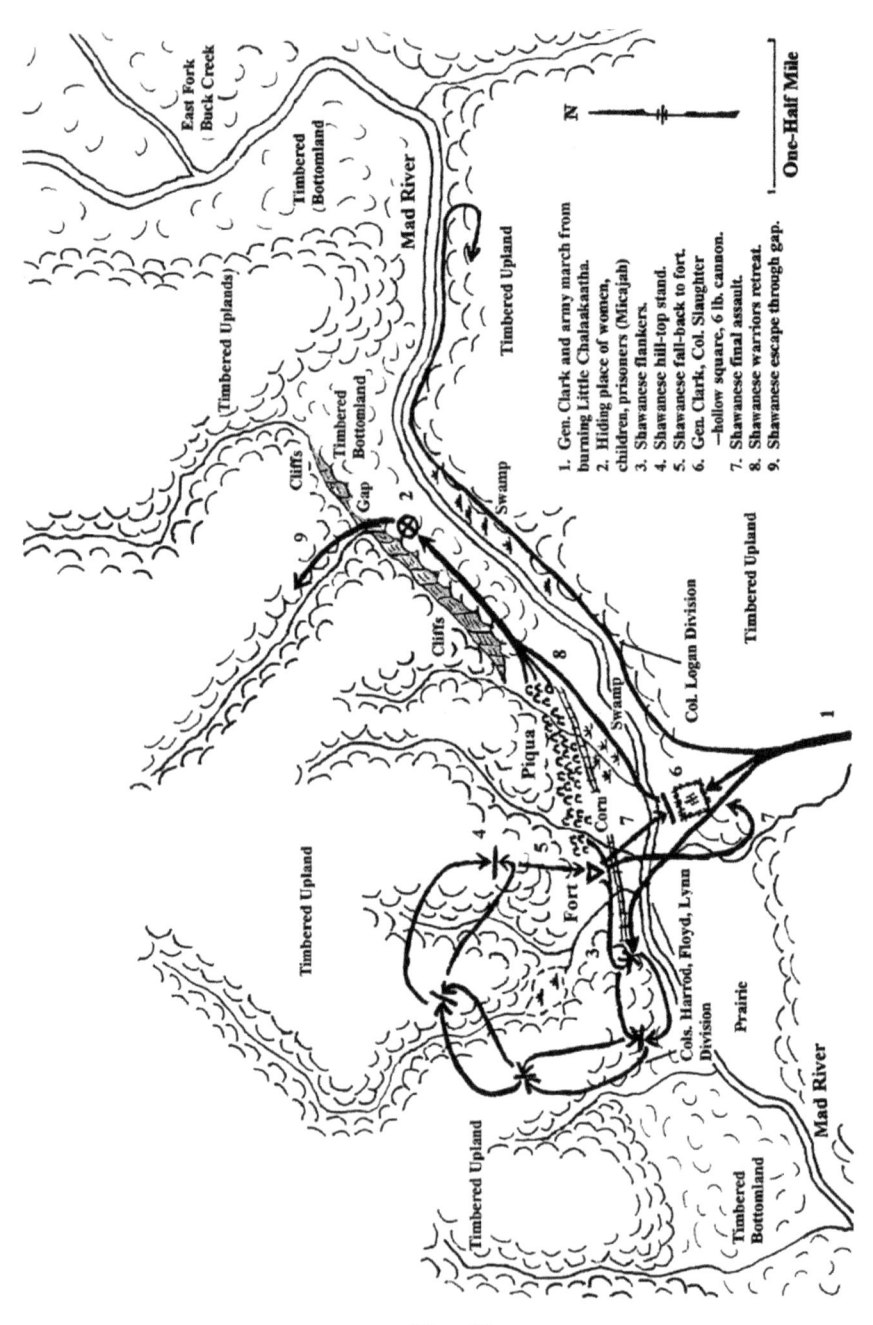

Map 12
The Battle of Piqua (1780)

Other Shawanese warriors had maintained a hot fire on Clark's frontal position from inside the Piqua fort and the sturdier of the nearby cabins while their comrades countered the flanking maneuver. The Shawanese chiefs gave orders around three o'clock in the afternoon for the surviving warriors behind the breastwork on the hill to fall back and join the other fighters in the Piqua fort and cabins. They hoped that a reinforcement of three hundred additional Shawanese, Mingo, Wyandot, and Delaware warriors would be arriving soon to join the fight.

Colonel Clark set up his six-pound cannon in a hastily constructed battery on high ground across the river from Piqua. He ordered his men to form a hollow square to protect the gun.[169] The cannon was loaded with grapeshot and fired several times with a booming report. Each shot splintered logs and ripped holes through the Piqua fort's stockade walls and cabins.[170]

The Shawanese chiefs divided their remaining warriors and surreptitiously dispatched half of them from the fort to sneak through the cornfields, across the river, and around to the rear of Clark's artillery battery. The remaining half opened the gate of the fort and brazenly marched out onto the open prairie below the battery, where they formed a battle line. It appeared at first that they were preparing to surrender, and Clark ordered the cannon to cease firing.

The concealed warriors to the rear of Clark then opened fire and attacked. Clark's men on the back side of the hollow square returned fire and stopped the Shawanese advance. The line of warriors on the prairie in front of the battery broke into a run and charged. They stood and fired when they were within range and then continued their charge. Clark ordered his men to hold their fire until the warriors were within forty yards. His men took cover behind trees.

The Long Knives opened fire with a tremendous volley, and several of the charging warriors were cut down. Clark ordered a second devastating volley. Several more warriors crumpled to the ground. The survivors were forced to fall back.[171]

Colonel Logan and his division came rushing back to aid Clark as the sound of gunfire intensified.[172] Their help was no longer required by the time they arrived. The surviving Shawanese warriors had melted away into the forest.[173]

The outnumbered Shawanese had bravely stood firm and fought back against greatly superior forces. Many years later an admiring old frontier veteran said, "The Indians stood at the Pickaway battle till they were powder burnt."[174]

MICAJAH HAD HEARD THE SOUNDS OF BATTLE through the trees during the course of the day. Wounded warriors limped and staggered into the camp as the battle continued and were immediately attended to by the women. The booms of the cannon shattered the air as Micajah paced, his mind racing with conflicting thoughts. Were his Callaway brothers here? He might have the opportunity to escape if he was alert. Did he want to? He tightened the grip on his rifle.

A small group of mounted warriors led by Nenessica galloped into the camp with the thunder of pounding hoofs. Nenessica summoned Micajah and the handful of warriors guarding the camp. He told them that the warriors had been driven from the field and were preparing to fall back and make a stand in the woods. They were prepared to treat for peace before they were utterly defeated and routed so that they could prevent their women and children from being captured or harmed.[175]

Nenessica turned to Micajah and asked him if he would be willing to serve as their interpreter. Micajah hesitated. He looked at Nenessica's wife and the other women and children in the crowd forming around them.

Micajah's heart was touched by the plight of these innocents. He made a momentous decision that he knew was right. He handed his rifle to Nenessica's wife and mounted a horse. He would be their interpreter. Nenessica and Micajah rode off together to join the surviving warriors preparing to make their final stand against the Long Knives.

The Long Knives did not pursue the Shawanese warriors into the forest, and there were no negotiations. The Shawanese slipped away through the gap in the limestone cliffs with the sound of a soft summer breeze upon meadow grass.

Clark's soldiers lingered in the town and took the time to prepare and eat a meal from the food left behind by the fleeing Shawanese. The Long Knives stripped Piqua of plunder, cut down all the corn in the fields, set the town on fire, and marched home.

Colonel Clark reported to the Virginia governor that the Long Knives had suffered losses of fourteen men killed and thirteen wounded. The Long Knives had found fourteen bodies of warriors near the Long Knife lines. Clark surmised that many more had been killed and retrieved.[176] Joseph ("Fish") Jackson later reported that no more than twenty had been killed.[177]

Alexander McKee and Captain Bird had returned to Detroit on August 4 from their expedition into Kentucky. They had received John Clary's report on August 5. Colonel Clark had struck the Shawanese Towns on August 7 and 8. McKee and Bird had not expected such rapid retaliation from Kentucky. The British and their Indian allies had been surprised once again by a lightning-quick counterstrike by Colonel Clark and his Long Knife soldiers.

Retrenchment in Wapatomica

AFTER THE DEPARTURE OF COLONEL CLARK'S ARMY, a Shawanese council was convened in the council house at Wapatomica on the west bank of the Mad River, some thirty miles to the north of Piqua.[178] The Wapatomica council house was built from split poles covered with bark. It was fifty yards long and twenty-five yards wide, with a height of about sixteen feet.[179]

Disheartened Shawanese chiefs sent a missive from Wapatomica to Major De Peyster in Detroit on August 22, 1780, and complained that the British had not come to their aid in a timely manner. They reported that they had heard that another Long Knife army would soon depart from Fort Pitt and attack the Indian towns as well as Detroit. They begged for more ammunition and protection.[180]

The Shawanese council considered the question of where the displaced Shawanese would live. They decided to permanently abandon the Little Chalaakaatha and Piqua sites because they were too close to the advancing Long Knife settlements.[181] The towns were never rebuilt there.[182]

A site for a new town for the Chalaakaatha division was selected on the Greater Miami River at the former location of the old British post at Pickawillany, about twenty-five miles to the west-southwest of Wapatomica. The rotting stockade walls of Pickawillany were still visible. The new town was called the "Standing Stone Village" by the British.

The new town site selected for the Piqua division was about three miles north of the Standing Stone Village on the Greater Miami River. It will be hereinafter referred to as "New Piqua."[183]

The Shawanese refugees faced a severe food shortage in the fast-approaching winter. The Long Knives had destroyed over 1200 acres of corn at Little Chalaakaatha and Piqua. It was now late summer, and there was no time to raise another crop before the onset of winter. Captain McKee and Simon Girty paid a visit to Wapatomica to offer British assistance. Other nations and villages promised to share what they could of their own corn crops. However, there was little to spare.

The Shawanese women used the small amount of corn that they had salvaged to feed their younger children. The adults relied totally upon hunting for their food. Large hunting parties were assembled and fanned out in a desperate search for meat. Micajah was called upon to contribute to the hunting effort. Fishing parties spread out along the Greater Miami River and its tributaries. There were few Shawanese raids into Kentucky that winter as they struggled for survival.

Nenessica decided to settle in the relative security of Wapatomica until the new Standing Stone Village was well established. Captain Snake and young War Chief Kekewapilathy (Tame Hawk) welcomed the refugees to their town.[184]

Nenessica and Micajah constructed a comfortable temporary cabin for Nenessica and his wife on the edge of Wapatomica. They built a smaller wegiwa for Micajah next to it.

Mackachack was located about five miles to the south of Wapatomica on a rise near the eastern banks of the Mad River. Micajah passed through Mackachack on his way down the river during a fishing trip in mid-September. Lamatumque lived with her husband Chief Moluntha in Moluntha's Town just across the Mad River from Mackachack.

Nenessica was a Makujay himself and told Moluntha and Lamatumque of Micajah's offer to interpret at the Battle of Piqua. He noted that Micajah was connected to the Callaway and Boone families and that he was a potential political asset for future negotiations.

Lamatumque saw Micajah passing through Mackachack on one of his fishing trips and asked if he would speak with her. She led him into the

The Bluegrass War

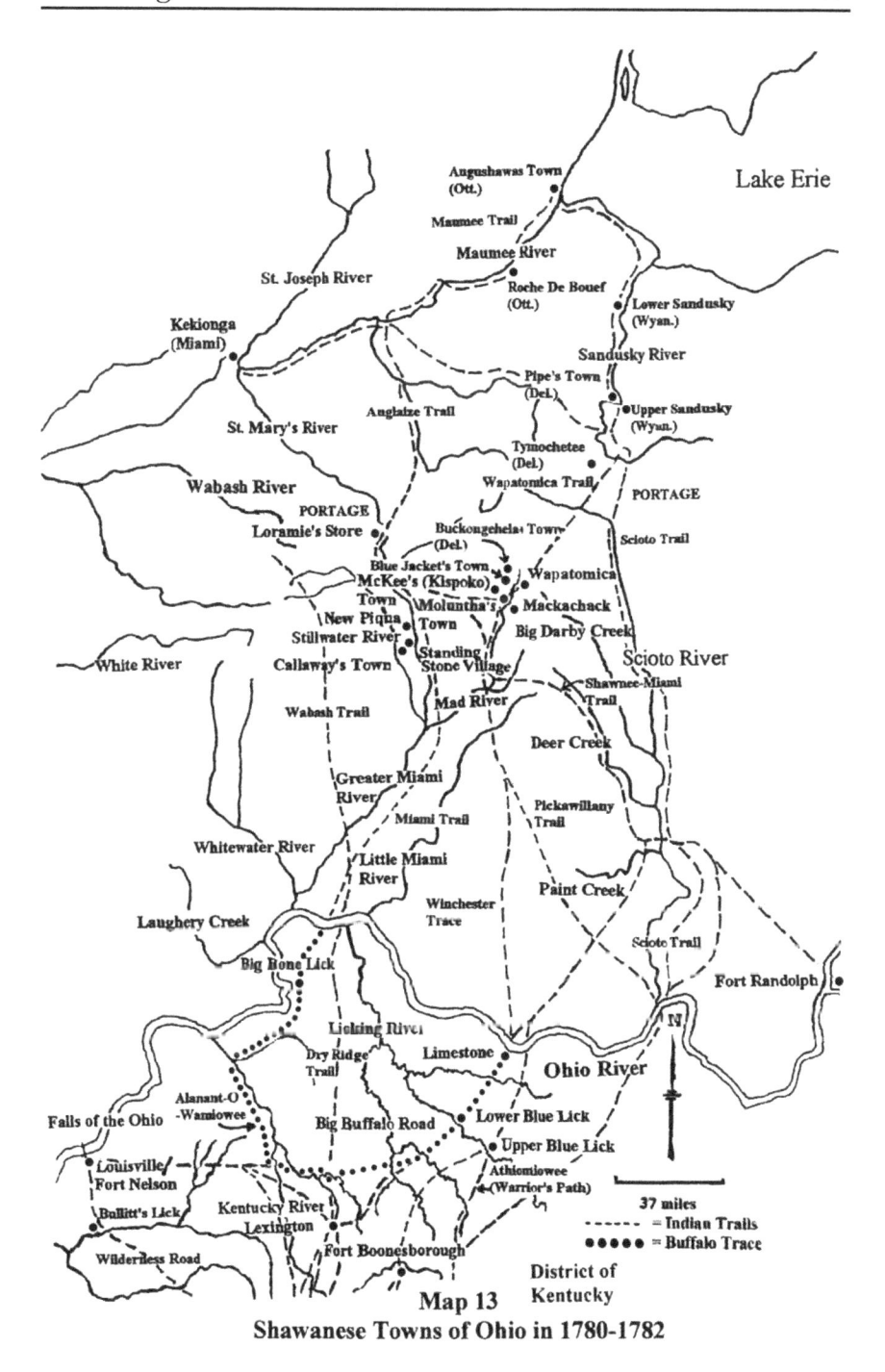

Map 13
Shawanese Towns of Ohio in 1780-1782

----- = Indian Trails
••••• = Buffalo Trace

Mackachack council house. It had an unusual design for a council house, since the roof only covered part of the structure. A sixteen-foot-tall pole was set up in the middle of the roofless portion. The pole sometimes served as a war pole.[185]

Lamatumque was highly respected among the Shawanese, despite her youth. She was gifted with beauty, intelligence, a strong will, and wisdom beyond her years. She and her mother, Headwoman Coitcheleh, and her Aunt Nonhelema were the most important women in the Shawanese Nation. It was an honor to speak with her.

Micajah and Lamatumque seated themselves on buffalo hides on the council house floor. They began their conversation with polite inquiries regarding the health and welfare of their respective families and discussed their adjustments to the recent upheavals from the war.

Lamatumque thanked Micajah for his willingness to help her people at Piqua. She invited him and his Shawanese family to attend the feast for the Autumn Bread Dance ceremony at Mackachack as guests of Chief Moluntha.

Nenessica and his wife and Micajah accepted the invitation and attended the ceremony in Mackachack a few weeks later. Lamatumque introduced Micajah to Moluntha before the ceremony began.

Moluntha shook Micajah's hand in the white man's fashion as they were introduced. Lamatumque described Micajah's generous action during the battle with the Long Knives at Piqua. Moluntha listened attentively and complimented Micajah on his courage and compassion.

The Autumn Bread Dance ceremonies began with Moluntha's prayer to Moneto. He climbed up on the Mackachack prayer rock and raised his arms high above his head. He gratefully thanked Moneto for the meager harvest that He had provided for the Shawanese Nation that year. Moluntha prayed for Moneto's protection and for a more bountiful harvest in the coming year.

Micajah was invited to stay with Moluntha's family for a few days after the ceremony. The invitation was a great honor. Micajah accepted with Nenessica's consent.

Moluntha invited Micajah into his cabin. They sat down on buffalo hides in front of his hearth fire. Moluntha tossed a small handful of tobacco into the fire and said a brief prayer to Moneto. He lit a calumet filled with tobacco and passed it to Micajah. Micajah inhaled the smoke and passed it back.

The aged sachem addressed Micajah after a period of silence and

The Bluegrass War

reflection. He explained how hard it was for an old man like him to carry the burden of leading his people in such troubled times. The Shawanese were at great risk of losing all of their lands and even being wiped entirely off of the face of the earth. It was very difficult to know what to do.

Moluntha passed the pipe back to Micajah who thoughtfully inhaled the smoke and nodded his head sympathetically. He wondered why Moluntha would speak to him so directly. He was hardly more than a boy.

Moluntha continued. He told Micajah that the Shawanese people had made a grievous error when they had believed that the British and French Kings would join to help them defend their lands against the Long Knives. The French had surprised them when they took the side of the Long Knives.

It now appeared that the British might lose the War for Independence. He was pondering what to do if that happened. He thought that the only hope lay in agreeing once and for all to abide by the old treaties that had ceded Kentucky, even though doing so would make many enemies within his own nation.

Micajah did not know what to say and took his time in responding. He knew that Nenessica was not ready to give up his dream of keeping their ancestral hunting grounds in Kentucky. However, Moluntha was probably being realistic. Micajah finally spoke and said that he would think about what Moluntha had said and might one day have some advice.

Moluntha was pleased. Micajah had blood ties to influential Long Knife families and could be a very useful ally in the future. He had shown tempered judgment and sympathy for the plight of the Shawanese people. Moluntha smiled warmly, shook Micajah's hand, and enthused, "Wessah! Wessah! (Very good! Very good!)"[186]

As Nenessica and his wife prepared for their return to Wapatomica, Micajah looked back at Lamatumque, who was busy nursing her child at her breast. She smiled approvingly.

Kentucky (August–December 1780)

THE SUMMER AND FALL OF 1780 ARE remembered as the time when the fortunes of the besieged settlers of Kentucky began to take a turn for the better. The Indian troubles temporarily subsided and another flood tide of thousands of new settlers came down the Ohio River and through the Cumberland Gap. There was an excellent corn crop and harvest that year, which provided an ample winter food supply for the old-timers as well as the newcomers. New stations, towns, and homesteads proliferated.

Kentucky County was divided into the three counties of Fayette, Lincoln, and Jefferson in November of 1780. The thriving town of Lexington was chosen over Boonesborough to serve as the seat of Fayette County.

Daniel Boone was appointed a Lieutenant Colonel in the Fayette County militia and elected to serve as the county's representative in the Virginia General Assembly. He also served the public as Justice of the Peace, Sheriff, and Deputy Surveyor.[187] He became increasingly involved in real estate speculation and surveying and spent less time hunting. Micajah's brother Chesley worked for Daniel on occasion as a survey chain-carrier.[188]

Eight | Micajah Callaway, White Shawanese

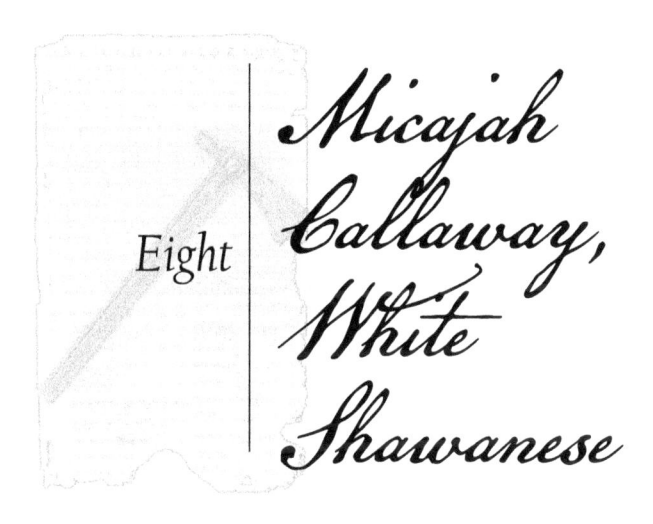

Wapatomica (January – August, 1781)

MICAJAH'S CHILDHOOD IN VIRGINIA WAS NOW A fading memory. He dreamed in the Shawanese language for the first time and found himself thinking in the Shawanese language with increasing frequency. English seemed awkward and unfamiliar when he had the occasion to speak it.

The suffering of the Shawanese Nation increased as the winter of 1780–1781 progressed. Micajah resorted to ice fishing in addition to hunting to obtain enough food to survive. He was forced to hunt for raccoons because larger game was increasingly scarce. His frost-damaged toes throbbed with pain during his longer winter hunts.

Starving Shawanese fathers and mothers sacrificed their own well-being for the sake of their children. They gave the children the remaining corn and the choicer portions of fresh meat. Micajah ate only fish.

The Shawanese women took to their fields with great determination as spring broke the icy grip of winter. They had managed to scrounge enough seed corn and vegetable seeds from their friends in the neighboring Indian nations to plant a large crop. Micajah helped extensively in the planting effort. The women slept in the fields to keep raccoons and other pests from destroying seeds and seedlings once their planting was complete.

Nenessica and his wife and Micajah attended the local Spring Bread Dance at Wapatomica that spring. It was marked by prayers and tobacco offerings to Grandmother Kokomthena for a good harvest and prayers to Moneto and the Thunderbirds to protect them from further Long Knife attacks. The corn crop thrived under the careful management of the women as the year unfolded.

A council of war was convened in Wapatomica in the Spring of 1781. The British and the Indian allies of the Shawanese attended as did all of the principal chiefs and warriors of the Shawanese Nation.

Captain McKee and Simon Girty addressed the Shawanese and encouraged them to be strong. They repledged the full support of Great Britain in the war effort. Several small war parties were sent off to Kentucky to secure prisoners and intelligence regarding the future intentions of the Long Knives.[1]

George Rogers Clark's Campaign of 1781

COLONEL GEORGE ROGERS CLARK WAS CONVINCED THAT the Americans had a window of opportunity to attack and destroy the British fortifications in Detroit.[2] He decided in late 1780 to prepare for an American military expedition to do so in the summer of 1781.

Clark also entered into a contract with Richard Chenoweth to construct a new, larger fort at the Falls of the Ohio to be named "Fort Nelson." Construction was completed in March of 1781.[3] Fort Nelson was second only to Fort Pitt in the Ohio River valley in size and sophistication.

In December of 1780, Colonel Clark traveled to Richmond via the Wilderness Road to obtain support for his invasion plan. General Washington and Governor Thomas Jefferson of Virginia approved and agreed to support it.

On January 2, 1781, the Virginia General Assembly approved a grant of 150,000 acres of land in the Illinois Country to Clark and his Illinois Regiment in recognition of their service.[4] The grant lands were located on the north shore of the Ohio River at the Falls of the Ohio and were commonly called "Clark's Grant."[5] Governor Jefferson also delivered a letter to George Rogers Clark on January 22, 1781, enclosing a new commission as Brigadier General.[6]

General Clark's plans for Detroit were disrupted when the British Royal Navy sailed up the James River and General Benedict Arnold and his British regular soldiers bombarded, sacked, and burned Richmond. Clark was pressed into service under the command of Major General Von Steuben in the desperate effort to defend Virginia. He was unable to detach himself from Von Steuben's command until mid-January.[7]

British and Indian Countermeasures

CAPTAIN ALEXANDER MCKEE OBTAINED INTELLIGENCE ABOUT GENERAL Clark's plans to attack Detroit from three prisoners captured by the Shawanese near the Falls of the Ohio. He informed Major De Peyster of this in a letter dated March 1, 1781.[8] The British decided to counter General Clark's offensive plans by keeping him on the defensive.

Captain Thompson of Butler's Corps of Rangers was dispatched to reinforce Wapatomica with a company of green-coated rangers. Captain McKee, Matthew Elliott, and the Girty brothers organized the Ohio Confederacy nations to join the rangers in offensive operations in Kentucky.

A council of the Principal War Chiefs of the Shawanese, Delaware, and Cherokee Nations was held at Detroit on April 5, 1781. Major De Peyster and Captain Henry Bird of the Royal Army and Captain Alexander McKee, Isodore Chene, and Jacques Duperon Bâby from the Indian Department represented Great Britain.[9] Shawanese War Chiefs Wryneck (Joshua Rennick) and Captain Snake demanded that the British provide the additional military assistance that Lieutenant Governor Hamilton had promised when the enemy approached their towns.[10]

Another council was held at Detroit on April 26, 1781. Chiefs and representatives of the Wyandot, Ottawa, Chippewa, and Pottawatomie Nations and the Six Nations were present.[11] The noted Mohawk warrior Theyaendinega—alias Captain Joseph Brant—brother-in-law of the late Sir William Johnson, was among them.

Captain Brant had commanded an army of one thousand Six Nations warriors and two hundred fifty Loyalist volunteers when American General Sullivan and four thousand Continental soldiers with artillery invaded and attacked the Iroquois homelands in August of 1779. Despite a heroic effort by Captain Brant and his outnumbered warriors, the Americans defeated the Six Nations and Loyalists at the Battle of Newtown.

Brant subsequently asked for a transfer from his New York duties and was ordered to report to Detroit to help the Ohio Indians. He and a loyal band of seventeen Mohawk warriors arrived in Detroit on April 8, 1781.[12]

Captain Snake addressed Major De Peyster and the assembled chiefs again on April 20. He repeated his previous demand for military assistance.[13] Major De Peyster promised to help and asked the Ohio Confederacy to join with the other nations and assemble their warriors into an army.

Old Mingo Vice Regent Guyashuta then spoke on four strings of white and black wampum:

> Brothers, I now greet you all and am much rejoiced to see you all assembled at our Fathers Council Fire. You have heard that we brown skins are one Body, and I now tell you that we the Six Nations are come here for to open your Ears to hear what is good, and to attend to whatever our Father may say—(On which delivers the 4 Strings.)

Captain Brant (Theyaendinega), addressed himself to the several Indian nations, and said:

> I am pleased to find that you are ready to assist your Brethren the Shawanese—You see me here, I am sent upon Business of importance to your several nations, I shall follow you and your Father to the camp that it is to be formed at St. Dusky, at which place I shall deliver you the Speeches of the Six Nations in presence of the Ohio Confederacy who will be there, I hope when you are acquainted with the contents of my Embassy it may furnish means to unite you more strongly in the cause we are mutually engaged, and continue our Friendly intercourse as the meeting will be general . . .[14]

The red tomahawk was circulated to Great Britain's Indian allies with a message calling upon them to assemble their warriors at the British Post at Upper Sandusky. The warriors of the Shawanese, Wyandot, Delaware, Mingo, and Six Nations gathered there, and Joseph Brant and Simon Girty were placed in command.

A party of warriors under Brant's command was dispatched from Upper Sandusky to the mouth of the Greater Miami River. They were to either intercept Clark on his way down the Ohio River from Fort Pitt or intercept any invasion forces moving toward the Ohio Country from the Falls of the Ohio and Kentucky. The war party included Brant's loyal band of Mohawk warriors and chiefs and warriors of the Delaware, Mingo, and Wyandot Nations.

George Girty, Nenessica and a small party of Shawanese warriors joined them. Nenessica asked Micajah to accompany them to serve as interpreter and to help carry booty and escort prisoners. Micajah agreed. He and George Girty were the only two white men in Joseph Brant's war party.[15]

Nenessica and his Shawanese warriors left Brant's party and crossed the Ohio River into Kentucky on June 26, 1781, to gather intelligence on the movements of the Kentucky militia. The British in Detroit received an alarming intelligence report on July 14 from "the Principal Warrior of Chillicothey" (Nenessica) reporting that his scouts had detected numerous signs of a large force of Kentucky militia estimated at about 1,200 men. An Ottawa party confirmed the information.[16]

Colonel Lochry's Defeat (August 24, 1781)

GENERAL CLARK WAITED IN VAIN AT FORT Pitt for the anticipated Pennsylvania and Virginia militia companies that had been promised for his campaign again Detroit. Virginia could not spare any troops: It continued to fight desperately for its very survival as Lord Cornwallis and his army joined the British invasion of Virginia. The Pennsylvania counties also did not meet their commitments as they were also focused on "home defense."

Clark decided to depart down the Ohio River in late June with the mere four hundred troops that he was able to assemble. He left a letter at Fort Pitt with instructions for Pennsylvania militia commander Colonel

Archibald Lochry (also sometimes spelled Laughery) to meet him farther down the river at Fort Henry in Wheeling.

The assembled troops, led by General Clark, proceeded down the river in a fleet of several boats. They fired a small swivel cannon at dawn each morning in order to intimidate any Indians considering an attack.

Colonel Lochry assembled a company of 107 mounted volunteers from Westminster County, Pennsylvania, and departed for Fort Pitt where he found the message from General Clark. He proceeded downriver on rafts as instructed, but was unable to catch up with General Clark. He began to run out of provisions and dispatched Major Cracraft and four men in a desperate attempt to overtake Clark.[17]

Nenessica and his band of Shawanese warriors rejoined Brant's war party after completing their scouting mission into the Bluegrass Region. Brant set up a forward base camp on the forested shore of the northwest corner of the confluence at the mouth of the Greater Miami River.

They lay there in concealment on the night of August 18, 1781, and heard the sounds of several boats passing by them on the Ohio River in the darkness. A cannon shot suddenly boomed out from one of the boats. It was General Clark's force. Captain Brant elected not to attack the boats and silently withdrew.

Joseph Brant and his men prepared to cross the river two days later to see if General Clark and his men were camped at the Big Bone Lick. Micajah and several of the warriors made elm bark canoes for the journey. The group then crossed the river and checked the woodlands and prairies around the Big Bone Lick. There were no signs of any Long Knives there.

Micajah stepped from the forest path into the large barren salt lick and beheld an astounding sight: five massive skeletons lay on the surface. The Indians called the great beast to which they belonged the "big buffalo." Their bones were far larger than any bones he had ever seen, and their tusks were ten to twelve feet long.

Nenessica told Micajah the legend of how the bones came to be there.[18] A herd of the enormous animals had come to the licks many, many years ago and had begun to destroy the bear, deer, elk, buffalo, and other animals that also used the licks. Moneto looked down and was angered by the destruction. He descended from Heaven and seated himself on a nearby hill, leaving

Micajah Callaway, White Shawanese

impressions that could still be seen. Moneto hurled lightning bolts at the animals and killed all but one big bull. The bull was wounded and escaped to the north of the Great Lakes, where he still lived.[19]

The warriors held a war dance around the central campfire that night. Micajah painted himself and danced to the throbbing water drum as they sang war songs.[20]

The war party arose before dawn on the following morning. The warriors stripped to their breechcloths and moccasins and painted themselves for battle. They canoed back over to the north shore of the Ohio River and marched east single-file along the river path. They set up an ambush on the river and captured Major Cracraft and the advance party for Colonel Lochry's regiment.[21]

Colonel Lochry and his starving troops had decided to stop at a grassy embankment on the north shore of the Ohio River on August 24, 1781, about ten miles below the mouth of the Greater Miami River at its confluence with Laughery's Creek. They had disembarked, turned their horses out to feed on the grass, and begun cutting bundles of the grass to take with them for the remaining 120-mile trip to the Falls.

Colonel Lochry had made the unfortunate decision to disembark at the precise location where Joseph Brant's war party waited in ambush. A volley of musket shots suddenly poured out of the adjoining woods onto the militiamen as the painted warriors attacked with a chorus of war whoops, and several soldiers were killed and wounded.

The hapless soldiers tried to escape in their boats, but they were blocked by warriors in five canoes hiding on the opposite shore. The warriors fired on the men as their boats floundered in the shallow water along the shore. More soldiers were killed and wounded. Colonel Lochry saw that his situation was hopeless and decided to surrender.

Joseph Brant accepted Colonel Lochry's surrender with Micajah at his side.[22] The prisoners were placed under guard and escorted to the Indian camp. Brant and the leadership of the war party withdrew into council to decide the fate of the prisoners.

The Delaware warriors in Brant's war party were eager for revenge. A force of Continental regulars and Pennsylvania militia under the command of Colonel Daniel Broadhead had attacked the Delaware capital of Coshocton in the spring of 1781. Several Coshocton Delaware were killed or captured and atrocities were committed by the Americans.

A warrior led Colonel Lochry to a log and ordered him to sit. The colonel sat as directed, and the warrior suddenly swung a tomahawk and struck him on the side of the head. The colonel fell forward on his face. The warrior reached down, lifted up one of his arms, and stabbed him in the chest with a knife.

A total of forty-two of Colonel Lochry's men were killed and scalped either during battle or in the first two days of their imprisonment.[23] Nenessica and his band of Shawanese warriors were given custody of five of the surviving prisoners to take back to the Shawanese towns. One of the prisoners was Ezekiel Lewis.

Micajah gruffly explained to the prisoners that the Shawanese warriors only carried a small amount of dried meat and parched corn in a pouch at their waist. There would be no food for the prisoners while they were on the trail unless they were able to kill some game along the way. Micajah told them that they would be killed if they complained or showed signs of weakness.

They reached Wapatomica after a five-day march. The starving and exhausted prisoners were greeted with the gauntlet when they approached the town. Micajah secured them in a cabin after their ordeal and provided them with their first meal since their capture. He advised them to show a hearty appetite and eat their fill so the warriors would not be tempted to kill them. The prisoners ate a full meal and that night suffered from severe nausea and diarrhea.[24]

The desertions of the militia during the long journey down the Ohio River and the loss of Colonel Lochry's forces left General Clark with a maximum of seven hundred men for his invasion force. They were not enough to accomplish the mission. General George Rogers Clark's 1781 campaign against Detroit had been thwarted.[25]

Captain Alexander McKee and Joseph Brant managed to hold a number of Indian Confederacy warriors together in a small army after Brant's victory. They divided into war parties and struck the Long Knife settlements in northern Kentucky. The raids were devastating and succeeded in terrorizing the countryside. Captain McKee estimated that over two hundred settlers were killed before the Indians returned to their homes.

Daniel Boone's battle-scarred brother, Squire Boone, had recently settled at his Painted Stone Station on Clear Creek, several miles to the southeast of Louisville and south of the Beargrass Stations. Squire was commissioned captain of a company of militia comprised of the twenty-three able-bodied men who lived at the station.

Captain Boone ordered the evacuation of the station as soon as he learned of the invading British and Indian war party. A convoy of wagons carrying the women and children departed on September 14, 1781, escorted by Bland Ballard and other mounted riflemen from the fort. Captain Boone and his family, along with the Hinton family, remained behind in the station.

The convoy was ambushed and most of the party was massacred. Bland Ballard managed to escape to Floyd's Station to get help. Colonel John Floyd assembled a force of about thirty men and set out to collect and bury the dead on September 15.

Captain McKee, Joseph Brant, and their warriors set up an ambush where the Painted Stone convoy had been massacred. Louis Lorimier was with them.[26] Colonel Floyd and his horsemen rode into the trap on September 16, 1781, and sixteen more Long Knives were killed. Colonel William Linn and Captain Samuel Wells were among the dead.

Colonel Floyd escaped the trap and returned to the Beargrass settlements. He assembled a force of three hundred mounted Long Knives. They searched in vain for the raiders. Squire Boone and his family abandoned the Painted Stone Station and moved to Louisville.[27]

Standing Stone Village and Callaway's Town

MICAJAH AND THE WAR PARTY RETURNED TO Wapatomica with their prisoners from Lochry's Defeat just in time for the Green Corn Festival. The Shawanese had much to be thankful for this year. They had preserved and harvested their corn crop and held the Long Knives at bay. Nenessica and his wife and Micajah traveled down the river to Mackachack to attend the festival.

On the first morning of the festival, the assembled Shawanese seated themselves on the grass in the clearing in front of the council house. They passed the calumet around until all had smoked it several times. Moluntha stepped up onto the sacred Prayer Rock and lifted his arms to the Heavens.

Moluntha thanked Moneto for smiling down on his brown children and for blessing them as the first and most honorable people among the human race. Moneto had given them the vast island stretching from the eastern waters where the sun rises to the great salt water beyond the mountains in the west, and from the sea of the north to the salt waters of the south. He had provided abundant corn for bread, and buffalo, deer, and bear for meat. For every illness, Moneto had provided a medicinal plant. Moluntha tossed a handful of tobacco into the fire to carry his prayer of thanks to the heavens.

Moluntha requested that his people show their gratitude to Moneto by enjoying their plentiful harvest and the sports and games of the festival. They all leapt to their feet with a great shout and began the celebration.[28]

The feast began around noon. The participants ate their fill of venison, squirrel stew, corn bread, beans, squash, and other foods. The calumet was passed around for another relaxing smoke after the feast. A variety of additional sports events took place in the early afternoon, after their meal had settled.

The dancing began in the late afternoon. The ceremonial Green Corn Dance came first and was followed by other traditional dances. The social dancing followed at nightfall and continued on through the night until morning light.

Nenessica decided to move his family to rejoin the Chaalakaatha division at the new Standing Stone Village not long after the festival. Micajah helped Nenessica and his wife pack and move their possessions once again.

They found Standing Stone Village filled with refugees from Little Chaalakaatha and old Piqua. It was smaller than either of the two former towns and reflected the declining Shawanese population in Ohio. The town was not fortified. Micajah renewed his acquaintance with Chiaxi and his other Chaalakaatha friends as well as Fish Jackson and other adopted whites living with the Chaalakaatha.

In late winter, Nenessica and his family moved again from the Standing Stone Village to a little village on the Stillwater River not far to the west-southwest from the Standing Stone Village. The Stillwater was a tributary stream of the Greater Miami River. A mixture of Chalaakaatha Shawanese, northern Cherokee, and Mingo lived there and had built a small council house. The village was known to some as Will's Town[29] and to others as Callaway's (Calaway's) Town.[30]

LORD CORNWALLIS SURRENDERED HIS ARMY TO THE Americans and French at Yorktown on October 19, 1781. Celebrations spontaneously erupted throughout the thirteen American colonies. The British Crown and Parliament considered the merits of continuing the war effort and decided to give it up. They initiated negotiations in Paris, France, to end the war in early 1782. The end of the long and bloody American War of Independence was at hand.

However, the war was not yet over in Kentucky and on the northwestern frontier of Virginia. News of the British defeat at Yorktown did not reach the isolated British post at Detroit until April of 1782. Major De Peyster instructed Captain McKee to withhold the information from their Indian allies until he received orders from Quebec.[31]

Virginia's resources had been exhausted by General Cornwallis's invasion of Virginia and the great American and French victory over the British at Yorktown. General Clark's men at Fort Nelson had not been paid for two years. They had been provided with no clothing and were virtually dressed in rags. Clark had used his own limited funds to pay for provisions for his men and had little left to give. Morale was low.

Benjamin Harrison was chosen to succeed Thomas Jefferson as Virginia's Governor. Governor Harrison ordered Clark to establish new forts and garrisons at the mouths of the Kentucky River, Licking River, and Limestone Creek but provided no funding to do so. Clark was unable to comply with the order without funding. He grew increasingly bitter over the unreasonable demands placed on him and requested that he be relieved of his command. Governor Harrison refused his request and continued to insist that he build the new forts.[32]

Colonel Crawford's Defeat (June 11, 1782)

IN LATE FEBRUARY 1782, THE BRITISH HELD a Grand Council in Detroit with the Shawanese, Delaware, Wyandot, and ten other Indian Nations.[33] There they developed a plan for two major campaigns into enemy territory during the coming summer. One campaign would penetrate Kentucky with the ultimate goal of capturing Fort Nelson. The goal of the other campaign was to capture and destroy Wheeling.

American soldiers from Fort Pitt commanded by Colonel David Williamson massacred and scalped ninety-six captive and bound Christian Moravian Delaware men, women, and children at the Moravian mission of Gnaddenhutten in March of 1782. These peaceful Delaware were the last of their nation in Ohio that were friendly to the Americans, who executed their allies by crushing their skulls with wooden mallets and burning their bodies afterward.

The massacre at Gnaddenhutten outraged and hardened the resolve of the Indian Confederacy to fight on against the hated Long Knives. The surviving Delaware and the other northwestern Indian nations responded with a series of ferocious raids on white settlements in western Pennsylvania and the Wheeling area.

The American settlers in the upper Ohio River Valley clamored for a follow-up to their "victory" at Gnaddenhutten. On May 22, 1782, a force of around five hundred Western Pennsylvania and Virginia militia soldiers commanded by Colonel William Crawford marched on the Wyandot towns on the Sandusky Plains. Colonel Crawford still served as General George Washington's personal land agent in the Ohio River Valley, as he had for many years.

Colonel Crawford's offensive campaign caused a temporary shift in the British and Indian plans for invading the Wheeling area in the summer of 1782. They redirected their forces to confront Colonel Crawford.

The outnumbered American forces engaged in a battle with an army of over one thousand Indian warriors and three companies of mounted British Rangers led by British Captain Caldwell, Matthew Elliott, and Simon Girty on June 6, 1782. One hundred forty mounted Shawanese warriors commanded by Captain Snake joined the attack on June 7.[34] Their faces and chests were painted in stripes and whirls of red, blue, and white paint.

The Americans were decisively defeated and routed from the field of battle. Colonel Crawford and several other officers and soldiers were captured. The implacable Delaware were determined to take revenge for the massacre at Gnaddenhutten. A Delaware council sentenced Colonel Crawford to be burned alive.

Crawford was taken to the Delaware village of Tymochtee for execution. He never screamed or begged for his life as he was tortured and burned to death.

Micajah may have been present at Crawford's execution. His son John H. Callaway described a very similar torture and execution witnessed by his father.[35]

The Shawanese convened a council at Wapatomica to determine the fate of the prisoners that had been sent there after the battle. Several prisoners were condemned and executed. It is very likely that Micajah witnessed these Shawanese executions.

Major John McClelland was burned at the stake at Wapatomica. Private William Harrison was shot to death after running the gauntlet. McClelland's and Harrison's bodies were mutilated and decapitated, and their heads were stuck on poles near the Wapatomica council house.[36] Young Ensign William Crawford (a nephew of the Colonel) and John Slover were taken to Mackachack. Crawford was burned at the stake there in the council house, but Slover managed to escape.[37]

Crisis in Kentucky.
The Fog of War

NEW SETTLERS CONTINUED TO POUR INTO KENTUCKY throughout 1782 despite the continuing hostilities. Captain Abraham Lincoln, his wife Bathsheba, sons Mordecai, Josiah, and Thomas, and daughters Mary and Nancy were among the new arrivals from Lacey Springs in Rockingham County, Virginia. They settled on an eight-hundred-acre tract on the Green River in Lincoln County in March or April of 1782. Abraham's youngest son, Thomas, future father of the president of the United States, was only four years old at the time of their arrival.[38]

The Virginia General Assembly enacted a law in 1782 establishing a new political subdivision of the State of Virginia to be known as the District of Kentucky. The district was comprised of the three western-most Virginia counties: Fayette, Jefferson, and Lincoln.[39] The new town of Danville, Kentucky, was selected as the district capitol.

General Clark decided in early March to post large armed row galleys at the confluence of the Greater Miami River and Ohio River in case the British attempted to invade Kentucky by boat down the Greater Miami River.[40] A single-row galley equipped with swivel cannon was completed and deployed in June of 1782. It was a sturdy vessel over seventy feet in length, had forty-six oars, and carried one hundred men. A company of Continental Marines commanded by Captain Benjamin Piatt was stationed on it. It patrolled between the Falls of the Ohio River and the mouth of the Licking River.[41]

On June 8, 1782 Captain Snake requested that the British Rangers at Lower Sandusky join the Shawanese warriors in the Shawanese villages on the Greater Miami River. Captain Snake said that if the enemy did not come into Ohio, the Indians were determined to attack them in Kentucky.[42]

The Shawanese hosted a council in Wapatomica beginning the third week of June. The Delaware and Wyandot convinced the Indian Confederacy leaders that their first priority was to attack Fort Henry at Wheeling as vengeance for the Gnaddenhutten massacre. Alexander McKee, Simon Girty, and a large force of confederacy warriors rendezvoused with Captain Caldwell's Rangers in Upper Sandusky and departed for Wheeling on July 15.

An urgent message from the Shawanese Towns overtook them as they marched. Shawanese Chief Blue Jacket and his scouting party had observed the new row galley near the mouth of the Licking River during a reconnaissance patrol. Based on that observation, Blue Jacket reported that the Long Knives were preparing an invasion of Ohio and that he had discovered their main invasion force.[43]

When they received Blue Jacket's report, the Shawanese warriors with the confederacy army refused to continue on the march to Wheeling and returned to their homes to defend them. Alexander McKee, Matthew Elliott, Captain Caldwell and his Rangers, and the Lake Indians agreed to join the Shawanese while a reduced war party continued on to Wheeling.

The Shawanese and their allies gathered at the former location of Piqua on the Mad River and assembled a force of 1,100 warriors. British Ranger scouts then reported to Captain Caldwell that the intelligence concerning General Clark was incorrect and that no invasion was underway. The Shawanese had overreacted to the row galley observed by Blue Jacket.

The Indian army disintegrated as the Lake Indians ridiculed the Shawanese, and the offended Shawanese chiefs and warriors dispersed. The

Micajah Callaway, White Shawanese 177

British struggled to salvage some gain from the extensive planning and preparations of the previous few months. Captain Caldwell and a company of his Rangers, Alexander McKee, Matthew Elliot, Simon and George Girty, three hundred Wyandot and Lake Indians, and a handful of Shawanese, Delaware, and Mingo warriors crossed the Ohio River and retraced Captain Bird's 1780 campaign trail into the Kentucky Bluegrass Region.[44]

The Long Knives had built no new stations in the Bluegrass Region and had not rebuilt Ruddle's Station, Martin's Station, Grant's Station, or Houston Station since their destruction in Captain Bird's campaign in 1780. Captain Caldwell and the Indian leaders targeted the remaining Bluegrass settlements in Kentucky as their primary objective. The destruction of Bryant's Station, Strode's Station, Boone's Station, and McGee's Station would sweep most of the traditional Shawanese hunting grounds free of intruders.

BRITISH BRIGADIER GENERAL POWELL SENT A LETTER to Major De Peyster in Detroit on August 15, 1782 requesting that he cease all offensive military operations against the Americans because of the recent progress made in the Paris peace negotiations. General Powell instructed that only defensive military measures would be supported by the British if the Americans should attack the Indians.

Major De Peyster sent a letter back to General Powell on August 27 acknowledging receipt of his August 15 letter. He noted that Captain Caldwell and the expedition of British Rangers and Indian Confederacy warriors had already left for Kentucky and could not be recalled in time to prevent attacks on the Kentucky settlements.[45] A small army of British Rangers and Indian Confederacy warriors led by Ranger Captain Andrew Bradt had also departed to attack Wheeling.

Captain John Holder's Defeat (August 15, 1782)

COLONEL RICHARD CALLAWAY'S WIDOW ELIZABETH AND HER seven-year old son Jacky had moved to Hoy's Station after Richard's death to live with Captain

William Hoy, her oldest son by her first marriage. Hoy's Station was located on a beautiful tract of land to the south of the Kentucky River on high ground between Tates Creek and Otter Creek. Captain Hoy had a nine-year old son named Jones Hoy.[46]

Captain Hoy and the other men at Hoy's Station went into the forest near their homes on August 14, 1782, to clear and construct a horse racetrack. Jacky and Jones asked if they could go and watch the men work, and Elizabeth gave her permission. The two young boys decided to stop at a neighbor's garden and pick up a watermelon on their way to the racetrack.[47]

A raiding party of seventy Shawanese warriors from Captain Caldwell's invasion force infiltrated the Bluegrass settlement area and crossed the Kentucky River without being detected. The brave young Shawanese warrior Wabapusito, beloved son of old Chief White Bark of the Piqua division, was among the leaders of the raiding party.[48]

The Shawanese raiders stealthily crept between Hoy's Station and the racetrack. As the two little boys were picking their watermelon, several warriors stepped out from the forest and caught them in the garden. The boys made a ruckus as they were captured, and their neighbors heard them. The warriors fled north across the Kentucky River and up the hunter's trace to Grassy Lick and beyond. The settlers quickly gathered a group of men to pursue the raiders.[49]

Wabapusito devised a clever plan for ambushing the anticipated pursuit party. The warriors carried the two boys along the trail to a sandbar in Battle Run Creek near the Upper Blue Lick.

One of the older warriors spoke English and asked the boys if they wanted to play a game. The old warrior showed the boys two colorful painted medicine sticks used in "medicine hunting." He said that he would throw each of the sticks and give a prize to the first boy to reach one.

The old man threw the sticks. One landed on each side of the sandy stream bed several dozen yards upstream. The boys raced to the sticks and picked them up. A warrior then stepped out from a hiding place beside each boy and asked him to follow. The boys obeyed and created diverging trails of footprints. The two separate traces would induce any pursuing rescue party to divide and weaken their force.[50]

Rear scouts alerted the raiders that a company of soldiers was in hot pursuit as anticipated. Jacky and Jones were left in the custody of women traveling with the war party and were hidden in the bushes. The warriors took cover behind trees to wait in ambush.[51]

Captain John Holder gathered what men he could find at Holder's Station when he learned of the boys' abduction and prepared to pursue the enemy. Captain Holder had married Colonel Richard Callaway's daughter Fanny after helping rescue her from her Indian abductors at Boonesborough in 1776. Little Jacky Callaway was his brother-in-law.[52]

Holder and his men joined thirty-five additional men at McGee's Station, including Captain John Fleming and William Cassidy.[53] Cassidy was a short and stocky Irishman and a pugnacious Indian fighter. He had a large scar across his forehead right above his eyes.[54]

The pursuit group totaled sixty-one men on horseback. They left McGee's Station and followed the trail of the warriors past Strode's Station and up the hunter's trace past Grassy Lick, and on to Battle Run Creek near the Upper Blue Lick, where they reached the sandbar where the trail of the boys divided.

It was obvious to them that a trap had been laid by the Shawanese. The captains conferred and decided that they had no choice but to divide their force and pursue both trails to ensure the rescue of both boys. Captain Holder and his men took the right-hand trail and a party commanded by William Cassidy took the left-hand trail.

Captain Holder's party was ambushed and driven from the field by superior forces. They were on the run by the time Cassidy reached them. The Indians turned their attention to Cassidy's party and also routed it. Captain Fleming was wounded and several men were killed in the ensuing fight.[55]

Wabapusito and a handful of his warriors approached an isolated cabin in the Kentucky wild lands on their return journey to Ohio. A young white woman and an African American slave were alone in the cabin. Wabapusito forced his way into the cabin. The powerful African American man slammed the door closed behind Wabapusito, grabbed him, and pinned his arms to his sides. The young woman attacked Wabapusito with a broad axe and killed him.[56]

The Battle of Lower Blue Licks (August 19, 1782)

CHARLES BEASLEY HAD ESCAPED FROM THE SHAWANESE towns and warned the occupants of Bryant's Station that the British Rangers and Indians planned to attack the fort and then lure pursuers from the fort to ambush them.[57] The forewarned residents secured their livestock and prepared for a siege.[58]

Bryant's Station had been strengthened over the years and by this time consisted of a strong rectangular stockade measuring fifty yards by two hundred yards. There was a two-story blockhouse at each of the four corners. Twenty cabins lined the stockade walls on the long axis of the rectangle while pickets formed the walls on the short axis. Heavy gates were located in each of the long walls.[59]

Captain Caldwell's Rangers and their Indian allies attacked Bryant's Station on August 17, 1782. The battle raged through the day as the Rangers and warriors took cover and fired at the fortified settlers. The settlers returned fire.

Thomas Bell and Nicholas Tomlinson slipped out of the fort and rode off to summon aid. They delivered their message to Colonels John Todd and Stephen Trigg at Lexington Fort.[60]

Colonel Todd had directed the construction of Lexington Fort in 1782. It was in the form of a quadrangle with a blockhouse bastion at each of the four corners. The fort was surrounded by a ditch that was eight feet wide and four to five feet deep. Rammed earth walls were built to a height of nine feet. They were seven feet thick at the base and five feet thick at the top. A six foot high timber picket wall was constructed on top of the rammed earth walls to provide cover from small arms. A powder magazine was sheltered inside.[61]

Colonels Todd and Trigg mustered a militia force at the Lexington Fort on August 18, 1782, and marched to the rescue of Bryant's Station on the morning of August 19. They were joined by Lieutenant Colonel Daniel Boone and a small company from Fort Boonesborough and Boone's Station as they left. The Long Knife commanders learned upon their arrival that the British and Indians had withdrawn from the siege on the morning of August 18 and disappeared up the Big Buffalo Road.

British Ranger Captain Caldwell and his force withdrew to the former

Micajah Callaway, White Shawanese

site of Ruddell's Station. Caldwell conferred there with the Indian war leaders. About one hundred Shawanese, Delaware, and Wyandot warriors decided to leave the main body and return to Wapatomica via Captain Bird's trail.

Captain Caldwell persuaded the rest of the warriors to march up the Big Buffalo Road with his Rangers and lay an ambush for their anticipated pursuers at the Lower Blue Licks. They set up the ambush at a strategic location on a ridge of high bluffs in the middle of the oxbow bend just east of where the Big Buffalo Road crossed the Licking River at the Lower Blue Licks. Their concealed battle line spanned from one point on the river over and across the top of the river bluffs to another point on the river, ensuring that they could not be flanked.[62]

The Long Knives set off up the Big Buffalo Road in hot pursuit. When they reached the top of the ridge to the west, above the Licking River crossing at the Lower Blue Licks, they spotted two Indian warriors walking back and forth along the edge of a clearing on top of the bluffs on other side of the crossing.

Daniel Boone and the majority of the commanders suspected a trap and recommended against a precipitous attack. Captain Hugh McGary accused them of cowardice, rode down the hill, and forged across the river. Against their better judgment, Daniel Boone and the others took up McGary's challenge and followed him.[63]

The Long Knives sent a small mounted advance party to draw enemy fire away from their main body, which pressed forward on foot. The British Rangers and Indians opened fire from ambush as the advance party climbed the ridge and drew near and closed around the main body of the Long Knives.

The Long Knives drove the enemy back on their left flank but their own right flank collapsed into their center which in turn collapsed into their left flank. Confusion reined as a melée of hand-to-hand combat with tomahawks and scalping knives ensued. The battle lasted only five minutes before the Long Knives were driven into a panicked retreat. The warriors shot several of the retreating men as they crossed over the river.[64]

Over seventy officers and soldiers were either killed or captured in the brief fire-fight. Colonels John Todd and Stephen Trigg were among the dead. Daniel Boone's beloved son Israel was gunned down and bled to death before Daniel's eyes. The victorious British Rangers and Indians took the scalps of the dead and withdrew across the Ohio River.

Colonel Benjamin Logan arrived at Lexington with his Lincoln County soldiers after the others had already left on their disastrous mission. Colonel Logan sent a letter to the Governor of Virginia and the Executive Council on August 31, 1782, and recommended an offensive campaign against the Indian towns.[65]

Callaway's Town (August - November, 1782)

MICAJAH WAS IN CALLAWAY'S TOWN WHEN THE warriors returned to New Piqua with their prisoners after the victory at the Lower Blue Licks, and he rode over to see them.

The Shawanese celebration of the Indian Confederacy victory was tempered by their grief for the deaths of several of their warriors. Wabapusito's mangled body was returned to his father Chief White Bark. The old chief was sick with grief and anger over the loss of his most beloved son.

Micajah joined the crowd that gathered to inspect the two young boys captured near Hoy's Station. He had known Jacky as an infant in Fort Boonesborough and easily recognized him. Jacky's resemblance to his father, Colonel Richard Callaway, was unmistakable. A flood of memories of his half-forgotten Callaway family flashed through Micajah's mind.

Micajah knew that Chief White Bark would probably take his revenge upon the boys for the death of his own son Wabapusito. He asked Nenessica to speak to Alexander McKee and request that the boys be protected.

Jacky and Jones Hoy were placed in the care of Chief White Bark's adopted daughter Margaret Pawley when they arrived in New Piqua.[66] The vengeful old chief announced his intention to place Margaret Pawley, Jacky Callaway, and Jones Hoy inside the cabin of his dead son and burn all three of them alive.

The fate of the prisoners was submitted to the Shawanese council convened in the New Piqua council house. Mrs. Pawley secretly listened in on the proceedings from just outside the door.[67] The council was divided.

Chief White Bark was the first speaker. He spoke tearfully about his loss and his just cause for revenge. His supports echoed his call for vengeange. Several Shawanese speakers under Captain McKee's influence pleaded to spare innocent Margaret and the two boys.[68]

Micajah's heart pounded as he stood up in the flickering firelight of the council fire to speak. He began by reviewing his life with the Shawanese beginning with his capture and adoption and continuing through his experiences during the war. He thanked Nenessica for his kindness and strength as a father. The chiefs and warriors murmured in appreciation of his gesture.

White Bark listened coldly as Micajah pleaded that the prisoners be spared and that the two boys be adopted into the nation. Other warriors spoke after Micajah. Some of them were in favor of adoption and others favored death. White Bark was unmoved and said so.

Then Micajah was allowed to make a final plea. He picked up his long rifle, put the stock on the ground, and leaned on the barrel. The firelight glinted off of its polished metal. He spoke eloquently in praise of Wabapusito as a fine son and a great warrior. He acknowledged White Bark's grief at his loss and said that he and the rest of the nation also grieved with him. Several Shawanese men murmured their assent.

Micajah bowed his head and paused several minutes before speaking again. He spoke softly and acknowledged that mere words could not compensate for Chief White Bark's loss. He stepped before the old chief, kneeled, and offered his rifle to him.

It was an impressive gesture. All eyes turned to White Bark. The elderly chief impassively held up his hand and pointed to the ground before him. Micajah laid the rifle on the ground and stepped back.

White Bark closed his eyes and meditated. The council house was quiet with the exception of the crackling council fire. After a long pause, old White Bark struggled to his feet and held out his hands. He had chosen mercy. Micajah picked up his rifle and handed it to him. Margaret and the boys had been spared.

Chief White Bark held the rifle high above his head in one hand, shook it, and cried out in a feeble but strident war whoop. Pandemonium broke loose in the council house as the other warriors joined him in an impromptu war dance. Old White Bark silently wept bitter tears of grief as he danced.[69]

Margaret took very good care of young Jacky and Jones after the crisis had passed. She had a young son of her own with her who was born not long after her capture in 1779. Jacky and her little son developed a friendship that lasted for many years.

Margaret made the boys bathe in the Greater Miami River every morning of every day of the year in the Shawanese fashion. They climbed a flexible sapling that bent and dipped them into the water. If their heads were dry after their bath, she made them bathe again. They sometimes returned to the cabin with ice in their hair in the winter.[70]

Micajah thought about his own future after he had assured himself of the immediate safety of the boys. He was once again troubled and torn by conflicting loyalties toward his friends and families on both sides of the war.

He had come to respect and even love many of the Shawanese. Their lifestyle suited him very well; however, he also deeply missed his own Callaway family. Seeing Jacky Callaway had brought them back to mind. Someday the war would be over, and he would have to choose which people to live with.

WORD OF THE DISASTROUS LONG KNIFE DEFEAT at the Lower Blue Licks traveled quickly to the east along the Wilderness Road. General George Washington sent a letter to Sir Guy Carleton on September 8, 1782, complaining about the persistent warfare in the northwestern territories.[71] Sir Guy responded to Washington on September 12, 1782, and reassured him that all war parties had been recalled.[72]

Major De Peyster sent a letter to General Haldimand on September 29, 1782, and explained his difficulties in limiting Indian military operations to purely defensive measures when the settlers of Kentucky continued to make war on the Indians. He expected that the warriors would continue their raids.[73]

General Clark's Campaign of 1782: Disaster in the Shawanese Towns

GENERAL CLARK TOOK COMMAND OF THE LONG Knife response to the defeat at the Battle of Lower Blue Licks. He met with Colonel Benjamin Logan

(County Lieutenant for Lincoln County), Colonel John Floyd (County Lieutenant for Jefferson County), and Colonel Daniel Boone (recently promoted to County Lieutenant for Fayette County) to organize and mobilize another Long Knife army.[74] Their military objective was to attack and destroy the Standing Stone Village and several nearby Shawanese towns.

General Clark issued orders drafting all able-bodied men in the District of Kentucky and directed them to rendezvous on November 1, 1782, at the stockade on the north shore of the Ohio River across from the mouth of the Licking River. The stockade had been maintained and periodically manned since Clark's 1780 campaign. They would march from there to the Shawanese towns.

Each man was ordered to bring his own provisions of parched corn and jerked meat. A packhorse was provided for every six men. General Clark bartered 3,500 acres of his own land for enough flour to feed the expedition. Colonel Floyd assumed the responsibility for repairing the twenty boats that would carry men and provisions up the Ohio River. Major Walls at Fort Nelson was ordered to ready his soldiers for the campaign and load the boats prepared by Colonel Floyd.[75]

General Clark served as the Commanding General of the army. Colonel Benjamin Logan assembled a division of troops from the interior of Kentucky composed of his own Lincoln County troops; the Fayette County militia commanded by Colonels Boone, Patterson, and Levi Todd; and a regiment from Harrodsburg commanded by Major Hugh McGary.

Colonel Logan's division marched from Lexington and fanned out to hunt and collect provisions for the campaign. They reassembled at Captain Henry Bird's abandoned stockade at the split of the South and North Forks from the Licking River. They marched on from there to rendezvous at the stockade at the mouth of that river.[76]

General Clark, Colonel Slaughter with eighty soldiers from the Illinois Regiment, Captain Piatt's Continental Marines, and Colonel Floyd's Jefferson County militia arrived at the rendezvous by boat. General Clark brought with them the six-pound cannon that he had used in his 1780 campaign. The boats used by Clark and Floyd for the voyage up the Ohio River from the Falls were used to ferry Colonel Logan's division across the river to the stockade.

The combined forces of General Clark and Colonel Logan totaled 1,050 men.[77] They set off on November 4, 1782, following the same route that they had used in Clark's 1780 campaign. They moved rapidly to once again gain the element of surprise.

The army approached the Shawanese towns on the Greater Miami River on November 10.[78] Major George Walls led an advance party of horsemen to probe for the enemy as they approached the Standing Stone Village from the south.

The advance party encountered two Shawanese men about four or five miles south of the town. The Shawanese turned and ran back to the village to warn their fellow tribesmen. General Clark gave orders for the main body of his army to accelerate their march to a trot when he learned that they had been discovered.[79]

The approaching Long Knife army could soon see the Standing Stone village across a prairie on the far side of the Greater Miami River. They had again caught the Shawanese by surprise. The town was a scene of pandemonium as women and children ran about screaming and scrambling to save a few precious possessions before fleeing.

The Shawanese custodians of the sacred bundles, sacred fire, and wampum belts slipped away with their charges as the women and children also melted away into the forest. A handful of warriors on foot covered their retreat and fired their muskets to delay the army before withdrawing themselves.

The Long Knives forded the Greater Miami River and marched into the town. It was completely deserted. The only sentries who remained were barking dogs. Food had been left on spits and in cooking pots.[80]

LAMATUMQUE RODE HER HORSE ALONG THE TRAIL from Callaway's Town toward the Standing Stone Village with her toddler son and six other mounted Shawanese women. One of them was an adopted white Shawanese woman named Mrs. McFall who had been taken prisoner two years earlier at Ruddle's Station.[81] Their packhorses were loaded with furs. They intended to take them on to Louis Lorimier's Store to trade for various necessities and items of adornment. Six mounted Shawanese warriors escorted the women.

The little party heard a scattering of gunfire as they came within sight of the Standing Stone Village. The warriors carefully checked their weapons and rode on. As they drew closer, they realized to their horror that the town was occupied by a huge army of Long Knives.

The Long Knives spotted them and opened fire with the roar of a hundred rifles discharging at once. The outnumbered warriors wheeled their horses and sped off down the trail. Mounted Long Knife soldiers immediately gave chase.

Lamatumque and the women wheeled their horses and sped off down the trail as well as they could with their heavily laden horses. They quickly fell behind the warriors. Lamatumque shouted to her female companions to ride as hard as they could and when the Long Knives drew near, to dismount, scatter on foot, and hide.

The Long Knife riders were quickly upon them. Her companions dismounted upon Lamatumque's command. Lamatumque and her child and four other women scattered into the tall prairie grass like quail and hid. Mrs. McFall and a young Indian girl ran for the edge of the forest.

Sergeant Henry Wilson scanned the tall grasses and ordered his men to spread out to find the women. They soon found them squatting in the grass and took them as prisoners.[82]

Lamatumque was dressed in some of her finest doeskin clothing ornamented with detailed and colorful quill and beadwork and covered with glittering silver brooches. She stood trembling like an aspen leaf before the Long Knives, protectively shielding her little boy.

Lamatumque's worst nightmare had come true. The ruthless Long Knives were known to take no Indian prisoners. Her tongue felt thick and clumsy as she began to chant her death song. She tried to reassure her weeping little son with gentle hugs and squeezes but then began to silently convulse with sobs herself.

One of the older soldiers dismounted and approached her. He cradled a primed long rifle in his arms and a tomahawk and scalping knife hung loosely from his belt. She prayed to Moneto and Grandmother Kokomthena to make their deaths swift and calmed herself. She looked at the sky and the trees and the nearby river. She gave her son a final gentle squeeze and awaited the fatal blow. She would die with dignity as befitted a Queen of her people.

The Long Knife soldier stopped before her and paused. He took off his hat, politely bowed his head, and identified himself as Sergeant Henry Wilson. He recognized that Lamatumque was a lady of high status and proceeded to treat her with great respect and kindness. Lamatumque slowly relaxed as it became apparent that death was not imminent.

The other two women in her party who had run for the forest were now seen at some distance off, moving along the riverbank. They were pursued by a small group of soldiers on horseback. One of the soldiers shouted for them to stop as they drew near. Mrs. McFall stopped on command. The other woman, a pretty young Shawanese girl of some sixteen years, ran down the bank and plunged into the river.

The water was waist deep. The girl did not know how to swim and made slow progress wading across the river. A soldier jumped in the water to chase and catch her. Her pursuer had almost reached her when another soldier shot her in the spine and killed her instantly. The soldier in the water dragged her limp body to the shore.[83]

Major Walls escorted Lamatumque and her son into Standing Stone Village where all of the soldiers and their prisoners were assembling. A total of six women and one child had been captured.[84]

GENERAL CLARK ORDERED A DETACHMENT UNDER THE command of Colonel Logan to march to Lorimier's Store and destroy it. A detachment under the command of Colonel Daniel Boone was ordered to march against Callaway's Town and destroy it.[85] Major McGary was placed in command of a detachment directed to lay waste to McKee's Town.

Colonel Logan stripped the packhorses, mounted about two hundred men on them, and pushed on up the river to seize the goods at Lorimier's Store before they could be removed. They would burn it after they plundered it. They reached the store not long after dusk. It was a very dark and cloudy night. Louis Lorimier had departed for Detroit just before the attack and his assistant Msr. Largeau escaped into the darkness as the Long Knives approached the store. The Long Knives looted the abandoned store, set it and surrounding dwellings on fire, and departed. They returned to Standing Stone Village on the following day.

Micajah was in Callaway's Town when the warriors who had been escorting Lamatumque rode into town and spread the alarm. They said that Lamatumque and her son and friends had been captured. The panic-stricken residents of the little village rushed about to salvage as many possessions and as much food as they could carry. Micajah pitched in and helped Nenessica's wife organize and pack her possessions.

Micajah was very upset at the news of Lamatumque's capture. He thought once again of escaping from the Shawanese. He might be able to help Lamatumque and her son in Kentucky if they were still alive.

The residents of Callaway's Town quickly loaded their possessions and as much corn and dried meat as they could carry into their elm bark canoes. They barricaded their cabins, boarded the canoes, and set off up the Stillwater River. Micajah grabbed a paddle and paddled furiously until his arm and shoulder muscles burned with fatigue.

CALLAWAY'S TOWN LAY ON THE STILLWATER RIVER to the southwest of the Standing Stone Village. John Sovereign assured Daniel Boone that the large, well-beaten road between the two towns was the only guide that they needed.

Daniel had heard of this town from escaped prisoners and knew that several white prisoners were living there, including Micajah. Some of the escaped prisoners were, in fact, calling it "Callaway's Town" after Micajah, a reflection of Micajah's growing stature within the Shawanese Nation. Daniel had volunteered for this specific mission, in part so that he could look after Micajah to make sure he didn't get killed by his own people.

Daniel Boone's detachment of soldiers consisted of ninety men. All of them were on foot except for five who rode the only five horses remaining in camp after Colonel Logan's departure to Lorimier's Store. Boone's foot soldiers marched in single file, while the horsemen were placed on the flanks of the column with three horses on one side and two on the other.

It sounded as if the Shawanese were still there as the Long Knives came within sight of the town. Dogs were baying, and chickens were crowing. Daniel immediately formed his company into three groups and ordered them to prime their rifles and surround the town on three sides, the fourth side being covered by the stream. He ordered them to attack at his signal. If the cabin doors were barred, the men were to break through with rails or anything else convenient. If they failed in that effort, they were to mount the bark roofs and gain access to the cabins through the flimsy bark.

The men surrounded the town and charged on Daniel's command. They found the cabin doors barricaded and the town deserted. The Shawanese occupants had been given a timely warning and had escaped. Strings of corn silk floating down the stream betrayed the direction of their flight. Boone decided not to pursue them.

The Long Knives set about plundering the buildings. They found stores of buckskins, peltry, brass kettles, and other trade articles. They even captured the chickens.

The Long Knives set the town on fire and marched off to their main camp with their booty. They reached the Long Knife camp at the Standing Stone Village soon after dusk. There they enjoyed a fresh chicken dinner.

GENERAL CLARK ISSUED THE ORDERS FOR THE first night's encampment. The camp was arranged in a hollow square with the horses, booty, military stores, artillery, and prisoners in the center. The front of the square faced the horseshoe bend of the river, and their campfires stretched along the sides and rear.

John Sovereign was directed to contact the Shawanese and request a parley that evening. Sovereign correctly assumed that Shawanese warriors were hiding across the river. General Clark dictated as Sovereign shouted his words.

Sovereign called out the names of all the Shawanese prisoners and assured the warriors that they would be treated well. He invited them to come to Fort Nelson at the Falls of the Ohio for an exchange of prisoners in half a moon. The signal for their peaceful intent upon approaching the fort would be a flag of truce.

The soldiers were awakened that night by the discharge of a volley of muskets from a party of warriors on the opposite bank of the stream. The musket balls struck the campfires and knocked hot coals upon the prostrate Long Knives and their blankets. Some of them jumped up and danced about brushing themselves off before taking cover. One man was mortally wounded by the volley.

General Clark ordered that a stronger sentry be posted. They had

Micajah Callaway, White Shawanese

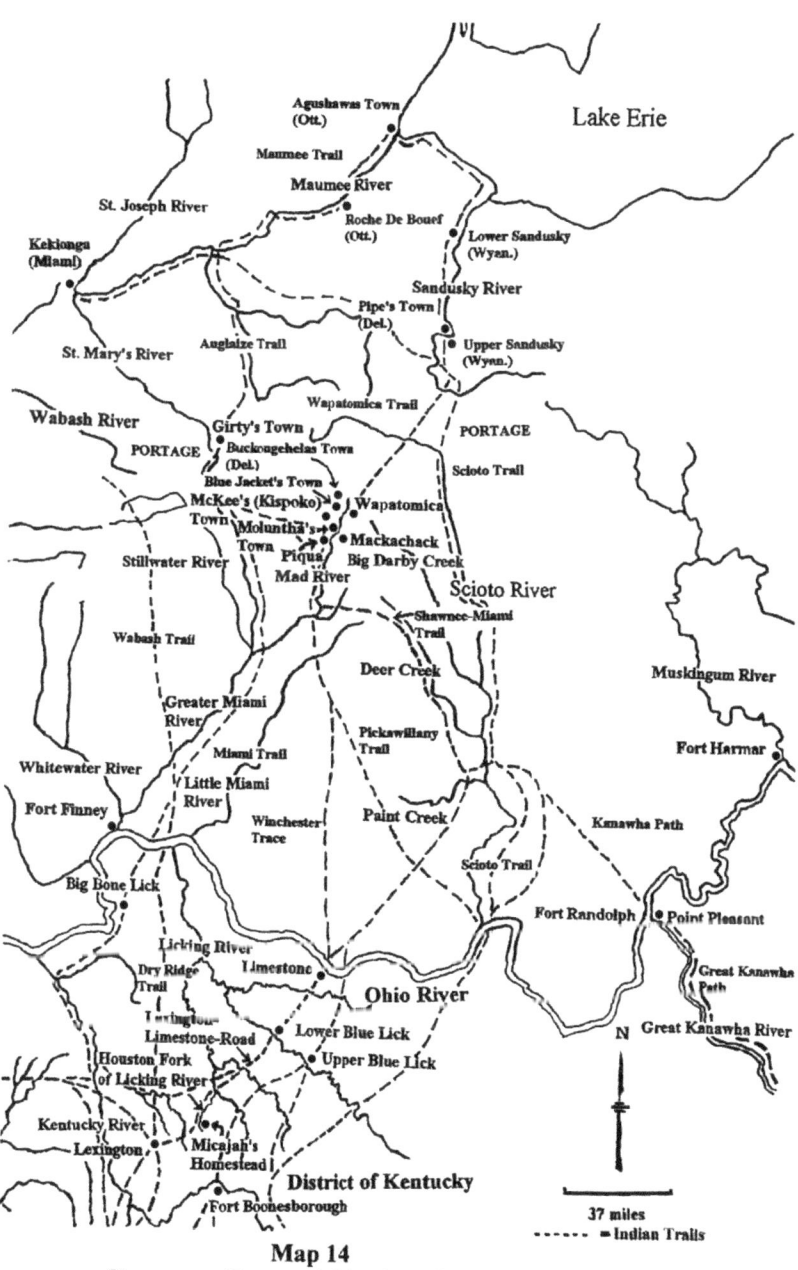

Map 14
Shawanese Towns of Ohio in 1782-1786

scarcely retired again to rest when George Girty and his warriors opened a sharp fire along the whole rear line. The Long Knives returned the Shawanese gunfire. Whenever the Shawanese discharged their muskets, the Long Knives fired their rifles at the muzzle flash in the darkness, and the Shawanese did the same. The moment a Long Knife or Shawanese warrior discharged his gun, he took the precaution to roll and change his position.

The night fighting continued for half an hour before a heavy rain put a stop to the action. General Clark ordered his men to keep their rifles and powder dry. None of General Clark's men were killed or wounded during the fighting.

Chief Moluntha rode a white horse onto the prairie about a fourth of a mile from the camp on the following day.[86] He shouted to Lamatumque and asked if she and their son were all right. She shouted back that they were fine and had been treated well. Old Moluntha then cursed the Long Knives.

Lamatumque shouted to him that he should come to meet with General Clark and make peace. The women would be taken back to Kentucky as prisoners if he did not agree to do so. Moluntha responded that he was too angry to make peace now and that if the Long Knives attempted to take her and his son and the other women to Kentucky, the Shawanese would attack and free them.[87]

On the following day, Lamatumque's mother Coitcheleh came alone into General Clark's camp and asked to exchange herself for her daughter and grandson. General Clark refused.[88] She then asked to join the other seven prisoners so that she could be with them. General Clark reluctantly granted her request.[89]

Moluntha returned on his white horse to parley again, but this time General Clark ordered that the cannon be fired at him. The cannon shot missed. Moluntha applied his whip to his horse and quickly withdrew, and did not appear again.[90]

Alexander McKee learned of the attack at midnight on November 11 and rode to the rescue from Wapatomica with seventy warriors. General Clark dispatched a party of three hundred horsemen across the river without detection. There, he outflanked and attacked McKee's Shawanese warriors from their rear. The Shawanese were routed and lost thirteen warriors. McKee retreated to Wapatomica and sent a plea for help to Detroit.

The Long Knives burned the Standing Stone Village and destroyed the

Micajah Callaway, White Shawanese

corn in the cribs on the day following their third night of encampment at the town site. They reserved some corn for their own use and commenced their return march.

The army marched in triple lines down along the Greater Miami River for some five miles, and then crossed over to the southeast shore. They proceeded to leave the established trails and cut a direct course to the mouth of the Licking River between the mouths of the Little Miami and Greater Miami Rivers.

The eight Shawanese captives were imprisoned at Fort Nelson at the Falls of the Ohio upon the return of the army to Kentucky. They were later moved to the new District of Kentucky log jailhouse in Danville, near John Crow's Station. The walls of the jail were over nine inches thick.[91]

On November 27, 1782, General Clark sent a report of the results of the campaign to the governor. It had been a relatively bloodless excursion. He reported a loss of only one man killed and one wounded, and counted ten Indians killed with two white prisoners retaken.

The main benefit of the campaign was the destruction of the towns and the corn, and the plundering of the valuable goods and personal property of the residents. The eight prisoners would also be useful in negotiating for the exchange of American prisoners. In addition to the destruction of the Standing Stone Village, Callaway's Town, and Loramier's Store, the Long Knives had also destroyed New Piqua and Wills Town.[92]

Retrenchment at Girty's Town

THE BRITISH HAD FAILED ONCE AGAIN TO provide timely support to their Shawanese allies. Major De Peyster sent a letter to McKee on November 21, 1782, blaming the Shawanese defeat upon poor surveillance by Shawanese lookouts. He said that he was unable to spare any Rangers to help them.[93]

The Shawanese chiefs reassembled their scattered people for a council in Wapatomica. It was now abundantly clear that the more southerly locations for the Shawanese towns were no longer safe from the increasingly powerful Long Knives. The council decided not to attempt to rebuild the destroyed towns. The displaced Shawanese would live in the remaining towns of Wapakoneta, Mackachack, Moluntha's Town, Wapatomica, and Blue Jacket's Town.

The Shawanese people were in desperate straits. Winter was rapidly approaching, and there was no shelter available for hundreds of men, women, and children. Once again the Long Knives had destroyed most of their food reserves.

Nenessica chose to relocate to a new village on the St. Mary's River, at the site of a new trading post opened by Simon Girty's brother James. Many of the Chaalakaatha Shawanese from the Standing Stone Village were moving there. The town was commonly called Girty's Town or New Chillicothy.[94]

The ensuing winter was cold and hard. Hunting parties were sent out to scour the countryside and bring in fresh meat, but they found little game, and the suffering increased as the weeks passed. The meager amount of corn that the Shawanese had salvaged and obtained from their allies was again rationed to the children. The starving men and women grew gaunt and weak. Many went to Detroit and camped outside the British post to beg for food and shelter. The women pleaded with the chiefs and warriors to make peace for the sake of their children.

Micajah helped with the hunting parties and ice-fished in the St. Mary's River. He subsisted almost exclusively on the few fish that he could catch and suffered along with the Shawanese.[95]

Nine | The War's End

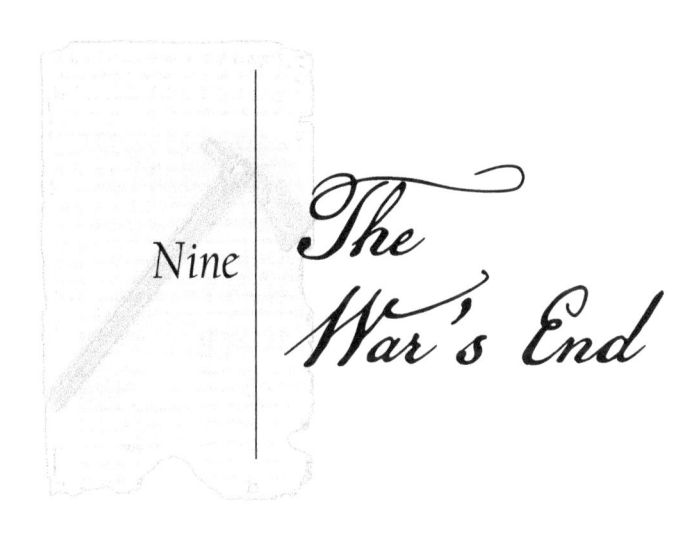

Cease Fire!

BRITISH AND AMERICAN REPRESENTATIVES HAD BEEN ENGAGED in negotiations to end the American War for Independence since shortly after the defeat of General Cornwallis at Yorktown in October of 1781. A preliminary treaty was finally signed in Paris on January 20, 1783, establishing a formal cessation of hostilities.

Great Britain's claims to the northwestern territories south of a line through the middle of the Great Lakes and east of the Mississippi River were ceded to the United States under the terms of the preliminary treaty. However, the treaty did not include any reference to the northwestern Indian nations or their rights or claims to the land.[1]

The combatants on both sides of the war between the Long Knives and Ohio Confederacy Indians had reached the point of exhaustion. The Shawanese had retreated and were entrenched in northern Ohio after their towns and corn crops were destroyed by General Clark, and were on the brink of starvation.

The Shawanese leadership was divided as to the best course of action. Some wanted to continue the war against the Long Knives, while others wanted to move to Detroit or to Spanish Louisiana on the other side of the Mississippi River. A third faction wanted to sue for a separate peace with the Americans and remain in Ohio.

General Clark's soldiers at Fort Nelson were in no better condition than the Shawanese. They were ill-equipped, poorly fed, and exhausted. The rapidly deflating Continental currency made it more and more difficult to feed and pay them.[2]

Governor Harrison decided to initiate peace negotiations between Virginia and the Shawanese without waiting for the final peace treaty with Great Britain. He sent a letter to General Clark on January 13, 1783, authorizing him to treat with the Shawanese and Wyandot.[3]

Queen Lamatumque's Mission of Peace

THE SHAWANESE HELD SEVERAL COUNCILS TO DEBATE and determine the proper course of action for their nation. The general population began to listen again to the remnants of the Makujay division leadership. The Makujay counseled for peace and Nenessica aligned himself with them even though he was a war chief. The militant war chiefs led by Captain Snake opposed them.

Chief Moluntha invited Micajah to his cabin in February of 1783. They sat down before the hearth fire and smoked a calumet together. Moluntha told Micajah that he was sending Chief Wryneck to the Long Knife fort at the Falls of the Ohio under a flag of truce to explore the offer to exchange prisoners that Clark had taken on the battlefield at Standing Stone three months earlier.[4]

Moluntha asked if Micajah would go to the Falls with Wryneck and serve as his interpreter, after Nenessica had given his permission. Micajah agreed to help, and Moluntha thanked him.[5]

Chief Wryneck and Micajah departed from Mackachack on horseback accompanied by a small escort of warriors. They arrived at the Falls of the Ohio and crossed over the river to Fort Nelson. They appeared before the fort gate under a flag of truce, as General Clark had instructed on the Standing Stone battlefield.

Micajah was surprised at the strength of the Fort Nelson fortifications. It enclosed a full acre and was surrounded by a ditch ten feet wide and eight feet deep with sharp wooden stakes in the bottom. The dirt from the ditch had been thrown into log pens which formed the fort's outer rammed-earth walls, and a sturdy log palisade formed the inner walls. The surrounding land had been cleared of trees for several hundred feet from the fort to deprive enemies of protective cover. The fort was armed with four cannon and a garrison of regular soldiers of the Virginia Line. It was the strongest American fort west of Fort Pitt.[6]

The fort sentries summoned Major George Walls to the ramparts. He appeared and shouted a greeting to the visitors. General Clark was notified of their arrival and appeared beside him. The General ordered that the fort gates be opened and that the Shawanese deputation be received with hospitality.

Clark met with the Shawanese party in a parley. He remembered Chief Wryneck from the Cahokia council in 1778 and recognized Micajah from Fort Boonesborough in 1777.

After the usual exchange of wampum and gifts and smoking the calumet, Clark repeated the offer that he had made at Standing Stone to exchange prisoners. He requested that the Shawanese deputies carry the offer back to their national council for consideration by the entire Shawanese Nation, and Wryneck agreed to do so.

Micajah was taken aside for a private meeting with General Clark at the conclusion of the parley. Clark had known members of the Callaway family for many years, and was familiar with Micajah's capture with Daniel Boone and the other saltboilers in 1778. General Clark offered Micajah his personal protection if Micajah would return to rejoin his family in Kentucky.

Micajah carefully considered General Clark's offer. His Shawanese friends had entrusted him with an important diplomatic mission, and he did not want to betray them. Yet, he also longed to see his mother and Flanders and his other siblings. He told General Clark that he was not then inclined to return to Kentucky but would think about his generous offer.

The appearance of the Shawanese deputation at Fort Nelson triggered a flurry of diplomatic activity in Kentucky. General Clark suggested that Micajah's mother be summoned to attend the next meeting to plead with the Shawanese for his return.[7]

A French trader named Bartholomew Tardinieu sent a letter to General Clark on March 12, 1783, on behalf of Lamatumque, stating in relevant part,

> Sir:
>
> ... One of the Indian squaws, your prisoner, conceits that if she was permitted to return to her people, in company of Mr. Sherlock, the Interpreter, she can easily bring her nation, and in all probability several others, to terms of peace; She offers to leave here her child as a pledge of her faith, and if she does not succeed promises to come back, and surrender herself as a prisoner for life. Now, Sir, I do not pretend to give any advice to those who are more knowing than myself; but as a well wisher to that country which I have adopted, give me leave to urge the reasons, which in my humble opinion, seem to point out that plan as a means to restore peace to our frontiers ...
>
> B. Tardineau.[8]

General Clark sent a letter to Governor Harrison on March 19, 1783, recommending that they accept Lamatumque's proposal.[9] Harrison responded on April 9 and approved it.[10]

Lamatamque was escorted from the Danville prison to Fort Nelson by a small guard of mounted horsemen not long after Governor Harrison's approval. Her mother Coitcheleh and son remained in the Danville jail under the care of one of the other female prisoners.

Lamatumque joined James Sherlock at Fort Nelson upon her arrival there. Sherlock was an Irishman who had been captured by the Six Nations when he was a young boy and had since gained a great deal of experience as an Indian interpreter for the colonial and American governments.[11] Major Walls gave Sherlock a letter to deliver to the Shawanese and paid him one hundred dollars for his services.[12]

Although many Shawanese were eager for peace, the war was not yet over for Captain Snake and the other militant Shawanese at Wapatomica. The warriors there raided Kentucky to avenge General Clark's destruction of their towns even as the Makujay peace movement gained momentum. Major De Peyster wrote a letter on April 20, 1783, praising Captain McKee's efforts to stop the raiders.[13]

Colonel John Floyd was ambushed and shot in the back by the Wapatomica raiders while riding with his brother Charles and a small party down the Wilderness Road from Floyd's Station to the salt works at Bullitt's Lick. He died on April 12, 1783, after lingering on for two days.[14]

Lamatumque and James Sherlock left Fort Nelson to deliver the proposal for a prisoner exchange to her husband Moluntha. A mounted Shawanese sentry spotted them as they approached Mackachack on May 26, 1783.

News of Lamatumque's return and the arrival of James Sherlock with a message from the Long Knife leaders quickly spread through the Shawanese towns. Micajah learned of their arrival as he was helping cultivate the newly sprouted corn in the fields near his home on St. Mary's River. An impromptu council was called in the Mackachack council house. Chief Moluntha was not present at the time.

Micajah attended the council with Nenessica. A vigorous debate ensued. Some of the chiefs and counselors argued that Lamatumque could no longer be trusted because she had been with the Long Knives too long. Captain Snake, Kekewapilathy, White Bark, Buffalo, and Captain Will were among this group.

Other chiefs and warriors protested that Lamatumque would never betray her people. Cornstalk's surviving family members and their influential Makujay allies supported her. Others argued that no decisions should be made without consulting with Alexander McKee.

The debate went on for some time before a decision was reached by the council. Lamatumque and Sherlock would be imprisoned, and Major Wall's letter would be delivered to Captain McKee. Lamatumque and Sherlock would be put to death if McKee said that the letter could not be trusted. They were imprisoned in a guarded cabin.

Sherlock was then taken to McKee's residence by an armed escort of painted warriors. McKee read the letter and told the Shawanese that it said that the "Great Captain" of Kentucky wanted to exchange prisoners and make peace. He believed that the Long Knives could be trusted. Sherlock and Lamatumque were subsequently released.

Moluntha returned from his business elsewhere and convened a Grand Council of the Shawanese Nation at the Mackachack council house. He presided with Lamatumque at his side. Moluntha and the Makujay chiefs argued that peace was the only choice for the survival of their people and the preservation of their Ohio homeland. Since the Shawanese could no longer count on the British for support, they should make their own separate peace with the Long Knives.

Captain Snake and the Wapatomica warriors continued to argue for war as the only choice left to them. He insisted that the Long Knives could not be trusted and would never cease their incursions into Shawanese territory until the Shawanese were exterminated or driven from their lands. Captain Snake maintained that the real choice for their nation was between continued war and the extermination of the Ohio Shawanese.

The council met again on May 28, and the Makujay advocates of peace prevailed. It was agreed that the Shawanese would suspend all hostilities and pursue a prisoner exchange as proposed by Major Walls. One white prisoner would be exchanged for each Shawanese prisoner. The Shawanese would count Lamatumque as a released prisoner as a gesture of good faith, and the Shawanese would release eight white prisoners.

Seven Shawanese chiefs were selected to go to the Falls of the Ohio under the white flag of James Sherlock. There do not appear to be any surviving records of their names but the following chiefs typically participated in such diplomatic exchanges during this time period: Moluntha, Wryneck, Aweecomy, Shade, Captain Johnny, and Blue Jacket.[15] Lamatumque undoubtedly accompanied them because her mother and son were among the Shawanese prisoners.

Moluntha chose Micajah to serve as his interpreter. Micajah agreed to help them, and fully intended to return to Ohio to live with the Shawanese at the conclusion of the negotiations.[16] Captain Alexander McKee sent a letter to Major George Walls on May 29, 1783, confirming the prisoner exchange.[17]

The Shawanese chiefs selected white prisoners for the exchange. One of them was a young man named William Johnson.[18] Micajah requested that

The War's End

Jacky Callaway and Jones Hoy be included among the prisoners who would be exchanged, but Moluntha and Lamatumque could not obtain the support of the other chiefs to include them.[19]

James Sherlock, the seven Shawanese chiefs, Micajah, and the white prisoners departed from Mackachack for the Falls of the Ohio on or about June 7, 1783. They traveled on horseback down the trail along the west bank of the Greater Miami River to the Ohio River.

It is doubtful that General Clark attended the prisoner exchange negotiations through to their conclusion because he left Fort Nelson to ride to Richmond, Virginia in early June. It is possible but doubtful that he remained at the fort long enough to greet the Shawanese delegations before departing, as he had arrived in Richmond by June 16, 1783.[20] In any event, he left Major Walls in charge of completing the negotiations and exchanging the prisoners.

On July 2, 1783, General Clark received a letter in Richmond from Governor Harrison relieving him of his command and thanking him for his services.[21] He sent a response the same day thanking the governor for the pleasure of having served his country.[22]

The Prisoner Exchange at the Falls of the Ohio River

A HUNTING PARTY OF FOUR CHALAAKAATHA DIVISION warriors left Girty's Town on a hunting expedition at about the same time that James Sherlock and his traveling companions left Mackachack bound for Fort Nelson. Three young white men from Kentucky dressed as Indians stole the hunting party's horses on the night of June 10, 1783. The warriors were furious and set off in hot pursuit. They followed the tracks of the horse thieves south to the north bank of the Ohio River and killed them there.

Captain Snake learned of the bloody encounter and dispatched a group of young warriors to intercept and stop Sherlock's party before it crossed the river. He directed the warriors to bring Sherlock back to him alive so that he could confront and question him.

The Shawanese warriors arrived at the ford at the Falls of the Ohio and discovered that Sherlock and his party had crossed the Ohio River just before they had reached the Falls. They turned back and reported to Captain Snake. He decided to register a complaint with the British Indian Department rather than send his warriors across the Ohio River into Kentucky.[23]

James Sherlock and the Shawanese chiefs rode up to the main gate of Fort Nelson. Sherlock hailed the sentries under a white flag of truce, and the sentries escorted Major Walls to the gate.

The Shawanese chiefs and Micajah made a fine impression as they sat on their horses before the fort. The proud leaders of the Shawanese Nation were dressed in their finest clothing and carried themselves with great dignity. Black ostrich plumes floated above their turbans and sunlight sparkled off their silver jewelry. Lamatumque's fine clothing and jewelry perfectly framed her natural beauty. They all held their heads high.

The Shawanese Nation had fought bravely and sometimes alone as they confronted the unceasing advances of the Long Knives of Virginia. They had fought the Long Knives to a standstill and had held the line of their encroachment at the Ohio River. The greatest commander of the Long Knives, General George Rogers Clark, had failed to subdue them and break their spirit. The cost of their resistance had been great and many valiant young warriors had died.

Micajah sat on his horse beside the others. His long hair was greased with bear grease and braided into a club. He wore a calico shirt, and a wide broadcloth breechcloth secured by a sash. Soft, single-seamed buckskin mocassins covered his feet.

Major Walls welcomed the Shawanese chiefs and invited them into the fort. Seven days of negotiations ensued.[24] Major Walls led the negotiations for the Long Knives. Chief Moluntha and Chief Wryneck probably served as the primary Shawanese spokesmen. James Sherlock interpreted for the Long Knives, and Micajah interpreted for the Shawanese.

Major Walls expressed his disappointment that only eight white prisoners had been delivered and requested the release of all prisoners. The Shawanese replied that they had not brought more because they only wanted to conduct a one-for-one exchange. They explained that the Long Knives had fewer prisoners than the Shawanese because the Long Knives usually killed Shawanese instead of capturing them.[25]

The prisoner exchange took place at the conclusion of the negotiations

The War's End

in mid to late June. It was held in a simple ceremony on the parade grounds of Fort Nelson.

Micajah's Aunt Elizabeth Callaway, the widow of Colonel Richard Callaway, was there.[26] She hoped that her son Jacky Callaway and grandson Jones Hoy would be among those released. Excitement filled the air.

Moluntha addressed Major Walls and held out the wampum peace belt that George Morgan had given to the Shawanese at Fort Pitt in 1776. He acknowledged that the foolish young men of his nation had "listened to bad birds" and had not heeded the belt. However, the Shawanese kings had never forgotten it and had always adhered to it. Micajah translated and Moluntha held the belt so Major Walls could inspect it and verify its authenticity. Moluntha handed the belt back to Lamatumque.

Lamatumque handed a white wampum peace belt to Moluntha with the beaded figure of a white man holding hands with the beaded figure of an Indian. Moluntha made a short and eloquent plea for peace and offered to exchange the prisoners as a gesture of good will. He invited the Long Knives to a council in Mackachack to negotiate a peace treaty. James Sherlock nodded in agreement with Micajah's translation.

Moluntha stepped forward to hand the belt to Major Walls. Major Walls accepted the belt and thanked Moluntha. He said that the Long Knives also wanted peace and were prepared to exchange prisoners. He accepted the invitation to Mackachack. James Sherlock translated his speech into Shawanese, and Micajah agreed with his translation. Major Walls then stepped forward and presented a finely crafted calumet and a pouch of Virginia's finest tobacco.[27]

Lamatumque tearfully welcomed her mother Coitcheleh and her little son and held them both to her bosom. The other freed Shawanese women joined the Shawanese party and were welcomed by the chiefs. They would soon be reunited with their families back in Ohio.

Elizabeth Callaway was disappointed that her son Jacky and grandson Jones Hoy were not among the released prisoners. A mother's love drove her on to force the issue. She spoke directly to the chiefs and asked for their help, but they would not agree to her request. She then pleaded with Micajah to return to Kentucky and work for the release of her son and grandson.

Micajah faced an agonizing decision. He stepped aside for a moment to collect his thoughts. He calmed his nerves and asked the chiefs to gather around him in a small circle.

Micajah told them that he was faced with a very difficult decision—whether to remain among his Shawanese family and friends or return to his first family, the family of his own blood. Seeing members of his Callaway family had persuaded him make the decision to rejoin them in Kentucky.

The chiefs were shocked. They had come to see Micajah as one of their own people. He had learned their ways and had been with them through one of the most difficult times that they had ever known. They pleaded with him not to leave them. Chief Moluntha offered him several horses and a choice parcel of land.[28]

Micajah firmly insisted that he had made up his mind. Lamatumque and Moluntha intervened to calm the other chiefs. Lamatumque stepped forward to shake Micajah's hand and wish him well. The other chiefs paused and sadly did the same.

The Shawanese chiefs had a brief final meeting with Major Walls in which they agreed that Lieutenant James McCulloch and James Sherlock would accompany them back to Mackachack to negotiate a formal treaty of peace.[29] Micajah asked them to explain his decision to Nenessica and his wife and assure them that he would visit them soon. The chiefs mounted their horses and rode off toward the ford at the Falls.

Micajah stood outside the gate of Fort Nelson and watched them leave. He had lived among the Shawanese for a total of five years and five months. Lamatumque and Moluntha turned to look back over their shoulders and slightly bowed their heads toward him and smiled. He nodded his head in acknowledgement.

Micajah walked over to Elizabeth and thanked her for helping him. If she felt any bitterness or suspicion toward him concerning Richard Callaway's death at the hands of the Shawanese, she did not show it. It appeared that all was forgiven.

They walked together back into the fort. Daniel Boone, Flanders and Jemima, and Micajah's brothers Edmund and John were waiting inside to greet him.[30] Micajah was overwhelmed at seeing them and could barely speak. His lips trembled and chest heaved. It had been so long since they had been together, and he had often supposed that he would never see them again. Tears flowed freely.

The Callaway brothers began to notice how the years had changed Micajah as they talked. He had been a gangly and naive young lad when they had seen him the last time. Micajah was now twenty-three years old but seemed much older. He had witnessed almost unimaginable acts of human depravity by both the Shawanese and the Long Knives and had come to suppress his feelings. He was slow to smile or laugh. Only time could heal the wounds upon his spirit.

Daniel told Micajah that Major Walls and some of the other officers wanted to talk to him before he left Fort Nelson.[31] They had a number of questions regarding Shawanese matters. He advised Micajah to choose his words very carefully when he met with Walls. Daniel would join Micajah during the interrogation as his former commander and his friend.

The Repatriation of Micajah Callaway

MICAJAH SHARED BREAKFAST WITH BOONE AND HIS family on the following morning. Flanders and Jemima asked Micajah to return with them to their Fayette County homestead and stay with them for a while. They also invited Daniel to stay with them for a few days. He could help Micajah with his transition back into white culture, since Daniel had faced the same challenge himself. Micajah shed his Shawanese clothing and changed into a hunting shirt and buckskin breeches provided by Flanders and Jemima.

Micajah and Daniel went to meet with Major George Walls and his officers. Boone formally introduced Micajah to the officers as a soldier from his Fort Boonesborough company who had been captured by the Shawanese at the Lower Blue Licks in February of 1778. He explained that he would like to attend the briefing as Micajah's former commanding officer, and Major Walls agreed.

Major Walls quickly got down to business after the introductions. He stated that General Clark had decided to take a chance with Micajah despite indications that he might have collaborated with the British and Shawanese during the war. He acknowledged that the reported collaboration may have been under duress and said that Virginia was willing to give Micajah the benefit of the doubt in exchange for his cooperation in future dealings with the Shawanese Nation. The major's specific question for Micajah was whether he was willing to serve Virginia as a spy so that they could monitor Shawanese intentions and movements.

Micajah pondered the question for several minutes and then agreed. He expressed his hope that he might help find a way to prevent more war. Major Walls expressed his satisfaction with Micajah's response and said that he would send a favorable report to Richmond.

The Callaways and Daniel Boone departed early the next morning on horseback. Micajah remarked at how large Louisville had grown as they rode through it. It had not even existed when he was captured. Kentucky's population had grown to twelve thousand settlers during the years that he had lived among the Shawanese.[32]

As they rode, Flanders and John updated Micajah on what had happened in their lives and the lives of their Callaway brothers and sisters. Flanders had spent much of the war scouting, hunting and defending his family at his homestead and the forts. His union with Jemima had produced a daughter, Sarah, in 1779, and a son, John, in 1781. Jemima was expecting another child in September.[33]

James Callaway Jr. was released from British imprisonment in New York on October 8, 1782.[34] He returned to Bedford County and rode west to Kentucky. There he obtained a patent on the land claim that Flanders had filed on his behalf on December 11, 1782.[35]

Dudley was living in Bedford County. He had married Martha ("Patty") Trent, the sister of Obadiah Trent, who had been Dudley's Sergeant during Lord Dunmore's War. Dudley fought in the Battle of Trenton, wintered at Valley Forge, and served under General Daniel Morgan as a rifleman in the critical American victory at the pivotal Battle of Saratoga. He had been promoted to captain in the Bedford County militia in 1778.[36]

Chesley had served in the Kentucky militia on the frontier and had fought in the battle of Guilford County Courthouse. He was presently staying in Bedford County where he had fallen in love with a young lady named Christina Galloway, and Flanders expected them to be married soon.[37]

Their sister Elizabeth was still married to Thomas Barnes and living in Bedford County. Sister Mary's first husband William North had died in 1782,

The War's End

and she was living with their mother in Bedford County for the time being.[38] Brother John said that he was living in Fayette County on the Hinkston Fork.[39]

Daniel Boone explained his current situation as they forded the Kentucky River at Devil's Hollow and continued on toward Lexington. Lexington had grown into the largest town in Kentucky and served as the "de facto" capital of the Bluegrass Region after its selection as the county seat of Fayette County.

Limestone (now Maysville) was now the preferred port of entry for immigrants coming down the Ohio River to move to Lexington and the Bluegrass Region. Daniel had visited Limestone with Flanders in October of 1782 to look for available land for settlement.[40]

The Fayette County Court directed Daniel Boone and several other men in early 1783 "to view and mark the most convenient way from Lexington to Lower Blue Licks to mouth of Limestone." The Big Buffalo Road was the logical choice for a right-of-way. Only minor modifications were required, and construction was underway.

Daniel seized on the financial opportunities presented by the new road and moved his family from Boone's Station to Limestone. He established a tavern and warehouse there on the banks of the Ohio River and became a merchant, trader, and innkeeper while he continued with his surveying and real estate businesses.[41] Micajah's younger brother Edmund Callaway worked for Boone as a survey chain carrier.[42]

Daniel built a house for his family at Limestone out of the materials salvaged from an old boat. His warehouse was constructed on the waterfront so that vessels could be loaded and unloaded there.

Flanders asked Jemima if she would stay at the neighbors' with the children for a bit longer while he and Daniel took Micajah on a short hunt. The three men continued to ride on to the east along the new Lexington-Limestone Road, past Bryant's Station and on to the ruins of Grant's Station. There they left the road and rode about four miles due east along a faint trace through the canebrake and forest.

Flanders paused and asked Micajah if he knew where they were. Micajah answered that he knew exactly where they were: They were at the headwaters of the Houston Fork, where they had hunted in the fall of 1777. Flanders complimented Micajah's memory and then reached into his saddlebag. He pulled out a document with a flourish and read it out loud:

December 11th, 1782

Surveyed for Micajah Callaway by virtue of the Certificate of Settlement &c a tract of Land Situate lying and being in the County of Fayette on the headwaters of Hustons fork of Licking and bounded as follows to wit, Beginning at a large Sugar tree at corner to Edward Walton thence NE sixty six degrees three hundred thirty four poles to a Buckeye and stooping hickory thence NW twenty four degrees one hundred ninety poles to a Hoopwood and Sugartree a corner of another tract of Edward Waltons thence along his line SW sixty six degrees three hundred thirty four poles to a Stake in the line of Waltons first Tract thence along the line SE twenty four degrees one hundred ninety poles to the Beginning containing four hundred acres by:

James Parberry, John Bruce, Chains.
James Forbes, Marker
B. Ashley, Deputy Surveyor Fayette County
J. Marshall, Surveyor Fayette County[43]

Flanders told Micajah that all he needed to do was finish the paperwork and get the patent deed, and the land would be his. James Jr. had already gotten the deed for a four-hundred-acre parcel that adjoined Micajah's on the western side.

Micajah was dumbfounded. He looked around at the beautiful forest and canebrakes. His old dream of a Kentucky home had finally come true. He struggled to keep his composure. For the moment, it didn't seem like he had been gone for so many years. He was speechless for several moments and then thanked his kind brother from the bottom of his heart.

They walked the survey boundaries between the corner trees of Micajah's parcel. Micajah invited them on a hunt on his property, and they all laughed together. It was the first time he had laughed in a very long time. Daniel laughed and pounded Micajah on the back.

They rode down Buchanan's Trace toward Flanders's and Jemima's

The War's End

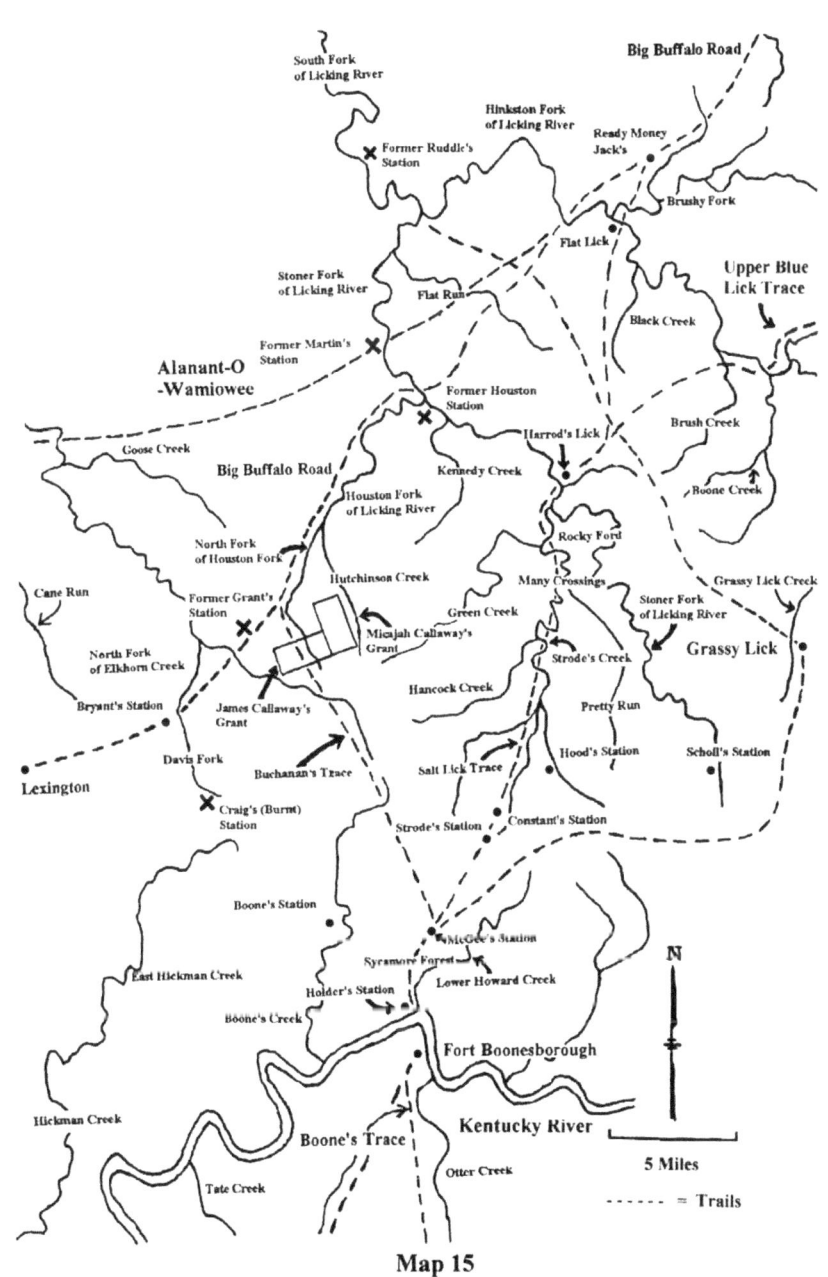

Map 15
Kentucky Bluegrass Region in 1783

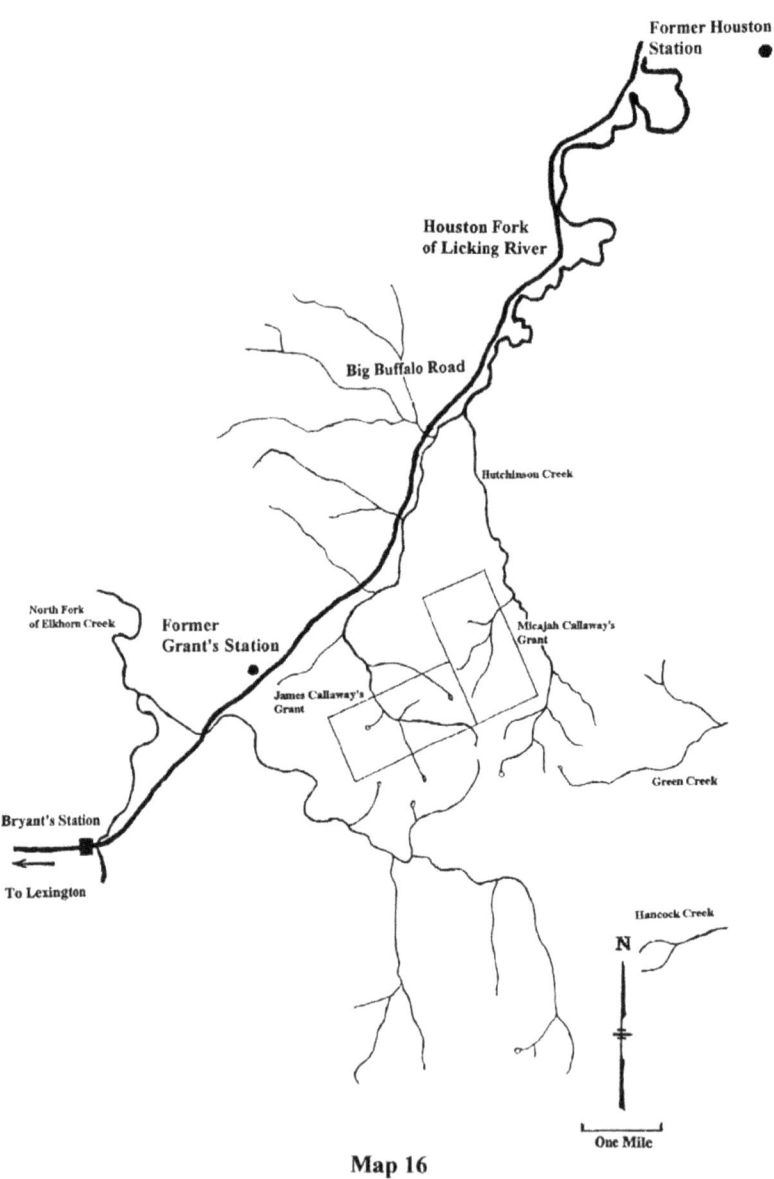

**Map 16
Micajah and James Callaway Jr. Land Grants in 1783**

The War's End

home on East Hickman Creek after they finished the tour of Micajah's property. Micajah told Flanders the unhappy story of seeing Uncle Richard's scalp in Little Chalaakaatha as they rode the final few miles, and Flanders was visibly saddened. He paused and said that Micajah should be prepared to deal with some ugly rumors about his behavior with the Shawanese. He would explain more later.

Flanders invited Micajah to stay at his home for as long as he needed to recover. They talked late into the night in the cabin that evening. Daniel and Micajah said good night to Flanders and Jemima and went to their half-faced lean-to and bedded down.

Daniel spoke as the sound of cicadas and crickets and other night sounds washed over them. He asked Micajah to forgive him for abandoning him when he escaped from Chief Black Fish. Micajah said that he understood why Daniel had done it and had already forgiven him years ago.[44] Daniel thanked him and said that he would do whatever he could to help Micajah get settled back into Kentucky.

Micajah did not fall asleep right away and lay on top of the buffalo hide bedding in his clothing with his hands clasped behind his head. He thought about the life-changing events of the last couple of days. He had hoped that his sense of purpose and direction would be clarified by his return to his Callaway family. Instead, he was finding that his joy over returning to Kentucky and his family was tempered, if not overshadowed, by his regret at having abandoned his Shawanese friends.

His initial exuberance was replaced by mixed emotions tinged with sadness. His parcel of land was in the very heart of the Bluegrass hunting grounds that the Shawanese had fought so desperately to recover during the war. He thought of Nenessica's whole-hearted devotion to that effort. The land was drenched in the blood of Shawanese warriors, and he could not easily forget that fact. Micajah drifted off into a troubled sleep.

Ten — The False Peace

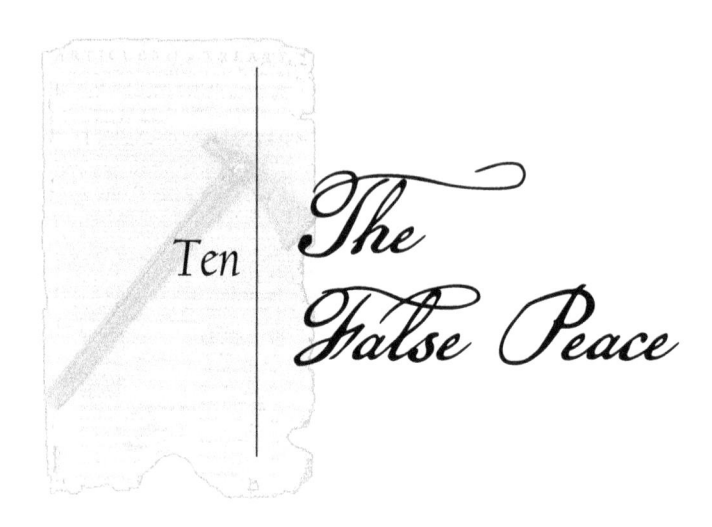

Queen Lamatumque's Quest

SHAWANESE PRINCIPAL CHIEF MOLUNTHA WAS VERY PLEASED with the prisoner exchange at Fort Nelson in late June of 1783 and the good treatment that his wife Lamatumque and the other Shawanese women and children had received during their imprisonment. They departed from Fort Nelson on the long journey back to their Ohio towns in high spirits.

Moluntha summoned the Shawanese chiefs and principal warriors to a council at Mackachak upon his arrival back in the Shawanese homeland. They considered the Long Knives' offer of peace. Lieutenant James McCullock of Harrodsburg represented Virginia in the negotiations and James Sherlock served as his interpreter.[1] Captain Snake and his militant faction openly challenged the sincerity and honesty of the Long Knives at the council proceedings.[2]

Chief Moluntha temporarily suspended the negotiations in order to search for and intercept any militant Shawanese hunting or raiding parties that might be prowling near the north shore of the Ohio River. Recently promoted Lieutenant Colonel De Peyster reported that the Principal Chief of the Shawanese was accompanied by interpreters during his search. Micajah may have been among them.[3]

Moluntha returned to Mackachack. The negotiations continued for five more days and culminated in a fragile preliminary agreement. The Long Knives

The False Peace

promised to stay to the south of the Ohio River, and the Shawanese promised to stay to its north. A final treaty would be negotiated at a later date to confirm treaty boundaries and resolve the final prisoner exchange issues. Lieutenant McCullock returned to Fort Nelson accompanied by James Sherlock.[4]

DURING THE AUTUMN OF 1783, MICAJAH SLOWLY readjusted to living among white people. He began to develop his new property, socialized with family and friends, and hunted. His brothers James Jr., Flanders, John, Edmund, and William all lived within a few miles of him in Fayette County. They had all started or were starting families, with the exception of John.

James Jr. settled with his wife Susan on the parcel next to Micajah's land. The two brothers helped each other build a small hunter's cabin on Micajah's land for him to live in over the winter and a larger one for James Jr. and his wife Susan. Micajah later obtained a patent for his four hundred acres on the Houston Fork on June 1, 1785, in a deed that was personally signed by Virginia Governor Patrick Henry.[5]

Micajah and his Kentucky bachelor friends would gather at one of their woodland homes for a social occasion from time to time. They would dress in the Indian fashion and spend the day drinking rum and whiskey, telling stories, and engaging in contests of skill and strength.[6]

Fellow saltboiler soldiers Richard Wade, John Brown, Nathaniel Bullock, Jesse Copher, William Hancock, Andrew Johnson, and Bartlett Searcey had all returned to settle in Kentucky after their own escape and repatriation. Only Joseph (Fish) Jackson remained with the Shawanese after the war.[7]

A sense of hope and optimism encouraged peace advocates on both sides of the Ohio River valley into early 1784. John Filson interviewed Daniel Boone and published "The Adventures of Colonel Daniel Boone" in 1784. The book became popular in America and Europe and began the process of mythologizing Boone as the prototypical American frontier hero.

A poignant quote from the book expresses Daniel's hope for peace at this time:

> My footsteps have been marked with blood . . . Two
> darling sons and a brother have I lost by savage hands,

which have also taken from me forty valuable horses, and abundance of cattle. Many dark and sleepless nights I have been a companion for owls, separated from the cheerful society of men, scorched by the summer's sun, pinched by the winter's cold—an instrument ordained to settle the land. But now the scene has changed: peace crowns the sylvan glade. I now live in peace and safety, enjoying the sweets of liberty, and the bounties of Providence, with my once fellow-sufferers, in this delightful country, which I have seen purchased with a vast expence of blood and treasure.[8]

Congress issued a Proclamation on September 22, 1783, claiming the "sole and exclusive right and power" under Article IX of the Articles of Confederation to govern Indian affairs and forbade settlement on lands claimed by Indians unless authorized by Congress.[9] Nonetheless, as notice and implementation of the federal Proclamation slowly unfolded, the Virginians persisted in pursuing their own separate peace treaty with the Shawanese.

The Shawanese chiefs continued to send delegations to the Falls of the Ohio through the end of the summer of 1783, expressing their desire to conclude this treaty.[10] The parties exchanged correspondence regarding the negotiations several times through the spring of 1784.[11]

Virginia finally abandoned its independent negotiations with the Shawanese to abide by the Congressional Proclamation, also in the spring of 1784. The State of Virginia formally ceded all of its claims to lands north of the Ohio River to the United States of America on March 1, 1784, and terminated all of its governmental functions and services there.[12]

Tensions between Virginia and the Shawanese had already begun to build again. Shawanese and Miami Confederacy scouts observed surveying parties in the Clark Grant to the north of the Falls of the Ohio River in early 1784. The Miami Confederacy nations along the Wabash River were directly threatened by the imminent settlement of the Clark Grant.[13] As a result, Miami warriors began raiding forays into Kentucky.

As the encroachments by Virginia escalated, Chief Moluntha and the other leaders of the Makujay Shawanese began to lose influence over their people. Militant Miami chiefs and warriors were finding common cause with the Shawanese militants.

The Shawanese appeared to be ready to release all of their remaining prisoners to James Sherlock in July of 1784. They then abruptly canceled the final exchange with little explanation. Sherlock returned to Fort Nelson with only a half-dozen prisoners.[14]

A few additional prisoners were ransomed and released through the intercession of French traders. Margaret Pawley (Erskine) had continued to care for Jacky Callaway and Jones Hoy during their captivity in New Piqua until she was freed in 1784. She and Jacky wept as they parted, and poor little Jacky exclaimed, "What shall I do now?"[15]

Jacky did not have long to wait for help. Daniel Boone secured his release in a private prisoner exchange, undoubtedly with Micajah's assistance.[16] Jacky was returned to Squire Boone's station in Kentucky. He was escorted from there to Fort Boonesborough by Squire's son Moses, where he was reunited with his mother Elizabeth.[17]

Raids into Kentucky by small parties of Shawanese militants resumed around the time of these final prisoner exchanges. The militants focused their attacks on isolated outlying homesteads and routes of travel into Kentucky such as the Ohio River and the Wilderness Road.

The Treaty of Paris, Joseph Brant's Confederacy, and the Beginnings of American Indian Policy

GREAT BRITAIN AND THE UNITED STATES OF America signed the final Treaty of Paris on September 3, 1783, formally ending the American War for Independence. Although this was cause for great celebration, the seeds for continued conflict between the United States and the northwestern Indian nations were sown in the treaty itself.

In the Treaty of Paris, the king of Great Britain ceded sovereignty over the lands in the Northwest Territory to the United States of America. The cession included the lands formerly lying in the British province of Quebec, to the east of the Mississippi River, and between the Ohio River and the southern shores of the Great Lakes. The treaty contained no mention of the Indian allies of the British who lived in the ceded territory, or their rights.

The treaty was also ambiguous regarding when the British would close their northwestern military posts, which now lay in United States territory. The British took advantage of the ambiguity, and their posts at Detroit, Mackinack, and Niagara remained intact and active after the end of the war. Alexander McKee, Matthew Elliott, Simon Girty, and the other British Indian Department agents and representatives in Detroit continued to maintain their relationship with the Indian nations living within the new boundaries of the United States.

The Six Nations and British Indian Department sponsored a Grand Council of the Indian nations at Lower Sandusky, beginning on September 6, 1783. The Six Nations and the Shawanese, Wyandot, Delaware, Creek, Cherokee, and Lake nations attended. Alexander McKee presided and Joseph Brant, Matthew Elliott, and Simon Girty were also present. Chief Wryneck represented the Shawanese Nation.

Joseph Brant and the British Indian Department encouraged the Indian nations lying within American territory to establish their own united confederacy for purposes of negotiating with the new American nation. They discouraged individual Indian nations from negotiating their own separate peace.[18]

A FEDERAL AMERICAN INDIAN POLICY BEGAN TO take form as the Treaty of Paris was signed and Joseph Brant met with the Indian nations in September of 1783. General Washington opined in a September 11, 1783, letter to a member of the Congressional Committee on Indian Affairs,

> . . . Policy and economy points very strongly to the expediency of being upon good terms with the Indians, and the propriety of purchasing their Lands in preference to attempting to drive them by force of arms out of their Country . . .[19]

The smooth words of General Washington masked an underlying ruthlessness in the implementation of the policy. The first round of American purchases by treaty would be negotiated under duress, at gunpoint.

Eleven — The Federal Treaties of Conquest

In the Federal Interest

THE GREATEST FINANCIAL AND MORAL DEBT OF the new United States was owed to the thousands of American veterans of the War for Independence who had fought and suffered for many years with little or no compensation for their service. Virginia successfully obtained Congressional approval for a four-million-acre tract called the Virginia Military District, from which to pay land bounties to Virginia veterans. This huge tract of land lay between the Scioto River and Little Miami River in the heart of the Shawanese territory in Ohio.[1]

Congress selected federal Commissioners Plenipotentiary on March 6, 1784, to negotiate treaties with the northwestern Indian nations on behalf of the United States of America.[2] The commissioners were tasked to negotiate for sufficient land cessions to cover the military land bounties and other existing obligations of the federal and state governments. All surveying and settlement north of the Ohio was prohibited by proclamation of Congress until the treaties were negotiated.

Generals Richard Butler, George Rogers Clark, and Samuel H. Parsons were selected as commissioners and formed the active quorum for conducting the business of the commissioners. General Butler had lived with the Shawanese for many years as a young trader and his Shawanese consort and their half-Shawanese children still lived among them. He had ended his service in the War for Independence as a highly respected and decorated officer, with the rank of Brigadier General in the Continental Army.[3]

General Clark was much less sympathetic toward the Indian nations than General Butler. He was eager to develop the Clark Grant north of the Falls of the Ohio.

The Commissioners Plenipotentiary decided that they would negotiate three treaties with the Indian nations in furtherance of the Congressional instruction to employ a "divide and conquer" approach.[4] The first treaty would be negotiated with the Six Nations of the Iroquois at Fort Stanwix. The commissioners would then move on to negotiate a second treaty with the Delaware and Wyandot and other invited nations at Fort McIntosh on Beaver Creek. They would negotiate the third treaty with the Shawanese, Miami Confederacy nations, and Mingo at the mouth of the Greater Miami River.

The American Commissioners Plenipotentiary arrived at Fort Stanwix to negotiate with the Six Nations, accompanied by a company of fully armed regular soldiers. The presence of the soldiers alarmed and disconcerted the Indian nations. A few Shawanese chiefs attended to observe.

General Butler served as the primary spokesman for the United States in the negotiations. He emphasized that the United States earnestly wanted peace and that only the commissioners were empowered by Congress to treat with the Indian nations. He said that the United States wanted only two things: 1) return of all prisoners of war, and 2) agreement by the Indians to sell land to the United States so that the veterans of the war could be rewarded with land bounties.[5]

The second Treaty of Fort Stanwix was signed by the Six Nations and Commissioners Plenipotentiary on October 22, 1784. The Six Nations were allowed to keep small reservations, and the rest of their vast territory was purchased by the United States for a nominal sum. They were required to provide hostages to the United States to secure the peace.

The American Commissioners Plenipotentiary moved on to negotiate the next treaty with the Wyandots, Delaware, Chippewa, and Ottawa Indians at Fort McIntosh on Beaver Creek. The Shawanese chiefs were invited to attend but refused the invitation. General Butler made speeches similar to those he had made at Fort Stanwix.

The Treaty of Fort McIntosh was signed on January 31, 1785.[6] The treaty purported to cede to the United States most of the southern two-thirds of the Ohio Country, to the south of McKee's Town and to the east of

The Federal Treaties of Conquest

the eastern banks of the Greater Miami River. A large portion of this land was the territory of the Shawanese and Miami Nations and the Mingo people who were not represented at the treaty negotiations. The Americans required that the Wyandot and Delaware Nations provide hostages to secure the peace.

Cornstalk's sister Nonhelema and her daughter Fanny were the only Shawanese who attended the negotiations at Fort McIntosh.[7] She brought with her a petition in which she asked the commissioners to present to Congress on her behalf a request for a grant of two thousand acres to her on the Scioto River. General Butler and General Clark endorsed her request. However, it does not appear that Congress ever answered her petition.[8]

Treaty at the Mouth of the Greater Miami River (Fort Finney) with the Shawanese Nation
January 31, 1786

UPON THE CONCLUSION OF THE TREATY OF Fort McIntosh, the Commissioners Plenipotentiary turned their attention to the impending treaty negotiations at the mouth of the Greater Miami River. There they faced a very difficult situation. The Shawanese and Miami Confederacy nations and Mingo were furious with the Americans and the Wyandot, Delaware, Chippewa, and Ottawa Nations because the Treaty of Fort McIntosh had directly affected their lands without their participation.[9]

Shawanese Chief Captain Johnny explained their grievances to Virginians in a council at Wapatomica on May 18, 1785:

> Indian Council Held at Wakitunikee. At a Council held at Wakitunikee, May 18, 1785. By the Chiefs of the Shawanese, Mingoes, Delawares, and Cherokees. Present. James Shirlock & four other Americans ...Capt. Jonny, a Shawanese chief, spoke on behalf of the three first mentioned nations in that Country ...

You know Brethren Virginians . . . we see your Intention—you are drawing close to us, and so near our bedsides that we can almost hear the noise of your axes felling our Trees and settling our Country. According to the Lines settled by our Forefathers, the Boundary is the Ohio River, but you are coming upon the ground given to us by the Great Spirit—we wish you to be strong and keep your people on that side of the River . . .—we remind you that you will find all the people of our Colour in this Island strong, unanimous, and determined to act as one man in Defence of it, therefore be strong and keep your people within Bounds, or we shall take up a Rod and whip them back to your side of the Ohio. It is now incumbent upon you to restrain your People and listen to us, otherwise the Consequence of what may happen hereafter will be your fault. . . .[10]

Former General George Washington recommended to Congress that a federal military force be formed and posted in the northwestern territory to counteract the hostile Indians and the perceived British influence there. Congress reluctantly agreed with his recommendations.

Colonel Josiah Harmar was selected to serve as the commandant of a force of three hundred regular federal soldiers who would be posted in the northwestern territory. Harmar assembled and deployed his force and proceeded to construct and garrison a string of fortifications at intervals from Fort Pitt down the Ohio River to the mouth of the Muskingum River. Captain Doughty reached the mouth of the Muskingum in late October where he constructed and garrisoned Fort Harmar on the north shore of the Ohio River.[11]

The Commissioners Plenipotentiary dispatched Majors Samuel Montgomery, John Boggs, Daniel Elliott, and James Rinken from Fort Pitt in August and September of 1785 to carry messages to the Delaware, Wyandot, Miami, and Shawanese Nations, inviting them to attend the impending treaty negotiation at the mouth of the Greater Miami River. The messengers

The Federal Treaties of Conquest

were well received by the Delaware and Wyandot. They were poorly received by the Miami Nation, and their horses were stolen during their visit.

Majors Montgomery, Rinken, and Elliot met with Shawanese chiefs at Mackachack on September 25 and 28 and October 2 and at Wapatomica on October 7. The American messengers reported to the commissioners that the Shawanese chiefs were unwilling to attend the impending treaty negotiations. The chiefs also refused to endorse or help deliver the American invitation to the Indian nations to the west of them.[12]

The Shawanese militants in Wapatomica, led by Captain Snake, pressed the Shawanese leadership to support the hard-line Miami Confederacy position and intensify their raids into Kentucky to deter white encroachment north of the Ohio River. The influence of Captain Snake was to some degree offset by the emergence of a younger, more moderate Wapatomica war chief named Kekewapilathy (Tame Hawk). Kekewapilathy was a tall and raw-boned warrior with a fierce countenance.[13] He was heavily involved in the council discussions and his eloquent words held great sway among his people. He favored peace through negotiations with the Americans but with a hard-line stance that the Ohio River must remain the northern boundary for the Long Knives.

On September 25, 1785, General Butler and a company of seventy soldiers departed from Fort Pitt for the mouth of the Greater Miami River. They were transported by a little fleet of twelve small keelboats and bateaux and two flatboats carrying their horses and provisions. He may have met Daniel Boone as he stopped briefly in Limestone on his passage down the Ohio River.[14]

Butler's party arrived at the mouth of the Greater Miami River on October 22. They disembarked on the narrow spit of low-lying land between the Greater Miami and Ohio Rivers and encamped a short distance up the spit.[15]

Micajah Callaway was hired to assist General Butler as his interpreter.[16] Butler was no doubt aware of Micajah's close relationships with Moluntha, Lamatumque, and Nenessica through his own close personal connection to the Shawanese Nation.

Butler expected Micajah to play a political role in the negotiations beyond his role as interpreter. The support of Moluntha and Nenessica would be needed in order to convince the Shawanese Nation to enter into a treaty. Nenessica was a highly respected and influential Makujay war chief who also had close connections to the Chalaakaatha division. His support could offset the influence of Captain Snake.

The commissioners sent messengers to press the Shawanese leadership to attend the treaty negotiations several more times over the next several weeks. It is likely that Micajah was one of the unnamed interpreters and assistants referred to in General Butler's and Lieutenant Denney's journals for this time period.

Generals Clark, Butler, and Parsons decided to remain at the mouth of the Greater Miami River during the winter and continue their efforts to persuade the Shawanese and the other reluctant northwestern nations to attend the treaty negotiations. They directed that Major William Finney construct a fort to house their soldiers through the winter.

Major Finney began construction of the fort on the low-lying narrow spit of land between the Greater Miami River and Ohio River where the boundaries of the States of Ohio, Indiana, and Kentucky now converge. It was nearly directly across the Greater Miami River from the location where Micajah had lain in ambush with Joseph Brant and his warriors in August of 1781 and heard General Clark's fleet pass in the night.

The construction of Fort Finney began on October 25, 1785. The fort was built in the shape of a quadrangle, with a strong blockhouse at each corner. The stockade walls, constructed of strong wooden pickets set firmly into the ground, were completed by November 8. A guardhouse and storehouse were then constructed under a single roof. The storehouse was filled with excellent trade goods designated for the treaty.

A council house measuring twenty feet by sixty feet was constructed within rifle-shot range of the fort by November 24. The anticipated treaty negotiations were to take place there. Brush was cleared from around Fort Finney and the council house for a considerable distance to eliminate cover for any marauders who might attack.[17]

American messengers returned to Fort Finney on November 24 accompanied by two Delaware chiefs; two Wyandot chiefs; and Captain Johnny, a young Shawanese chief named Micanimsica, Nonhelema, and her daughter Fanny.[18] Captain Johnny and Micanimsica carried a personal message from Moluntha.

Moluntha reported that the Shawanese leaders had determined that

The Federal Treaties of Conquest

they had been deceived by the British in Detroit and were now in agreement with the boundaries of the Treaty of Fort McIntosh. They apologized for recent raids by young Shawanese warriors and blamed the British for encouraging them.

General Butler was optimistic that the Shawanese would attend the negotiations by the end of November. Moluntha had stopped just short of agreeing to attend. The Shawanese needed one final push to induce them to come. The commissioners dispatched Captain Johnny, Micanimsica, and Fanny back to the Shawanese towns on December 1 carrying an American demand that the Shawanese provide their final answer to the American invitation to the treaty within fifteen days.

Fanny and her brother Morgan returned to Fort Finney on December 19, 1785, with two other Shawanese and a message from their nation stating that they had finally decided they would attend the treaty negotiations. They delivered two strings of black and white wampum and Shawanese tobacco to the Commissioners.[19]

The main body of the Shawanese approached Fort Finney on January 14 and sent a messenger in advance announcing their intention to salute the Americans with three rounds of gunfire per warrior. The American commissioners agreed to honor the "proud little nation" in kind.

The Shawanese approached and entered the cleared grounds at Fort Finney in single file. The commissioners and Major Finney's soldiers stood at attention to receive them. Micajah and John Sovereign stood next to the Commissioners.

Moluntha led the Shawanese procession onto the grounds. He was beating a small water drum and leading the entire Shawanese party in a song. He was followed by two dancing young warriors, both of whom carried a calumet with a painted stem decorated with wampum and bald eagle feathers. They were followed by a small group of young warriors, also dancing.

Old Makujay War Chief Aweecomy followed the dancers and was in turn followed by other Shawanese chiefs and warriors, including Nenessica, Captain Johnny, Captain Wolf, Blue Jacket, Kekewapilathy, Chiaxi, Tecumseh, and Tecumseh's brother Chiksika. Captain Snake and his militant Wapatomica followers were conspicuously absent.

Headwoman Coitcheleh ("Cawechile") followed the warriors. She was in turn followed by her daughter Lamatumque, her sister Nonhelema, and the other headwomen. The remainder of the women and children followed behind them.

The Shawanese party totaled one hundred eight men, eighty-eight women, twenty-one boys, thirty girls, and five infants. The entire party was elegantly painted and dressed in their finest Shawanese style.[20]

The American Commissioners invited the Shawanese chiefs to join them in the council house. The commissioners entered first and took their seats at a small table in the front and center of the council house. The Shawanese men paused to dance at the western door as a sign of respect and followed them in. Moluntha beat his drum and the two pipe dancers danced in front of the commissioners and waved their feathered calumets over them as the other chiefs and warriors filed in and took their places in the western end. The women then entered through the eastern door and took their seats on the eastern end with elegant form and grace.

Moluntha stopped beating his drum and the dancers withdrew when all were seated. He rhetorically asked who among the Americans the commissioners were. Captain Johnny answered him and pointed to the three generals at the table. Moluntha led a brief song and then called upon Kekewapilathy to speak.

Kekewapilathy addressed the commissioners through John Sovereign. His speech was short, pathetic, and reasonable. He said that the Shawanese delegation had come to the American council fire despite the advice of many in their nation. They had brought their women and children with them. They hoped that the Americans would be strong, would take pity upon their women and children, and would pursue the good work of peace.[21]

The Americans replied with their own positive speech. The commissioners had directed American soldiers to prepare a feast for the Shawanese chiefs and principal warriors to be served in the council house. As the soldiers walked in to serve the food, the Shawanese chiefs and warriors laughed at the soldiers and mocked them, "There come the old women with warriors' coats on!" Micajah sat next to General Butler and translated when necessary.[22]

The commissioners met with the chiefs and Captain Johnny on January 15 to plan the course of the negotiations. When asked why the Shawanese had not responded to the initial invitation to treat at Fort

The Federal Treaties of Conquest

Stanwix in 1784 with all of the Indian nations, they said that the British had warned them not to attend as the Americans intended to cheat them. Moluntha said that the British had advised the Shawanese to kill the American commissioners.

The Shawanese occupied the council house and used it for dancing every day beginning on January 16. Nonhelema met with Lieutenant Denney to assist him in preparing a written vocabulary of the Shawanese language at the request of General Butler. Nonhelema saw this as an important task to help build understanding between their two people. They labored together for many hours and produced an excellent written vocabulary of over four hundred Shawanese words and phrases.[23]

Micajah met with Nenessica several times during the ensuing two weeks. Nenessica was very concerned about American intentions and did not trust the situation. He was still smarting from Moluntha's decision to give up Shawanese aspirations of reclaiming Kentucky, and now feared that the Americans would try to force the Shawanese to give up Ohio. Micajah tried to reassure him that the Americans primarily wanted to secure the peace in the treaty and would only request minor cessions of Ohio land. Nenessica remained skeptical.

The commissioners met with the Shawanese chiefs in a private council on January 28, 1786. They explained through their interpreters that they were going to present the general principles of the treaty in a public council so that the young warriors would be impressed with the seriousness of the occasion.

All of the Shawanese and commissioners assembled in the council house later in the day. General Butler made an opening speech for the American side, interpreted through Micajah. His speech was similar to the one he had delivered at Fort McIntosh. He berated the Shawanese Nation for their part in the late war and for their depredations against the Americans. He stated that Great Britain had ceded sovereignty over the Indian lands to the United States and had abandoned their Indian allies.

The General softened his tone. He emphasized that the Americans wanted peace. The United States wished to buy a portion of the land from them to repay its veteran Revolutionary soldiers. He warned that the consequence of failure to agree to peace on these terms would be war. The negotiations were adjourned so that the chiefs could consider what they had heard. Nenessica would not look at Micajah as he left the council.

The negotiations resumed in the council house on the following day, January 29. Chief Kekewapilathy made a speech in reply to the commissioners. He acknowledged that the Shawanese warriors had brought much grief to the Long Knife people and expressed regret for their past actions. The Shawanese warriors now would show their leadership by returning American prisoners just as they had shown leadership in capturing them.

Captain Johnny then stood up to speak for the Shawanese. He produced a large wampum belt and road belt that had been provided to Cornstalk at the Treaty of Fort Pitt in 1775. He said,

> ... These belts I only show you that it may bring the friendship which has been mentioned fresh to your memories. These are belts which our kings have kept by them. They are the belts received from the thirteen fires at the beginning of the war; and although some of our young people have been led astray by the evil advice of the British, and have done you much mischief, our kings never gave their consent or advice for the war, but have sat still as they promised; they have also kept the road belt, and although the road has been stopped for some time, we have now wiped it clean, and nothing shall stop it in the future, and we shall still hold fast these belts.[24]

The Commissioners sent for the Shawanese chiefs on January 30 to present to them the specific terms of the Articles of the treaty. The proposed treaty provided for the cession to the United States of all Shawanese claims to lands to the south and east of a proposed boundary line beginning on the north with the southern east-west boundary line of the Treaty of Fort McIntosh with the Wyandot and Delaware Nations and running west to where that line intersected with the main branch of the Greater Miami River. The line continued south down the Greater Miami River to the fork of the river just below the site of old Fort Pickawillany (1752). It ran west from

The Federal Treaties of Conquest

there in a straight line to the head of the River de la Panse (a tributary of the Wabash River known today as Wild Cat Creek) and west down that river to its mouth on the Wabash River.[25]

It appeared that all of the Shawanese towns except for Girty's Town on St. Mary's River might be located within the area that the Americans were asking the Shawanese to cede under the treaty. Some of the Shawanese thought that perhaps they had misunderstood. Again, Nenessica left the council house without looking at Micajah.

The commissioners summoned the full Shawanese council to the council house to present the specific terms of the treaty to all of them. The council house was soon packed with Shawanese counselors and spectators. The commissioners were sitting at a small table in the center along one of the long walls of the council house.

General Butler spoke on behalf of the commissioners. He expressed through Micajah the sincere hope of the American people for peace and their joy at hearing the great Shawanese desire for peace and regret over past transgressions. He then proceeded to present the details of each one of the articles of the treaty to the assembled Shawanese.

Chief Kekewapilathy rose to speak when General Butler was finished. He asked the commissioners if the Great Spirit had himself given the United States the power to divide the land in this manner. The Shawanese did not believe that the Great Spirit had done so. The Shawanese would agree to nothing less than the Ohio River as the boundary. It was up to the Americans to decide if it was to be peace or war. Kekewapilathy concluded his speech by laying a mixed belt of black and white wampum upon the table before the commissioners.[26] Restless young warriors stirred in the council house.

When General Butler stood up and responded through Micajah, he was visibly angry. He reminded the Shawanese again of their breach of their treaties with the Americans at Fort Pitt in 1775 and 1776. He had negotiated the 1775 treaty with Cornstalk himself and his personal anger at the Shawanese breach of that treaty was clearly evident to the Shawanese in the council house. There was no need for an interpreter.

General Butler noted the many atrocities that the Shawanese had committed against American prisoners. He reminded them that they had allied themselves to the British who had lost the war and had surrendered the country to the Americans. The Americans considered the Shawanese to be a conquered people. The terms of the proposed treaty were non-negotiable and would not be altered in any way. It was up to the Shawanese to decide if it would be peace or war.

General Clark had observed Kekewapilathy's speech with a casual, disdainful demeanor as he rested his head in his left hand, his elbow propped upon the table. He casually raised his walking cane with his right hand and flipped the wampum belt onto the floor.[27] Shocked, every Shawanese in the room started from their seats. Nenessica and some of the other men reached for their tomahawks. Micajah stepped closer to General Butler and rested his hand on the head of his own tomahawk. The American soldiers glanced nervously at the priming on their muskets.

General Clark leapt to his feet and stood ramrod-straight before the Shawanese crowd. His eyes bore down with fiery defiance, and his red hair seemed as if it were aflame. He stamped on the sacred wampum belt and ground it into the floor with his bootheel as he looked directly into Kekewapilathy's eyes. The warriors prepared to pounce, and the soldiers held their guns at the ready.

General Butler interceded and told the Shawanese through Micajah that they were fortunate that the Thirteen Fires did not wish for war. The Americans would give the Shawanese two days to reconsider their position. If they did not agree to the terms of the treaty within that time period, six days of grace and provisions would be provided for their return to their villages. They should then take care because they would certainly face the full power of the armed forces of the United States of America.[28]

The Shawanese left the council house in consternation and disarray. They faced imminent destruction if they did not concede to the American terms. This was not a peace negotiation. It was an ultimatum and a land grab. The Americans could hear the Shawanese debating in their camps in the forest near the fort well into the afternoon.

Old Moluntha approached the commissioners in the late afternoon and pleaded for another meeting. The parties reassembled in the council house. Nenessica was pale and stared at the ground, occasionally shaking his head. Kekewapilathy made a short, contrite speech and sued for peace on the Americans' terms. He apologetically presented a white string of wampum signifying peace. The young Shawanese warriors were shamed by his actions.[29]

The Treaty at the Mouth of the Greater Miami River was signed on February 1, 1786. It read as follows:

ARTICLES of a TREATY

Concluded at the Mouth of the GREAT MIAMI, on the north-western Bank of the Ohio, the thirty-first of January, one thousand seven hundred and eighty-six, between the COMMISSIONERS PLENIPOTENTIARY of the United States of America, of the one Part, and CHIEFS and WARRIORS of the Shawanoe Nation of the other Part.

Article 1. Three hostages shall be immediately delivered to the commissioners, to remain in the possession of the United States, until all the prisoners, white and black, taken in the late war from among the citizens of the United States, by the Shawanoe nation, or by any other Indian or Indians residing in their towns, shall be restored.

Art. 2. The Shawanoe nation, do acknowledge the United States to be the sole and absolute sovereign of all the territory ceded to them by a treaty of peace made between them and the King of Great Britain, the fourteenth day of January, one thousand seven hundred and eighty four.

Art. 3. If any Indian or Indians of the Shawanoe nation, or any other Indian or Indians residing in their towns, shall commit murder or robbery on, or do any injury to the citizens of the United States, or any of them, that nation shall deliver such offender, or offenders to the officer commanding the nearest post of the Untied States to be punished according to the ordinances of Congress; and in like manner any citizen of the United States who shall do an injury to any

Indian of the Shawanoe nation, or to any other Indian or Indians residing in their towns, and under their protection, shall be punished according to the laws of the United States.

Art. 4. The Shawanoe nation having knowledge of the intention of any nation or body of Indians to make war on the citizens of the United States, or of their counselling together for that purpose, and neglecting to give information thereof to the commanding officer of the nearest post of the United States, shall be considered as parties in such war, and be punished accordingly; and the United States shall in like manner inform the Shawanoes of any injury designed against them.

Art. 5. The United States do grant peace to the Shawanoe nation, and do receive them into their friendship and protection.

Art. 6. The United States do allot to the Shawanoe nation, lands within their territory to live and hunt upon, beginning at the fourth line of the lands alloted to the Wiandots and Delaware nations, at the place where the main branch of the great Miami, which falls into the Ohio intersects said line - then down the river Miami, to the fork of that river, next below the old fort, which was taken by the French in 1752; thence due west to the River de la Panse; -then down that river to the river, Wabash, beyond which lines none of the citizens of the United States shall settle, nor disturb the Shawanoe in the settlement and possessions; and the Shawanoes do relinquish to the United States, all title, or pretence of title they ever had to the lands east, west, and south, of the east, west, and south lines before described.

Art. 7. If any citizen or citizens of the United States, shall presume to settle upon the lands allotted

The Federal Treaties of Conquest

to the Shawanoes by this treaty, he or they shall be put out of the protection of the United States.

In TESTIMONY WHEREOF, the Parties hereunto have affixed their Hands and Seals, the Day and Year first above mentioned

Attest, ALEXANDER CAMPBELL, Secr'y to Commissioners

W. FINNEY, Maj. B.B.	G.R. CLARKE, (L.S.)
THOS. DOYLE, Capt. B.B.	RICHD. BUTLER, (L.S.)
NATHAN McDOWELL, Ens.	SML. H. PARSONS, (L.S.)
JOHN SAFFENGER,	
HENRY GOVY,	AWEECONY, X ( ) his mark.
KAGY GALLOWAY, X his mark.	KAKAWILPILATHY, X ( ) his mark.
JOHN BOGGS,	
SAM. MONGOMERY,	
DANIEL ELLIOT,	MALUNTHY, X ( ) his mark.
JAMES RINKER,	
NATHA. SMITH,	MUSQUAUCONOCAH, X ( ) his mark.
JOS. SUFFREIN, X or KEMEPENO SHAWNO, his mark.	
ISAAC ZANE, (a Wiandot) X his mark.	MEANYMSECAH, X ( ) his mark.
The HALF-KING of the WIANDOTS,) X X their marks. The CRANE of the WIANDOTS,)	WAUPAUCOWELA, X ( ) his mark.
Capt. PIPE of the DELAWARES, X his mark.	NIHIPEEWA, X ( ) his mark.
Capt. BOHONGEHELAS, X his mark.	
TETEBOCKSHIEKA, X his mark.	NIHINESSICOE, X ( ) his mark.
The BIG CAT of the DELAWARES, X his mark.	
PIERE DROULLAR,	

ARTICLES of a TREATY,

Concluded at the Mouth of the GREAT MIAMI, on the north-western Bank of the Ohio, the thirty-first of January, one thousand seven hundred and eighty-six, between the COMMISSIONERS PLENIPOTENTIARY of the United States of America, of the one Part, and the CHIEFS and WARRIORS of the Shawanoe Nation of the other Part.

Article 1. THREE hostages shall be immediately delivered to the commissioners, to remain in the possession of the United States, until all the prisoners, white and black, taken in the late war from among the citizens of the United States, by the Shawanoe nation, or by any other Indian or Indians residing in their towns, shall be restored.

Art. 2. The Shawanoe nation, do acknowledge the United States to be the sole and absolute sovereigns of all the territory ceded to them by a treaty of peace, made between them and the King of Great-Britain, the fourteenth day of January, one thousand seven hundred and eighty-four.

Art. 3. If any Indian or Indians of the Shawanoe nation, or any other Indian or Indians residing in their towns, shall commit murder or robbery on, or do any injury to the citizens of the United States, or any of them, that nation shall deliver such offender, or offenders to the officer commanding the nearest post of the United States, to be punished according to the ordinances of Congress; and in like manner any citizen of the United States who shall do an injury to any Indian of the Shawanoe nation, or to any other Indian or Indians residing in their towns, and under their protection, shall be punished according to the laws of the United States.

Art. 4. The Shawanoe nation having knowledge of the intention of any nation or body of Indians to make war on the citizens of the United States, or of their counselling together for that purpose, and neglecting to give information thereof to the commanding officer of the nearest post of the United States, shall be considered as parties in such war, and be punished accordingly: and the United States shall in like manner inform the Shawanoes of any injury designed against them.

Art. 5. The United States do grant peace to the Shawanoe nation, and do receive them into their friendship and protection.

Art. 6. The United States do allot to the Shawanoe nation, lands within their territory to live and hunt upon, beginning at the south line of the lands allotted to the Wiandots and Delaware nations, at the place where the main branch of the great Miami which falls into the Ohio intersects said line--then down the river Miami, to the fork of that river, next below the old fort, which was taken by the French in 1752; thence due west to the River de la Panse;--then down that river to the river, Wabash, beyond which lines, none of the citizens of the United States shall settle, nor disturb the Shawanoes in their settlement and possessions; and the Shawanoes do relinquish to the United States, all title, or pretence of title they ever had to the lands east, west and south, of the east, west and south lines before described.

Art. 7. If any citizen or citizens of the United States, shall presume to settle upon the lands allotted to the Shawanoes by this treaty, he or they shall be put out of the protection of the United States.

In TESTIMONY WHEREOF, the Parties hereunto have affixed their Hands and Seals, the Day and Year first above mentioned.

Attest, ALEXANDER CAMPBELL, Secr'y to Commissioners.

Witnesses.

W. FINNEY, Maj. B. B.
THOS. DOYLE, Capt. B. R.
NATHAN M'DOWELL, Ens.
JOHN SAFFENGER,
HENRY GOVY,
    his
KAGY GALLOWAY, ×
    mark.
JOHN BOGGS,
SAM. MONTGOMERY,
DANIEL ELLIOT,
JAMES RINKER,
NATHA. SMITH,
   his
JOS. SUFFREIN, or KEMPENO SHAWNO,
  mark.   his
ISAAC ZANE, (a Wiandot) ×
    mark.   their
The HALF-KING of the WIANDOTS,
The CRANE of the WIANDOTS,) marks.
        his
Capt. PIPE of the DELAWARES,
    mark.
      his
Capt. BOHONGEHELAS,
     mark.
    his
TETEBOCKSHIEKA,
   mark.
      his
The BIG CAT of the DELAWARES,
PIERRE DROULLAR.   mark.

(Signed,)
G. R. CLARKE,   (L.S.)
RICHD. BUTLER,   (L.S.)
SAML. H. PARSONS,   (L.S.)
    his
AWEECONY, × ( )
   mark.
    his
KAKAWIPILATHY, × ( )
    mark.
   his
MALUNTHY, × ( )
   mark.
     his.
MUSQUAUCONOCAH, × ( )
     mark.
    his
MEANYMSECAH, × ( )
    mark.
    his
WAUPAUCOWELA, × ( )
    mark.
   his
NIHIPEEWA, × ( )
   mark
    his
NIHINESSICOE, × ( )
    mark.

Treaty at the Mouth of the Greater Miami (1786)

[Courtesy of the Library of Congress]

The Federal Treaties of Conquest

Micajah placed his "x" at the place indicated by those supervising the signature process.[31] John Sovereign also signed with his "x." Chiefs Moluntha, Kekewapalithy, Aweecomy, Nenessica (Nihinessicoe), and Musquaconah (Red Pole) and three other chiefs signed for the Shawanese. The three commissioners and Major Finney and his subordinate officers signed for the Americans.

It is unclear if the Shawanese chiefs who signed the treaty fully understood the precise location of the proposed boundary and near-total cession of their homeland to the United States. Moluntha and Red Pole later denied that they did. One could understand how hard it would have been to believe that the Americans were bold enough to demand everything.

The Shawanese produced six hostages to be held at Fort Finney to secure the treaty: Nenessica (Nohinissica), Mithawano and his brother Wewessicanpawie, Mannashcommiqua, Mianimissica, and Methoto.[32] They were taken into custody.

The rest of the humiliated Shawanese did not linger long after the treaty was signed. They accepted treaty gifts and provisions from the Americans and loaded them onto their horses and their backs and prepared to depart.

Micajah sought out Moluntha and Lamatumque in order to bid them farewell and wish them well. The old chief was exhausted and seemed to have shrunken in on himself. He looked at Micajah with a trace of a tear in his eye and silently held out his wizened hand. Micajah shook it. Lamatumque stepped up to her husband's side. She seemed stunned and confused. Nonhelema joined them and stood on Moluntha's other side. She was smoldering with anger at the American betrayal of her trust.

Moluntha told Micajah that he had failed his nation. His people would not accept the treaty, and there would be war. They would lose their lands and might possibly be destroyed. Micajah mumbled something about hoping that they could appeal to higher authorities but it sounded weak and apologetic. Lamatumque and Nonhelema each gently placed a hand on Moluntha's shoulders, and they turned and walked away.

Lamatumque looked back over her shoulder in a brief glance back at Micajah as they left. Their gaze locked for an intense moment. She had tried with every fiber of her being to bridge the gulf between her people and Micajah's people in the name of love, family, and shared humanity. Slowly she turned away to face the uncertain future.

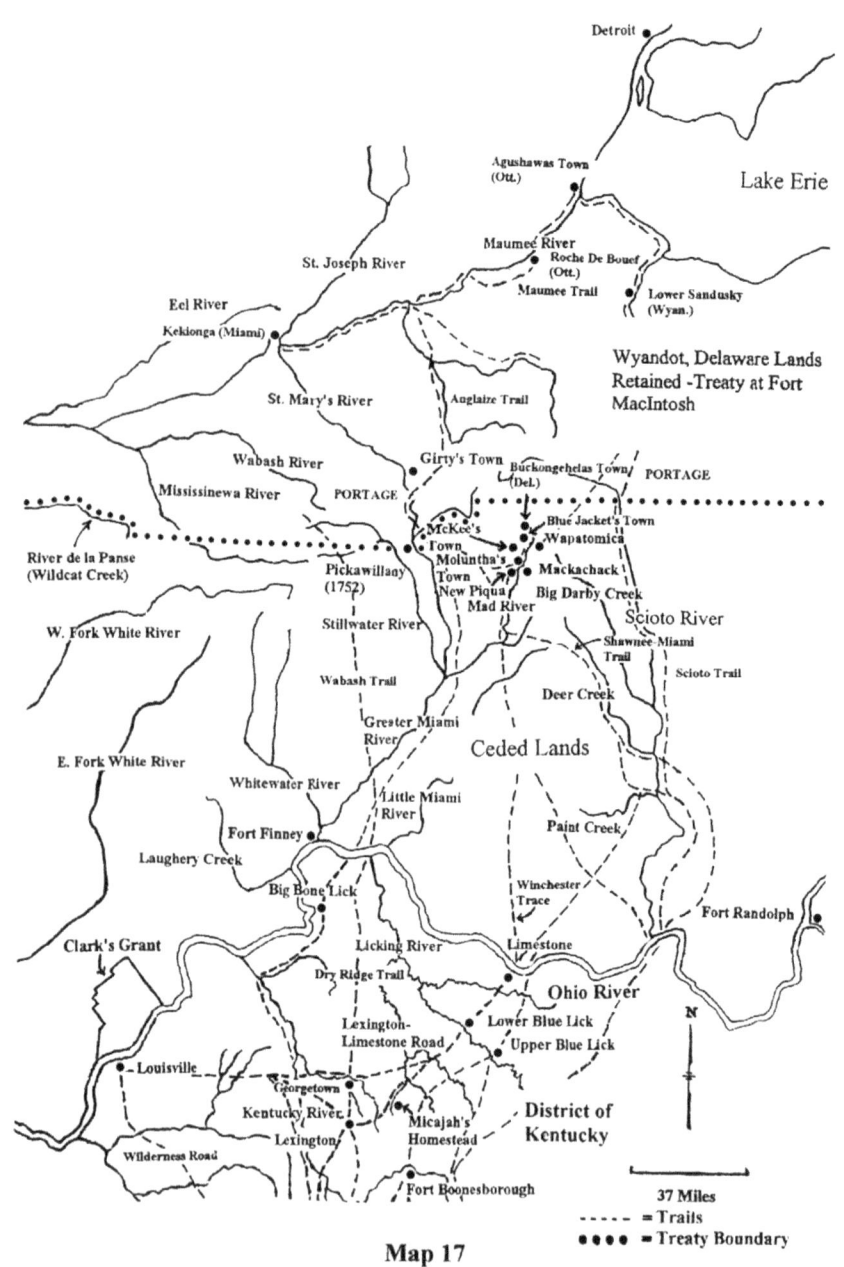

Map 17
**Boundaries of Treaty at the Mouth of the Greater Miami River
(January 1786)**

Micajah felt a lump in his throat as he watched them disappear up the trail. He was ashamed. He knew that old Moluntha was right. Many Shawanese were too proud to accept the American terms and would fight the Long Knives to retain their lands rather than surrender them. There would be more misery for both peoples—more prisoners and more death—and Micajah would have to go to war against his Shawanese friends.

Twelve: War in the Wabash Country

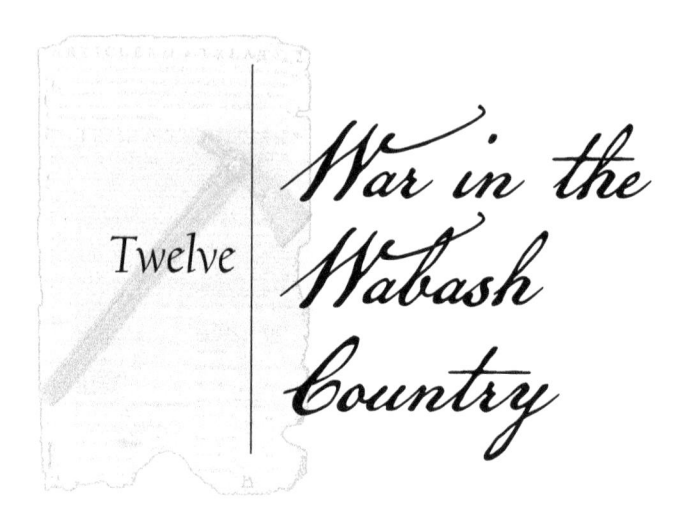

THE AMERICAN COMMISSIONERS PLENIPOTENTIARY DEPARTED FROM THE mouth of the Greater Miami River in early February. Micajah was paid for his interpreting and scouting services at Fort Finney and met with Nenessica for a final visit before leaving for home.

Nenessica smiled and his eyes narrowed slightly as Micajah was let into the brig. They made small talk for a few minutes, and Nenessica casually asked a few questions concerning General Butler's and General Clark's plans. Micajah was intentionally vague in his responses.

Nenessica paused and stroked his chin. He confided to Micajah that the Shawanese chiefs were going to present the treaty to their old friends in the British Indian Department and ask their help in interpreting it. Then they would decide what to do.

The tall and rangy Nenessica smiled and placed his hands on Micajah's shoulders. Micajah steadily returned his father's gaze and smiled back. Micajah extended his hand. Nenessica accepted it and firmly shook it. Nenessica promised that they would meet again in better days.

MICAJAH STOPPED BY LIMESTONE TO VISIT BRIEFLY with Daniel Boone and then rode on down the Lexington-Limestone Road toward his cabin at the head of the Houston Fork. He paused briefly en route at Ready Money Jack's trading post for a gill of whisky. Micajah had his interpreter's pay ready, and Jack served up the drink. He slammed the whisky down in one gulp.

General Butler and General Parsons journeyed back up the Ohio River

War in the Wabash Country

and arrived in the Carlisle, Pennsylvania area thirty-four days later. There they publicly announced the successful conclusion of the treaty negotiations, and reported that the surveying and conveyance of the lands purchased in the treaty could now begin without threat of attack by the Shawanese.[1]

The land speculators responded immediately and General Parsons was foremost among them. A group of wealthy investors formed a new Ohio Company in early March for the purpose of purchasing and developing property in the Ohio Country. The Board of Directors was comprised of General Samuel Parsons, General Rufus Putnam, and Manassah Cutler. Winthrop Sargent was elected as the Secretary. Many of the new nation's foremost men were investors.

Moluntha and the other Makujay chiefs who had signed the treaty were severely chastised by Captain Snake and his militant followers upon their return to the Shawanese Towns. Most of the Shawanese war chiefs and warriors simply refused to comply with the treaty. Moluntha struggled to retain the support of his people while honoring his agreement with the Americans.

Nenessica and the other Shawanese hostages held at Fort Finney escaped on March 24, 1786. John Sovereign's family was taken captive by the escaping Shawanese hostages while Sovereign was off hunting.[2] Micajah sighed when he heard the news, but he was not surprised.

Makujay Chiefs Moluntha, Shade, and Red (Painted) Pole sent a plea for help to King George III on March 27:

> Father: Last Fall the Americans our Brethren called us to the Big Miamis, when we arrived they told us they had something to communicate for our future welfare and that of our Children after us. But alas we heard nothing good from them, they told us that our Father had given us to them with our Lands likewise . . . We were not sensible of the error we committed, till our friend Elliott explained it to us.
>
> Father: We request you'll be strong and give us the best advice you are capable of, in our present situation, you see we never have been in more need of

your friendship and good offices, we have been cheated by the Americans, who are still striving to work our destruction, and without your assistance they may be able to accomplish their ends. You have too much wisdom not to be convinced of this truth, as well as we are. We earnestly request you will consider and send us a speedy answer. In the mean time, we salute you & remain your steady friend. Signed: Maloontha, Shade, Painted Pole, Principal Chiefs of the Shawanese.[3]

David Duncan sent a letter to Colonel Harmar on March 28 forwarding intelligence gathered during a four month trip through Detroit and the Ohio Indian country. He stated that the war chiefs of the Wyandot, Delaware and Shawanese nations did not agree with the treaty terms and would fight to the last man to defend their land. Duncan advised that his intelligence report should be forwarded to Congress.[4]

Miami Confederacy raiding parties had been stealing horses in Kentucky since the previous autumn.[5] Pursuit parties of Kentucky horsemen had added to the escalating tensions by chasing the raiders back across the Ohio River.

In early 1786, the Miami Nation and the other nations of the Miami Confederacy held a Grand Council at Ouiatenon and issued a declaration of war against the United States of America.[6]

The Miami Nation and their Miami Confederacy allies were populous and prosperous. They had not participated heavily in the War for Independence, and their resources and manpower had not been drained by that conflict. They had many more warriors than the remnants of the Ohio Shawanese and were well equipped and well led by their brilliant War Chief Little Turtle.

Captain Snake and other militant Shawanese war chiefs accelerated their diplomatic exchanges with the Miami Confederacy and pressed for an alliance with the powerful nations along the Wabash River. The Shawanese did not vacate their Ohio towns as mandated by the new treaty. Militant Shawanese warriors once again resumed their raids on remote Kentucky settlements.

War in the Wabash Country

Abraham Lincoln, grandfather of the future president, was in the process of relocating his family in May of 1786 from their former Lincoln County homestead to property he had purchased near Hughes Station in Jefferson County, Kentucky. One day that month Abraham was planting corn in a field near their new cabin.

A small Shawanese raiding party crossed the Ohio River and crept up through the forest to the edge of the cornfield. A warrior fired a shot from the edge of the forest and killed Abraham. His eight-year-old son Tom, father of the future president, stood next to his father's body as the warrior ran up to take Abraham's scalp. Tom's fifteen-year-old brother Mordecai sent thirteen-year-old brother Josiah to Hughes Station for help and ran to the cabin to get his father's gun.

The warrior grabbed Tom and prepared to scalp Abraham as Mordecai reached the cabin. Mordecai found the gun, took careful aim at a medallion on the warrior's chest, and fired one shot. The warrior dropped dead to the ground. A rescue party from Hughes Station arrived and drove the rest of the warriors away.[7]

The security of Americans living in and around Vincennes deteriorated as their Miami neighbors became increasingly hostile. The federal government had taken no steps to provide a substitute for the Virginia system of government following Virginia's final cession of its lands north of the Ohio River on March 1, 1784.[8] The Articles of Confederation did not provide authority to establish law enforcement, courts, or a militia system in the Northwest Territory. There was no executive leadership or legislature. Vincennes and the rest of the Northwest Territory was a lawless frontier zone loosely governed by informal citizen associations.

General Clark sent a letter to the president of Congress on June 8, 1786, informing Congress of the declaration of war by the Miami Confederacy ("Wabash") Indians. He noted that the Kentucky militia forces were prohibited from leaving their state to protect Vincennes or attack the Indian towns after Virginia's cession. Clark concluded with a recommendation that a federal military expedition be undertaken to intimidate and silence the Indians.[9]

On June 21, 1786, Americans who lived in and around Vincennes were attacked. Captain Daniel Sullivan dragged a peaceful Indian into the American fort where the wife of a wounded American man shot and scalped him.[10]

French militia Colonel J.M.P. Legras demanded that the Americans leave the fort at Vincennes, but the Americans refused to leave. A deputation from several Indian nations arrived at the fort on the night of July 13, 1786. They informed the colonel that a party of four or five hundred warriors was encamped a few miles away and intended to exterminate all of the Americans at Vincennes.

Colonel LeGras sent a long letter to General Clark from Vincennes on July 22, 1786. The colonel upbraided the Americans and opined that their barbarity far exceeded that of the Indians. He demanded that Clark remove the bad element from among the Americans in Vincennes.[11] Colonel LeGras persuaded the Miami army to disband and give him time to address their grievances.

Shawanese warriors increased the frequency and severity of their raids into Kentucky and Pennsylvania. American Captain Saunders reported that he had observed two raiding parties leave the Shawanese Towns. The Buffalo and nine warriors had raided the Limestone area and returned to New Piqua with three scalps. Another party of ten had gone to the mouth of the Great Kanawha and had been unsuccessful in their search for scalps. However, they did manage to steal horses from Limestone on their return trip.[12]

A party of forty-seven Shawanese warriors led by Chief Black Wolf invaded the Abbs Valley in western Pennsylvania in July and attacked the settlement of Captain James Moore. Captain Moore and four children were killed during the initial attack. Mrs. Moore and her daughter Jane were taken back to Wapatomica where their legs were chopped off, and they were burned to death. Daughter Polly survived as a prisoner in the Shawanese towns until she was released.[13]

Captain Snake was identified as the leader of another Shawanese raid into Kentucky. He and four warriors crossed the Ohio River and captured a white settler near the settlement of Washington, Kentucky, just to the south of Limestone and stole several horses before returning to the Ohio Country.[14]

CONGRESS ENACTED THE LAND ORDINANCE OF 1785 to establish orderly procedures for the surveying, recordation, and disposition of lands in territories of the United States purchased from the Indians outside of the boundaries of the original thirteen states. Alexander McKee had learned of the ordinance by August 6, 1785, and undoubtedly informed his Indian friends.[15]

The new law required that, wherever possible, the purchased lands were to be surveyed into six-mile-square townships delineated by lines running due north and south and others crossing from east to west at right angles. East/west numbers were identified by "Range" and north/south numbers by "Township," all measured off of specified base lines and meridian lines.

Captain Thomas Hutchins was appointed by Congress to serve as Geographer General and organize survey teams to implement the ordinance. They began surveying the lands ceded in the Treaty at Fort McIntosh and the Treaty at the Mouth of the Greater Miami River on July 21, 1786.[16] Their first step was to survey the primary "Geographer's Line" running due west from the point where the Ohio River intersected the western Pennsylvania boundary. The surveyors would proceed from there to survey the first four of seven planned north-south Ranges in the Ohio Country running parallel to the Pennsylvania border.[17] An intelligence report received in Fort Pitt on September 14, 1786, from a former prisoner of the Wyandot described ominous preparations by the Shawanese war chiefs and their Ohio Indian allies in response to the ongoing surveys:

> ... They frequently inquire if Captain Hutchins is out; they say that the moment they hear of his beginning to survey, seven hundred men will march from the Shawanese Towns to cut him off. That this will be the case, the informant verily believes, for they all seem greatly exasperated; they are more united, & better prepared in all respects for war than they ever were during the time of his residence among them ...
>
> He further says that thirteen scalps and four prisoners were brought into the Shawanese Towns that two of them, women, were burned; they were mother & daughter of the name of Moore—their names were known by papers found with them.[18]

Captain Hutchins temporarily suspended surveying work on

October 23, 1786, because of the Indian hostilities. Surveys for four of the planned initial seven ranges had been completed by then.[19]

Other spies informed the Americans that the Shawanese planned to divide their warriors into three groups to attack the Long Knives. One group would attack Wheeling, another group Fort Harmar, and the third would join forces with the Miami Confederacy nations along the Wabash River in their confrontation with General Clark. The Shawanese war chiefs decided to send the largest portion of their army to help the Miami Confederacy.[20]

The Executive Council of Virginia issued an Executive Order directing that the field officers of the District of Kentucky meet to "concert some system for their own defense" subject to the militia laws of Virginia and Article VI of the Articles of Confederation. District of Kentucky Attorney General Harry Innes issued a legal opinion interpreting Article VI and the Executive Order to provide the authority for a punitive military expedition into the Wabash Country. Action quickly followed.[21]

A Board of Officers at War selected General Clark to command an expedition of Kentucky militia to rendezvous at Clarksville, march from there to Vincennes, and destroy the towns and villages of the Miami Confederacy ("Wabash") Indians.[22] Colonel Levi Todd was selected to command the Fayette County troops and Colonel Benjamin Logan chosen to command the Lincoln County troops.[23]

Micajah joined the Fayette County troops under Colonel Todd. His Houston Fork property was located within the boundaries of the new Bourbon County which had been formed in 1785 but had not yet established its own independent county militia.[24]

Major John Holder from Holder's Station served as Colonel Todd's field major. Captain John Saunders from the Houston Fork area commanded one of Colonel Todd's companies and may have been Micajah's company commander.[25]

Micajah prepared his weapons and packed some extra clothing and parched corn into his knapsack. The recent federal treaty negotiations had been very unpopular with many Kentuckians, particularly among those involved in the New State movement who felt such matters should be subject to local control. This was a chance to demonstrate his loyalty to Virginia and the United States. He knew that many of the Shawanese warriors were joining forces with the Miami Confederacy nations,

War in the Wabash Country

and he expected he would have to fight some of his Shawanese family and friends.

Over 1,200 soldiers had rendezvoused and encamped at Clarksville by September 10, 1786. Many were spurred to volunteer by an open letter to the young men of Kentucky from a frightened young lady living in Vincennes asking for their help.

The Board of Officers held a council of war at the rendezvous on September 13, 1786. The board decided that most of the troops as well as three small brass cannon would travel over land from Clarksville to Vincennes. They would drive a herd of cattle with them. The balance of the troops, larger pieces of ordnance, and provisions (including dried beef and flour) would be transported by nine keelboats up the Wabash River to Vincennes.[26]

On September 14, 1786, General Clark ordered Colonel Benjamin Logan to gather additional Lincoln County troops and attack the Shawanese Ohio towns. He noted that the Shawanese would not then be expecting an attack on their Ohio towns from Kentucky. Colonel James Barnett took over command of the Lincoln County troops that would remain with Clark's expedition.

The divisions of the Long Knife army taking the overland route from Clarksville to Vincennes marched from Clarksville on September 17, 1786. Micajah served as an advance scout and helped the army find its way through the wilderness of what was later to become southern Indiana.

The army generally followed the old winding Buffalo Trace between Clarksville and Vincennes. The army's first destination was a mineral spring near the Buffalo Trace named French Lick, which was located mid-way between Clarksville and Vincennes. The salt lick was heavily used by buffalo and other wild game.

The cannon proved to be difficult to transport because of the narrowness of the trail, and progress was slow. Moving the herd of cattle proved to be almost impossible. The herd would break up in the thickets and scatter. The soldiers were constantly searching for the strays, rounding them up, and bringing them back to the main herd. They lost more and more cattle in the forest as the march progressed.

The troops encamped for a brief rest at French Lick. Micajah and the other scouts and hunters killed several buffalo in the forest around the licks to supplement their provisions.[27]

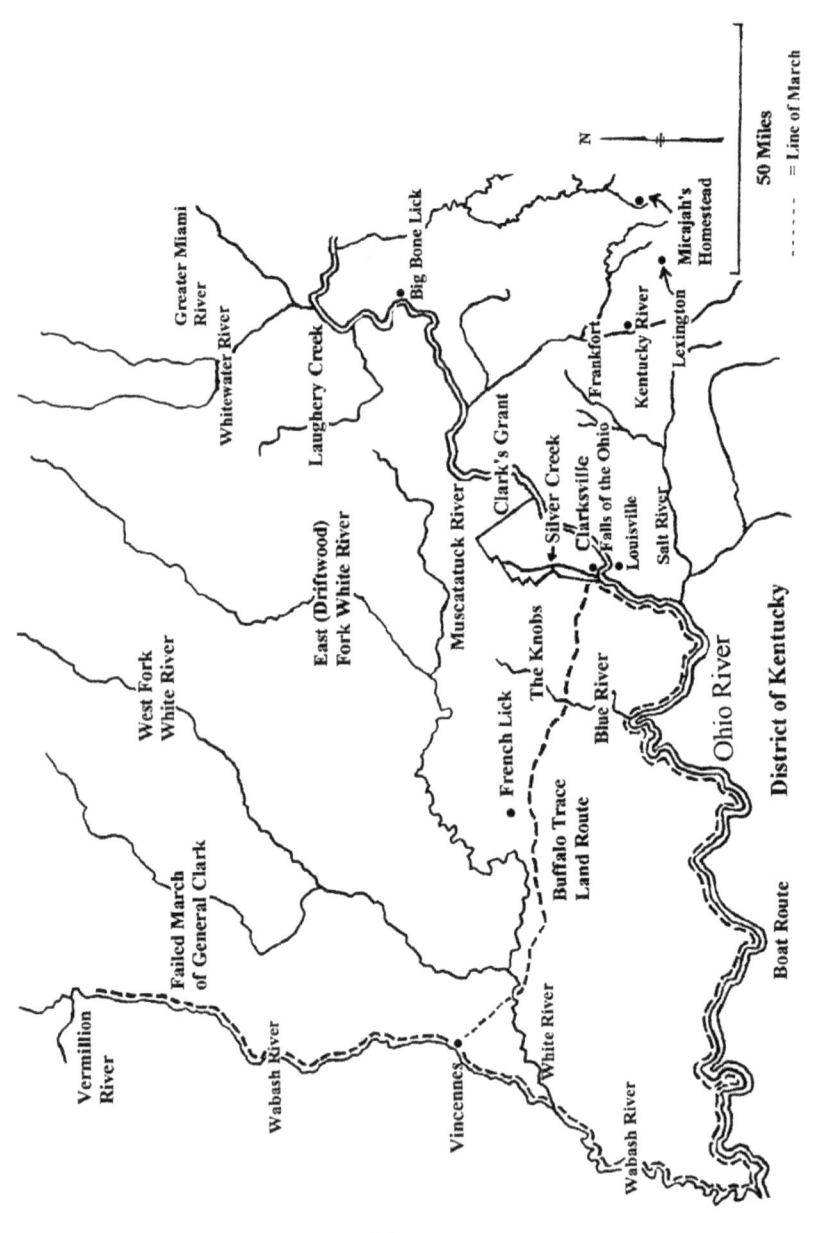

Map 18
General George Rogers Clark's Campaign of 1786

War in the Wabash Country

The army arrived in Vincennes on September 25. The French and American occupants there were overjoyed to see General Clark and his troops and greeted them warmly. The soldiers encamped within the fort and the adjacent area.

Micajah had never visited Vincennes before and took the opportunity to explore it. The well-established French village was now over eighty years old. The Americans variously referred to it as "St. Vincents," "Post Vincents," or, most frequently, the "O'Post."

Some of the original French buildings were still in use. The original St. Francis Xavier Catholic Church was built when the town was founded in 1702. The church had moved into a new log building measuring ninety by forty-two feet in 1785. The original structure was converted to a residence for the clergy. The earlier French fort was still standing and served as the American military post.

The old French houses in the town were constructed of vertical timbers plastered with adobe, which had been white-washed. The roofs of the houses were thatched with straw. They were half-hidden behind arbors of mature grapevines with fruit trees planted around them. The French residents used small two-wheeled carts pulled by a single horse called "calesches" to transport themselves and small loads throughout the town.[28]

Many nations and cultures met and mixed in the "O'Post." French traders came and went through the fort and the town accompanied by Indians from various nations. The Spanish government maintained a consulate there. There were a number of ragged young American adventurers hanging about, many of them veterans of the late war seeking their fortunes on the frontier.

General Clark's army lingered at Vincennes for eight days beyond the date initially planned for their departure. The reasons for the delay were not communicated to the soldiers and they began to speculate.

Rumors had circulated widely in Virginia for at least the past three years that General Clark had developed an alcohol problem. The rumors had made their way to the highest levels of the federal and state government. Congressman James Monroe had complained publicly about the alleged problem as early as January of 1783.[29]

General Clark had a legitimate reason to remain in Vincennes. The summer of 1786 was very dry, and the water level in the Wabash River was subsequently quite low. The keelboats were held up by the sand and gravel bars at several locations. The dried beef in the keelboats got wet in the course of the protracted effort and spoiled in the intense heat.

The Long Knives were facing a logistical disaster. The beef on the boats was lost and eight days of other precious rations had been wasted while the army waited in Vincennes for the boats to arrive. The keelboats only delivered five days of flour rations.[30]

Despite the shortage of provisions, General Clark pressed his army to march up the Wabash river valley toward the Wea towns. Micajah probed ahead of the main body of the army with the other advance scouts, looking for Indian sign. Colonel Barnett's Lincoln County men mutinied and refused to go any farther when the army had progressed about eighty miles toward the Wea towns and was approaching the mouth of the Big Vermilion River.

General Clark wept as he pleaded with them to continue with his army.[31] He asked for only two more days so that they could reach the Wea towns at full strength. He agreed that they could leave then with his blessing if provisions had not been procured by that time.

The Lincoln County men were adamant and refused to go on. They began to shout, "Who's for home?" At first a few turned to go, but then more joined in, until most of them were gone.[32]

General Clark assembled Colonel Todd's loyal Fayette County officers and soldiers into a circle and asked who was willing to continue on with him and fight.[33] Micajah and a handful of other men stepped forward into the circle.[34]

The senior officers reviewed the situation carefully with General Clark. They regretfully concluded that they had an insufficient number of men to continue the campaign and decided to return to the O'Post. All remaining semblance of discipline in the remnants of General Clark's army broke down. Most of the remaining rank-and-file soldiers stopped obeying their commanders and left to find their own way back to the Falls of the Ohio.

General Clark remained in Vincennes in order to attempt to salvage some good from his failed Wabash Campaign. He placed Major Holder in charge of a small O'Post garrison of loyal Fayette County militia.[35]

Clark sent emissaries to the Miami Confederacy nations and their allies in October and invited them to treat for peace. He met with them near

Vincennes and through sheer force of his personality bluffed and persuaded them to accept a temporary peace and disband their army. He managed to conceal the fact that his own army had abandoned him. The chiefs agreed to meet and treat with him at Clarksville on November 20, 1786, for a permanent peace.[36]

The Shawanese had sent a body of four hundred chiefs and warriors to join their Miami allies against the Long Knife army.[37] The Miami had already agreed to the interim peace with General Clark and were disbanding by the time the Shawanese warriors arrived to join them.

General Clark proceeded to make his already difficult situation worse. Spain had unilaterally imposed a ban on American navigation on the Mississippi River from the Spanish territory in Missouri to the Gulf of Mexico. The Spanish seized a boat belonging to inhabitants of the Ohio River country in late 1786 as it neared Spanish territory on the Mississippi River.

General Clark retaliated by arresting and trying three Spanish citizens in Vincennes in a military court of his own creation on charges of illegally trading in American territory.[38] He also ordered the seizure of two Spanish vessels moored on the Wabash River at Vincennes.[39] A group of Kentucky citizens sent a petition to the governor of Virginia informing him of General Clark's unauthorized seizure of the Spanish vessels. The petitioners complained that he was levying recruits, nominating officers, and impressing provisions without any authority to do so.[40]

Virginia Governor Randolph issued a proclamation on February 28, 1787, "solemnly disavowing" General Clark's actions.[41] Congress enacted a resolution on April 24, 1787, directing the secretary of war to take immediate and efficient measures "for dispossessing a body of men who had, in a lawless and unauthorized manner, taken possession of Post Vincennes in defiance of the proclamation and authority of the United States."[42]

Secretary of War Henry Knox ordered recently promoted General Harmar to march to Vincennes and employ force if necessary to disperse Clark's Fayette County garrison.[43] General Harmar and six companies of regular soldiers dutifully marched from the Falls of the Ohio up the Buffalo Trace to Vincennes and drove Major John Holder and his garrison of Fayette County militiamen out of the town. The federal troops occupied the fort there from July 17 to 25, 1787.[44]

Congress and the state of Virginia narrowly averted a war with both Spain and France by taking these measures. This incident, coming quickly on the heels of allegations of alcoholism and his failed 1786 campaign against the Wabash Indians, effectively ended the public service career of George Rogers Clark.

Thirteen — Col. Benjamin Logan's Expedition

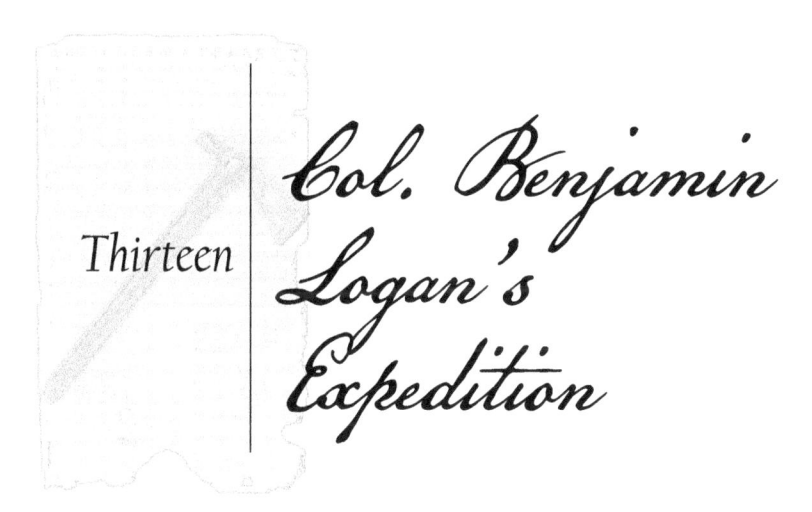

COLONEL BENJAMIN LOGAN'S ARMY OF EIGHT HUNDRED militia volunteers rendezvoused at Limestone on September 29, 1786, to prepare for the expedition against the Ohio Shawanese towns.[1] They crossed the Ohio River on September 30 and marched to the towns. They arrived at their destination at noon on October 6.[2]

The majority of the Shawanese warriors in the towns had departed a few days earlier for the Wabash River valley to support their Miami allies in the anticipated battle against General Clark, and had not yet returned. The Makujay chiefs who led the Shawanese peace faction, women and children, and a handful of warriors were all that remained in the Ohio towns.[3]

The Six Nations and British had called for a Grand Council in Wapatomica to restore unity among the northwestern nations after the disastrous results of the Treaty at the Mouth of the Greater Miami River. The council was hosted by Chief Moluntha.

The first delegations from the various nations had arrived at Wapatomica when the Long Knives attacked the Shawanese towns. Joseph Brant and almost all of the chiefs and warriors were out hunting near Wapatomica at the time of the attack and managed to escape without being detected.[4]

Colonel Logan's men first attacked Mackachack and Moluntha's Town. Chief Moluntha and his family were in Mackachack at the time, including his wife Lamatumque and her son.[5] Headwoman Coitcheleh, Nonhelema and her daughter Fanny, and Chief Wryneck's widow Tecumapease and their son, Spemica Lawba,[6] were also present, as was the late Chief Cornstalk's young son, Peter Cornstalk,[7] and Makujay Chiefs Aweecomy and Shade.

The Shawanese received a brief warning of the impending attack and were still scattering and fleeing into the forest when the Long Knives arrived. A small group of warriors quickly escorted the sacred bundle, sacred fire, and wampum belts to safety.

Gallant old Aweecomy and Shade and a handful of warriors put up a spirited resistance but were all killed. The Long Knife soldiers fell upon the defenseless old men, women, and children like wolves.[8]

The American Commissioners Plenipotentiary had given Moluntha a safe conduct pass at the Treaty at the Mouth of the Greater Miami. Moluntha picked up the pass at his cabin and calmly gathered his friends and family about him to wait for the Americans in front of the council house. They hung an American flag on the side of the council house. Nonhelema stood protectively at Moluntha's side with her hand on her tomahawk.[9]

Simon Kenton and the advance party of Logan's army rode up to the little group. Kenton placed Moluntha and his family in the custody of armed guards and sent for Colonel Logan.

Moluntha presented the safe conduct pass to Colonel Logan. Daniel Boone rode up, dismounted, and engaged in conversation with Moluntha. The old chief started a pipe of tobacco and passed it around the assembled officers and soldiers as scattered gunshots continued elsewhere in the town.

Lamatumque and her son were desperately trying to work their way through the village to the council house through the chaos of attacking soldiers and fleeing Shawanese. She darted out of the bark wegiwa in which she had initially taken refuge with her young son and dashed into a sturdier cabin next door, where a number of women and children were already hiding.

Lamatumque took charge of the group and directed that on her signal they should run across a clearing toward another cabin closer to the council house. She could see Moluntha and Nonhelema and other family members standing there.

The women and children burst from the cabin on Lamatumque's signal just as Colonel Thomas Kennedy rode up on his horse with his heavy saber drawn.[10] Colonel Kennedy wheeled his horse and slashed into the group of women and children with his saber, cutting down one after another. He partially decapitated one woman just below her brain case with a powerful stroke.

Kennedy then rode straight at Lamatumque and her son, drawing his saber back for a vicious cut. Lamatumque placed her son behind her and raised her hand to ward off the blow as Kennedy slashed at her head. She partially deflected the blow but three of her fingers were severed and sent flying through the air. Her skull was cracked by the glancing blow with a sickening, cracking sound.

Blood instantly spurted from her finger-stumps as she fell stunned to the ground, and blood poured from a deep gash in her head.[11] Her little boy bravely stood beside her and tried to help her to her feet. One of her friends ducked through an opening as Kennedy's horse spun around and half-dragged the semiconscious Lamatumque and her son across the clearing.

Other soldiers had observed Kennedy's cowardly acts and began tauntingly shouting at him, "Who hacked the squaws? Who hacked the squaws?" Kennedy withdrew to another part of the slaughter grounds and continued his blood sport.[12]

The women tended to Lamatumque's wounds, pressing clumps of buzzard's down against her finger stumps and head wound to stop the bleeding. The blood matted on one side of her hair. A searing pain pounded in her head and her hand with each beat of her heart, and she felt faint and nauseated from shock.

Major Hugh McGary walked up to the group of prisoners and their guards at the council house. McGary asked Moluntha if he had been at the Battle of the Lower Blue Licks. Moluntha understood very little English and did not understand McGary's question. He smiled and bobbed his head up and down affirmatively, but he had not been at the battle.

McGary exclaimed, "I'll give you Blue Lick's play!" He picked up Nonhelema's tomahawk. McGary first struck Moluntha's head with the poll of the axe and knocked him to his knees. He then buried the blade in the side of his skull, killing him instantly.[13] Moluntha convulsed briefly and lay still with the safe conduct pass still clutched in his hand. McGary quickly scalped him before the shocked bystanders. The last hope for peace died with Moluntha.[14]

Daniel Boone and the guards rushed forward and restrained McGary before he could harm anyone else. McGary venomously threatened to kill anyone who tried to prevent him from killing more Indians.[15] Colonel Logan placed McGary under arrest.

Logan's army marched on from Mackachack and Moluntha's Town to plunder and burn New Piqua, Wapatomica, Blue Jacket's Town, McKee's (Kispoko) Town, Pigeon Town, and Mingo Town. They killed ten chiefs and warriors and captured thirty-two prisoners.[16] The dead included Chiefs Moluntha, Aweecomy, and Shade.[17] Only three soldiers in Colonel Logan's army were killed.[18]

The Shawanese prisoners included Nonhelema and her daughter Fanny, Lamatumque and her son, Lamatumque's mother Coitcheleh, Cornstalk's widow Wasekakotha, Tecumapease, Spemica Lawba, young Peter Cornstalk, and a Frenchman, his wife and their two children. Colonel Logan sent a message to the surviving chiefs of the Shawanese inviting them to a prisoner exchange.[19]

Hugh McGary was tried in a court-martial on March 20, 1787, and was convicted of the murder of Moluntha. He was punished by one year of suspension from the militia.[20]

Fourteen | Prisoner Exchange at Limestone

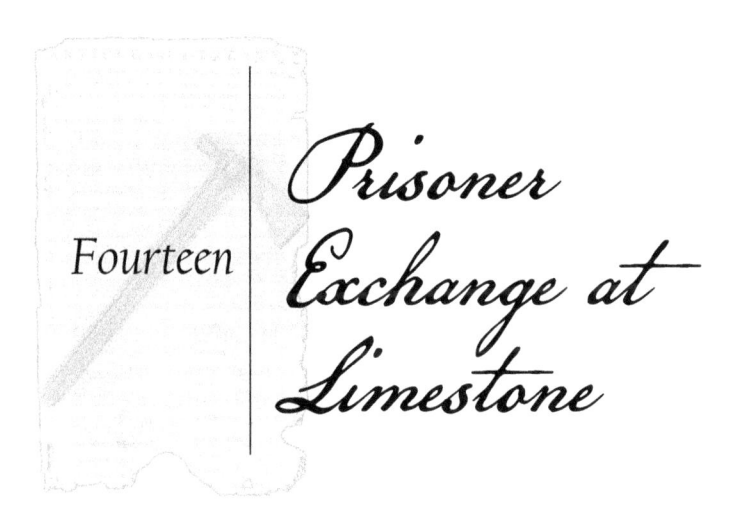

AT THE CONCLUSION OF GENERAL CLARK'S 1786 campaign, Micajah said farewell to the last of his companions on the long trek back from Vincennes. He unpacked and stored his gear in his Bourbon County cabin and retrieved his horse from Flanders and Jemima the following day.

He was heartsick when he learned from Flanders about the outcome of Colonel Logan's raid and rode off into the dusky evening at a full gallop. Daniel Boone was sitting on a puncheon stool by the front door of his house in Limestone when Micajah rode up and greeted him early the next day. He told Micajah what had happened after the prisoners were captured.

Colonel Logan had passed through Limestone on the return march to Kentucky and left the Shawanese prisoners in Daniel's custody. The prisoners stayed there for several days. Boone fed them and provided them with nineteen gallons of whisky. Lamatumque was severely injured, but was expected to live.[1]

The prisoners were removed to the District of Kentucky jail in Danville so that they would not be within easy reach of Shawanese rescue parties. They arrived there on October 21. Colonel Robert Patterson of Fayette County was placed in charge of the care of the prisoners, and John Crow was appointed to serve as their commissary.[2]

The Kentucky militia commanders looked to Daniel to follow up on the prisoner exchange that Colonel Logan had offered to the Shawanese. Daniel asked Micajah to assist him in the negotiation of the exchange, and Micajah agreed.

MICAJAH LEFT LIMESTONE EARLY THE NEXT MORNING and rode hard down the Lexington-Limestone Road through Bourbon County and Lexington. He was determined to see the prisoners to make sure that they were well cared for. He arrived at Danville two days later and received permission from Colonel Patterson to visit them.

Two soldiers guarded the door of the log jailhouse, which was covered by a large hanging buffalo hide. Micajah explained the purpose of his visit to the guards and stepped through the door.

There were no windows, so the jailhouse was dark inside even during the day. Fires in two fireplaces flickered and smoldered. Micajah could see a group of children quietly playing in a group near one of the fires as his eyes adjusted to the gloomly scene. The women were wrapped in blankets and huddled near the fires.

Micajah picked out Lamatumque sitting with her little boy next to one of the fires. He greeted her, and she looked up at him in dull surprise. Micajah squatted down next to her and warmed his hands. The remnant of a monstrous bruise was still evident on her upper forehead. Her hands trembled and her speech was slurred. She hid her maimed hand under her blanket.

Lamatumque told Micajah that the prisoners had been fed well, but they were all worried since they had no idea of what was going to happen to them.

Micajah slipped her a gift of a small packet of smoked buffalo tongue, and gave her son a small carving of a bear that he had made for him. Lamatumque smiled at him and thanked him as tears misted her eyes. She began to weep silently. Micajah awkwardly took his leave as his own eyes filled with tears, and resolved to help her.

MICAJAH SPENT THE NEXT COUPLE OF MONTHS hunting buffalo and deer and curing some of the meat. The personal property lists for 1787 for Fayette County confirmed that he lived alone. The only personal property listed under his name was a horse.[3]

Micajah returned to Limestone in early January of 1787. Daniel Boone opened the prisoner exchange negotiations by sending the captured

Prisoner Exchange at Limestone

Frenchman, his wife, and their two children to the Shawanese chiefs as a gesture of good faith. They carried an invitation to a prisoner exchange to be held at Limestone. Daniel directed the Frenchman to pass on his request that the Shawanese give up an important young prisoner named Robert Clark in their own gesture of good faith. Further exchanges would then follow.

Robert Clark was the son of the George Clark who had scouted for Colonel Bowman in 1778 and 1779. Young Clark had been captured in September of 1786 while plowing a cornfield near the new town of Washington, on the North Fork of the Licking River.[4]

Daniel hired Micajah and another man to serve as armed escorts for the Frenchman and his family.[5] They departed for the Shawanese towns on February 2, 1787, and arrived at the ruins of Mackachack without incident.

Captain Johnny had succeeded Moluntha as Principal Chief of the Shawanese Nation and greeted Micajah upon their arrival at Mackachack. He told Micajah that he was pleased to hear the good talk from their old friend Sheltowey (Daniel Boone). He said that he intended to send a response with a chief named Noamohouoh after meeting with the council.[6] Micajah thanked him and returned to Limestone.

It was a risky time to be viewed as a despised "Indian lover." Micajah kept a low profile but continued his efforts in earnest. Lamatumque had helped him return to his people, and he was obligated to do the same for her.

Indian raiders continued to attack the Kentucky settlements as the negotiations continued. A small war party from either the Miami or Shawanese Nation struck on the Lexington-Limestone Road near Micajah's cabin in February of 1787, and Tim Peyton was killed while riding up the road.[7]

Captain John Saunders's thirteen-year old daughter Betty Saunders was walking down the road at about the same time that Peyton was killed. Her parents had sent her to a neighbor's house to borrow a cup of sugar. She was tomahawked and scalped, and her mutilated body was left lying in the road. A militia pursuit party lost the trail of the raiders at the Upper Blue Licks.[8]

Chief Noamohouoh met with Daniel and Micajah at the mouth of Limestone Creek on March 4 to organize the prisoner exchange. Boone hired Micajah as an interpreter and provided lodging for him and Noamohouoh at his Limestone inn for the next twenty days.[9] He paid Micajah six pounds for his services.[10]

Noamohouoh stated that Captain Johnny wanted to exchange Robert Clark for two prisoners in an initial exchange and would deliver the rest of the prisoners at Limestone in one month.[11] He insisted that Lamatumque and her little son be released in the initial exchange of prisoners.

Boone sent a letter to Colonel Patterson at Danville on March 16 requesting that he release Lamatumque ("I flater myself you Will be of the Same opinion as the author's opinion and Send the Indian Woman With the bearer.")[12]

Colonel Patterson agreed and delivered Lamatumque, her little boy, and two other Shawanese prisoners to Limestone as Boone had requested. There they were exchanged for Robert Clark and two children.

Micajah walked up to Lamatumque and her son as they prepared to leave. Lamatumque took his hands and thanked him for helping again to arrange for her release from captivity with her son. She would be forever grateful. He asked when he would see her again. She smiled weakly and said that she would always consider him to be a true friend. She regretted that they had come to know each other in a time of war between their peoples when they could not enjoy their friendship.

Lamatumque and her son boarded an elm-bark canoe and crossed the Ohio River with Noamohouoh and a small Shawanese escort. Micajah watched until he could no longer see them, then turned away and rode home to his cabin.

The exchanges of prisoners continued as the year unfolded. Daniel paid another interpreter named Peter for his services for those exchanges. Captain Wolf and a party of seven other Shawanese arrived at Limestone on April 27 with seven more prisoners to trade for Coitcheleh and Nonhelema and their kin. Ten more white prisoners were released during a series of exchanges through May 17, 1787.[13]

The fighting continued through the year. Colonel Levi Todd assembled a company of 170 militiamen at Lexington and Washington in May and set off on a punitive expedition to Old Chalaakaatha and nearby Shawanese camps along the Scioto River and Paint Creek. They attacked two Indian camps near the north fork of Paint Creek.

Captain Spencer Records described the attack on the second camp:

> They rode up to the camp, alarmed the dogs; the men all made their escape, so that they only took three

Prisoner Exchange at Limestone

squaws prisoner. Flanders Callaway shot an old squaw which he should not have done. I saw her lying on her face with her back naked . . . [14]

On August 10, Captain Johnny and a party of about sixty Shawanese chiefs and warriors arrived on the shores of the Ohio River opposite Limestone, accompanied by their white prisoners.[15] They set up a camp and settled in for the duration of the negotiations. Captain Snake, Captain Wolf, Blue Jacket, Manemsecho (Nianimsica?), Lathenfecho, and Pemenaway were among the chiefs who were present.[16] Daniel Boone sent two young Indian prisoners over to the Shawanese camp escorted by his son Daniel Morgan Boone as a gesture of good faith.

Captain Johnny made a speech to Colonel Logan on August 20, 1787:

> . . . If we want peace we shall have peace, to which we are agreed, to come back to where our old town was burnt and live like brothers. These Indians who are for war, they will be always out on the Wabash, and we will make a distinction between them and ourselves, to let our brother the big knife know we are really for peace. Here will be five little towns of us that will be for peace, and will trade with our brother big knife, and use all industry we can, to get as many prisoners as possible . . .

Colonel Logan answered:

> . . . Brothers, there are a great many designing men in this country and some may encourage you to go to war, because they know if you do, that you will be driven out of the country that you now inhabit, and then they can live where you now live, and laugh to think how they have fooled you. This will surely be the case, and it is you and us that must fight the battle . . . I have no more to say to you, only advise you to

go home and live at peace, and I will assure you no army will march against you from Kentucky . . . .[17]

The Long Knives decided to keep ten of the prisoners in Danville for future negotiation leverage, including Wasekakotha and her thirteen-year old son Peter Cornstalk. Thomas Ball loaded the rest of the Shawanese prisoners into a wagon on August 12 for the long ride to Limestone, and delivered them to Daniel Boone on August 24.

A large number of Virginians had gathered at Limestone to witness the exchange. Colonel Benjamin Logan was there, as were the families of the captives, Simon Kenton and a number of rough frontiersmen and rowdies.

The Shawanese sent a messenger to the Long Knives, inviting them to cross the Ohio River with their prisoners. Daniel Boone and the other Virginians ferried across and met the Shawanese at a site near the river. The exchange began after brief speeches by the leaders of both sides. There were many emotional scenes as the prisoners rejoined their families.

Daniel Boone invited the Shawanese back over the river to his Limestone inn for a feast when the prisoner exchange was completed, and the Shawanese accepted. Puncheon tables were set up and kegs of whisky were opened. Two cows were slaughtered and roasted on spits over large outdoor cooking fires. Spirits ran high as old friendships were renewed.

But convivial feelings were not shared by all. Captain Calvin said that he recognized a horse in the possession of one of the Shawanese that had been stolen from a needy widow named Mrs. McGuiness. He threatened to take it away by force if necessary. Daniel Boone and Simon Kenton saw trouble brewing, so they bought the mare from the Indian owner for a keg of whisky, and gave it to Captain Calvin to return to the widow.

Several of the Shawanese warriors in attendance were offended by Captain Calvin's confrontational behavior. They painted their faces black and stalked menacingly through the crowd. An old warrior began to beat a rhythm with a stick on a pair of old saddlebags, and the painted warriors began to dance the war dance.[18]

Friendly conversations between the Long Knives and Shawanese tapered off, and individuals drifted back to stand with their respective peo-

Prisoner Exchange at Limestone 259

ples. Daniel and Captain Johnny agreed that it was time to end the festivities before there was real trouble. They shook hands, and the Shawanese recrossed the river and returned to Ohio.

A TOTAL OF 1,200 SHAWANESE MEN, WOMEN and children remained in Ohio. Frenchman Louis Lorimier convinced a large contingent of them to move west with him and join their tribesmen already living in Spanish Louisiana. They settled in two new villages on Apple Creek, about eighteen miles above Cape Girardeau on the west bank of the Mississippi River.

The new Shawanese towns were located just to the north of the new expatriate American settlement of New Madrid. This was on the west bank of the Mississippi River a few miles below the mouth of the Ohio River. New Madrid had been founded by former American Indian Agent George Morgan, who left the United States in disgust because of its inhumane treatment of the Indian nations.[19]

The majority of the remaining Ohio Shawanese elected to stay in the Ohio Country to make a stand. They abandoned their towns on the Greater Miami River and Mad River and moved farther north to the shores of the Maumee River and its tributaries. There they would be outside the boundaries of the Treaty at the Mouth of the Greater Miami and would be closer to their British and Miami friends.

The Shawanese established several new towns near the Maumee. The Chalaakaatha division, led by Nenessica (Black Beard), established a town three miles east of the Miami capital of Kckionga at the headwaters of the Maumee River. Their town was called New Chillicothe by the whites. Captain Snake, Captain Johnny, and Blue Jacket each established their own towns near the confluence of the Auglaize River and the Maumee River.[20]

The Shawanese war chiefs defied the efforts of Captain Johnny and the surviving Makujay leaders to negotiate a peaceful resolution of the conflict. They began to take command of their nation's affairs in preparation for military action to block the impending Long Knife invasion of Ohio.

The war chiefs put their women, children, and old men behind their backs and faced their enemy. Lamatumque and the surviving Makujay head

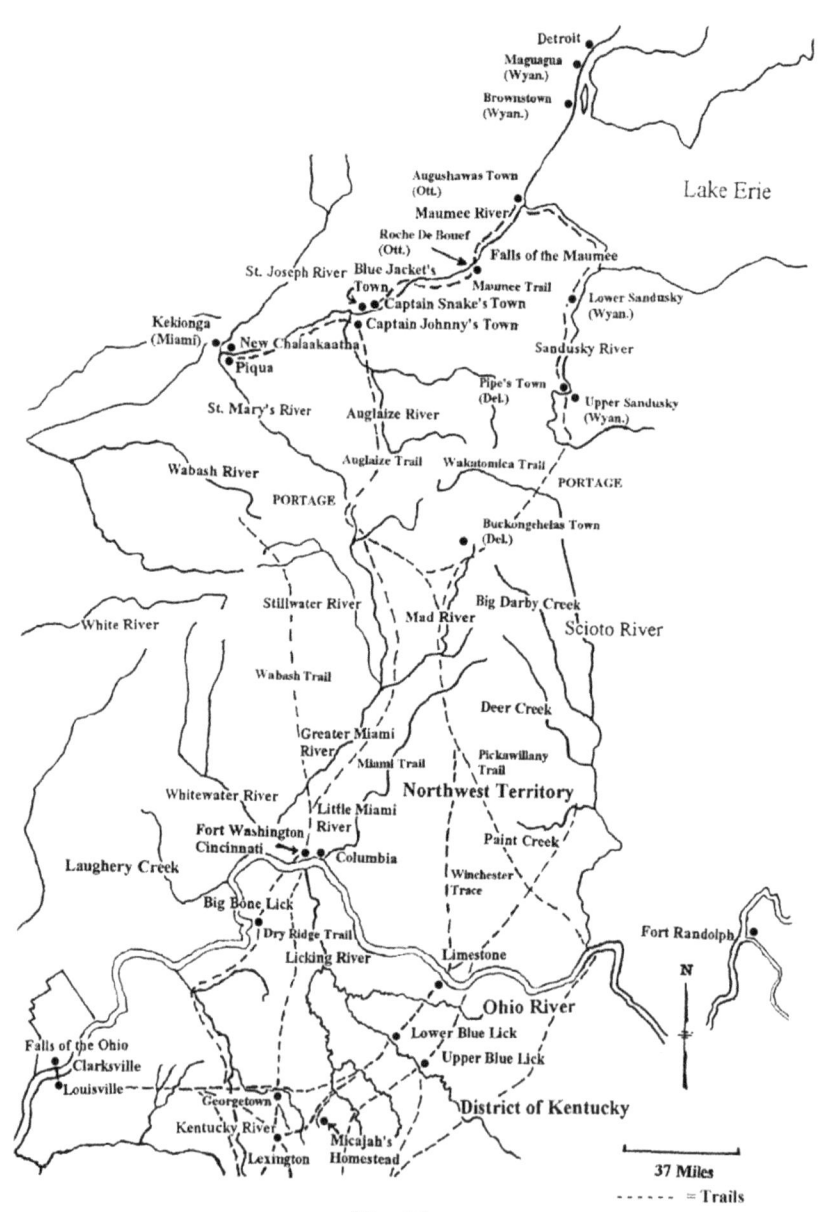

Map 19
Shawanese Towns of Ohio in 1787-1791

women disappeared from the historical record behind the protective shield of their nation's defenders.

Captain Snake and a young war chief who had resurrected the honored name of Black Fish competed for the role of Principal War Chief of the Shawanese.[21] Blue Jacket's star rose rapidly as he led successful raiding parties into Kentucky and along the Ohio River.

The military leaders of the Ohio Shawanese strengthened their alliances with the other northwestern Indian nations as they retrenched. Their future preservation depended upon the support of the powerful Miami Nation and Confederacy under the leadership of Chiefs Pacanne, Little Turtle, and Le Gris (Little Turtle's brother-in-law).[22]

Fifteen

The Northwest Ordinance & Ensuing Indian War

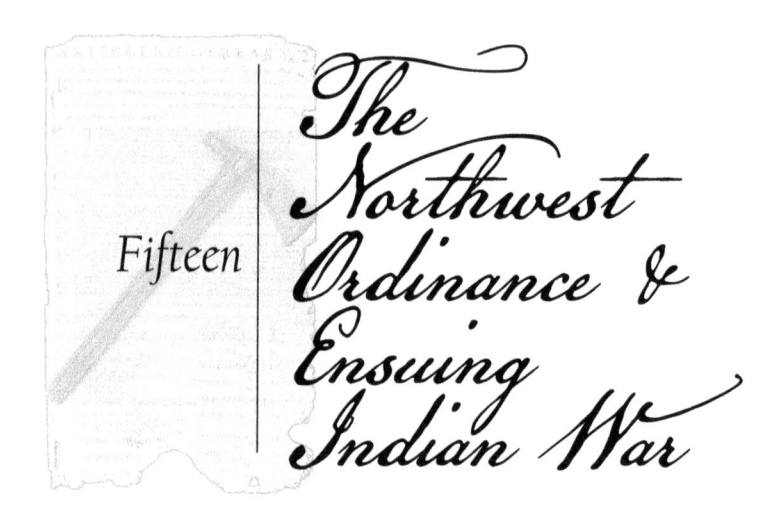

The Northwest Ordinance of 1787

HENRY LEE DECLARED ON THE FLOOR OF Congress that General George Rogers Clark's campaign into the Northwest in 1786 had been justified by "the imbecilities of the federal government." He argued that it was "indispensably necessary immediately" to extend civil government into the Northwest Territory.[1]

Two great European powers were well positioned to take possession of the territory if the United States should prove unable to govern and hold it. Spain possessed the massive Louisiana Territory and continued to block navigation on the Mississippi River. Great Britain still ruled Canada and maintained illegal military posts at Detroit, Niagara, and Mackinac.

Congress enacted the Northwest Ordinance on July 13, 1787, just before General Harmar and his troops drove Major John Holder and the rest of General Clark's men out of Vincennes and occupied the town.[2] The ordinance provided that the Northwest Territory would be governed as a single territory until further territorial subdivisions were established. It provided for the appointment of a governor for a term of three years, an elected General Assembly, and a judicial system whose judges were empowered to adjudicate disputes.

A GRAND COUNCIL OF THE RENEWED INDIAN Confederacy was held between November 28 and December 18, 1786, under the general leadership and direction of Joseph Brant. The Iroquois Confederacy, Lake Confederacy,

Shawanese, Wyandot, Delaware, Miami Confederacy, and Cherokee nations reviewed their failures in negotiating the three "treaties of conquest" with the Americans and renewed their pledge to work as a united body in future negotiations.[3] The Indian Confederacy endorsed and submitted a petition to Congress on December 18, 1786, proposing to meet again with the United States to renegotiate a comprehensive treaty.[4]

Former General Arthur St. Clair was selected by Congress to serve as governor of the Northwest Territory on October 5, 1787.[5] Congress directed him to initiate the negotiation of a new general treaty with as many of the Indian nations in the Northwest Territory as possible.[6] The new treaty would supersede the three failed "treaties of conquest."

Major land development enterprises had already begun surveying and settling north of the Ohio River without waiting for the outcome of negotiations with the Indian nations. A large group of Ohio Company settlers founded the town of Marietta next to Fort Harmar. Governor St. Clair arrived at Marietta in July of 1788 and established the seat of government for the Northwest Territory there.

Northwest Territory Justice John Cleves Symmes and his associates purchased a one million-acre tract of Ohio land from the federal government on October 15, 1788. The huge tract was located between the Greater Miami River and Little Miami River and was commonly called "the Miami Purchase."[7]

Colonel Robert Patterson of Lexington, Kentucky, and John Filson cut a new road from Lexington to the mouth of the Licking River in the late summer of 1788. They surveyed lots for a new town site on the north shore across the Ohio River from the mouth of the Licking River and named it "Losantiville."

Shawanese militants continued their aggressive opposition to the expanding white settlements to the north and south of the river as preparations for general treaty negotiations inched forward. Colonel Harmar's troops counted 631 boats carrying a total of 12,205 passengers passing by Fort Harmar between October 10, 1786, and June 15, 1788. The population of Kentucky soared to 62,000 people in 1788.[8]

A war party of a hundred Shawanese, Cherokee, and Mingo warriors led by Captain Snake, Nenessica, and Kakinathucca attacked five flatboats on March 21, 1788, just above the mouth of the Greater Miami River. The war party killed several travelers and captured several more.[9] Micajah Callaway's declaration in support of his Revolutionary War pension application indicates that he served as a scout in defense of the Kentucky settlements through the late 1780s and into the early 1790s.[10] Although no specific records of his service as a scout during this time period have been located, there are records of many incidents of conflict with the Shawanese. It is highly probable that Micajah was involved in some of them.

The Treaty of Fort Harmar and the Miami Purchase

GOVERNOR ST. CLAIR SENT INVITATIONS TO THE Indian Confederacy nations to attend a council at the Falls of the Muskingum River to renegotiate a treaty with the United States in July of 1788. Joseph Brant initially played a leading role in the negotiations. Brant and the Iroquois, the Wyandot Nation, and the Three Fires (Ottawa, Pottawatomie, and Chippewa) supported cession of lands north of the Ohio River and east of the Muskingum River. This included Fort Harmar and other lands that the Ohio Company were already settling and did not include any Shawanese or Miami lands.

The Shawanese and Miami Confederacy insisted that the Ohio River boundary established in the 1768 Treaty of Fort Stanwix be reaffirmed as the boundary in any treaty with the Americans. They were prepared to declare for war if necessary to defend their position.[11]

Joseph Brant and his supporters were unable to persuade the militants to accept the Muskingum boundary. Brant and the Six Nations gracefully relinquished their traditional leadership of the Indian Confederacy to the Shawanese and Delaware Nations and Miami Confederacy in the fall of 1788.[12]

Governor St. Clair subsequently entered into two treaties: one with with unauthorized representatives of the Six Nations and a second with the Wyandot, Delaware, Ottawa, Chippewa, Pottawatomie, and Sauk Nations, on January 9, 1789. The 1785 Treaty of Fort McIntosh boundary was adopted with little change. The Shawanese Nation and Miami Confederacy did not attend the negotiations. Moravian missionary John Heckewelder later asserted in 1792 that he could not find "the name of even one Great Chief" amid the signatories of the treaty.[13]

The American Eagle

WHEN THE TREATY NEGOTIATIONS WERE CONCLUDED, JUDGE Symmes established the town of Northbend on the north shore of the Ohio River four miles above the mouth of the Greater Miami, and settled there with his family.[14]

Nenessica (Black Beard) and a Shawanese delegation visited Judge Symmes at Northbend in late February, accompanied by an interpreter named George (possibly George Girty). Nenessica asked if Symmes had been sent by the "Thirteen Fires." Symmes replied that he had indeed been sent by them and showed Nenessica the federal seal on his commission that displayed an American Eagle.

Nenessica responded:

> That he could not perceive any intimations of peace from the attitude the Eagle was in; having her wings spread as in flight; when folding of the wings denoted rest and peace. That he could not understand how the branch of a tree could be considered as a pacific emblem, for rods designed for correction were always taken from the boughs of trees. That to him the Eagle appeared from her bearing a large whip in one claw, and such a number of arrows in the other, and in full career of flight, to be wholly bent on war & mischief.[15]

Nenessica exchanged several hundred furs and skins for nearly all of the spun cloth that Symmes had brought with him. He and his entourage departed on apparently good terms after a stay of four weeks. Judge Symmes later opined that the true purpose of Nenessica's visit had been to gather intelligence concerning the strength and disposition of the Americans settling the new communities to the north of the river.

The United States of America reformed and strengthened its national government as their relationship with the northwestern Indian nations crumbled. A new Constitution for the United States was ratified in January of 1789 which established a powerful new executive position called

"President of the United States." The president was empowered to execute the laws enacted by Congress and enter into treaties with other nations, including the Indian nations. The president was also the commander-in-chief of the armed forces of the United States.

Congress ordered national elections to be held in January of 1789. George Washington was elected and inaugurated into office in New York City on April 30, 1789, as the first American president.

Washington was the ultimate Virginian. He and his Virginia associates had dedicated their lives to achieving their vision of a vast American continental empire stretching west to the Pacific Ocean and perhaps beyond. To the Indians he was a proven leader and a great warrior who had conquered the powerful armies of the king of Great Britain in battle. But this steely Long Knife leader was not a friend of the Indian nations; he saw them as a potential threat to the future of the American empire.

The militant war chiefs and warriors of the Shawanese Nation consolidated their own power as the new leaders of the Indian Confederacy as George Washington rose to power. Their loyal Miami Confederacy, Mingo friends and War Chief Buckongahelas' Delaware warriors stood firmly with them.

The Shawanese Nation was well-equipped for its new leadership role. It had made many useful contacts among the Indian nations to the east of the Mississippi River during its years of wandering and fighting. The Shawanese set about strengthening the Indian Confederacy in preparation for the final defense of their homelands. In a June 15, 1789, report, Secretary of War Henry Knox warned President Washington that the outbreak of general hostilities with the northwestern Indian nations in the Northwest Territory was imminent. The Indian nations could muster up to two thousand warriors, and Secretary Knox estimated that it would take a professional army of two thousand five hundred soldiers to subdue them by force. The United States only had six hundred troops quartered in the territory.

Judge Symmes confirmed the growing threat. He reported to Congressman Dayton that Isaac Freeman had arrived in Northbend with an alarming report that the Miami and Shawanese Nations and their Delaware allies were engaged in major preparations for war. Freeman had observed five hundred pounds of gunpowder and lead and a hundred muskets being delivered by the British to Blue Jacket's home. A prisoner told Freeman that the

The Northwest Ordinance & Ensuing Indian War

Indians planned to drive the settlers out of Ohio.[16]

General Harmar initiated the construction of a massive new federal fort named Fort Washington next to the new community of Losantiville in June of 1789. He moved four companies of infantry and one company of artillery from Fort Harmar to the new fort. Timbers from flatboats and keelboats abandoned at Limestone were used in its construction.

Governor St. Clair relocated the seat of the Northwest Territory government from Marietta to Fort Washington on January 1, 1790. He also persuaded the residents of Losantiville to change the name of the village to Cincinnati in honor of the Roman consul and dictator Cincinattus.[17]

Several additional new stations were founded on the Miami Purchase in late 1789 and early 1790. The new stations included Dunlap's Station, twelve miles up the Greater Miami River; Ludlow's Station on Mill Creek, five miles north of Cincinnati; and Covalt's Station on the Little Miami River, nine miles north of Columbia.

The Shawanese and their allies intensified their raids on Ohio River boat traffic through 1789. There were many casualties among the occupants of the boats.

The citizens of Kentucky had reached the point where they had absorbed as much punishment as they cared to take from the incessant Miami and Shawanese raids over the previous five years. Large volunteer militia forces were mustered and began retaliatory raids into the Wabash Country in 1789.

Governor St. Clair was powerless to control or stop the Kentucky raiders. He wrote to President Washington on September 14, 1789, noting that the Kentuckians were retaliating "without attending precisely to the nations from which the injuries are received." The Kentucky raiders drove the neutral nations into the arms of the Shawanese, Miami, Delaware, and Mingo militants, and the conflict began escalating.[18]

On July 7, 1790, Judge Harry Innes sent the following estimates of the damage caused by Indian depredations in the District of Kentucky between 1783 and 1790 to Secretary Knox:

> I can venture to say that above fifteen hundred souls have been killed and taken in the district and migrating to it; that upwards of twenty thousand horses

> have been taken and carried off, and other property, such as money, merchandise, household goods, and wearing apparel have been carried off and destroyed ... to at least fifteen hundred dollars.

Secretary Knox later incorporated these figures into an informational broadside on the "Causes of the Indian War" which was circulated to the general public at the request of President Washington.[19]

The Defeats of General Josiah Harmar and General Arthur St. Clair

CHIEF BLUE JACKET ASCENDED TO THE RANK of Principal War Chief of the Shawanese Nation over old Captain Snake after the death of young Chief Blackfish in 1790.[20] Blue Jacket's half-brother Red Pole had emerged as one of the senior Shawanese Civil Chiefs in the Makujay division. The half-brothers worked closely together and formed a very effective team.

Blue Jacket invited American envoys to his house to confer. He told the Americans:

> ... the Shawanese nation was in doubt of the sincerity of the Big Knives, so called, having been already deceived by them . . . Moreover, that some other nations were apprehending that offers of peace would, may be, tend to take away, by degrees, their lands, and would serve them as they did before: a certain proof that they intend to encroach on our lands, is their new settlement on the Ohio. If they don't keep this side (of the Ohio) clear, it will never be a proper reconcilement with the nations Shawanese, Iroquois, Wyandots, and perhaps many others.[21]

Governor St. Clair, in consultation with General Harmar, concluded that there could be no prospects for peace and decided to send a strong expedition against the Indians. General Harmar and the Kentuckians assembled a force of 1,133 militia and 320 regular federal soldiers at Fort Washington to march on the Indian towns.[22]

The northwestern Indian nations chose Chiefs Blue Jacket and Little Turtle to lead their combined forces against the Americans. Kekionga and the Shawanese Towns were abandoned and burned in anticipation of the American invasion.

The American expeditionary force set out from Fort Washington on September 30, 1790. General Harmar sent a six hundred-man advance detachment under Colonel Hardin to attack and destroy Kekionga, but Hardin found Kekionga burning upon his arrival. He nonetheless took possession of the town and was soon joined by the remainder of General Harmar's forces.

On October 14, General Harmar divided his force and sent a detachment commanded by Colonel Hardin to attack a group of Indians fifteen miles to the west of Kekionga. The Indian warriors ambushed and unleashed a shower of arrows on Colonel Hardin's detachment and then attacked with their tomahawks and scalping knives. The Americans were routed with a loss of nearly one hundred lives.[23]

General Harmar reformed his forces and destroyed what was left of Kekionga, nearby New Chalaakaatha, and the other Miami Towns. He then began the return march to Fort Washington on the morning of October 21. He divided his forces again as his troops marched south, and sent a detachment of over three hundred men back to Kekionga to attack any Indians who may have gathered there after the American departure.

The Indians again concentrated their forces, and destroyed the isolated detachment in a brilliant display of military tactics. Eighty more soldiers were killed by bows and arrows, tomahawks, and knives. The surviving American army panicked and fled in disarray back to Fort Washington. Their abandoned supplies were quickly appropriated by the Indians.[24]

Americans living in the Northwest Territory and Kentucky were shocked and frightened by General Harmar's defeat. All of the northwestern Indian nations enthusiastically pledged their full support for a general war against the Americans. Blue Jacket played upon the Indian victory to encourage the British to provide more assistance.[25]

Indian raids upon the new American settlements in the Ohio Territory intensified after General Harmar's Defeat. Night raiders stalked through Cincinnati up to the walls of Fort Washington. Deaths were reported on a daily basis, but the settlers grimly held their ground in their fortified communities and refused to abandon them.[26]

Shawanese raids on boat traffic on the Ohio River intensified. The Jacob Greathouse boat party was captured and brutally massacred. The warriors apparently recognized Greathouse as the killer and mutilator of Mingo Chief Logan's sister seventeen years earlier. Greathouse was disemboweled and forced to walk and wrap his small intestine around a sapling until he expired.[27]

Governor St. Clair was commissioned a major general in the United States Army on March 14, 1791, and took command of preparations for a second major American expedition against the Indian Confederacy.[28] Major General Richard Butler was selected to be second-in-command of the federal army. President Washington personally warned General St. Clair to be very careful to avoid a surprise attack by the Indians.

Micajah apparently made the decision to return to "old" Virginia to regroup and reassess his life as preparations for General St. Clair's campaign progressed.[29] On September 16, 1791, he sold his four hundred acres on the Houston fork to his brother John for five hundred pounds,[30] and relocated to Amherst County, Virginia.[31] Micajah's older brother Dudley owned property there and it appears likely that Micajah lived with him for a brief period of time upon his arrival.[32]

General St. Clair assembled an army of 2,300 soldiers at Fort Washington. The army was comprised of a few hundred American regular soldiers with the balance made up of Kentucky militia volunteers. A huge amount of equipment was assembled at Fort Washington, including eight cannon and a large quantity of munitions.[33]

The Americans planned to construct a chain of forts linked by wagon roads into the heart of the confederacy homelands. The first in the chain was built on the banks of the Greater Miami River some twenty miles to the north of Fort Washington and was named Fort Hamilton. Advanced parties stockpiled provisions there.

The main body of the army departed from Fort Washington on October 4 and marched north to occupy the new fort. The second fort in the chain, Fort Jefferson, was constructed forty-four miles to the north of Fort Hamilton and occupied on October 13. The army left Fort Jefferson on October 24, marched an additional six miles, and camped at the current location of Greenville, Ohio, remaining there for about a week.

The Indian Confederacy prepared to meet General St. Clair's army. Over a thousand Shawanese, Miami, Delaware, Mingo, Cherokee, Wyandot, Ojibway, Ottawa, and Pottawatomie warriors assembled at Kekionga.

Blue Jacket and Little Turtle were chosen as the joint commanders. It is not clear whether one of them was ranked higher than the other; however, the weight of evidence supports the conclusion that Blue Jacket was the ultimate commander.[34] Little Turtle placed Miami adoptee William Wells in charge of a special unit of three hundred sharpshooting warriors equipped with rifles.[35]

Oliver M. Spencer, an Indian captive, described Blue Jacket's appearance around this time:

> . . . he was dressed in a scarlet frock coat, richly laced with gold, and confined around his waste with a party-colored sash, and in red leggings and moccasins ornamented in the highest style of Indian fashion. On his shoulders he wore a pair of gold epaulets, and on his arms broad silver bracelets, while from his neck hung a massive silver gorget and a large medallion of His Majesty, George III.[36]

On October 30, General St. Clair's army marched on from their weeklong encampment for seven more miles. One hundred fifty Kentucky militiamen deserted on October 31 and threatened to plunder the supply trains moving up from the rear. A regiment of three hundred regular troops was dispatched to protect the provisions from the turncoat militia. This reduced the main body of the army to fourteen hundred men.[37]

The army marched on, halting on November 3 on the east bank of the Wabash River near the Ohio/Indiana boundary. Kentucky scouts observed increasing numbers of Indians in the area, and Indian scouts in turn reported back to their own leaders that they had located the enemy.

St. Clair's army set up their encampment on the east bank of the river.

The troops were exhausted and cold after marching through ice and snow. Some of the officers anticipated an attack in the morning but General St. Clair did not heed their warnings. The cannon were set up in two batteries, and militia sentries were posted around the perimeter of the camp. The officers and men slept heavily that night.

The Indian army encamped for the night about a mile from the Long Knife camp. Blue Jacket assembled his warriors for a fire-light speech:

> Our fathers used to do as we now do. Our tribe used to fight other tribes. They could trust to their own strength and their numbers. But in this conflict we have no such reliance. Our power and our numbers bear no comparison to those of our enemy, and we can do nothing unless assisted by our Great Father above. I pray now,' continued Blue Jacket, raising his eyes to the heaven, 'that he will be with us tonight, and' (it was now snowing) 'that tomorrow he will cause the sun to shine out clear upon us, and we will take it as a token of good, and we shall conquer.'[38]

The Indian army awakened an hour before dawn on November 4, 1791. The warriors stripped down to their breechcloths and painted their faces, and readied their weapons for battle.

Blue Jacket set off toward the Long Knife camp at the head of the army dressed in his scarlet military jacket while singing a sacred war song. The warriors quietly encircled the Long Knife camp and waited for the signal to attack.[39]

The attack began in the pre-dawn twilight with the eerie keening sound of the scalp halloo. The warriors first attacked the camp of the Kentucky militia advance guard with a heavy barrage of musket fire. The militia panicked at the sound of these first shots and retreated pell-mell into the main camp, pursued by a large party of painted warriors. The militiamen ran through two ranks of regular soldiers only to find that the warriors had encircled the entire camp, thus cutting off any means of escape.

The warriors ceased the scalp halloo and silently advanced tree-to-tree

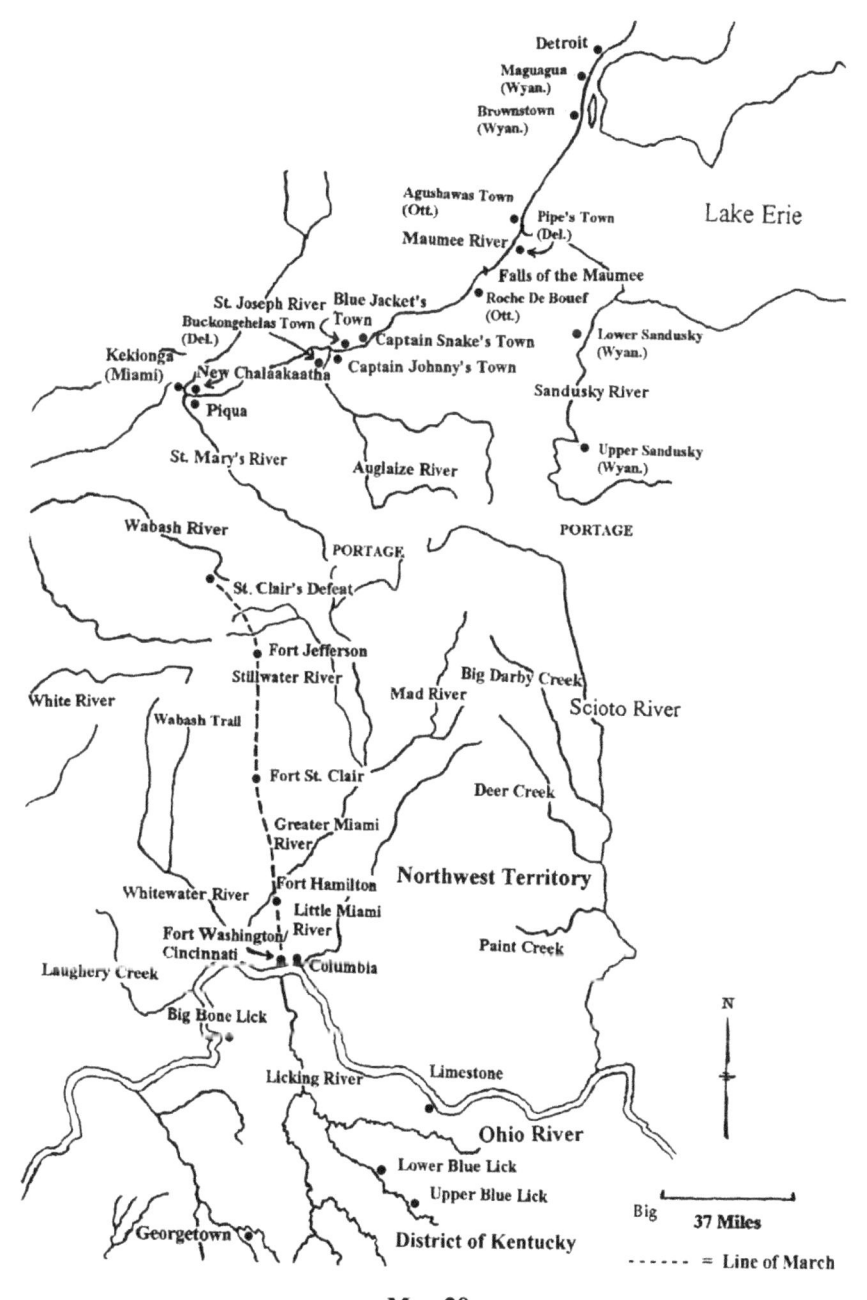

The Northwest Ordinance & Ensuing Indian War 273

Map 20
General Arthur St. Clair's Defeat

firing their guns and arrows as they tightened the circle. They poured a tremendous volume of musket and rifle fire and arrows into the camp of the now-trapped soldiers, and the screams and moans of the wounded and dying soon filled the air.

The American artillerymen ran to their batteries and desperately loaded their cannon. A hot volley of artillery fire drove the warriors back. Blue Jacket rallied them to press on in a renewed wave of assaults. William Wells and his sharpshooting Miami riflemen opened fire and decimated the ranks of the officers and artillerymen.[40] All but one of the American officers was killed, and the artillery was silenced within an hour and a half. Two horses were shot from under General St. Clair.

St. Clair ordered Colonel Darke and his division of regular soldiers to charge with bayonets in an attempt to break the encirclement. The warriors faded back into the trees before the advance, only to return fire when the American charge slowed. Lieutenant Ebenezer Denny later reported, "They seemed not to fear anything we could do. They could skip out of reach of the bayonet and return as they pleased. They were visible only when raised by a charge."[41] The Americans fell back.

Wyandot and Mingo warriors broke through into the American camp during Colonel Darke's sortie and weighed in with tomahawks and scalping knives. General Butler's men and Darke's returning division drove them back in fierce hand-to-hand combat.

General Butler was severely wounded by musket fire and fell from his horse. He staggered to a tree and continued loading and firing his pistols as he leaned against it.[42] He died on the battlefield from a tomahawk blow.

The Indians pressed their attack again and were repulsed by another counterattack with bayonets, but this American counterattack was weaker than the one before. The fight continued for three more hours until nearly all of the officers and half of the American troops had been killed. Confusion and chaos spread among the surviving soldiers as Indian warriors swarmed into the camp with tomahawks and scalping knives. The warriors cut them down without mercy.

General St. Clair ordered the able survivors to muster for a concerted effort to break out of the death trap. He directed a final desperate charge on the point of the encirclement closest to the road back to Fort Jefferson. The soldiers charged, and the warriors fell back before them. The frantic survivors flooded through the gap and fled from the field of battle down the road to Fort Jefferson. The Indians warriors harassed their rear for three or four miles before finally giving up the chase.

General St. Clair was among the survivors that reached Fort Jefferson. The Indians remained at the scene of slaughter, taking scalps, collecting plunder, and leaving the bodies to rot in the forest. They celebrated with war dances and dutifully performed the post-battle purification rituals required by their religion.

The defeat of General St. Clair and his army was the single greatest Indian victory over the armed forces of the United States in American history. Over seven hundred Americans were killed, and eight cannon were captured and hidden in the forest.

The Americans had been crushed and humiliated. It was unequivocally clear that the Indian Confederacy had evolved to a higher level of military capability. The numbers of American battlefield casualties in the Indian Wars were now being measured by the hundreds instead of dozens. An American major general had been killed on the battlefield. And the worst for the Americans might well lie ahead as the Indian Confederacy now possessed heavy artillery.

Great Britain and Spain would perceive General St. Clair's disastrous defeat as a sign of American weakness. This would encourage them to engage in intrigue and mischief on the western frontier and perhaps endeavor to wrest the Northwest Territory from the United States by force. The credibility of the United States of America and the future of the Northwest Territory hung in the balance as the new nation faced its first national emergency.

President Washington, Secretary Knox and their advisors embarked on an urgent search for a new commander for the American armed forces. President Washington selected one of the most disciplined and aggressive of his former senior officers in the War for Independence: General "Mad Anthony" Wayne. Wayne was commissioned a major general in April of 1792 and replaced Arthur St. Clair as the commander of the western American forces.

Congress authorized and appropriated funding for the creation of an army of 2,500 regular soldiers to be named the Legion of the United States. General Wayne immediately departed for Fort Pitt to assemble and train his new army. The Legion of the United States was the true beginning and foundation of the permanent standing army of the United States of America.

Sixteen | Battle of Fallen Timbers

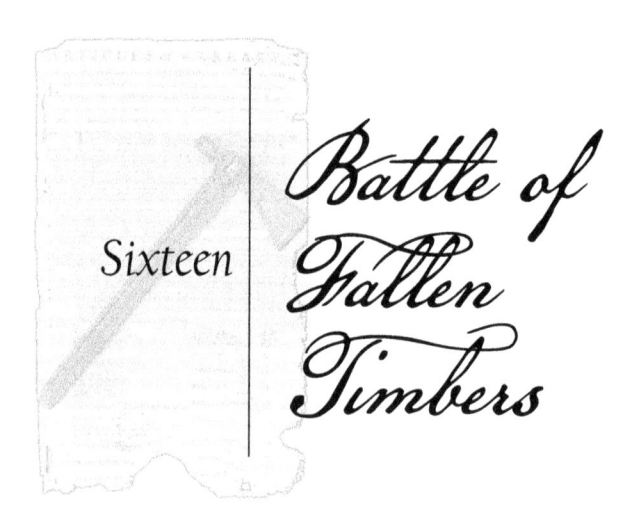

General Anthony Wayne's Campaign and the Battle of Fallen Timbers (1793-1794)

Prelude to Battle

THE MIAMI, SHAWANESE, AND DELAWARE NATIONS ABANDONED the Miami Towns in early 1792 in anticipation of American retaliation for General St. Clair's defeat. Many members of the Miami Confederacy nations moved farther west into the Wabash River valley. The Shawanese, Delaware, and remainder of the Miami Nations consolidated near the mouth of the Auglaize River on the Maumee River at a location called "the Grand Glaize."[1] The Ohio Indian nations would be able to muster a larger army on shorter notice by concentrating their numbers in a smaller area, since eight hundred warriors lived within ten or fifteen miles of the Grand Glaize and could be assembled in a few hours. Several hundred additional Wyandot and Ottawa warriors were available farther down the Maumee River and near Detroit.[2]

Blue Jacket's new town was located on the north side of the Maumee River one mile below the mouth of the Auglaize River in July of 1792. Captain Snake's Town was situated eight miles downstream from Blue Jacket's Town. Miami Chief Little Turtle's town was a short distance up Bean Creek, a tributary of the Maumee River entering it from the north about two miles above the mouth of the Auglaize River. Delaware War Chief Buckongahelas'

Battle of Fallen Timbers

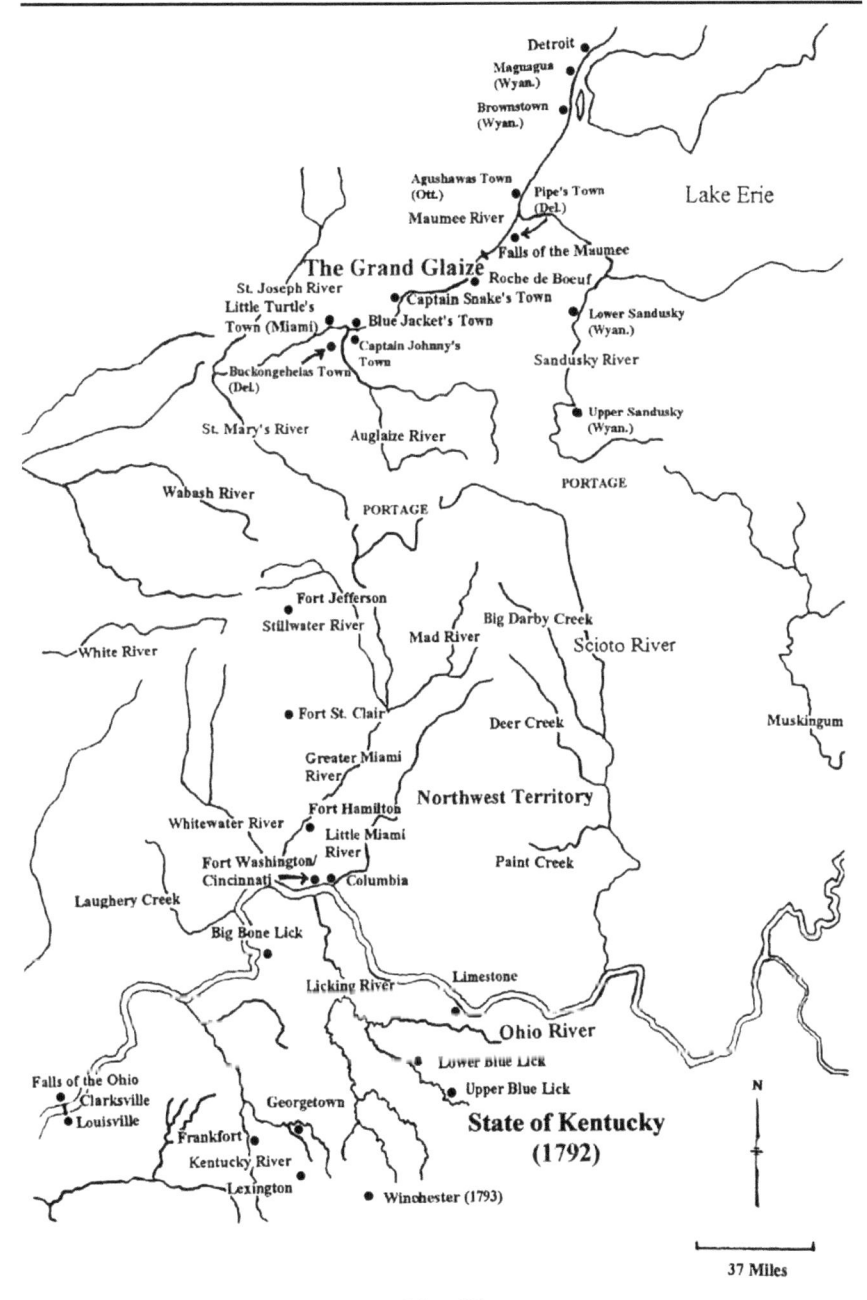

Map 21
Shawanese Towns of Ohio: The Grand Glaize in 1792

Town was sited on the west bank of the Auglaize River across from Captain Johnny's Town, about a mile above the mouth of the river.[3]

The Shawanese chiefs launched a major diplomatic effort to persuade more nations to join them in their struggle. Blue Jacket carried a war calumet throughout the Great Lakes and Mississippi River valley to plead his cause to the nations that had not yet joined and invite them to a Grand Council of the Indian Confederacy. It was to be held at the Grand Glaize. Shawanese Chief Red Pole said: "All the nations are now of one mind and resolved and able to defend themselves."[4]

The Grand Council was relocated to the foot of the rapids of the Maumee River. The following nations assembled there in September of 1792: the Delaware, Shawanese, Miami, Wea, Chippewa, Ottawa, Wyandot, Munsey, Connoy, Nantikoke, Mohican, Pottawatomie, Sauk, Fox, Cherokee, and Creek, and the Ohio Mingo. For the first time, the Indian nations of the north, south, east, and west had united together in common cause.

Chiefs Blue Jacket and Captain Johnny appointed Shawanese Chief Red Pole to serve as the master of ceremonies for the Grand Council.[5] Red Pole welcomed the delegates at the opening session on September 30, 1792. Alexander McKee attended on behalf of the British Indian Department.

The Grand Council continued for ten days and was a resounding Shawanese success. The assembled nations endorsed the Ohio River boundary and pledged themselves to the cause of Pan-Indian unity.[6] Red Pole was dispatched to the south on a critical diplomatic mission to gain firmer commitments from the southern nations to support the confederacy.[7]

THROUGH LATE 1792, GENERAL WAYNE HAD METHODICALLY assembled and trained a formidable military force of 2,500 regular soldiers at his "Legionville" training camp near Fort Pitt. He selected a talented young ensign named William Henry Harrison to serve as his aide-de-camp. Harrison was the twenty-year-old son of former Virginia Governor Benjamin Harrison who had approved Queen Lamatumque's peace initiative in 1783.

General Wayne drilled his men in military tactics and strict obedience to their commanding officers. Discipline was imposed and reinforced through a continuously sitting court-martial proceeding with floggings administered for disciplinary infractions and a sentence of death by hanging for desertion.

The general procured handsome uniforms for his men. The privates and non-commissioned officers of the legion were provided with attractive navy-blue uniforms. The facings (lapels and sleeves) of their coats were red and a red stripe ran down the pantlegs. Wide white straps criss-crossed their chests. They wore tall black bearskin hats with a cockade above the left ear—the cockades of the First Sublegion were white, the Second Sublegion red, the Third Sublegion yellow, and the Fourth Sublegion green.

The captains wore a navy blue coat faced with red, a white sash across the chest, white pants, and knee-high shiny black leather boots. A navy blue bicorn hat with a red cockade on the left-hand side of its front completed their uniform. The captains and other commissioned officers were each provided with a saber.[8]

Blue Jacket dispatched young Tecumseh and his band of warriors to spy on General Wayne's preparations. They reported that the soldiers drilled daily in mock battles to perfect techniques for countering Indian tactics. Their potent artillerymen honed their skills and refined their accuracy. A large fleet of boats was assembling along the banks of the Ohio River. Sentries were posted everywhere and were on alert around the clock. The Indian scouts searched for some breach of vigilance, some fatal flaw that they could exploit, but could find none.

In the spring of 1793, the Legion of the United States departed down the Ohio River in a freshwater fleet of keelboats and flatboats and arrived at Fort Washington several days later. They established a training camp near the fort named "Hobson's Choice." The Chickasaw Nation sent a contingent of warriors to serve as American scouts.[9]

The Indian nations of the northwest turned to Blue Jacket and Little Turtle to again serve as the co-leaders of the defense of the Indian Confederacy homelands. However, Little Turtle declined to lead the Indian forces and advised that the Indians negotiate for peace rather than fight. Blue Jacket was then chosen as the sole commander of the allied Indian forces.

Micajah's Resolve

MICAJAH RETURNED TO KENTUCKY IN EARLY 1793 after spending a little over a year with his brother Dudley in Amherst County, Virginia. He settled in Clark County, Kentucky, which had been formed in 1792 out of portions of Fayette County and Bourbon County. The new town of Winchester was selected as the county seat. The tax rolls of Clark County list Micajah Callaway as a resident from 1793 to 1797.[10]

A party of thirty-five Shawanese warriors attacked Morgan's Station in Clark County on Monday, April 1, 1793, and brutally assaulted the families living there.[11] Nineteen women and children were captured and twelve of the prisoners were killed and mutilated.

A militia pursuit party of 150 armed men was formed and pursued the warriors on April 2, but failed to catch up with them. The pursuit party included several Clark County militiamen with whom Micajah served in General Wayne's campaign a year later, so it is likely that Micajah was a member of this group. However, no confirming records have been found.[12]

Micajah and his Long Knife friends and family hardened their resolve to bring the seemingly endless war with the Shawanese Nation and their allies to a conclusive end. The raid on Morgan's Station emphasized the grim reality that the lives of their families and loved ones depended upon this. Several of Micajah's siblings lived in the area, and he had many young nieces and nephews who were at risk.

The Final Negotiations

THE LEADERS OF THE INDIAN CONFEDERACY REFUSED to agree to enter into final negotiations with the Americans in the summer of 1793 unless the Americans first agreed to the Ohio River boundary as a pre-condition to further discussions. On July 31, 1793, American Commissioners attended a preliminary council at Matthew Elliot's home at the mouth of the Detroit River to address the issue.

The American Commissioners conceded that their predecessors had made an error of law in the "conquest" Treaties of Fort Stanwix, Fort McIntosh, and the Mouth of the Greater Miami River in 1785 and 1786:

> REPLY OF THE COMMISIONERS OF THE
> UNITED STATES TO THE INDIANS . . .
>
> BROTHERS,
>
> We are determined that our whole conduct shall be marked with openness & sincerity. We therefore frankly tell you that we think those Commissioners put an erroneous construction on that part of our treaty with the King—as he had not purchased the country of you, of course he could not give it away. He only relinquished to the United States his claim to it. That claim was founded on a right acquired by Treaty with other white Nations to exclude them from purchasing or settling in any part of your country; and it is this right which the King granted to the United States . . .
>
> BROTHERS,
>
> We now concede this great point: We by the express authority of the President of the United States acknowledge the property or right of soil of the great country above described to be in the Indian Nations so long as they desire to occupy the same. We only claim particular tracts in it as beforementioned and the general right granted by the King as above stated & which is well known to the English & Americans and called the right of pre-emption or the right of purchasing of the Indian Nations disposed to sell their lands to the exclusion of all other white People whatever . . .

The Commisioners explained that the United States of America could not agree to the Ohio River boundary regardless of their error of law because of the importance to the white man of protecting the investments already made in developing real estate to the north of the river:

BROTHERS,

You are men of understanding & if you consider the customs of white people, the great expenses which attend this settling in a new country, the nature of their improvements, in building houses & barns, and clearing & fencing their lands, how valuable the Lands are thus rendered, & thence how dear they are to them. You will see that it is now impracticable to remove our people from the northern side of the Ohio. Your Brothers the English know the natures of white People, and they know that under the circumstances which we have mentioned, the United States cannot make the Ohio the Boundary between you & us . . ."

At Capt. Elliot's at the Mouth of the Detroit River, this thirty first day of July 1793.

        B. Lincoln   )
        Beverly Randolph) Commrs.[13]
        Timothy Pickering)

The chiefs of the confederacy replied to the American Commissioners on August 13, 1793:

REPLY OF THE INDIANS TO THE
COMMMISSIONERS OF THE UNITED STATES.

To the Commissioners of the United States.

BROTHERS,

You have talked to us about concessions. It appears strange, that you should expect any from us, who have only been defending our just rights, against your invasions; we want peace: Restore to us our Country and we shall be Enemies no longer.

BROTHERS,

You make one concession to us by offering us your money, and another by having agreed to do us justice, after having long & injuriously withheld it: We mean in the acknowledgement you have now made, that the King of England never did, nor ever had a right to give you our Country by the Treaty of Peace. And you want to make this act of common justice a great part of your concession and seem to expect that because you have at last acknowledged our independence, we should for such a favor surrender to you our Country . . .

BROTHERS,

. . . We desire you to consider Brothers, that our only demand is the peacable possession of our once great country. Look back & view the Lands from whence we have been driven, to this Spot. We can retreat no further because the Country behind barely affords food for its present Inhabitants; and we have therefore resolved to leave our bones, in this small place to which we are now confined.

BROTHERS,

We shall be persuaded that you mean to do us justice if you agree that the Ohio shall remain the boundary line between us; if you will not consent thereto, our meeting will be altogether unnecessary. This is the great point which we hoped would have been explained, before you left your homes, as our message last fall was principally directed to obtain that information . . .[14]

Captain Wolf signed the reply on behalf of the Shawanese with his mark. The commissioners provided their final response to the confederacy on August 16, 1793:

COMMISSIONERS OF THE UNITED STATES TO THE CHIEFS OF THE INDIAN NATIONS

To the Chiefs & Warriors of the Indian Nations, assembled at the foot of the Miamis Rapids.

BROTHERS,

We have just received your answer dated the 13th instant to our Speech of the 31st of last month which we delivered to your Deputies at this place. You say it was interpreted to all your Nations; and we presume it was fully understood. We therein explicitly declared to you, that it was now impossible to make the River Ohio the boundary between your lands & the Lands of the United States. Your answer amounts to a declaration that you will agree to no other boundary but the Ohio. The negotiation is therefore at an end.

We sincerely regret that peace is not the result, but knowing the upright and liberal views of the United States, which as far as you gave us opportunity, we have explained to you, we trust that impartial judges will not attribute the continuance of war to them.

Done at Captain Elliots at the mouth of the Detroit River, the Sixteenth day of August 1793.

        B. Lincoln   )
        Beverly Randolph) Commrs.[15]
        Timothy Pickering)

The Warpath

GENERAL WAYNE BEGAN HIS FINAL PREPARATIONS FOR war when he was informed that the negotiations had failed. He planned to strike the Grand Glaize in the autumn of 1793 before the winter weather arrived.

The Americans estimated that approximately thirteen hundred Shawanese, Delaware, Miami, Wyandot, Ottawa, Munsee, Pottawatomie, and Cherokee warriors could be assembled to meet the legion in battle.[16] General Wayne could field two thousand regular troops to meet the enemy. That number fell several hundred short of the numbers that were required to guarantee victory. The United States could not afford to gamble and lose.

General Wayne did not trust the Kentucky militia but resigned himself to making use of them. He decided that they would serve best as light cavalry. However, they would have to serve directly under the discipline of his command.

Kentucky had been admitted into the Union on June 1, 1792, as the fifteenth state of the United States, and Isaac Shelby served as the first governor. President Washington had designated a Kentucky Board of War comprised of Isaac Shelby, Congressman John Brown, Benjamin Logan, Charles Scott, and Harry Innes in 1791. The board issued a muster call for mounted Kentucky volunteers to join a federal campaign against the towns of the Grand Glaize for sixty days' service beginning on October 1, 1793. The volunteers would serve under the command of Major General Charles Scott of the Kentucky militia.

The Kentucky volunteers didn't complete their muster at Hobson's Choice until October 23, 1793. Compounding General Wayne's problems from that delay, the legion was wracked by an outbreak of influenza and many soldiers were too sick to fight.

General Wayne decided to postpone the campaign against the Grand Glaize until the following year, when his complete force would be healthy and well prepared. He redirected his efforts for the remainder of the year to establishing a major new forward post.

The federal legion marched north from Hobson's Choice on October 7, 1793, and followed the path taken by General St. Clair's army two years earlier. A large contingent of Chickasaw warriors served as American scouts. The legion marched six miles past Fort Jefferson where General Wayne ordered the construction of Fort Greenville.

General Wayne used the additional time provided by the delay in his campaign to concentrate on gathering intelligence on enemy plans and movements. He turned to local scouts who had the knowledge and contacts that could help him.

Captain Ephraim Kibbey was one of the original settlers of Columbia, Ohio, at the mouth of the Little Miami River. He had established a militia company of scouts and spies called the Columbian Scouters. They were assigned to serve General Wayne as federal scouts and spies for special intelligence operations.[17]

William Wells had been convinced to abandon the Miami Nation and return to his white family during prisoner exchange negotiations in Cincinnati and Louisville in 1792. He volunteered to serve as a spy and interpreter for General Wayne.[18] Wells was given command of his own elite special unit of federal spies within the Columbian Scouters.[19]

In 1791 the British had established a fort named Fort Miamis near Colonel McKee's trading post at the foot of the rapids of the Maumee River, in order to protect Detroit. Lord Dorchester sent a letter to Upper Canada Lieutenant Governor John Graves Simcoe on February 17, 1794, ordering that the fortifications and garrison at Fort Miamis be strengthened.

The British refurbished and reinforced Fort Miamis in May. The war chiefs of the Indian Confederacy interpreted the British actions as evidence that the British would join them to fight against the Americans.

SPAIN JOINED GREAT BRITAIN AS AN ALLY in the ongoing European war against the revolutionary French Republic. The French in turn courted an alliance with the United States through the efforts of their ambassador, Citizen Genet.

Genet's agents pressed former General George Rogers Clark to form an army of Kentucky frontiersmen to attack Spanish Louisiana and "liberate" the Frenchmen living there under Spanish rule. Clark agreed to do so and began to assemble a "private" army with the aid of Colonel John Montgomery.[20]

Louisiana Governor Baron de Carondelet learned of the French plot and Clark's activities. He established a blockade of six heavily armed row galleys at the mouth of the Ohio River. The Baron reminded the Shawanese led by Louis Lorimier that they would lose their Spanish land grant at Cape Girardieu if the Spanish were driven away. He sent them a war calumet and belt of black wampum for them to deliver to the British in Canada.

Louis Lorimier organized a force of six hundred Shawanese warriors and marched from Cape Girardeau into Kentucky to attack Colonel Montgomery's post. They drove Montgomery and his men out of their post to a refuge at Red Rock.[21]

The well-informed and shrewd Shawanese leaders saw an opportunity for their Indian Confederacy to form a military alliance with Spain and Great Britain against the United States. They might succeed in preserving the Ohio River boundary or perhaps even drive the Americans back east over the mountains if they could gain the support of these two world powers.

The Louisiana Shawanese sent emissaries carrying the Spanish war calumet and belt to their Ohio Shawanese kinsmen at the Grand Glaize. They arrived there in May and delivered the Spanish calumet and belt, which were passed on to the British in Detroit. The Spanish asked the British to attack the American legion.[22] Nenessica was dispatched to visit the southern Indian nations on a secret mission of great importance.[23]

President George Washington firmly believed that his fledgling nation could not afford to become entangled in another major European war and took action to preserve American neutrality. Secretary Knox tasked General Wayne to resolve the brewing conflict and reassure Spain of the peaceful intentions of the United States. General Wayne dispatched Major Thomas Doyle with a detachment of sixty soldiers to reoccupy old French Fort Massac and stabilize the increasingly dangerous political situation on the lower Ohio River.[24]

Major Doyle thwarted General Clark's and Colonel Montgomery's plans, and the threat on the lower Ohio River and Mississippi River began to subside. The Americans and Spanish never came to blows.[25]

A member of the British Cabinet wrote a letter to Lieutenant Governor Simcoe on July 4, 1794, and informed him that negotiations with American ambassador John Jay were nearing a successful conclusion. The British expected to enter into a treaty to turn their northwestern posts over to the Americans. The Indians were not informed of the contents of this letter or the improving prospects for the preservation of peace between the United States and Great Britain.[26]

GENERAL WAYNE SENT A LETTER TO KENTUCKY Governor Isaac Shelby asking for one thousand mounted volunteers to strengthen his force in preparation for his 1794 campaign. The governor responded with a call for more volunteers and over fifteen hundred mounted men reported for duty.[27] They were organized into two brigades commanded by Brigadier Generals Robert Todd and John Barbee. Battalions were formed in Todd's brigade under the command of Majors John Caldwell, William Price, Notley Conn, and William Russell III.[28]

Joshua Baker Jr. was commissioned a captain in Major Conn's Battalion in command of a company of scouts and spies from Mason County, Bourbon County, and Clark County. William Sudduth of Clark County was commissioned as Captain Baker's Lieutenant and Michael Cassidy of Clark County was commissioned as his ensign. Sudduth was an athletic schoolteacher and Indian fighter.[29]

Micajah and Edmund Callaway volunteered together in late June to serve as privates in Captain Baker's company.[30] The federal government paid the scouts and spies five Virginia shillings per day for their services.

Callaway family records indicate that Micajah served as "principal scout and spy" for General Wayne. This is likely a reflection of a *de facto* leadership role. Micajah was held in high regard as one of the best scouts and spies in Kentucky.[31] He knew the Shawanese language and customs, and the geography and terrain of their homeland. Many of the other volunteer scouts and spies had never even lived in the Indian country.

Simon Kenton did not respond to this call for volunteers.[32] Some historical accounts maintain that he was sick at the time with recurring bouts of malaria. Other accounts say that he was upset at not receiving a commission as a major.[33] Micajah's detailed knowledge of Shawanese territory and tactics would offset the impact of Kenton's absence.

The Kentucky volunteers were ordered to rendezvous in Georgetown, Kentucky, in early July. The Clark County volunteers mustered there on July 16 and were paid fifteen dollars in advance money. Micajah and Edmund went to Pitts Tavern in Georgetown and joined the rest of their Clark County friends for a rowdy night of drinking shots of Bourbon County whiskey.[34]

Major Conn received orders from General Todd to report for duty at Fort Washington on July 18, so the volunteers set off for Cincinnati early the next morning. They crossed the Ohio River by boat on July 19, 1794. Major Conn was ordered to depart for Fort Greenville and transport military supplies on July 21, 1794.[35]

The battalion approached Fort Greenville on the fourth day of their march and encamped with the rest of General Todd's forces about a mile in advance of Fort Greenville. They were joined there by General Barbee's brigade two days later.

Major General Scott reorganized his forces on July 27, 1794. Major William Price was ordered to form and command a special corps consisting of two companies of Kentucky volunteer scouts and spies to report directly to General Wayne. It was named the "Corps of Guides and Spies" (hereinafter referred to as the "Corps").[36] The Corps would work with and complement the federal legion's company of Columbian Scouters under the command of Captain Kibbey.

Major Price was ordered to select scouts and spies from Brigadier General Todd's brigade to form one company. He selected Captain Joshua Baker Jr. and his company with little hesitation. General Scott ordered that a second company of scouts and spies be handpicked by Captain John Arnold from Brigadier General Barbee's brigade.

General Wayne issued his General Orders to the legion concerning the "Line of March, Signals, Encampment, and Order of Battle" on July 21, 1794. The infantry was to advance in two columns. The artillery and the contractors' supply wagons, packhorses, and cattle were to move in between the two columns. Troops of dragoons and riflemen would flank the two columns with expert woodsmen posted further out on the flanks to look for signs of the enemy.

Fortified encampments were to be formed each afternoon at the end of a day's march. This would begin with the delineation of a square of specified dimensions. The legionnaires would then construct a breastwork of felled trees and brush on the square to provide cover from enemy fire. Four strong redoubts were to be constructed three hundred yards out from the corners of the encampment and occupied by picket guards.[37]

The main body of the Legion of the United States and General Todd's brigade prepared to leave Fort Greenville on July 28, 1794.[38] General Todd's brigade was at its full strength of seven hundred Kentucky volunteers. General Barbee's brigade of eight hundred volunteers would remain at Fort Greenville to await the arrival of additional provisions and advance forward to the main body of the army at a later date.

A cannon was fired from the east bastion of Fort Greenville to signal the beginning of the march to battle on the morning of July 28. The Kentucky volunteers followed the legion in the order of march. The army encamped for the first night on the banks of the Stillwater River after an advance of twelve miles.

Micajah and Tecumseh began a game of cat-and-mouse that would last up to the day of battle. Micajah had lived with the Shawanese in Callaway's Town on the Stillwater River in 1782 and remembered the detailed lay of the land. He and his scouts found subtle signs that at least two small parties of Tecumseh's scouts were shadowing the progress of the American army.[39]

Micajah gave a pre-arranged signal to the sentries at the Kentucky volunteer camp upon their return at the end of the day. The scouts were admitted into the encampment and reported their findings to Captain Baker who in turn passed them up the chain of command. The scouts then tended to their horses' needs, which was part of their nightly ritual.

The American army arrived at Fort Recovery on the night of July 29 and camped about a mile above the fort on the Wabash River. The Kentucky volunteers camped in a separate unfortified encampment about half a mile from the legion's camp.

MAJOR HENRY BURBECK HAD BEEN DISPATCHED BY General Wayne with six companies to construct Fort Recovery on the site of the defeat of General St. Clair. They gathered several hundred skulls and thousands of bones from the casualties of St. Clair's defeat from the forest and buried them in a mass grave. William Wells helped the Americans locate and recover the cannon that the Indians had captured from General St. Clair's army and hidden in the surrounding forest.

An army of 1,434 warriors attacked Fort Recovery on June 30, 1794, and failed to capture it. The Americans suffered 21 soldiers killed, 29 soldiers wounded, and one Chickasaw scout slain. The Indians sustained a loss of 25 warriors.

GENERAL WAYNE'S LEGIONNAIRES AND KENTUCKY VOLUNTEERS FOUND a few more skulls and bones from St. Clair's Defeat when they encamped on July 29 and buried them in the mass grave with the others. The sentinels gave several alarms that night.

The army marched on through rugged, uneven terrain and ravines covered by nettles and brush on the following day. They passed through a large abandoned Indian encampment where the Indians had prepared for their attack on Fort Recovery. A discarded bag of war paint was found among the trees.

An advance party of pioneers was sent ahead of the main force to construct a bridge across Beaver Creek and to clear the road to the St. Mary's River. They were unable to complete the bridge during the day and were still working on it when the army arrived at the crossing after a march of twelve miles.

That night, the army camped next to Beaver Creek near the bridge construction site. The surrounding land was a wet and swampy beech forest swarming with large, hungry mosquitoes. Tecumseh's scouts fired ten shots into the Kentucky volunteers' camp that night and small parties were heard moving around their encampment in the darkness. Construction of the bridge took longer than planned and the legion camped along Beaver Creek again on the night of July 31.

The army arose early in the morning of August 1, broke camp, and crossed the bridge. They marched from there across a large open plain. The entire legion and the mounted Kentucky volunteers were visible along the trail. The vivid colors of the legion uniforms created a splendid sight in the summer sunlight.

The legion camped that night on the shores of St. Mary's River after another march of twelve miles. The Kentucky volunteers camped in the ruins of Girty's Town, where Micajah had lived in 1783. Some of the troops caught salmon and pike from the St. Mary's River to supplement their diet.

Micajah organized a scouting expedition through the surrounding countryside in the late afternoon to look for signs of Indians on the old trails that he recalled from his many hunting trips through the area. His scouts reported more traces left by Tecumseh's elusive spies.

A legion surveyor named Newman disappeared that night and the Americans did not know if he was killed or captured as a prisoner. The Americans would later learn on August 12 that he had fled to the Indians and British and had provided them with a complete description of the American forces and their plans. Micajah and his men detected the tracks of a party of four Indian scouts near the camp.

The legion remained at their encampment along St. Mary's River through August 2 in order to construct a fort named Fort Adams. General Barbee's brigade caught up with the main body of the army that day with more provisions.

The construction of Fort Adams continued into August 3. A tree felled in the course of construction toppled over onto General Wayne and injured one of his knees and his abdomen in the groin area. He passed blood in his urine and stools for the duration of the campaign and needed help to mount his horse on the most painful days.

Micajah had never served with such a disciplined force. Some of his more free-spirited compatriots from Kentucky bristled at the constraints of General Wayne's rigorous regimen. Micajah understood the effectiveness of this approach to fighting the Indians and supported it. This well-trained and well-equipped army would not be surprised and would not run from battle.

The force departed from Fort Adams on August 4 and followed a branch of the Auglaize River called Upper Delaware Creek. They passed through rugged terrain covered by thick forests and heavy brush. They continued to follow this course on August 5 and 6.

Major Price's Corps was ordered to deploy far in advance of the main body of the American army on August 6 to range all the way down the Auglaize River to its mouth and ascertain the location of the Indians. Micajah, Edmund, and their comrades in the Corps discovered that the Grand Glaize towns at the mouth of the Auglaize River were abandoned and burning. Reports of their findings were passed up the chain of command. The tracks of a party of twenty Indians were detected during the day's scout.

The main body of the American army marched onward on August 7 and arrived at the main branch of the Auglaize River. It was nearly one hundred yards wide at that point. They passed a recently abandoned Delaware Town, cornfields, and large Indian sugar camps in groves of sugar maples as they marched along the river.

The army marched down the Auglaize River for nine more miles on the following morning of August 8. They passed through cultivated cornfields for seven of those miles and arrived at the Grand Glaize at midday. The cabins of the British and French traders who had lived there were in smoldering ruins. They found abundant fields of ripe corn, beans, cucumbers, potatoes, and other vegetables.

General Wayne congratulated his troops on taking possession of the "Grand Emporium of the hostile Indians of the Northwest." One gill of whisky (about four ounces) was issued as a reward to every non-commissioned officer and soldier in the legion. American scouts reported that night that the main body of enemy warriors had encamped along the Maumee River about two miles above Fort Miamis, near Alexander McKee's post at the foot of the rapids of the Maumee River.

General Wayne ordered that a large fort be constructed and garrisoned at the confluence of the Maumee River and Auglaize River. It was named "Fort Defiance." The Corps was ordered to constantly patrol five to ten miles out from the main body of the army during their encampment at the forks. General Wayne forbade troops from swimming in the river for security reasons.[40]

As construction of Fort Defiance progressed, parties of Kentucky volunteers were ordered out from the encampment to forage for food from the surrounding Indian cornfields and gardens. The foraging parties were to contain at least ten soldiers and, for the time being, were forbidden from burning the Indian huts that remained.

Enormous quantities of corn and vegetables were harvested by the volunteers, and most of the cornfields were destroyed. Micajah could not help but think of the hard work and loving care that the Indian women had put into cultivating their bountiful fields and gardens, only to have their harvest stolen to provide sustenance for their mortal enemies.

On August 10, William Wells and a party of eleven federal scouts were sent in advance of the army to reconnoiter down the Maumee River to the old Ottawa town of Roche de Bout and attempt to capture prisoners. Roche de Bout was adjacent to a small rocky island by the same name. It was crowned with cedar trees at the head of the Rapids of the Maumee River about eight miles upstream of British Fort Miamis.

Wells' scouts found a party of sixty Indians camped there and skirmished with them. Wells and his scouts killed several warriors and captured an old Shawanese man and woman before they fled. Wells was wounded and his injury was serious enough to take him out of the campaign.⁴¹

General Wayne issued a general order on August 11, directing that from that date forward Major Price's Corps would parade for action and await orders on their own ground, separate from the main army.⁴² The Corps was directed to leave their encampment before sunrise each morning, to take up and maintain a position five to twelve miles in advance of the main body of the army. If they encountered and were attacked by a large number of hostile Indians as they advanced, they were to immediately send express messengers back to the legion to warn them to prepare for action, briefly skirmish to delay the Indians, and then retreat to the main body. They were ordered not to rejoin the main body in the evening until it was encamped and fortified.

Major Price ordered the Corps to advance, deployed in a broad linear front linked by close communications. Each officer in the Corps from major down to ensign commanded a small division. The divisions were spaced in a line at distances of one hundred yards, each within sight and shouting distance of its adjoining divisions. Express riders ran messages up and down the advancing line as needed. Reports were forwarded up the chain of command to Major Price who sent any necessary communiqués directly to General Wayne.

One division on each flank roamed far to the side of the line with orders to fire warning shots if they should encounter a body of hostile warriors. Each division was preceded by two advance scouts ranging one hundred yards ahead of their division.⁴³

General Wayne dispatched the Corps down the Maumee River to the site of Captain Snake's Town on August 12. About five miles down the river path, they met the wounded William Wells and his scouting party on the return from their mission to Roche de Bout.

After briefly conferring with Wells, Major Price and the Corps continued for another five miles down the river path to Captain Snake's Town. The town was abandoned and had been burned, and they found fields of ripe corn, beans, muskmelons and unripened watermelons all along the path. They returned to Fort Defiance at the end of the day.

The Shawanese prisoners captured by Wells's party were interrogated

Battle of Fallen Timbers

by the Americans. General Wayne sent the old Shawanese man back to the Indian Confederacy leadership on August 13 with a written peace proposal and a request that the confederacy respond to the proposal within four days. Christopher Miller, from William Wells's groups of scouts, accompanied him.

The general ordered all heavy baggage to be secured within Fort Defiance "so that the Army may move as light and unencumbered as possible." Each man in the army was provided with twenty-four rounds of ammunition.

On August 15, the American army left Fort Defiance and resumed their line of march. They crossed the Maumee River and continued down the river path toward the Roche de Boute, the Rapids of the Maumee River, and Fort Miamis.

From this point forward, General Wayne and the Kentucky officers looked to Micajah to provide senior leadership to the scouts and spies on the campaign. Simon Kenton and William Wells were both out of the action and no one was left who had more knowledge and experience of the Indian country and Indian warfare than Micajah. He had already proven his value during the long march.

Micajah began to patrol before dawn every morning during the campaign. He arose earlier than most of the scouts in order to consult with the officers during their formulation of the day's plan of action and obtain orders.

The Corps ranged far in advance of the legion while the Columbian Scouters served as the immediate advance guard to "mark the best way" for the pioneers cutting the road for the main body of the legion. Micajah and the other Corps scouts discovered and observed several small parties of Indians four or five miles in advance of the main body of the army.

The Corps divisions returned to their encampment next to the fortified encampment of the legion at Captain Snake's Town toward dusk. As he drifted off to sleep that night, Micajah recalled Captain Snake's stirring speech and war song as the Shawanese marched off to join Captain Bird in the invasion of Kentucky in 1780.

On August 16, the leadership of the Indian Confederacy nations held a Grand Council on the banks of the Maumee River to consider General Wayne's final peace proposal. Miami Chief Little Turtle and young Chief Kinjoino of the Ottawa Nation counseled for peace.[44] Little Turtle eloquently expressed his reservations:

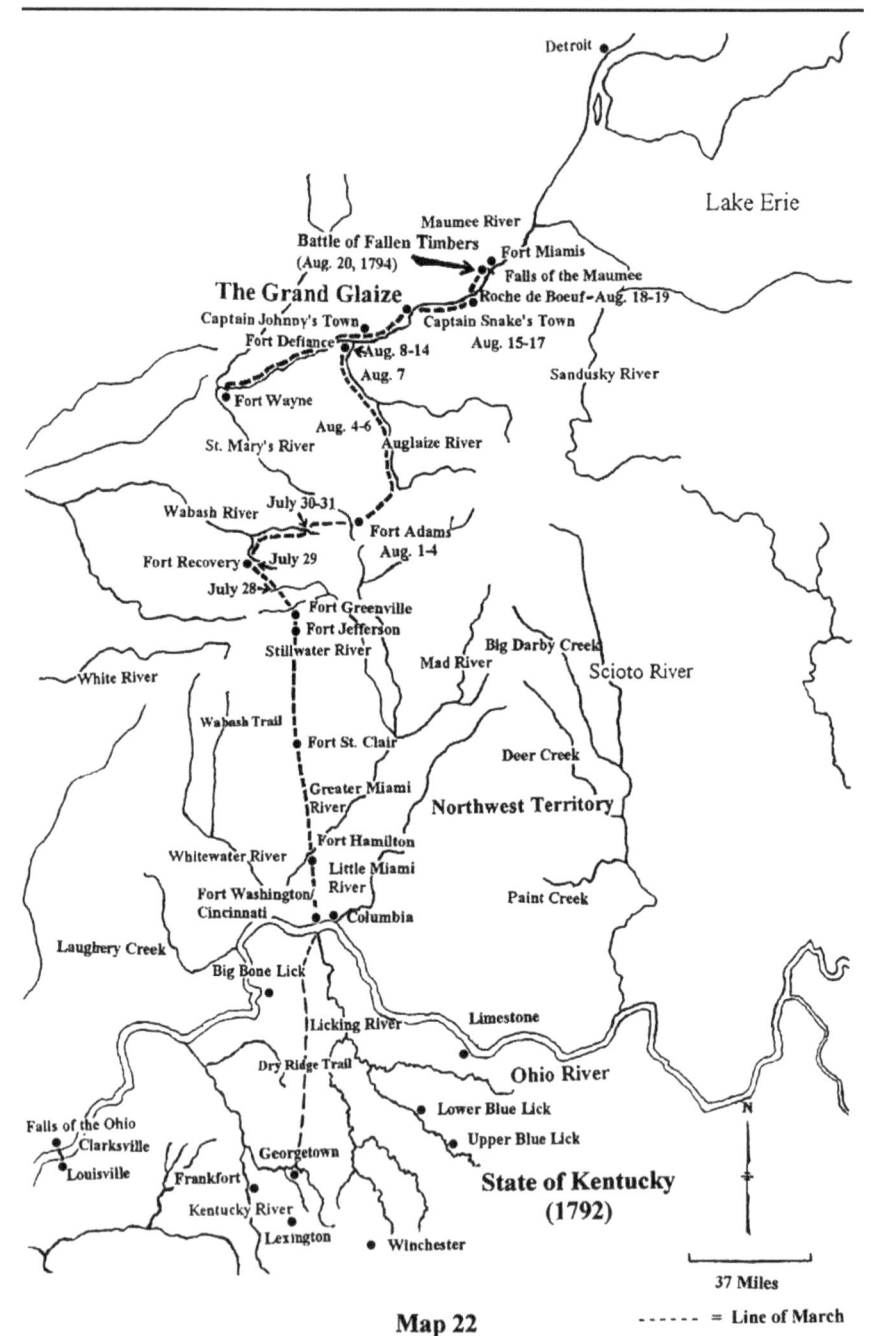

Map 22
General Anthony Wayne's Campaign of 1794

> We have beaten the enemy twice under separate commanders. We cannot expect the same good fortune always to attend us. The Americans are now led by a chief who never sleeps. The night and the day are alike to him; and during all the time that he has been marching upon our villages, notwithstanding the watchfulness of our young men, we have never been able to surprise him. Think well of it. There is something whispers it would be prudent to listen to his offers of peace.[45]

Nonetheless, the militant faction prevailed over the moderates led by Little Turtle and confirmed Blue Jacket as the sole commander-in-chief of the Indian Confederacy army. As the inevitable battle loomed, they decided that the confederacy would stall for time by negotiating. Meanwhile they would reinforce their army with late-arriving contingents of warriors from the more distant confederacy nations.

Christopher Miller returned to Captain Snake's Town late in the day on August 16 and communicated the Indian response to General Wayne. General Wayne decided that the confederacy's offer was not made in good faith. He did not respond and prepared for the final march to battle.

The Battle of Fallen Timbers

A SMALL PARTY OF INDIANS FIRED ON the Corps' advance scouts on August 17 and injured a horse. William May was captured and taken to Fort Miamis as a prisoner. He informed the British and Indians that the Americans planned to attack on the following day. The historical record does not tell us whether May did this under torture, in fear for his life, or willingly; regardless, he was reportedly executed in the British garrison the day after his capture.

On August 18, the legion marched from Captain Snake's Town for ten miles to the Roche de Bout at the head of the Rapids of the Maumee River.

298   Tomahawks & Treaties

The river there flowed over a large sheet of rock which formed the rapids. It was bordered on both sides by a verdant prairie of tall grass over a quarter of a mile wide. As one moved away from the river bottom to the north and west, the land rose into bluffs that were eighty to a hundred feet high. The timber was sparse at the crest of the bluffs and grew denser as one moved farther away from the bluffs onto the upland plains.

One of the Corps divisions came upon an area of open space in the timber at the crest of the bluffs, where the main body of the Indians had formed a line of battle early in the morning and withdrawn. The site was located just a short distance back from the top of the northern side of a deep ravine cut into the bluffs by a small stream flowing from the uplands. The stream cut directly through the bluffs at roughly a right angle to the river. Major Price reported their findings to General Wayne and his officers.

The legion paused at Roche de Bout through August 19 to construct a fortification to hold their reserves of provisions. It was named "Camp Deposit" by General Wayne.

The Corps was deployed again in advance of the army on the morning of August 19. The Kentucky scouts spread out in their divisions and moved forward. Major Price and Captain Baker and their divisions were on the right flank, with Lieutenant William Sudduth and Captain Arnold and their divisions on the left. Micajah's division was commanded by Lieutenant McKenney, an officer with relatively little experience in scouting and Indian fighting.[46]

Micajah and Edmund took the advance scout positions for their division as the Corps rode forward through the forest on the bluffs above the Maumee River. Edmund was on Micajah's left. Micajah carefully guided his horse through the forest litter and attempted to avoid making noise. The enemy was very near. They could clearly see through the scattered trees to Alexander McKee's store across the grassy bottomlands and r iver on their far right. Fort Miamis was only a couple of miles farther down the river.

They rode on through the ravine and up through the clearing where the Indian battle line had been discovered on August 18. They continued to advance for roughly another half-mile.

Micajah spotted a Shawanese warrior partially obscured by the underbrush, his face painted black. Their eyes locked, and Micajah's hair stood on end on the back of his neck. He shouted the alarm, took aim at the warrior, and pulled the trigger. The forest erupted with the explosive sound of crashing gunfire and scalp halloos. Hundreds of painted warriors sprang from cover with their tomahawks drawn and ready.

The Kentucky scouts up and down the line fired their long rifles and retreated back through the ravine on the command of Major Price. At the top of the southern edge of the ravine they paused to reload and fired down into the advancing horde of warriors. The Corps fell back again and met with General Todd's brigade, who had been following them to provide protection. The Indians skirmished briefly with forward elements of the brigade and retired from the battlefield.

Major Price reported directly to General Wayne that the enemy had made a stand to receive them. The sentry was doubled that night and orders were issued to shoot anyone seen outside the lines of the encampment without prior warning.[47]

CHIAXI LED HIS BAND OF WARRIORS BACK to the Indian encampment after their brief skirmish with the Long Knives. He had recognized Micajah and some of the other Kentucky scouts. He rued the day that the Shawanese had taught them so much about their homelands, customs, and fighting style.

The intelligence reports that the Indians received from their Shawanese scouts were ominous. The army of the legion and the Long Knives was nearly three times the size of the Indian force. They were well-equipped and disciplined. The intelligence extracted from William May indicated that the Americans were determined for war; the opportunity for negotiations had passed. The importance of the impending battle was obvious to all of the Indian chiefs and warriors.

The Indian army had been gathering for several weeks in a large encampment near the Shawanese, Delaware, and Ottawa towns across the river from Fort Miamis. A total of over thirteen hundred warriors were assembled. The Delaware, Miami, Shawanese, Ottawa, and Wyandot Nations contributed the largest contingents of the warriors, with the Mingo, Pottawatomie, and Chippewa Nations providing smaller numbers. Colonel

England had provided additional artillery and a force of seventy Canadian militia commanded by Captain Caldwell.[48]

Chiaxi had arrived at Fort Miamis by canoe, accompanied by his young family. He had married Polly Butler, the daughter of late American General Richard Butler and his Shawanese consort. Chiaxi and Polly had a young son named Chaguska (Spy Buck) and a baby daughter.[49] Most of Micajah's surviving friends and acquaintances among the Shawanese chiefs and warriors were present.

The war chiefs set up their line of battle on August 18 in the expectation that the Americans would quickly engage them as indicated by the intelligence extracted from William May. They had carefully chosen the location for the battle line on the high ground in an area of timber above the bluffs of the river. A large tornado had recently touched down in the uplands, knocking down a long swath of the timber into a jack-straw jumble of tree trunks and branches.

On August 18, the Indian battle line was deployed a short distance in advance of the fallen timbers and behind a large ravine through which a small stream flowed. It extended two miles inland from the crest of the bluffs and slanted slightly diagonally away from the river in the upstream direction. Their flanks were slightly advanced over the center.

The line was divided into three segments. The Wyandot, Canadian militia, and Ottawa anchored the right-hand segment farthest upland. The central segment was composed of Mingo and Buckongahelas' Delaware warriors. The left-hand segment, closest to the river, was composed of Shawanese and Pottawatomie, with the Chippewa on the far left flank reaching to the crest of the river bluffs.

The Americans surprised the Indians by pausing to construct Fort Deposit instead of attacking on August 18, contrary to Mays's intelligence. The warriors were forced to continue their traditional pre-battle fasting for another day.

The Indian army set up their line of battle again on August 19, but closer to the fallen timbers. However, the American advance party broke off their initial engagement.

The warriors had now been fasting for two days and some of them were showing signs of physical distress from hunger. Several large groups were dispatched to Fort Miamis and the Swan Creek encampment to bring

Battle of Fallen Timbers

food forward. Their fighting force on the battlefield was reduced to eight hundred warriors.

War dances were held around the campfires of the assembled warriors that night, and prayers for victory were sent to Moneto and the Thunderbirds on wisps of tobacco smoke. Blue Jacket moved restlessly through the camp, exhorting his chiefs and warriors, consulting with the various chiefs, and finalizing their battle plan. Chiaxi slept fitfully that night.

The Indian army awoke before dawn on August 20 and deployed again in their battle line near where the line had been located on the morning of August 18. The day began with a very heavy thunderstorm in the early morning. The morning became hot, sunny, and humid after the storm had passed.

Chiaxi was light-headed from hunger as he took up his battle station behind a large tree. He checked with his band of warriors to see that they were properly deployed. Tecumseh's little band and two of his brothers were nearby.

THE KENTUCKY CORPS OF SCOUTS AND SPIES also arose before dawn on August 20 with orders to precede Captains Cooke and Steel and their legion vanguard by four hundred yards. Major Price was directed to give timely notice to the main body of the army as soon as the Corps made their first contact with the enemy.

The main body of the legion received orders to follow two hundred yards behind its vanguard. The legion itself was formed into three major components for deployment on the field of battle. The right wing was comprised of the First and Third Sublegions and commanded by Brigadier General James Wilkinson. The Third Sublegion was initially deployed behind the First. The lines of both sublegions were doubled, forming a narrow, deep front. The left wing was comprised of the Second and Fourth Sublegions and commanded by Colonel John F. Hamtramck. The Fourth Sublegion was deployed behind the Second, their files also doubled. The center column was comprised of the artillery, provision train, and companies of dragoons and light infantry under the direct command of General Wayne.

The morning thunderstorm delayed the departure of the Corps until eight o'clock. Even the most battle-hardened of the scouts were tense as they waited to deploy. Micajah's thoughts turned to his family and his hopes for

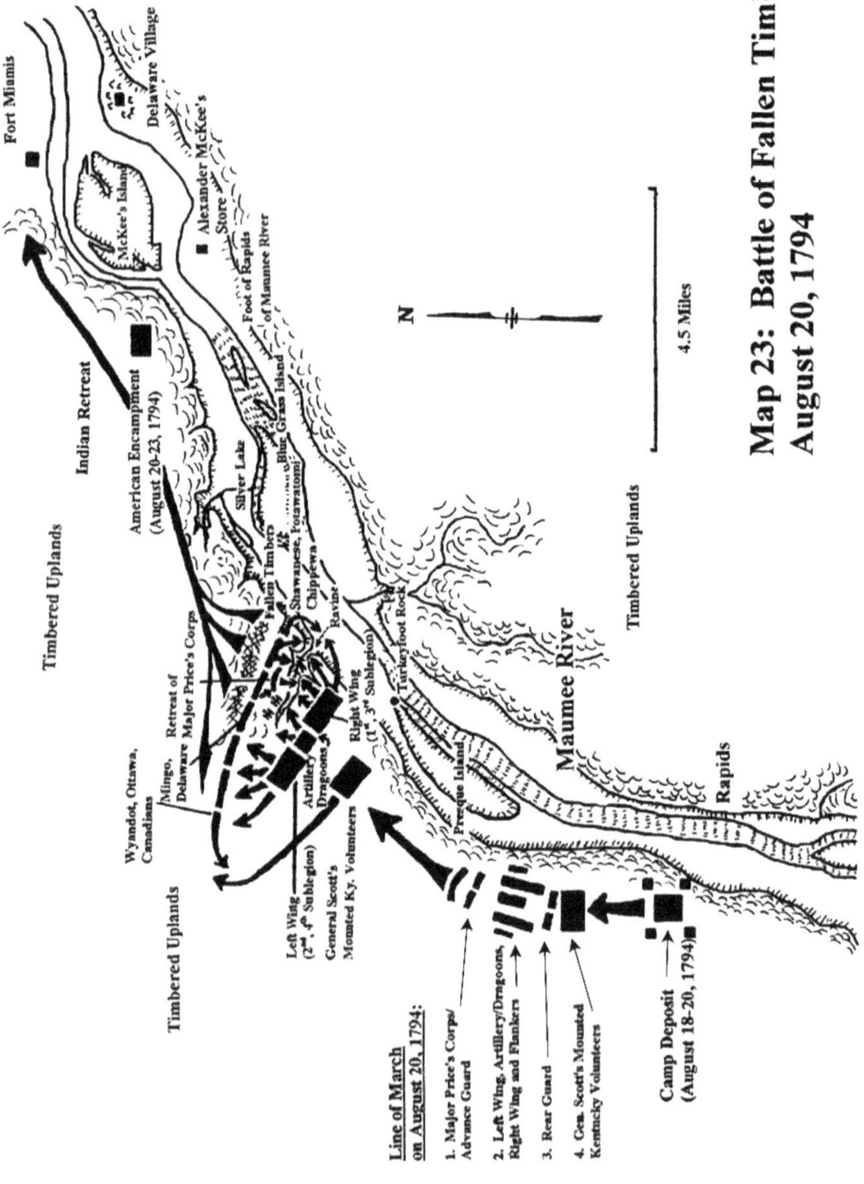

Map 23: Battle of Fallen Timbers
August 20, 1794

the future. Micajah was not a particularly religious man, but this morning he prayed to God that he and Edmund would both survive.

Major Price and the Corps ventured out after carefully checking their powder and priming to make sure it was dry. They deployed into their divisions and proceded to the southern edge of the large ravine beyond which lay the Indian battle line of August 18. The legion vanguard and main body followed.

Micajah and Edmund were again the advance scouts for their division. They dismounted when they reached the top of the ravine and crept down toward the bottom. Micajah spotted two painted warriors standing near the banks of the stream just ahead. The brothers withdrew back into some bushes and observed the Indians closely. Micajah drew upon all of his knowledge of Indian behavior. These two warriors were bait for battle, just as he and Edmund were. The main body of the Indians waited in ambush immediately ahead.

Micajah and Edmund quietly backed through the brush, remounted their horses, and rode over to Lieutenant McKenney to report their observations. They recommended that Captain Baker, Major Price, and the legion be informed that they had located the main body of the Indians. The lieutenant scoffed at Micajah's report of an ambush and accused him of "Shawnee Fever."

Lieutenant McKenney ordered his division to proceed across the stream without reporting Micajah's sighting. The two warriors had disappeared. The scouts moved on up and out of the ravine to the Indian battle line, and then spread out into the opening just beyond the top of the ravine.[50] Micajah and Edmund kept their rifle hammers cocked and ready for action.

Lieutenant William Sudduth and his division advanced with the Corps on Micajah's left. They came to the stream at the bottom of the ravine and stopped to dismount, drink, and strip off unnecessary clothing.

The Lieutenant sent Privates Thomas Moore and William Steele through the ravine and onto the uplands to probe for the enemy. Chiaxi gave the command to his warriors to open fire before the two scouts had gone a hundred yards. Moore and Steele were both blown out of their saddles.

The forest surrounding the Corps once again erupted with the roar of gunfire and the sound of hundreds of painted warriors screaming the scalp halloo. Blue Jacket, Tecumseh, Captain Snake, Chiaxi, and the other Shawanese chiefs and warriors drew their tomahawks and surged forward with their Pottawatomie and Chippewa allies.[51]

Micajah, Edmund, Lieutenant McKenney, and the rest of their division were exposed in the open when the Indians opened fire. The lieutenant looked around in surprise as the Indian guns barked their reports and staggered as he was struck by a musket ball. Major Price gave the order for his Corps to fire and retreat.[52]

The Corps' divisions pulled together into a tighter formation as they retreated. Tecumseh helped lead the Shawanese charge and fired his gun repeatedly until he mistakenly jammed a musket ball into the barrel before the powder charge, rendering his musket useless. He borrowed a fowling piece from a friend and continued to fight.

The course of the Corps' retreat led them to the left along the Indian battle line directly in front of the Shawanese. They rode like the wind down the line of battle as the warriors fired on them. They soon passed Chiaxi and his band and rode head-on into another body of Shawanese footmen led by several chiefs on horseback.

Major Price ordered his outnumbered men to stand and fight when he realized that there was nowhere to retreat. Micajah, Edmund, and the others reined in their horses and quickly reloaded their guns. The Shawanese horsemen fired from only forty steps away, and several scouts were struck and fell from their horses.

Micajah, Edmund, and the surviving Long Knives returned the fire point-blank, killing one Shawanese horseman and wounding several more. The Shawanese footmen then poured very heavy fire into the Long Knives. More scouts fell.

Micajah's horse screamed as a musket ball tore through its breast. It reared up on its hind legs and fell over backwards, nearly crushing him. He managed to roll away and hang onto his rifle, but lost sight of the other scouts.[53]

Above the din of battle, Major Price shouted another command to retreat. Lieutenant Sudduth recalled, "I could see into the muzzle of many of their guns where they raised them to fire on us. The bark of the trees flew in our faces."[54] The retreating Kentucky volunteers drew the Indian battle line forward toward the advancing vanguard and right wing of the legion commanded by General Wilkinson.

Edmund hung back in the rear of the retreating Corps and looked for

Micajah, but he could not find him. The advancing Shawanese focused on Edmund as their main target and sent a hail of musket balls toward him like a swarm of angry bees. Edmund ducked, wheeled his horse, hugged its neck, and galloped after the Corps. He scanned the forest for signs of Micajah as he rode, hoping he would spot him. Micajah sprinted through the forest as musket balls tore into the foliage around him, ignoring the pain in his frostbite-scarred feet. The warriors were hot on his trail. He reloaded his gun as he ran, treed, fired, and then ran on. He recognized some of the warriors pursuing him. They would not be kind to him if they caught up with him. Micajah reloaded on the run again and ran on with his rifle in one hand and tomahawk drawn in the other.

The Corps scouts who remained mounted picked up and rescued as many wounded as they could and sped back toward the main body of the legion. They approached the front line of the legion commanded by Captain John Cooke and Captain Steele. The vanguard mistook the scouts for Indians and opened fire on them.

The Shawanese warriors reached the legion advanced guard and engaged them in a hot firefight. The vanguard retreated for about a hundred yards. This drew the Indian charge close to the main body of the right wing of the legion, which had not yet fully formed into a battle line.

Blue Jacket and Tecumseh capitalized on the confusion caused by the retreating scouts and vanguard and directed their warriors to attempt to flank the Americans through the grassy plains below the bluffs. The surge of flanking warriors drove Micajah and a group of the retreating men down the side of the bluffs and out onto the grassy plain next to the river.[55]

General Wilkinson directed the Light Infantry Company of Lieutenant Bernard Gaines to form a skirmish line and return fire while commanding the main body of the right wing of the legionnaires to rapidly form its battle line and prepare to advance. He dispatched Captain Uriah Springer's First Sublegion rifle company down into the prairie grass on the bottomlands to intercept and block the flanking maneuver.

General Wilkinson's countermeasures stalled the advancing Indian line and stopped the flanking maneuver. Micajah finally reached the right wing of the legion, his lungs burning from the exertion.[56] General Wayne rallied the retreating volunteers and exhorted them to stand with the legion and fight.

The skirmish line of the right wing began their advance across the stream and up the northern side of the ravine toward the main Indian battle line. Mr. Eliot, the American contractor, reformed a group of dismounted Corps scouts and led them back into the fray alongside the advancing legionnaire skirmishers.[57] Micajah was among them.

Chiaxi and his warriors treed and fired their rifles and muskets at the soldiers in a barrage of deadly lead. The legion skirmishers maintained their discipline under the withering fire and advanced slowly, methodically firing, reloading, and shooting their bayoneted rifles again and again. Soldiers dropped as they were killed or wounded.

The Indians fell back before the advancing skirmish line and took cover within the fallen timbers. The warriors stood up from their cover to fire and then dropped back down among into the protection of the timbers to reload before standing and firing again. From their natural fortress a skirmish line advanced, forcing the Americans to fall back about eighty yards toward their main force.

As the skirmishers battled, the main body of the legion advanced toward the fallen timbers.

Riflemen and infantrymen reinforced the skirmish line. Four companies of artillery were deployed from the central column to support the both the right wing and left wing.

American artillery supporting the right wing, under the command of Captain John Price, opened fire and blasted into the warriors with their howitzers. They started their firing with regular shells and then switched to grape and canister shot. The Indians retreated again into the timbers as the main body of the American army began to roll forward. The artillery was moved forward to keep pace and opened fire on the Indian stronghold. The downed trees were splintered and human bodies shattered as the howitzers kept up an unrelenting fire. Indian casualties mounted.[58] Chiaxi would later describe the sound of the howitzers as, "Waugh! Waugh!"[59]

On General Wayne's direct order, Captain MisCampbell and his company of dragoons charged the Indian line in an effort to reach the grassy plain along the river and turn the Indians' left flank. The dragoons slashed from behind the American center to the right, down through the large ravine and

Battle of Fallen Timbers

up the other side, past the line of American skirmishers and into the line of Shawanese, Pottawatomie, and Chippewa warriors.

The Indians along the battle line opened fire on the attacking dragoons with their rifles and muskets. Captain MisCampbell and several of his troops were shot out of their saddles and killed. The balance fled back to the American line.

The battle had been raging for about an hour when General Wayne ordered Major General Scott and his mounted volunteers to ride in a wide circle to the Americans' left in order to turn the Indian's right flank. General Wayne then ordered his legionnaires to consolidate the First and Third Sublegions into a single battle line on the right wing and the Second and Fourth Sublegions into a single line on the left wing. The Second Sublegion was ordered to form the line by moving to the left of the Fourth Sublegion to help block the Indians' flanking maneuver on the American left flank.

General Wayne waited until the main battle lines had formed and then gave the order to advance. He ordered his troops to save their shot until the Indians rose from their cover to fire. The soldiers were then to fire and immediately attack with their bayonets before the warriors could reload. The Americans would dig the warriors out of the fallen timbers with their bayonets.[60]

As the main battle line of the legion advanced, Chiaxi and his surviving warriors had fallen back from their advanced skirmish line into the timbers with the other entrenched warriors. A dense line of determined blue-coated soldiers extended in both directions as far as he could see. The Americans did not raise their guns to shoot as they marched forward. Chiaxi shouted encouragement to his warriors as they prepared for the main engagement.

Blue Jacket's army stood and fired their muskets and rifles together in a coordinated barrage when the soldiers drew close. The soldiers stopped to return fire as the warriors exposed themselves. The Americans then gave a shout and broke into a running bayonet charge.

The warriors in the timbers frantically tried to reload as the legionnaires descended on them. They simply ran out of time. Many threw their rifles and muskets down to stand and fight against the bayonets with their tomahawks and scalping knives. Others fell back to reload. Micajah and the other dismounted Kentucky volunteers who had joined the advancing legion drew their tomahawks and scalping knifes from their belts and weighed into hand-to-hand combat.

It was an uneven match. The warriors who were not killed were driven from the fallen timbers by the bayonet charge and began to fall back.[61] Chiaxi kept his musket, fired, fell back, treed, reloaded, fired, and fell back again as he retreated with the survivors in his band.[62]

Lieutenant Covington and a small group of his dragoons pursued the retreating warriors.[63] Chiaxi and his band bore the brunt of Covington's attack. His warriors fired their muskets as the dragoons sped toward them, then threw them down and drew their tomahawks and scalping knives. The dragoons were upon them in an instant with sabers drawn.

The Shawanese warriors showed great courage and stood their ground as the dragoons attacked, but their tomahawks and scalping knives were no match for sabers in hand-to-hand combat. The Dragoons mercilessly slashed off the heads and arms of several warriors and pressed onward with their attack. Chiaxi later recounted the battle and imitated how the headless forms of his slain warriors flopped backward onto the ground.[64] The dragoons cut the Indian left flank in half, and the Indians fell back in full retreat.[65]

As the Indian warriors retreated on their left flank, the focus of battle shifted deep into the wooded uplands on the Indian right flank. Indian commanders directed a final desperate effort to flank the American's left wing. The Wyandots, Ottawas, and Canadians led a flanking maneuver which continued for another hour with sporadically heavy fighting. Colonel Hamtramck's Second Sublegion extended far to the American left flank in order to block the enemy. The Long Knife horsemen of General Todd's brigade at last arrived and turned the right flank of the Indians.

A shrill howl was heard from the Indians and passed on down their lines as soon as the warriors were outflanked. The warriors melted away into the woods. All firing ceased within two minutes. The legion had pushed the Indian line back for two miles into the wooded uplands before they disengaged. The Americans did not pursue them farther.[66]

The retreating warriors gathered at Fort Miamis and pleaded for the British to open the gates and help them, but the British kept the fort gates

Battle of Fallen Timbers

barred. Blue Jacket later reported that Major Campbell looked down from the top of the stockade upon the warriors gathering at the gate and said, "I cannot let you in! You are painted too much, my children!" The Indians were furious. Blue Jacket later said, "It was then that we saw the British dealt treacherously with us."[67]

Chiaxi ever after referred to them as the "damned British," and hated them for the rest of his life. He picked up his young family at Swan Creek and fled by canoe down the Maumee River.[68]

The victorious Americans possessed the field of battle. They had resoundingly defeated the Indian Confederacy. General Wayne congratulated the officers and soldiers of the legion and Kentucky volunteers and rewarded them all with a half-gill of whiskey. Micajah and Edmund joined a group of their friends in the Corps and celebrated.

The casualties on both sides were surprisingly light for a major battle. The total American casualties were approximately thirty-three killed and one hundred wounded. In Major Price's Corps, Captain Baker's company suffered five killed and Captain Arnold's company six wounded but none killed. Lieutenant McKenney was seriously wounded, and he never again questioned Micajah's judgment.[69]

Thirty Indians had been killed and seven wounded. The Wyandot Nation suffered the greatest losses on the right flank of the Indian army. Eight of their chiefs had been killed. The great Ottawa War Chief Turkey Foot was among the dead, as well as Ottawa Chief Little Otter.

Aftermath of Battle

THE AMERICAN ARMY REMAINED CAMPED ON THE banks of the Maumee River for the following three days and nights. General Wayne confronted Major Campbell, commander of the British garrison at Fort Miamis, and demanded that he surrender his post, but Campbell refused. Wayne decided to withdraw and end the confrontation without a battle. He had achieved the most important of his objectives.[70]

On August 22, the Corps was ordered to destroy the corn and other crops around Fort Miamis and burn the outbuildings. Micajah and his comrades burned the home of Alexander McKee at the foot of the rapids.

General Wayne assembled his forces at the American encampment on August 23. He congratulated them on their courage and great achievement. Three rounds of artillery were fired at noon in a ceremony to celebrate the victory and honor the dead.

The Americans departed on August 24 and reversed the order of march for their return journey. Major Price's Corps served as the rear guard. Corps scouts circled in a wide arc out from the marching army early in morning of August 25 and back toward their August 24 campsite. They attacked a small party of warriors who had entered the abandoned campsite. They killed one, wounded two, and drove the others away.

As the Corps marched, raiding parties were sent out to destroy all of the Indian villages and cornfields on either side of the Maumee River for fifty miles. The American army reached Fort Defiance on August 28. They spent a couple of weeks there improving the fortifications. General Todd's brigade, including Major Price's Corps with Micajah and Edmund, left for Fort Recovery the following day to pick up additional provisions for the legion. They returned with a number of bullocks and flour on September 10.

The legion's pioneers were deployed on September 12 to prepare a road for the legion to march from Fort Defiance up the Maumee River valley to the abandoned site of Kekionga. General Wayne planned to build and garrison a huge fortification there that would dominate the entire region.

The legion and Kentucky volunteers took up the line of march for Kekionga on September 14 under the cover of Captain Kibbey's advance scouts. A garrison of three hundred men was left at Fort Defiance under the command of Major Burbeck.

The legion arrived at the former location of Kekionga, at the confluence of the St. Joseph's and St. Mary's Rivers, on September 17. General Wayne selected the site for the new fort the next day. Construction of the new fort began immediately. On September 21, General Todd's brigade, including Micajah and Edmund, left for Fort Greenville to obtain another load of provisions. They returned with about 150 bullocks on September 28.

The Kentucky volunteers in General Todd's and Barbee's brigades grew restless as the weeks rolled by. They did not want to tarry longer sim-

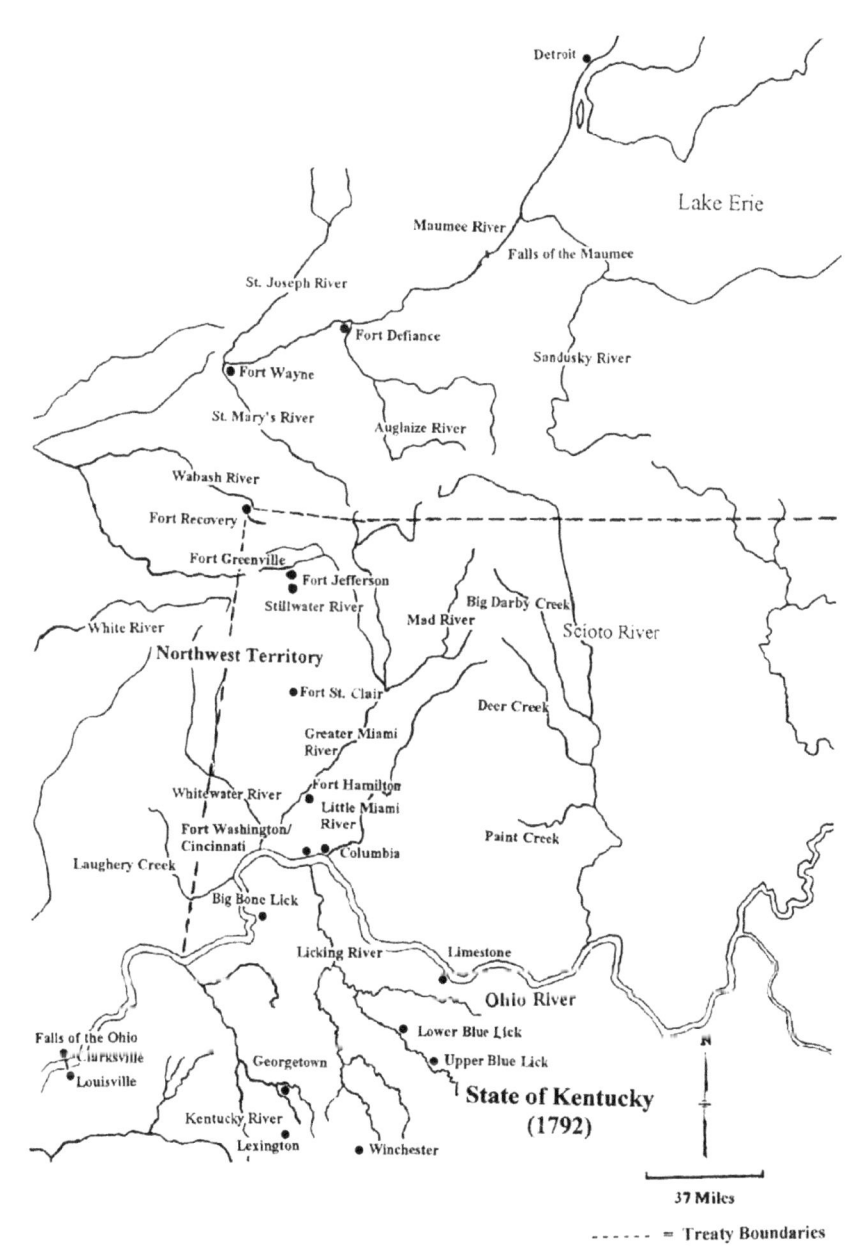

**Map 24
Boundaries of the Treaty of Greenville (1795)**

ply to serve as escorts for shuttling provisions from Fort Recovery and Fort Greenville up to the new fort.

Construction of the fort was completed by October 12 as the weather continued to cool. General Wayne finally directed Major General Scott to return to Fort Washington on October 13 for the purpose of discharging his Kentucky volunteers within fourteen days. He thanked General Scott and the volunteers for their soldierly conduct during the campaign. The new fort was occupied and named "Fort Wayne" in a ceremony with a fifteen-gun salute on October 22.

The Kentucky volunteers assembled at Fort Greenville and marched for Fort Washington and Cincinnati on October 20. Lieutenant William Sudduth completed the discharge papers for both Captain Joshua Baker Jr.'s and Captain John Arnold's companies of spies and scouts.[71] Micajah and Edmund arrived at Georgetown on October 26 and were discharged from service.

The military power of the Indian nations of the Northwest Territory had been shattered at the Battle of Fallen Timbers. The survivors wintered at Swan Creek after their defeat. Lieutenant Governor Simcoe visited them there in September of 1794 and found over three thousand men, women, and children in residence. British provisions were inadequate and many suffered from hunger.

John Jay successfully completed the negotiation of Jay's Treaty on November 19, 1794. The British committed to finally closing their posts in Detroit, Niagara, and Mackinack and turning them over to the Americans. The treaty was ratified by Congress on January 22, 1795.

General Wayne summoned the northwestern Indian nations to a treaty negotiation to be held at Greenville, Ohio, on June 15, 1795.[72] The Wyandot Nation was the first of the Indian Confederacy nations to accept the invitation. The remainder followed their lead and assembled at Fort Greenville on June 16. Eleven hundred chiefs and warriors attended the treaty negotiations. One hundred forty-two Shawanese were present.

The United States of America and the Indian Confederacy nations signed the Treaty of Greenville on August 3, 1795. The Principal Chiefs of the Wyandot, Delaware, Shawanese, Ottawa, Chippewa, Pottawatomie, Miami, Eel River, Wea, Kickapoo, Piankeshaw, and Kaskaskia Nations all signed. The Indian Confederacy nations ratified the boundaries established in the

Treaty of Fort Harmar and ceded all of their lands to the east and south of the "Greenville Treaty Line."

Chiefs Blue Jacket, Black Hoof, Red Pole, Long Shanks, Captain Reed, Kay-fe-wa-e-fe-kah, Wey-tha-pa-mat-tha, Nia-num-fe-ka, and Ne-que-taugh-aw signed the treaty on behalf of the Shawanese Nation. Ever true to the oath that he had pledged to his late father Pucksinwah, after the Battle of Point Pleasant twenty years before, Tecumseh refused to attend the negotiations or agree to make peace with the Americans.

Blue Jacket addressed General Wayne at the conclusion of the treaty:

> Elder brother, and you my brothers present. You see me now present myself as a war chief to lay down that commission and place myself in the rear of the village chiefs, who, for the future will command us. Remember brothers, you have all buried your war hatchets. Your brothers the Shawanoes now do the same good act. We must think of war no more.[73]

The British honored Jay's Treaty and abandoned Detroit and their remaining posts in United States territory in 1796. The British Indian Department, including Alexander McKee, Matthew Elliott, and the Girty brothers, relocated to Amherstberg, Upper Canada, on the Canadian eastern shore of the Detroit River about seventeen miles south of Detroit.

Captain Johnny, Nenessica (Black Beard), Buffalo, Kakinathucca, and their militant Shawanese faction moved to the island of Bois Blanc near Amherstberg. Shawanese from the peace faction established a new town named Wapakoneta on the upper Auglaize River just north of the Greenville Treaty line. Tecumseh and his militant band moved to the headwaters of the Whitewater River in the Indiana Territory.[74]

On November 28, 1796, Chief Blue Jacket and his half-brother Red Pole traveled to Philadelphia and met with President Washington. Red Pole became ill and died in Pittsburgh on January 28, 1797, during their return journey. He was buried in the cemetery of Trinity Church in Pittsburgh.[75]

The aging Virginia veterans of the War for Independence settled in the Virginia Military District and other territory ceded with finality by the

Treaty of Greenville. In 1796, Nathaniel Massie surveyed and founded the town of Chillicothe, at the mouth of Paint Creek on the Scioto River near the former location of the Old Chalaakaatha town. Chillicothe grew rapidly and was ultimately chosen as the capital of the new state of Ohio when it was formed in 1803. The population of Ohio reached 230,000 by 1810.[76]

Thomas Spottswood Hinde hosted Blue Jacket during a visit to Chillicothe in September 1807. He found Blue Jacket standing on his porch gazing over the Scioto River valley with tears streaming down his cheeks. Blue Jacket said that he had been thinking about the many Shawanese chiefs and warriors that he had known who died defending their Ohio homeland: "It affects my heart and fills it with sorrow. Now, I am a very old man, and will soon pass away like all the rest. I desire to live and die in peace!"[77]

MICAJAH HAD MET A YOUNG WOMAN NAMED Mary Arnold just before leaving with the Kentucky volunteers to join General Wayne's Campaign.[78] His thoughts had turned to her frequently since then. Micajah proposed to her upon his return to Kentucky after the campaign, and they were married in early 1796.[79] The newlyweds lived in Clark County after their marriage.[80]

Micajah tried to continue to make a living by hunting and trapping. However, the game population was in steep decline in the Kentucky Bluegrass region and throughout the Ohio River Valley. To make matters worse, skin and fur prices were falling on the world market. Micajah supplemented his income by helping his brothers and neighbors in their tobacco fields, delivering express messages, working on surveying crews, and taking any other work he could find and get paid for.

Many of Micajah's friends and acquaintances among the original settlers in Kentucky had lost or were losing their lands in the 1790s in disputes over defective titles. Daniel Boone was involved in a great deal of land title litigation as a result of his work as a surveyor and real estate broker in the 1770s and 1780s. Micajah found himself drawn into some of these disagreements.

Micajah served as a witness for depositions by Flanders Callaway and Samuel Boone in title litigation between William Scholl and Enos Hardin. Each of the two depositions was followed by the statement:

The foregoing Deposition taken before us the Commissioners Appointed by the County Court of Clarke at a spring on the North East side of a small Branch and a red Oak anciently marked DB (D reversed) called for in Daniel Boones Entry in the presence of Paul Hulse and Micajah Callaway, Disinterested Witnesses and have caused a red Oak Tree to be marked with the letter Y given under our hands this 18th of November 1796. Wm. Payne, Abraham Miller.

                          Paul Hulse
                                his
                     Micajah (X) Callaway
                              mark.[81]

Seventeen — The Pioneer Expatriates

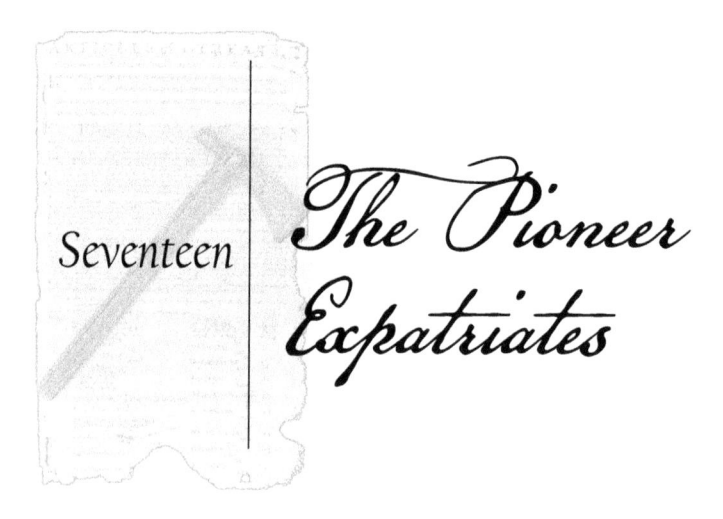

The Louisiana Territory

THE UNITED STATES AND SPAIN RESOLVED THEIR differences over navigation on the Mississippi River in 1795, in the Treaty of San Lorenzo. The government of Spain circulated handbills throughout the western frontier beginning in 1796, offering cheap land concessions (grants) in the Spanish Louisiana Territory.

Daniel Boone, his family, and close friends were intrigued by the possibility of fresh start in Spanish Louisiana. Daniel's son Daniel Morgan ("M.") Boone visited Spanish Lieutenant Governor Zenon Trudeau in Saint Louis at his father's request and was favorably impressed by the opportunities described by the governor.[1]

Trudeau expedited the grant of a land concession to Daniel M. It was located in a beautiful little valley along a stream named the Femme Osage River in the St. Charles District. The Femme Osage joined the Missouri River on its north shore several miles upstream of the confluence of the Missouri and Mississippi Rivers at St. Louis.

Daniel Boone and his son Nathan decided to move to Missouri and join Daniel M. in the Femme Osage River valley.[2] Other members of their extended family and friends joined the growing immigration party, including Flanders and Micajah Callaway and their families.

The large, noisy "Boone Party" assembled at Limestone in early September of 1799. Flanders, Jemima, Micajah, Mary, and their children and several other families traveled up the Lexington-Limestone Road to meet

The Pioneer Expatriots

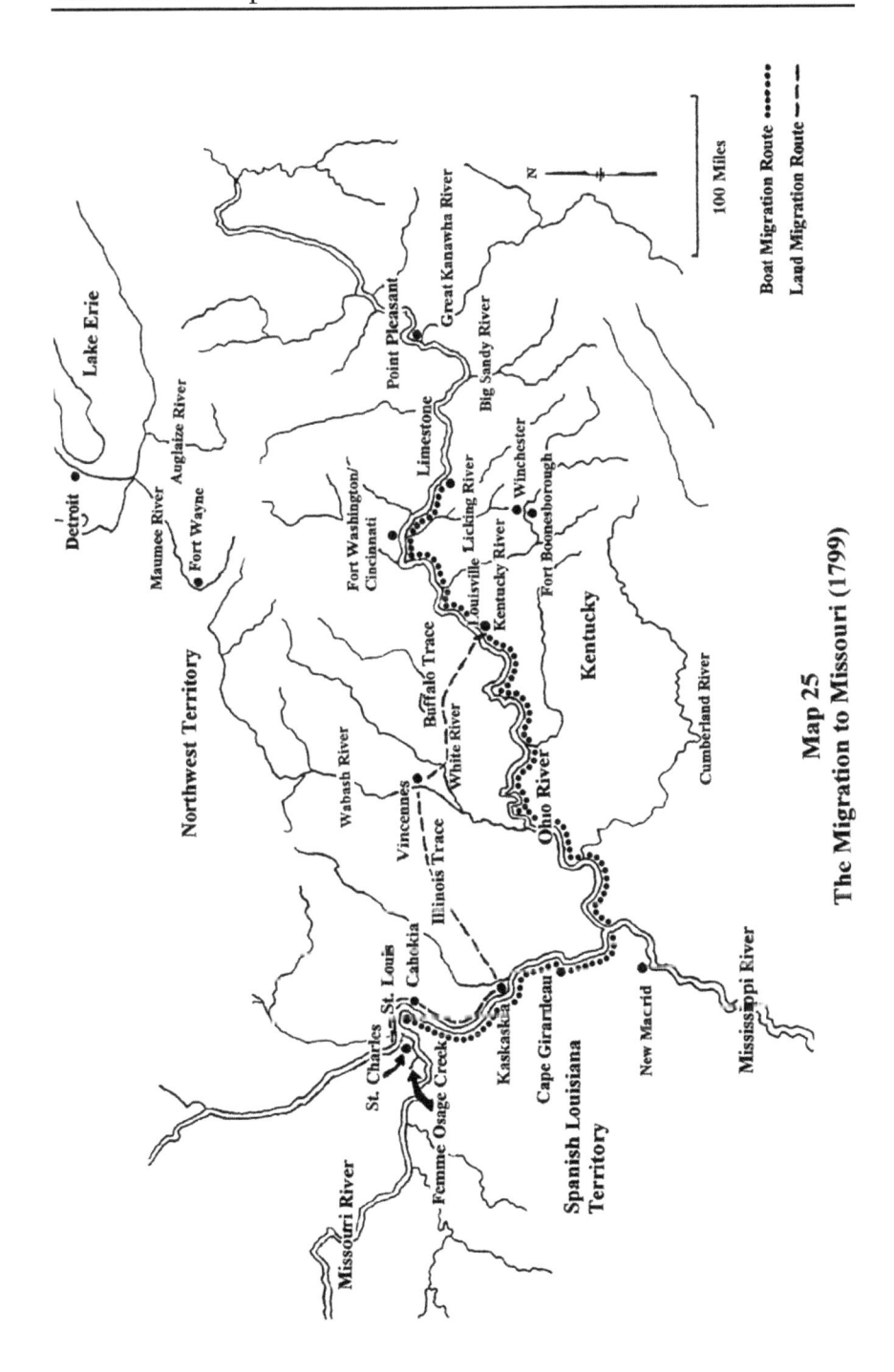

Map 25
The Migration to Missouri (1799)

them. Micajah was thirty-nine years old. Flanders's oldest son John was then eighteen years old and his second oldest son James was sixteen years old.[3]

Daniel and the other leaders decided that a group of men (the land party) should drive the families' cattle, horses, sheep, and hogs overland to St. Louis. The rest of the party (the boat party) would travel by boat to rendezvous with the livestock drovers in St. Louis. Daniel Boone would then meet with Lieutenant Governor Trudeau there to obtain the land concessions for the settlers before moving on to settle in the Femme Osage River valley.

The land party was comprised of Daniel Boone, Flanders Callaway and his sixteen-year-old son James Callaway, Forest Hancock, Isaac VanBibber, and William Hays Sr. and Jr. They would drive the livestock along the Ohio River path until they reached the Falls of the Ohio. There they would cross the Ohio River and then follow the old Buffalo Trace to Vincennes. They planned to ford the Wabash River there and travel on to St. Louis via the Illinois Trace.

The boat party was comprised of the rest of Daniel Boone's family, Squire Boone's family, Flanders Callaway's family, Micajah and Mary Callaway, and several other families. They would travel down the Ohio River and up the Mississippi River to St. Louis in a small fleet of boats.

Mary and Micajah had conceived a child in the early part of the year, and Mary was in the sixth or seventh month of her term as the pioneers assembled at Limestone. Micajah wanted to stay with her on the rugged journey. They joined Jemima and the rest of Flanders's family in a large pirogue carved from a single massive poplar tree log. The other families traveled in various pirogues, flatboats, and keelboats.

The immigrants left Limestone and set off down the river for Missouri in mid-September 1799 on a journey which lasted several weeks. The land party crossed over the Mississippi River and reached St. Louis in the latter part of October. The boat party arrived soon afterward.[4]

Daniel Boone met with Trudeau and Don Charles Dehault Delassus after their arrival in St. Louis. Delassus would soon succeed Zénon Trudeau as the new lieutenant governor. The Spanish officials welcomed and paid tribute to the world-renowned Colonel Daniel Boone in a military ceremony filled with pomp and circumstance. The Spanish garrison paraded both the American and Spanish flags.[5]

The Pioneer Expatriots

Trudeau consulted with Delassus to ensure that his prior commitments made to Daniel Boone would be honored.[6] Boone and Trudeau compiled a list of the heads of household in the Boone party including Flanders and Micajah Callaway.[7]

Don Charles Dehault Delassus provided Daniel Boone with blank concession forms allowing him to designate parcels of land to each of the listed heads of households. Zénon Trudeau advised Boone to backdate the forms to the time when they had exchanged correspondence over the prospects of settlement in Missouri. Spain and France were negotiating a retrocession of the Louisiana Territory back to France. Backdating the forms would help ensure that the concessions would be honored in the event that the retrocession was consummated.[8]

The Missouri River

DANIEL BOONE LEFT THE OFFICES OF THE lieutenant governor when the transactions were completed, mounted his horse, and set off with his flock of pioneers.[9] He and some of the men in the party crossed east back over the Mississippi River to retrieve their herds of livestock, then drove the animals down the eastern bank of the Mississippi River and crossed to the western shore just above the mouth of the Missouri River.

The Boone party reassembled and set off to the west up the river trail on the north shore of the Missouri River. They passed through the French frontier town of St. Charles and arrived at Daniel M. Boone's property at the mouth of the Femme Osage River. The settlers set up a temporary camp there and prepared for the winter while the heads of household went about locating their land concessions.[10]

Mary gave birth to a baby boy in the settlers' encampment very soon after their arrival, and the couple named him James in honor of Micajah's father and brother.[11]

Flanders and Micajah were awarded neighboring concessions of eight hundred arpens (approximately six hundred fifty acres) located along the Femme Osage River. Their parcels were located between Nathan Boone's and Daniel M.'s properties at the mouth of a branch of the river that came to be known as Callaway's Fork.[12] Daniel Boone located his concession near Daniel M.'s property, a couple of miles downstream from Micajah's land near the mouth of the Femme Osage River.[13]

Micajah's concession application was completed and backdated to January 23, 1798.[14] The date of the decree approving his application was backdated to January 24, 1798. His survey was conducted as Survey No. 32 on December 24, 1799. Daniel M.'s survey of six hundred arpens was listed as Survey No. 33, and Daniel Boone's survey of one thousand arpens was listed as Survey No. 34.[15]

Micajah completed construction of a temporary cabin by the first day of the new century and his little family moved in. Micajah and Mary were very pleased with their snug little home. The bottomlands of their concession were fertile and well irrigated. Forests covered the hills to the north and wild game was plentiful. Through the remainder of the winter season, Micajah alternated clearing the trees from his land and hunting with Flanders and the other men.

Micajah began work on a larger, permanent log house the next spring. He plowed his virgin fields, planted his first crop of corn, and cleared more land for a larger crop the next season. Flanders and Micajah traded labor by alternately helping each other clear and cultivate their respective land. Daniel Boone frequently dropped by as he came and went to visit his children and grandchildren. Mary became pregnant again that summer.

It appears that Micajah made at least one trip back to Kentucky in 1800. Bourbon County, Kentucky, tax records for 1800 show him as entering seven hundred acres of land on behalf of James Callaway (Jr.) and James's son Abraham that year.[16]

Micajah may have learned of the death of his elderly Uncle Thomas Callaway from Callaway cousins on this trip. Thomas was the last surviving son of English immigrant Joseph Callaway Jr. at the time of his death in 1800. He had seen Virginia expand its dominion and influence from the frontiers of Essex and Spotsylvania County to the Missouri River and beyond in his long and eventful life. He was buried in the Callaway Cemetery in West Jefferson, North Carolina. Many years earlier Daniel Boone had carved the initials "T.C." into the long gray stone that serves as Thomas' tombstone.[17]

The French Republic entered into the Treaty of San Ildefonso with His

The Pioneer Expatriots

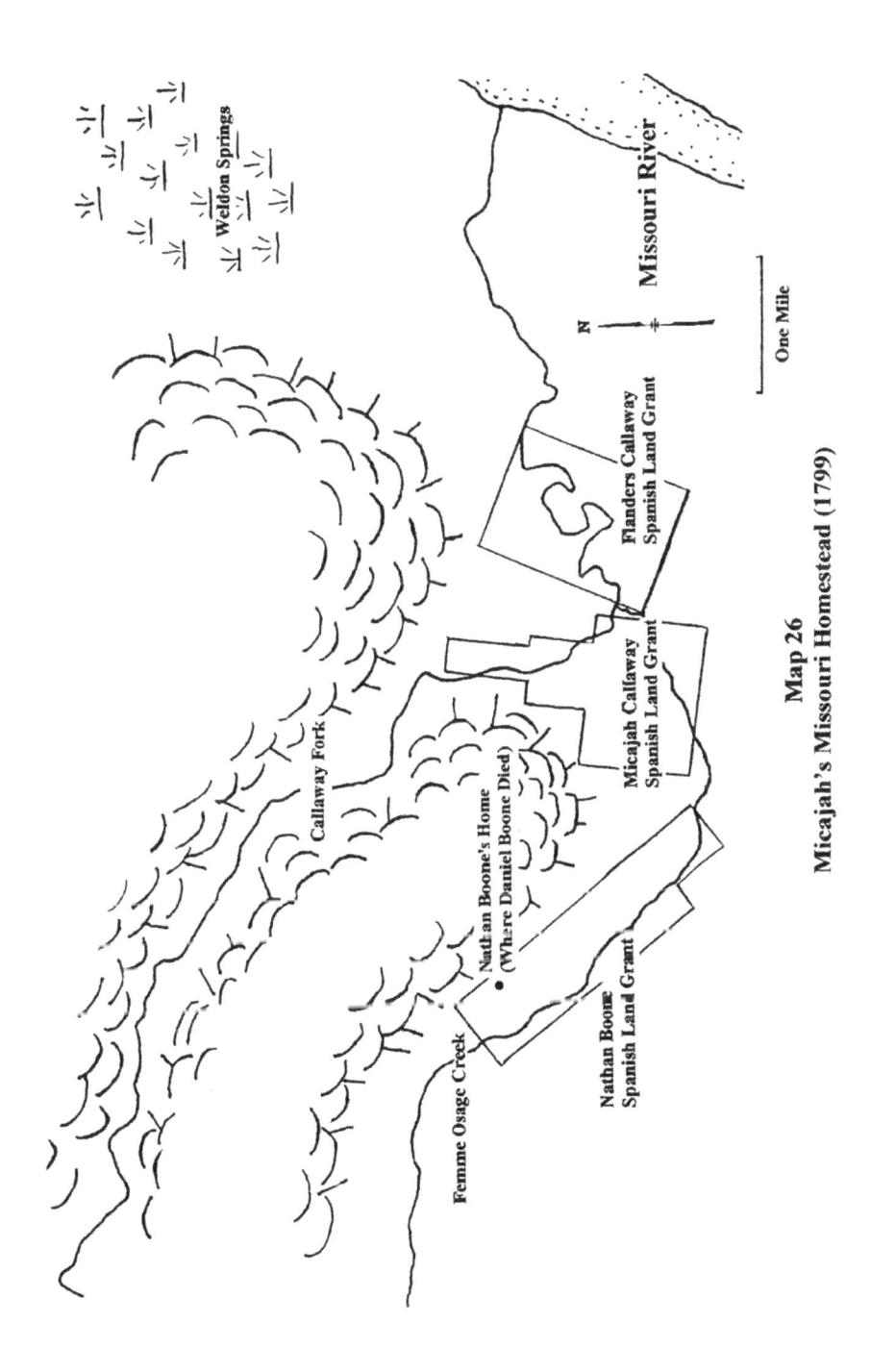

Map 26
Micajah's Missouri Homestead (1799)

Catholic Majesty, the King of Spain, on October 1, 1800, providing for the retrocession of the Louisiana Territory from Spain back to France. The Boones, Callaways, and other American immigrants in Missouri thus became residents of the French Republic.

Micajah continued to improve his property and hunt locally with Daniel and Flanders through the winter of 1801–1802. A second son named Edmund was born in early 1801. Micajah planted a larger corn crop in the spring and diligently tended it through the summer. Mary became pregnant again at the end of the summer of 1802.

Micajah basked in happiness. He had a loving wife and family to share his life with, and owned several hundred acres of fresh, unspoiled, fertile land . . . yet adventure was still at his doorstep. The nearby Missouri River was like a great beckoning highway carrying travelers from the Gulf of Mexico as well as distant Indian Nations from the Great Plains, the Rocky Mountains, and beyond. The troubled times in Kentucky and the Northwest Territory seemed distant and long ago.

Daniel Boone, Flanders Callaway, Flanders's son James, William Hays, and Derry went to the Niango River in October of 1802 for an extended fall and winter hunt. The Callaways formed one hunting party and Boone and Hays the other. The two parties separated and trapped beaver in the areas around the base camp. They rapidly accumulated beaver pelts and cached them in hiding places for safekeeping.

The hunters returned to their homes with two hundred beaver pelts. Flanders and his son James delivered them to Lexington, Kentucky, on horseback and sold them there. They procured household supplies in Lexington and packed them back to Missouri. This became an annual ritual for Flanders.[18]

Daniel Boone and Rebecca moved into a small cabin on their son Nathan's property on the Femme Osage River sometime in late 1802 or early 1803, and once again became neighbors of Micajah and his family. A baby girl was born to Micajah and Mary in the spring of 1803, and they named her Margaret.[19]

President Thomas Jefferson and the United States of America entered into the Louisiana Purchase with the French Republic on April 30, 1803, and as a result obtained the entire Louisiana Territory. Daniel Boone and the American settlers along the Femme Osage River were once again residents of the United States. They were pleased, but uncertain about what impact the change would have on the land titles that they had obtained from the Spanish government.

Micajah, Mary, and Margaret were all stricken with malaria not long after the Louisiana Purchase was concluded. According to the medical lore of the time, malaria was a result of the "bad air" (also called marsh effluvia or miasmata) that hung about swamps. Micajah's property was located not far to the west of a large area of wetlands to the northeast of the mouth of the Femme Osage River on the Missouri River. The Callaways were no doubt bitten by malaria-carrying mosquitoes originating from those wetlands. Little James and Edmund were spared.

Flanders and Jemima moved the three stricken Callaways and their two little boys into their home next door and cared for them. Micajah, Mary, and tiny Margaret suffered greatly from recurring bouts of high fever and delirium. They rapidly declined to the edge of death. Jemima did her best to break their fevers with home remedies.

The ravages of the disease were too much for Mary and Margaret, and they both succumbed. Micajah suffered as many as three severe recurrences of the fever in less than twenty-four hours, and barely survived.

Flanders buried Mary and baby Margaret on Micajah's land. Micajah was still ill and leaned on Flanders at the funeral. He was devastated and wept bitter tears. The two surviving little boys were not yet acquainted with death and were bewildered.

Jemima nursed Micajah back to health, but he remained in a melancholy mood after his recovery. He had experienced so much death and hardship in his lifetime on the frontiers of Virginia, Kentucky, and Missouri, but the loss of his beloved Mary and little daughter was the hardest loss of all. He struggled alone to operate his farm and household through the summer farming season as he grieved. Jemima helped care for his two little boys.

Micajah could not let his grief overwhelm him. It took two people to run a frontier household, and he needed to find a new mother for the boys. There weren't many available single women in the little Femme Osage settlement. He decided to return to Kentucky and make new plans for the future, so he sold his Femme Osage land to Thomas Smith early in 1804.[20]

Flanders's twenty-three year old son John agreed to accompany

Micajah and his children on the journey. John would add a helpful second rifle in case they encountered hostile Indians or bandits.[21] Two packhorses would carry provisions and only the most irreplaceable of their worldly possessions. Everything else would be sold or given away.

Micajah made two oversized buffalo-hide saddlebags to carry little James and Edmund. He put the soft buffalo wool on the inside of the saddlebags to provide a cushion for his little ones.[22]

It was time for Micajah to say goodbye to Flanders, Daniel, Rebecca, and Jemima and their children. It was hard to leave them. They had shared so much of life for so many years. Daniel Boone was now seventy years old and Flanders Callaway was fifty-six. Micajah, who had always been "the kid" among the three, was forty-four. Time was slowly slipping away.

PRESIDENT THOMAS JEFFERSON WAS DETERMINED TO PUSH forward to realize Virginia's dream of a continental empire. The next logical step after the Louisiana Purchase was to explore the Missouri River to its source and beyond. He dispatched an expedition led by Virginians Meriwether Lewis and William Clark to travel up the Missouri to its source, cross the Continental Divide, and follow the Columbia River to the Pacific Ocean.

The Lewis and Clark expedition passed by the mouth of the Femme Osage River on May 23, 1804, as the time for Micajah's departure from Missouri approached. In his journal, William Clark noted the community of thirty to forty American families living along the Femme Osage River.[23]

Return to Kentucky

MICAJAH LOADED HIS BOYS INTO THE SADDLEBAGS and walked his small horse-train over to Flander's home, where his family and friends had gathered. They sat down to one last breakfast together, and reminisced about past adventures and old friends and enemies. They toasted the memory of Richard Callaway, Black Fish, Moluntha, and Lamatumque and the many brave settlers and Shawanese who had died in the battles of olden times.

When they were finished eating, they walked to Flanders's front yard

The Pioneer Expatriots 325

where the tethered horses waited. Micajah and his sons shook hands with the men and kissed the ladies. He loaded his little boys into the saddlebags, and set off down the trail with John. He glanced over his shoulder one last time. The little group waved to him, and he waved back.

Micajah, John, and the boys passed through St. Charles and reached the Mississippi River just above the mouth of the Missouri four days later. James and Edmund quietly played with their homemade toys down inside the giant saddlebags. Their little heads occasionally popped up to peer over the edges to look at their surroundings with eyes round with curiosity.

Micajah located a flatboat ferry, and they were ferried across the Mississippi River. They rode south down the river trail to Kaskaskia where they rested and re-provisioned, and then headed east from there on the Illinois Trace, reaching Vincennes in six days without incident.[24] The travelers took a rest in Vincennes before continuing on their journey.

Micajah learned that the town had grown considerably in importance since his stay there during General Clark's Campaign of 1786. Vincennes had been established as the capital for the new Indiana Territory on May 7, 1800. The Indiana Territory included all of the former Northwest Territory except for the new State of Ohio. The boundary line between Indiana and Ohio was surveyed in 1803 to run due north from the mouth of the Greater Miami River where Micajah had served as interpreter in the 1786 treaty negotiations with the Shawanese.[25]

Vincennes had also been selected to serve as the capitol of the newly acquired Louisiana Territory.[26] A monthly postal service was established on the old Buffalo Trace between Vincennes and Clarkville to improve the speed and reliability of communications between the territorial capital and the Ohio River.[27]

William Henry Harrison, General Wayne's former aid-de-camp at Fallen Timbers, had been appointed to serve as the governor of the new Indiana Territory in May 1800. He lived in Vincennes.[28] He was married to Anna Symmes, daughter of Judge John Cleves Symmes. Governor Harrison's Grouseland estate consisted of a fine tract of land along the Wabash River with a solid two-story brick mansion facing it.[29]

In June of 1803, Governor Harrison, at the direction of President Jefferson, negotiated a treaty of cession at Fort Wayne with the Miami,

Kickapoo, Pottawatomie, Delaware, and Shawanese Nations. The treaty reconfirmed the cession of a tract of land called the "Vincennes Tract" which had been ceded to the United States in the 1795 Treaty of Greenville.[30]

Governor Harrison planned to request that the Delaware Nation enter into another treaty to cede its interests in all lands to the south of a diagonal line running between the Wabash River and Ohio River just to the north of the Buffalo Trace.[31] The Delaware had claimed these lands since the Miami Confederacy nations had given them permission to settle there around 1770.[32]

Micajah, John, and the boys crossed the Wabash River at Vincennes and set off down the Buffalo Trace. The trace was still quite rugged and only two feet wide in most places despite the recent improvements. The Callaway party arrived at Clarksville and crossed over the Ohio River at the Falls of the Ohio by ferry into Louisville. The journey from Vincennes had taken four days. They made their way through the streets of Louisville to the Louisville Trace and arrived at James Callaway Jr.'s Bourbon County plantation two days later.

James Jr. and his family warmly welcomed Micajah, his sons and John. Micajah and his boys initially stayed with James Jr. and his family while he decided where to settle.

Old Nenessica (Black Beard) and two other Shawanese men visited Bourbon and Clark Counties about the time of Micajah's return to Kentucky. They reportedly came from Bourbon County through Grassy Lick and into the "Old Fields" area around the former site of Eskippakithiki. Nenessica had lived in Eskippakithiki as a boy and shouted with joy to once again see the old village site and beloved hunting grounds. He and his two companions reportedly camped a night near Eskippakithiki and then rode on to visit Pilot Knob and the Red River.

Nenessica did not explain the purpose of his visit to curious settlers. He and his companions reportedly returned north through Bourbon County and visited former Shawanese prisoner Stephen Ruddle, who lived there.[33] Perhaps they also visited Micajah.

MICAJAH FELL IN LOVE WITH FRANCES ("FRANKIE") Hawkins and married her in Garrard County on April 4, 1805. The marriage was recorded in Lancaster,

Kentucky and James Davis co-signed the marriage bond for the amount of fifty pounds.[34] James Davis was married to Frankie Hawkins's sister Nancy.[35]

Garrard County tax records show Micajah living in Garrard County as head of a household with three dependents (Frankie and little James and Edmund) in 1806.[36] Micajah and his family apparently relocated again early that year to Bourbon County, to live near Micajah's brother James Jr. on the Houston Fork. A son, John Hawkins ("Hawk") Callaway, was born to them in Bourbon County on February 22, 1806. Another son, Noble, was born there on March 15, 1809.[37]

Eighteen

The Indiana Territory

Another New Beginning

Governor Harrison signed the final Treaty of Grouseland with the Delaware, Miami, Eel River, Wea, Kickapoo, and Pottawatomie Nations on August 21, 1805. The Delaware and Miami Nations sold and ceded all of their claims to lands between the White River and the Ohio River to the west of the western boundary of the Clark Grant.[1] This opened a vast tract of land in the southern part of the Indiana Territory for American settlement.

On March 3, 1807, a land office was established in Jeffersonville, Indiana. The Federal government conducted initial surveys in the area in 1806 and early 1807.[2] In late summer of 1809, Micajah packed his scouting gear and set off to search for land to purchase in the ceded area. He decided to focus his search on lands near a small salt lick named Royse's Lick, located in the headwaters of the Blue River valley. It was located about thirty miles to the north-northwest of the Falls of the Ohio River in the newly-formed Harrison County, which had been formed out of portions of Knox and Clark Counties in 1808.

The headwaters of the Blue River drained from the northern and eastern edges of a large upland plateau called the Norman Uplands, which sloped gently to the west. The eastern edge of the upland plateau was formed by the "Knobstone Escarpment." This escarpment was created from the same erosion-resistant hard Devonian limestone that had formed the Falls of the Ohio River.

The Indiana Territory

North-flowing tributaries of the Muscatatuck River had deeply eroded the northeastern edge of the Norman Uplands, creating a series of very large forested hills cut through with deep ravines. The large hills were called "The Knobs." One could see spectacular views of the Muscatatuck River valley to the north from their five-hundred-foot summits. The hills reminded Micajah of his boyhood home in Bedford County in the foothills of the Blue Ridge Mountains. The Delaney Creek and Elk Creek watersheds were particularly rugged.

Royse's Lick was located in the upper reaches of a fork of the Blue River near the northern edge of the upland plateau. It was named after a settler and Indian trader named Frederick Royse, who had started a small saltworks and trading post there in 1802.[3] Royse moved his family there in 1805 where they squatted until the land was opened for surveying and purchase.[4]

Micajah probably crossed the Ohio River on Marston G. Clark's flatboat ferry from the mouth of the Beargrass River just east of Louisville to the new town of Jeffersonville on the north shore. Marston Clark was the son of George Rogers Clark's uncle Benjamin Clark and a brother of the William Clark who surveyed Clark's Grant in Indiana.[5]

Micajah rode on from Jeffersonville to the head of the Buffalo Trace on the western outskirts of Clarksville and camped for the night. He followed the trace to its ford at the Blue River, then followed a well-traveled horse path that headed to the north from the ford and paralleled the western banks of the river. The path swung to the northeast along the river and continued to Royse's Lick.

Micajah approached Royse's Lick and rode into a small clearing along the river where the little saltworks had been established. Large kettles of boiling salt water were set up on stacks of flat limestone rocks framed around roaring wood fires, and a column of thick white smoke billowed into the air. A small ramshackle cabin stood near the saltworks, serving both as Royse's working quarters and as a salt storage room. His family cabin was nearby.

Micajah met there with Frederick Royse and Dr. Simeon Lamb and learned that several families had already settled in the area since the Jeffersonville Land Office had opened in 1807. A self-sufficient community of settlers was slowly taking shape around Royse's Lick. The nearby hills

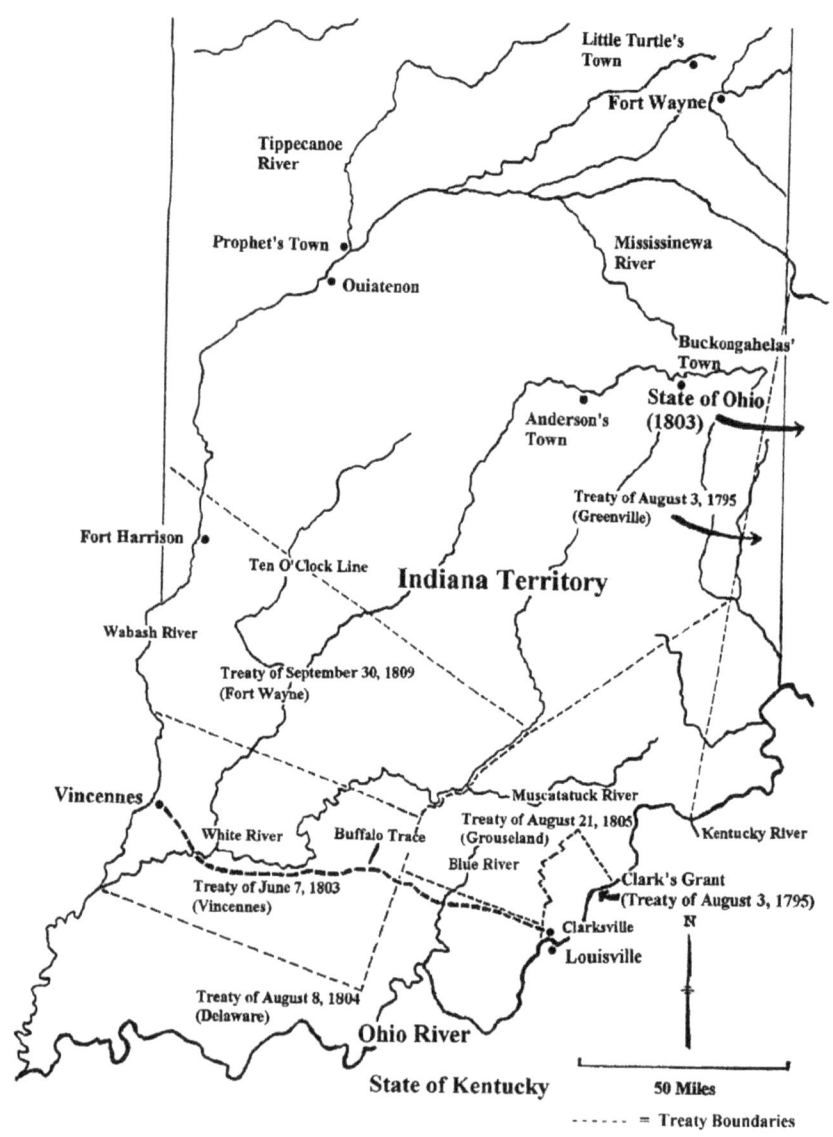

Map 27
The Indiana Territory and Indian Treaty Boundaries
(1804-1809)

literally echoed with the sounds of axes as the settlers cleared their land and built cabins.

George Brock and his sons-in-law Fred Neidiffer and Adam Barnett and their families had settled near Royse's Lick in 1807, followed by Robert Thompson, William Gordon, Philbert Wright, and Benjamin Brewer and their families. Brock was a blacksmith and had opened a small shop on his property. Henry Dawalt had just arrived from Pennsylvania and began building a small blockhouse just to the east of Royse's Lick early in 1809. Other settlers were arriving on almost a daily basis.

There was still good land available for purchase and location to the north of George Brock's homestead up along the Crest of the Knobs. Royse suggested that Micajah explore the property there near a small salt lick called Deer Lick (also known as Evans Lick) about a half-hour ride to the north and west of Royse's Lick. It was a favorite hunting spot for both the local Delaware Indians and white settlers.

Micajah ended his search for a homestead site about a mile to the east of Deer Lick on a large terrace of land on the top of a ridge gently sloping north from the Crest of the Knobs. A small, bubbling spring of clean, cool water emerged from a shelf of limestone at the edge of the terrace and flowed down into a deep ravine below.

The terrace was covered with large, mature hackberry, sugar maple, ash, elm, hickory, chestnut, and tulip poplar trees. Deep ravines sloped down from both sides of the ridge, draining away from the Knobs toward Delaney Creek, a couple of miles to the north. The surrounding forest teemed with game. This seemed like a perfect place to settle with his young family.

Micajah returned to Royse's Lick on the following day to learn more about the local Indian population. Delaware Chief Ox's hunting camp was located just to the west of Royse's Lick on the Blue River floodplain.[6] His main village was on the Muscatuck River to the north. A mix of Delaware and a few Shawanese refugees lived there.

Delaware Indians had settled in the White River valley beginning about 1770 with permission of the Miami Nation. In 1772, the survivors of Delaware Chief Captain Bull's band moved from their village on the Little Kanawha River to a new location eighteen miles up the White River. Several additional villages were established nearby in 1773.[7] The Delaware settled there aligned themselves with the British during the War for Independence and battled with George Rogers Clark and his men in 1779. Hostilities had continued until at least 1782.[8] It seems plausible that Captain Bull and the elderly Chief Ox were the same individual.

Micajah introduced himself to Chief Ox in the Delaware language and mentioned some of his Delaware acquaintances through the years, including Buckongahelas, the Big Cat, and George White Eyes. Chief Ox's face lit up with a broad smile as he stepped forward to shake Micajah's hand. He introduced Micajah to his elderly wife, his son Towhead, and his son-in-law, a white scout named Silas McCullough.[9]

There were a number of other small Delaware villages in the general area that served as bases for large hunting parties from the main Delaware villages up on the West Fork of the White River. There was a small village at the mouth of Salt Creek down the East (Driftwood) Fork of that river. A descendant of the great Delaware Chiefs Netawatwes and Captain Killbuck, known as "Little Killbuck," had established a small Delaware village about ten miles to the southeast of Royse's Lick.[10]

Micajah carefully steered the conversation with Chief Ox and his family toward the subject of the messianic Shawanese "Prophet" and his militant brother Tecumseh. Micajah had lived near them in the Shawanese Ohio towns when they were children and had matched wits with Tecumseh and his scouts during the Wayne Campaign. He had followed their recent rise to power with great concern. They now lived in Prophet's Town in the northern part of the Indiana Territory and were threatening the new settlements in that area. Micajah did not want to move his family into a dangerous and unmanageable situation.

The Shawanese Prophet

TECUMSEH'S YOUNGER BROTHER LOWALUWAYSICA HAD BEEN A useless and violent alcoholic for most of his early adult life. He fell into a trance on a November night in 1805 while lighting his pipe and dreamed that Moneto transported his spirit up to Heaven.

In Lowaluwaysica's dream, Moneto told him that if the Indians lived as warriors as their ancestors had done and returned to their traditional ways, He would lead the Indians through Lowaluswaysica to take their ancestral lands back from the white people. Moneto would bring forth all of the animals ever created to repopulate the forests and restore the dead friends of the living Indians. Their enemies would be destroyed and the Indians would be the masters of the land again.

However, the Indian people would be destroyed if they did not obey Moneto's wishes. Those who did not agree with the Lowaluwaysica's vision were witches and were to be put to death.

Lowaluswaysica dreamed that Moneto told him that he should change his name to "Tenskwatawa"—the "Open Door." He came to be known to white people as "the Prophet."

The Prophet presented his religious vision to a Shawanese council in Wapakoneta late in November of 1805. The vision struck a responsive chord and provided hope to the increasingly despondent northwestern Indian peoples who had lost so much of their homeland to the advancing whites and were rapidly losing their cultural heritage. Their only hope now was divine intervention and the Prophet offered to bring it to them.

The Prophet was a magnetic speaker and captured the hearts and minds of many who heard him. His message spread quickly and galvanized the people of the northwestern Indian nations. Thousands of them abandoned their white clothing, artifacts, and cabins and returned to the forests to live as their fathers and grandfathers had done. Indian witches were sought out and burned to death.[11]

Tecumseh was a great war leader and spellbinding orator in his own right. He set about re-establishing and strengthening military and political alliances among the Indian nations as his brother spread his religious message. Tecumseh, like his pan-Indian movement predecessors Guyasuta, Pontiac, Joseph Brant, Blue Jacket, and Red Pole, strove to unite the Indian nations under the vision that they were one people and could stand up to the whites and drive them back south of the Ohio River and perhaps even to the east of the mountains . . . if they would only stand together.

Old Makujay Chief Black Hoof had become the Principal Chief of the remaining Ohio Shawanese in 1801. Most of them were pro-American and lived in the towns of Wapakoneta and Lewistown. Black Hoof's faction was adamantly opposed to Tecumseh and the Prophet and refused to follow their leadership.

The Prophet and Tecumseh traveled tirelessly across the vast landscape to spread their religious and political vision among the northwestern Indian nations. The Prophet converted many doubters among the Shawanese and neighboring nations when he successfully predicted a solar eclipse in the summer of 1806.

In the spring of 1808, Tecumseh and the Prophet and their followers established a new town they named "Tippecanoe" on the Wabash River in the Indiana Territory. It was located three miles below the mouth of the Tippecanoe River and approximately one hundred twenty miles upstream from Vincennes. The Americans called it "Prophet's Town."

British Deputy Superintendent General William Claus met with Shawanese Chiefs Buffalo, Nenessica (Black Beard), and Captain Johnny on March 25, 1808. They discussed a renewed alliance as another war between Great Britain and the United States loomed in the near future.[12]

Aged Nenessica had returned to Ohio in 1800 from Bois Blanc and was living in Wapakoneta among the faction that opposed the Prophet and Tecumseh in 1805–1807.[13] He was once again dispatched on a long-distance secret mission to carry a message to the Cherokee Nation regarding the possibility of a renewed Indian Confederacy. He returned in 1809 and was reportedly exhausted by the effort.[14]

A WAVE OF FRATRICIDAL WITCH-HUNTING SET in motion by the Prophet was sweeping through the main Delaware towns on the West Fork of the White River at the time of Micajah's visit to Royse's Lick. Nearly a dozen suspected witches had been killed that year, and the Delaware Nation teetered on the brink of civil war. The local Delaware bands living in the southern Indiana Territory reflected the internal divisions within their nation.

Chief Ox's son Towhead spoke out passionately in support of Tecumseh and the Prophet. Towhead railed against the Treaty of Grouseland. He predicted that there would someday be a day of reckoning between the Indians and the white settlers along the Muscatatuck and Blue Rivers. He and Little Killbuck hoped to join Tecumseh and the Prophet at Tippecanoe.

The Indiana Territory

Chief Ox shook his head sadly, looked at Micajah, and said that he did not agree with his son. He was doing all that he could to keep the peace.

Micajah's return trip to Kentucky was uneventful. He reported his findings to Frankie and James and Nancy Davis. They all agreed that the location near Deer Lick sounded ideal. Micajah's discovery of sympathizers to the cause of the Prophet and Tecumseh among the local Delaware concerned them all.

Micajah Callaway, James Davis and their wives decided together to move forward with their plans to move to the Indiana Territory and settle near Royse's Lick, despite the increasing tension on the frontier. Perhaps they did not fully appreciate the intensity of the coming storm.

James Davis traveled to the Jeffersonville Land Office following their return to Kentucky and on June 25, 1810, purchased a quarter-section parcel of 160 acres on the Crest of the Knobs. It was located at the southwest quarter of section 27 of the third township north of the "Base Line" and the fourth range east of the "Principal Meridian" at Jeffersonville.[15]

Hoosiers

GOVERNOR HARRISON AND VILLAGE CHIEFS OF THE Delaware, Miami, and Pottawatomie Nations entered into the Treaty of Fort Wayne not long after Micajah's visit to Royse's Lick. Miami, Eel River, and Delaware chiefs agreed to sell and cede three million acres of land to the United States along the Wabash River to a point sixty miles to the north of Vincennes. This was half the distance from Vincennes to Prophet's Town.

The tensions between the Americans and northwestern Indian nations reached the brink of open warfare as the Callaway and Davis families made their final preparations to relocate to the Indiana Territory. Tecumseh and the Prophet were infuriated by the Treaty of Fort Wayne. Governor Harrison sent a letter to the secretary of war on April 25, 1810, noting that the "Shawnee Prophet" was inciting hostilities against the whites and that he could muster up to four hundred Kickapoo and Winnebago warriors at Prophet's Town. Harrison noted that the British were beginning to supply the warriors with arms and ammunition.[16]

Tecumseh sent messengers to the northwestern Great Lakes and western nations summoning them to a Grand Council to be held in the summer of 1810 to organize opposition to the Treaty of Fort Wayne. The Grand Council convened on the St. Joseph River in May 1810. The majority of those in attendance were firmly opposed to war.[17]

In July 1810, the Prophet dispatched a band of Creek warriors from Prophet's Town to visit and terrorize the Indiana Territory settlers in Vallonia and the nearby Long Knife settlements on the Muscatatuck and Blue River. The Creek warriors killed cattle and hogs, robbed and plundered several homesteads, and warned the settlers to move back south of the Ohio River or they would be killed. Several families in the settlements abandoned their homesteads and fled south of the Ohio River. Those that remained began to "fort up" and prepare for the worst.[18]

The Prophet's threat to kill all the settlers in Vallonia and nearby settlements was specifically directed at the very location where Micajah planned to move his family and establish his new home. Micajah conferred again with James Davis and both their wives when he learned of the threat, but they all remained committed to moving ahead with their plans. All agreed that construction of a fortified blockhouse would be the first order of business upon their arrival in the Indiana Territory.

Governor Harrison met with Tecumseh and seventy-five warriors in a tense council at his Grouseland estate in Vincennes, which began on August 15, 1810, and lasted for several days. They met a final time on August 21, 1810, and Tecumseh drew the line:

> Brother, we want to save that piece of land. We do not wish you to take it. It is small enough for our purpose. If you do take it, you must blame yourself as the cause of the trouble between us and the tribes who sold it to you. I want the present boundary line to continue. Should you cross it, I assure you it will be productive of bad consequences.[19]

Micajah, James Davis, and their families finished closing out most of their affairs in Kentucky and departed for the Indiana Territory in the early

The Indiana Territory 337

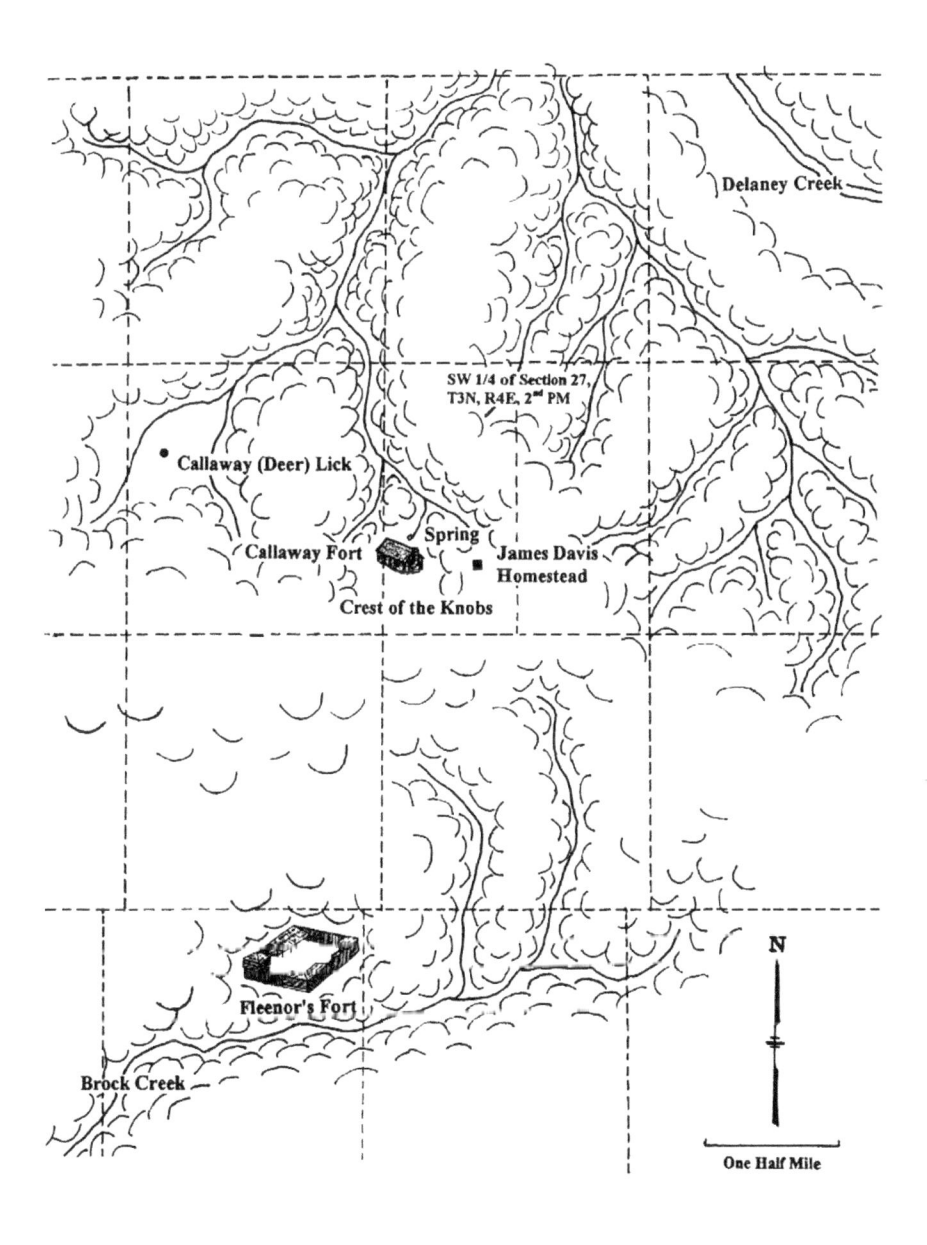

**Map 28
Callaway Fort -1810**

autumn of 1810. They most likely took the more established Vallonia Trace/Cincinnati Trace route from Jeffersonville to their destination. Micajah noticed the heavy boat traffic on the Ohio River as they ferried across. One hundred ninety-seven flatboats and fourteen keelboats descended the Falls of the Ohio in the two month period between November 24, 1810, and January 24, 1811.[20]

The Callaway/Davis party reached their new home on the Crest of the Knobs after a four-day journey. Micajah and James Davis quickly chose a location for the blockhouse next to the freshwater spring in the western half of the quarter-section that Davis had purchased. They planned to build a second cabin near a spring in the western half of the quarter-section after the blockhouse had been constructed. The Callaway family would occupy the blockhouse, and the Davis family would occupy the second cabin. In times of danger, the Davis family and other neighbors would take refuge together in the blockhouse.

Micajah and James Davis chopped down a number of large tulip poplar trees with their felling axes. The sturdy, straight trunks were ideal for the fortified structure that Micajah envisioned, and they used broadaxes to hew the heavy logs into thick, squared beams. As they lay out and constructed the walls, they built a large hearth and stick-and-clay chimney at one end.

Funnel-shaped gun portals were built into the ends and sides of the blockhouse, with the small end of the funnel shape on the inside wall of the house. The small aperture afforded the defenders protection and the large end of the funnel allowed a wider field of fire for their long rifles.

They installed a well-constructed puncheon floor in the blockhouse—a relative luxury compared to the bare dirt floors that were common among settlers' first cabins.[21] The blockhouse was completed with the addition of a stable for the horses against the backside.

As they labored, the two men hunted and killed deer, black bear, turkey, and other game for food for their families. They would be dependent upon wild game for food until they had planted and harvested their first crop.

They hunted at the Deer Lick and nearby wooded Knobs within range of hearing of a gunshot from their homestead. Frankie and Nancy were to fire a pistol to alert their husbands if they were in danger. The families carefully brought all of the guns and axes into the partially completed blockhouse

The Indiana Territory 339

every night and barred the door from the inside.[22] The local people came to call the blockhouse the "Callaway Fort."[23]

Micajah preferred to hunt with a partner for safety reasons. Moses Thompson was one of his frequent hunting partners. His homestead was located about four miles to the east of Micajah's, on the Crest of the Knobs near the headwaters of a tributary of Elk Creek. The rugged Knobs and ravines of the Elk Creek watershed stretched below his home to the east and north.

Micajah rode over to Moses Thompson's homestead to join him on an elk hunt early one morning before dawn in the spring of 1811. A number of elk lived in the canebrakes along the Elk Creek bottomland below Thompson's property.[24] Micajah and Moses had scouted there and discovered a particularly large and dominant bull.

The duo rode down to the bottomland, dismounted, spread out within view of each other, and slowly crept to the edge of a clearing. The magnificent bull stood on the other side of the clearing not thirty yards away, facing to Micajah's left. The thick neck of the great beast rose from powerfully muscled shoulders to its head, which was crowned by a huge rack of antlers. Micajah had never seen any elk approaching this size in a lifetime of hunting on the frontier.

Micajah and Moses raised their long rifles together. As they did so, the bull elk turned to look at them with its enormous, dignified brown eyes. At Moses' signal, they fired with a loud retort.

As the thick black-powder smoke drifted away from their gun barrels in the morning light, they could see that the bull was still standing. He had not changed his position at all. The bull calmly turned and lowered his head as if to graze on the grass. After a seemingly interminable pause, his knees buckled, and he collapsed onto his knees. The old patriarch turned to stare at Micajah. Then he lay his chin down on the ground as if to sleep. His spirit fled with a great shuddering sigh.

Micajah and Moses reloaded and stepped out from the edge of the clearing. They looked at each other and back at the bull. Neither had ever seen such a large and beautiful creature before.

The meat from the elk bull fed the Callaway, Thompson, and Davis families for several weeks. Moses decided that they should keep the magnificent rack of antlers as a trophy so that future residents of Indiana could appreciate the natural bounty that the first Hoosier settlers had discovered upon their arrival.[25] The bull's antlers were reportedly preserved and displayed for many years at an Indiana University museum in Bloomington, Indiana.[26]

The Prophet's War and the Battle of Tippecanoe

IN JUNE 1811, GOVERNOR HARRISON SENT A final plea to Tecumseh for peace:

> Brothers, what can be the inducement for you to undertake an enterprise when there is so little probability of success? Do you really think that the handful of men that you have about you are able to contend with the Seventeen Fires, or even that the whole of the tribes united could contend against the Kentucky Fire alone? Brothers, I am myself of the Long Knife Fire. As soon as they hear my voice you will see them pouring forth their swarms of hunting-shirt men, as numerous as the mosquitoes on the shore of the Wabash. Brothers, take care of their stings . . .[27]

Tecumseh approached the territorial capital of Vincennes on June 27, 1811, accompanied by three hundred warriors. He sent a message to Harrison stating that he wanted another parley.[28]

They met on the outskirts of Vincennes. Tecumseh professed his peaceful intentions. He said that he would be leaving the Indiana Territory to visit the southern Indian nations to persuade them to join the renewed Indian Confederacy. He then intended to travel to Washington, D.C., to personally negotiate a peace with the president of the United States on behalf of the entire confederacy.

Tecumseh left the Indiana Territory with twenty warriors and traveled south to meet with the Cherokee, Creek, and other southern nations. Governor Harrison wrote admiringly of Tecumseh's vision and energy:

The Indiana Territory   341

> If it were not for the vicinity of the United States, he would perhaps be the founder of an empire that would rival in glory that of Mexico or Peru. No difficulties deter him. His activity and industry supply the want of letters. For four years he has been in constant motion. You see him today on the Wabash, and in a short time hear of him on the shores of Lake Erie or Michigan, or on the banks of the Mississippi, and wherever he goes he makes an impression favorable to his purpose. He is now upon the last round to put a finishing stroke on his work. I hope, however, before his return that that part of the fabrick, which he considered complete will be demolished and even its foundations rooted up.[29]

While Tecumseh was absent on his journey to the south, the Prophet impetuously unleashed Pottawatomie warriors to attack unprotected white settlements in the Illinois Territory. The Indian Confederacy was not yet prepared for the confrontation that followed.

On July 17, 1811, President James Madison instructed the secretary of war to authorize Governor Harrison to call out the militia and attack Prophet's Town if necessary.[30] A company of volunteers from the upper Blue River valley and Royse's Lick, led by Captain John Beck of Beck's Mill, were among the forces that responded to Governor Harrison's call for volunteers. John Fleenor was one of the volunteers in Beck's company.[31] Fleenor had arrived in Royse's Lick in 1811 and purchased a quarter-section tract of land about a mile and a half south-southwest of Micajah's Callaway Fort.[32] Micajah and James Davis did not volunteer, because they did not want to leave their wives and young children unprotected in their isolated wilderness homes.

Governor Harrison and his army marched from Vincennes on September 26, 1811. The army was comprised of 250 regular federal soldiers under the command of Colonel Boyd, 600 militia volunteers from the Indiana Territory, and about 60 volunteers from Kentucky.[33] Marston Clark served Governor Harrison as his brigade major.[34]

On October 3, Harrison and his army encamped just to the north of an old Wea village where Terre Haute, Indiana, now stands and built a fort there. They completed construction and garrisoned "Fort Harrison" on October 28 and marched for Prophet's Town on October 29.

The American army approached Prophet's Town on November 6, 1811, and encamped. Governor Harrison ordered the men to sleep with their clothing and battle gear on and weapons at the ready.[35]

Seven hundred warriors surrounded Harrison's army during the night. The majority of them were from the Kickapoo and Winnebago Nations, although the Shawanese, Pottawatomie, and Sauk Nations were also represented by a few warriors.

The Indians attacked the Americans in their camp at 4:45 a.m. in the chilly morning of November 7, 1811, while most of the soldiers were still sleeping.[36] Against all odds, the Americans rallied to decisively defeat the warriors and drove them from the field of battle. The Americans suffered sixty-eight dead and one hundred twenty wounded. Approximately fifty warriors were killed. The Americans marched into Prophet's Town and burned it to the ground on November 8, 1811.[37]

Forting Up in the Blue River Country

JOHN FLEENOR SET ABOUT CONSTRUCTING A LARGER stockade fortification for the use of his family and neighbors upon his return from the Battle of Tippecanoe. Micajah and James Davis offered to help Fleenor build his new fort in exchange for his agreement that they could live there with their families for the duration of the anticipated hostilities, since it would be safer in a larger fort with more armed men.

Fleenor's Fort was constructed as a classic fortified frontier station. The stockade walls enclosed about an acre of land and were constructed from heavy vertical timbers set deep in the ground. The stockade timbers stood fifteen to sixteen feet tall. Cabins for the residents lined the inner wall. A large two-story blockhouse was constructed within the enclosure.

The following families moved into Fleenor's Fort upon its completion and lived there for the next two years:

The Indiana Territory 343

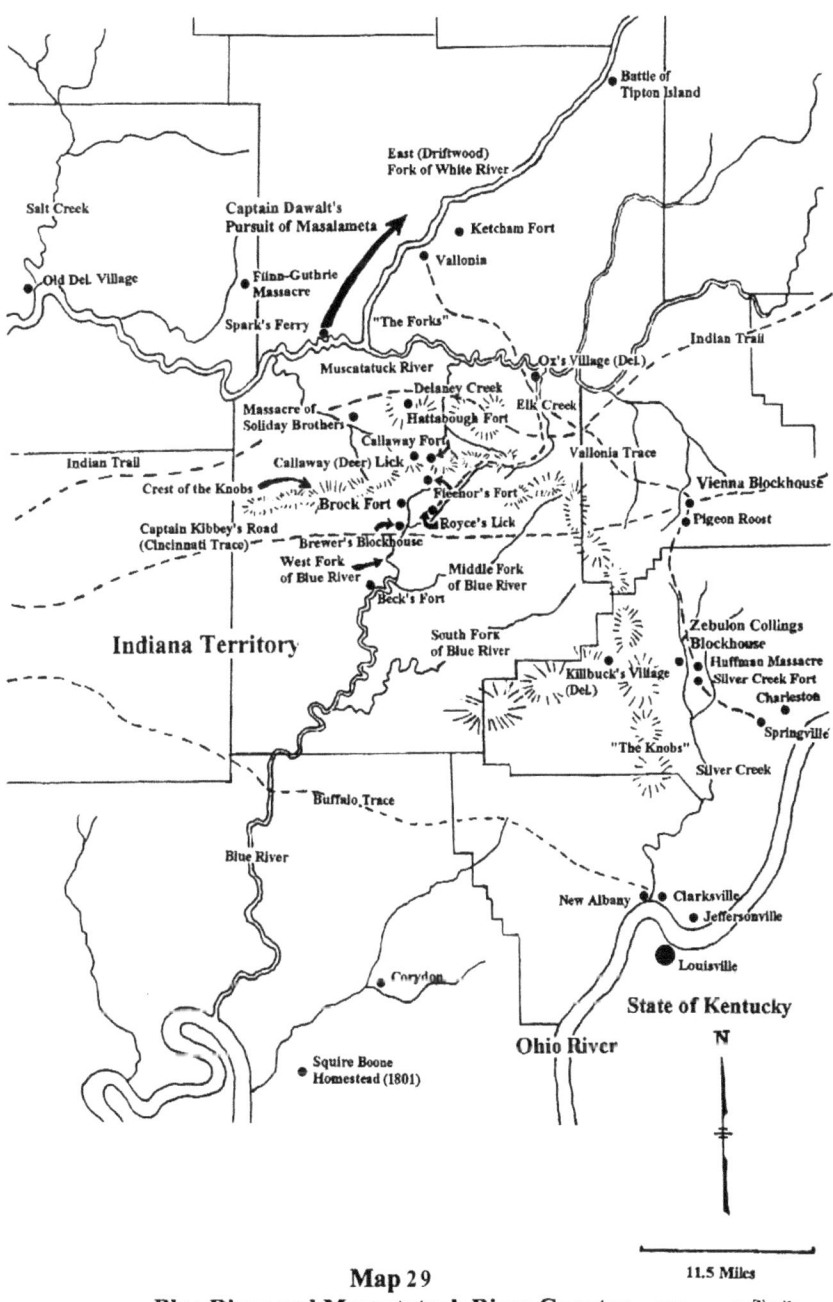

Map 29
Blue River and Muscatatuck River Country
(1810-1813)

John Fleenor and his wife and nine or ten children.
Micajah Callaway and his wife and five children.
James Davis and his wife and five children.
Arch Johnson and his wife, Mary, and nine children.
George House and his wife and two children.
Charles Carter and his wife and an unknown number of children.
Elisha Denny and his wife, Polly, and two children.[38]

They built a magazine for storing gunpowder and lead. Quantities of dried meat, flour, and barrels of water were stockpiled and stored. Pens for livestock were constructed and a garden was tilled and cultivated inside the fort. The men rotated duty manning the fort defenses, working in small armed groups at their outlying homestead farms, scouting, and hunting.

Several other forts were constructed in the upper Blue River valley in the Royse's Lick area. Brock Fort was constructed by George Brock and his neighbors about three miles to the south of Callaway Fort. The Brewer Blockhouse was built by Benjamin Brewer on Brock Creek at the current location of Salem, Indiana. Brock and Brewer were both veterans of the War for Independence.

The settlers in the Forks of the White River and Muscatatuck River (commonly called "the Forks") also built fortifications. They included Fort Vallonia, Ketcham Fort, and Huff's Fort.[39]

A band of Kickapoo warriors came up the White River during the winter of 1811–1812, and established a hidden camp of forty wegiwas just inland from the northern shore about four miles below the Forks and about ten miles to the northwest of Callaway and Fleenor Forts.[40] Kickapoo warriors crossed the river on the eve of Good Friday, 1812, and killed Daniel and Jacob Soliday. A man named Hinton was killed at the Forks on the same day.

The men of Fleenor's Fort assembled in a war council when they learned of the attacks and prepared to defend the fort. The men and boys were assigned to posts on the stockade and in the blockhouse. The women calmed and distracted the frightened children. Micajah and John Fleenor scouted the surrounding countryside.

Captain Henry Dawalt mustered a force of forty Royse's Lick militiamen and set off in pursuit of the Kickapoo marauders. Captain Dawalt and his men followed the war party for two days until calling off the chase on the rain-swollen banks of Bean Blossom Creek, not far from the current location of Bloomington, Indiana.[41]

The peaceful Delaware at Ox's Village sent messengers with white flags to the white settlements ten days later to confirm that the raiders were Kickapoo and reaffirm that the local Delaware wanted to live in peace.[42] Governor Harrison advised that the Delaware living there should be treated well as they had pledged their friendship with the Americans and had not yet shown any sign of disloyalty to them.[43]

About seventy families lived at the Forks of the White River and Muscatatuck River before the Soliday brothers and Hinton were killed. Only fifteen to eighteen families stayed to make a stand after the killings.[44] Governor Harrison ordered the construction of additional blockhouses at the Forks on April 16, 1812.[45]

A company of federal volunteers for the defense of northwestern Harrison County was raised in Corydon, Indiana, and placed under the command of Major Paul French. The company was divided into four units that were stationed at new Forts Alexander, Defiance, Pleasant and a fourth fort near Vallonia and the Forks.

Captain Jacob Zenor commanded one of the four federal units and was posted at Fort Pleasant. Captain Zenor and his men, including young Ensign John Tipton, patrolled down through the Royse's Lick area on May 20, July 5, and July 20, 1812.[46]

TECUMSEH RETURNED TO THE INDIANA TERRITORY FROM his southern journey in January of 1812. He was furious with his brother, the Prophet, and the Pottawatomies for their blunder in attacking the whites before the confederacy was at its full strength.

A major Indian council was held at an Indian village on the Mississinewa River in May of 1812. The chiefs of the Wyandot, Chippewa, Ottawa, Pottawatomie, Delaware, Miami, Eel River, Wea, Piankeshaw, Shawanese, Kickapoo, and Winnebago Nations attended. The chiefs of the assembled nations declared themselves in favor of peace with the whites.

Tecumseh denied that he had sought war and placed the blame for the Battle of Tippecanoe on the Pottawatomie. The Pottawatomie blamed the Shawanese individual "who pretended to be" a Prophet.

THE BRAVE SETTLERS WHO REMAINED IN THE upper Blue River valley continued making improvements on their property during the summer of 1812 despite the frequent Indian alarms. A settler named William Gordon decided to construct a larger home to replace his little cabin. A dog treed a black bear about a hundred yards from the site of the house-raising. Two young men named Joseph and Samuel Young each took a shot at the bear with their rifles. The bear glowered down at them as if unaffected.

    Micajah stepped forward with his old long rifle. He was dressed in his raccoon skin cap, hunting shirt, buckskin leggings, and moccasins. He raised the long rifle to his shoulder, cocked the hammer, took aim down the long barrel, and fired. The black bear tumbled from the tree to the ground, kicked spasmodically, and lay dead. The bear weighed three hundred pounds when fully dressed.[47] The hide, meat, and bear oil were shared among several families.

Nineteen: The War of 1812

The Rise of Tecumseh and the Fall of Forts Detroit, Mackinac, and Dearborn

TECUMSEH AND THE PROPHET AND THEIR FOLLOWERS rebuilt Prophet's Town in late May of 1812.[1] A force of seven to nine hundred Winnebago and Shawanese warriors assembled there. An additional force of eight hundred allied Kickapoo warriors assembled in the Peoria Towns in the Illinois Territory.

The Prophet remained at Prophet's Town, and Tecumseh went to Upper Canada to join the British at Fort Malden in early June as the United States and Great Britain slid inexorably toward war.[2] Tecumseh hoped that if the Shawanese helped the British, they would reward them by restoring the Ohio River as the boundary between the Indians and Americans if they were victorious.

Revolutionary War hero William Hull was the governor of the Michigan Territory in 1812 as tensions were rising along the American border with Upper Canada. He was commissioned the first commanding general of the new United States Army of the Northwest and took command in Urbana, Ohio, in the spring of 1812. The army mustered there and immediately marched for Detroit. The Wapakoneta Shawanese provided a group of scouts commanded by Spemica Lawba to aid the Americans.

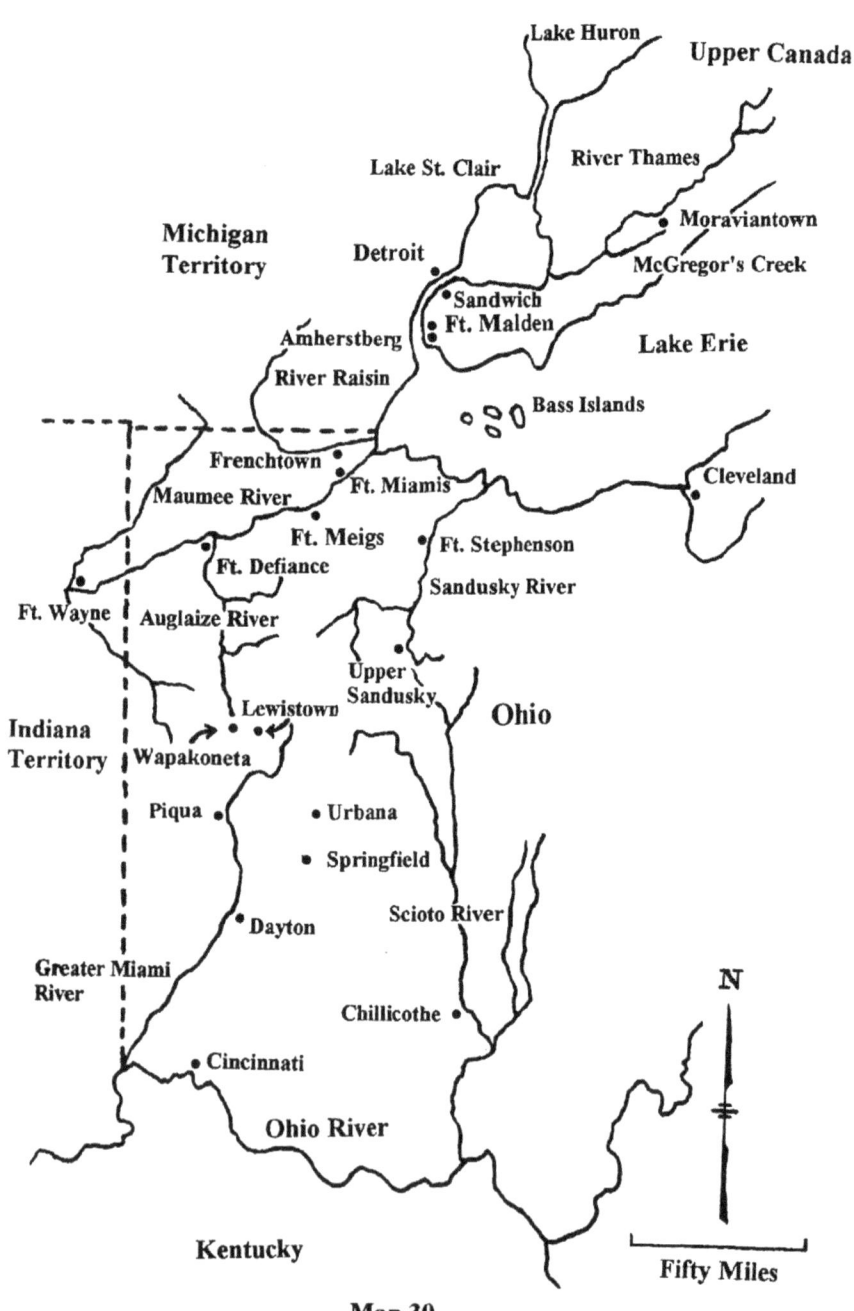

Map 30
The War of 1812 in Ohio and Upper Canada

The War of 1812 officially began on June 18, 1812, with a Declaration of War by the Congress of the United States against Great Britain. General Hull was notified on July 1, and arrived at Fort Detroit with his army on July 6.[3]

Tecumseh sent a large red war belt from Amherstberg to summon all of the warriors of the Indian nations to war against the United States of America. His messengers canvassed the Indian towns throughout Ohio and the Indiana Territory in search of volunteers.[4]

On July 21, General Hull led the Army of the Northwest across the Detroit River into the Canadian town of Sandwich and set up an armed encampment. He issued a menacing proclamation demanding that Canadians surrender to the Americans or face destruction.

Fort Mackinac was then captured by the British in a surprise attack. General Hull began to lose his already frayed nerves and sent an urgent message to Fort Dearborn and the adjacent Chicago trading post urging the Americans there to withdraw to the safety of Detroit. He ordered his army to retreat from Sandwich and retrench at Fort Detroit on August 11.[5]

Tecumseh and his painted warriors were victorious in a series of bloody surprise attacks launched on American supply trains and their escorts intending to re-supply Detroit. The Army of the Northwest was effectively cut off from the rest of the United States and blockaded.

News of Tecumseh's victories and successful blockade spread to the Indian towns to the south and west and additional warriors began to join him. By August 15, his Indian army had grown to nearly six hundred warriors.

British Major General Isaac Brock and a regiment of regular infantry and artillery under his command arrived at Fort Malden on August 13. Old Colonel Matthew Elliot introduced him to Tecumseh. General Brock's aide described Tecumseh's appearance at their first meeting:

> Tecumseh's appearance was very prepossessing; his figure light and finely proportioned; his age I imagined to be about five and thirty; in height, five feet nine or ten inches; his complexion, light copper; countenance, oval with bright hazel eyes beaming cheerfulness, energy and decision. Three small silver crowns, or coronets, were suspended from under the

cartilage of his aquiline nose; and a large silver medallion of George the Third . . . was attached to a mixed coloured wampum string, and hung round his neck. His dress consisted of a plain, neat uniform, tanned deerskin jacket, with long trousers of the same material, the seams of both being covered with neatly cut fringe; and he had on his feet leather mocassins, much ornamented with work made from the dyed quills of the porcupine.[6]

General Brock and his army marched into Sandwich on August 15. The troops were comprised of three hundred British regulars from Fort Malden, thirty artillerymen, four hundred Canadian militiamen, and six hundred warriors under Tecumseh's command. Brock sent a messenger to General Hull demanding that he surrender or be attacked, but Hull refused to surrender.

On August 16, the British force and Tecumseh's warriors crossed the Detroit River less than a mile downstream from Fort Detroit and landed unopposed. Tecumseh led his warriors in single file along the edge of the forest clearing to the west of Fort Detroit where they could easily be observed from the ramparts of the fort. As the warriors reached the end of the line, they covertly circled back through the forest and marched along the line once again. This fueled rumors among the Americans that Tecumseh led a huge force of several thousand Indian warriors.

As British artillery bombarded Fort Detroit, General Hull was paralyzed by fear, confusion, and indecision. He cowered in the fortifications and decided to surrender. The American offer of surrender was carried to the British command under a white flag. The British accepted, immediately marched into the fort, and took possession of it.

As he had prepared for the battle at Detroit, Tecumseh had already set plans in motion for broadening the Indian offensive on other fronts along the northwestern frontier. He sent messages in late July directing Pottawatomie Chief Chaubenee and Winnebago Chief Sauganash to quietly gather their warriors in the vicinity of Fort Dearborn and Chicago and attack in mid-August.

Captain Nathan Heald commanded the American garrison at Fort Dearborn. General Hull's orders to abandon Fort Dearborn somehow made it through Tecumseh's blockade and reached him. The Americans left the fort and were attacked by a large group of Pottawatomie warriors in the sand dunes about an hour and a half's ride east of Chicago. Eighty-six Americans from Fort Dearborn and Chicago were massacred. American Indian agent William Wells was among those killed.[7]

War in the Indiana Territory

TECUMSEH'S NEXT MILITARY OBJECTIVE WAS TO CAPTURE and reduce Fort Harrison and Fort Wayne. Tecumseh would lead the Pottawatomie, Ottawa, and British in the attack on Fort Wayne. The Prophet would lead his remaining Shawanese, Kickapoo, Winnebago, and Pottawatomie followers in the attack on Fort Harrison.

The Americans were not idle as Tecumseh carried the war into American territory. The secretary of war sent a letter to Indiana Territory Governor Harrison on July 9, 1812, requesting that he in turn request that Kentucky Governor Isaac Shelby muster the Kentucky militia for the defense of the northwestern frontier.[8]

Governor Harrison was commissioned by Governor Shelby as a brevet major general of the Kentucky militia and was authorized to call up Kentucky volunteers in early August of 1812. General Harrison established his forward field headquarters at the Piqua Indian Agency in the town of Piqua, Ohio.

The Indian assaults on Fort Harrison and Fort Wayne began on September 3 and 4, 1812, respectively. General Harrison issued another "Call for Volunteers" on September 5. Two thousand Kentucky volunteers and seven hundred Ohio volunteers responded and marched to the Piqua Agency to join him. Harrison asked Black Hoof's Ohio Shawanese for their assistance, and they agreed to help.

On September 6, General Harrison and his army departed from Piqua and marched to relieve Fort Wayne, accompanied by their Ohio Shawanese allies.[9] Spemica Lawba commanded a group of Shawanese scouts serving with the Americans, including Captain John, Captain White Feather, Anthony Shane, Chiaxi, Bright Horn (Waseweela), Spy Buck (Chaguska), John Coldwater (Pamota), and Waywaylapea.[10]

The American army reached Fort Wayne on September 12, 1812. Pottawatomie and Ottawa warriors besieging the fort fled without a fight. General Harrison ordered his troops to burn all of the Indian villages within sixty miles of Fort Wayne, making no distinction between neutral and hostile Indian nations. The Pottawatomie and Miami fled to British Fort Malden.

The assault on Fort Harrison had begun around 11:00 p.m. on the night of September 4. Captain Zachary Taylor defended the fort with his little garrison of fifty regular soldiers against a much larger force of Prophet's Town warriors.[11] The battle continued throughout the night until 6:00 a.m. on September 5, when the Indians withdrew.[12]

Frustrated Winnebago warriors left Prophet's Town for their Illinois homes while bands of Kickapoo and Miami warriors headed toward the White River country to attack the small new settlements there. Colonel William Russell III arrived at Fort Harrison with 1,200 Kentucky volunteers on September 16 and relieved the defenders of Fort Harrison.[13]

Between Hope and Despair along the Muscatatuck River

THE PROPHET INSTRUCTED HIS WAR CHIEF AND adviser, Masalameta, to handpick a small band of hardened Shawanese warriors to strike terror deep into the vulnerable new Long Knife settlements developing just to the north of the Falls of the Ohio River. Masalemeta led his band of ten Shawanese warriors from Prophet's Town down to the Forks of the White River and Muscatatuck River as Tecumseh and the Prophet were preparing for the attacks on Fort Wayne and Fort Harrison.[14]

Masalameta sent two warriors down into the Delaware village at the Forks upon their arrival in the adjacent hills, in order to reconnoiter and gather intelligence from sympathetic local Delaware such as Towhead and Little Killbuck. The Shawanese spies learned that the settlers at the Forks and the upper Blue River valley were securely fortified and on constant alert.

However, security was lax at a settlement on Pigeon Roost Creek, about seventeen miles due east of Royse's Lick, since the settlers there had not fortified their settlement.

Pigeon Roost Creek was named after a huge rookery of passenger pigeons that had roosted in the white oak trees at its headwaters from time immemorial. The numbers that roosted there were so vast that they sometimes broke the limbs of mature trees.

On the morning of September 3, 1812, Masalemeta and his warriors set out for the Pigeon Roost Settlement with Little Killbuck as their guide. They found Henry Collings working alone in his fields. Collings spotted them and fled back toward his homestead through a cornfield. Little Killbuck shot him in the back of the head and left him for dead. Henry's pregnant wife Rachel was killed by a hunting knife plunged through her throat. She was scalped and disemboweled. Her fetus was cut out of her womb, scalped, and placed at her bosom.

The Shawanese raiders killed and mutilated twenty-three men, women, and children at the Pigeon Roost Settlement and fled after their bloody work was completed. A militia rescue party found the dying Henry Collings in hiding the next day. He whispered that he was certain that the Indian that shot him was Little Killbuck.[15]

Captain Dawalt brought word of the massacre to the Royse's Lick community early on the day after the killings. The residents of Fleenor's Fort prepared to repel any attack. Micajah and the other men and boys manned the stockade and blockhouse with primed and loaded rifles. The women sharpened the men's knives and tomahawks and molded a surplus of bullets from the fort's lead stockpile. The livestock was secured in the pens in the fort, and the younger children were shuttered inside the fort cabins. Micajah's wife Frankie took care not to unduly frighten Little Hawk, Noble, and Elizabeth.

Captain Dawalt mustered a small company of Royse's Lick mounted volunteer rangers to pursue the fleeing Shawanese warriors. They rode north to the banks of the Muscatatuck River where they located and followed the trail of the marauders. The rangers crossed the river in canoes and continued their pursuit up the valley of the Driftwood Fork of the White River toward the northeast.[16]

The rangers rapidly overtook and overshot the trail of the war party at Chestnut Ridge, near Rockford in Jackson County. They discovered the

Indian camp soon after doubling back.

Captain Dawalt and his men crept up on the camp and attacked on the captain's signal. The Shawanese warriors were completely surprised. They abandoned their plunder, treed, and returned fire as they withdrew. Three of the Indians were wounded in the firefight and were carried away by their companions. John Zink was wounded and died on September 6 on the trail between Ketcham's Fort and Fort Vallonia.[17]

Masalameta and his warriors rode far to the north and finally stopped their flight at the Prophet's temporary headquarters on the Kankakee River. Here they celebrated their victory with a war dance.

Micajah was disappointed with his adoptive Indian nation when it became known that the Shawanese had been responsible for the massacre of the women and children at Pigeon Roost. Were their once proud and principled warriors now reduced to murdering helpless women and children? His sympathy for their plight was sorely tested. He reminded himself that there were many good Shawanese warriors who would not stoop so low.

News of Henry Collin's identification of Little Killbuck at the Pigeon Roost massacre spread quickly through the southern Indiana settlements and caused many settlers to blame the Delaware for the atrocity.[18] General Harrison directed Indian Agent John Johnston to order the White River Delaware to leave the Indiana Territory and move to Ohio to live under Johnson's protection at the Piqua Agency.

By January 1, 1813, the principal Delaware towns on the West Fork of the White River had been abandoned and their residents had moved to Piqua. Chief Ox and most of the members of his Elk Creek band were probably among the Delaware refugees at Piqua as they were reported to have fled from southern Indiana after the Pigeon Roost Massacre.

Kentucky Governor Isaac Shelby reported that hundreds of settlers were fleeing the Indiana Territory and crossing the Ohio River into Kentucky. He expressed his concern in a September 5, 1812, letter to the Secretary of War: "... we shall, I fear, for a time have the Ohio River for a barrier, from the mouth of Kentucky to the junction of Ohio and the Mississippi." Micajah and Frankie Callaway both decided that they would not leave and would stand their ground with their brave friends and defend their new home.

Absolom Buskirk and Robert Sturgeon were killed by Indian raiders near Fort Vallonia in late September. Although there were no further killings in the area for the rest of the fall and through the winter of 1812–1813, horse raids and Indian alarms were frequent.[19]

General William Henry Harrison was commissioned a major general in the United States Army and commander of the Army of the Northwest on February 27, 1813. Thomas Posey was appointed to replace him as governor of the Indiana Territory on March 3, 1813.[20]

As the 1813 campaign season unfolded, the main body of the American Army of the Northwest and their Indian allies battled the main body of the British army and their Indian allies in Michigan and Ohio. An American force commanded by General Winchester was defeated at the community of Frenchtown on the River Raisin in southern Michigan. Hundreds of American prisoners were massacred by Great Britain's Indian allies.[21]

The embattled and besieged Americans held out in the First Siege of Fort Meigs, Second Siege of Fort Meigs, and Siege of Fort Stephenson as General Harrison pressed the federal government and state of Kentucky to provide more soldiers and logistical support. The Americans were methodically gathering their strength.

Indian depredations and killings resumed with renewed intensity in March 1813 in the southern Indiana Territory, in the Forks and northern Clark and Harrison Counties. The assaults were part of a deliberate strategic campaign by the British and Tecumseh to discourage Kentuckians from marching north to help General Harrison from fear of leaving their homes and families exposed to Indian raids.

The Indians attacked the Pigeon Roost country again in March. They killed a Mr. Huffman, wounded his wife and daughter, and captured his grandson. The marauders also stole horses from the Elk Creek neighborhood of Cadwallader Jones just to the north of the Royse's Lick community.[22]

On March 16, 1813, Pottawatomie warriors attacked Flinn's settlement a few miles to the west of Fort Vallonia. A Harrison County militia ranger named George Doom was killed and three others were wounded near Fort Ketcham on March 18.

Major John Tipton and his Harrison County militia rangers set out from Fort Vallonia and cornered an Indian raiding party on Tipton's Island not far to the north of Fort Vallonia on March 25. The rangers drove the warriors into the river, killing and wounding several of them without sustaining any casualties themselves.[23]

Two men were killed about eight miles to the southwest of Fort Vallonia on April 16. Major Tipton commented on the state of morale in the isolated Long Knife outposts in an April 1813 letter to John Gibson: "The citizens are living between hope and despair, waiting to know their doom."[24]

The occupants of the forts and blockhouses in the Forks and the Royse's Lick settlements maintained a constant state of alertness and preparedness. They were rewarded for their vigilance as the Indians limited their attacks to isolated individuals, travelers, and homesteads and did not attack a single fort or blockhouse in the Indiana Territory in 1813.[25]

Colonel William Russell III organized a force of 573 men in late July of 1813 which included federal rangers, Indiana Territory volunteers, and one hundred volunteers from Kentucky. The objective of the expedition was to destroy the group of Indian towns located where the Mississinnewa River emptied into the Wabash River.[26]

Colonel Russell was from Fayette County, Kentucky, and in 1808 had been appointed colonel of the Seventh Infantry of the United States Army by President Madison.[27] He was the son of the Colonel William Russell II who had hired Daniel Boone to guide his expedition to settle in Kentucky in 1773.[28] He had subsequently fought in the War for Independence and in the Battle of Fallen Timbers.

There is some evidence indicating that Micajah may have served as principal scout on this expedition.[29] However, his son James told frontier historian Lyman Draper that Micajah did not go out on any campaigns in the War of 1812.[30]

Colonel Russell's army marched north and passed through most of the Indian towns in Indiana, finding that all of them were deserted. The Indians had apparently moved their families out of the Indiana Territory while their warriors went to Canada to join with Tecumseh's forces. Nonetheless, the army destroyed everything they found in the towns.[31]

The Invasion of Canada and Battle of the Thames River

GENERAL HARRISON SENT A LETTER TO KENTUCKY Governor Isaac Shelby on July 20, 1813, requesting that he assemble a large force of Kentucky militia in preparation for an invasion of Canada.[32] Governor Shelby issued a call for volunteer mounted Kentucky riflemen on July 31.

Sixty-two-year-old Governor Shelby, hero of the Battle of Point Pleasant and the Battle of Lookout Mountain, would command the volunteer army himself. He asked fifty-eight-year-old Simon Kenton to accompany him as his personal advisor.[33]

The courageous stand of young Major George Croghan during the American victory at the Siege of Fort Stephenson had inspired the patriotic spirit of the Long Knives.[34] Nearly 3,500 mounted volunteers flooded the recruiting stations to join Governor Shelby's Long Knife army.

Micajah's cousin Jack Callaway was commissioned a colonel and mustered the Eighth Regiment of Kentucky Mounted Volunteer Militia on August 3, 1813, in response to Governor Shelby's call to arms. Colonel Callaway's light cavalry regiment was popularly known by the name "Callaway's Regiment."[35]

Jack was the grown-up son of Micajah's late uncle, Colonel Richard Callaway. There was little trace left in him of the little "Jacky" Callaway who had been captured and held prisoner by the Shawanese from 1782 to 1784.[36] Jack had grown up to become a strapping big man of six feet three inches with a booming, commanding voice. He closely resembled his father in appearance and was a successful farmer and community leader in Henry County, Kentucky.[37]

Jack reportedly became sullen and silent when asked about his childhood captivity.[38] His son James said, "He was one of the most inveterate enemy [sic] of the Indian. He could not discourse about the Indians with any degree of complacency."[39]

Jack Callaway had followed the military tradition of his father in the Kentucky militia. He was commissioned a captain in the Kentucky militia in 1800, a major in 1807, and a full colonel in 1813.

Fate now impelled Jack Callaway toward the final confrontation between the Long Knives and the last battle-hardened cadre of proud Shawanese warriors. Perhaps he was seeking revenge for the death of his father at the hands of the Shawanese over thirty years earlier.

Micajah's younger brother Edmund was also among the host of Kentucky volunteers. Edmund served as a lieutenant in Captain James Sympson's company of Clark County militia, in Colonel John Donaldson's Regiment of Kentucky Mounted Volunteers.[40]

Governor Shelby and his volunteers crossed the Ohio River at Newport, Kentucky, on September 1, 1813, and began their long march to rendezvous with General Harrison. They paused at Urbana, Ohio, to organize themselves. The Kentuckians formed into two divisions, one commanded by Major General Joseph Desha and the other by Major General Henry. On September 11, they marched on to rendezvous with General Harrison at the mouth of Portage River on Lake Erie.[41]

General Harrison increased the overall strength of his army to over five thousand men with the arrival of the Kentucky volunteers. Over two hundred Ohio Shawanese joined his forces under the leadership of venerable old Chiefs Black Hoof and Captain Snake.[42] Harrison's preparations for the invasion of Canada were nearing completion. All that remained was to gain control of the Great Lakes.

British Naval Commander Robert Barclay had sailed from Amherstburg with his Lake Erie Squadron on September 9, 1813, to search Lake Erie for the fleet of American Master Commandant Oliver Hazard Perry and destroy it. He located Perry's fleet on September 10 and prepared to engage.

The Americans were victorious in the brief but bloody naval battle that ensued. Master Commandant Perry's famous message to General Harrison said, "We have met the enemy and they are ours."[43] The Americans controlled the Great Lakes. Upper Canada, Fort Malden, and Amherstburg lay exposed before them.

General Harrison issued his final orders. Colonel Richard Johnson was ordered to lead his regiment of one thousand mounted Kentucky volunteers via an overland route to attack and recapture Detroit. General Harrison and the balance of the American force would invade Upper Canada in an amphibious assault.

General Harrison and his army embarked on their voyage on September 22, 1813. Sixteen ships and one hundred smaller boats were used to carry the soldiers. They completed an unopposed amphibious landing on September 24, at Bar Point, on the shores of the Detroit River about three miles below Fort Malden. Chiaxi accompanied General Harrison as his bodyguard.[44]

British General Procter abandoned Fort Malden and Amherstberg on the day the Americans landed. The Americans marched into Amherstberg to the tune of "Yankee Doodle."

General Procter and the British withdrew rapidly before the advancing Americans. The Americans re-occupied and garrisoned Fort Detroit on September 28, 1813. Tecumseh was infuriated by the lack of British resolve to fight.[45]

On October 2, General Harrison, with a force of three thousand Kentucky volunteers and 120 regular American soldiers, crossed the Detroit River to Sandwich to pursue the fleeing British and Indians. Colonel Jack Callaway and Lieutenant Edmund Callaway were among them.[46]

Tecumseh and his remaining 1,200 warriors harassed the advancing Americans to cover the British retreat as the British withdrew up the Detroit River, Lake St. Claire, and the Thames River.[47]

The British commander ordered his forces to prepare to receive the Americans on October 3, 1813, on an open field of firm ground lying between the Thames River and the Backmetack Marsh, about one and a half miles below the Moravian Town of Delaware Indians. The field was about two hundred fifty yards wide and interspersed with maple and beech trees. The 450 British soldiers formed two battle lines in the fields.[48]

Tecumseh deployed his warriors in a line along the edge of Backmetack Marsh to set up an attack on the left flank of the approaching American army. He commanded the left segment of the warriors' line while Chippewa Chief Oshawahnah led the warriors on the right. The Prophet, Tecumseh's son Pacheta, and his brother-in-law Wasegaboah were also present as were Winnebago Chiefs Naw Kaw and Four Legs, Ottawa Chief Naiwash, Pottawatomie Chief Mad Sturgeon, Wyandot Chief Splitlog, and Sauk Chief Black Hawk.

General Harrison ordered Colonel Richard Johnson's regiment of mounted Kentucky volunteers to prepare to attack the British in a frontal cavalry charge. Three brigades of reserves were drawn up into parallel lines facing the British, and the remainder of the reserves formed a division under the command of Major General Desha to face the warriors in Backmetack Marsh.[49]

Colonel Richard Johnson's regiment of Long Knife horsemen began their charge against the regular British forces shortly before 4:00 p.m. with the sound of bugles and the resounding battle cry, "Remember the Raisin!" The fearless Long Knife cavalry charge crushed the British line and gained the rear of the British force in less than three minutes.

General Procter rode between the British lines as they fell back in confusion, exhorting his soldiers and crying "For shame 41st Regiment! Halt, 41st! Shame on you!" Procter barely avoided being captured. The British soldiers surrendered after only two volleys.[50]

Tecumseh and his brave warriors made a valiant last stand against their Long Knife enemies in Backmetack Marsh. Colonel Johnson called for twenty volunteers to form a small company to charge the left flank of the Indian line. They were to draw the fire of the Indians in order to allow the rest of the Kentucky troops to attack before the Indians could reload. Twenty men stepped forward, a group that later came to be known as "The Forlorn Hope."

Old Kentucky Colonel William Whitley volunteered to lead the Forlorn Hope to their almost certain doom. He raised his saber and led his company in a wild, frontal charge into the muzzles of the Indian muskets. Hundreds of rounds of musket fire greeted them. Fifteen of the Forlorn Hope were killed instantly, including Whitley. Four others fell wounded to the ground. Only one survived unhurt.

Colonel Johnson led the remainder of his cavalry in a massive frontal assault on the Indian line before the Indians could reload. His Long Knife soldiers fired their long rifles and surged into the Backmetack Marsh with tomahawks and scalping knives drawn. Tecumseh was shot in the chest and killed on the battlefield as he led his warriors. The Long Knives captured his big blue battle flag with a British ensign in the corner. The surviving warriors withdrew from the field and melted away into the marsh.[51]

Tecumseh had honored the oath that he made to his father Pucksinwah and his people so many years before and died as a warrior, on his feet, defending his people and their homeland against the Long Knife enemy.

The Battle of the Thames was the culmination of the long struggle between the Long Knives and the Shawanese Nation which had begun nearly sixty years earlier during the French and Indian War. The sheer duration of the conflict was a tribute to the skill, cunning, and determination of the many Shawanese diplomats, battlefield commanders, and warriors who had served their people over three generations of conflict. Rarely have so few fought so well for so long against so many.

The Battle of the Thames marked the end of major conflicts between the United States and the Indian nations of the Old Northwest, although the War of 1812 continued with great intensity at other locations. General Harrison retired from military service on May 31, 1814. Chiaxi attended Harrison's retirement ceremony wearing Scottish plaids that he had obtained during the Thames River campaign.[52]

The last major battle of the War of 1812 between the United States and Great Britain took place in New Orleans. On January 8, 1815, General Andrew Jackson led four thousand defenders in successfully repulsing the British main attack on New Orleans. The Treaty of Ghent, which ended the war, was ratified by Congress on February 17, 1815.

Hostilities continued with the Sauk Indians in the Missouri Territory into early 1815. In March, Captain James Callaway, the popular oldest son of Flanders and Jemima Callaway and Daniel Boone's grandson, was killed in a Sauk ambush. Daniel, Flanders, and Jemima were devastated.[53] Callaway County, Missouri, was subsequently named in his honor.

Twenty | White Wampum

THE UNITED STATES OF AMERICA WAS NOW able to proceed with the settlement and development of the Indiana Territory with little further interference from the northwestern Indians. The last Indian horse-stealing raids in the Royse's Lick area was in the autumn of 1814 or 1815. Chief Ox and his Delaware band appear to have left the Muscatatuck River country for good by late 1814.[1]

Washington County was created from the northern portion of Harrison County on December 21, 1813.[2] The citizens of the county decided to found a new town named Salem to serve as the county seat. They chose to locate it at the confluence of Royse's Fork of the Blue River and Brock Creek.[3] The new town site was about four miles south and a mile west of Callaway Fort.

Colonel John Depauw had purchased the land for the Salem town site on March 18 and March 21, 1814, and a plat consisting of 142 town lots was surveyed on April 4, 1814.[4] Colonel Depauw's father Charles was a boyhood friend of the Marquis de Lafayette and had fought at Lafayette's side in the American War for Independence.[5] Charles later served as one of Citizen Genet's French agents in Kentucky in 1793–1794.[6]

Micajah and his family moved out of Fleenor's Fort and back into Callaway Fort. He purchased the western half (eighty acres) of James and Nancy Davis's quarter-section of land for $160 on February 15, 1815, a tract that included Callaway Fort and his improvements.[7]

Micajah was at last free to enjoy the dream that he had pursued for much of his life. The wars were over. He owned his own land, with a forest for hunting and ample fields to farm, and had been blessed with a fine and loving family.

The Indiana Territorial Census counted the population of Washington County as 7,317 by 1815. The total population of the Indiana Territory was 62,697—sufficient to qualify for statehood. The state of Indiana was admitted to the Union on December 11, 1816.

English author Morris Birkbeck included a reassuring report of the beginnings of Hoosier hospitality in a travelogue of his journey across southern Indiana in the summer of 1816:

> I have good authority for contradicting a supposition that I have met with in England, respecting the inhabitants of Indiana; -that they are lawless, semi-barbarous vagabonds, dangerous to live among. On the contrary, the laws are respected, and are effectual; and the manners of the people are kind and gentle, to each other, and to strangers.[8]

On September 8, 1815, the United States of America entered into another treaty with the Shawanese and the other northwestern Indian nations. The chiefs and warriors who had engaged in hostilities during the War of 1812 were pardoned and the terms of the 1795 Treaty of Greenville were renewed. The treaty was signed for the Shawanese by old Chiefs Black Hoof and Captain Snake and six younger chiefs.

The Ohio Shawanese signed the Treaty of Fort Meigs in 1817. In that treaty they ceded the bulk of their remaining lands in the northern third of Ohio and retained reservations totaling eighty three square miles at Wapakoneta, Hog Creek, and Lewistown, Ohio.[9]

Micajah's last known contact with the Shawanese occurred at about this time. He was working on the farm one day with his oldest sons James and Edmund when one of the boys shouted to his father that he saw seven Indian warriors riding down the lane from the Crest of the Knobs toward their home. Micajah told them to get their rifles and hide in the loft of the barn to cover him through the second-floor portholes.

Micajah strode down the path to greet his visitors. He easily recognized his aged Indian father Nenessica.[10] It had been many years since they had seen each other, but Micajah could never forget that rangy form and beard, even though the form was now frail and stooped with age, and the beard white. He did not recognize the accompanying six warriors.

The old man dismounted with the help of one of his companions. His eyes lit up with joy as he stepped toward Micajah with hand extended. Micajah grasped it and shook it warmly. Nenessica murmured that he had told Micajah that they would meet again in better days. Since the wars were over, could all now be forgiven?

Micajah silently guided the warriors down the path past the fort to his

Photograph of James A. Callaway, grandson of Micajah Callaway, son of Noble Callaway, and great-grandfather of the author

[author's personal collection]

spring, where they watered their horses. Nenessica asked him, "Tanakaywa (Where is your wife)?" Micajah said that his wife and children were visiting neighbors and were not home. He did not know or trust the other warriors and did not want them to know too much about him.

Nenessica told Micajah that he was living with Black Hoof's group in Wapakoneta. His wife had passed away recently, and he was lonely in his old age. He hoped that he and Micajah could visit each other freely now that the wars had ended. Micajah responded with a noncommittal nod. Nenessica reminded Micajah that he was still one of them. Micajah smiled.

The old man reached into his pouch and pulled out a string of white wampum (wahcanaquah pettawakay). He asked Micajah what the white man called the land around them. Micajah said it was called "Indiana." Nenessica snorted contemptuously and proudly said that all of the land along the Ohio River was once the land of the Shawanese people. First Kentucky, then Ohio, and then "Indiana" had been taken away from them. He and Micajah had lived and struggled through it all.

Nenessica offered the string of white wampum to Micajah, and he accepted it. Nenessica then raised his frail arms and prayed to Moneto that Micajah and his children would enjoy the blessings of peace forever and that they would never forget those who had lived upon the land before them. Micajah thanked him.

Micajah showed the Shawanese the way back to the trail to Royse's Lick when they were finished watering their horses. As they parted, Nenessica offered his hand again and tearfully said, "Nepaukeche, kelaqueulemela nequatto (Farewell, dear son)!" Micajah took his hand, shook it, and responded, "Nepaukeche, kelaqueulemela nothaw (Farewell, dear father)!"[11]

One of the warriors helped Nenessica up onto his horse. He stopped at the top of the Crest, turned in his saddle, and waved. Micajah returned his wave and watched as they disappeared over the Crest. James and Edmund climbed down from the loft when the Shawanese were gone and looked upon their father with a mixture of awe and curiosity.[12]

THE LIVES OF MICAJAH AND HIS FAMILY followed the natural cycles and rhythms of farm life as the ensuing years passed. They began each spring with plowing and planting the fields and tending the new-born livestock. They tilled crops through the summer and harvested them in the fall along with walnuts, chestnuts, hickory nuts, persimmons, pawpaw fruit, and other bounty of the forest. They enjoyed many a kettle of tea brewed from the roots of the sassafras tree. Autumn and winter brought the hunting season. The years passed by so quickly that they seemed to blur together.

Daughters Sarah and Lucy were born in 1814 and 1815.[13] James, Edmund, John, and Noble helped with planting, plowing, and weeding the fields, gathering and chopping firewood, cleaning the stables, and milking the cows. Little Elizabeth helped Frankie with spinning and weaving, tending to the livestock, cooking, and washing.

Micajah developed a circle of friends in Washington County who were also veterans of the War for Independence and the frontier Indian Wars. Three of them were Murphy D. Still, Arthur Parr, and James Garrison.[14]

He also regaled his family at the dinner table and before the hearth with tales of his adventures on the frontier and in the Indian Wars. He described the suffering and cruelty that he had witnessed and "seared it into their brains."[15]

Micajah continued to live the life of a frontier hunter and farmer as the sweeping technological revolution of the steam age arrived in the cotton mills in Salem in the 1820s. He still wore his combination of Indian and white frontier clothing. His frost-scarred feet became increasingly tender with the advancing years, and he continued to wear soft and supple Shawanese-style mockeethena (mocassins).[16]

The wild game populations in the Knobs and Delaney Creek and Elk Creek basins collapsed precipitously as the forests were cleared and hunting pressure from Micajah and his neighbors increased. The elk and passenger pigeons were the first to follow the buffalo into local extinction and the last of the wolves and black bears in the area were killed off by 1825.[17]

Micajah continued to hunt white-tailed deer at the old Deer Lick for many years. The local people came to refer to Deer Lick as "Callaway Lick."[18] Micajah's son Noble eventually purchased the property containing Callaway Lick.[19]

Hawk, Micajah's youngest son, never married and continued to live with Micajah and Frankie into their old age at Callaway Fort. He ran the farm and cared for his aging parents.[20] He idolized Micajah and did much to preserve the stories of his experiences on the frontier.

Micajah would occasionally hear news from and receive visits from his siblings and old friends in Missouri, Kentucky, Virginia, and Ohio as the years passed by. Although he could not read or write letters himself, others would read and write for him.

Edmund, Micajah's brother, died in Clark County, Kentucky, in 1818. In 1806, John had moved from Kentucky back to Virginia to live in Campbell County, but eventually returned to Kentucky, where he died in 1821.[21] James Jr. died in 1835 in Howard County, Missouri, where he had moved not long after Micajah's move to Indiana. Dudley lived in Amherst County, Virginia until his death in 1844. Chesley died at his No Creek homestead in Ohio County, Kentucky on February 13, 1846.[22] Mary survived until 1852 when she died in Owen County, Kentucky.

Micajah's friends and family members in Missouri remained there for the rest of their lives. Daniel Boone and Flanders Callaway hunted and trapped well into their old age. The old frontiersmen traveled up the Missouri River all the way to the Yellowstone River in the autumn of 1810. They were gone for six months and returned with a load of valuable beaver pelts. Their last long hunt into the Rocky Mountains foreshadowed the lives of the mountain men of the following decades.[23]

Daniel Boone passed away in his son Nathan's house in the Femme Osage River valley on September 26, 1820. Flanders and Jemima were at his side. He was buried next to his beloved Rebecca on the banks of Teque Creek in Charette, Missouri. Flanders died in Charette in 1824. Jemima lived on until 1829. They were buried near Daniel and Rebecca. The remains of Daniel and Rebecca were moved and reinterred in a cemetery in Frankfort, Kentucky, in a magnificent ceremony on September 13, 1845.[24]

THE ADVANCING YEARS WERE NOT KIND TO Micajah's adopted Shawanese Nation. President Andrew Jackson committed the executive branch of the federal government to a policy of removing the remaining Eastern Woodland Indian nations to a special Indian Territory to be created to the west of the Mississippi River, beyond the boundaries of existing states. He offered the

Indian nations the choice of either accepting the authority of the states over their traditional lands or moving to the new Indian Territory.[25]

A fierce debate ensued between those who supported Jackson's removal policy and those who supported Indian rights. Congressman Freylinghuysen of New Jersey was an eloquent advocate for the rights of the eastern Indians and defended those of the Cherokee Nation against the encroachments of the State of Georgia in a speech on April 6, 1830:

> It is a subject full of grateful satisfaction, that, in our public intercourse with the Indians, ever since the first colonies of white men found an abode on these Western shores, we have distinctly recognized their title; treated with them as owners, and in all our acquisitions of territory, applied ourselves to these ancient proprietors, by purchase or cession alone, to obtain the right of soil. Sir, I challenge the record of any other or different pretension . . .
>
> We were aware of the potency of any edict that sprang from the deliberations of the council fire; and when we desired land, or peace, or alliance, to this source of power and energy, to this great lever of Indian government we addressed our proposals—to this alone did we look; and from this alone did we expect aid or relief.
>
> Every administration of this Government, from President Washington's, have, with like solemnities and stipulations, held treaties with the Cherokees; treaties, too, by almost all of which we obtained further acquisitions of their territory. Yes, sir, whenever we approached them in the language of friendship and kindness, we touched the chord that won their confidence; and now, when they have nothing left with which to satisfy our cravings, we propose to annul every treaty—to gainsay our word—and, by violence and perfidy, drive the Indian from his home. . . .[26]

The efforts of the Indians and their Congressional allies were to no avail. Congress enacted the Indian Removal Act and President Andrew Jackson signed it into law on May 28, 1830.[27] Negotiations were initiated under the Act to force the eastern Indian nations to sign treaties to give up their remaining lands east of the Mississippi River in exchange for land to its west.

Shawanese Principal Chief Black Hoof stubbornly contested every effort to force the 400 Shawanese remaining in Ohio to leave their reservations. He refused to sign a treaty of cession for the reservations and used every legal means short of war to resist. Black Hoof died in 1831 at the remarkable age of 110 years old without approving this final concession to the Long Knives.

Without the iron will and leadership of Chief Black Hoof, the Shawanese remaining at the Wapakoneta, Hog Creek, and Lewistown reservations finally yielded to the unrelenting pressure from the whites.[28] They ceded the Wapakoneta and Hog Creek reservations on August 8, 1831, and the Lewistown reservation on July 20, 1831.[29] Chiaxi died in Wapakoneta around 1833.[30] Captain Snake died in Kansas in 1838 at the age of one hundred years.[31]

The last lingering group of Shawanese to leave Ohio prepared for their final departure in 1838. They leveled the graves of their fathers, mothers and children and covered them with sod. They said farewell to the bones and spirits of Paxinosa, Kishenosity, Black Fish, Aweecomy, Nimwha, Moluntha, White Bark, Black Hoof, Chiaxi, and the many thousands of Shawanese who left their remains in Ohio soil.

The Shawanese emigrants mounted their horses and boarded their wagons. The chief shaman took a position at the head of the migration party and blew a Shawanese ceremonial "trumpet." The party set off for their new homes in the west with solemnity and sadness.[32] There were no Shawanese left living in their ancestral Ohio homeland by the end of 1838, with the exception of a handful that had intermarried with the whites or elected to live among them.

MICAJAH CONTINUED WITH HIS LIFE-LONG PASSION of hunting well into his old age. His hunting trips became shorter and the game smaller and less plentiful as the years advanced. The pain in his frost-bitten feet worsened. When he could no longer walk well enough or mount a horse to hunt, Micajah sat in Callaway Fort and shot turkeys through the gun-port in the wall next to the chimney.[33] One day he leaned his now antique long rifle in the corner of Callaway Fort for the last time as the effort to hunt had become too exhausting.

Micajah's health declined as he entered his mid-eighties and his hearing began to fail. His once powerful muscles shrank away and his rangy frame became stooped.

Old white-haired Micajah would sit on the puncheon bench in the shade just outside the front door of Callaway Fort for hours, dozing and dreaming about the old days. Friends and family would drop by to visit with him and listen patiently to his reminiscences.

Lyman C. Draper, the famed historian of the northwestern frontier, learned that Micajah was still alive in early 1849. Micajah was now the last survivor of Daniel Boone's company of saltboiler soldiers, and Draper was preparing to write biographies of Daniel Boone and George Rogers Clark.

Mr. Draper sent a letter to Micajah on March 12, 1849, and asked him to respond to a long series of questions about his experiences. The letter began,

> I have been over ten years engaged in collecting materials for two separate works upon western history & biography—one to be entitled *The Life & Times of General George Rogers Clark*—the other, *The Life of Colonel Daniel Boone*. I have lately learned that you were one of the party of salt boilers under Col. Boone captured at the Blue Licks, in Feb. 1778—& hence I infer, that you have it in your power to give me a great deal of very desirable information. I hope your health & memory will enable you to gratify me.[34]

Mr. Leonard Bliss responded to Mr. Draper on behalf of Micajah with a letter dated April 9, 1849. Micajah's sons had told Bliss that Micajah was very feeble and as helpless as an infant. He was hard of hearing and barely able to speak. His son Hawk offered to try to answer some of Draper's questions.[35]

Micajah died of natural causes in his bed at Callaway Fort on April 11, 1849, surrounded by his loving family.[36] Lyman Draper never had the opportunity to interview him directly, but he later interviewed Micajah's sons, who helped answer some of his many questions.

The first steam locomotive for the New Albany and Salem Railroad was delivered at New Albany, Indiana, in the late spring of 1849.[37] The powerful engine of American civilization surged onward after Micajah Callaway's quiet passing. It transformed the Ohio River Valley that he and his fellow Virginians had explored, conquered, and settled at such great cost to themselves and the Indian peoples that they displaced.

Epilogue

Micajah Callaway is buried in the pioneer Peugh Cemetery next to Seldom Seen Lake Road, about four miles to the north of Salem, Indiana. The little cemetery is located in a quiet pastoral setting on the gently rounded crest of a ridge at the head of a heavily forested ravine that falls away to the east toward the Clark State Forest. Cow pastures surround the cemetery on three sides. The peaceful Indiana countryside belies its bloody history.

Micajah lies in a family group with his wife Frankie and their sons Noble, Edmund, and Hawk. Edmund's tombstone is now gone but the weathered pale gray limestone tombstones of the other family members still stand as they slowly dissolve in centuries of rainfall. Micajah and Frankie share an elaborately carved tombstone that was purchased for them by their sons. The words "Father and Mother" are lovingly carved on two sides of it. The tombstone is also inscribed with an epitaph noting the searing event that indelibly marked Micajah's life:

"Held Prisoner by Indians 5 Yrs. 7 Mos."

I sat alone in the silence of the pastures on one unforgettable evening visit to the cemetery as the sun slowly set in the west. The receding sun cast a rosy glow on the pale tombstones of Micajah and his family. The simple scene led me to reflect upon the sharp contrast between their turbulent lives and the silence of their peaceful resting place. They had rested there for a cen-

Epilogue

Micajah Callaway's tombstone in Peugh Cemetery near Salem, Indiana
[author's personal collection]

tury and a half and eternity stretched endlessly before them. One day I would inevitably join them.

That simple perception triggered an epiphany that moved me to the core of my soul. I clearly saw eternity waiting for me. The significance of the sometimes overwhelming passions and conflicts in my own life faded away before the vastness.

I found great comfort in this silent lesson from my ancestors. With tears in my eyes, I thanked Micajah and his family for their courage and fortitude and for the gift of life that they had so carefully preserved to pass on to me.

As the sun set, I imagined the spirits of Micajah's Shawnee friends calling to him from the darkening forest of the ravine, asking him to go buffalo hunting with them. Micajah's spirit rose up in my vision dressed in fringed hunting shirt, loin-cloth, leggings, and mocassins. He picked up his long rifle and tomahawk and silently strode down into the forest to hunt with them once again. You will not be forgotten, Micajah! Sleep well, old scout!

List of Principal Characters

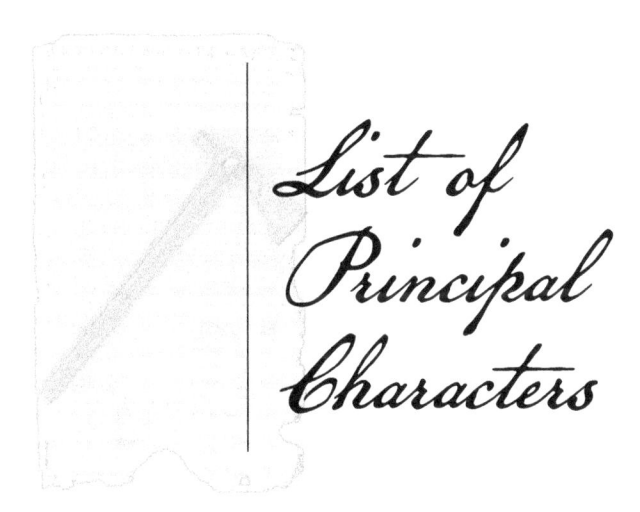

Bâby, Jacques Duperon - French Canadian partisan married to Shawanese woman; fought on the side of French in French and Indian War as a captain; served in British Indian Department in Detroit during War for Independence.

Bird, Henry - British Army captain who commanded British/Indian expedition against settlers of Kentucky in 1780.

Blue Jacket (Weyapiersenwah) - Piqua Shawanese; warrior and Principal War Chief of Shawanese Nation in the early 1790s.

Black Beard (Nenessica) - Makujay Shawanese; war captain during War for Independence who adopted Micajah Callaway after his capture at the Lower Blue Licks in 1778; civil village chief and senior diplomat later in life.

Black Fish (Chiungalla) - Chalaakaatha Shawanese; warrior and Principal War Chief of Shawanese Nation from 1776–1780.

Black Hoof (Catchecassa) - Makujay Shawanese; war captain through course of Ohio River valley Indian wars; principal civil chief of Shawanese Nation for three decades in early nineteenth century.

Boone, Daniel - The famous Kentucky frontier explorer, hero, and leader; also founder of Fort Boonesborough settlement.

Boone, Rebecca (Bryan) - Daniel Boone's wife.

Boone, Squire - Daniel Boone's brother and fellow explorer.

Bowman, John - Appointed to serve as "Colonel of the Militia of Kentucky County" by Governor Patrick Henry on December 21, 1776. Commanded Virginia militia force sent to reinforce the Kentucky settlements in 1777; led the attack on Little Chalaakaatha in Bowman's Campaign of 1779.

Braddock, Edward - British major general defeated by French and Indian forces at Fort Duquesne and killed on the battlefield in 1755.

Brant, Joseph (Theyaendinega) - Mohawk warrior; secretary of British Indian Department; captain in British army; provided military assistance to Ohio Indians in 1781.

Brock, Isaac - British major general in command of combined British and Indian forces during siege of Detroit in 1812.

Buckongahelas - Delaware; war chief allied with Shawanese militants in the 1770s-1790s.

Butler, Richard - Pennsylvania Indian trader living with Shawanese in early 1770s; father of Shawanese children through his Shawanese consort; served as American Indian agent for American Northern Department in 1775–1776; served as U.S. Commissioner Plenipotentiary in 1786 Treaty at the Mouth of the Greater Miami River; served as Major General in U.S. Army in St. Clair's defeat when he was killed on the battlefield (1791).

Butler, William - Pennsylvania Indian trader; partner and brother of Richard Butler.

Caldwell, William - British captain in command of company of Butler's Rangers helping defend Shawanese during War for Independence.

Callaway, Chesley - Micajah Callaway's brother.

Callaway, Edmund - Micajah Callaway's brother.

Callaway, Edmund - Micajah Callaway's son.

Callaway, Flanders - Micajah Callaway's oldest brother.

Callaway, Francis "Frankie" (Hawkins) - Micajah Callaway's second wife.

Callaway, John - Micajah Callaway's brother.

Callaway, John ("Jack") - Micajah Callaway's first cousin and son of Colonel Richard Callaway.

Callaway, John Hawkins ("Hawk") - Micajah Callaway's son.

Callaway, James - Micajah Callaway's oldest son.

Callaway, James, Sr. - Micajah Callaway's father; brother of Thomas, William, Richard, and Francis Callaway.

Callaway, James, Jr. - Micajah Callaway's brother.

Callaway, Jemima (Boone) - Wife of Flanders Callaway and daughter of Daniel Boone.

Callaway, Mary (Arnold) - Micajah Callaway's first wife.

List of Principal Characters

Callaway, Micajah - The subject of this book; great-great-great grandfather of the author.

Callaway, Noble - Micajah Callaway's son; great-great grandfather of the author.

Callaway, Richard - Micajah Callaway's uncle; militia colonel in Bedford County, Virginia during French and Indian War and in Kentucky County during War for Independence; one of the two first Kentucky County representatives in the Virginia General Assembly; brother of Thomas, William, Francis, and James Callaway Sr.

Callaway, Thomas - Micajah Callaway's uncle; militia captain in Halifax County, Virginia during French and Indian War; eldest brother of William, Richard, Francis, and James Callaway Sr.

Callaway, Sarah (Bramlett) - Micajah Callaway's mother; wife of James Callaway Sr.

Callaway, William - Micajah's uncle; County Lieutenant of Bedford County, Virginia militia during French and Indian War; Bedford County representative in Virginia House of Burgesses; brother of Thomas, Richard, Francis, and James Callaway Sr.

Callaway, Zachariah - Colonel Richard Callaway's eldest son.

Captain Snake - Kispoko Shawanese; Principal War Chief during War for Independence.

Captain Johnny - Makujay Shawanese; principal civil chief of Shawanese Nation after death of Moluntha from 1786 through mid-1790s.

Captain Tommy (Chiaxi) - Chalaakaatha Shawanese; warrior and war captain from 1770s to the War of 1812; personal bodyguard of Major General William Henry Harrison during War of 1812.

Carleton, Sir Guy - British Governor General and Commander-in-Chief of the Province of Quebec from 1768 to 1778 when he was replaced by Frederick Haldimand; Commander-in-Chief of all British forces in North American in 1782 and 1783.

Clark, George Rogers - Aggressive Virginia militia colonel and then brigadier general in command of the Illinois Regiment; generally credited for successfully defending Kentucky and militarily seizing and holding the Old Northwest for the United Colonies during War for Independence.

Clark, Marston - First cousin of George Rogers Clark; ferryman at the Falls of the Ohio; General Harrison's brigade major in Battle of Tippecanoe; first Indiana representative in the Electoral College.

Clark, William - Brother of George Rogers Clark; one of the leaders of the Lewis and Clark Expedition to the Pacific Ocean.

Coitcheleh - Makujay Shawanese; sister of Cornstalk; head woman of the Shawanese Nation during the War for Independence.

Cornstalk (Hokoleskwa or Colesque) - Makujay Shawanese; Principal War Chief before, during, and after Lord Dunmore's War until his death in 1777.

Christian, William - Popular colonel of Botetourt County, Virginia militia.

Crawford, William - Friend and land agent for George Washington; colonel in Virginia militia who was captured and executed by the Delaware in 1782.

Depauw, Charles - French aide-de-camp to the Marquis de Lafayette and later an agent for the French Republic in Kentucky in 1793 - 1794; settled in Salem, Indiana in 1814.

De Peyster, Arent - British major in command at Detroit after capture of Lieutenant Governor Hamilton during the latter part of the War for Independence.

Elliott, Matthew - Indian trader; friend of Simon Girty; interpreter and agent for British Indian Department in Detroit.

Fleenor, John - Militia volunteer serving in Battle of Tippecanoe; Micajah Callaway's neighbor in Harrison County (later incorporated into Washington County), Indiana Territory, during War of 1812; organized and constructed Fleenor's Fort where Micajah and his family lived for two years with six other families during the war.

Fleming, William - County Lieutenant of Botetourt County, Virginia militia in Dunmore's War and War for Independence.

Floyd, John - Highly respected captain and later colonel in Virginia militia.

Gibault, Father Pierre - French Catholic Jesuit priest in Kaskaskia, Illinois; aided Colonel George Rogers Clark in the conquest of the Old Northwest and capture of Vincennes.

Gibson, John - Pennsylvania Indian trader; married to Mingo Chief Logan's sister; later became a frontier military leader during the War for Independence; and ultimately, acting governor of Indiana during the War of 1812.

Girty, George - Brother of Simon Girty.

List of Principal Characters

Girty, James - Brother of Simon Girty.

Girty, Simon - Indian agent and interpreter working for British Indian Department in Detroit during War for Independence and the ensuing Ohio River Valley Indian wars.

Haldimand, Sir Frederick - British Governor General and Commander-in-Chief of the Province of Quebec after Sir Guy Carleton (from 1778 to 1786).

Hamilton, Henry - British lieutenant governor and commandant in Detroit during early part of War for Independence until his capture by George Rogers Clark.

Harmar, Josiah - Colonel and later general in command of U.S. Army in Ohio River basin after War for Independence; badly defeated by Indians in "Harmar's Defeat" in 1790.

Harrison, Benjamin - Governor of Virginia following Thomas Jefferson's term at the end of the War for Independence; father of William Henry Harrison.

Harrison, William Henry - Son of Benjamin Harrison; aid-de-camp to General Anthony Wayne during Wayne's Campaign in 1794; first Governor of Indiana Territory; major general of the U.S. Army of the Northwest; and ninth president of the United States.

Harrod, James - Founder of Harrodsburg, the first settlement in Kentucky.

Henderson, Judge Richard - North Carolina judge and founder of Transylvania Colony in Kentucky.

Henry, Patrick - Political firebrand and governor of Virginia at the inception of the War for Independence.

Holder, John - Captain and later colonel of Kentucky militia; married Colonel Richard Callaway's daughter Fanny.

Hull, William - American major general who surrendered to the British in Detroit in 1812.

Jefferson, Thomas - Virginia political activist, drafter of Declaration of Independence, governor of Virginia during War for Independence, and third president of the United States.

Johnson, Guy - Nephew of Sir William Johnson and his successor as superintendent of the Northern Department of the British Indian Department.

Johnson, Sir William - Superintendent of the Northern Department of the British Indian Department based in Albany, New York; friend of the Mohawk Nation and Iroquois Confederacy.

Kenton, Simon - Explorer, frontiersman and Indian fighter extraordinaire; commanded company of "first responders" counter-attacking and pursuing Indian raiding parties during 1770s-1790s; later became a senior commander of Ohio militia.

Kishenosity ("Hard Man") - Makujay Shawanese; principal civil chief of Shawanese Nation during Lord Dunmore's War and the War for Independence until his death in 1778.

Knox, Henry - President George Washington's Secretary of War.

Lamatumque - Makujay Shawanese; daughter of head woman Coitcheleh; niece of Cornstalk; and wife of Moluntha.

Lernoult, Richard - British major in command of British forces at Detroit during early part of War for Independence.

Lewis, Andrew - County Lieutenant of Augusta County, Virginia and commander of Southern Division during Dunmore's War.

Little Turtle - Miami war chief and principal civil chief for many years.

Logan, Benjamin - Kentucky militia colonel and leader of early settlement at Logan's Fort.

Logan (Taghahjute) - Mingo chief; befriended British and Americans; and then turned against them after Virginia frontiersmen massacred his family in 1774.

Lorimier, Pierre-Louis de ("Louis Lorimier") - An influential French Indian trader who married a Shawanese woman and lived among and traded with the Shawanese.

McGary, Hugh - A highly volatile Kentucky militia major who is blamed for rashly goading the Kentucky militia into their bloody defeat at the Lower Blue Licks in 1783 and the murder of Shawanese Principal Chief Moluntha in 1786.

McKee, Alexander - A captain in the British Indian Department in Detroit; British deputy Indian agent and Indian agent; and devoted friend of the Shawanese Nation.

Moluntha - Makujay Shawanese; principal civil chief of the Shawanese Nation during much of the War for Independence after the death of his predecessor Chief Nimwha in 1779; murdered by Hugh McGary in 1786.

Morgan, George - American Indian agent for Northern Department following resignation of Richard Butler; highly respected and trusted by Shawanese.

List of Principal Characters

Murray, John - The fourth Earl of Dunmore, Viscount Fincastle, and Baron of Blair, Monlin and Tillimet; British Royal Governor of Virginia during Dunmore's War against the Shawanese and at the outbreak of the War for Independence.

Nimwha (Munseka) - Makujay Shawanese; brother of Cornstalk; briefly served as principal civil chief of Shawanese Nation between Kishenosity's death in 1778 and his own death in 1779.

Nonhelema - Makujay Shawanese; sister of Cornstalk; village chief; warrior; diplomat; and friend of the Americans during and after the War for Independence.

Ox - Delaware; village chief of Ox's Village on the Muscatuck River near the Forks of the White River in the southern Indiana Territory; also kept dwelling at Royse's Lick, future site of Salem, Indiana in Washington County.

Pauling, Henry - Captain in the Botetourt County, Va. militia during Lord Dunmore's War and War for Independence; later in life served as Kentucky's representative at the Constitutional Convention.

Price, William - Major in Kentucky militia during General Anthony Wayne's Campaign of 1794 commanding Kentucky Corps of scouts and spies, including Micajah and Edmund Callaway.

Pucksinwah - Kispoko Shawanese; war chief and father of Tecumseh and Tenskwatawa.

Red Pole (Musquaconah) - Makujay Shawanese; civil chief; half-brother of Blue Jacket; played key role in forming Indian Confederacy to confront the Americans in General Anthony Wayne's Campaign of 1794.

Rennick, Joshua (Chief Wryneck) - Piqua Shawanese; captured in Virginia and adopted into the Shawanese Nation during French and Indian War; senior Shawanese war chief during War for Independence.

Scott, Charles - Major general of Kentucky militia in command of Kentucky volunteers in General Anthony Wayne's Campaign of 1794.

Shelby, Isaac - Militia commander; hero of the Battle of Point Pleasant and Battle of King's Mountain; first governor of the state of Kentucky.

Silverheels - Makujay Shawanese; brother of Cornstalk.

St. Clair, Arthur - Pennsylvania trader; officer in the Continental Army during War for Independence; first governor of the Northwest Territory;

American major general in disastrous "St. Clair's Defeat" on the shores of the Wabash River in 1791.

Symmes, John Cleves - New Jersey politician, Northwest Territory judge and real estate investor; sponsor and land developer of the Miami Purchase.

Tame Hawk (Kekewapilathy) - Kispoko Shawanese; war chief from Wapatomica who spoke on behalf of the Shawanese Nation during negotiation of the Treaty at the Mouth of the Greater Miami River (1786).

Tecumseh - Kispoko Shawanese; son of war chief Pucksinwah; legendary and visionary Shawanese warrior and leader of auxiliary Indian forces fighting alongside the British against the Americans in the Old Northwest and southern Canada in the War of 1812.

Tenskwatawa (the Shawanese Prophet) - Kispoko Shawanese; brother of Tecumseh; visionary prophet who rallied Indian resistance to American occupation of Indiana and Ohio immediately before the War of 1812.

Walls, George - Major in the Illinois Regiment; second-in-command to General George Rogers Clark at Fort Nelson in 1783 and presided over prisoner exchange at Fort Nelson in 1783.

Washington, George - Commander of Virginia colonial militia during French and Indian War; Commanding general of the Continental Army during the War for Independence; and first president of the United States.

Wayne, Anthony - Major general in command of U.S. Army and Kentucky militia in military campaign to subdue and break the military power of the northwest Indians in 1794.

Wells, William - Captured by Miami raiders in Kentucky as a child and adopted into a Miami family; led Miami riflemen in St. Clair's Defeat; defected to Americans and served as American spy in General Anthony Wayne's Campaign of 1794; served as an American Indian agent in Chicago at outset of War of 1812 where he was killed.

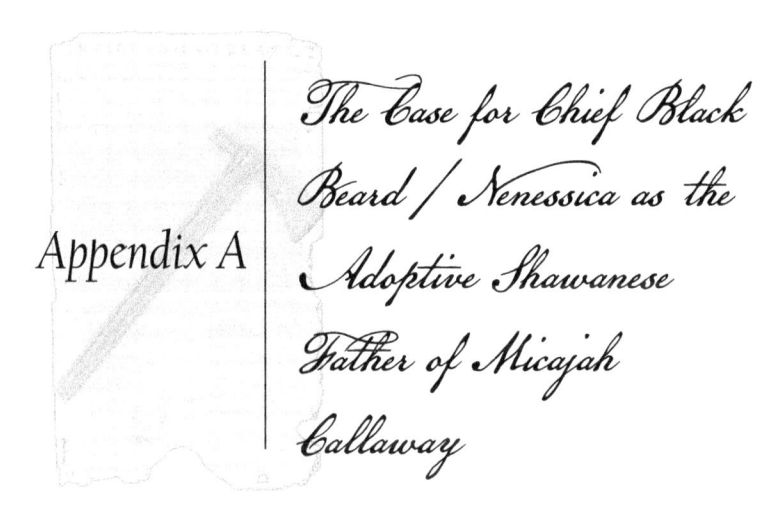

Appendix A: The Case for Chief Black Beard / Nenessica as the Adoptive Shawanese Father of Micajah Callaway

MICAJAH CALLAWAY WAS IN DANIEL BOONE'S COMPANY of soldiers that were captured by a Shawanese war party led by Chief Black Fish while they were processing salt at the Lower Blue Licks in Kentucky in February of 1778. Micajah's sons and "saltboiler" Joseph ("Fish") Jackson stated that Micajah was adopted as a son by one of his captors. However, they did not provide the name of his adoptive parent.

I believe that the weight of the available evidence supports the conclusion that a Shawanese chief known to the Virginians as "Black Beard" was the adoptive Shawanese father of Micajah, since their lives touched and intertwined in many ways over the course of the Indian Wars.

Black Beard's Shawanese name was "Nenessica." He was a senior leader of the Makujay Shawanese division but lived with the Chalaakaatha division in their town of Little Chalaakaatha at the time that Micajah was captured.[1]

Nenessica was raised in Ekippakithiki as a boy.[2] Therefore, he was probably associated with half-Shawanese Peter Chartier's pro-French Makujay warriors who lived there in the 1740s and early 1750s. His connection to the French is also evident from his apparent blood relationship to French trader Louis Lorimier's half-French Shawanese wife, Charlotte "Pemanpieh" Bougainville.[3]

Peter Chartier and his warriors moved south to live with the Creek Nation during the French and Indian War. This would explain why Nenessica was selected for diplomatic missions to the southern Indian nations later in his life.

There are fragmentary descriptions of Nenessica in the record indicating that he was a tall and rangy man. One would expect from his English name that he also wore a black beard during at least a part of his life. Shawanese men generally plucked facial hair and had no beards. Therefore, his beard suggests again that he had some French ancestry. He must have been in his fifties during the American War for Independence because he is described as being very old thirty years later.

Nenessica was an important Shawanese chief in his time.[4] He played a key role in both the military and diplomatic affairs of his nation for over thirty years. As a Makujay living with the Chalaakaatha division, he served as an important connecting link between the two divisions who often disagreed over national policy. He was very shrewd and understood the use of military and political power to serve the ends of his people. The British described him as "a very confidential man."[5]

The Shawanese war party that captured Daniel Boone and his saltboiler soldiers was seeking revenge for Makujay Chief Cornstalk's murder. Chalaakaatha Principal War Chief Black Fish led the war party, and Cornstalk's Makujay brother Nimwha (Munseka) accompanied it.[6] French trader Louis Lorimier was also among them.[7]

Nenessica was one of Black Fish's senior war "captains" at the time and was undoubtedly among the mixed band of warriors from the Chalaakaatha, Makujay, and other Shawanese divisions that captured Boone and the saltboilers. He served as a war captain under Chief Black Fish at the siege of Fort Boonesborough in September of 1778, only seven months after their capture.[8] He and Black Hoof shared command of the Little Chalaakaatha warriors after Black Fish was severely wounded in the attack on Little Chalaakaatha during Bowman's Campaign in May of 1779.[9] It appears that Nenessica became the Principal War Chief of the Chalaakaatha division following the death of Black Fish.

Micajah's military pension declaration documents that he relocated to the same sites that the Chalaakaatha division relocated to as they were displaced several times during the War for Independence. This is a clear indication that his adoptive father lived with the Chalaakaatha division.[10] It is also clear that Micajah worked closely with the Makujay division leadership fol-

Appendix A

lowing the War for Independence as an interpreter in peace and prisoner exchanges involving Makujay prisoners.[11]

Why was Micajah selected and trusted by the Makujay division to play such an important role for the Shawanese Nation at the end of the war? The leaders of the Makujay division lived in separate towns from the Chalaakaatha division. How did they become acquainted with him? The key is Nenessica. He was in a unique position to facilitate the development of the relationship between Micajah and the senior Makujay leadership.

It appears that Nenessica decided to bury his tomahawk and join his Makujay kin in their effort to conclude a final peace treaty with the new United States of America in 1785 - 1786. Nenessica (Nihinessicoe) was one of the Makujay chiefs who signed the Treaty at the Mouth of the Greater Miami River in January 1786 for the Shawanese.[12] Micajah served as federal interpreter for American General Richard Butler in those negotiations.[13]

The Shawanese produced six hostages to secure the treaty after it was signed, including Nenessica (Nohinissica).[14] He was the only chief to sign the document and also serve as a hostage.

Nenessica and Micajah found themselves on opposite sides of an escalating military conflict and drifted apart over the next ten years. A war party including Nenessica attacked five flatboats on March 21, 1788, just above the mouth of the Greater Miami River, and several travelers were killed and captured.[15]

In the early 1790s, Nenessica became the village chief of a New Chalaakaatha town three miles east of the Miami capital of Kekionga, at the headwaters of the Maumee River.[16] He visited Judge John Cleves Symmes at Northbend, Ohio, in late February 1789 accompanied by an interpreter named George (George Girty?).[17] Nenessica's nuanced speech to the judge about the double meaning of the menacing symbolism of the arrow-grasping American Eagle is unforgettable.[18]

In May-June 1794, Nenessica was dispatched by the Shawanese leadership to visit the southern Indian nations on a secret mission of great importance in the final months before the fateful Battle of Fallen Timbers.[19] He joined the militant Shawanese who refused to negotiate with the Americans after the battle.[20] He moved to Bois Blanc, near Amherstberg, Ontario, in 1796 with Captain Johnny, the Buffalo, and Kakinathucca.[21]

Micajah moved to Missouri with Daniel Boone in 1799 and returned to Kentucky in 1804. Nenessica returned to Ohio in 1800 and was living in Wapakoneta among the Shawanese peace faction that opposed the Prophet and Tecumseh in 1805–1807.[22]

Old Nenessica and two other Shawanese men paid a mysterious visit to Bourbon County and Clark County, Kentucky, in 1804–1805, about the time of Micajah's return to that part of Kentucky from Missouri.[23] Perhaps they visited Micajah then.

British Deputy Superintendent General William Claus met with Shawanese Chiefs Buffalo, Nenessica (Black Beard), and Captain Johnny on March 25, 1808, to discuss a renewed alliance.[24] Nenessica was once again dispatched on a long-distance secret mission to carry a message to the Cherokee Nation regarding the impending war. He returned in 1809 and was reportedly exhausted by the effort.[25]

Some historians believe that Nenessica died not long after his return from the south although direct evidence confirming this hypothesis has not been presented. A Shawanese man named Naneskaka was still living in Wapakoneta in 1817.[26] The number of syllables, sound, and "rhythm" of the name "Naneskaka" is very similar to "Nenessica."

Micajah's adoptive Indian father cared enough to pay a final visit to him at his homestead near Salem, Indiana, around 1816. The Indian Wars were over at last, and their peoples were no longer enemies. Nenessica and Micajah met briefly, then said farewell forever.[27]

Endnotes

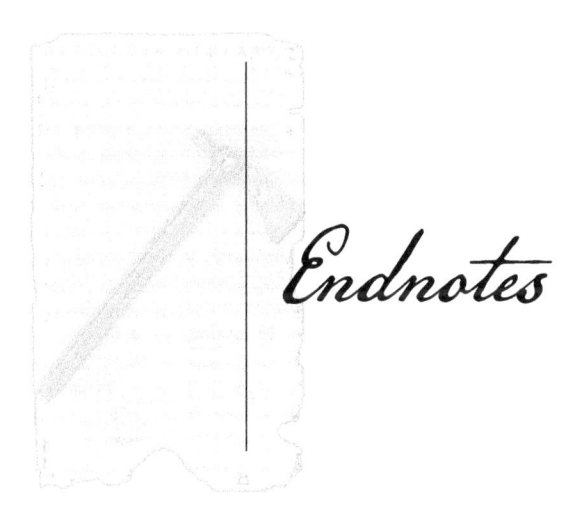

A Note to the Reader

1. James H. Howard, *Shawnee: The Ceremonialism of a Native American Tribe and its Cultural Background*, (Athens, Oh.: Ohio University Press, 1981), 24.
2. Alexander Scott Withers, *Chronicles of Border Warfare*, (Cincinnati: Stewart & Kidd Company, 1895), 194 ftnt.

Chapter One

1. Richard L. Powell, *Geology of the Falls of the Ohio River (Indiana Geological Survey Circular 10)*, (Bloomington, Ind.: Indiana University, 1970, updated 1999), 13–15.
2. There is no public record of the date of Micajah Callaway's birth. The best estimate is July 1760. Micajah's sons Noble and James stated that he was seventeen years old when he was captured by the Shawanese in February, 1778, which would establish a birth date of 1760 or 1761 (Lyman Copeland Draper, *Draper Manuscript Collections (Draper Mss.)* (microfilm edition). State Historical Society of Wisconsin, Madison, Wisc., "Statement of James Callaway, Son of Micajah Callaway," *Draper Mss.* 25S257–261, and "Statement of Noble Callaway, Son of Micajah Callaway," *Draper Mss.* 23S124). This information is corroborated by a July 22, 1776, Bedford County, Virginia Court Order pursuant to which Micajah was "bound out" by Anglican church wardens as an orphan apprentice (*Bedford County, Virginia Order Book 6*, July 22, 1776, 112, and William Waller Hening, *The Statutes at Large being a Collection of All the Laws of Virginia from the First Session of the Legislature in the Year 1619*, Vol. 5, (Richmond: Franklin Press, 1819), 449–454). Although other secondary sources indicate a possible date of birth in 1756 or 1758, it is doubtful that a young man of eighteen to twenty years old would be addressed in a court order intended to address the welfare of orphaned children. If one presumes that Micajah was "bound out" at a time near his sixteenth birthday, this would establish a birthdate in July 1760. Micajah would have been sixteen years old when he enlisted in the Virginia militia in April 1777 and this is consistent with an age of seventeen when he was captured.
3. Andrew Gallup, ed., *The Celeron Expedition to the Ohio Country 1749*, (Bowie, Md.: Heritage Books, Inc., 1997), 83, n.3.
4. The name "Shawanese" is used throughout this book to refer to the ancestors of the modern-day Shawnee people because the term "Shawanese" was used in most contemporary British and American records of the late eighteenth and early nineteenth century. See "A Note to the Reader" at the end of the Preface of this book for further explanation.

5. Helen Hornbeck Tanner, *Indians of Ohio and Indiana Prior to 1795: The Greenville Treaty 1795*, Vol. I, (New York and London: Garland Publishing Inc., 1974), 176, 177.
6. Withers, Chronicles, 194 ftnt.
7. Willard Rouse Jillson, "The Discovery of Kentucky," *The Register of the Kentucky State Historical Society* 20, No. 59 (1922): 125.
8. Frank G. Speck, "The Delaware Indians as Women: Were the Original Pennsylvanians Politically Emasculated?" *The Pennsylvania Magazine of History and Biography* 70, No. 4 (1946): 379.
9. George P. Donehoo, "The Shawnee in Pennsylvania," *The Western Pennsylvania Historical Magazine* 7. No. 3 (1924): 179.
10. Lucien Beckner, "Eskippakithiki: The Last Indian Town in Kentucky." *The Filson Club Quarterly* 6, No. 4 (1932), 358, 362, 365.
11. C. Hale Sipe, *The Indian Chiefs of Pennsylvania*, (Butler, Pa.: The Ziegler Printing Co., 1927), 114, and John A. Jakle, "The American Bison and the Human Occupance of the Ohio Valley," *Proceedings of the American Philosophical Society* 112, No. 4 (198): 302.
12. T.P. Field, *Kentucky and the Southwest Territory (Map)*, (Lexington: Dept. of Geography, University of Kentucky, 1965).
13. George R. Wilson, *Early Indiana Trails and Surveys*, (Indianapolis: Indiana Historical Society, 1986), 369–371.
14. Powell, *Geology*, 1–3.
15. Beckner, "Eskippakithiki," 368–370.
16. C. Hale Sipe, *The Indian Wars of Pennsylvania, Book One*, (Bowie, Md.: Facsimile Reprint by Heritage Books, Inc., 2000), 34.
17. Hayes Baker-Crothers, *Virginia and the French and Indian War* (Chicago: University of Chicago Press, 1928), 5–6; Lewis Preston Summers, *History of Southwest Virginia, 1746–1786*, (Baltimore, Md.: Regional Publishing Company, 1979), 47; Kenneth P. Bailey, *Christopher Gist*, (Hamden, Conn.: Archon Books, an imprint of the Shoestring Press, Inc., 1976), 26.
18. Summers, *History of Southwest Virginia*, 47.
19. Michael N. McConnell, *A Country Between, The Upper Ohio Valley and its Peoples, 1724–1774*, (Lincoln: University of Nebraska Press, 1992), 100.
20. Bailey, *Christopher Gist*, 86–88.
21. Alan Fitzpatrick, *Wilderness War on the Ohio, The Untold Story of the Savage Battle for British and Indian Control of the Ohio Country During the American Revolution*, (Benwood, W.Va.: Fort Henry Publications, 2003), 89–90.
22. *Minutes of the Provincial Council of Pennsylvania*, Vol. 8, (Harrisburg: Theo Fenn & Co., 1852), 293.
23. Near the present location of Blacksburg, Va. See F.B. Kegley, *Kegley's Virginia Frontier*, (Roanoke, Va.: The Southwest Virginia Historical Society, 1938), 209–210.
24. Patricia Givens Johnson, *William Preston and the Allegheny Patriots*, (Pulaski, Va.: B.D. Smith & Bros., Printers, Inc., 1976), 48–49.
25. Withers, *Chronicles*, 90.
26. *Draper Manuscript Collection*, "Appendix, Captivity of the Renick Family, 1757" (Draper Mss. 21U126).
27. *Draper Manuscript Collection*, Draper Mss. 11CC93.
28. Kegley, *Virginia Frontier*, 264.
29. *Minutes of the Provincial Council of Pennsylvania*, Vol. 8, 126–127 and Joseph S. Walton, *Conrad Weiser and the Indian Policy of Colonial Pennsylvania*, (Philadelphia: George W. Jacobs & Co., 1900), 368–369.
30. Withers, *Chronicles*, 172, ftnt. 2, "'Sketch of Cornstalk' Draper Mss. 3D, Chapter XVIII," *Ohio Archaeological and Historical Publications* 21 (1912): 245–246, and Charles E. Kemper, ed., "Documents Relating to the French and Indian War, 1755–1762," *The Virginia Magazine of History and Biography* 15, No. 3 (1908): 255–256.
31. Jeff Carskadden and James Morton, *Where the Frolics and War Dances are Held, the Indian Wars and the Early European Exploration and Settlement of Muskingum County and the Central Muskingum Valley*. (Baltimore: Gateway Press, Inc., 1997): 120.
32. Moravian missionaries reported that Paxinosa had been married for thirty-eight years in the

Endnotes

year 1755 placing the date of his marriage in 1717. See George Henry Loskiel, *History of the Mission of the United Brethren Among the Indians of North America*, (London: Brethren's Society for the Furtherance of the Gospel, 1794), 160. Cornstalk was believed to be in his 50s around the time of the Battle of Point Pleasant in 1774. If that is the case, there would not be enough time for another generation to have existed between Paxinosa and Cornstalk.

33. Daniel K. Richter and James H. Merrell, "Peoples 'In Between' the Iroquois and the Ohio Indians, 1720-1768," In *Beyond the Covenant Chain* (Syracuse, New York: University Press, 1987), 107-109

34. Typical wampum belts were four or five inches wide and three to four feet long. The color black often signified war. White signified peace, prosperity, and health. Violet signified tragedy, death, and sorrow. Stick figures and geometric designs were used to make the message plainer. Metaphoric expressions were conveyed by symbols such as a raised hatchet for war, a buried hatchet for peace, covered bones for forgiveness, kindling a fire for initiating negotiations, a clear path between nations for peace, a warpath for war; etc.

35. Milton W. Hamilton, ed., *The Papers of Sir William Johnson*, Vol. 12, (New York: The University of the State of New York, 1957), 1090-1091, and Vernon Kinietz and Erminie W. Voegelin, eds., *Shawanese Traditions, C.C. Trowbridge's Account*, (Ann Arbor, Mich.: University of Michigan Press, 1939), 11.

36. "'Sketch of Cornstalk,'" 246-252; Joseph A. Waddell, *Annals of Augusta County, Virginia from 1726 to 1871*, (Harrisonburg, Va.: C.J. Carrier Company, 1972), 168-176.

37. Randolph C. Downes, *Council Fires on the Upper Ohio: A Narrative of Indian Affairs in the Upper Ohio River Valley Until 1795*, (Pittsburgh: University of Pittsburgh Press, 1940), 121-122, 134-135.

38. Howard, *Shawnee: Ceremonialism*, 25-32.

39. Carskadden and Morton, *Where the Frolics and War Dances are Held*, 121-123, 242-243.

40. McConnell, *Country Between*, 262-263.

41. Schaaf, Gregory, *Wampum Belts*, 136-137.

42. Colin G. Calloway, "Chapter 6: Maquachake: The Perils of Neutrality in the Ohio Country." In *The American Revolution in Indian Country*, (New York: Cambridge University Press, 1995): 162.

43. Schaaf, *Wampum Belts*, 68, 131, 163, and *Draper Manuscript Collections*, "Interview Notes from Joseph Jackson," Draper Mss. 11C62(1).

44. Schaaf, *Wampum Belts*, 68, 131.

45. William Albert Galloway, *Old Chillicothe: Shawnee and Pioneer History, Conflicts and Romances in the Northwest Territory*, (Xenia, Oh.: The Buckeye Press, 1934), 283, 287, and *Draper Manuscript Collections*, Draper Mss. 5S11. There is some doubt among some researchers as to whether these two individuals were the biological children of Nonhelema. Nonhelema did not live a traditional female Shawanese lifestyle. Also, Fanny and Morgan may have been adopted by Nonhelema.

46. Reuben Gold Thwaites and Louise Phelps Kellogg, *Documentary History of Dunsmore's War, 1774*, (Madison, Wisc.: Wisconsin Historical Society, 1905), 242, fnt. 70, 427 and C. Hale Sipe, *The Indian Wars of Pennsylvania, Book Two*, (Bowie, Md.: Facsimile Reprint by Heritage Books, Inc, 2000), 104.

47. Alexander C. Flick, ed., *The Papers of Sir William Johnson*, Vol. 7, (Albany: The University of the State of New York, 1921-1962), 182.

48. Ibid., 184-185

Chapter Two

1. Virgil A. Lewis, *History of the Battle of Point Pleasant Fought Between Indians and White Men at the Mouth of the Great Kanawha River, (now Point Pleasant, West Virginia) Monday, October 10, 1774*, (Westminster, Md.: Reprint by Willow Bend Books, 2000), 55, and E.O. Randall, "The Dunmore War," *Ohio Archaeological and Historical Publications* 11 (1903): 169, and Thwaites and Kellogg, *History of Dunsmore's War*, 425-426.

2. Willard Stern Randall, *George Washington, A Life*, (New York: Henry Holt and Company, 1997), 248, and Warren Skidmore and Donna Kaminsky, *Lord Dunmore's Little War of 1774, His Captains and Their Men who Opened Up Kentucky & the West to American Settlement*, (Bowie, Md.: Heritage Books, Inc., 2002), 2, ftnt. 18.
3. McConnell, *Country Between*, 264.
4. Edna Kenton, *Simon Kenton, His Life and Period, 1755–1836*, (North Stratford, N.H.: Reprint, Ayer Publishers, Inc., 1999), 42–43, 73.
5. Robert B. McAfee, "The Life and Times of Robert B. McAfee and his Family and Connections," *The Register of the Kentucky State Historical Society* 25, No. 73 (1927): 7, 13–14.
6. "Letters of Colonel George Croghan," *Pennsylvania Magazine of History and Biography* 15, No. 4 (1892): 434, and Nancy O'Malley, *Stockading Up*, (Frankfort: Kentucky Heritage Council, 1994), 121.
7. Edward G. Williams, "The Journal of Richard Butler, 1775 Continental Congress' Envoy to the Western Indians," *The Western Pennsylvania Historical Magazine* 46, No. 4 (1963): 381–383, and Erminie Wheeler-Voegelin, *Indians of Ohio and Indiana Prior to 1795: Ethnohistory of Indian Use and Occupancy of Ohio and Indiana Prior to 1795*, Vol. 2, (New York & London: Garland Publishing, Inc., 1974), 52–55.
8. Henry Howe, ed., *Historical Collections of Ohio*, Vol. 1 (Cincinnati: C.H. Krehbiel & Co., 1902), 301, and *Draper Manuscript Collections*, "Statement of Judge Christopher Woods," Draper Mss. 8BB125.
9. McAfee, "Life and Times of Robert B. McAfee," 13–23, and O'Malley, *Stockading Up*, 14.
10. McAfee, "Life and Times of Robert B. McAfee," 18–23.
11. Ibid., 18–23.
12. Hamilton, *Papers of Sir William Johnson*, Vol. 12, 1032–1033.
13. Robert L. Kincaid, "Boone and Russell Graves in Lee County, Virginia," *The Virginia Magazine of History and Biography* 60, No. 1 (1952): 172.
14. Jack M. Sosin, "The British Indian Department and Dunsmore's War," *The Virginia Magazine of History and Biography* 74, No. 1 (1966): 43, and Neal O. Hammon, "The Fincastle Surveyors at the Falls of the Ohio, 1774," *The Filson Club History Quarterly* 47, No. 1 (1973): 14.
15. Walter R. Hoberg, "Early History of Colonel Alexander McKee," *The Pennsylvania Magazine of History and Biography* 58 (1934): 29–30, and Kathrine Wagner Seineke, *The George Rogers Clark Adventure in the Illinois*, (New Orleans, La.: Polyanthos, Inc., 1981), 143.
16. Downes, *Council Fires on the Upper Ohio*, 158–160, and Farragher, *Daniel Boone*, 99.
17. Downes, *Council Fires on the Upper Ohio*, 162.
18. Sipe, *Indian Wars of Pennsylvania*, Book Two, 502.
19. Charles A. Hanna, *The Wilderness Trail*, (New York: G.P. Putnam's Sons, 1911), 71–73.
20. Neville B. Craig, ed., *The Olden Times*, Vol, 2. (Pittsburgh: Wright & Charlton, 1847. Reprint, Millwood, N.Y.: Kraus Reprint Co., 1976), 10–11.
21. Downes, *Council Fires on the Upper Ohio*, 165.
22. Thwaites and Kellogg, *History of Dunsmore's War*, 66–67.
23. Thomas Jefferson, *Notes on the State of Virginia*, (Boston: Thomas & Andrews, J. West, West & Greenleaf, et al. 1801. Reprinted with Introduction and Notes by William Peden, ed. Chapel Hill and London: North Carolina University Press, 1982 (Page references are to the 1982 edition.)), 247.
24. Downes, *Council Fires on the Upper Ohio*, 167.
25. Thwaites and Kellogg, *History of Dunsmore's War*, 36, and Downes, *Council Fires on the Upper Ohio*, 174.
26. A County Lieutenant in colonial Virginia was commissioned as a Colonel and was the official commander of all county militia. He was responsible for procuring and organizing logistical support for the troops and was authorized to place all males over eighteen years of age into service, appoint Captains, and hold courts martial. See Marshall Wingfield, *A History of Caroline County Virginia*, (Baltimore, Md.: Reprinted for Clearfield Company, Inc. by Genealogical Publishing Co., Inc., 1991).
27. Sosin, "British Indian Department," 45–46.
28. Withers, *Chronicles*, 176–177.
29. Randall, "Ohio in Early History," 406, and Randall, "The Dunmore War," 168.

Endnotes

30. Randall, "Ohio in Early History," 407.
31. John Romeyn Broadhead, ed. *Documents Relative to the Colonial History of the State of New York*, Vol. 8 (Albany: Weed, Parsons and Company, 1857), 471-473.
32. Fitzpatrick, *Wilderness War on the Ohio*, 157, 164.
33. Thwaites and Kellogg, *History of Dunsmore's War*, 97-98.
34. Lewis, *Battle of Point Pleasant*, 23.
35. Seineke, *George Rogers Clark Adventure*, 150-151.
36. Sipe, *Indian Wars of Pennsylvania, Book One*, 317-320.
37. Col. William Fleming's regiment included Capt. Henry Pauling's company; Dudley Callaway was included on the Muster Roll of Captain Henry Pauling's company. *Draper Manuscript Collections*, Draper Mss. 2ZZ71(1) and (17).
38. Emily Foster, *The Ohio Frontier: An Anthology of Early Writings*, (Lexington: the University Press of Kentucky, 1996), 41.
39. Lewis, *Battle of Point Pleasant*, 31.
40. Randall, "The Dunmore War," 177, and Thwaites and Kellogg, *History of Dunsmore's War*, 212-214.
41. Col. William Fleming's regiment includes Capt. Henry Pauling's company; Dudley Callaway was included on the Muster Roll of Captain Henry Pauling's company. *Draper Manuscript Colections*, Draper Mss. 2ZZ71(1) and (17). See also Thwaites and Kellogg, *History of Dunsmore's War*, 411.
42. Thwaites and Kellogg, *History of Dunsmore's War*, 340, ftnt. 57.
43. Lewis, *Battle of Point Pleasant*, 35-36.
44. Randall, "The Dunmore War," 178; Sosin, "British Indian Department," 46, and Thwaites and Kellogg, *History of Dunsmore's War*, 425-426.
45. Chief Pluggy was the chief of a village on the Scioto River upstream from the Lower Shawanese Towns and was commonly described as a Mingo.
46. Olmstead, *David Zeisberger*, 227.
47. Lewis, *Battle of Point Pleasant*, 41, and Carskadden and Morton, *Where the Frolics and War Dances are Held*, 121-123, 242-243.
48. Kenton, *Simon Kenton*, 51.
49. Lewis, *Battle of Point Pleasant*, 43.
50. J.T. McAllister, "Battle of Point Pleasant," *The Virginia Magazine of History and Biography* 10 (1903): 75.
51. Skidmore and Kaminsky, *Lord Dunmore's Little War*, 187.
52. *Draper Manuscript Collections*. "The Battle of Point Pleasant, Oct. 10, 1774" by S. Eliot Land, D.D., Draper Mss. 15J96.
53. Kegley, *Virginia Frontier*, 622.
54. G. Melvin Herndon, "George Mathews, Frontier Patriot," *The Virginia Magazine of History and Biography* 77, No. 3 (1969)," 312; McAllister, "Battle of Point Pleasant," 77; and Lewis, *Battle of Point Pleasant*, 46, 48.
55. Thwaites and Kellogg, *History of Dunsmore's War*, 287, 293, and Randall, "The Dunmore War," 180-187.
56. Lewis, *Battle of Point Pleasant*, 34, and Thwaites and Kellogg, *History of Dunsmore's War*, 302, ftnt. 15.
57. Lewis, *Battle of Point Pleasant*, 54.
58. Galloway, *Old Chillicothe*, 289.
59. Randall, "The Dunmore War," 188-190, and Lewis, *Battle of Point Pleasant*, 94.
60. Thwaites and Kellogg, *History of Dunsmore's War*, 288-289, 350-352.
61. Lewis, *Battle of Point Pleasant*, 56.
62. Randall, "The Dunmore War," 193-194.
63. Thwaites and Kellogg, *History of Dunsmore's War*, 303-304.
64. "'Sketch of Cornstalk,'" 256.
65. Lewis, *Battle of Point Pleasant*, 92-93.

Chapter Three

1. Flanders was selected as a juryman on July 28, 1769, placing his probable date of birth in 1748 on the assumption that he was then 21 years old. See *Bedford County, Virginia Order Book 3*, "July 28, 1769," 559.
2. The heavy oznaburg fabric of flax and hemp fibers was the perfect material for the cold, wet weather. See John S. Salmon and Emily J. Salmon, *Franklin County Virginia 1786–1796*, (Rocky Mount, Va.: Franklin County Bicentennial Commission, 1993), 45.
3. Harriette Simpson Arnow, *Seedtime on the Cumberland*, (Lincoln: University of Nebraska Press), 150–151.
4. Other nicknames used by family and friends for Micajah were "Cage," "Caja," and "Cager."
5. See *Draper Manuscript Collections*, "Letter from Elijah Callaway to Lyman Draper," Draper Mss. 5DD20. Joseph Callaway Jr. and his father Joseph Sr. immigrated to Virginia in 1687 and 1690 (Nell Martin Nugent, *Cavaliers and Pioneers: Abstracts of Virginia Land Patents and Grants, 1666–1695*, Vol. 2, (Richmond: Virginia State Library, 1977), 306, 342). Joseph Callaway Jrs.' six sons and daughters Elizabeth and Ann were born on their father's one hundred acre tobacco plantation in the Rappahannock River valley in Caroline County (John Frederick Doorman, *Essex County, Virginia Deeds and Wills No. 13*, (Washington, D.C.: John Frederick Doorman, 1963), 120). Joseph Jr., his wife, and his son Joseph III died from dysentery in 1732 (Sherrill Williams, "The Callaways in Early America," *Callaway Family Association Journal* 4 (1979): 10–12; *Draper Manuscript Collections*, "Letter from Elijah Callaway to Lyman Draper," Draper Mss. 5DD20; and Louis B. Wright, *The Prose Works of William Byrd of Westover, Narratives of a Colonial Virginian*, (Cambridge, Mass.: The Belknap Press of Harvard University Press, 1966), 345). Thomas led his orphaned younger brothers in a bold move west to Spotsyvania County where Thomas and William purchased land along Swift Run on the eastern flanks of the Blue Ridge Mountains in 1734 (John Frederick Doorman, ed. *Orange County Virginia Deed Books 3 and 4: 1738–1741*. (Washington, D.C.: John Frderick Doorman, 1966),60). The six Callaway brothers and their young families relocated in the 1742–1744 time period to areas that later became Bedford County and Halifax County, Virginia. They were among the first English settlers to settle in that area (Sherrill Williams, "Colonel Richard Callaway of Virginia and Kentucky," *Callaway Family Association Journal* 6 (1981): 75; Kegley, *Virginia Frontier*, 112–113; and Maud Carter Clement. *The History of Pittsylvania County, Virginia*. (Clearfield Company, Inc., 1929. Reprint, Baltimore: Genealogical Publishing Co., 1999), 42). They served in the Bedford County and Halifax County militias against Shawanese and Cherokee raiders during the French and Indian War (William Waller Hening, *The Statutes at Large being a Collection of All the Laws of Virginia from the First Session of the Legislature in the Year 1619*, Vol. 7, (Richmond: Franklin Press, 1819), 204–211 and 219).
6. "New London, Bedford County, VA., Deed Book A, p. 434," *The Virginia Magazine of History and Biography* 19 (1911): 431–432.
7. Lucy Evans, "Bedford County, Virginia Records," *Callaway Family Association Journal* 2,(1977), 41.
8. See John S. Salmon and Emily J. Salmon, *Franklin County Virginia 1786–1796*, (Rocky Mount, Va.: Franklin County Bicentennial Commission, 1993), 29, and Clement, *History of Pittsylvania County*, 69. Fort Vause was located in the Blue Ridge Mountains to the south and west of Bedford County. Captain Callaway and his company of soldiers pursued the war party through the southwest Virginia and Kentucky wilderness all of the way to the Ohio River before giving up their pursuit (Johnson, *William Preston*, 48–49; *Draper Manuscript Collections*, "Letter from Elijah Callaway to Lyman Draper," Draper Mss. 5DD20; and Kegley, *Virginia Frontier*, 231–232). Thomas briefed young Colonel George Washington at Fort Trial during Washington's famous tour of the western Virginia forts in 1756 (Kegley, *Virginia Frontier*, 237–245).
9. *The Courier Journal (Louisville, Ky.)*, March 16, 1896, and Lucy Evans, *The Boone Scout* 7, No. 1, (Seattle: The Boone Family Association of Washington, October 1962).
10. Ruth Sparacio and Sam Sparacio, *Virginia County Court Records; Deed & Will Abstracts of Albemarle County, Virginia 1748–1752*, (McLean, Va.: The Antient Press, 1990), 104–105.

Endnotes

11. Nancy Callaway Russell, "Micajah Callaway," *Callaway Family Association Journal* 20 (1995), 53.
12. *Bedford County, Virginia Order Book 3 (1763–1771)*, June 15, 1769, 310.
13. Richard Callaway served as a commissioned Colonel and second-in-command to his brother William as the senior field commander of the Bedford County militia during the French and Indian War. He was about six feet tall, weighed about one hundred and eighty pounds, and had dark eyes and long dark hair (*Draper Manuscript Collections*, "Letter to Lyman Draper from Col. Callaway's grandson, Richard Holder," Draper Mss. 24C29; "Lyman Draper Tribute to Col. Richard Callaway," Draper Mss. 5B56; and "Letter to Lyman Draper from John Redd," Draper Mss. 10NN104).
14. *Draper Manuscript Collections*, "Statement of Capt. Samuel Boone, son of George Boone," Draper Mss. 22S271.
15. Horace Heffren, "Pioneer Pickings No. 36." (Salem, Ind.: *The Salem Democrat*, January 19, 1876. Reprint, *Pioneer Pickings*. Salem, Ind.: James E. Bolding, 1993), 7.
16. Williams, "Colonel Richard Callaway," 76.
17. *Draper Manuscript Collections*, "Letter from Elijah Callaway lto Lyman Draper," Draper Mss. 5DD20.
18. Williams, "Colonel Richard Callaway," 77.
19. Lowell H. Harrison and James C. Kotter, *A New History of Kentucky* (Lexington: The University of Kentucky Press, 1997), 28, and Williams, "Colonel Richard Callaway." 77.
20. *Bedford County, Virginia Deed Book 5 (1773–1778)*, "June 28, 1773," 89, and *Bedford County, Virginia Deed Book 5 (1773–1778)*, "November 15, 1774," 268.
21. Williams, "Colonel Richard Callaway," 76–77.
22. Harrison and Kotter, *New History of Kentucky*, 28, and Williams, "Colonel Richard Callaway," 77.
23. Bobbie L. Callaway, "Flanders: Legend and His Legacy." *The Callaway Journal* 10 (1985): 18, and *Bedford County, Virginia Deed Book 5 (1773–1778)*, February 3, 1775, 324.
24. Harrison and Kotter, *New History of Kentucky*, 28, and Williams, "Colonel Richard Callaway," 77.
25. O'Malley, *Stockading Up*, 15.
26. *Draper Manuscript Collections*, "Ledger A (of the Henderson Company), Hart's Ledgers, & Co., Capt. Nathaniel Hart," Draper Mss. 17CC189.
27. Julian Boyd, ed. *The Papers of Thomas Jefferson*, Vol. 2 (Princeton, N.J.: University Press, 1950), 85, 87, 88, 105.
28. Arnow, *Seedtime on the Cumberland*, 201.
29. Thwaites and Kellogg, *History of Dunsmore's War*, 60, ftnt. 2.
30. Jakle, "American Bison," 302.
31. Wendell H. Rone, Sr., *An Historical Atlas of Kentucky and her Counties*, (Central City, Ky.: Rev. Wendell Sandefur, 1965), 25.
32. John Mack Faragher, *Daniel Boone: The Life and Legend of an American Pioneer*, (New York: Henry Holt and Company, 1992), 117.
33. George W. Ranck, *Boonesborough, Its Founding, Pioneer Struggles, Indian Experiences, Transylvania Days, and Revolutionary Annals*, (Louisville: John P. Morton & Company, 1901), 19–21.
34. Neal O. Hammon, "The First Trip to Boonesborough," *The Filson Club History Quarterly* 45, No. 3 (1971): 260.
35. Charles W. Bryan, Jr., "Richard Callaway, Kentucky Pioneer." *The Filson Club History Quarterly* 9, No. 1 (1935): 43.
36. Williams, "Colonel Richard Callaway," 78, and Hammon, "First Trip to Boonesborough," 260.
37. *Draper Manuscript Collections*, "Proceedings of the First Transylvania Convention held at Boonesboro, May 23, 1775," Draper Mss. 1CC, and "Letter from Col. Floyd," Draper Mss. 17CC180.
38. Daniel Boone and Richard Callaway left Boonesborough on June 13 to collect their families and move them to Boonesborough. Faragher, *Daniel Boone*, 126.
39. "Descendants of Joseph Callaway of Virginia through One of His Sons: Richard Callaway." *Callaway Family Association Journal* 5 (1980): 70.
40. *Draper Manuscript Collectiions*, "Statement of Simon Kenton," Draper Mss. 7S123.
41. O'Malley, *Stockading Up*, 23–27.

42. Captain Logan was born to Scotch-Irish parents in Augusta County, Virginia in 1743 and served as a Sergeant in General Bouquet's campaign of 1764. He settled on the Holston River in 1771 and then served as a Lieutenant in the Battle of Point Pleasant. Captain Logan was a tall man with a thin visage and spare frame. See Thwaites and Kellogg, *History of Dunsmore's War*, 82, ftnt. 31.
43. O'Malley, *Stockading Up*, 241–244.
44. Ibid., 292–293.
45. *Draper Manuscript Collections*, "McAfee's Kentucky Sketches," Draper Mss. 4CC92; Bryan, "Richard Callaway," 44; and Williams, "Colonel Richard Callaway," 80.
46. *Draper Manuscript Collections*, Draper Mss. 12C27; *Draper Manuscript Collections*, "McAfee's Kentucky Sketches," Draper Mss. 4CC92; and Williams, "Colonel Richard Callaway,," 80–81.
47. Carskadden and Morton, *Where the Frolics and War Dances are Held*, 242–243.
48. Located two miles south of the present-day location of Zanesfield, Ohio. See Wheeler-Voegelin, *Indians of Ohio and Indiana*, Vol. 2, 269.
49. "Wapatomica" will be used to refer to the relocated capital from this point forward in the text.
50. Located two and a half miles southeast of present-day location of Bellefontaine and about four miles west of Zanesfield, Ohio. See Wheeler-Voegelin, *Indians of Ohio and Indiana*, Vol. 2, 276.
51. Located at present-day location of Bellefontaine, Ohio. See Wheeler-Voegelin, *Indians of Ohio and Indiana*, Vol. 2, 276.
52. Also called "Old Town" and "Old Chillicothe." Located three miles north of present Xenia, Ohio. See Wheeler-Voegelin, *Indians of Ohio and Indiana*, Vol. 2, 259.
53. Pierre-Louis ("Louis") de Lorimier and his father Captain Claude-Nicolas-Guillaume de Lorimier de la Riviere, Chevalier de Saint-Louis, established a trading post on Loramie's Creek near the former location of Pickawillany in 1769 and began a thriving trade with the Miami Confederacy nations. Captain de Lorimier died in 1770 and his son Louis continued to operate the trading post. See Paul L. Stevens, *Louis Lorimier in the American Revolution: A Memoire by an Ohio Indian Trader and British Partisan. (Center for French Colonial Studies Extended Publications Series Number 2)*, (Naperville, Ill.: The Center for French Colonial Studies, Inc.), 3–4; Beverly W. Bond, Jr., "The Captivity of Charles Stuart, 1755–57." *The Mississippi Valley Historical Review* 13 (1926–1927) 19, ftnt. 61; and Milo M. Quaife, "The Ohio Campaigns of 1782," *The Mississippi Valley Historical Review* 17 (1930–1931): 528.
54. Four and one-half miles west of present-day location of Springfield, Ohio. See Wheeler-Voegelin, *Indians of Ohio and Indiana*, Vol. 2, 260.
55. *Draper Manuscript Collections*, "Statement of Henry Wilson," Draper Mss. 9J62.
56. Fitzpatrick, *Wilderness War on the Ohio*, 168.
57. Olmstead, *David Zeisberger*, 239–241.
58. Reuben Gold Thwaites and Louise Phelps Kellogg, *The Revolution on the Upper Ohio, 1775–1777*, (Madison, Wisc.: Wisconsin Historical Society, 1905), 61.
59. Thwaites and Kellogg, *Revolution on the Upper Ohio*, 34, 43–44, 47.
60. Williams, "Journal of Richard Butler," 383, 385.
61. Calloway, "Maquachake," 164.
62. Schaaf, *Wampum Belts*, 68, 131.
63. Edward G. Williams, "The Journal of Richard Butler, 1775 Continental Congress' Envoy to the Western Indians," *The Western Pennsylvania Historical Magazine* 47, No. 2 (1964), 148–149.
64. Schaaf, *Wampum Belts*, 151.
65. Calloway, "Maquachake," 164.
66. Craig, *Olden Times*, Vol. 2, No. 11, 520.
67. "Treaty Between Virginia and the Indians at Fort Dunsmore (Pittsburgh) June, 1775," *The Virginia Magazine of History and Biography* 14 (1907): 54–58, reprint Millwood, New York: Krause Reprint Corporation, 1968.
68. O'Malley, *Stockading Up*, 292–293.

Endnotes

Chapter Four

1. Jack M. Sosin, "The Use of Indians in the War of American Revolution: A Re-Assessment of Responsibility," *The Canadian Historical Review* 46, No. 2 (1965): 119.
2. Craig, *Olden Time*, Volume 2, No. 3, 99.
3. Schaaf, *Wampum Belts*, 151.
4. Ibid., 155.
5. William L. Saunders, ed., *The Colonial Records of North Carolina*, Vol. 10, (New York: AMS Press, Inc., 1968), 773–774.
6. Schaaf, *Wampum Belts* 150, 168, 179.
7. Saunders, *Colonial Records*, Vol. 10, 776–779.
8. Ibid., 776–779.
9. Ibid., 661.
10. Downes, *Council Fires on the Upper Ohio*, 190.
11. Anne Crabb, *Carried Off by the Indians*. (Richmond, Ky.: Anne P. Crabb, 1991), 8–9.
12. Some later Callaway family histories state that Micajah was present at the capture and rescue of the girls. However, none of the accounts by participants in this famous event in the Draper Manuscripts or by their descendants mention his name. These accounts place the date of the girls' capture and rescue in early July 1776. The available records indicate that Micajah was in Bedford County at that time preparing for his gunsmith apprenticeship to Zachariah Callaway.
13. *Draper Manuscript Collections*, "Letter to Lyman Draper from Nathaniel Reed, Jr.," Draper Mss. 10NN147; "Statement of Mrs. Susan Howell, daughter of Flanders and Jemima Boone Callaway," Draper Mss. 23S228; and "Statement of Colonel Richard Callaway, Jr., son of Colonel Richard Callaway," Draper Mss. 23C48.
14. Hening, *Statutes at Large*, Vol. 5, 449–454.
15. *Bedford County, Virginia Order Book 6*, July 22, 1776, 112.
16. John Hawkins Callaway's recollection of his father Micajah Callaway: "He never learned to read or write. Was not religious—but was never known to utter an oath." *Draper Manuscript Collections*, "Interview Notes from John Hawkins Callaway, Son of Micajah Callaway," Draper Mss. 25S124.
17. Robert John Holden, *The Hunting Pioneers, 1720–1840*, (Bowie, Md.: Heritage Books, Inc., 2000), 76–77.
18. Robert L. Scribner, *Revolutionary Virginia, The Road to Independence*, Vol. 7, Part Two, (Richmond, Va.: University Press of Virginia, 1983), 568.
19. "Virginia Militia in the Revolution," *The Virginia Magazine of History and Biolgraphy* 7 (1900), reprint, New York: Kraus Reprint Corporation, 1968): 150, 152; Callaway, "Virginia Kentucky-Missouri," 30; Williams, "Colonel Richard Callaway," 81; and "Pension File No. S 30917, Revolutionary War Chesley Callaway."
20. Saunders, *Colonial Records of North Carolina*, Vol. 10, 671.
21. "September 2, 1776 Letter from Lieutenant Governor Hamilton to Lord Dartmouth," *Historical Collections: Pioneer and Historical Society of the State of Michigan*, Vol. 10, (Lansing: Thorp & Godfrey, 1888), 269.
22. William H. Engle, "The Indian Treaty at Fort Pitt in 1776," *The Pennsylvania Magazine of History and Biography* 5, No. 4 (1881): 484, and Schaaf, *Wampum Belts*, 164, 184.
23. Calloway, "Maquachake," 166.
24. *Draper Manuscript Collections*, "June 20, 1776 Memorial of the Kentucky Committee to Convention of Virginia," Draper Mss. 14S7.
25. *Draper Manuscript Collections*, "Deposition of Simon Kenton," Draper Mss. 6BB24, and *Draper Manuscript Collections*, Draper Mss. 15CC159.
26. Boyd, *Papers of Thomas Jefferson*, Vol. 2, 82, 108.
27. Williams, "Colonel Richard Callaway," 81, 86.

28. *Draper Manuscript Collections*, Draper Mss. 15CC160.
29. The present-day location of Maysville, Kentucky.
30. *Draper Manuscript Collections*, "Interview Notes from Noble Callaway and John Hawkins Callaway, Sons of Micajah Callaway," Draper Mss. 25S124.
31. *Draper Manuscript Collections*, "Interview Notes from Noble Callaway, Son of Micajah Callaway," Draper Mss. 25S124.
32. *Draper Manuscript Collections*, "Interview Notes from James Callaway, Son of Micajah Callaway," Draper Mss. 25S257–161.
33. *Draper Manuscript Collections*, "Interview Notes from James Callaway, Son of Micajah Callaway," Draper Mss. 25S257–161 and "Interview Notes from Morgan Bryan," Draper Mss. 6S300–302.

Chapter Five

1. Randall, *George Washington*, 320.
2. "March 12, 1777, Letter from Lord Germain to General Guy Carleton," *Historical Collections: Pioneer and Historical Society of the State of Michigan*, Vol. 9, (Lansing: Thorp & Godfrey, 1886), 347.
3. Seineke, *George Rogers Clark Adventure*, xix.
4. *Draper Manuscript Collections*, "Statement of James Wade," Draper Mss. 12CC40.
5. Mary B. Kegley, *Wythe County, Virginia, a Bicentennial History*, (Marceline, Mo.: Walsworth Publishing Inc., 1989), 38–39.
6. *Draper Manuscript Collections*, "Letter from Gov. Patrick Henry to Col. William Fleming," Draper Mss. 15ZZ5.
7. Faragher, *Daniel Boone*, 138.
8. *Draper Manuscript Collections*, "Declaration of Joseph Kennedy," Draper Mss. 29C103.
9. Because of disputes between the Transylvania Company and its settlers, the fort was not fully completed until 1778. *Draper Manuscript Collections*, "Interview with Mrs. Elizabeth Pogue," Draper Mss. 12C27(15).
10. *Draper Manuscript Collections*, "Statement of Nathaniel Hart," Draper Mss. 17CC195.
11. *Draper Manuscript Collections*, "Statement of Josiah Collins," Draper Mss. 12CC74, 97.
12. *Draper Manuscript Collections*, "Excerpt from Kentucky Historical Society Journal," Draper Mss 15CC161–162; "Declaration of Joseph Kennedy," Draper Mss. 29C103; and "Statement of Col. William Whitley," Draper Mss. 9CC21.
13. *Draper Manuscript Collections*, "Excerpt from Kentucky Historical Society Journal," Draper Mss. 15CC162.
14. Kenton, *Simon Kenton*, 86.
15. *Draper Manuscript Collections*, "Interview with John Gass," Draper Mss. 11CC12.
16. Kenton, *Simon Kenton*, 88.
17. William Waller Hening, *The Statutes at Large being a Collection of All the Laws of Virginia from the First Session of the Legislature in the Year 1619*, Vol. 9, (Richmond: J. & G. Cochran, 1821), 317.
18. Statement of John Gass: "We removed to Estill's S., the spring after Pemberton Rollins and Col. Callaway were taken (killed). He (Col. C.) was the worst barbequed man I ever saw. Cut his head bones up. They stripped him stark naked and rolled in a mud-hole. It was said that Cajah Callaway was along with the Indians. Some of the prisoners said, he had threatened revenge on his uncle. Cajah was of those taken at the salt-making. His uncle had whipped him before he was taken. There was not a bone as big as your hand." *Draper Manuscript Collections*, Draper Mss. 11CC15.
19. *Draper Manuscript Collections*, "Interview Notes from John Hawkins Callaway, Son of Micajah Callaway," Draper Mss. 25S124, and Russell, "Micajah Callaway," 56.
20. The pension application Declarations of both Micajah and James Callaway (Micajah Callaway, "Declaration of Micajah Callaway, September 29, 1832," in *Micajah Callaway Pension Application File*. Washington, D.C.: National Archives Trust Fund, Pension File Designation No. W6646, BLWT26660-160-55, and *Draper Manuscript Collections*, Draper Mss. 21C75) both indicate that

Endnotes

they enlisted with Captain Paulding in April, 1777. Fort Boonesborough was attacked and Captain Boone badly wounded on April 24, 1777. The fort was attacked again on May 23 and July 4 before the Shawanese and Mingo invasion force returned to Ohio (Faragher, *Daniel Boone*, 147–151). A December 18, 1850 letter from Leonard Bliss to Lyman Draper (*Draper Manuscript Collections*, Draper Mss. 14C119) and notes of Lyman Draper (*Draper Manuscript Collections*, Draper Mss. 1R379) indicate that Micajah fought in two sieges of Fort Boonesborough after his arrival there. See also March 12, 1849, letter from Lyman Draper to Micajah Callaway (*Draper Manuscript Collections*, Draper Mss. 14C117). These two sieges must be the May 23 and July 4, 1777 sieges. See also *Draper Manuscript Collections*, "Excerpt from Kentucky Historical Society Journal," Draper Mss. 15CC162, and Kenton, *Simon Kenton*, 89.

21. Bryan, "Richard Callaway," 45.
22. *Draper Manuscript Collections*, "Statement by John Gass to Lyman Draper," Draper Mss. 24C73, and Callaway, "Flanders," 21.
23. Faragher, *Daniel Boone*, 150.
24. *Draper Manuscript Collections*, "Statement of Susan Howell," Draper Mss. 23S227.
25. *Draper Manuscript Collections*, "Deposition of Arabia Brown," Draper Mss. 9C44(2).
26. *Draper Manuscript Collections*, "Statement of Nathan Reid," Draper Mss. 10NN147.
27. Frank Wilcox, *Ohio Indian Trails*, (Kent, Oh.: The Kent State University Press, 1933), 113–114.
28. Jakle, "American Bison," 302.
29. Galloway, *Old Chillicothe*, 102.
30. Michael L. Cook and Bettie A. Cook. *Fayette County Kentucky Records*. Vol. 1, (Evansville, Ind.: Cook Publications, 1985), 283–290, 294.
31. Cook and Cook, *Fayette County*, Vol. 1, 157, 283–290, 294, 162–163, and 244.
32. Cook and Cook, *Fayette County*, Vol. 1, 268–269.
33. *Draper Manuscript Collections*, "Statement of Josiah Collins," Draper Mss. 13CC171, and O'Malley, *Stockading Up*, 249.
34. Callaway, "Virginia-Kentucky-Missouri," 30; Williams, "Colonel Richard Callaway," 83; and "Pension File No. S 30917, Revolutionary War, Chesley Callaway."
35. Williams, "Colonel Richard Callaway," 83.
36. Dudley Callaway and Jess Reynolds. "A Campaine of Souldiers." *The Virginia Genealogist* 20, No. 3 (1976): 223–224.
37. Ranck, *Boonesborough*, 62.
38. Cook and Cook, *Fayette County*, Vol. 1, 288.
39. *Draper Manuscript Collections*, "Petition of Inhabitants of Kentucky, November 25, 1777," Draper Mss. 13S13.
40. Calloway, "Maquachake," 167–168.
41. "'Sketch of Cornstalk," 256–258.
42. *Draper Manuscript Collections*, Draper Mss. 25CC12.
43. Calloway, "Maquachake," 168.
44. Kegley, *Virginia Frontier*, 636–638.
45. Kinietz and Voegelin, *Shawnese Traditions*, 17.
46. Calloway, "Maquachake," 168–169.
47. Ranck, *Boonesborough*, 65; Schaaf, *Wampum Belts*, 68, 131, 163; and *Draper Manuscript Collections*, "Interview Notes from Joseph Jackson," Draper Mss. 11C62(1) and (10).

Chaper Six

1. Williams, "Colonel Richard Callaway," 83.
2. *Draper Manuscript Collections*, "Declaration/Pension Statement of Ansel Goodman," Draper Mss. 15C28(1).
3. "... He then volunteered under Colonel Boone and in February, 1778, he was stationed at the Blue Licks, with others, making salt; and whilst there he was taken prisoner, with 26 others,

Colonel Boone among the number, and conveyed with the others to the Little Miami. James Callaway, Jesse Copher, Nathaniel Bullock, John Holley, William and Samuel Brooks were among the prisoners. He remained a prisoner with said Tribe of Indians from that time for five years & five months—during which time he moved with sd. Tribe to different places in Ohio: After the tribe were driven from Little Miami by a party from Kentucky, it took its station on Mad River, & remained there about one year, then moved up the Big Miami about 20 miles— remained there some time—then moved to a small stream emptying into Miami; & from that place was driven by a party under Genl. George Rogers Clark, seven of the Indians being taken prisoner there, the Queen of the nation being among the number (her name Lamatumque) the tribe then took their station on St. Mary's remained there about 3 months . . ." Excerpt from Callaway, "Micajah Callaway Declaration."

4. The muster roll of the company was:

Daniel Boone	John Holley
Daniel Asbury	William Humphries
Samuel Brooks	Joseph Jackson
William Brooks	William Jackson
James Callaway	Micajah Callaway
Andrew Johnson	John Brown
Benjamin Kelly	Nathaniel Bullock
Jonathan Ketcham	James Mankins
John Morton	Jesse Copher
James Robson	Jack Dunn
Bartlett Searcy	Thomas Foot
Ansel Goodman	William Tracey
William Hancock	Richard Wade
George Hendricks	William Cradelbaugh
Stephen Hancock	Jesse Hodges

See Ted Franklin Belue, "Terror in the Canelands: The Fate of Daniel Boone's Salt Boilers." *The Filson Club History Quarterly* 68, No. 1 (1994): 3.

The following soldiers, in addition to Micajah and James Callaway Jr., were from Bedford County, Virginia and had arrived with Captain Gwatkins company of reinforcements: Joseph Jackson, Daniel Asbury, Benjamin Kelly, John Brown, William Humphries, Jesse Hodges, John Morton, Ansel Goodman, Stephen Hancock, William Hancock, Richard Wade, John Holley, William Tracy, and Jesse Copher.

5. Ranck, *Boonesborough*, 64, 70.
6. Cook and Cook, *Fayette County*, Vol. 1, 286.
7. *Draper Manuscript Collections*, "Interview Notes from Noble Callaway, Son of Micajah Callaway," Draper Mss. 25S124.
8. *Draper Manuscript Collections*, "Statement of Simon Kenton," Draper Mss. 7S123.
9. *Draper Manuscript Collections*, "Interview Notes from John Hawkins Callaway, Son of Micajah Callaway," Draper Mss. 25S124.
10. *Draper Manuscript Collections*, "Interview with Col. Nathan Boone, Daniel Boone's Son," Draper Mss. 6S108.
11. Ranck, *Boonesborough*, 65; Schaaf, *Wampum Belts*, 68, 131, 163; and *Draper Manuscript Collections*, "Interview Notes from Joseph Jackson," Draper Mss. 11C62(1).
12. *Draper Manuscript Collections*, "Draper Notes," Draper Mss. 11S81.
13. See Appendix A for discussion of the likely identity of Micajah Callaway's captor and adoptive Shawanese father.
14. See Bond, "Captivity of Charles Stuart" 19, ftnt. 61; Quaife, "Ohio Campaigns of 1782," 528; and Stevens, *Louis Lorimier*, 15, 31.
15. Oliver M. Spencer, *The Indian Captivity of O.M. Spencer*, (Chicago: R.R. Donnelley and Sons, 1917), 89–93.
16. *Draper Manuscript Collections*, "Interview with Col. Nathan Boone, Daniel Boone's Son," Draper Mss. 6S104.

Endnotes

17. *Draper Manuscript Collections*, "Declaration/Pension Statement of Ansel Goodman," Draper Mss. 15C28(1).
18. *Draper Manuscript Collections*, "Draper Notes," Draper Mss. 11C83.
19. *Draper Manuscript Collections*, "Interview with Col. Nathan Boone, Daniel Boone's Son," Draper Mss. 6S105–107, and "Interview Notes from Joseph Jackson," Draper Mss. 11C62(3) and (5).
20. *Draper Manuscript Collections*, "Interview Notes from Joseph Jackson," Draper Mss. 11C62(6).
21. *Draper Manuscript Collections*, "Interview with Col. Nathan Boone, Daniel Boone's Son," Draper Mss. 6S108; "Interview Notes from John Hawkins Callaway, Son of Micajah Callaway," Draper Mss. 25S124; and "Declaration/Pension Statement of Ansel Goodman," Draper Mss. 15C28(1). The term "Little Chalaakaatha" was used by the Shawanese to distinguish the town on the Little Miami River from the previous town by that name on the Scioto River which they called "Old Chalaakaatha." When they relocated Chalaakaatha to the Greater Miami River after George Rogers Clark's Campaign of 1780, they called that town "New Chalaakaatha" also known as "Standing Stone Village." The author will use these Shawanese names throughout the text, although some of the old soldiers and settlers tended to call "Little Chalaakaatha" by the name "Old Chalaakaatha."
22. "Packed Mr. Callaway with kettles so as to harden & chalice his shoulders, as he expressed it, half an inch thick." *Draper Manuscript Collections*, "Interview Notes from James Callaway, Son of Micajah Callaway," Draper Mss. 25S257–261.
23. *Draper Manuscript Collections*, "Interview Notes from Joseph Jackson," Draper Mss. 11C62(9).
24. "At nights going from Blue Licks to the Shawanese towns, Indians would scrape away the snow, & fasten down the prisoners, & tie bells to them—so if they moved, it would give the alarm—& nearly froze." *Draper Manuscript Collections*, "Interview Notes from James Callaway, Son of Micajah Callaway," Draper Mss. 25S257–261.
25. See Appendix A for discussion of the likely identity of Micajah Callaway's captor and adoptive Shawanese father.
26. John Sugden, *Blue Jacket: Warrior of the Shawnees*, (Lincoln: University of Nebraska Press, 2000), 282, Note 4.
27. "At nights, Indians would scrape away the snow—& drive a bent stick like a half hoop with the points deep into the ground, thus fastening down each prisoners ankles as in the stocks. Could sit up but didn't move his feet." *Draper Manuscript Collections*, "Interview Notes from John Hawkins Callaway, Son of Micajah Callaway," Draper Mss. 25S124.
28. *Draper Manuscript Collections*, "Interview with Col. Nathan Boone, Daniel Boone's Son," Draper Mss. 6S111.
29. *Draper Manuscript Collections*, "Interview Notes from John Hawkins Callaway, Son of Micajah Callaway," Draper Mss. 25S124.
30. Ebenezer Denny. *Military Journal of Major Ebenezer Denny, An Officer in the Revolutionary and Indian Wars*. (Philadelphia: J. B. Lippincott & Co., 1859. Reprint, Arno Press Inc., 1971), 281.
31. *Draper Manuscript Collections*, "Interview Notes from Joseph Jackson," Draper Mss. 11C62(8–9).
32. Galloway, *Old Chillicothe*, 102.
33. *Draper Manuscript Collections*, "Interview Notes from John Hawkins Callaway, Son of Micajah Callaway," Draper Mss. 25S124, and "Interview Notes from James Callaway, Son of Micajah Callaway," Draper Mss. 25S257–261.
34. *Draper Manuscript Collections*, "Interview Notes from Noble Callaway, Son of Micajah Callaway," Draper Mss. 25S124.
35. Denny, *Military Journal*, 279–281.
36. *Draper Manuscript Collections*, "Interview Notes from John Hawkins Callaway, Son of Micajah Callaway," Draper Mss. 25S124.
37. Thomas Ridout, "An Account of my Capture by the Shawanese Indians," *Western Pennsylvania Historical Magazine* 12, No. 1 (1929): 23.
38. Reverend David Jones, *A Journal of Two Visits Made to Some Nations of Indians on the West Side of the Ohio in the Years 1772 and 1773*, (Fairfield, Wash.: Ye Galleon Press, 1973), 55, 63, and *Draper Manuscript Collections*, "Interview Notes from Joseph Jackson," Draper Mss. 11C62(17).
39. *Draper Manuscript Collections*, "Statement of Henry Wilson," Draper Mss. 9J10; Bond, "Captivity of Charles Stuart," 19, ftnt. 61; and Quaife, "Ohio Campaigns of 1782," 528.

40. Howard, *Shawnee: Ceremonialism*, 81.
41. Ibid., 362.
42. Carskadden and Morton, *Where the Frolics and War Dances are Held*, 152.
43. *Draper Manuscript Collections*, "Statement of Henry Wilson," Draper Mss. 9J10; Bond, "Captivity of Charles Stuart," 19, ftnt. 61; and Quaife, "Ohio Campaigns of 1782," 528.
44. *Draper Manuscript Collections*, "Declaration/Pension Statement of Ansel Goodman," Draper Mss. 15C28(2).
45. Howard, *Shawnee: Ceremonialism*, 125.
46. This traditional welcome for returning warriors and their prisoners was not technically "the gauntlet," and, therefore, was not specifically covered by Boone's agreement with Black Fish. *Draper Manuscript Collections*, "Draper Interview Notes from Mrs. Susan Howell, Daughter of Flanders Callaway and Jemima Boone Callaway," Draper Mss. 23S232.
47. A water drum was typically constructed from a crockery pot which was partially filled with water before a hide drum top was stretched over the top and tied down. A piece of charcoal was put in the water in the drum to "hold the water." The hide was periodically dampened to improve the tone. The drumstick was typically carved from walnut wood with a knob on each end to facilitate holding it when it became wet (Howard, *Shawnee: Ceremonialism*, 235, 282, 339, 408).
48. Joseph Jackson stated that a War Dance was held at Little Chalaakaatha upon the return of the warriors with their prisoners (*Draper Manuscript Collections*, "Interview Notes from Joseph Jackson," Draper Mss. 11C62(9)). Although there are no detailed accounts of this particular War Dance, I have included a brief description of the customary ceremonies relating to prisoners and the War Dance on the assumption they were followed in this instance (Kinietz and Voegelin, *Shawnese Traditions*, 19; Denny, *Military Journal*, 71–72; Kenton, *Simon Kenton*, 111; and Howard, *Shawnee: Ceremonialism*, 120, 235, 276–277, 282, 337, 339.
49. *Draper Manuscript Collections*, Draper Mss. 11YY33.
50. *Draper Manuscript Collections*, Draper Mss. 23S174 and 23S168.
51. Howard, *Shawnee: Ceremonialism*, 216–217, and Denny, *Military Journal*, 280.
52. Howard, *Shawnee: Ceremonialism*, 121.
53. Available records indicate that at least the following three men were forced to run the gauntlet despite the Shawanese agreement with Daniel Boone: Ansel Goodman (*Draper Manuscript Collections*, "Declaration/Pension Statement of Ansel Goodman," Draper Mss. 15C28(2)), James Callaway Jr. (*Draper Manuscript Collections*, "Interview Notes from Morgan Bryan." Draper Mss. 6S302–303), and William Hancock (*Draper Manuscript Collections*, "Statement of Robert Hancock," Draper Mss. 24C17(1–3).
    It is possible that Micajah may have also been forced to run the gauntlet, although the available information is conflicting. Micajah's son John Hawkins Callaway told Lyman Draper that Micajah was not forced to run the gauntlet (*Draper Manuscript Collections*, "Interview Notes from John Hawkins Callaway, Son of Micajah Callaway," Draper Mss. 25S124). Micajah's son James Callaway told Lyman Draper that Micajah was forced to run the gauntlet two or three times during his stay with the Shawanese, although he does not specify when (*Draper Manuscript Collections*, "Interview Notes from James Callaway, Son of Micajah Callaway," Draper Mss. 25S257–261).
54. *Draper Manuscript Collections*, "Declaration of James Callaway in Support of Revolutionary War Pension Application," Draper Mss. 21C75.
55. *Draper Manuscript Collections*, "Interview Notes from Joseph Jackson," Draper Mss. 11C62(10), and "Statement of D. Thompson," Draper Mss. 12CC200.
56. "Some of the prisoners were taken to Detroit, soon afterwards, but John Brown and myself remained until after they were done planting corn." *Draper Manuscript Collections*, "Declaration of Richard Wade," Draper Mss. 11C33.
57. Stevens, *Louis Lorimier*, 31.
58. James Callaway Jr. remained a prisoner of the British from the date of his capture until December 24, 1781. He was imprisoned in Detroit, Fort Niagara, Quebec and St. Paul's Bay before being released in New York. He then returned to Bedford County, Virginia. *Draper Manuscript Collections*, "Declaration of James Callaway in Support of Revolutionary War Pension Application," Draper Mss. 21C75.

Endnotes 401

59. *Draper Manuscript Collections*, "Declaration/Pension Statement of Ansel Goodman," Draper Mss. 15C28(2).
60. Stevens, *Louis Lorimier*, 31.
61. Ibid., 4
62. James Galloway observed the remains of a blacksmith hearth, including cinders, in the ruins of Little Chalaakaatha. *Draper Manuscript Collections*, "Dec. 1839 Letter from James Galloway to Lyman Draper," Draper Mss. 8J262, and "Map with Jan. 23, 1849 Letter," Draper Mss. 8J299. *Draper Manuscript Collections*, See Draper Mss. 1NN2, 22J193, and 1R379 for references to Caesar.
63. William L. McDowell, Jr., ed., *Colonial Records of South Carolina, Documents Relating to Indian Affairs, 1754–1765*, (Columbia, S.C.: South Carolina Archives Department, 1958), 368–369.
64. She is described as the "Shawanese Queen" in a number of references in the *Draper Manuscript Collections*, including "Declaration of Micajah Callaway," Draper Mss. 100147. See also Callaway, "Declaration of Micajah Callaway." She was married to Chief Moluntha (*Draper Manuscript Collections*, "Interview Notes from Joseph Jackson," Draper Mss. 11C62(38)).
65. Calloway, "Maquachake," 169.
66. *Draper Manuscript Collections*, "Statement of D. Thompson," Draper Mss. 11C81.
67. *Draper Manuscript Collections*, "Statement of Josiah Collins," Draper Mss. 12CC105.
68. Sugden, *Blue Jacket*, 275, Note 2.
69. *Draper Manuscript Collections*, "Interview Notes from Joseph Jackson," Draper Mss. 11C62(10).
70. There appear to be no surviving records of Micajah's Shawanese name.
71. *Draper Manuscript Collections*, Draper Mss. 14J34–37, 4BB73, and 9BB63.
72. *Draper Manuscript Collections*, "Statement of Col. Nathan Boone, Daniel Boone's Son," Draper Mss. 6S118–121.
73. "Cage Callaway used to relate that Col. Boone could have escaped from the Indians much sooner than he did, but remained in the hope of getting Callaway away with him, but both could not set off together. Col. Boone at length ascertained that some 400 Indians were gathering to go to Boonesborough." *Draper Manuscript Collections*, "Interview Notes with Joseph Scholl, Jr, Grandson of Daniel Boone," Draper Mss. 24S209–211.
74. *Draper Manuscript Collections*, Draper Mss. 22C14(12).
75. *Draper Manuscript Collections*, "Interview Notes from Joseph Jackson," Draper Mss. 11C62(11), and "Interview Notes from John Hawkins Callaway, Son of Micajah Callaway," Draper Mss. 25S124.
76. *Draper Manuscript Collections*, "Statement of Stephen Cooper," Draper Mss. 11C97–99.

Chapter Seven

1. Heffren, "Pioneer Pickings No. 36," 7
2. Arnow, *Seedtime on the Cumberland*, 144
3. *Draper Manuscript Collections*, "Statement of John Gass," Draper Mss. 11CC15.
4. Helen Hornbeck Tanner, *Atlas of the Great Lakes Indian History*, (Norman, Okl.: University of Oklahoma Press, 1987), 82, and Seineke, *George Rogers Clark Adventure*, 55.
5. Kenton, *Simon Kenton*, 58.
6. Helen Hornbeck Tanner, "The Glaize in 1792: A Composite Indian Community," *Ethnohistory* 25 (1978): 27.
7. Seineke, *George Rogers Clark Adventure*, 234–235.
8. Ibid., 246–251.
9. "List of Officers, Interpreters, &ca., in the Indian Department, District of Detroit, Sept'r 5th, 1778"
    Jehu Hay, Esq.-Deputy Agent
    Alexander McKee-Captain and Interpreter
    Duperon Baby-Ditto
    Charles Reume-Ditto
    Isidore Chesne-Ditto
    Jacob Schieffelin-Lieutenant

Frontenay Dequindre-Ditto
Antoine Dequindre-Ditto
Francois Dequindre-Ditto
Francois Chabert-Ditto
Louis Joncaire-Ditto
Claude Labat-Ditto
Joseph Bondy-Ditto
William Tucker-Interpreter for the Ottawas & Chippewas
Pierre Drouillard-Interpreter for the Hurons
Simon Girty-Interpreter for the Six Nations
Medard Gamelin-Storekeeper
Etienne Ballard-Smith
Augustin Lefoi-Extra ditto"
See *Historical Collections*, Volume 10, 470.

10. *Draper Manuscript Collections*, "Interview Notes with James Callawa, Son of Micajah Callaway," Draper Mss. 25S257–261.
11. Bryan, "Richard Callaway," 46.
12. *Draper Manuscript Collections*, "Deposition of William Buchanan," Draper Mss. 14S18–19.
13. Ted Franklin Belue, "Did Daniel Boone Kill Pompey, the Black Shawnee, at the 1778 Siege of Fort Boonesborough?" *The Filson Club History Quarterly* 67, No. 1 (1993): 8.
14. "Letters from the Canadian Archives," *Collections of the Illinois State Historical Society* 1 (1903): 339–397.
15. Seineke, *George Rogers Clark Adventure*, 282–284.
16. Stevens, *Louis Lorimier*, 31.
17. Williams, "Colonel Richard Callaway," 84.
18. *Draper Manuscript Collections*, "Excerpt from Deposition of Jesse Hodges, Nov. 20, 1817," Draper Mss. 11C65.
19. Kenton, *Simon Kenton*, 98; John Bradford, *John Bradford's Historical & c. Notes on Kentucky* (San Francisco: The Grabhorn Press, 1932), 41; and Williams, "Colonel Richard Callaway," 84.
20. *Draper Manuscript Collections*, "Interview Notes from Joseph Jackson," Draper Mss. 11C62(16).
21. Bradford, *Historical & c. Notes*, 41.
22. Faragher, *Daniel Boone*, 183.
23. *Draper Manuscript Collections*, "Statement of John Gass," Draper Mss. 11CC11–12.
24. Faragher, *Daniel Boone*, 184, and *Draper Manuscript Collections*, "Statement of Josiah Collins," Draper Mss. 12CC74.
25. *Draper Manuscript Collections*, "Statement of Nathaniel Hart," Draper Mss. 17CC198.
26. *Draper Manuscript Collections*, "Statement of Susan Howell," Draper Mss. 23S224.
27. *Draper Manuscript Collections*, "Journal of Daniel Trabue," Draper Mss. 57J.
28. *Draper Manuscript Collections*, Draper Mss.S 11CC94(44) and 12CC205.
29. *Draper Manuscript Collections*, "Statement of Levena Howell," Draper Mss. 23S239.
30. *Draper Manuscript Collections*, "Journal of Daniel Trabue," Draper Mss. 57J26.
31. *Draper Manuscript Collections*, "Statement of Susan Howell," Draper Mss. 23S225 and "Statement of Levena Howell," Draper Mss. 23S239.
32. *Draper Manuscript Collections*, "Statement of Elijah Bryan," Draper Mss. 23S242, and "Statement of Levena Howell," Draper Mss. 23S239–240.
33. *Draper Manuscript Collections*, "Statement of Richard French," Draper Mss 12CC205.
34. *Draper Manuscript Collections*, "Statement of Capt. Nathaniel Hart," Draper Mss. 17CC197, and Williams, "Colonel Richard Callaway," 84.
35. Bryan, "Richard Callaway," 46.
36. Faragher, *Daniel Boone*, 195–196.
37. *Draper Manuscript Collections*, "Statement of Susan Howell," Draper Mss. 23S222.
38. *Draper Manuscript Collections*, Draper Mss. 6S132.
39. *Draper Manuscript Collections*, "Statement of Levena Howell," Draper Mss. 23S239.
40. *Draper Manuscript Collections*, "Statement of John Gass," Draper Mss. 11CC11.

Endnotes

41. Williams, "Colonel Richard Callaway," 84.
42. Ranck, *Boonesborough*, 93.
43. Williams, "Colonel Richard Callaway," 84.
44. *Draper Manuscript Collections*, "Statement of John Gass," Draper Mss. 11C11, and "Journal of Daniel Trabue," Draper Mss. 57J27.
45. Faragher, *Daniel Boone*, 198.
46. *Draper Manuscript Collections*, "Journal of Daniel Trabue," Draper Mss. 57J32-33.
47. *Draper Manuscript Collections*, "Statement of Henry Wilson," Draper Mss. 9J6-7, 27.
48. Howard, *Shawnee: Ceremonialism*, 44-47.
49. Ibid., 64-65
50. Lamatumque is described as the "Shawanese Queen" in a number of references in the Draper manuscripts including, including *Draper Manuscript Collections*, "Declaration of Micajah Callaway," Draper Mss. 100147. See also Callaway, "Declaration of Micajah Callaway." She was married to old Chief Moluntha (*Draper Manuscript Collections*, "Interview Notes from Joseph Jackson," Draper Mss. 11C62(38)). It appears that Lamatumque may have been a daughter of Cornstalk's sister, the Shawanese Headwoman Coitcheleh (Schaaf, *Wampum Belts*, 68, 131, and Craig, *Olden Times*, Vol. 2, No. 11, 512). Lamatumque's mother reportedly walked into General George Rogers Clark's camp by herself following Lamatumque's capture in 1782 and was recognized and treated with great respect as a head Shawanese woman. This is consistent with Coitcheleh's status as well as her trust of and fearlessness among Americans—a rare trait. She asked to exchange herself for her daughter and infant grandson but General Clark refused. She then asked to join the other seven prisoners in order to be with her daughter and grandson. General Clark reluctantly accepted. See *Draper Manuscript Collections*, Draper Mss. 23S174 and 23S168 and "Statement of Josiah Collins," Draper Mss. 12CC105.
51. Kenton, *Simon Kenton*, 108.
52. *Draper Manuscript Collections*, "Interview Notes from Joseph Jackson," Draper Mss. 11C62(24), and Draper Mss. 17S60.
53. Howe, *Historical Collections of Ohio*, Vol. 1, 378-382.
54. Kenton, *Simon Kenton*, 112-133.
55. These soldiers were to act and be paid as militia and not as regular soldiers. E.O. Randall, "Clark's Conquest of the Northwest," *Ohio Archaeological and Historical Quarterly* 12, No. 1 (1903): 72.
56. Henry S. Cauthorn, *A History of the City of Vincennes Indiana from 1702 to 1901*. (Bowie, Md.: Heritage Books, Inc., 2001), 84.
57. Ted Reese, *Soft Gold, A History of the Fur Trade in the Great Lakes Region and Its Impact on Native American Culture*, (Bowie, Md.: Heritage Books, Inc., 2001), 49-50.
58. Thwaites and Kellogg, *Revolution on the Upper Ohio*, 43-44, 47.
59. Sugden, *Blue Jacket*, 53.
60. *Draper Manuscript Collections*, "January 12, 1778 Letter from Patrick Henry to Colonel George Rogers Clark," Draper Mss. 46J12.
61. Cauthorn, *Vincennes Indiana*, 88-90.
62. Seineke, *George Rogers Clark Adventure*, 92-96.
63. Cauthorn, *Vincennes Indiana*, 89.
64. Seineke, *George Rogers Clark Adventure*, xxvii-xxviii, 373-376.
65. *Draper Manuscript Collections*, "December 20, 1778 Message Received by Captain John Thillbush from Captain Pipe and the Wyandot Half King," Draper Mss. 1H16-17.
66. *Draper Manuscript Collections*, "Statement of Elizabeth Callaway, Daughter-in-law of James Callaway," Draper Mss. 24S142, and "Statement of Mrs. Leana Swearingen, Daughter of James Callaway," Draper Mss. 23S141.
67. *Draper Manuscript Collections*, "Statement of Col. Nathan Boone, Son of Daniel Boone," Draper Mss. 6S116-117, and "Sept. 20, 1785, Declaration of Daniel Boone," Draper Mss. 29C108.
68. Seineke, *George Rogers Clark Adventure*, 29-30.
69. Cauthorn, *Vincennes Indiana*, 95-96.
70. The route taken was called the "St. Louis Trace" at the time, leaving Kaskaskia, passing through

Sparta, Oakdale, Nashville, Walnut Hill, Salem, Olney, and Lawrenceville, Illinois, and ending at Vincennes. See Randall, *Clark's Conquest*, 86, ftnt.
71. Holden, *Hunting Pioneers*, 81.
72. Seineke, *George Rogers Clark Adventure*, xxxiv.
73. Williams, "Colonel Richard Callaway," 86.
74. Herndon, "George Mathews," 319.
75. "March 26, 1779 Letter from Captain Lernoult," *Historical Collections*, Vol. 9, 429.
76. *Draper Manuscript Collections*, "Deposition of George Rogers Clark (April 27, 1805)," Draper Mss. 29J47, and Seineke, George Rogers Clark Adventure, xxii, 79.
77. Fitzpatrick, *Wilderness War on the Ohio*, 325.
78. Sugden, *Blue Jacket*, 59.
79. *Draper Manuscript Collections*, "Interview Notes from Joseph Jackson," Draper Mss. 11C62(17), and Thomas L. McKenney and James Hall, *The History of the Indian Tribes of North America, with Biographical Sketches and Anecdotes of the Principal Chiefs*, (Philadelphia: E.C. Biddle, 1836–1844), 18.
80. "Bowman's Expedition Against Chillicothe. Draper Mss. 5D." *Ohio Archaeological and Historical Publications* 19 (1910): 453.
81. Ibid., 453.
82. Calloway, "Maquachake," 171, and *Draper Manuscript Collections*, "Interview Notes from Joseph Jackson," Draper Mss. 11C62(32).
83. Jones, *Journal of Two Visits*, 71.
84. *Draper Manuscript Collections*, Draper Mss. 23S170, 19S245.
85. Howard, *Shawnee: Ceremonialism*, 175–176.
86. Kinietz and Voegelin, *Shawnese Traditions*, 2–3, 41.
87. Howard, *Shawnee: Ceremonialism*, 173–174.
88. Kinietz and Voegelin, *Shawnese Traditions*, 55–56.
89. Howard, *Shawnee: Ceremonialism*, 180–181, 212–217.
90. John McDonald, *Biographical Sketches of Nathaniel Massie, General Duncan McArthur, Captain William Wells, and General Simon Kenton*, (Cincinnati: M. Morgan and Son, 1828), 52–53.
91. Howard, *Shawnee: Ceremonialism*, 57.
92. Howe, *Historical Collections of Ohio*, 294.
93. Howard, *Shawnee: Ceremonialism*, 52, 58, 245–262.
94. *Draper Manuscript Collections*, "Statement of Josiah Collins," Draper Mss. 12CC66–67; "Declaration of Josiah Collins," Draper Mss. 18J84; and "A Provision Return of James Trabue, Commissary to Col. John Bowman," Draper Mss. 17J32, and Charles Gano Talbert, "Kentucky Invades Ohio, - 1779," *The Register of the Kentucky Historical Society* 51, No. 176 (1953): 231.
95. *Draper Manuscript Collections*, "Captain Holder Company Muster Roll," Draper Mss. 17J29, and "Statement of Bland Ballard," Draper Mss. 8J150.
96. "Bowman's Campaign of 1779, Draper Mss., The Bedinger Papers, 'A,' Volume 1." *Ohio Archaeological and Historical Publications* 22 (1913): 502.
97. Withers, *Chronicles*, 271, ftnt. 1.
98. "Bowman's Campaign of 1779," 515, and "Bowman's Expedition," 451.
99. Wilcox, *Ohio Indian Trails*, 113–114.
100. *Draper Manuscript Collections*, "Interview Notes from Joseph Jackson," Draper Mss. 11C62(19).
101. Talbert, "Kentucky Invades Ohio, -1779," 230.
102. "Bowman's Expedition,," 452.
103. *Draper Manuscript Collections*, "Statement of Josiah Collins," Draper Mss. 12CC66–67.
104. "Bowman's Campaign of 1779," 504, 505, 516.
105. *Draper Manuscript Collections*, "Interview Notes from Joseph Jackson," Draper Mss. 11C62(18) and (22).
106. *Draper Manuscript Collections*, "Statement of Josiah Collins," Draper Mss. 12CC104.
107. *Draper Manuscript Collections*, "Declaration of Josiah Collins," Draper Mss. 18J84, and "Statement of Henry Wilson," Draper Mss. 9J10.
108. "Bowman's Expedition," 453.
109. *Draper Manuscript Collections*, "Interview Notes from Joseph Jackson," Draper Mss. 11C62(17), (20), and (21).

Endnotes

110. *Draper Manuscript Collections*, "Declaration of Josiah Collins," Draper Mss. 18J84; "Statement of Josiah Collins," Draper Mss. 12CC66-67; "Statement of Col. William Whitley," Draper Mss. 9CC17-60; "Interview Notes from Joseph Jackson," Draper Mss. 11C62(22); and "Bowman's Campaign of 1779," 507.
111. Holden, *Hunting Pioneers*, 85.
112. "Bowman's Expedition," 455-456.
113. *Draper Manuscript Collections*, "Interview Notes from Joseph Jackson," Draper Mss. 11C62(22).
114. "A young man, a prisoner then, told me in 1783, at the falls of the Ohio, that about 40 were killed, and died of their wounds, on the part of the Indians. He was then living at the Old Chillicothe town. Was exchanged in 1783 for some squaw prisoners that we took in 1782." See *Draper Manuscript Collections*, "Statement of Josiah Collins," Draper Mss. 12CC67. (*Note*: Lyman Draper's notes regarding this statement indicate that he believed that this young man was Micajah).
115. "Bowman's Campaign of 1779," 511, and *Draper Manuscript Collections*, "Interview Notes from Joseph Jackson," Draper Mss. 11C62(23), and "Statement of Josiah Collins," Draper Mss. 12CC66-67, 104.
116. *Draper Manuscript Collections*, "Interview Notes from Joseph Jackson," Draper Mss. 11C62(23).
117. Fitzpatrick, *Wilderness War*, 324.
118. The British built the forts for the Shawanese after the Bowman Campaign of 1779. From the first-hand accounts of the battle in the *Draper Manuscript Collections*, it is obvious that there were no fortifications in Chalaakaatha other than the Council House during the May 1779 attack by Colonel Bowman and his troops. However, by the time of the 1780 George Rogers Clark campaign against the Shawanese towns, both Chalaakaatha and Piqua were fortified. See *Draper Manuscript Collections*, "Feb. 13, 1833 Interview with Simon Kenton," Draper Mss. 4BB125; "Dec. 1839 Letter from James Galloway to Lyman Draper," Draper Mss. 8J262-863; "Map with Jan. 23, 1849 Letter," Draper Mss. 8J299-300; and "Letter from Colonel Brady," Draper Mss. 15S227-228. See also Seineke, *George Rogers Clark Adventure*, 442-443.
119. Sugden, *Blue Jacket*, 62.
120. James Galloway observed the remains of a Blacksmith hearth, including cinders, in the ruins of the fort. See *Draper Manuscript Collections*, "Dec. 1839 Letter from James Galloway to Lyman Draper," Draper Mss. 8J262, and "Map with Jan. 23, 1849 Letter," Draper Mss. 8J299.
121. Fitzpatrick, *Wilderness War on the Ohio*, 251.
122. Seineke, *George Rogers Clark Adventure*, 413.
123. "The Certificate Book of the Virginia Land Commission of 1779-1780." *The Register of the Kentucky State Historical Society* 21, No. 61 (1923): 4-5.
124. O'Malley, *Stockading Up*, 178-187.
125. "Certificate Book of Virginia Land Commission," 85-86, and Callaway, "Flanders," 19.
126. Bryan, "Richard Callaway," 48, and William Waller Hening, *The Statutes at Large being a Collection of All the Laws of Virginia from the First Session of the Legislature in the Year 1619*, Vol. 10, (Richmond: Franklin Press, 1819), 143-144, 196-197.
127. *Draper Manuscript Collections*, "Journal of Daniel Trabue," Draper Mss. 57J38.
128. Bryan, "Richard Callaway," 48.
129. Cook and Cook, *Fayette County*, Vol. 1, 300.
130. *Draper Manuscript Collections*, "Interview Notes from Joseph Jackson," Draper Mss. 11CC62(28).
131. *Draper Manuscript Collections*, "Statement of John Gass," Draper Mss. 11CC15.
132. *Draper Manuscript Collections*, "Statement of Nathan Hart, Jr." Draper Mss. 17CC192-193. Micajah later learned that Captain Johnny Holder had led the party that had brought Uncle Richard's body back to Fort Boonesborough. *Draper Manuscript Collections*, "Statement of Bland Ballard," Draper Mss. 8J179. See also Williams, "Colonel Richard Callaway," 87-89.
133. Some whites in Kentucky believed that Micajah had joined the Shawanese and become a Tory renegade. Micajah was identified by witnesses as accompanying two war parties in a supporting role (bearing booty and escorting prisoners). See *Draper Manuscript Collections*, "Statement of Rhoda Ground," Draper Mss. 29J18 and "Statement by Ezekiel Lewis," Draper Mss. 30J79.

    This obviously provides a basis for speculation about his loyalties. However, there is no evidence that he ever took up arms against Kentucky as a warrior. Such an action would be contrary to the obvious affection that he felt for his family and that his family felt for him as indicated on the record. The Shawanese would not force prisoners to fight against their own people. See *Draper Manuscript Collections*, "Interview Notes from Joseph Jackson," Draper Mss. 11C63.

Micajah's reputation as a renegade as well as some complaints he appears to have made about his Uncle Richard to some fellow prisoners while a captive, appear to have given rise to the speculation that he may have participated in Colonel Richard Callaway's death. See *Draper Manuscript Collections*, "Statement of John Gass," Draper Mss. 11CC15: "We removed to Estill's S., the spring after Pemberton Rollins and Col. Callaway were taken (killed). He (Col. C.) was the worst barbequed man I ever saw. Cut his head bones up. They stripped him stark naked and rolled in a mud-hole. It was said that Cajah Callaway was along with the Indians. Some of the prisoners said, he had threatened revenge on his uncle. Cajah was of those taken at the salt-making. His uncle had whipped him before he was taken. There was not a bone as big as your hand."

134. *Draper Manuscript Collections*, "Letter from Capt. David Gess (Gass)," Draper Mss. 50J18.
135. Callaway County, Kentucky was named in honor of Colonel Richard Callaway in 1820. *Draper Manuscript Collections*, "Newspaper Article," Draper Mss. 12CC204.
136. Milo M. Quaife, ed., "When Detroit Invaded Kentucky." *The Filson Club History Quarterly*, Vol. 1, No. 2 (1927): 55–56.
137. Ridout, "An Account of my Capture," 27–28.
138. "Ruddell's Station Taken, June, 1780. The Indians first came and attacked the Station, & were repulsed. Sometime afterward they came again, & with cannon, & attacked with the cannon - an old man named Goodnight was killed -Simon Girty & Micajah Callaway were with the enemy." See *Draper Manuscript Collections*, "Statement of Rhoda Ground," Draper Mss. 29J18. For confirmation of Micajah's participation in this campaign, see also *Draper Manuscript Collections*, "Interview Notes from James Callaway, Son of Micajah Callaway," Draper Mss. 25S257–161, and "Interview Notes from John Hawkins Callaway, Son of Micajah Callaway," Draper Mss. 25S124.
139. "June 4, 1780 Letter from Alexander McKee to Major De Peyster," *Historical Collections: Pioneer and Historical Society of the State of Michigan*, Vol. 19, (Lansing: Robert Smith & Co., 1892), 530.
140. Otis K. Rice, *Frontier Kentucky*, (Lexington: The University Press of Kentucky, 1993), 99–104.
141. "July 8, 1780 Letter from Captain Alexander McKee to Major De Peyster," *Historical Collections*, Vol. 19, 541.
142. "July 1, 1780 Letter from Captain Bird to Major De Peyster," *Historical Collections*, Vol. 19, 538.
143. Kenton, *Simon Kenton*, 153, and Charles Gano Talbert, *Benjamin Logan: Kentucky Frontiersman*, (Lexington: The University of Kentucky Press, 1962), 104–107.
144. *Draper Manuscript Collections*, "Letter from Perrin to Draper," Draper Mss. 13J21.
145. *Draper Manuscript Collections*, "Capt. Hinkston's Narrative," Draper Mss. 16J82.
146. *Draper Manuscript Collections*, "Interview Notes from John Hawkins Callaway, Son of Micajah Callaway," Draper Mss. 25S124.
147. *Draper Manuscript Collections*, "Captain Hinkston's Narrative," Draper Mss. 16J82, and Draper Mss. 29J23–24.
148. "July 8, 1780 Letter from Captain Alexander McKee to Major De Peyster," *Historical Collections*, Vol. 19, 541–542.
149. *Draper Manuscript Collections*, "Statement of Rhoda Ground," Draper Mss. 29J18.
150. *Draper Manuscript Collections*, "Capt. Hinkston's Narrative," Draper Mss. 16J82.
151. *Draper Manuscript Collections*, "Letter from Fort Pitt, Aug. 18 (1780). Maryland Journal," Draper Mss. 29J20.
152. "July 8, 1780 Letter from Captain Alexander McKee to Major De Peyster," *Historical Collections*, Vol. 19, 541, and *Draper Manuscript Collections*, "Letter to Draper from Mr. P. Parkinson, Jr.," Draper Mss. 29J22.
153. *Draper Manuscript Collections*, Draper Mss. 29J23–24; Draper Mss. 18S114; and "Statement of John M. Ruddell," Draper Mss. 22S41, and "July 24, 1780 Letter from Captain Bird to Major De Peyster," *Historical Collections*, Vol. 19, 545.
154. "July 8, 1780 Letter from Captain Alexander McKee to Major De Peyster," *Historical Collections*, Vol. 19, 541.

Endnotes

155. Charles Gano Talbert, "Kentucky Invades Ohio -1780," *The Register of the Kentucky Historical Society* 52, No. 181 (1954): 294, and *Draper Manuscript Collections*, "'Sketches of Border Life: Narrative of Abraham Thomas,' The Troy Times (Ohio)," Draper Mss. 8J241.
156. J. Martin West, ed., *Clark's Shawnee Campaign of 1780*, (Springfield, Oh.: The Clark County Historical Society, 1975), 15; Holden, *Hunting Pioneers*, 85; Mary A. Skardon, *The Battle of Piqua, August 8, 1780*, (Springfield, Oh.: Clark County Historical Society, 1964), 21; and Talbert, "Kentucky Invades Ohio -1780," 294.
157. This was the future site of Cincinnati, Ohio. See *Draper Manuscript Collections*, "'Sketches of Border Life: Narrative of Abraham Thomas,' The Troy Times (Ohio)," Draper Mss. 8J241.
158. Talbert,"Kentucky Invades Ohio -1780," 294–295; "Intelligence from John Clairy an American Deserter," *Historical Collections*, Vol. 19, 554; and Stevens, *Louis Lorimier*, 34–35.
159. Seineke, *George Rogers Clark Adventure*, 453.
160. West, *Clark's Shawnee Campaign*, 17, and Skardon, *Battle of Piqua*, 24.
161. *Draper Manuscript Collections*, "Dec. 1839 Letter from James Galloway to Draper," Draper Mss. 8J263; "Map with Jan. 23, 1949 Letter," Draper Mss. 8J300; and "Newspaper Article Titled, 'The Siege of the Old Indian Town of Piqua'" Draper Mss. 8J210.
162. *Draper Manuscript Collections*, "Dec. 1839 Letter from James Galloway to Draper," Draper Mss. 8J263; "Map with Jan. 23, 1949 Letter," Draper Mss. 8J300; and "Statement of Henry Wilson," Draper Mss. 9J26.
163. C.W. Butterfield, *History of the Girtys.* (Cincinnati: Robert Clarke & Co., 1890), 86–91.
164. *Draper Manuscript Collections*, "Statement by Mr. Moorman," Draper Mss. 18S92.
165. *Draper Manuscript Collections*, "Dec. 1839 Letter from James Galloway to Draper," Draper Mss. 8J262; "Map with Jan. 23, 1849 Letter," Draper Mss. 8J299; and "Statement of W. Clinkenbeard," Draper Mss. 11CC66.
166. *Draper Manuscript Collections*, "'Narrative by John Bradford, Participant,' in Columbus State Journal, Dec. 14, 1826," Draper Mss. 7J139.
167. *Draper Manuscript Collections*, "'Sketches of Border Life: Narrative of Abraham Thomas,' from The Troy Times (Ohio)," Draper Mss. 8J241.
168. Skardon, *Battle of Piqua*, 22–24.
169. Ibid., 24.
170. *Draper Manuscript Collections*, "Statement of Bland Ballard," Draper Mss. 8J150.
171. McAfee, Robert B., "Life and Times of Robert B. McAfee," 32–33.
172. Skardon, *Battle of Piqua*, 24–25.
173. *Draper Manuscript Collections*, "'Narrative by John Bradford, Participant,' in Columbus State Journal, Dec. 14, 1826," Draper Mss. 7J139, and "'Sketches of Border Life: Narrative of Abraham Thomas' from The Troy Times (Ohio)," Draper Mss. 8J241.
174. *Draper Manuscript Collections*, Interview with Mrs. John Morrison (Draper Mss. 11C153).
175. *Draper Manuscript Collections*, "Statement of Henry Wilson," Draper Mss. 9J26.
176. *Draper Manuscript Collections*, "August 20, 1780 Report on 1780 Campaign from General Clark to Virginia Governor," Draper Mss. 8J136.
177. *Draper Manuscript Collections*, "Interview Notes from Joseph Jackson," Draper Mss. 11C62(29).
178. *Draper Manuscript Collections*, "Interview Notes from Joseph Jackson," Draper Mss. 11C62(29), and Wheeler-Voegelin, *Indians of Ohio and Indiana*, Vol. 2, 269.
179. C.W. Butterfield. *Historical Account of the Expedition Against Sandusky under Colonel William Crawford in 1782* (Cincinnati: Robert Clarke & Co., 1873), 347.
180. "August 22, 1780 Speech of the Delawares and Shawnese Assembled at the Upper Shawanese Village to their Father Major De Peyster, Commandant of Detroit," *Historical Collections*, Vol. 10, 420.
181. Wheeler-Voegelin, *Indians of Ohio and Indiana*, Vol. 2, 260.
182. Reverend John D. Shane, "Reverend John D. Shane's Interview with Pioneer William Clinkenbeard," *The History Quarterly* 2, No. 3 (1928): 128.
183. Wheeler-Voegelin, *Indians of Ohio and Indiana*, Vol. 2, 261–265, and *Draper Manuscript Collections*, "Interview Notes from Joseph Jackson," Draper Mss. 11C62(29), and "October 2, 1848 letter from John Johnston to Draper," Draper Mss. 11YY34. The town of Piqua, Ohio is now at this location.

184. Craig, *Olden Times*, Vol. 2, No. 11, 513.
185. Butterfield, *Expedition Against Sandusky*, 354.
186. Denny, *Military Journal*, 281.
187. *Draper Manuscript Collections*, "Statement of Colonel Nathan Boone, Son of Daniel Boone," Draper Mss. 6S159.
188. Chesley Callaway served as a chain carrier for Daniel Boone in Dec. 13, 1782, survey of Evan Shelby property. See Samuel M. Wilson, *Catalogue of Revolutionary Soldiers and Sailors of the Commonwealth of Virginia to Whom Land Bounty Warrants Were Granted by Virginia for Military Services in the War for Independence*, (Greenville, S.C.: Southern Historical Press, Inc., 1994), 108.

Chapter Eight

1. "March 1, 1781, Letter from Captain McKee to Major De Peyster," *Historical Collections*, Vol. 19, 597.
2. *Draper Manuscript Collections*, "Deposition of George Rogers Clark (April 27, 1805)," Draper Mss. 29J47.
3. Nelson L. Dawson. "Louisville's Fort Nelson." In *Kentucky History Highlights from the Filson Club*, edited by Katherine L. House (Louisville: Filson Club, 1992), 104.
4. *Draper Manuscript Collections*, "Proceedings Relating to the Illinois Grant," Draper Mss. 61J161–268.
5. Dr. Dorothy Libby, *An Anthropological Report on the Piankashaw Indians–(Miami Archives, Before the Indian Claims Commission, Dockett 99 (ca. 1776-ca. 183)*. (Bloomington, Ind.: Indiana University). http://www.gbl.indiana.edu/archives/dockett_99/d99toc.html
6. Seineke, *George Rogers Clark Adventure*, 473.
7. Fitzpatrick, *Wilderness War on the Ohio*, 392.
8. "March 1, 1781, Letter from Captain McKee to Major De Peyster," *Historical Collections*, Vol. 19, 597.
9. Fitzpatrick, *Wilderness War on the Ohio*, 403.
10. "Indian Council, held at Detroit April 5th 1781, with a Deputation of Principal Chiefs of the Shawanese, Delawares & Cherokees," *Historical Collections*, Vol. 10, 463–465.
11. "Indian Council, held at Detroit 5th April 1781, by Major De Peyster Commanding Detroit and its Dependencies, with the Several Nations," *Historical Collections*, Vol. 10, 472.
12. Fitzpatrick, *Wilderness War on the Ohio*, 401.
13. "Indian Council, held at Detroit 26th April 1781, by Major De Peyster Commanding Detroit and its Dependencies, with the Several Nations," *Historical Collections*, Vol. 10, 473–474.
14. "Indian Council, held at Detroit 26th April 1781, by Major De Peyster Commanding Detroit and its Dependencies, with the Several Nations," *Historical Collections*, Vol. 10, 475–476.
15. Micajah was identified by Ezekiel Lewis as being present among the small Shawanese contingent that accompanied Brant and George Girty. Nenessica was then the senior War Chief for the Chalaakaatha division and undoubtedly brought Micajah with him on this expedition. Fitzpatrick, *Wilderness War on the Ohio*, 415.
16. "Intelligence from the Shawnese," *Historical Collections*, Vol. 19, 646.
17. *Draper Manuscript Collections*, "Statement of William Cracraft," Draper Mss. 14J129, and "Notes on Conversation with Genl. Robert Orr," Draper Mss. 6NN138.
18. Vine Deloria, Jr. *Red Earth, White Lies*. (Golden, Col.: Fulcrum Publishing, 1997), 104–105.
19. Jefferson, *Notes on the State of Virginia*, 43.
20. *Draper Manuscript Collections*, "Statement by Ezekiel Lewis," Draper Mss. 30J79, and Fitzpatrick, *Wilderness War on the Ohio*, 423.
21. "August 21, 1781, Letter from Captain Joseph Brant to Captain Alexander McKee," *Historical Collections*, Vol. 19, 655.
22. "A party of Clark's men deserted, & Lochry apprehended them, sixteen in number. With these, Lochry's whole force consisted of 102 men. Of this number 42 were killed when taken & sub-

Endnotes 409

sequently—possibly only 40 ... The first notice Lochry's men had of Indians was, a heavy fire from them—said to have been one hundred of them under Joseph Brant, 'Cage Callaway—no other whites recollected. Don't recollect particularly about Colo. McKee—perhaps he came next day with Simon Girty's large party of four or five hundred. Callaway was the worst savage amongst them. When Girty and his party came the next day, Girty deplored the death of Col. Lochry—who was a mason, as was Girty, and said Lochry would not have been killed if he had been there." *Draper Manuscript Collections*, "Statement by Ezekiel Lewis," Draper Mss. 30J79.

23. *Draper Manuscript Collections*, "Notes of Conversation with Genl. Robert Orr," Draper Mss. 6NN138.
24. "Cage Callaway was of a small party that took Lewis and four others to a town on Big Miami, and were five days marching there without any food; & when they reached there Callaway said they must eat all that was given them, or they would be killed; & thus they stuffed, and overloaded their stomachs, and that night they thought they would die of their distress." *Draper Manuscript Collections*, "Statement by Ezekiel Lewis," Draper Mss. 30J79.
25. *Draper Manuscript Collections*, "Deposition of George Rogers Clark (April 27, 1805)," Draper Mss. 29J47.
26. Stevens, *Louis Lorimier*, 16, 17, 40, and 41.
27. Ted Igleheart, "Squire Boone, The Forgotten Man," *The Filson Club History Quarterly* 44, No. 4 (1970): 363; Paul A. Hutton, "William Wells: Frontier Scout and Indian Agent," *Indiana Magazine of History* 74, No. 3 (1978): 183; and *Draper Manuscript Collections*, "April 26, 1781, Letter from Colonel John Floyd," Draper Mss. 17CC135-137.
28. Howard, *Shawnee: Ceremonialism*, 269-271.
29. *Draper Manuscript Collections*, "Statement of Col. Nathan Boone, Son of Daniel Boone," Draper Mss. 6S158.
30. *Draper Manuscript Collections*, "Declarations of Beal Kelly," Draper Mss. 32J431; "Draper Notes," Draper Mss. 1R366 and 1R372; and "Letter from Lyman Draper to Micajah Callaway dated March 12, 1849," Draper Mss. 14C117.
31. "April 3, 1782, Letter from Major De Peyster to Captain McKee," *Historical Collections*, Vol. 10, 565.
32. James Alton James, "Significant Events During the Last Year of the Revolution in the West," *Proceedings of the Mississippi Valley Historical Association* 6 (1913): 240, 242-244.
33. James, "Significant Events," 243.
34. James, "Significant Events," 247, and Sugden, *Blue Jacket*, 62.
35. The weight of documentary evidence tends to support the conclusion that Micajah was present at the capture and death of Colonel Crawford. A detailed account of the death by torture of a militia officer by Micajah's son John Hawkins Callaway very closely matches the description of the death of Col. Crawford provided by other eyewitness. Although the date given by John Hawkins Callaway was 1779, this was undoubtedly an error. See Russell, "Micajah Callaway," 57. See also *Draper Manuscript Collections*, "Statement of Col. John Johnston," Draper Mss. 11YY12; "Statement of Capt. Marcus Richardson," Draper Mss. 12CC125-127; "Statement of Stephen Shelton," Draper Mss. 11CC267-269; and "Memoirs of Margaret Erskine, Draper Mss. 8ZZ30.
36. Butterfield, *Expedition Against Sandusky*, 346. See also *Draper Manuscript Collections*, "Interview Notes from Joseph Jackson," Draper Mss. 11C62(34).
37. Hugh H. Brackinridge, ed. *Indian Atrocities: Narratives of the Perils and Sufferings of Dr. Knight and John Slover, Among the Indians During the Rebvolutionary War, with Short Memoirs of Colonel Crawford and John Slover* (Cincinnati: U.P. James, 1867), 53.
38. Charles H. Coleman, "Lincoln's Lincoln Grandmother." *Journal of the Illinois State Historical Society* 52, No. 1 (1959): 60, 68, and 70.
39. Charles Gano Talbert, "Kentucky Invades Ohio -1782," *The Register of the Kentucky Historical Society* 53, No. 185 (1955): 288.
40. *Draper Manuscript Collections*, "March 5, 1782 Letter from General George Rogers Clark," Draper Mss. 11J17.
41. James, "Significant," 245, and *Draper Manuscript Collections*, "Declaration of John Searcy," Draper Mss. 32J29.
42. "June 8, 1782, Message from the Mingos, Shawanese and Delawares to Major De Peyster signed by Captain Snake," *Historical Collections*, Vol. 10, 583.

43. Sugden, *Blue Jacket*, 63; and Stevens, *Louis Lorimier*, 43.
44. Fitzpatrick, *Wilderness War on the Ohio*, 500-506.
45. "August 27, 1782, Letter from Major De Peyster to Brig. Gen. Powell," *Historical Collections*, Vol. 10, 633.
46. W.H. Perrin, J.H. Battle, and G.C. Kniffin, *Kentucky. A History of the State*, (Louisville: F.A. Battey and Company, 1887), 182; Anne Crabb, "'What shall I do now?' The Story of the Indian Captivities of Margaret Paulee, Jones Hoy, and Jack Callaway, 1779-ca. 1789." *The Filson Club History Quarterly* 70, No. 4 (1996): 386; and *Draper Manuscript Collections*, "Statement of John Sappington," Draper Mss. 12CC188.
47. *Draper Manuscript Collections*, "Statement of John Sappington," Draper Mss. 12CC188, and "Letter to Draper from James Callaway (1857)," Draper Mss. 24C67.
48. R.S. Cotterill, "Battle of Upper Blue Licks." *The History Quarterly* 2, No. 1 (1927): 29; Crabb, "What shall I do now?" 364; and *Draper Manuscript Collections*, "Memoirs of Margaret Erskine," Draper Mss. 8ZZ30.
49. *Draper Manuscript Collections*, "Statement of Capt. Samuel Boone, Son of George Boone," Draper Mss. 22S242-243.
50. *Draper Manuscript Collections*, "Statement of Thomas Jones," Draper Mss. 21S229.
51. Crabb, "What shall I do now?" 388.
52. Shane, " William Clinkenbeard," 119; A. Goff Bedford, *Land of Our Fathers: History of Clark County, Kentucky* (Mt. Sterling, Ky.: Dr. A. Goff Bedford, 1958), 104-105; and O'Malley, *Stockading Up*, 155-156.
53. Cotterill, "Battle of Upper Blue Licks," 29.
54. Lucien Beckner, "John D. Shane's Interview with Benjamin Allen, Clark County." *The Filson Club History Quarterly* 5, No. 2 (1931): 85.
55. Shane, "William Clinkenbeard," 123; *Draper Manuscript Collections*, "June 3, 1845 Letter from Col. Cave Johnson to Draper," Draper Mss. 9J157; "Statement of Josiah Collins," Draper Mss. 12CC107-108; and "Statement of Thomas Jones," Draper Mss. 21S230-231.
56. Crabb, "What shall I do now?" 389.
57. *Draper Manuscript Collections*, "Statement of Major John H. Craig," Draper Mss. 9J112-113, and "Statement of Captain Benjamin Briggs," Draper Mss. 9J191-198.
58. *Draper Manuscript Collections*, "Statement of Major John H. Craig," Draper Mss. 9J112-113.
59. O'Malley, *Stockading Up*, 183-185.
60. *Draper Manuscript Collections*, "Statement of Maj. John H. Craig," Draper Mss. 9J120.
61. O'Malley, *Stockading Up*, 24.
62. Fitzpatrick, *Wilderness War on the Ohio*, 511-513; Leroy V. Eid, "'A Kind of Running Fight': Indian Battlefield Tactics in the Late Eighteenth Century," *The Western Pennsylvania Historical Magazine* 71, No. 2 (1988), 155-156; and Quaife, "The Ohio Campaigns of 1782," 527.
63. *Draper Manuscript Collections*, "Interview of Jacob Stevens," Draper Mss. 12CC133-138, and "Letter from Elijah Callaway," Draper Mss. 5DD20.
64. Quaife, "The Ohio Campaigns of 1782," 526.
65. *Draper Manuscript Collections*, "August 31, 1782 Letter from Col. Benjamin Logan to Governor, Council re Defeat at Blue Licks," Draper Mss. 11S10.
66. John H. Moore, "A Captive of the Shawnees, 1779-1784," *West Virginia History: A Quarterly Magazine* 23, No. 4 (1962): 287.
67. Crabb, "What shall I do now?" 390.
68. *Draper Manuscript Collections*, "Memoirs of Margaret Erskine," Draper Mss. 8ZZ30.
69. There are two slightly varying accounts of the conclusion of the proceedings. In one version an eloquent warrior pleads for their lives and offers to give his fine rifle to White Bark to appease him in exchange for sparing the boys. White Bark accepted the rifle and spared their lives. See Crabb, "What shall I do now?" 391.

    In the other version, White Bark asks a white interpreter to trade his handsome rifle for their lives. The interpreter readily agreed, and White Bark was appeased. See Moore, "A Captive of the Shawnees," 292-293, and Crabb, "What shall I do now?" 391, ftnt. 39. It is probable that this warrior/interpreter was Micajah. He lived nearby and undoubtedly would have seen and rec-

Endnotes 411

ognized Jacky. It is likely that he was present at the Council and would have interceded to save his cousin Jacky and the others.

70. Moore, "A Captive of the Shawnees," 293, and *Draper Manuscript Collections*, "Interview from Richard French (Grandson of Col. Richard Callaway)," Draper Mss. 12CC202–203.
71. *Draper Manuscript Collections*, "September 8, 1782, Letter from General George Washington to Sir Guy Carleton," Draper Mss. 11J13.
72. *Draper Manuscript Collections*, "September 12, 1782, Letter from Sir Guy Carleton to General George Washington," Draper Mss. 11J14.
73. "September 29, 1782, Letter from Major De Peyster to General Haldimand," *Historical Collections*, Vol. 10, 649.
74. Talbert, "Kentucky Invades Ohio -1782," 289.
75. James, "Significant Events," 252; Talbert, "Kentucky Invades Ohio -1782," 289; and *Draper Manuscript Collections*, "'Sketches of Border Life: Narrative of Abraham Thomas,' The Troy Times (Ohio)," Draper Mss. 8J242, and "Statement of Henry Wilson," Draper Mss. 9J61–74.
76. Kenton, *Simon Kenton*, 160.
77. Talbert, "Kentucky Invades Ohio -1782," 291, and *Draper Manuscript Collections*, "Statement of Henry Wilson," Draper Mss. 9J61–74, and "General George Rogers Clark's Official Report of 1782 Campaign," Draper Mss. 8J320.
78. *Draper Manuscript Collections*, "General George Rogers Clark's Official Report of 1782 Campaign." Draper Mss. 8J320.
79. *Draper Manuscript Collections*, "Statement of Josiah Collins," Draper Mss.12CC71, and "Statement of Capt. Benjamin Briggs," Draper Mss. 9J191–198.
80. *Draper Manuscript Collections*, "Statement of Henry Wilson," Draper Mss. 9J61–74, and Draper Mss. 11DD42.
81. *Draper Manuscript Collections*, "'Sketches of Border Life: Narrative of Abraham Thomas,' The Troy Times (Ohio)," Draper Mss. 8J242, and Draper Mss. 18S114.
82. "... & from that place the tribe was driven by a party under George Rogers Clark, seven of the Indians being taken prisoners there, the Queen of the nation being among the number (her name Lamatumque)." See Callaway, "Declaration of Micajah Callaway." See also *Draper Manuscript Collections*, "Notes Regarding Capture of Moluntha's Wife," Draper Mss. 1R145, and "Interview Notes from Joseph Jackson," Draper Mss. 11C62(30).
83. *Draper Manuscript Collections*, "Statement of Henry Wilson," Draper Mss. 9J61–74.
84. *Draper Manuscript Collections*, "Statement of William Clinkenbeard," Draper Mss. 11CC65.
85. *Draper Manuscript Collections*, "Statement of Col. Nathan Boone, Son of Daniel Boone, Draper Mss. 6S158. and "Declaration of Beal Kelly," Draper Mss. 32J43 and 10054.
86. The account of the Chief on a white horse is from *Draper Manuscript Collections*, "Interview from Maj. John Craig," Draper Mss. 9J129–130. Joseph Jackson identified Moluntha as the husband of Lamatumque in *Draper Manuscript Collections*, "Interview Notes from Joseph Jackson," Draper Mss. 11C62(30)
87. *Draper Manuscript Collections*, "Statement of Josiah Collins," Draper Mss. 12CC106.
88. *Draper Manuscript Collections*, Draper Mss. 23S174 and 23S168.
89. *Draper Manuscript Collections*, "Statement of Josiah Collins," Draper Mss. 12CC106.
90. *Draper Manuscript Collections*, "Interview from Maj. John Craig," Draper Mss. 9J129–130.
91. O'Malley, *Stockading Up*, 109.
92. *Draper Manuscript Collections*, "General George Rogers Clark's Report of 1782 Campaign," Draper Mss. 8J320 and Wheeler-Voegelin, *Indians of Ohio and Indiana*, Vol. 2, 264–266. .
93. "November 21, 1782, Letter from Major De Peyster to Captain McKee," *Historical Collections*, Vol. 11, 323.
94. Wheeler-Voegelin, *Indians of Ohio and Indiana*, Vol. 2, 264.
95. *Draper Manuscript Collections*, "Interview Notes from John Hawkins Callaway, Son of Micajah Callaway," Draper Mss. 25S124.

Chapter Nine

1. *Draper Manuscript Collections*, "April 6, 1783 Letter from John Campbell to General Clark," Draper Mss. 52J82.
2. *Draper Manuscript Collections*, "Letter from Major Walls to Colonel Davies," Draper Mss. 11S206.
3. *Draper Manuscript Collections*, "January 13, 1783 Letter from Governor Benjamin Harrison to General Clark," Draper Mss. 52J94.
4. *Draper Manuscript Collections*, "Statement of Henry Wilson," Draper Mss. 9J73.
5. Micajah Callaway's sons told an interviewer that Micajah accompanied the Shawanese on two trips to the Falls of the Ohio to serve as their interpreter in negotiations for a peace treaty and prisoner exchange at the end of the War for Independence. See *Draper Manuscript Collections*, "December 18, 1850, Letter from Leonard Bliss to Lyman Draper," Draper Mss. 14C119. It is clear that the second visit occurred during a prisoner exchange in July of 1783. However, the timing of his earlier visit is not as clear. It is likely that he made this first visit in conjunction with an initial Shawanese contact with General Clark following up on Clark's November 1782 battlefield offer to parley for peace at the Falls of Ohio. This initial visit probably occurred sometime between January and March of 1783 after the January 13, 1783, Indian Council in Detroit and Governor Harrison's letter of the same date. The author believes that Chief Wryneck was a logical choice to serve as the initial Shawanese emissary to Clark. Wryneck was an adopted former Virginian named Joshua Rennick, spoke English, and had been chosen as the Shawnese emissary to Clark in Clark's first meeting with the northwestern Indian nations at Cahokia, Illinois in 1778. Wryneck was also documented as being very active in Shawanese diplomatic affairs in 1783–1784.
6. Dawson, "Fort Nelson," 104.
7. This activity can be inferred from subsequent events discussed later in the text.
8. *Draper Manuscript Collections*, "March 12, 1783 Letter from Bartholomew Tardineau to General Clark (translation from French)," Draper Mss. 52J105.
9. "If a peace was made in the face of an army, in their own country, it would be the more valuable. Much depends on the manner of introducing them to a treaty, and management of them afterwards. I have often experienced it. I have for some time been inclined to temporize with the Shawanees through the means of a prisoner woman who has a child by sending her pretending to negotiate an exchange of prisoners without mentioning anything about peace. Perhaps it might be an introduction to something of more consequence. But I am not afraid her child would be a sufficient security for her returning, as they know our levity is such that we would not put it to death. I wish I knew your sentiments on the subject. However, it can't be attended with bad consequences, as she will know nothing of the situation of the country to its prejudice, & her loss would be but trifling." See *Draper Manuscript Collections*, "March 19, 1783 Letter from General Clark to Governor Benjamin Harrison," Draper Mss. 14S77.
10. "I like your proposal of sending the Indian woman to the Shawnees to sound them on the subject of peace. Your prudence will suggest to you not to appear too forward in this business, lest it should encourage them to continue the war." See *Draper Manuscript Collections*, "April 9, 1783 Letter from Governor Harrison to General Clark," Draper Mss. 13S165, 170.
11. *Minutes of the Provincial Council of Pennsylvania*, Vol. 8, 630.
12. "June 5, 1783, Letter from Lieutenant Colonel De Peyster to Alexander McKee," *Historical Collections*, Vol. 11, 366, and *Draper Manuscript Collections*, "Statement of Josiah Collins," Draper Mss. 12CC107.
13. "April 20, 1783, Letter from Major De Peyster to Captain McKee," *Historical Collections*, Vol. 11, 359.
14. *Draper Manuscript Collections*, Draper Mss. 13CC9-18.
15. "He was then employed as an Interpreter on behalf of sd. Tribe to go to the Falls of the Ohio to treat on the subject of exchange of prisoners: Seven Indians went with him to that place, for that purpose. Genl. Clark being there at the time, by whose assistance this declarant was released at that time." See Callaway, "Declaration of Micajah Callaway."

Endnotes 413

The list of seven Chiefs is not set forth in Micajah's application or any other single document but list in the text is plausible if not likely. The author developed it based on the following reasoning: 1) These Chiefs were prominent in the Shawanese Nation at the time and were associated with the peace faction, 2) most of them are Makujays who traditionally lead treaty negotiations for the tribe or other chiefs (such as Wryneck) who frequently represented the Shawanese in parleys, 3) Moluntha was the Principal Chief and his child was still a hostage of the Long Knives, 4) Moluntha's wife Lamatumque was an important Headwoman and she was there for her child, 5) Aweecomy, Shade, and Captain Johnny were Makujay Chief that frequently signed treaties in this time-period, 6) Blue Jacket was less militant than other Piqua Chiefs and supported peace before Moluntha's assassination in 1786, and 7) Wryneck had been a participant in parleys with the Americans and British and was later mentioned as a leader of the 1783 and 1784 negotiations (*Draper Manuscript Collections*, "March 20, 1784 Speeches of the Shawanese & Wyndots," Draper Mss. 12S4).

16. *Draper Manuscript Collections*, "Interview Notes from John Hawkins Callaway, Son of Micajah Callaway," Draper Mss. 25S124; "Interview Notes from Noble Callaway, Son of Micajah Callaway," Draper Mss. 25S124; and "Interview Notes from James Callaway, Son of Micajah Callaway," Draper Mss. 25S257-261.

17. "May 29, 1783, Letter from Capt. Alexander McKee to Major Walls," *Historical Collections: Pioneer and Historical Society of the State of Michigan*, Vol. 20, (Lansing: Thorp & Godfrey; Robert Smith & Co., 1892), 125.

18. William Johnson is the only white prisoner released in this exchange that is identified in the documentation reviewed by the author. *Draper Manuscript Collections*, "September 8, 1783 Maryland Journal," Draper Mss. 11J26. In his statement regarding the prisoner exchange, Josiah Collins mentions a young "Jimmie" or "Dick" Callaway (probably a reference to Jackie Callaway) and Jones Hoy as prisoners exchanged at this time (*Draper Manuscript Collections*, "Statement of Josiah Collins," Draper Mss. 12CC107). See also Draper Inquiries to Major Ballard for further indication that Johnny (aka Jacky) Callaway was exchanged then (*Draper Manuscript Collections*, Draper Mss. 8J182). Other documentation indicates that Johnny (Jacky) Callaway was not released until mid-1784 (*Draper Manuscript Collections*, "Statement of Richard French," Draper Mss. 12CC205; "Statement of John Rankings," Draper Mss. 11CC81; and "Memoirs of Margaret Erskine," Draper Mss. 8ZZ30).

Other possible candidates for the prisoners who were released at this exchange are a group of men captured during the Battle of Blue Licks that were released about his time—Hugh Cunningham, Lewis and Martin Rose, and John McMurty (*Draper Manuscript Collections*, "Statement of J. Stevens," Draper Mss. 12CC136) and the wife and four children of Captain Charles Gatliff, captured at Ruddle's Station in 1780 (*Draper Manuscript Collections*, Draper Mss. 29J40).

19. There is no specific record of these discussions but it is likely the topic was discussed.

20. Although both Micajah Callaway and Josiah Collins, state that the prisoner exchange occurred in July, the author believes it took place in mid- to late-June, 1783. Assuming that Sherlock and the Chiefs left Mackachack on June 7, they would have arrived in Fort Nelson in about a week (June 14). The negotiations then reportedly lasted for seven days (June 21). It also appears that General Clark was in Richmond by June 16, apparently having delegated responsibility for completing the negotiations to Major Walls (*Draper Manuscript Collections*, Draper Mss. 52J86).

21. *Draper Manuscript Collections*, "July 2, 1783 Letter from Governor Harrison to General Clark," Draper Mss.11J25.

22. *Draper Manuscript Collections*, "July 2, 1783 Letter from General Clark to Governor Harrison," Draper Mss. 11J26.

23. "Indian Council at Detroit, July 30, 1783," *Historical Collections*, Vol. 20, 153. The Chalaakaatha division resided in Girty's Town at this time.

24. Callaway, "Declaration of Micajah Callaway."

25. *Draper Manuscript Collections*, "Statement of Josiah Collins," Draper Mss. 12CC107.

26. There are accounts of a woman purporting to be Micajah's mother browbeating the Shawanese into releasing Micajah. See Colonel Durrett's correspondence about a women scolding the Shawanese for the release of a prisoner—doubtless Micajah Callaway—after being prompted

to do so by General Clark (*Draper Manuscript Collections*, "Draper Notes regarding Gen. G.R. Clark—1783," Draper Mss. 32J77–79). The author does not belive that the woman referenced in this note was Micajah's mother Sarah Callaway, because there is no corroboration in Callaway family records and it appears that she still lived far to the east in Bedford County at the time of the prisoner exchange. However, it is fairly likely that Micajah's Aunt Elizabeth was there in the hope of recovering her son Jacky and grandson Jones Hoy. The author believes that Elizabeth was probably the woman noted in Colonel Durrett's correspondence.

27. The author was unable to locate any specific surviving records of the actual prisoner exchange transaction. The account in the previous paragraphs is modeled upon the protocol for such matters as reflected in accounts of many other diplomatic exchanges between Virginia and the Shawanese.
28. *Draper Manuscript Collections*, "Interview Notes from John Hawkins Callaway, Son of Micajah Callaway," Draper Mss. 25S124; "Interview Notes from Noble Callaway, Son of Micajah Callaway," Draper Mss. 25S124; and "Interview Notes from James Callaway, Son of Micajah Callaway," Draper Mss. 25S257–261.
29. *Draper Manuscript Collections*, "Statement of Henry Wilson," Draper Mss. 9J61–74, and "Pension Declaration of James McCullock," Draper Mss. 16J10.
30. The author found no specific information indicating that Daniel Boone was present at the exchange but believes that it is likely that he was there, given Boone's relationship with Micajah and Jacky Callaway, the history of his past dealings with the Shawanese, and his access to General Clark as an officer in the Fayette County militia.
31. Although there are no surviving records of Micajah's debriefing upon his return to Kentucky, it is certain to have occurred. Daniel Boone was a likely participant as Micajah's commanding officer at the time of his capture.
32. Harry G. Enoch, *In Search of Morgan's Station and 'The Last Indian Raid in Kentucky,'* (Bowie, Md.: Heritage Books, Inc., 1997), 1.
33. Callaway, "Flanders," 21.
34. Chris McHenry, *Rebel Prisoners at Quebec: 1778–1783*, (Louisville: Filson Club, 1981), 55.
35. *Draper Manuscript Collections*, "Declaration of James Callaway," Draper Mss. 21C75, and "Virginia Land Patent Records," *Callaway Family Association Journal* 13 (1988): 58.
36. *Amherst County, Va. Will Book 3 (1786–1800)*, 397–398; Callaway and Reynolds, "A Campaine of Souldiers," 223–224; and *Bedford County, Virginia Order Book* 6, p. 187.
37. Callaway, "Virginia-Kentucky-Missouri," 30.
38. Callaway, "Flanders," 19.
39. "Certificate Book of the Virginia Land Commission," 76, 101, and 111.
40. G. Glenn Clift. *History of Maysville and Mason County.* (Lexington, Ky.: Transylvania Printing Company, 1936), 42.
41. Faragher, *Daniel Boone*, 235.
42. *Draper Manuscript Collections*, "March 10, 1784 Survey for Thomas Austin by Daniel Boone," Draper Mss. 14C4.
43. Deed for Original Survey No. 2134. See Joan E. Brookes-Smith, ed. *Master Index Virginia Surveys and Grants 1774–1791* (Frankfort, Ky.: Kentucky Historical Society, 1976), 30.
44. *Draper Manuscript Collections*, "Interview Notes from John Hawkins Callaway, Son of Micajah Callaway," Draper Mss. 25S124, and "Interview Notes from James Callaway, Son of Micajah Callaway," Draper Mss. 25S257–261.

Chapter Ten

1. *Draper Manuscript Collections*, "Statement of Henry Wilson," Draper Mss. 9J61–74, and "Pension Declaration of James McCullock," Draper Mss. 16J10.

Endnotes

2. "Indian Council at Detroit, July 30, 1783, Haldimand Papers," *Historical Collections*, Volume 20, 153. The Chalaakaatha division resided in Girty's Town at this time.
3. "August 1, 1783, Letter from Lt. Col. De Peyster to Brig. Gen. Allan MacLean," *Historical Collections*, Vol. 20, 157.
4. Although Henry Wilson's statement indicates a peace treaty was agreed to after a five day council, subsequent events in August and September indicate that a final written peace treaty was apparently never concluded. *Draper Manuscript Collections*, "Statement of Henry Wilson," Draper Mss. 9J61-74, and "Pension Declaration of James McCullock," Draper Mss. 16J10.
5. Michael L. Cook and Bettie A. Cook. *Kentucky Court of Appeals, Deed Books V-Z*. Vol. 4. (Evansville, Ind.: Cook Publications, 1985), 580-581, and Deed for Original Survey No. 2134. See Brookes-Smith, *Virgina Surveys and Grants*, 30.
6. Bedford, *Land of Our Fathers*, 190.
7. Belue, "Terror in the Canelands," 3-34.
8. John Filson, *The Discovery, Settlement and Present State of Kentucke, 1784. Appendix, The Adventures of Col. Daniel Boon*, (Reprint, New York: Corinth, 1962). This publication began the process of deification of Daniel Boone into the archetype of the American pioneer spirit and experience. See Faragher, *Daniel Boone*, 2-7.
9. Francis Paul Prucha, *Documents of United States Indian Policy*, (Lincoln: University of Nebraska Press, 1990), 3.
10. *Draper Manuscript Collections*, "September 7, 1783 Maryland Journal," Draper Mss. 11J26" and "October 11, 1783 New York Royal Gazette," Draper Mss. 16J90.
11. William P. Palmer, *Calendar of Virginia State Papers and Other Manuscripts*, Vol. 3, (Richmond: James E. Goode, 1883), 530, and *Draper Manuscript Collections*, "Gen. Wilkinson's Speech to the Shawanese dated Feb. 7. 1784," Draper Mss. 12S1, and "Speeches by the Shawanese and Wyandots received by William Coleman on March 20, 1784," Draper Mss. 12S4.
12. Cauthorn, *Vincennes Indiana*, 36, 82-83.
13. *Draper Manuscript Collections*, "July 27, 1784 Letter from Richard Butler to George Rogers Clark," Draper Mss. 53J12.
14. *Draper Manuscript Collections*, "Extract of July 25, 1784 Letter from Danville," Draper Mss. 11J30. Although there is no direct evidence that Daniel Boone and Micajah were present at the time of the squabble, it is quite possible given their prior and subsequent involvement in prisoner exchange matters.
15. Moore, "Captive of the Shawnees," 295.
16. *Draper Manuscript Collections*, "Statement by Johnny (Jacky) Callaway's Brother-in-law Richard French," Draper Mss. 12CC205: "Jack was kept 2 Years." Jacky was captured in August 1782 so would have been released in the July-August 1784 time period. See also *Draper Manuscript Collections*, "Statement of John Rankins," Draper Mss. 11CC81: "Jack Callaway, a younger brother, that was taken out of the watermelon patch at Hoy's Station, I saw when he was exchanged & brought in; the same summer we came (1784)." and *Draper Manuscript Collections*, "1857 Letter from James Callaway, Son of Johnny (Jacky) Callaway," Draper Mss. 24C67: "Colonel Boone made an exchange with Indians for my father."
17. *Draper Manuscript Collections*, "Statement of Judge Moses Boone, Son of Squire Boone," Draper Mss. 19C41.
18. "Indian Council at Lower Sandusiky on September 6, 1783," *Historical Collections*, Volume 20, 176.
19. Joyce G. Williams and Jill E. Farrelly, *Diplomacy on the Indiana-Ohio Frontier 1783-1791*, (Bloomington, Ind.: Indiana University Bicentennial Committee, 1976), 12, ftnt. 27.

Chapter Eleven

1. McDonald, *Biographical Sketches*, 24.
2. *Draper Manuscript Collections*, "Election of Indian Commissioners," Draper Mss. 53J6.
3. *Draper Manuscript Collections*, "Statement of Jesse Bledsoe," Draper Mss. 15CC45, and "The Butler Brothers," Draper Mss. 4JJ, Book A.

4. Thomas B. Wait, "March 19, 1784 Entry," *Secret Journals of the Acts and Proceedings of Congress, Vol. I Domestick Affairs*, (Boston, Mass., 1821).
5. *Draper Manuscript Collections*, "Captain Brant's report to British on Fort Stanwix Treaty Negotiations," Draper Mss. 23U.
6. "Articles of Agreement Between the United States and Indians, January 21, 1785," *Historical Collections: Pioneer and Historical Society of the State of Michigan*, Vol. 25, (Lansing: Robert Smith & Co., 1896), 687.
7. Williams and Farrelly, *Diplomacy on the Indiana-Ohio Frontier*, 15, ftnt. 35.
8. *Draper Manuscript Collections*, "Petition of Grenadier Squaw," Draper Mss. 14S158, and Galloway, *Old Chillicothe*, 292-293.
9. *Draper Manuscript Collections*, "Message from Shawnee Chiefs to Colonel McKee," Draper Mss. 23U.
10. "Transcript of Indian Council at Wakatomica on May 18, 1785," *Historical Collections*, Vol. 25, 691.
11. *Draper Manuscript Collections*, "October 3, 1785 Letter from Colonel Harmar to Captain John Doughty," Draper Mss. 1W94.
12. *Draper Manuscript Collections*, "October 1785 Report from Samuel Montgomery," Draper Mss. 14S174-195, and "October 1785 Report from Daniel Elliott, James Rinken (Messengers)," Draper Mss. 14S195.
13. Denny, *Military Journal*, 72-73, and *Draper Manuscript Collections*, "From the Notes of an Old Soldier" National Gazette, Oct. 18, 1820," Draper Mss. 11J52, and "February 12, 1786 Letter from Major Finney to Colonel Robert Patterson," Draper Mss.11J73.
14. The "Captain, a clever kind of a man" that Butler describes meeting at Limestone was Daniel Boone. See Craig, *Olden Times*, Vol. 2, No. 10, 451.
15. Denny, *Military Journal*, 59; Craig, *Olden Times*, Vol. 2, No. 10, 446-447; and Beverley W. Bond, Jr., *The Correspondence of John Cleves Symmes, the Founder of the Miami Purchase* (New York: The Macmillan Company, 1926), 61-65.
16. "(Micajah) Was employed as interpreter in making a treaty at Limestone for the Exchange of prisoners: & also at the mouth of Big Miami he acted as interpreter for Gen. Sinclair and Genl. Butler." See Callaway, "Declaration of Micajah Callaway."
17. Denny, *Military Journal*, 59.
18. Lieutenant Denny identies one of the Shawanese as "Captain Johnny" while General Butler identifies the two Shawanese as John Harris and Micanimsica or "Mr. Wappan." From these two statements by well-respected American officers, it appears to be very possible that Captain Johnny and John Harris were the same individual. See Denny, *Military Journal*, 60, and Craig, *Olden Times*, Vol. 2, No. 11, 486, 490. See Endnote 49 regarding doubt about whether Fanny and Morgan were the biological children of Nonhelema. It is possible that they were probably adopted.
19. Craig, *Olden Times*, Vol. 2, No. 11, 500. See also *Draper Manuscript Collections*, "December 21, 1785, Letter from Commissioner Published in 'Pennsylvania Packet' on March 28, 1786," Draper Mss. 11J43. See Endnote 49 regarding doubt about whether Fanny and Morgan were the biological children of Nonhelema. It is possible that they were adopted.
20. Craig, *Olden Times*, Vol. 2, No. 11, 512, 531 and Denny, *Military Journal*, 69-70.
21. Craig, *Olden Times*, Vol. 2, No. 11, 513.
22. Denny, *Military Journal*, 69-70.
23. Ibid., 277-281.
24. Craig, *Olden Times*, Vol. 2, No. 11, 520.
25. E.Y. Guernsey, *Indiana: The Influence of the Indians Upon its History–with Indian and French Names for Natural and Cultural Locations (Publication No. 122)*, (Indianapolis: Indiana Department of Natural Resources, 1933)–a Map.
26. Denny, *Military Journal*, 72-73, and "February 12, 1786, Letter from Major Finney to Colonel Robert Patterson," Draper Mss.11J73.
27. Craig, *Olden Times*, Vol. 2, No. 11, 527.
28. Craig, *Olden Times*, Vol. 2, No. 11, 523, and Denny, Military Journal, 72-73.
29. Denny, *Military Journal*, 72-73; Craig, *Olden Times*, Vol. 2, No. 11, 524-525; and *Draper Manuscript Collections*, "'From the Notes of an Old Soldier,' National Gazette, Oct. 18, 1820," Draper Mss. 11J52, and "Draper Notes," Draper Mss. 11J39.
30. *Journals of the Continental Congress*, 529, Continental Congress Broadside Collection, Library of Congress.

Endnotes 417

31. Micajah's name was misspelled on the treaty as "Kagy Galloway." Micajah's nickname was "Cagey" and "Kagy" is obviously a misspelling of "Cagey." The surname "Galloway" is commonly confused with the surname "Calloway" or "Callaway." Micajah did not know how to read or write so could not check the spelling. The name of Joseph Sovereign, the other interpreter who marked the treaty, was also misspelled as "Suffrein"; he also could neither read nor write.
32. Craig, *Olden Times*, Vol. 2, No. 12, 529.

Chapter Twelve

1. *Draper Manuscript Collections*, "April 11, 1786 'Pennsylvania Packet,'" Draper Mss 33J55.
2. *Draper Manuscript Collections*, "May 19, 1786 'Maryland Journal'" Draper Mss. 11J49, and Denny, *Military Journal*, 80.
3. *Draper Manuscript Collections*, "March 27, 1786, Message from Shawanese Chiefs to King of England," Draper Mss. 23U.
4. *Draper Manuscript Collections*, "March 28, 1786, Letter from David Duncan to Colonel Harmar," Draper Mss. 1W115.
5. *Draper Manuscript Collections*, "December 20, 1785, Letter from Fort Harmar Officer," Draper Mss. 33J52.
6. *Draper Manuscript Collections*, "Letter from George Rogers Clark to Congress," Draper Mss. 14S207.
7. Coleman, "Lincoln's Lincoln Grandmother," 78–80.
8. L.C. Helderman, "The Northwest Expedition of George Rogers Clark, 1786–1787," *The Mississippi Valley Historical Review* 25, No. 3 (1938): 321.
9. *Draper Manuscript Collections*, "Letter from George Rogers Clark to Congress," Draper Mss. 14S207.
10. Helderman, "Northwest Expedition," 323, and *Draper Manuscript Collections*, "Narrative by John Filson," Draper Mss. 10CC1–23, and "July 22, 1786, Letter from Colonel J.M.P. Legras to General George Rogers Clark," Draper Mss. 16S96.
11. *Draper Manuscript Collections*, "July 22, 1786, Letter from Colonel J.M.P. Legras to General George Rogers Clark," Draper Mss. 16S96.
12. *Draper Manuscript Collections*, "July 17, 1786, Letter from Major Finney," Draper Mss. 11J74(1); "July 22, 1786, Letter from Major Finney to General Harmar," Draper Mss. 1W139; "July 24, 1786, Letter from Captain Saunders," 1W185; and "July 29, 1786, Letter from Major Finney," Draper Mss. 11J76.
13. "Preston Papers, February 21, 1783 Letter from James Moore to William Preston," *The Virginia Magazine of History and Biography* 29, No. 1 (1921): 29, ftnt. 1; Wheeler-Voegelin, *Indians of Ohio and Indiana*, Vol. 2, 270; and *Draper Manuscript Collections*, "Extract of September 26, 1786, Letter in October 24, 1786 'Maryland Journal'" Draper Mss. 11J121.
14. Wheeler-Voegelin, *Indians of Ohio and Indiana*, Vol. 2, 303.
15. *Draper Manuscript Collections*, "August 6, 1785 Letter from Colonel McKee(?)," Draper Mss. 23U.
16. *Draper Manuscript Collections*, "Letter from Thomas Hutchins dated July 21, 1786," Draper Mss. 1W144.
17. George W. Geib, "The Land Ordnance of 1785: A Bicentennial Review," *Indiana Magazine of History* 81, No. 1 (1985): 9.
18. *Draper Manuscript Collections*, September 14, 1786 Intelligence Report (Draper Mss. 1W276).
19. Geib, "Land Ordnance of 1785," 9.
20. *Draper Manuscript Collections*, "September 17, 1786, Letter from Colonel Harmar to Congress," Draper Mss. 11J128, and "Extract of September 13, 1786, Letter Published in October 3, 1786 'Maryland Journal,'" Draper Mss. 11J48.
21. *Draper Manuscript Collections*, Draper Mss. 12S123–124.
22. Helderman, "Northwest Expedition," 326, and George R. Wilson and Gayle Thornbrough, *The Buffalo Trace*, (Indianapolis: Indiana Historical Society, 1946), 197.

23. *Draper Manuscript Collections*, "Statement of Major John H. Craig," Draper Mss. 9J135-137.
24. William Henry Perrin, *History of Bourbon, Scott, Harrison and Nicholas Counties, Kentucky*, (Chicago: O.L. Baskin & Co., 1882), 40-91.
25. Cave Johnson, "Reminiscences from the Life of Col. Cave Johnson," *Register of the Kentucky State Historical Society* 20, No. 59 (1922).
26. John W. Monette, M.D., *History of the Discovery and Settlement of the Valley of the Mississippi*, (New York: Harper & Brothers, 1846), 152, and *Draper Manuscript Collections*, "'Columbia Magazine,' October 1786," Draper Mss. 33J32, and "October 1844 Statement of Elijah Farris," Draper Mss. 9J236.
27. Wilson and Thornbrough, *Buffalo Trace*, 186, 198, and 202; Joseph S. Karol, "The French at French Lick: Fact or Fiction?" *Indiana Magazine of History* 50, No. 2 (1954): 139-140; and *Draper Manuscript Collections*, "Statement of Major John H. Craig," Draper Mss. 9J135-137.
28. Cauthorn, *Vincennes Indiana*, 24, 39, 42-44, and 114.
29. *Draper Manuscript Collections*, "January 5, 1783 Letter from James Monroe," Draper Mss. 52J69-70.
30. *Draper Manuscript Collections*, "Statement of S. Robard," Draper Mss. 11J; "Statement of Major John H. Craig," Draper Mss. 9J135-137; and "Dec. 17, 1833 Letter from B. Gaines," Draper Mss. 9J238.
31. "Clarke's Wabash Expedition—Callaway served on this expedition. He said Clark and men lay long (3 months says informant—but it was not so long) at Vincennes, drinking & drunk & ate up the provisions. Clark harangued the men, appealing to all who would go & fight the Indians under his leadership to advance forward from the ranks—only fifteen did so—Callaway among them. Clark wept like a child and said he was ruined. He finally told the men that they must get back to the Falls as best they could -& did so." See *Draper Manuscript Collections*, "Interview from John Hawkins Callaway, Son of Micajah Callaway," Draper Mss. 25S124.
32. Helderman, "Northwest Expedition," 327.
33. *Draper Manuscript Collections*, "Fall 1846 Statement of Moses Boone," Draper Mss. 9J236.
34. *Draper Manuscript Collections*, "Interview Notes from John Hawkins Callaway, Son of Micajah Callaway," Draper Mss. 25S124.
35. *Draper Manuscript Collections*, "Dec. 17, 1833 Letter from B. Gaines," Draper Mss. 9J238, and "Statement of Major John H. Craig," Draper Mss. 9J135-137.
36. *Draper Manuscript Collections*, "Message from General Clark to the Wabash Indians," Draper Mss. 14S201.
37. *Draper Manuscript Collections*, "Statement of Colonel William Sudduth," Draper Mss. 12CC79.
38. Helderman, "Northwest Expedition," 329.
39. *Draper Manuscript Collections*, "February 20, 1787 'Pennsylvania Packet,'" Draper Mss. 11J148.
40. See also John B. Dillon. *A History of Indiana from its Earliest Explorations to the Close of the Territorial Government in 1816.* (Indianapolis: Bingham & Doughty, 1859), 197-199, and *Draper Manuscript Collections*, "December 22, 1786, Letter to Governor Randolph," Draper Mss.13S176.
41. *Draper Manuscript Collections*, "February 28, 1787 Proclamation by Virginia Governor Randolph," Draper Mss.5J(?)65
42. Dillon, *History of Indiana*, 202.
43. *Draper Manuscript Collections*, Draper Mss. 1W290.
44. Helderman, "Northwest Expedition," 330-331, and *Draper Manuscript Collections*, "Statement of Major John H. Craig," Draper Mss. 9J135-137.

Chapter Thirteen

1. Talbert, *Benjamin Logan*, 209, and *Draper Manuscript Collections*, "October 27, 1786, Letter from Gentleman in Danville to his Correspondent in Richmond," Draper Mss. 33J36, and "Statement of Colonel William Sudduth," Draper Mss. 12CC79.
2. Talbert, *Benjamin Logan*, 209. *Draper Manuscript Collections*, "Statement of Colonel William Sudduth," Draper Mss. 12CC79; "October 9, 1786 Message of Colonel Benjamin Logan to Shawanese Chiefs," Draper Mss. 23U; and Draper Mss. 19S72.

Endnotes 419

3. *Draper Manuscript Collections*, "Statement of Colonel William Sudduth," Draper Mss. 12CC79, and Denny, *Military Journal*, 93–94.
4. Williams and Farrelly, *Diplomacy on the Indiana-Ohio Frontier*, 46; "Indian Speech to the Congress of the United States, December 18, 1786," *Historical Collections*, Vol. 11, 467; and "October 13, 1786 Letter from W. Ancrum," *Historical Collections: Pioneer and Historical Society of the State of Michigan*, Vol. 24 (Lansing: Robert Smith & Co., 1895), 37.
5. *Draper Manuscript Collections*, "Interview Notes from Joseph Jackson," Draper Mss. 11C62(32–33), and "Statement of Judge Christopher Woods," Draper Mss. 8BB38.
6. Joshua Rennick married Tecumseh's sister Tecumseh and they had two children, James and John. See *Draper Manuscript Collections*, "January 30, 1847, Letter from Felix Rennick to Draper," Draper Mss. 7U131; "Statement of John McDonald," Draper Mss. 7U128; "March 16, 1867 and May 6, 1867 Letters from Wm. Renick to Draper," Draper Mss. 4CC119; and "Statement of Mrs. John Poage," Draper Mss. 13CC213–215.
7. *Draper Manuscript Collections*, "Statement of Charles Tucker," Draper Mss. 23S175, and see also Draper Mss. 23S168 and 23S161.
8. Henry Clay Alder, *A History of Jonathan Alder, His Captivity and Life with the Indians*, (Akron: University of Akron Press, 2002), 92, and "October 11, 1786 Letter from Simon Girty to Captain McKee," *Historical Collections*, Vol. 24, 34.
9. Faragher, *Daniel Boone*, 252, and *Draper Manuscript Collections*, "Interview Notes from Joseph Jackson," Draper Mss. 11C62(32–33) and see also Draper Mss. 9BB55.
10. *Draper Manuscript Collections*, "Statement of Judge Christopher Woods," Draper Mss. 8BB37.
11. *Draper Manuscript Collections*, "Interview Notes from Joseph Jackson," Draper Mss. 11C62(33), and "Statement of Judge Christopher Woods," Draper Mss. 8BB38.
12. *Draper Manuscript Collections*, "Statement of Abner Bryan," Draper Mss.4C50.
13. *Draper Manuscript Collections*, "Statement of Isaac Clinkenbeard," Draper Mss. 11CC3, and Draper Mss. 9BB57.
14. *Draper Manuscript Collections*, "Statement of Captain James McDowell in Courtsmartial of Hugh McGary," Draper Mss. 12S134.
15. Talbert, *Benjamin Logan*, 212.
16. *Draper Manuscript Collections*, "British Transmittal Letter for October 9, 1786, Message of Colonel Benjamin Logan to Shawanese Chiefs," Draper Mss. 23U, and Wheeler-Voegelin, *Indians of Ohio and Indiana*, Vol. 2, 269–276, 279, 287, and 288–289.
17. "October 11, 1786 Letter from Simon Girty to Captain McKee," *Historical Collections*, Vol. 24, 34.
18. *Draper Manuscript Collections*, "December 8, 1786, New York Newspaper," Draper Mss. 33J37
19. *Draper Manuscript Collections*, "October 9, 1786, Message of Colonel Benjamin Logan to Shawanese Chiefs," Draper Mss. 23U.
20. Talbert, *Benjamin Logan*, 213–214. See also *Draper Manuscript Collections*, Draper Mss. 12S133

Chapter Fourteen

1. Faragher, *Daniel Boone*, 255, and David I. Bushnell, Jr., "Daniel Boone at Limestone, 1786–1787," *The Virginia Magazine of History and Biography*, Volume XXV, January, 1917, 3.
2. Talbert, *Benjamin Logan*, 213; Bushnell, "Daniel Boone at Limestone," 2, 10–11; and *Draper Manuscript Collections*, "Statement of David Crouch," Draper Mss. 12CC229; "Statement of Mrs. John Poage," Draper Mss. 13CC213–215; and "October 27, 1786, Letter from Gentleman in Danville to his Correspondent in Richmond," Draper Mss. 33J36.
3. Netti Schreiner-Yantis and Florene Love, *The Personal Property Tax Lists for the Year 1787 for Fayette, County, Virginia (Now Kentucky)*, (Springfield, Va.: Genealogical Books in Print, 1985), 17.
4. Whitley Papers (Draper Mss. 9CC2).
5. Statement of Cornelius Washburn (Draper Mss. 19S82) and Bushnell, "Daniel Boone at Limestone," 1–11. There is no direct evidence that Micajah was one of the guards but this is likely given his familiarity with the Shawanese and his later involvement in the prisoner exchange.

6. It is possible if not likely that Noamohouoh was former saltboiler soldier Joseph Jackson. Jackson still lived among the Shawanese at this time and would have been a logical choice to coordinate the exchange with Daniel Boone and Micajah. Jackson had been named "Fish" by the Shawanese. Nonhelema told Major Ebenezer Denny that the Shawanese word for "fish" was: "Noameatha" (Denny, *Military Journal*, 279). Chief Black Hoof told C.C. Trowbridge that their word for "fish" was: "Nemaathau" (Kinietz and Voegelin, *Shawanese Traditions*, 69). There are obvious similarities between these two spellings and "Noamohouoh."
7. O'Malley, *Stockading Up*, 200.
8. *Draper Manuscript Collections*, Statement of John F. Shrylock (sp?) (Draper Mss. 11CC168).
9. David Bushnell states that Daniel Boone's voucher dated Aptil 27, 1787 was probably for Noamohouoh's visit to Limestone in Bushnell, "Daniel Boone at Limestone," 4.
10. "(Micajah) Was employed as interpreter in making a treaty at Limestone for the Exchange of prisoners . . ." See Callaway, "Declaration of Micajah Callaway." See also "Daniel Boone's 'Voucher of the Contingent Fund' dated August 27, 1787 for "Micagy Callaway Served twenty days as an Interpreter . . . 6 Pounds." found at Bushnell, "Daniel Boone at Limestone," 5.
11. Bushnell, "Daniel Boone at Limestone," 1–2.
12. *Draper Manuscript Collections*, "March 16, 1787, Letter from Daniel Boone to Colonel Patterson," Draper Mss. 26C176.
13. John Winter, *A Narrative of the Sufferings of Massy Harbison from Indian Barbarity*, (Beaver, 1836), 164; and *Draper Manuscript Collections*, "July 20, 1787 'New Haven Gazette,'" Draper Mss. 14C73; "May 17, 1787, Letter from Colonel Logan to Governor Randolph," Draper Mss. 33J108; and "June 11, 1787, Letter from Colonel Walter Crockett to Governor Randolph," Draper Mss. 33J94.
14. Jarod C. Lobdell, ed. *Further Materialson Lewis Wetzel and the Upper Ohio Frontier, the Historical Narrative of George Edginton, Peter Henry's Account, The Narrative of Spencer Records, The Reminiscences of Stephen Burkham*,(Bowie, Md.: Heritage Books, Inc., 1994), 67–68.
15. Bushnell, "Daniel Boone at Limestone," 6.
16. John Bakeless, *Daniel Boone: Master of the Wilderness* (New York: William Morrow & Company, 1939), 321, Kenton, *Simon Kenton*, 188, and *Draper Manuscript Collections*, "'The Kentucky Gazette,' August 25th, 1787," Draper Mss. 33S17–25.
17. *Draper Manuscript Collections*, "'The Kentucky Gazette,' August 25th, 1787," Draper Mss. 33S17–25.
18. *Draper Manuscript Collections*, "Statement of Judge Christopher Woods," Draper Mss. 8BB57–58, and "Statement of Cornelius Washburn," Draper Mss. 19S82.
19. Bond, *Correspondence of John Cleves Symmes*, 92.
20. Wheeler-Voegelin, *Indians of Ohio and Indiana*, Vol. 2, 224–226.
21. *Draper Manuscript Collections*, "Statement of Judge Christopher Woods," Draper Mss. 8BB70.
22. Sugden, *Blue Jacket*, 79–80.

Chapter Fifteen

1. Helderman, "Northwest Expedition," 332.
2. Ibid., 332.
3. Faragher, *Daniel Boone*, 257.
4. "Indian Speech to the Congress of the United States, December 18, 1786," *Historical Collections*, Vol. 11, 467.
5. Dillon, *History of Indiana*, 212–214.
6. Williams and Farrelly, *Diplomacy on the Indiana-Ohio Frontier*, 62–63.
7. Randall, "Ohio in Early History," 416–420, and Dillon, *History of Indiana*, 210–214.
8. John Sugden, *Tecumseh, A Life*, (New York: Henry Holt and Company, 1997), 49, and Helen Hornbeck Tanner, "Cherokees in the Ohio Country," *Journal of Cherokee Studies* 3, No. 2 (1978): 99.
9. Ridout, "An Account of my Capture," 7–27.
10. Callaway, "Declaration of Micajah Callaway," and Russell, "Micajah Callaway," 54.
11. Williams and Farrelly, *Diplomacy on the Indiana-Ohio Frontier*, 65, 67–68, and Sugden, *Blue Jacket*, 84.

Endnotes

12. Ernest A. Cruikshank, ed. *The Correspondence of Lieutenant Governor John Graves Simcoe*, Vol. 2. (Toronto: Ontario Historical Society, 1923–1931), 13–15.
13. Williams and Farrelly, *Diplomacy on the Indiana-Ohio Frontier*, 68–70; "Abstract of a Treaty at Fort Harmar," *Historical Collections*, Vol. 24, 41; and Randolph C. Downes, *Frontier Ohio, 1788–1803*, (Columbus: The Ohio State Archaeological and Historical Society, 1935), 10.
14. Bond, *Correspondence of John Cleves Symmes*, 61–65.
15. Ibid., 74–75.
16. Bond, *Correspondence of John Cleves Symmes*, 103–106.
17. John W. Van Cleve, "Van Cleve's Memoranda," *American Pioneer* 2, No. 4 (1843): 148 and Dillon, *History of Indiana*, 222–223.
18. Dillon, *History of Indiana*, 217–218, 220.
19. Wheeler-Voegelin, *Indians of Ohio and Indiana*, Vol. 2, 321, ftnt. 42.
20. *Draper Manuscript Collections*, "Statement of Judge Christopher Woods," Draper Mss. 8BB70.
21. Dillon, *History of Indiana*, 231.
22. Dillon, *History of Indiana*, 232–233, and Basil Meek, "General Harmar's Expedition," *Ohio Archaeological and Historical Quarterly* 20, No. 1 (1911), 77–79.
23. Meek, "General Harmar's Expedition," 79, 82–84, 91–92, 104–106, and "Additional News from Detroit (February, 1791)," *Historical Collections*, Vol. 24, 160.
24. Tanner, "The Glaize in 1792," 16; "Information of Captain Matthew Elliott (November 29, 1790)," *Historical Collections*, Vol. 24, 134; and Meek, "General Harmar's Expedition," 85–87, 106–107.
25. "Information of Blue Jacket (November 29, 1790)," *Historical Collections*, Vol. 24, 134, and Erminie Wheeler-Voegelin, *Indians of Northwest Ohio: An Ethnohistorical Report on the Wyandot, Potawatomi, Ottawa, and Chippewa of Northwest Ohio*, (New York & London: Garland Publishing, Inc., 1974), 229.
26. Van Cleve, "Van Cleve's Memoranda," 149.
27. Kenton, *Simon Kenton*, 202–203.
28. "Instructions given by H. Knox, Secretary of War, for the Protection of the Frontiers in the Ensuing Campaign," *Historical Collections*, Vol. 24, 186.
29. ". . . thinks he (Micajah) was not with Harmar, St. Clair, Scott nor Wilkinson—but in considerable scouting." See "Statement of James Callaway, Son of Micajah Callaway," Draper Mss. 25S257–261.
30. Cook and Cook, *Kentucky Court of Appeals*, Vol. 4, 580–581.
31. Micajah is identified as a resident of Amherst County in a September 16, 1791, indenture of his Bourbon County property to his brother John. See Cook and Cook, *Kentucky Court of Appeals*, Vol. 4, 580–581.
32. "Callaway Names Found in Virginia Personal Property Tax Lists, 1782–1800." *The Callaway Journal* 1 (1976): 35–36, and Ruth Sparacio and Sam Sparacio, *Virginia County Court Records: Amherst County, Virginia Land Tax Books 1789–1791*, (McLean, Va.: The Antient Press, 1997), 16, 51, and 87.
33. Hutton, "William Wells," 188.
34. Sugden, *Blue Jacket*, 118.
35. Hutton, "William Wells," 188.
36. Spencer, *Indian Captivity*, 89–93.
37. "Letter from William Darke to Mrs. Sarah Darke (November 1, 1791)," *Historical Collections*, Vol. 24, 331.
38. Sugden, *Blue Jacket*, 121–122.
39. Ibid., 123.
40. Hutton, "William Wells," 188.
42. Sugden, *Blue Jacket*, 124.

Chapter Sixteen

1. Wheeler-Voegelin, *Indians of Northwest Ohio*, 236–237.
2. Wheeler-Voegelin, *Indians of Northwest Ohio*, 245, and Sugden, *Blue Jacket*, 132.
3. Wheeler-Voegelin, *Indians of Northwest Ohio*, 270–272.
4. Sugden, *Blue Jacket*, 130.
5. Ibid., 134.
6. "Proceedings of a General Council of Indians (September 30-October 9, 1792," *Historical Collections*, Vol. 24, 483–498, and Wheeler-Voegelin, *Indians of Northwest Ohio*, 237–238.
7. Sugden, *Blue Jacket*, 138.
8. Colonel John R. Elting, *Military Uniforms in America: The Era of the American Revolution, 1755–1795*, (San Rafael, Ca.: Presidio Press, San Rafael, Ca., 1974), 122–123, 129–133.
9. Sugden, *Tecumseh, A Life*, 238.
10. "Kentucky County Tax Lists," *Callaway Family Association Journal* 9 (1984): 80–81.
11. Roseann R. Hogan, ed., "Buffaloes in the Corn: James Wade's Account of Pioneer Kentucky," *The Register of the Kentucky Historical Society* 89, No. 1 (1991): 21.
12. Enoch, In Search of Morgan's Station, 98–100.
13. "Reply of the Commissioners of the United States to the Indians," Historical Collections, Vol. 24, 579–585.
14. "Reply of the Indians to the Commissioners of the United States," *Historical Collections*, Vol. 24, 587–592.
15. "Commissioners of the United States to the Chiefs of the Indian Nations," *Historical Collections*, Vol. 24, 592–593.
16. Wheeler-Voegelin, *Indians of Northwest Ohio*, 241–242.
17. R.C. McGrane, "William Clark's Journal of General Wayne's Campaign," *The Mississippi Valley Historical Review* 1 (1915): 421, ftnt. 13.
18. Hutton, "William Wells," 189–190.
19. McDonald, Biographical Sketches, 183–185.
20. Corbitt and Corbitt, "Papers from the Spanish Archives," 93.
21. Leland R. Johnson, "The Doyle Mission to Massac, 1794," *Journal of the Illinois Historical Society* 73, No. 1 (1980): 2–3, and Corbitt and Corbitt, "Papers from the Spanish Archives," 93, ftnt. 36.
22. Sugden, *Blue Jacket*, 160, and Johnson, "Doyle Mission to Massac," 5.
23. Ernest A. Cruikshank, ed. "The Diary of an Officer in the Indian Country in 1794." *Magazine of Western History* 11, 384–385.
24. Richard C. Knopf, ed., "Wayne's Western Campaign, The Wayne-Knox Correspondence 1793–1794, Part II," *The Pennsylvania Magzine of History and Biography* 78, No. 4 (1954): 425.
25. Johnson, "Doyle Mission to Massac," 9–16.
26. Downes, *Frontier Ohio*, 40–41.
27. Paul David Nelson, *Anthony Wayne: Soldier of the Early Republic*, (Bloomington, Ind.: Indiana University Press, 1985), 258; Murtie June Clark, *American Militia in the Frontier Wars*. (Baltimore: Genealogical Publishing Co., 1990), 42; and *Draper Manuscript Collections*, "July 16, 1794 order from General Wayne to General Todd re First Division of Mounted Kentucky Volunteers -Orderly Book, p. 36," Draper Mss. 16U.
28. *Draper Manuscript Collections*, "July 18, 1794 Letter from Gen. Todd to Gen. Wayne -Orderly Book, p. 40," Draper Mss. 16U.
29. Clark, *American Militia*, 42, and *Draper Manuscript Collections*, "Statement of Colonel William Sudduth," Draper Mss. 12CC90.
30. Micajah and his brother Edmund are both listed as privates on the muster role of Captain Joshua Baker's Company of spies and scouts in Major Notley Conn's Battalion (Clark, *American Militia*, 43). Micajah's Pension Application states that he served as a spy under General Wayne for four months (*Draper Manuscript Collections*, Draper Mss. 100147). The Kentucky mounted volunteers that enlisted in June 1794 were discharged in October 23, 1794, a period of four months (*Draper Manuscript Collections*, Draper Mss.16U107).

Endnotes 423

31. Heffren, "Pioneer Pickings No. 36," 7.
32. Kenton, *Simon Kenton*, 231.
33. *Draper Manuscript Collections*, "Statements of Colonel William Sudduth," Draper Mss. 12CC63 and 12CC90.
34. *Draper Manuscript Collections*, "Statement of Colonel William Sudduth," Draper Mss. 12CC90; "Orderly Book," Draper Mss. 16U46; and "Journal of Nathaniel Hart," Draper Mss. 5U93.
35. *Draper Manuscript Collections*, "July 12, 1794, Order from Gen. Todd to Maj. Price -Orderly Book, p. 32," Draper Mss. 16U, and "July 19, 1794 Order from Gen. Todd to Maj. Conn -Orderly Book, p. 43–44," Draper Mss. 16U.
36. *Draper Manuscript Collections*, "July 27, 1794 General Order for the Volunteers from Maj. Gen. Scott -Orderly Book, p. 26," Draper Mss. 16U60,66. See also *Draper Manuscript Collections*, "Statement of Colonel William Sudduth," Draper Mss. 12CC91.
37. "General Anthony Wayne's General Orders, 1792–1797," *Historical Collections: Pioneer and Historical Society of the State of Michigan*, V01.34 (Lansing: Robert Smith & Co., 1905), 530–532.
38. McGrane, "William Clark's Journal," 419.
39. John S. Williams, ed., "Daily Journal of Wayne's Campaign," *The American Pioneer, a Monthly Periodical* 1, No. 7 (1844): 315.
40. McGrane, "William Clark's Journal," 424, and *Draper Manuscript Collections*, "Orders for August 10, 1794. Orderly Book, p. 48," Draper Mss. 16U69, and "Orders for August 12, 1794. Orderly Book, p. 52," Draper Mss. 16U.
41. McGrane, "William Clark's Journal," 424–425; McDonald, *Biographical Sketches*, 193; and *Draper Manuscript Collections*, "Statement of William Curry, Jr.," Draper Mss. 13CC150–151, and "Statement of Colonel William Sudduth," Draper Mss. 12CC90.
42. *Draper Manuscript Collections*, "Orders for August 11, 1794. Orderly Book, p. 51," Draper Mss. 16U.
43. *Draper Manuscript Collections*, "Statement of Colonel William Sudduth," Draper Mss. 12CC91.
44. Dresden W.H. Howard, "Battle of Fallen Timbers as told by Chief Kin-jo-i-no," *Northwest Ohio Quarterly* 20, No. 1 (1948): 40–48.
45. Howe, *Historical Collections of Ohio*, Vol. 1, 300–301.
46. Micajah Callaway recounted that his immediate, first-level commanding officer had been seriously wounded in the battle and that his second-level commanding officer was not informed by the first level officer when Micajah discovered the main body of the Indians on August 20. See Russell, "Micajah Callaway," 55–56. The only officers below the rank of Captain that were injured among the Kentucky volunteers were Lieutenant McKenney and Ensign Duncan, according to General Wayne's report of the engagement to Secretary Knox. See Dillon, *History of Indiana*, 347–350. As the officer described by Micajah does not appear to be as junior as an Ensign, Lieutenant McKenney appears likely to have been the officer who commanded Micajah's unit during the battle.
47. McGrane, "William Clark's Journal," 427, and *Draper Manuscript Collections*, "Statement of Colonel William Sudduth," Draper Mss. 12CC91.
48. Historian John B. Dillon stated that the total number of warriors was fourteen hundred broken down by Indian nation as follows: Four hundred and fifty Delaware, one hundred and seventy five Miamis, two hundred and seventy five Shawanese, two hundred and seventy five Ottawas, two hundred and seventy five Wyandots and smaller numbers of Chippewas, Potawatomis, and Senecas. See Dillon, *History of Indiana*, 349, ftnt.
49. *Draper Manuscript Collections*, Draper Mss. 19S255 and 11YY2, and "Statement of Reverend Charles Blue Jacket," Draper Mss. 23S170.
50. Russell, "Micajah Callaway," 55–56.
51. *Draper Manuscript Collections*, "Statement of Colonel William Sudduth," Draper Mss. 12CC91–93.
52. Dillon, *History of Indiana*, 348.
53. Accounts of Micajah's retreat describe him as running rather than riding his horse. As he was a member of the mounted Corps of volunteer scouts and spies, the fact that he ran appears to indicate that he probably lost his horse during the battle. *Draper Manuscript Collections*, "Interview Notes from John Hawkins Callaway, Son of Micajah Callaway," Draper Mss. 25S124.
54. *Draper Manuscript Collections*, "Statement of Colonel William Sudduth," Draper Mss. 12CC92.

55. Dwight L. Smith, *From Greenville to Fallen Timbers*, (Indianapolis: Indiana Historical Society, 1952), 289–290.
56. *Draper Manuscript Collections*, "Interview Notes from John Hawkins Callaway, Son of Micajah Callaway," Draper Mss. 25S124.
57. Smith, *Greenville to Fallen Timbers*, 297.
58. *Draper Manuscript Collections*, "Journal of Captain Thomas T. Underwood, p. 31," Draper Mss. 16U130.
59. *Draper Manuscript Collections*, Draper Mss. 19S255.
60. Dillon, *History of Indiana*, 348–349.
61. Milo M. Quaife, "General James Wilkinson's Narrative of the Fallen Timbers Campaign," *The Mississippi Valley Historical Review* 16 (1929–1930), 84.
62. *Draper Manuscript Collections*, Draper Mss. 19S246.
63. Smith, *Greenville to Fallen Timbers*, 293.
64. *Draper Manuscript Collections*, Draper Mss. 19S255–256.
65. Alder, *History of Jonathan Alder*, 115.
66. *Draper Manuscript Collections*, "Statement of Colonel William Sudduth," Draper Mss. 12CC92–93.
67. Sugden, *Tecumseh, A Life*, 90.
68. *Draper Manuscript Collections*, Draper Mss. 19S246.
69. Russell, "Micajah Callaway," 55–56.
70. Dillon, *History of Indiana*, 351, 354, 355.
71. *Draper Manuscript Collections*, "Statement of Colonel William Sudduth," Draper Mss. 12CC94.
72. Cruikshank, *Correspondence of Simcoe*, Vol. 3, 294.
73. *Draper Manuscript Collections*, Draper Mss. 11YY169.
74. Sugden, *Tecumseh, A Life*, 97.
75. Sugden, *Blue Jacket*, 214–216.
76. McDonald, *Biographical Sketches*, 60–64, and Sugden, *Blue Jacket*, 205.
77. Sugden, *Blue Jacket*, 253.
78. Mary Arnold's date of birth and the identity of her parents and siblings are not clear. It is possible that she was the Mary Arnold who was the daughter of Humphrey Arnold, a resident of Lincoln County at this time who lived near the Dicks River in the general vicinity of Logan's Fort. A James Arnold owned a station where the Alanantowamiowee Trail crossed the Kentucky River to the east of Lafayette County. See O'Malley, *Stockading Up*, 213–215.
79. Records regarding the exact date and location of their marriage have not been found. Indirect evidence indicates that it probably took place in 1796 in either Clark County or the adjacent Fayette County. See Russell, "Micajah Callaway," 57.
80. "Kentucky County Tax Lists," 80.
81. "Early Settlements in Clark County." *The Winchester (Kentucky) Sun*, June 14, 1923.

Chapter Seventeen

1. Gary W. Beahan, "Bound for the Promised Land: Tracing the Migration to Missouri, 1799–1849," *Callaway Family Association Journal* 10 (1985): 12–13, and *Draper Manuscript Collections*, "Statement of Colonel Nathan Boone, Son of Daniel Boone," Draper Mss. 6S213.
2. *Draper Manuscript Collections*, "Statement of Colonel Nathan Boone, Son of Daniel Boone," Draper Mss. 6S214–215.
3. Callaway, "Flanders," 21.
4. *Draper Manuscript Collections*, "Statement of Colonel Nathan Boone, Son of Daniel Boone," Draper Mss. 6S215, 221–222.
5. Bakeless, *Daniel Boone*, 360.
6. *Draper Manuscript Collections*, "Statement of Colonel Nathan Boone, Son of Daniel Boone," Draper Mss. 6S223.
7. *Draper Manuscript Collections*, "List of Associates of Daniel Boone (in French)," Draper Mss. 27C68.

Endnotes

8. *Draper Manuscript Collections*, "Statement of Colonel Nathan Boone, Son of Daniel Boone," Draper Mss. 6S223.
9. Bakeless, *Daniel Boone*, 360.
10. *Draper Manuscript Collections*, "Statement of Colonel Nathan Boone, Son of Daniel Boone," Draper Mss. 6S223–224.
11. The estimated date of birth of Micajah Callaway's son James Callaway in late 1799 is deduced from the 1850 and 1860 censuses in Bartholomew County, Indiana, and the 1870 census in Jackson County, Indiana. In each of those censuses he is identified as fifty, sixty and seventy years old, respectively, with the location of his birth listed as Missouri.
12. Callaway, "Flanders," 22. See also statement that Nathan Boone property was four miles upstream from Daniel Morgan Boone's property (Hurt, *Nathan Boone*, 31).
13. Faragher, *Daniel Boone*, 280.
14. Micajah Callaway, "Application for Land in Spanish Louisiana, January 23, 1798," Records of the Missouri Historical Society.
15. "Registre de Arpentage pour les terres St. Charles, du Missour river, gauche A, 1799." In *French and Spanish Land Grants, Territory of Louisiana, Vol. A*.
16. "Kentucky County Tax Lists," 80.
17. "Calloway Cemetery, Inc." *The Callaway Journal* 1 (1976), 25.
18. *Draper Manuscript Collections*, "Statement of Nathan Boone Son of Daniel Boone," Draper Mss. 6S230–231, and "Statement of Mrs. Susan Howell," Draper Mss. 23S221.
19. Russell, "Micajah Callaway," 58.
20. Ibid., 58.
21. Callaway, "Flanders," 20.
22. Russell, "Micajah Callaway," 55, 58.
23. Elliot Coves, ed. *The History of the Lewis and Clark Expedition*. Vol. 1. (Francis P. Harper, 1893), 7–8.
24. Wilson and Thornbrough, *Buffalo Trace*, 217.
25. George Pence and Nellie C. Armstrong, *Indiana Boundaries: Territory, State and County*, (Indianapolis: Indiana Historical Bureau, 1967), 2–3.
26. Dillon, *History of Indiana*, 414.
27. The Buffalo Trace followed a winding course from Vincennes to Clarksville. See Wilson and Thornbrough, *Buffalo Trace*, 217, 229.
28. Erminie Wheeler-Voegelin, Emily J. Blasingham, and Dorothy R. Libby, *Miami, Wea, and Eel-River Indians of Southern Indiana: An Anthropological report on the Miami, Wea, and Eel-River Indians*, (New York & London: Garland Publishing, Inc., 1974), 242.
29. Cauthorn, *Vincennes Indiana*, 25–29.
30. Wheeler-Voegelin, Blasingham, and Libby, *Miami, Wea, and Eel-River Indians*, 250–251, 255.
31. Wilson and Thornbrough, *Buffalo Trace*, 222.
32. Libby, *An Anthropological Report*, http://www.gbl.indiana.edu/archives/dockett_99/d99toc.html and Tanner, *Atlas*, Map 18.
33. "Statement of Cuthbert Combs," *Draper Manuscript Collections*, Draper Mss. 11CC80, and "Statement of Major Ben Daniels," *Draper Manuscript Collections*, Draper Mss. 11CC92–93.
34. Callaway, "Marriage Bond."
35. Micahel L. Cook. *Lincoln County Kentucky Records*. Vol. 1. (Evansville, Ind.: Cook Publications, 1987), 50.
36. "Records of County Tax Collector, Garrard Co. Ky., 1797–1806," Film # 000 7988, LDS Library, Salt Lake City S-599.
37. "Kentucky County Tax Lists," 80, and Russell, "Micajah Callaway," 58.

Chapter Eighteen

1. Wheeler-Voegelin, Blasingham, and Libby, *Miami, Wea, and Eel-River Indians*, 266-274.
2. John D. Barnhart and Dorothy L. Riker, *Indiana to 1816: The Colonial Period* (Indianapolis: Indiana Historical Bureau and Indiana Historical Society, 1971), 364, and Warder W. Stevens, *Centennial History of Washington County Indiana*, (Indianapolis: B.F. Bowen & Company, Inc., 1916), 69, 75.
3. Stevens, *Centennial History*, 73, 153, 545-546.
4. Ruth Dinn and Chelsea Dinn. *Frederick Royse, 1750-1825, Revolutionary War Militiaman*. (Franklin, Ind.: Ruth & Chelsea Dinn), 1, 18, 46-47.
5. *Draper Manuscript Collections*, "Statement of Lucy Clark," Draper Mss. 25S118 and 25S134.
6. *Archaeological and Historical Survey of Indiana, 1924, Washington Township, Washington County, Book I*, (Indianapolis: Indiana Historical Commission and The Division of Geology of the Department of Conservation, 1924), 41.
7. Paul L. Stevens, *Louis Lorimier in the American Revolution: A Memoire by an Ohio Indian Trader and British Partisan. (Center for French Colonial Studies Extended Publications Series Number 2)*, (Naperville, Ill.: The Center for French Colonial Studies, Inc.), 49-50.
8. Stevens, *Louis Lorimier*, 50
9. Stevens, *Centennial History*, 228, and Nellie Armstrong Robertson and Dorothy Riker, *The John Tipton Papers*, Vol. 1, (Indianapolis: Indiana Historical Bureau, 1942), 92, ftnt. 63.
10. Guernsey, *Indiana: Influence of the Indians Upon its History*, a Map.
11. Howard, *Shawnee: Ceremonialism*, 199-203.
12. "Proceedings of a Private Meeting with the Shawenoes, Amherstburgh, 25th March 1808," *Historical Collections*, Vol. 25, 242-244.
13. Sugden, *Tecumseh, A Life*, 120, and Sugden, *Blue Jacket*, 282, ftnt. 4.
14. Sugden, *Tecumseh, A Life*, 173, and Sugden, *Blue Jacket*, 282, ftnt. 4.
15. Janet C. Cowen, *Jeffersonville Land Entries 1808-1818*. (Utica, Ky.: McDowell Publications, 1984), 31.
16. Logan Esarey, ed., *Governors Messages and Letters: Messages and Letters of William Henry Harrison*, VOl.1, (Indianapolis: Indiana Historical Commission, 1922), 417-419.
17. Sugden, *Tecumseh, A Life*, 195.
18. Esarey, *Governors Messages and Letters*, Vol. 1, 453-454, 458.
19. Dillon, *History of Indiana*, 446.
20. Harlow Lindley, *Indiana as Seen by Early Travelers*, (Indianapolis: Indiana Historical Commission, 1916), 31.
21. *Indiana History Bulletin: Archaeological and Historical Survey of Washington County*, (Indianapolis: William B. Burford, 1924), 45.
22. *Indiana History Bulletin*, 45.
23. Ibid., 45.
24. Stevens, *Centennial History*, 498, 542, and Horace Heffren, "Pioneer Pickings No. 82," Salem, Ind.: *The Salem Democrat*, January 3, 1877. Reprint, *Pioneer Pickings*. Salem, Ind.: James E. Bolding, 1993), 101-102.
25. The term "Hoosiers" has been a term used for the residents of the State of Indiana since early pioneer times. The origin of the term is obscure and has never been identified with any certainty or consensus.
26. Stevens, *Centennial History*, 498.
27. Dillon, *History of Indiana*, 451-452.
28. Ibid., 453.
29. Esarey, *Governors Messages and Letters*, Vol. 1, 548.
30. Dillon, *History of Indiana*, 456-457.
31. Horace Heffren, "Pioneer Pickings No. 95," (Salem, Ind.: *The Salem Democrat*, April 4, 1877. Reprint, *Pioneer Pickings*. Salem, Ind.: James E. Bolding, 1993), 127-128.
32. Stevens, *Centennial History*, 196.
33. Esarey, *Governors Messages and Letters*, Vol. 1, 699, and Dillon, *History of Indiana*, 461-463.
34. Robertson and Riker, *John Tipton Papers*, Vol. 1, 134, ftnt. 30, and Stevens, *Centennial History*, 234.

Endnotes

35. Esarey, *Governors Messages and Letters*, V01.1, 699, and Dillon, *History of Indiana*, 461–463, 465.
36. John Tipton, "John Tipton's Tippecanoe Journal," The *Indiana Quarterly Magazine of History* 2 (1906, Reprint, New York: Kraus Reprint Corporation, 1967): 180–181.
37. C.A. Weslager, *The Delaware Indians: A History*, (New Brunswick, N.J.: Rutgers University Press, 1972), 345.
38. *Indiana History Bulletin*, 46.
39. Esarey, *Governors Messages and Letters*, Vol. 2, 274, 276, and Guernsey, "Indiana: Influence of the Indians Upon its History," Map.
40. Esarey, *Governors Messages and Letters*, Vol. 2, p. 275.
41. Stevens, *Centennial History*, 523–526; Esarey, *Governors Messages and Letters*, Vol. 2, 274; and Guernsey, "Indiana: Influence of the Indians Upon its History," Map.
42. Esarey, *Governors Messages and Letters*, Vol. 2, 275.
43. Dillon, *History of Indiana*, 482.
44. Esarey, *Governors Messages and Letters*, Vol. 2, 276.
45. Robertson and Riker, *John Tipton Papers*, Vol. 1, 91, ftnt. 59.
46. Ibid., 91–95.
47. Horace Heffren, "Pioneer Pickings No. 99," (Salem, Ind.: *The Salem Democrat*, May 2, 1877. Reprint, *Pioneer Pickings*. Salem, Ind.: James E. Bolding, 1993), 135–136.

Chapter Nineteen

1. Esarey, *Governors Messages and Letters*, Vol. 2, 58–59.
2. Tanner, *Atlas*, 116, and Dillon, *History of Indiana*, 486.
3. C. Edward Skeen, *Citizen Soldiers in the War of 1812*, (Lexington, Ky.: The University Press of Kentucky, 1999), 80, and Tanner, *Atlas*, 116.
4. Sugden, *Tecumseh, A Life*, 283–284.
5. Pierre Berton, *The Invasion of Canada, Vol. 1: 1812–1813* (Boston: Little, Brown and Company, 1980), 174–175, and Dillon, *History of Indiana*, 487–488.
6. Sugden, *Tecumseh, A Life*, 300.
7. Logan Esarey, ed., *History of Indiana from its Exploration to 1922*. (Dayton: Dayton Historical Publishing Co., 1923), 217, and Hutton, "William Wells," 218–220.
8. Esarey, *Governors Messages and Letters*, Vol. 2, 71.
9. Esarey, *Governors Messages and Letters*, Vol. 2, 117.
10. *Draper Manuscript Collections*, "Statement of James Chambers," Draper Mss. 22S80, and "Statement of Charles Tucker," Draper Mss. 23S175–177. See also Draper Mss. 17S272.
11. Berton, *Invasion of Canada*, 271–273, 278.
12. Dillon, *History of Indiana*, 489–491.
13. Esarey, *History of Indiana*, 221.
14. Sugden, *Tecumseh, A Life*, 316; Guernsey, *Indiana: Influence of the Indians Upon its History*, a Map; Constance A. Hackman, Leona M. Lawson, and Kenneth R. Scott, *The Collings, Richeys and the Pigeon Roost Massacre*, (Alice Rebecca Scott, 1980), 33; and Stevens, *Centennial History*, 50.
15. Hackman, Lawson, and Scott, *Pigeon Roost Massacre*, 2, 3, 10–13, 17–21, 33–41, and Stevens, *Centennial History*, 493.
16. Stevens, *Centennial History*, 493–494, 544–545, 555–556.
17. Esarey, *Governors Messages and Letters*, Vol. 2, 277.
18. Hackman, Lawson, and Scott, Pigeon Roost Massacre, 9.
19. Esarey, *Governors Messages and Letters*, Vol. 2, 277.
20. Ibid., 377–378.
21. Berton, *Invasion of Canada*, 285–299.
22. Stevens, *Centennial History*, 542.
23. Robertson and Riker, *John Tipton Papers*, Vol. 1, 105–106, and Esarey, *Governors Messages and Letters*, Vol. 2, 280–281.
24. Robertson and Riker, *John Tipton Papers*, Vol. 1, 107–108.

25. Dillon, *History of Indiana*, 520–525.
26. This is just north of present-day Lafayette, Indiana. See Horace Heffren, "Pioneer Pickings No. 48," (Salem, Ind.: *The Salem Democrat*, March 22, 1876. Reprint, *Pioneer Pickings*. Salem, Ind.: James E. Bolding, 1993), 31, and Esarey, *Governors Messages and Letters*, Vol. 2, 497.
27. Anderson Chenault Quisenberry, *Kentucky in the War of 1812*, (Baltimore: Genealogical Publishing Company, 1969), 158–159.
28. Faragher, *Daniel Boone*, 89–96.
29. Heffren, "Pioneer Pickings No. 48," 31
30. *Draper Manuscript Collections*, "Interview Notes from James Callaway, Son of Micajah Callaway," Draper Mss. 25S257–161.
31. Dillon, *History of Indiana*, 524–525; Barnhart and Riker, *Indiana to 1816*, 405; and Esarey, *Governors Messages and Letters*, Vol. 2, 497–498.
32. Dorothy Burne Goebel, *William Henry Harrison: A Political Biography*, (Indianapolis: Historical Bureau of the Indiana Library and Historical Department, 1926), 174.
33. Kenton, *Simon Kenton*, 284.
34. James Wallace Hammack, Jr., *Kentucky and the Second American Revolution: The War of 1812*, (Lexington: The University Press of Kentucky, 1976), 78.
35. Quisenberry, *Kentucky in the War of 1812*, 189, and *Draper Manuscript Collections*, "Letter from James Callaway to Lyman Draper (1857)," Draper Mss. 24C67.
36. *Draper Manuscript Collections*, "Letter from James Callaway to Lyman Draper (1857)," Draper Mss. 24C67.
37. *Draper Manuscript Collections*, Draper Mss. 31CC218.
38. *Draper Manuscript Collections*, "Interview from Richard French (Grandson of Col. Richard Callaway)," Draper Mss. 12CC202–203.
39. *Draper Manuscript Collections*, "Letter from James Callaway to Lyman Draper (1857)," Draper Mss. 24C67–68.
40. Quisenberry, *Kentucky in the War of 1812*, 187.
41. Micah Taul, "Memoirs of Micah Taul," *The Register of the Kentucky State Historical Society* 27, No. 79 (1929): 377–378.
42. Sandy Antal, *Wampum Denied: Procter's War of 1812*, (Ottawa: Carleton University Press, 1997), 317.
43. Goebel, *William Henry Harrison*, 179.
44. *Draper Manuscript Collections*, Draper Mss. 19S245
45. Goebel, *William Henry Harrison*, 180; Antal, *Wampum Denied*, 316; and Quisenberry, *Kentucky in the War of 1812*, 102–103.
46. Quisenberry, *Kentucky in the War of 1812*, 102–103, and Hammack, *Kentucky and War of 1812*, 81.
47. Goebel, *William Henry Harrison*, 182.
48. Antal, Wampum Denied, 334–337.
49. Hammack, *Kentucky and War of 1812*, 82, and Antal, *Wampum Denied*, 340.
50. Goebel, *William Henry Harrison*, 182; Antal, *Wampum Denied*, 340–344; Quisenberry, *Kentucky in the War of 1812*, 102–105, 187, and 189; and *Draper Manuscript Collections*, Draper Mss. 31CC218.
51. Hammack, *Kentucky and War of 1812*, 82–83, and Antal, *Wampum Denied*, 346–348.
52. *Draper Manuscript Collections*, Draper Mss. 19S247.
53. Faragher, *Daniel Boone*, 306.

Chapter Twenty

1. Stevens, *Centennial History*, 542, 544, 581.
2. Charles M. Franklin, *Indiana Territorial Pioneer Records: 1801–1820*. Vol. 2, (Indianapolis: Heritage House, 1985,),
3. *Salem Indiana through One Hundred and Seventy-Five Years*, (Salem, Ind.: Salem Historical Society, Leader Publishing Company, 1989), 7.
4. Robert M. Taylor, *Indiana: A New Historical Guide*. (Indianapolis: Indiana Historical Society, 1989), 172.

Endnotes

5. Robertson and Riker, *John Tipton Papers*, Vol. 1, 111, ftnt. 9.
6. Richard Lowitt, "Activities of Citizen Genet in Kentucky 1793-1794," *The Filson Club History Quarterly* 22, No. 4 (1948): 258-261.
7. *Washington County, Indiana, Deed Book A*, 378-379.
8. Morris Birkbeck, *Notes on a Journey in America from the Coast of Virginia to the Territory of Illinois* (London: Severn & Co., 1818), 91.
9. S.S. Knabenshue, "Indian Land Cessions in Ohio," Ohio Archaeological and Historical Quarterly 11, No. 2 (1902): 254.
10. Nenessica (Naneskaka) was still living in Wapakoneta in 1816 See Toni Jollay Prevost, *The Delaware and Shawnee Admitted to Cherokee Citizenship and the Related Wyandott and Moravian Delaware*, (Bowie, Md.: Heritage Books, Inc., 1993), 3.
11. Denny, Military Journal, 277-281.
12. *History of Washington County, Indiana, 1916-1976*, (Evansville, Ind.: Washington Cunty Historical Society, Unigraphic, Inc. 1976), 513-514. The story of the visiting Indians is also a Callaway family oral tradition passed on to the author by Roy Callaway, a direct descendant of Micajah and Edmund Callaway. The account of Micajah's conversation with Nenessica and the white wampum string is fictitious and was included for symbolic effect.
13. Russell, "Micajah Callaway," 59.
14. Horace Heffren, "Pioneer Pickings No. 90," (Salem, Ind.: *The Salem Democrat*, February 28, 1877. Reprint, *Pioneer Pickings*. Salem, Ind.: James E. Bolding, 1993), 117.
15. Russell, "Micajah Callaway," 56.
16. Denny, *Military Journal*, 279.
17. Stevens, *Centennial History*, 192, 548.
18. *Indiana History Bulletin*, 59.
19. *Map of Washington County, Indiana*. (New York: P. O'Beirne & Co., 1860).
20. Russell, "Micajah Callaway," 58-59.
21. Michael L. Cook and Bettie A. Cook. *Kentucky Court of Appeals Deed Books H-N*. Vol. 2. (Evansville, Ind.: Cook Publications, 1985), 218, and Evans, *Boone Scout* 7, No. 1.
22. James E. Calloway, "Virginia-Kentucky-Missouri." *The Callaway Journal* 10 (1985): 33.
23. Faragher, *Daniel Boone*, 294-295.
24. Ibid., xiv, 358-359.
25. Prucha, *Documents of United States Indian Policy*, 47.
26. Ibid., 50-51.
27. Ibid., 52.
28. *Draper Manuscript Collections*, "'The Siege of the Old Indian Town of Piqua,' Springfield Republic, June 17, 1859," Draper Mss. 8J210.
29. Knabenshue, "Indian Land Cessions," 254.
30. *Draper Manuscript Collections*, "Statement of Ka-che-qua or Mrs. Carpenter," Draper Mss. 23S164' "Statement of Rev. Charles Blue Jacket," Draper Mss. 23S170, and "Statement of Charles Tucker," Draper Mss. 23S173.
31. *Draper Manuscript Collections*, "Statement of Moses Silverheels," Draper Mss. 23S165, and "Statement of Rev. Charles Blue Jacket," Draper Mss. 23S167.
32. Howe, *Historical Collections of Ohio*, Vol. 1, 299.
33. Russell, "Micajah Callaway" 55.
34. *Draper Manuscript Collections*, "March 12, 1849 Letter from Lyman Draper to Micajah Callaway," Draper Mss. 14C117.
35. *Draper Manuscript Collections*, "April 9, 1849 Letter to Lyman C. Draper from Leonard Bliss," Draper Mss. 24C118.
36. Russell, "Micajah Callaway," 59.
37. *Salem Indiana*, 36.

Appendix A

1. Sugden, *Blue Jacket*, 282, Note 4.
2. *Draper Manuscript Collections*, Draper Mss. 11CC80, 92–93.
3. Stevens, *Louis Lorimier*, 4.
4. *Draper Manuscript Collections*, Draper Mss. 11YY37(3) and 11C62(16).
5. Sugden, *Blue Jacket*, 282, Note 4.
6. Ranck, *Boonesborough*, 65; Schaaf, *Wampum Belts*, 68, 131, 163; and *Draper Manuscript Collections*, "Interview Notes from Joseph Jackson," Draper Mss. 11C62(1) and (10).
7. Stevens, *Louis Lorimier*, 15, 31.
8. *Draper Manuscript Collections*, "Statement of Joseph Jackson," Draper Mss. 11C62(16).
9. *Draper Manuscript Collections*, "Statement of Joseph Jackson," Draper Mss. 11C62(22).
10. Callaway, "Declaration of Micajah Callaway."
11. Callaway, "Declaration of Micajah Callaway."
12. *Journals of the Continental Congress*, 529, Continental Congress Broadside Collection, Library of Congress.
13. Callaway, "Declaration of Micajah Callaway."
14. Craig, *Olden Times*, Vol. 2, 529.
15. Ridout, "An Account of my Capture," 7, 14.
16. Wheeler-Voegelin, *Indians of Northwest Ohio*, 224.
17. Bond, *Correspondence of John Cleves Symmes*, 74–75.
18. Sugden, *Blue Jacket*, 86.
19. Cruikshank, "Diary of an Officer," 384–385.
20. Sugden, *Blue Jacket*, 199.
21. Ibid., 212.
22. Sugden, *Tecumseh, A Life*, 120, and Sugden, *Blue Jacket*, 282, ftnt. 4.
23. *Draper Manuscript Collections*, Draper Mss. 11CC80, 92–93.
24. "Proceedings of a Private Meeting with the Shawenoes, Amherstburgh, 25th March 1808," *Historical Collections*, Vol. 25, 242–244.
25. Sugden, *Tecumseh, A Life*, 173, and Sugden, *Blue Jacket*, 282, ftnt. 4.
26. Prevost, *Delaware and Shawnee*, 3.
27. *History of Washington County, Indiana*, 513–514.

Bibliography

Alder, Henry Clay. *A History of Jonathan Alder, His Captivity and Life with the Indians.* Akron: University of Akron Press, 2002.

Amherst County, Va. Will Book 3 (1786–1800).

Antal, Sandy. *A Wampum Denied: Procter's War of 1812.* Ottawa: Carleton University Press, 1997.

"Archaeological and Historical Survey of Indiana, 1924, Washington Township, Washington County, Book I." Indianapolis: Indiana Historical Commission and The Division of Geology of the Department of Conservation, 1924.

Arnow, Harriette Simpson. *Seedtime on the Cumberland.* Lincoln: University of Nebraska Press, 1960.

Bailey, Kenneth P. *Christopher Gist.* Hamden, Conn.: Archon Books, an imprint of the Shoestring Press, Inc., 1976.

Bakeless, John. *Daniel Boone: Master of the Wilderness.* New York: William Morrow & Company, 1939.

Baker-Crothers, Hayes. *Virginia and the French and Indian War.* Chicago: University of Chicago Press, 1928.

Barnhart, John D. and Dorothy L. Riker. *Indiana to 1816: The Colonial Period.* Indianapolis: Indiana Historical Bureau and Indiana Historical Society, 1971.

Beahan, Gary W. "Bound for the Promised Land: Tracing the Migration to Missouri, 1799–1849." *Callaway Family Association Journal* 10 (1985): 11–17.

Beckner, Lucien. "John D. Shane's Interview with Benjamin Allen, Clark County." *The Filson Club History Quarterly* 5, No. 2 (1931): 63–98.

___. "Eskippakithiki: The Last Indian Town in Kentucky." *The Filson Club Quarterly* 6, No. 4 (1932). 355–382.

Bedford, A. Goff. *Land of Our Fathers: History of Clark County, Kentucky.* Mt. Sterling, Ky.: Dr. A. Goff Bedford, 1958.

Bedford County, Virginia Deed Book 5.

Bedford County, Virginia Order Book 3.

Bedford County, Virginia Order Book 6.

Belue, Ted Franklin. "Did Daniel Boone Kill Pompey, the Black Shawnee, at the 1778 Siege of Fort Boonesborough?" *The Filson Club History Quarterly* 67, No. 1 (1993): 5–22.

___. "Terror in the Canelands: The Fate of Daniel Boone's Salt Boilers." *The Filson Club History Quarterly* 68, No. 1 (1994): 3–34.

Berton, Pierre. *The Invasion of Canada, Vol. 1: 1812–1813.* Boston: Little, Brown and Company, 1980.

Birkbeck, Morris. *Notes on a Journey in America from the Coast of Virginia to the Territory of Illinois.* London: Severn & Co., 1818.

Bond, Beverley W., Jr., ed. *The Correspondence of John Cleves Symmes, Founder of the Miami Purchase.* New York: The Macmillan Company, 1926.

___. "The Captivity of Charles Stuart, 1755–57." *The Mississippi Valley Historical Review* 13 (1926–1927): 58–81.

"Bowman's Expedition Against Chillicothe. Draper Mss. 5D." *Ohio Archaeological and Historical Publications* 19 (1910): 446–459.

"Bowman's Campaign of 1779, Draper Mss., The Bedinger Papers, 'A,' Volume 1." *Ohio Archaeological and Historical Publications* 22 (1913): 502–519.

Boyd, Julian, ed. *The Papers of Thomas Jefferson*. Vol. 2. Princeton, N.J.: University Press, 1950.

Brackinridge, Hugh H., ed. *Indian Atrocities: Narratives of the Perils and Sufferings of Dr. Knight and John Slover, Among the Indians During the Revolutionary War, with Short Memoirs of Colonel Crawford and John Slover*. Cincinnati: U.P. James, 1867.

Bradford, John. *John Bradford's Historical & c. Notes on Kentucky*. San Francisco: The Grabhorn Press, 1932.

Broadhead, John Romeyn, ed. *Documents Relative to the Colonial History of the State of New York*. Vol. 8. Albany: Weed, Parsons and Company, 1857.

Brookes-Smith, Joan E., ed. *Master Index Virgina Surveys and Grants 1774–1791*. Frankfort, Ky.: Kentucky Historical Society, 1976.

Bryan, Charles W., Jr. "Richard Callaway, Kentucky Pioneer." *The Filson Club History Quarterly* 9, No. 1 (1935): 35–50.

Bushnell, David I., Jr. "Daniel Boone at Limestone, 1786–1787." *The Virginia Magazine of History and Biography* 25 (1917):1–11.

Butterfield, C.W. *Historical Account of the Expedition Against Sandusky under Colonel William Crawford in 1782*. Cincinnati: Robert Clarke & Co., 1873.

___. *History of the Girtys*. Cincinnati: Robert Clarke & Co., 1890.

Callaway, Bobbie L. "Flanders: Legend and His Legacy." *The Callaway Journal* 10 (1985): 18–22.

Callaway, Dudley and Jess Reynolds. "A Campaine of Souldiers." *The Virginia Genealogist* 20, No. 3 (1976): 222–225.

Callaway, Micajah. "Application for Land in Spanish Louisiana, January 23, 1798." -in French Language. Records of the Missouri Historical Society.

___. "Declaration of Micajah Callaway, September 29, 1832." In *Micajah Callaway Pension Application File*. Washington, D.C.: National Archives Trust Fund, Pension File Designation No. W6646, BLWT26660-160-55. See also *Draper Manuscript Collections*, Draper Mss. 10047.

___. "Marriage Bond." In *Micajah Callaway Pension Application File*. Washington, D.C.: National Archives Trust Fund, Pension File Designation No. W6646, BLWT26660-160-55.

"Callaway Names Found in Virginia Personal Property Tax Lists, 1782–1800," *The Callaway Journal* 1 (1976): 35–36.

Callaway, Colin G. "Chapter 6: Maquachake: The Perils of Neutrality in the Ohio Country." In *The American Revolution in Indian Country*. New York: Cambridge University Press, 1995.

"Calloway Cemetery, Inc." *The Callaway Journal* 1 (1976): 25.

Calloway, James E. "Virginia-Kentucky-Missouri." *The Callaway Journal* 10 (1985): 30–34.

Carskadden, Jeff and James Morton. *Where the Frolics and War Dances are Held, The Indian Wars and the Early European Exploration and Settlement of Muskingum County and the Central Muskingum Valley*. Baltimore: Gateway Press, Inc., 1997.

Cauthorn, Henry S. *A History of the City of Vincennes Indiana from 1702 to 1901*. Bowie, Md.: Heritage Books, Inc., 2001.

"The Certificate Book of the Virginia Land Commission of 1779–1780." *The Register of the Kentucky State Historical Society* 21, No. 61 (1923): 3–87.

Clark, Murtie June. *American Militia in the Frontier Wars*. Baltimore: Genealogical Publishing Co., 1990.

Clement, Maud Carter. *The History of Pittsylvania County Virginia*, Clearfield Company, Inc., 1929. Reprint, Baltimore: Genealogical Publishing Co., 1999.

Clift, G. Glenn. *History of Maysville and Mason County*. Vol. 1. Lexington, Ky.: Transylvania Printing Company, 1936.

Coleman, Charles H. "Lincoln's Lincoln Grandmother." *Journal of the Illinois State Historical Society* 52, No. 1 (1959): 59–90.

Continental Congress. *Journals of the Continental Congress*, 529, Continental Congress Broadside Collection, Library of Congress.

Bibliography

Cook, Michael. *Lincoln County Kentucky Records.* Vol. 1. Evansville, Ind.: Cook Publications, 1987.
Cook, Michael L. and Bettie Cook. *Kentucky Court of Appeals Deed Books H-N.* Vol. 2. Evansville, Ind.: Cook Publications, 1985.
Cook, Michael L. and Bettie A. Cook. *Fayette County Kentucky Records.* Vol. 1. Evansville, Ind.: Cook Publications, 1985.
___. *Kentucky Court of Appeals Deed Books V-Z.* Vol. 4. Evansville, Ind.: Cook Publications, 1985.
Corbitt, D.C. and Corbit, Roberta, eds., "Papers from the Spanish Archives Relating to Tennessee and the Old Southwest." In *East Tennessee Historical Society Publications, No. 39.* Knoxville: East Tennessee Historical Society, 1967.
Cotterill, R.S. "Battle of Upper Blue Licks." *The History Quarterly* 2, No. 1 (1927): 29–33.
The Courier Journal (Louisville, Ky.), March 16, 1896.
Coves, Elliott,ed. *The History of the Lewis and Clark Expedition.* Vol. 1. Francis P. Harper: 1893.
Cowen, Janet C. *Jeffersonville Land Entries 1808–1818.* Utica, Ky.: McDowell Publications, 1984.
Crabb, Anne. *Carried Off by the Indians.* Richmond, Ky.: Anne P. Crabb, 1991.
___. "'What shall I do now?' The Story of the Indian Captivities of Margaret Paulee, Jones Hoy, and Jack Callaway, 1779-ca. 1789." *The Filson Club History Quarterly* 70, No. 4 (1996): 363–404.
Craig, Neville B., ed. *The Olden Times.* Vol. 2. Pittsburgh: Wright & Charlton, 1847. Reprint, Millwood, N.Y.: Kraus Reprint Co., 1976.
Cruikshank, Ernest A., ed. "The Diary of an Officer in the Indian Country in 1794." *Magazine of Western History* 11 (1889–1990): 383–388.
___. *The Correspondence of Lieutenant Governor John Graves Simcoe,* 5 vols. Toronto: Ontario Historical Society, 1923-1931.
Dawson, Nelson L. "Louisville's Fort Nelson." In *Kentucky History Highlights from the Filson Club,* edited by Katherine L. House. Louisville: Filson Club, 1992, 104–107.
Deloria, Vine, Jr. *Red Earth, White Lies.* Golden, Col.: Fulcrum Publishing, 1997.
Denny, Ebenezer. *Military Journal of Major Ebenezer Denny, An Officer in the Revolutionary and Indian Wars.* Philadelphia: J.B. Lippincott & Co., 1859. Reprint, Arno Press Inc., 1971.
"Descendants of Joseph Callaway of Virginia through One of His Sons: Richard." *Callaway Family Association Journal* 5 (1980): 70
Dillon, John B. *A History of Indiana from its Earliest Exploration to the Close of the Territorial Government in 1816.* Indianapolis: Bingham & Doughty, 1859.
Dinn, Ruth and Chelsea Dinn. *Frederick Royse, 1750–1825, Revolutionary War Militiaman.* Franklin, Ind.: Ruth & Chelsea Dinn, 1971.
Donehoo, George P. "The Shawnee in Pennsylvania." *The Western Pennsylvania Historical Magazine* 7. No. 3 (1924): 178–187.
Doorman, John Frederick, ed. *Essex County, Virginia Deeds and Wills No. 13,* Washington, D.C.: John Frederick Doorman, 1963.
Doorman, John Frederick, ed. *Orange County Virginia Deed Books 3 and 4: 1738–1741.* Washington, D.C.: John Frederick Doorman, 1966.
Downes, Randolph C. *Frontier Ohio, 1788–1803.* Columbus: The Ohio State Archaeological and Historical Society, 1935.
___. *Council Fires on the Upper Ohio: A Narrative of Indian Affairs in the Upper Ohio River Valley Until 1795.* Pittsburgh: University of Pittsburgh Press, 1940.
Draper, Lyman Copeland. *Action at the Galudoghson, December 14, 1742.* Bowie, Md.: Heritage Books, Inc., 1995.
___. Draper Manuscript Collection (microfilm edition). State Historical Society of Wisconsin, Madison, Wisc.
"Early Settlements in Clark County." *The Winchester (Kentucky) Sun,* June 14, 1923.
Eid, Leroy V. "'A Kind of Running Fight': Indian Battlefield Tactics in the Late Eighteenth Century." *The Western Pennsylvania Historical Magazine* 71, No. 2 (1988): 147–171.
Elting, Colonel John R. *Military Uniforms in America: The Era of the American Revolution, 1755–1795.* San Rafael, Ca.: Presidio Press, San Rafael, Ca., 1974.
Engle, William H. "The Indian Treaty at Fort Pitt in 1776." *The Pennsylvania Magazine of History and Biography* 5, No. 4 (1881): 484–485.

Enoch, Harry G. *In Search of Morgan's Station and "The Last Indian Raid in Kentucky."* Bowie, Md.: Heritage Books, Inc., 1997.
Esarey, Logan, ed. *Governors Messages and Letters: Messages and Letters of William Henry Harrison*, 2 vols. Indianapolis: Indiana Historical Commission, 1922.
___. *History of Indiana from its Exploration to 1922.* Dayton: Dayton Historical Publishing Co., 1923.
Evans, Lucy. "Bedford County, Virginia Records." *Callaway Family Association Journal* 2 (1977): 40–47.
___. *The Boone Scout* 7, No. 1, The Boone Family Association of Washington, Seattle, Wash., October 1962.
Faragher, John Mack *Daniel Boone: The Life and Legend of an American Pioneer.* New York: Henry Holt and Company, 1992.
Field, T.P. *Kentucky and the Southwest Territory, 1794 (Map).* Lexington: Dept. of Geography, University of Kentucky, 1965.
Fitzpatrick, Alan. *Wilderness War on the Ohio, The Untold Story of the Savage Battle for British and Indian Control of the Ohio Country during the American Revolution.* Benwood, W. Va.: Fort Henry Publications, 2003.
Filson, John. *The Discovery, Settlement and Present State of Kentucke, 1784. Appendix, The Adventures of Col. Daniel Boon.* Reprint, New York: Corinth, 1962.
Flick, Alexander C., ed. *The Papers of Sir William Johnson.* 13 vols. Albany: The University of the State of New York, 1921–1962.
Foster, Emily. *The Ohio Frontier: An Anthology of Early Writings.* Lexington: The University Press of Kentucky, 1996.
Franklin, Charles M. *Indiana Territorial Pioneer Records: 1801–1820.* Vol. 2. Indianapolis: Heritage House, 1985.
Galloway, William Albert. *Old Chillicothe: Shawnee and Pioneer History, Conflicts and Romances in the Northwest Territory.* Xenia, Oh.: The Buckeye Press, 1934.
Gallup, Andrew, ed. *The Celeron Expedition to the Ohio Country 1749.* Bowie, Md.: Heritage Books, Inc., 1997.
Geib, George W. "The Land Ordinance of 1785: A Bicentennial Review." *Indiana Magazine of History* 81, No. 1 (1985): 1–13.
"General Anthony Wayne's General Orders, 1792–1797," *Historical Collections of the Michigan Pioneer and Historical Society* 34 (1905): 503–547.
Goebel, Dorothy Burne. *William Henry Harrison: A Political Biography.* Indianapolis: Historical Bureau of the Indiana Library and Historical Department, 1926.
Guernsey, E.Y. *Indiana: The Influence of the Indians Upon its History -with Indian and French Names for Natural and Cultural Locations (Publication No. 122).* Indianapolis: Indiana Department of Natural Resources, 1933.–a Map.
Hackman, Constance A., Leona M. Lawson, and Kenneth R. Scott. *The Collings, Richeys and the Pigeon Roost Massacre.* Alice Rebecca Scott, 1980.
Hamilton, Milton W., ed. *The Papers of Sir William Johnson.* Vol. 12. New York: The University of the State of New York, 1957.
Hammack, James Wallace, Jr. *Kentucky and the Second American Revolution: The War of 1812.* Lexington: The University Press of Kentucky, 1976.
Hammon, Neal O. "The Fincastle Surveyors at the Falls of the Ohio, 1774." *The Filson Club History Quarterly* 47, No. 1 (1973): 14–23.
___. "The First Trip to Boonesborough." *The Filson Club History Quarterly* 45, No. 3 (1971): 249–263.
Hanna, Charles A. *The Wilderness Trail.* 2 vols. New York: G.P. Putnam's Sons, 1911.
Harrison, Lowell H. and James C. Kotter. *A New History of Kentucky.* Lexington: The University of Kentucky Press, 1997.
Heffren, Horace. "Pioneer Picking No. 36." *The Salem Democrat*, January 19, 1876. Reprint, *Pioneer Pickings.* Salem, Ind.: James E. Bolding, 1993.
___. "Pioneer Picking No. 48." *The Salem Democrat*, March 22, 1876. Reprint, *Pioneer Pickings.* Salem, Ind.: James E. Bolding, 1993.
___. "Pioneer Picking No. 80." *The Salem Democrat*, December 13, 1876. Reprint, *Pioneer Pickings.* Salem, Ind.: James E. Bolding, 1993.

Bibliography

___. "Pioneer Picking No. 90." *The Salem Democrat*, February 28, 1877. Reprint, *Pioneer Pickings*. Salem, Ind.: James E. Bolding, 1993.
___. "Pioneer Picking No. 92." *The Salem Democrat*, January 3, 1877. Reprint, *Pioneer Pickings*. Salem, Ind.: James E. Bolding, 1993.
___. "Pioneer Picking No. 95." *The Salem Democrat*, April 4, 1877. Reprint, *Pioneer Pickings*. Salem, Ind.: James E. Bolding, 1993.
___. "Pioneer Picking No. 99." *The Salem Democrat*, May 2, 1877. Reprint, *Pioneer Pickings*. Salem, Ind.: James E. Bolding, 1993.
Helderman, L.C. "The Northwest Expedition of George Rogers Clark, 1786–1787." *The Mississippi Valley Historical Review* 25, No. 3 (1938): 317–334.
Hening, William Waller. *The Statutes at Large being a Collection of All the Laws of Virginia from the First Session of the Legislature in the Year 1619*. Vols. 5, 7, and 10. Richmond: Franklin Press, 1819.
___. *The Statutes at Large being a Collection of All the Laws of Virginia from the First Session of the Legislature in the Year 1619*. Vol. 9. Richmond: J. & G. Cochran, 1821.
Herndon, G. Melvin. "George Mathews, Frontier Patriot." *The Virginia Magazine of History and Biography* 77, No. 3 (1969): 307–328.
Historical Collections: Pioneer and Historical Society of the State of Michigan, Vols. 9, 10, 11, 19, 20, 24, 25, 34. Lansing: Thorp & Godfrey; Robert Smith & Co. (1886–1896, 1905).
History of Washington County, Indiana 1916–1976. Evansville, Ind.: Washington County Historical Society, Unigraphic, Inc., 1976.
Hoberg, Walter R. "Early History of Colonel Alexander McKee." *The Pennsylvania Magazine of History and Biography* 58 (1934): 26–36.
Hogan, Roseann R., ed. "Buffaloes in the Corn: James Wade's Account of Pioneer Kentucky." *The Register of the Kentucky Historical Society* 89, No. 1 (1991): 1–31.
Holden, Robert John. *The Hunting Pioneers, 1720–1840*. Bowie, Md.: Heritage Books, Inc., 2000.
Howard, Dresden W.H. "The Battle of Fallen Timbers as Told by Chief Kin-jo-i-no." *Northwest Ohio Quarterly* 20, No. 1 (1948): 37–49.
Howard, James H. *Shawnee: The Ceremonialism of a Native American Tribe and its Cultural Background*. Athens, Oh.: Ohio University Press, 1981.
Howe, Henry, ed. *Historical Collections of Ohio*. Cincinnati: C.J. Krehbiel & Co., 1902.
Hunter, W.H. "First Battle of the American Revolution." *Ohio Archaeological and Historical Publications* 11 (1903): 93–105.
Hurt, R. Douglas. *Nathan Boone and the American Frontier*. Columbia, Mo.: University of Missouri Press, 1998.
Hutton, Paul A. "William Wells: Frontier Scout and Indian Agent." *Indiana Magazine of History* 74, No. 3 (1978): 183–222.
Igleheart, Ted. "Squire Boone, The Forgotten Man." *The Filson Club History Quarterly* 44, No. 4 (1970): 356–366.
Indiana History Bulletin: Archaeological and Historical Survey of Washington County. Indianapolis: William B. Burford, 1924.
Jakle, John A. "The American Bison and the Human Occupance of the Ohio Valley." *Proceedings of the American Philosophical Society* 112, No. 4 (1968): 299–305.
James, James Alton. "Significant Events During the Last Year of the Revolution in the West." *Proceedings of the Mississippi Valley Historical Association* 6 (1913): 239–257.
Jefferson, Thomas. *Notes on the State of Virginia*. Boston: Thomas & Andrews, J. West, West & Greenleaf, et al. 1801. Reprinted with Introduction and Notes by William Peden, ed. Chapel Hill and London: North Carolina University Press, 1982. Page references are to the 1982 edition.
Jillson, Willard Rouse. "The Discovery of Kentucky." *The Register of the Kentucky State Historical Society* 20, No. 59 (1922): 117–129.
Johnson, Cave. "Reminiscences from the Life of Col. Cave Johnson." *Register of the Kentucky State Historical Society* 20, No. 59 (1922).
Johnson, Leland R. "The Doyle Mission to Massac, 1794." *Journal of the Illinois Historical Society* 73, No. 1 (1980): 2–16.

Johnson, Patricia Givens. *William Preston and the Allegheny Patriots.* Pulaski, Va.: B.D. Smith & Bros., Printers, Inc., 1976.

Jones, Reverend David. *A Journal of Two Visits Made to Some Nations of Indians on the West Side of the River Ohio in the Years 1772 and 1773.* Fairfield, Wash.: Ye Galleon Press, 1973.

Karol, Joseph S. "The French at French Lick: Fact or Fiction?" *Indiana Magazine of History* 50, No. 2 (1954): 139–144.

Kegley, F.B. *Kegley's Virginia Frontier.* Roanoke, Va.: The Southwest Virginia Historical Society, 1938.

Kegley, Mary B. *Wythe County, Virginia, a Bicentennial History.* Marceline, Mo.: Walsworth Publishing Inc., 1989.

Kemper, Charles E., ed. "Documents Relating to the French and Indian War, 1755–1762." *The Virginia Magazine of History and Biography* 15, No. 3 (1908): 247–258.

Kenton, Edna, *Simon Kenton, His Life and Period, 1755–1836.* North Stratford, N.H.: Reprint, Ayer Publishers, Inc., 1999.

"Kentucky County Tax Lists." *Callaway Family Association Journal* 9 (1984): 80–81.

Kincaid, Robert L. "Boone and Russell Graves in Lee County, Virginia." *The Virginia Magazine of History and Biography* 60, No. 1 (1952): 170–172.

Kinietz, Vernon and Erminie W. Voegelin, eds. *Shawnese Traditions, C.C. Trowbridge's Account.* Ann Arbor, Mich.: University of Michigan Press, 1939.

Knabenshue, S.S. "Indian Land Cessions in Ohio." *Ohio Archaeological and Historical Quarterly* 11, No. 2 (1902): 249–255.

Knopf, Richard C., ed. "Wayne's Western Campaign, The Wayne-Knox Correspondence 1793–1794, Part II." *The Pennsylvania Magazine of History and Biography* 78, No. 4 (1954): 424–452.

"Letters from the Canadian Archives." *Collections of the Illinois State Historical Society* 1 (1903): 339–397.

"Letters of Colonel George Croghan." *Pennsylvania Magazine of History and Biography* 15, No. 4 (1892): 429–439.

Lewis, Virgil A. *History of the Battle of Point Pleasant Fought Between Indians and White Men at the Mouth of the Great Kanawha River, (now Point Pleasant, West Virginia) Monday, October 10, 1774.* Westminster, Md.: Reprint by Willow Bend Books, 2000.

Libby, Dr. Dorothy. *An Anthropological Report on the Piankashaw Indians-(Miami Archives, Before the Indian Claims Commission, Dockett 99 (a part of Consolidated Docket No. 315): Piankashaw Locations (ca. 1776-ca.1783).* Bloomington, Ind.: Indiana University. http://www.gbl.indiana.edu/archives/dockett_99/d99toc.html

Lindley, Harlow. *Indiana as Seen by Early Travelers.* Indianapolis: Indiana Historical Commission, 1916.

Lobdell, Jared C., ed. *Further Materials on Lewis Wetzel and the Upper Ohio Frontier, The Historical Narrative of George Edgington, Peter Henry's Account, The Narrative of Spencer Records, The Reminiscences of Stephen Burkham.* Bowie, Md.: Heritage Books Inc., 1994.

Loskiel, George Henry. *History of the Mission of the United Brethren Among the Indians of North America.* London: Brethren's Society for the Furtherance of the Gospel, 1794.

Lowitt, Richard. "Activities of Citizen Genet in Kentucky 1793–1794." *The Filson Club History Quarterly* 22, No. 4 (1948): 252–267.

Map of Washington County, Indiana. New York: P. O'Beirne & Co., 1860.

McAfee, Robert B. "The Life and Times of Robert B. McAfee and his Family and Connections." *The Register of the Kentucky State Historical Society* 25, No. 73 (1927): 5–37.

McAllister, J.T. "The Battle of Point Pleasant." *The Virginia Magazine of History and Biography* 10 (1903): 75–82.

McConnell, Michael N. *A Country Between, The Upper Ohio Valley and Its Peoples, 1724–1774.* Lincoln: University of Nebraska Press, 1992.

McDonald, John, *Biographical Sketches of Nathaniel Massie, General Duncan McArthur, Captain William Wells, and General Simon Kenton.* Cincinnati: M. Morgan and Son, 1828.

McDowell, William L., Jr., ed. *Colonial Records of South Carolina, Documents Relating to Indian Afffairs, 1754–1765.* Columbia, S.C.: South Carolina Archives Department, 1958.

McGrane, R.C. "William Clark's Journal of General Wayne's Campaign." *The Mississippi Valley Historical Review* 1(1915): 418–444.

McHenry, Chris. *Rebel Prisoners at Quebec: 1778–1783.* Louisville: Filson Club, 1981.

Bibliography

McKenney, Thomas L. and James Hall. *The History of the Indian Tribes of North America, with Biographical Sketches and Anecdotes of the Principal Chiefs.* Philadelphia: E.C. Biddle, 1836–1844.
Meek, Basil. "General Harmar's Expedition." *Ohio Archaeological and Historical Quarterly* 20, No. 1 (1911): 74–108.
Minutes of the Provincial Council of Pennsylvania. Vol. 8. Harrisburg: Theo. Fenn & Co., 1852.
Monette, John W., M.D. *History of the Discovery and Settlement of the Valley of the Mississippi.* New York: Harper & Brothers, 1846.
Moore, John H. "A Captive of the Shawnees, 1779–1784." *West Virginia History: A Quarterly Magazine* 23, No. 4 (1962): 287–296.
Nelson, Paul David. *Anthony Wayne: Soldier of the Early Republic.* Bloomington, Ind.: Indiana University Press, 1985.
"New London, Bedford County, VA., Deed Book A, p. 434." *The Virginia Magazine of History and Biography* 19 (1911): 431–432.
Nugent, Nell Marion. *Cavaliers and Pioneers: Abstracts of Virginia Land Patents and Grants, 1666–1695*, Vol. 2. Richmond: Virginia State Library, 1977.
Olmstead, Earl P. *David Zeisberger: A Life Among the Indians.* Kent, Oh.: The Kent State University Press, 1997.
O'Malley, Nancy. *Stockading Up.* Frankfort: Kentucky Heritage Council, 1994.
Palmer, William P. *Calendar of Virginia State Papers and Other Manuscripts.* Vol. 3. Richmond: James E. Goode, 1883.
Pence, George and Nellie C. Armstrong. *Indiana Boundaries: Territory, State and County.* Indianapolis: Indiana Historical Bureau, 1967.
Perrin, W.H., J.H. Battle, and G.C. Kniffin. *Kentucky. A History of the State.* Louisville: F.A. Battey and Company, 1887.
Perrin, William Henry. *History of Bourbon, Scott, Harrison and Nicholas Counties, Kentucky.* Chicago: O.L Baskin & Co., 1882.
Powell, Richard L. *Geology of the Falls of the Ohio River (Indiana Geological Survey Circular 10).* Bloomington, Ind.: Indiana University, 1970, updated 1999.
"Preston Papers, February 21, 1783 Letter from James Moore to William Preston." *The Virginia Magazine of History and Biography* 29, No. 1 (1921): 29, ftnt. 1.
Prevost, Toni Jollay. *The Delaware and Shawnee Admitted to Cherokee Citizenship and the Related Wyandotte and Moravian Delaware.* Bowie, Md.: Heritage Books, Inc., 1993.
Prucha, Francis Paul. *Documents of United States Indian Policy.* Lincoln: University of Nebraska Press, 1990.
Quaife, Milo M., ed. "When Detroit Invaded Kentucky." *The History Quarterly* 1, No. 2 (1927): 53–67.
___. "General James Wilkinson's Narrative of the Fallen Timbers Campaign." *The Mississippi Valley Historical Review* 16 (1929–1930): 81–90
___. "The Ohio Campaigns of 1782," *The Mississippi Valley Historical Review* 17 (1930–1931): 515–529.
Quisenberry, Anderson Chenault. *Kentucky in the War of 1812.* Baltimore: Genealogical Publishing Company, 1969.
Ranck, George W. *Boonesborough, Its Founding, Pioneer Struggles, Indian Experiences, Transylvania Days, and Revolutionary Annals.* Louisville: John P. Morton & Company, 1901.
Randall, E.O. "Clark's Conquest of the Northwest." *Ohio Archaeological and Historical Quarterly* 12, No. 1 (1903): 67–94.
___. Randall, E.O. "The Dunmore War." *Ohio Archaeological and Historical Publications* 11 (1903): 167–195.
___. "Ohio in Early History and During the Revolution." *Ohio Archaeological and Historical Quarterly* 10, No. 4 (1902): 395–421.
Randall, Willard Stern, *George Washington, A Life*, New York: Henry Holt and Company, 1997
"Records of County Tax Collector, Garrard Co. Ky., 1797–1806." Film # 000 7988, LDS Library, Salt Lake City S-599.
Reese, Ted. *Soft Gold, A History of the Fur Trade in the Great Lakes Region and Its Impact on Native American Culture.* Bowie, Md.: Heritage Books, Inc., 2001.
"Registre de Arpentage pour les terres St. Charles, du Missouri river, gauche A, 1799." In *French and Spanish Land Grants, Territory of Louisiana, Vol. A.*

Rice, Otis K. *Frontier Kentucky*. Lexington: The University Press of Kentucky, 1993.
Richter, Daniel K. and James H. Merrell. "Peoples 'In Between,' the Iroquois and the Ohio Indians, 1720–1768." *Beyond the Covenant Chain*. Syracuse, New York: University Press, 1987.
Ridout, Thomas. "An Account of my Capture by the Shawanese Indians." *Western Pennsylvania Historical Magazine* 12, No. 1 (1929): 3–31.
Robertson, Nellie Armstrong and Dorothy Riker. *The John Tipton Papers*. Vol. 1. Indianapolis: Indiana Historical Bureau, 1942.
Rone, Wendell H. Sr. *An Historical Atlas of Kentucky and her Counties*. Central City, Ky.: Rev. Wendell Sandefur, 1965.
Russell, Nancy Callaway. "Micajah Callaway." *Callaway Family Association Journal* 20 (1995): 53–60.
Salem Indiana through One Hundred and Seventy-Five Years. Salem, Ind.: Salem Historical Society, Leader Publishing Company, 1989.
Salmon, John S. and Emily J. Salmon. *Franklin County Virginia 1786–1796*. Rocky Mount, Va.: Franklin County Bicentennial Commission, 1993.
Saunders, William L., ed. *The Colonial Records of North Carolina*. Vol. 10. New York: AMS Press, Inc., 1968.
Schaaf, Gregory. *Wampum Belts & Peace Trees, George Morgan, Native Americans, and Revolutionary Diplomacy*. Golden, Col.: Fulcrum Publishing, 1990.
Schreiner-Yantis, Netti and Florene Love. *The Personal Property Tax Lists for the Year 1787 for Fayette County, Virginia (Now Kentucky)*. Springfield, Va.: Genealogical Books in Print, 1985.
Scribner, Robert L. *Revolutionary Virginia, The Road to Independence*. Vol. 7, Part Two. Richmond, Va.: University Press of Virginia, 1983.
Seineke, Kathrine Wagner. *The George Rogers Clark Adventure in the Illinois*. New Orleans, La.: Polyanthos, Inc., 1981.
Shane, Reverend John D. "Reverend John D. Shane's Interview with Pioneer William Clinkenbeard." *The History Quarterly* 2, No. 3 (1928): 95–128.
Sipe, C. Hale. *The Indian Chiefs of Pennsylvania*. Butler, Pa.: The Ziegler Printing Co., 1927.
___. *The Indian Wars of Pennsylvania, Book One*. Bowie, Md.: Heritage Books, Inc., 2000.
___. *The Indian Wars of Pennsylvania, Book Two*. Bowie, Md.: Heritage Books, Inc., 2000.
Skardon, Mary A. *The Battle of Piqua, August 8, 1780*. Springfield, Oh.: Clark County Historical Society, 1964.
Skeen, C. Edward. *Citizen Soldiers in the War of 1812*. Lexington: The University Press of Kentucky, 1999.
"'Sketch of Cornstalk' Draper Mss. 3D, Chapter XVIII." *Ohio Archaeological and Historical Publications* 21 (1912): 245–262.
Skidmore, Warren and Donna Kaminsky. *Lord Dunmore's Little War of 1774, His Captains and Their Men who Opened Up Kentucky & the West to American Settlement*. Bowie, Md.: Heritage Books, Inc., 2002.
Smith, Dwight L. *From Greenville to Fallen Timbers*. Indianapolis: Indiana Historical Society, 1952.
Sosin, Jack M. "The British Indian Department and Dunsmore's War." *The Virginia Magazine of History and Biography* 74, No. 1 (1966): 34–50.
___. "The Use of Indians in the War of American Revolution: A Re-Assessment of Responsibility." *The Canadian Historical Review* 46, No. 2 (1965): 101–121.
Sparacio, Ruth and Sam Sparacio. *Virginia County Court Records; Deed & Will Abstracts of Albemarle County, Virginia 1748–1752*. McLean, Va.: The Antient Press, 1990.
___. *Virginia County Court Records: Amherst County, Virginia Land Tax Books 1789–1791*. McLean, Va.: The Antient Press, 1997.
Speck, Frank G. "The Delaware Indians as Women: Were the Original Pennsylvanians Politically Emasculated?" *The Pennsylvania Magazine of History and Biography* 70, No. 4 (1946): 377–389.
Spencer, Oliver M. *The Indian Captivity of O.M. Spencer*. Chicago: R.R. Donnelley and Sons, 1917.
Stevens, Paul L. *Louis Lorimier in the American Revolution: A Memoire by an Ohio Indian Trader and British Partisan. (Center for French Colonial Studies Extended Publications Series Number 2)*. Naperville, Ill.: The Center for French Colonial Studies, Inc., 1997.
Stevens, Warder W. *Centennial History of Washington County Indiana*. Indianapolis: B.F. Bowen & Company, Inc., 1916.
Sugden, John. *Blue Jacket, Warrior of the Shawnees*. Lincoln: University of Nebraska Press, 2000.
___. *Tecumseh, A Life*. New York: Henry Holt and Company, 1997.

Bibliography

Summers, Lewis Preston. *History of Southwest Virginia, 1746–1786*. Baltimore: Regional Publishing Company, 1979.
Talbert, Charles Gano. *Benjamin Logan: Kentucky Frontiersman*. Lexington: The University of Kentucky Press, 1962.
___. "Kentucky Invades Ohio, -1779." *The Register of the Kentucky Historical Society* 51, No. 176 (1953): 228–235.
___. "Kentucky Invades Ohio, -1780." *The Register of the Kentucky Historical Society* 52, No. 181 (1954): 291–300.
___. "Kentucky Invades Ohio -1782." *The Register of the Kentucky Historical Society* 53, No. 185 (1955): 288–300.
Tanner, Helen Hornbeck. *Atlas of the Great Lakes Indian History*. Norman, Okl.: University of Oklahoma Press, 1987.
___. "Cherokees in the Ohio Country." *Journal of Cherokee Studies* 3, No. 2 (1978): 94–102.
___. "The Glaize in 1792: A Composite Indian Community." *Ethnohistory* 25 (1978): 15–39.
___. *Indians of Ohio and Indiana Prior to 1795: The Greenville Treaty 1795*. Vol. 1. New York and London: Garland Publishing Inc., 1974.
Taul, Micah. "Memoirs of Micah Taul." *The Register of the Kentucky State Historical Society* 27, No. 79 (1929): 343–380.
Taylor, Robert M. *Indiana: A New Historical Guide*. Indianapolis: Indiana Historical Society, 1989.
Thwaites, Reuben Gold and Louise Phelps Kellogg. *Documentary History of Dunsmore's War, 1774*. Madison, Wisc.: Wisconsin Historical Society, 1905.
___. *The Revolution on the Upper Ohio, 1775–1777*. Madison, Wisc.: Wisconsin Historical Society, 1908.
Tipton, John. "John Tipton's Tippecanoe Journal." *The Indiana Quarterly Magazine of History* 2 (1906), Reprint, New York: Kraus Reprint Corporation, 1967):170–184.
"Treaty Between Virginia and the Indians at Fort Dunsmore (Pittsburg) June, 1775." *The Virginia Magazine of History and Biography* 14 (1907): 54–79, reprint Millwood, New York: Krause Reprint Corporation, 1968.
Van Cleve, John W. "Van Cleve's Memoranda." *American Pioneer* 2, No. 4 (1843): 148–153.
"Virginia Land Patent Records." *Callaway Family Association Journal* 13 (1988): 58.
"Virginia Militia in the Revolution," *The Virginia Magazine of History and Biography* 7 (1900), reprint, New York: Kraus Reprint Corporation, (1968): 250, 252.
Waddell, Joseph A. *Annals of Augusta County, Virginia from 1726 to 1871*. Harrisonburg, Va.: C.J. Carrier Company, 1972.
Wait, Thomas B. "March 19, 1784 Entry." *Secret Journals of the Acts and Proceedings of Congress, Vol. I. Domestick Affairs*, Boston, Mass., 1821.
Walton, Joseph S. *Conrad Weiser and the Indian Policy of Colonial Pennsylvania*. Philadelphia: George W. Jacobs & Co., 1900.
Washington County, Indiana, Deed Book A.
Weslager, C.A. *The Delaware Indians: A History*. New Brunswick, N.J.: Rutgers University Press, 1972.
West, J. Martin, ed. *Clark's Shawnee Campaign of 1780*. Springfield, Oh.: The Clark County Historical Society, 1975.
Wheeler-Voegelin, Erminie. *Indians of Northwest Ohio: An Ethnohistorical Report on the Wyandot, Potawatomi, Ottawa, and Chippewa of Northwest Ohio*. New York & London: Garland Publishing, Inc., 1974.
___. *Indians of Ohio and Indiana Prior to 1795: Ethnohistory of Indian Use and Occupancy of Ohio and Indiana Prior to 1795*. Vol. 2. New York & London: Garland Publishing, Inc., 1974.
Wheeler-Voegelin, Erminie, Emily J. Blasingham, and Dorothy R. Libby. *Miami, Wea, and Eel-River Indians of Southern Indiana: An Anthropological Report on the Miami, Wea, and Eel-River Indians*. New York & London: Garland Publishing, Inc., 1974.
Wilcox, Frank. *Ohio Indian Trails*. Kent, Oh.: The Kent State University Press, 1933.
Williams, Edward G. "The Journal of Richard Butler, 1775 Continental Congress' Envoy to the Western Indians." *The Western Pennsylvania Historical Magazine* 46, No. 4 (1963): 381–395.
Williams, John S., ed. "Daily Journal of Wayne's Campaign." *The American Pioneer, A Monthly Periodical* I, No. 7 (1844): 315–322.
Williams, Joyce G. and Jill E. Farrelly. *Diplomacy on the Indiana-Ohio Frontier 1783–1791*. Bloomington, Ind.: Indiana University Bicentennial Committee, 1976.

Williams, Sherrill. "The Callaways in Early America." *Callaway Family Association Journal* 4 (1979): 10–12.

___. "Colonel Richard Callaway of Virginia and Kentucky." *Callaway Family Association Journal* 6 (1981): 75–89.

Wilson, George R. *Early Indiana Trails and Surveys.* Indianapolis: Indiana Historical Society, 1986.

Wilson, George R. and Gayle Thornbrough. *The Buffalo Trace.* Indianapolis: Indiana Historical Society, 1946.

Wilson, Samuel M. *Catalogue of Revolutionary Soldiers and Sailors of the Commonwealth of Virginia to Whom Land Bounty Warrants Were Granted by Virginia for Military Services in the War for Independence.* Greenville, S.C.: Southern Historical Press, Inc., 1994.

Wingfield, Marshall. *A History of Caroline County Virginia.* Baltimore, Md.: Reprinted for Clearfield Company, Inc. by Genealogical Publishing Co., Inc., 1991.

Winter, John. *A Narrative of the Sufferings of Massy Harbison from Indian Barbarity.* Beaver, 1836.

Withers, Alexander Scott. *Chronicles of Border Warfare.* Cincinnati: Stewart & Kidd Company, 1895.

Wright, Louis B. *The Prose Works of William Byrd of Westover, Narratives of a Colonial Virginian.* Cambridge, Mass.: The Belknap Press of Harvard University Press, 1966.

Index

Alanant-O-Wamiowee, 44, 79, 80
Allegheny Mountains, 10-11
Amherst County, 270, 280, 367
Amherstburg, (Ontario) 313, 349, 358-59, 385
Appalachian Mountains, 49
Apple Creek, 259
Arbuckle, Matthew, 84
Arnold, Benedict, 164
Arnold, John, 289, 312
Arthur, Gabriel, 4
Articles of a Treaty, 229
Articles of Confederation, 214, 239, 242
Asbury, Daniel, 104
Ashley, Marker B., 208
Athiawiomee, 42, 57-58, 70
Athiawiowee, 6
Aubrey's 47th Regiment of Foot, 142
Augusta County, 30, 60
Baby, Jacques Duperon, 9, 38, 49, 121, 142, 164
Backmetack Marsh, 359-360
Bailey, William, 111
Baker, Joshua, 288, 290, 298, 303, 309
Baker, Joshua Jr., 288-89, 312
Baker, Joshua Sr., 20
Bald Eagle Creek, 58
Ball, Thomas, 258
Ballard, Bland, 171
Barbee, John, 288-89, 292, 310
Barclay, Robert, 357
Barnes, Thomas, 206

Barnett, Adam, 331
Barnett, James, 243, 246
Battle of Fallen Timbers, 276, 297, 312, 325, 356, 385
Battle of Lookout Mountain, 357
Battle of Newtown, 165
Battle of Piqua, 158
Battle of Point Pleasant, 23, 27-29, 33-34, 36, 313, 357
Battle of Saratoga, 206
Battle of the Thames, 357-59, 361
Battle of Tippecanoe, 334, 340, 342, 346
Battle of Trenton, 206
Battle Run Creek, 178-79
Battles of Lexington and Concord, 46, 48
Bean Blossom Creek, 345
Bean Creek, 276
Beargrass Stations, 139, 148, 171
Beasley, Charles, 180
Beaubien, Charles, 89, 104
Beaver Creek, 218, 291
Beaver Wars, 2, 4, 14
Beck, John, 341
Beck's Mill, 341
Bedford County, 37-38, 44, 46, 59, 66, 70, 72, 75, 83, 96, 106, 111, 129, 141, 206-07, 329
Bedford County Militia, 38, 70, 206
Bell, Thomas T., 180
Biaseka (the Wolf), 35
Big Cat, 332

Big Knives, 268
Big Sandy Island, 4
Bird, Henry, 136, 142-48, 157, 165, 177, 181, 185, 295
Birkbeck, Morris, 363
Bliss, Leonard, 370
Blue Jacket's Town, 48, 194, 252, 276
Blue Ridge Mountains, 8, 23, 38, 67, 96, 329
Bluegrass Region, 78, 137-41, 144, 146, 168, 177-78, 207
Bluegrass War, 109
Boggs, John, 220
Bois Blanc, 313, 334, 385
Boone, Cyrus, 139
Boone, Daniel, 15-16, 18-19, 29, 40-43, 56-59, 64, 69, 71-74, 77-79, 83, 87, 89-95, 100, 102-08, 112-118, 124, 138-139, 148, 162, 170, 180-81, 185, 188-90, 197, 204-08, 211, 213, 215, 221, 236, 239, 230-31, 233-59, 314-16, 318-20, 322, 324, 356, 361, 367, 370
Boone, Daniel Morgan, 82, 257, 316
Boone, Elizabeth, 215
Boone, Israel, 181
Boone, James, 19
Boone, Jemima, 56-59, 69, 72, 77, 106, 112, 114-17, 139, 204-08, 211, 253, 316, 318, 323-24, 361, 367
Boone, Moses, 215
Boone, Nathan, 316, 319, 322, 367

Boone, Rebecca, 324, 367
Boone, Samuel, 314
Boone, Squire, 15, 43, 70, 115-17, 139, 148, 170-71, 215, 318
Boone's Creek, 139
Boone's Station, 139, 177, 180, 207
Boone's Trace, 42, 46, 70
Boston Harbor, 22
Boston Port Act, 22
Boston Tea Party, 22
Botetourt County, 18, 24, 32, 60, 66, 118
Bouquet, Henry, 11
Bouquet's Treaty, 24
Bourbon County, 242, 253-54, 280, 288, 320, 326-27
Bowman, John, 64, 66, 77, 82, 87, 111, 118-19, 120, 131, 134, 141, 255
Braddock, Edward, 9
Braddock's Campaign, 15
Bradt, Andrew, 177
Brant, Joseph, 23, 165, 166-71, 215-16, 222, 249, 262, 264, 333
Brashear's Station, 139
Brewer Blockhouse, 344
Brewer, Benjamin, 331, 344
Bright Horn (Waseweela), 352
British Indian Department, 9, 14-15, 23, 53, 110, 121, 202, 216, 236, 278, 313
British Rangers, 174, 176-77, 181, 193
Brock Creek, 344, 362
Brock, George, 331
Brock, Isaac, 349-350
Brooks, Samuel, 104, 124
Brooks, Thomas, 57, 87
Brooks, William, 104
Brown, John, 104, 213, 285
Bruce, John, 208
Bryant, William, 137
Bryant's (aka Bryan's) Station, 137, 139, 148-49, 177, 180, 207
Buchanan, William, 57, 115
Buchanan's Trace, 208
Buckongahelas, 300, 331
Buffalo Trace, 243, 247, 318, 325, 326, 329
Buford, Richard, 34, 60
Bullitt, Thomas, 18-19, 199
Bullock, Nathaniel, 57, 104, 213

Burbeck, Henry, 290, 310
Burgoyne, John, 83
Buskirk, Absolom, 355
Butler, John, 136
Butler, Polly, 18, 300
Butler, Richard, 18, 21, 49-51, 54, 217-19, 221-25, 227-228, 231, 236, 270, 274, 300
Butler, William, 18, 20-21
Butler's Rangers, 136
Cahokia, 121-23, 143, 197
Caldwell, John, 288
Caldwell, William, 136, 174, 176-78, 180-81, 300
Callaway Cemetery, 320
Callaway County (Kentucky) 142,
Callaway County (Missouri) 361
Callaway Fort, 339, 341, 344, 362, 366, 370-71
Callaway, Abraham, 320
Callaway, Betsy, 56, 58
Callaway, Caleb, 57
Callaway, Chesley, 38, 59, 60-61, 65-66, 82-83, 162, 206, 367
Callaway, Dudley, 24, 26, 29, 32, 34, 38, 59, 270, 280
Callaway, Edmund, 38, 111, 204, 207, 213, 288, 292, 298, 303-05, 309-10, 312, 322-25, 327, 358-59, 363, 365-67, 372
Callaway, Elizabeth, 38, 44, 117, 177, 203-04, 353, 366
Callaway, Fanny, 14, 56, 58-59, 179, 219, 222-23, 252
Callaway, Flanders, 37-38, 40-41, 44, 46, 57-59, 69, 72-75, 77-79, 82-83, 87, 89, 111-12, 115-16, 137, 139, 141, 197, 204-08, 211, 213, 253, 257, 314, 316, 318-19, 320, 322-24, 361, 367
Callaway, Frances 'Frankie', 327, 335, 338, 353-54, 366, 372
Callaway, Francis, 38
Callaway, James, 38, 60, 83, 206, 318-19, 322, 325, 357, 361, 363, 365
Callaway, James Jr., 38, 65-67, 70, 72, 75-79, 82, 87, 91, 93-96, 100-101, 103-04, 124, 137, 208, 213, 320, 326-27, 366
Callaway, John (Micajah's brother), 38, 59, 111, 113, 131,

132, 134, 213, 270
Callaway, John (Micajah's uncle), 38
Callaway, John / 'Jackie' / 'Jack' / 'Jacky' (Micajah's first cousin), 44, 179, 182-84, 201, 203, 215, 318, 324-326, 357, 359
Callaway, John Hawkins / 'Hawk', 175, 327, 366, 370, 372
Callaway, Joseph Jr., 38, 320
Callaway, Lucy, 366
Callaway, Margaret, 322-323
Callaway, Mary, 318, 323, 366
Callaway, Mary (Polly), 38
Callaway, Noble, 327, 353, 364, 366, 372
Callaway, Richard, 37-38, 40-41, 43-44, 46, 56-59, 64, 70, 74-78, 82-83, 110-18, 125, 127, 138-41, 148, 177, 179, 182, 203-04, 211, 324, 357
Callaway, Sarah, 38, 44, 59, 66-67, 82, 111, 366
Callaway, Susan, 213
Callaway, Susannah, 59
Callaway, Thomas, 38, 40-41, 320
Callaway, William, 38, 111, 213
Callaway, Zachariah 'Zack', 59-61, 65-67, 75
Callaway's Fork, 320
Callaway's Regiment, 356
Camp Charlotte, 34, 48
Camp Charlotte Treaty, 35
Camp Deposit, 298
Campaign Creek, 28
Campbell County, 367
Campbell, Alexander, 231
Captain Logan, 134
Carleton, Guy, 48, 68, 184
Carter, Charles, 344
Cassidy, Michael, 288
Cassidy, William, 179
Castle's Wood, 19
Cavelier, Robert, 2
Chaguska (Spy Buck), 300
Chalaakaatha (Shawnee Town), 18, 22, 48, 80, 94, 98, 103-08, 112-13, 118-120, 126, 131, 133-37, 143, 146, 148-51, 157-58, 211, 256, 269, 314
Chartier, Peter, 8, 129

Index

Chartier's Town, 6
Chene, Isodore, 164
Chenoweth, Richard, 164
Chenusaw (the Judge), 35
Cherokee Expedition, 59-61, 65-66
Chiksika, 32, 223
Chillicothe, 2, 314
Chiswell Mines, 60, 138
Chote, 55-57, 60
Christian, William, 60
Cincinnati Trace, 338
Clark County, 280, 288, 314, 358, 367
Clark County Militia, 358
Clark County Militiamen, 280
Clark State Forest, 371
Clark, Benjamin, 329
Clark, George, 120, 131
Clark, George Rogers, 20, 24, 63-65, 73, 75, 82, 111, 120-26, 141, 143-44, 146-53, 155-57, 163-65, 167-68, 170, 173, 175-76, 184-86, 188, 190, 192-93, 195-98, 201-02, 205, 214, 217-19, 222, 228, 236, 239-40, 242-43, 245-49, 255-56, 262, 286-88, 329, 332, 370
Clark, Marston G., 329, 341
Clark, William, 324, 329
Clark's Grant, 164, 214, 328-29
Clarksville, 242-43, 247, 326, 329
Clary, John, 149, 157
Claus, William, 334
Clear Creek, 139, 170
Coitcheleh, 13, 50, 120, 160, 192, 198, 203, 223, 249, 252, 256
Collings, Henry, 353
Collings, Rachel, 353
Collins, Josiah, 133
Collins, William, 117
Colonial Land Office, 136
Commissioners Plenipotentiary, 217-20, 229, 236, 250
Committee of West Fincastle, 63
Confederacy of Western Indians, 61
Congressional Committee on Indian Affairs, 216
Conn, Notley, 288
Connolly, Dr. John, 19-21

Continental Congress, 49-51, 62, 122
Continental Congress, Second, 49
Continental Divide, 324
Cooke, John, 305
Copher, Jesse, 104, 213
Corn Island, 122, 126
Cornstalk, Peter, 252
Cornwallis, Lord Charles, 167, 172-73, 195
Corps of Rangers, 136, 164
Covalt's Station, 267
Covenant Chain Alliance, 4, 8, 14
Cracraft, Charles, 168-69
Crawford, William, 27, 36, 173-75
Cresap, Michael, 20
Crest of the Knobs, 331, 335, 338-39, 363
Croghan, George, 357
Crooked Creek, 27, 29, 32-33
Crow's Station, 193
Cumberland Gap, 19, 42, 69-70, 125, 161
Cumberland Mountains, 42, 69, 138
Cutler, Manassah, 237
Cuttenwa (Cuttemwha), 35
Cyclone Person, 128
Danville Prison, 198
Dartmouth, Earl of, 61
Davis, James, 327, 335-36, 338, 339, 341-42, 362
Davis, Nancy, 327, 335-36, 344, 362
Dawalt, Henry, 331, 344-45, 353-54
de Belestre, Francois-Marie Picot, 38
de Carondelet, Baron, 286
de Peyster, Arent, 126, 157, 164, 165, 166, 173, 177, 184, 193, 199
de Quindre, Fontenoy, 112
Delaney Creek, 329, 331, 366
Delassus, Don Charles Dehault, 318-19
Denny, Ebenezer, 274
Denny, Elisha, 344
Denny, Polly, 344
Depauw, Charles, 362
Depauw, John, 362
Desha, Joseph, 358, 360

Dickson, Josiah, 124
Donaldson, John, 358
Doom, George, 355
Doyle, Thomas, 231, 287
Drake, Ephriam, 139
Drake, Joseph, 139
Draper, Lyman C., 356, 370-71
Drouillard, Pierre, 112, 121
Dry Ridge Trail, 44
Duncan, David, 238
Dunlap's Station, 267
Dunn, Jack, 106
Dunn, John, 103
East Hickman Creek, 139, 211
Elinipsico, 84
Elk Creek, 26, 34, 329, 338, 353-54, 365
Elliot, Matthew, 34, 110-11, 136, 165, 174, 176-77, 216, 221, 280, 282, 313, 349
Elliott, Daniel, 220
Eskippakithiki, 6-9, 14-15, 43, 73, 129, 326
Essex County, 320
Fairfax, Thomas, 23
Fallen Timbers, 325
Falls of the Ohio, 2, 4, 7, 18, 121, 126, 131, 139, 143, 146, 148, 164-65, 167, 176, 190, 193, 196, 200-01, 214, 218, 246-47, 318, 326, 328, 338, 352
Fayette County, 162, 175, 185, 205, 207-08, 213, 242, 246-47, 253-54, 280, 356
Fayette County Court, 207
Fayette County Militia, 246-47
Federal Treaties of Conquest, 217
Field, John, 30
Filson, John, 213, 263
Fincastle County, 17, 19, 36, 64
Findley, John, 15
Finney, William, 222-23, 233
Fleenor, John, 340-42
Fleming Mountain, 37-38
Fleming, John, 179
Fleming, William, 24, 27, 30, 66, 67, 118-119
Floyd, John, 20, 44, 57, 82, 139, 153, 171, 185, 199
Floyd's Station, 139, 171, 199
Foote, Thomas, 139
Forbes, James, 208
Forbes, John, 9

Forlorn Hope, The, 360
Forts
  Adams, 292
  Alexander, 345
  Blair, 36
  Boonesborough, 43, 46, 56-57, 64-66, 68-70, 73-80, 82-83, 87, 89-91, 93, 104, 107-08, 110-13, 118-19, 125, 131, 137-41, 162, 179-80, 182, 197, 205, 215
  Brock, 344
  Callaway, 344, 362
  Chiswell, 60, 69
  Dearborn, 347, 349-51
  Defiance, 293-95, 310, 345
  Detroit, 7, 53, 262, 347, 349-350, 358
  Dunmore, 20, 23, 26, 48, 49
  Duquesne, 9, 10
  Finney, 219, 222-23, 233, 236-37
  Fleenor's, 342, 344, 353, 362
  Fort-on-Shore, 126
  Gower, 27
  Granville, 24
  Greenville, 285, 288-89, 310, 312
  Hamilton, 270, 271
  Harmar, 220, 263-64
  Harrison, 342, 351-52
  Henry, 168, 176
  Huff's, 342
  Jefferson, 143, 271, 274-75, 285
  Ketcham, 344, 354-55
  Lexington, 180
  Logan's, 44, 65, 73, 76, 87, 118
  Mackinac, 347, 349
  Malden, 347, 349-350, 352, 358-59
  Massac, 122, 287
  McIntosh, 218-219, 225-26, 241, 264
  Meigs, 355, 363
  Miami, 7, 286, 293, 295, 297, 298-300, 308-09
  Moore's Fort, 19
  Nelson, 164, 173, 185, 190, 193, 195-99, 201, 202-05, 212-13, 215
  Niagara, 53-54, 262
  Ouiatenon, 7
  Patrick Henry, 60, 69
  Pickawillany, 226
  Pitt, 19, 21, 24, 36, 49, 50-51, 53-54, 61-62, 64, 85, 110-111, 121, 157, 164, 167-68, 174, 197, 203, 220-21, 227, 241, 275-78
  Pleasant, 345
  Randolph, 36, 48, 84-85
  Recovery, 290-91, 310, 312
  Sackville, 122, 124-25, 148
  St. Louis, 4
  Stanwix, 14, 85, 218
  Stephenson, 355, 357
  Trial, 38
  Vallonia, 344-45, 354-56
  Vause, 38
  Vincennes, 7
  Washington, 267, 269-70, 279, 288, 312
  Wayne, 312, 325, 336, 351-52
Freeman, Isaac, 266
French and Indian War, 8, 10, 14, 17, 38, 107, 121, 129, 361
French, Paul, 345
Gage, Thomas, 48
Gaines, Bernard, 305
Galloway, Christina, 206
Garrard County, 326-27
Garrison, James, 366
Gass, David, 131, 141
Gates, Horatio, 82
Genet, Citizen, 286, 362
George White Eyes, 332
Germain, George, 68
Gibault, Pierre, 122, 125
Gibson, John, 20, 34, 355
Girty, George, 24, 110-11, 142, 150, 165, 167, 177, 192, 265
Girty, James, 24, 110, 142, 194
Girty, Simon, 24, 29, 110-12, 134, 142, 144, 150, 158, 163-64, 167, 174, 176-77, 194, 216
Girty's Town, 193-94, 201, 227, 291
Gnaddenhutten (Moravian Mission), 174
Gnaddenhutten Massacre, 176
Goodman, Ansel, 103, 106
Gordon, William, 331, 346
Graden, William, 65
Grand Council, 10, 18, 23, 28, 61, 110, 173, 200, 216, 238, 249, 278, 295, 336
Grand Glaize, 276, 278, 284-85, 287, 292
Grant's Station, 146, 177, 207
Great Britain, 8-11, 14, 22, 51, 61-62, 85, 121-122, 125, 163, 165, 196, 225, 262, 275, 287, 334, 347, 349, 355, 361
Greathouse, Daniel, 20
Greathouse, Jacob, 20, 270
Green Creek, 82
Greenville Treaty Line, 313
Grenadier Squaw Town, 13, 34
Guilford County Courthouse, 206
Gwatkins, Charles, 41, 66, 82
Halifax County Militia, 38
Hamilton, Henry, 53, 61, 68, 86, 104, 110, 113-14, 124-26, 165
Hamtramck, John F., 301
Hancock Creek, 82
Hancock, Forest, 318
Hancock, Stephen, 115
Hancock, William, 103, 106, 108, 115, 131, 139, 213
Hand, Edward, 84
Hanging Maw, 57
Hardin, Enos, 314
Harmar, Josiah, 220, 238, 242, 247, 262, 263, 267-70, 313
Harrison County, 328, 345, 355, 362
Harrison County Militia, 355
Harrison, William Henry, 278, 325, 355
Harrison, Benjamin, 173, 278
Harrison, William, 173, 175, 196, 198, 201, 278, 325-28, 335-36, 340-42, 345, 351-52, 355, 357-59, 361
Harrod, James, 44, 65, 73, 131-32, 134, 138, 153
Harrod's Creek, 80
Hawkins, Frances "Frankie", 326-27
Hawkins, Nancy, 327
Hays, William, 322
Hays, William Jr., 318
Hays, William Sr., 318
Heald, Nathan, 351
Heckewelder, John, 264
Helm, Leonard, 122
Henderson, Richard, 40-43, 117
Henderson, Samuel, 57-58, 139
Hendricks, George, 103, 106
Henry County, 357
Henry, Patrick, 20, 51, 53, 59, 63-64, 68, 85, 121, 213

Index 445

Hesse, Emanuel, 143
Hinde, Thomas Spottswood, 314
Hinkston Fork, 58, 80, 82, 88-90, 207
Hinkston, John, 44, 52
Hinkston's Station, 44, 52, 65
Hobson's Choice, 279, 285
Hockhocking Creek, 21
Hodges, Jesse, 57
Hog Creek, 362, 368
Holder, John, 57-58, 111, 113, 117, 131-32, 134, 137, 141, 177, 179, 242, 247, 262
Holder's Station, 179, 242
Holley, John, 103, 106
House of Burgesses, 22, 38, 48-49
House of Lords, 17
House, George, 344
Houston Station, 146, 177
Howard County, 366
Hoy, Jones, 178, 182, 201, 203, 215
Hoy, William, 178
Hoy's Station, 178, 182
Hughes Station, 239
Hughey, Joseph, 29
Hull, William, 347, 349-51
Hulse, Paul, 315
Hunter's Trace, 58
Hutchins, Thomas, 241
Illinois Regiment, 111, 121, 125, 148, 164, 185
Illinois Territory, 341, 347
Illinois Trace, 318, 325
Indian Chiefs and Warriors
  Aweecorny, 200, 223, 233, 250, 252, 369
  Beaver, 9
  Big Apple Tree, 26
  Black Fish, 13, 35, 57-58, 69, 73-74, 85-87, 89-91, 94-95, 98, 100-04, 106-08, 111-15, 132, 135, 211, 261, 324, 369
  Black Hawk, 359
  Black Hoof (Catehecassa), 6, 9, 92, 101, 113, 132, 150, 313, 333, 351 358, 363, 365, 369
  Black Stump, 126
  Black Wolf, 240
  Blackfish, 268
  Blue Jacket, 48, 89-90, 92, 101-102, 176, 200, 223, 257,

259, 261, 267-69, 271-72, 274, 276, 278-79, 297, 301, 303, 305, 307, 309, 313-14, 333
Buckongahelas, 266, 276
Buffalo, 334
Captain Bull, 330-31
Captain John / Johnny, 200, 219, 222-24, 226, 255-57, 259, 278, 313, 334, 352
Captain Killbuck, 332, 334
Captain Pipe, 18
Captain Reed, 313
Captain Snake, 13, 35, 101-02, 135, 142-44, 158, 165, 174, 176, 196, 198-99, 200-02, 212, 221-23, 237-38, 240, 257, 259, 261, 263, 268, 276, 294-95, 303, 358, 363, 369
Captain White Eyes, 20, 26, 85
Captain White Feather, 351
Captain Will, 16, 48, 89-90, 106, 108, 199
Captain Wolf, 223, 256-57, 283
Chaubenee, 350
Chiaxi, 101, 127, 150, 172, 223, 299, 300-01, 303-04, 306-09, 352, 359, 361, 369
Chief Splitlog, 359
Conneodico, 51
Cornstalk, 10-11, 13, 18-19, 21-22, 27-30, 32-33, 35, 48, 50-52, 54, 61-62, 84-85, 89, 101, 105-106, 120, 126, 199, 219, 226-227, 250, 252, 258
Custaloga, 26
Dragging Canoe (Chincanacina), 42, 55, 59-60
Four Legs, 358
Guyasuta, 10, 23, 165, 333
Kakinathucca, 263, 313
Kakowatchecky, 13
Kay-fe-wa-e-fe-kah, 313
Kekewapilathy, 158, 199, 221, 223-24, 226-28, 233
King Opessah, 4
King Shingas, 9-10
Kinjoino, 295
Kishenosity, 13, 20, 49, 62, 85, 105-06, 126, 369
Kishkalwa, 126
Lamatumque, 106, 120, 158,

160-61, 186-89, 192, 196, 198-204, 212, 221, 224, 233, 249-56, 259, 278, 324
Lathenfecho, 257
Le Gris, 261
Little Killbuck, 332, 334, 352-54
Little Otter, 309
Little Turtle, 238, 261, 269, 271, 276, 279, 295, 297
Logan / Taghahjute, 20-21, 35, 55, 270
Long Shanks, 313
Lowaluwaysica, 332-33
Mad Sturgeon, 359
Manemsecho, 257
Mannashcommiqua, 233
Masalameta, 352, 354
Methoto, 233
Micanimssica, 222-23, 233
Milkman, 49
Mithawano, 233
Moluntha / Maluntha, 85, 101, 106, 113-14, 120, 126, 158, 160-61, 171-72, 192, 196, 199, 200-04, 212, 214, 221-25, 228, 233, 235, 237-38, 249-52, 255, 324, 369
Musquaconah (Red Pole), 233, 268, 278, 313, 333
Naiwash, 359
Naw Kaw, 359
Nenessica, 6, 89, 95-97, 101, 104-06, 109, 112-13, 119-20, 128-29, 132-33, 135, 141-42, 145, 149-50, 156, 158, 160-61, 163, 167-68, 170-72, 182-83, 189, 194, 196, 199, 204, 211, 221, 223, 225-28, 233, 236-37, 259, 263, 265, 287, 313, 326, 334 363-65
Ne-quetaugh-aw, 313
Netawatwes, 332
Newa / Newau, 35
Nia-num-fe-ka, 313
Nimwha, 13, 62, 86, 89, 101, 106, 126, 369
Noamohouoh, 255-56
Nonhelema, 10-11, 13-14, 34, 84-85, 160, 219, 222, 224-25, 233, 249-52, 256
Oshawahnah, 359
Ox, 331-32, 334-35, 345, 354 362

Pacanne, 261
Pacheta, 359
Pappiqua, 89
Paxinosa, 9, 10, 13, 369
Pemenaway, 257
Pluggy, 26, 36, 50-51, 55, 64-65, 69, 72
Pontiac, 10, 332
Prophet, The / Tenskwatawa, 332-36, 341-42, 345-47, 351-352, 354, 359
Pucksinwah, 13, 27, 32, 313, 360
Red (Painted) Pole, 237-238
Red Hawk, 84
Sauganash, 349
Shade, 49, 200, 237-238, 250, 252
Shawanese Ben, 49
Silverheels, 13, 21-22
Snake, 49
Spemica Lawba, 249, 252, 347, 351
Spy Buck (Chaguska), 351
Stone, 51
Tamenatha, 18
Tecumapease, 249, 252
Tecumseh, 32, 223, 279, 290-91, 301, 303-05, 313, 332-36, 340-41, 345-46, 347, 349-352, 355-56, 359-60
Wasegaboah, 359
Wasekakotha, 101, 252, 258
Waywaylapea, 352
Wewessicanpawie, 233
Wey-tha-pa-mat-tha, 313
White Bark, 13, 33, 35, 131, 150, 178, 182-183, 199, 368
White Fish (Koketha), 62
Wryneck, 13, 107, 113, 123, 150, 165, 196-97, 200, 202, 216, 249
Yellow Hawk, 13, 98, 126, 133
Indian Confederacy, 10, 14, 68, 111, 143, 170, 174, 176-77, 182, 263-64, 266, 270-71, 275, 278-79, 286-87, 295, 297, 309, 312, 334, 340-41
Indian Nations (other than Shawanese/Shawnee)
Catawba, 6, 9, 10, 129
Cherokee, 4, 6, 10, 15, 19-20, 22, 40-42, 46, 55-57, 59-60, 62, 165, 172, 216, 263, 271,
278, 284, 334, 340, 368
Chickasaw, 279, 285, 290
Chippewa, 62, 122, 165, 218-219, 264, 278, 299, 300, 303, 307, 312, 345, 358-59
Connoy, 278
Creek, 4, 216, 278, 336, 340
Delaware, 4, 8-10, 15, 18-19, 22, 24, 26, 49-50, 54-55, 62, 84-85, 111, 155, 165, 167, 169, 173-74, 176-77, 181, 216, 218-22, 226, 230, 238, 263-64, 266-67, 271, 276, 278, 284, 292, 299-300, 312, 326-27, 328, 331-32, 334-35, 345, 352, 354, 359, 362
Eastern Woodland Algonquin, 2, 4, 10, 14, 367
Eel River, 312, 328, 335, 345
Fox, 122, 278
Huron, 2
Iroquois, 4, 8, 165, 218, 262, 264, 268
Kickapoo, 122, 312, 326, 328, 335, 342, 344-45, 347, 351-52
Lenape, 55
Miami, 10, 38, 46, 79-80, 94, 98, 214, 218-21, 238-40, 242, 247, 249, 255, 259, 261, 264, 266-67, 269, 271, 274, 276, 278, 284, 286, 299, 312, 325-26, 328, 331, 335, 345, 352
Mingo, 8, 10, 20-23, 26, 35-36, 50-52, 54-55, 62, 64, 69, 72-73, 76-77, 89, 91, 111, 118, 150, 155, 167, 172, 177, 218-19, 252, 263, 266-67, 271, 274, 278, 300
Mohawk, 4, 9, 23, 48, 55, 165-167
Mohican, 62, 278
Munsee (Munsey), 18, 62, 278, 284
Nantikoke, 55, 278
Ojibwa, 10
Ojibway, 271
Osage, 122, 318
Ottawa, 10, 50, 55, 122, 165, 167, 218-19, 264, 271, 276, 278, 284, 293, 295, 299-300, 309, 312, 345, 351-52, 359
Piankeshaw, 122, 312, 345
Pottawatomie, 10, 62, 122, 165, 264, 271, 278, 284, 299-
300, 303, 307, 312, 326, 328, 335, 341-42, 345-46, 350-52, 355, 359
Sauk, 122, 264, 278, 342, 359, 361
Shawanoe, 229-30
Wea, 246, 278, 312, 327, 341, 344
Winnebago, 122, 335, 342, 345, 347, 350-52, 359
Wyandot, 10, 26, 46, 49-50, 54, 61-62, 111, 121, 142, 155, 165, 167, 173-74, 176-77, 181, 196, 216, 218-22, 226, 238, 241, 263-64, 268, 271, 274, 276, 278, 284, 299-300, 308-09, 312, 345, 359
Indian Removal Act, 369
Indiana Territorial Census, 362
Indiana Territory, 313, 325, 328, 332, 334-36, 340-41, 345, 349, 351, 354-56, 362-63
Innes, Harry, 242, 267, 285
Iroquois Confederacy Nations, 4, 262
Cayuga, 4
Onandaga, 4
Oneida, 4
Seneca, 4, 10, 22
Tuscarora, 4x
Ivy Creek, 37-38, 41
Jackson County, 353
Jackson, Andrew, 361, 367-69
Jackson, Joseph, 103, 106, 157, 213, 383
Jay, John, 287, 312
Jay's Treaty, 312-13
Jefferson County, 162, 175, 185, 239
Jefferson County Militia, 186
Jefferson, Peter, 8
Jefferson, Thomas, 8, 20, 164, 173, 322, 324
John Coldwater (Pamota), 352
Johnson, Andrew, 107-08, 213
Johnson, Arch, 344
Johnson, Guy, 23, 48, 53
Johnson, Mary, 344
Johnson, Richard, 358-60
Johnson, Sir John, 23
Johnson, Sir William, 23, 165
Johnson, William, 9, 14-15, 19, 200
Johnston, John, 354

Index

Jones, Cadwallader, 355
Jones, John Gabriel, 63-65
Kaskaskia, 121-22, 125, 312, 325
Kekionga, 259, 269, 271, 310
Kelly, Benjamin, 103, 106
Kennedy, Thomas, 250-51
Kenton, Simon, 24, 29, 44, 52, 64, 65, 73-74, 113, 120-21, 148, 250, 258, 288, 295, 357
Kentucky Board of War, 285
Kentucky County, 63-64, 73, 75-77, 82-83, 138, 162
Kentucky County Militia, 73, 77, 82, 111, 144, 148, 167, 206, 239, 242, 253, 270-72, 285, 351, 358
Kentucky Mounted Volunteer Militia, 357
Kibbey, Ephraim, 285
King George III, 11, 17, 49, 61, 68, 121, 237, 271
King George's War, 8
King's Eighth Regiment, 142
Kirkham, Rob, 133
Kispoko Town, 18, 48
Knobs Creek, 366
Knox County, 327
Knox, Henry, 247, 266-68, 275, 287
Kokomthena, 127-29, 131, 163, 188
Lafayette, Marquis de, 362
Lake St. Claire, 359
Lakes
 Erie, 2, 53, 341, 358
 George, 9
 Great, 195, 215, 278, 336, 358
 Huron, 53
Lamb, Simeon, 329
Land Ordinance of 1785, 240
Lee, Richard Henry, 51
Legras, J.M.P., 240
Lewis and Clark Expedition, 324
Lewis, Andrew, 23-24, 26-30, 32, 34, 36
Lewis, Charles, 30
Lewis, Ezekiel, 170
Lewis, Meriwether, 324
Lick(s)
 Big Bone, 7, 79, 168
 Big Flat, 42, 70
 Deer, 331, 335, 338, 366
 Drennon's, 7, 18, 79

Evans, 331
Flat, 80, 83, 88-89
French, 243
Grassy, 58, 178-179, 326
Harrod's, 80, 83, 88
Lower Blue, 7, 44, 65, 80, 87-88, 113, 139, 180-82, 184, 205, 207, 251
Royse's, 328-29, 331-32, 334-35, 341, 344-45, 353, 355-56, 362, 365
Upper Blue, 7, 58, 178-79, 255
Limestone, 52, 64, 80, 94, 97, 173, 207, 221, 236, 240, 249, 253-58, 267, 316, 318
Limestone Creek, 255
Limestone Crossing, 52, 64, 80, 94, 97
Lincoln County, 162, 175, 182, 185, 239, 242-43, 246
Lincoln, Abraham, 131, 175, 239
Lincoln, Bathsheba, 175
Lincoln, Josiah, 175, 239
Lincoln, Mary, 175
Lincoln, Mary Todd, 131
Lincoln, Mordecai, 175, 239
Lincoln, Nancy, 175
Lincoln, Thomas, 175
Lincoln, Tom, 239
Linn, William, 153, 171
Linn's Station, 139
Little Chalaakaatha, 48, 105, 107
Lochry, Archibald, 167-70
Logan, Benjamin, 44, 73, 82, 118, 131, 132, 148-49, 152-53, 155, 182, 184-86, 188-89, 242-43, 249-50, 252-53, 257-58, 285
Logan's Camp, 20
Logstown, 6
Long Hunter, 15, 42
Long Island, 41-42, 59-60, 69
Long Knives/Knife, 1, 13-14, 21-22, 26-30, 32-34, 36, 48-50, 60, 69, 73-74, 78, 91, 105, 110, 112-113, 115-18, 124-27, 131-36, 139-41, 144, 146, 148-53, 155, 156-57, 160-61, 164, 168, 171, 174, 176-77, 181, 186-90, 192-95, 199-203, 205, 212, 221, 226, 235, 242-43, 246-47, 249-50, 258-59, 266, 272, 280, 299, 304, 308, 336, 340, 352, 356-58, 360-61, 369

Loramie Creek, 48, 142
Lord Dunmore, 17, 19-24, 26-29, 33-36, 46, 48, 51, 66, 206
Lorimier, Charlotte "Pemanpieh", 104
Lorimier, Louis, 48, 89, 98, 104, 106, 112, 119, 121, 133, 135, 142, 149, 171, 186, 188-89, 259, 286
Losantiville, 263, 267
Louisiana Purchase, 322-24
Lower Howard Creek, 80, 88
Lower Shawnee Town, 6, 14, 28, 33
Loyal Land Company, 8
Ludlow's Station, 267
Mackachack, 85, 106, 150, 158, 160, 171, 175, 194, 196, 199, 200-01, 203-04, 212, 221, 249, 252, 255
Madison, James, 341, 356
Martin's Station, 42, 69, 145-46, 177
Mason County, 288
Massie, Nathaniel, 314
Massies Creek, 48, 98
Mathews, George, 33
May, Richard, 131
May, William, 297, 299-300
McAfee, Robert, 18, 19
McClelland, John, 44, 52, 65, 175
McClelland's Station, 44, 52, 65, 72, 80
McCullock, James, 212-13
McCullough, Silas, 331
McDowell, Nathan, 231
McGary, Hugh, 133, 148, 181, 185, 188, 251, 252
McGee's Station, 177, 179
McKee, Alexander, 14-15, 19-21, 26, 53-54, 110-12, 125, 136, 143-44, 146, 157-58, 163-64, 170-71, 173, 176-77, 182-83, 192-93, 199-200, 216, 218, 241, 252, 278, 286, 293, 298, 310, 313
McKee's Town, 48, 188
Miami (Wabash) Confederacy, 62
Miami Confederacy, 214, 238-39, 242, 246, 261, 263-64, 276, 326
Miami Purchase, 263-64, 267
Michigan Territory, 347, 355

Mill Creek, 267
Miller, Abraham, 315
Miller, Christopher, 295, 297
Mocassin Gap, 42
Moluntha's Town, 194
Moneto (The Great Spirit), 2, 6-7, 127-29, 160, 163, 168-69, 172, 187, 301, 332-33, 365
Monroe, James, 245
Montgomery, John, 286-87
Montgomery, Samuel, 220-21
Mooney, James, 26, 29
Moore, James, 240
Moore, Jane, 240
Moore, Polly, 240
Moore, Thomas, 303
Morgan, Daniel, 206
Morgan, George, 54-56, 61-62, 203, 259
Morgan's Station, 280
Murray, John, 17
Neidiffer, Fred, 331
New Chillicothe (Chillicothy), 194, 259
No Creek, 367
Norman Uplands, 328-29
North American Fur Trade, 2
North Elkhorn Creek, 82
North, William, 206
Northbend, 265-66
Northern Indian Department, 9, 23, 53
Northwest Ordinance, 262
Northwest Ordinance of 1787, 262
Ohio Company, 8, 237, 263-264
Ohio Confederacy, 8, 54, 62, 69, 143, 165-66, 195
Old Yie, 84
Otter Creek, 43, 178
Owen County, 367
Paint Creek, 48, 107-08, 113, 256, 314
Painted Stone Station, 139, 148, 170-71
Parberry, James, 208
Parr, Arthur, 366
Parsons, Samuel H., 217, 236-37
Patterson, Robert, 253, 263
Pauling, Henry, 24, 26, 30, 32, 34, 66, 69-70, 72, 74-75, 82, 87, 118
Payne, William, 315
Penn, John, 24

Penn, William, 4
Perry, Oliver Hazard, 358
Peter, John, 9, 10
Peyton, Tim, 255
Piatt, Benjamin, 176, 185
Pickawillany, 48, 157
Pickering, Timothy, 282, 284
Pigeon Roost Creek, 353-55
Pigeon Roost Massacre, 353-55
Pigeon Roost Settlement, 353
Pigeon Town, 252
Pimmepesy, 107
Piqua (Shawnee Town), 48, 107, 110, 134-36, 148-152, 155-57, 160, 172, 176
Piqua, New (Shawnee Town), 158, 160, 182, 193, 215, 240, 252, 354
Piqua (Ohio), 351
Piqua Indian Agency, 351, 354
Pleistocene Epoch, 1
Point Pleasant, 27-29, 33-34, 36, 84
Pommepesy, 107
Pontiac's War, 11
Posey, Thomas, 355
Post St. Louis, 148
Powell Mountains, 18
Preston, William, 19
Price, John, 306
Price, William, 288-89, 292, 294, 298-99, 301, 303-04, 309-10
Proclamation of 1763, 17, 19
Prophet's Town, 332, 334-36, 341-342, 347, 352
Putnam, Rufus, 237
Quebec Act, 22-23, 121
Randolph, Beverly, 282, 284
Reed, Nathaniel, 57
Regiment of Kentucky Mounted Volunteers, 357-58
Rennick, Joshua, 9
Rennick, Robert, 9
Rinken, James, 220-21
Rivers
 Allegheny, 6
 Auglaize, 142, 259, 276, 278, 292-93, 313
 Beargrass, 329
 Big (Ohio), 55
 Big Vermilion, 246
 Blue, 328-29, 331, 334, 336, 341-42, 344, 346, 352, 362

Chattahoochee, 4
Chickamauga, 60
Clinch, 18
Columbia, 324
Cumberland, 4, 41-42, 122
de la Panse, 227, 230
Detroit, 53, 124, 142, 280, 282, 284, 313, 349-50, 359
Dick's, 44
Elkhorn, 44, 137
Femme Osage, 316, 318-20, 322-24, 367
Great Kanawha, 6, 11, 18-19, 24, 26-27, 29, 33-34, 62, 240
Greater Miami, 48, 142-44, 146, 157-58, 167-69, 172, 175-76, 184, 186, 193, 201, 218-22, 226, 236, 259, 265, 267, 325
Green, 175
Greenbrier, 24
Hockhocking, 23, 27, 29
Holston, 8, 15, 42, 44, 59, 69
Illinois, 4, 23
James, 9, 164
Kankakee, 354
Kentucky, 4, 7, 18, 40-43, 57, 73, 78-80, 88, 113, 138, 140, 148, 173, 178, 207
Licking, 7, 44, 58, 73, 79-80, 82, 87, 91, 112, 131, 137, 144-46, 148, 173, 176, 181, 185, 193, 255, 263
Little Kanawha, 20, 331
Little Miami, 48, 106, 131-32, 151, 193, 217, 263, 267
Mad, 46, 48, 85, 106-07, 136, 143, 149-50, 152, 157-58, 176, 259
Maumee, 48, 142, 259, 276, 278, 286, 293-95, 297-98, 309-10
Mississinewa, 345
Mississippi, 22, 121-22, 195, 215, 247, 259, 262, 266, 278, 287, 316, 318-19, 325, 341, 354, 367, 369
Missouri, 316, 319-20, 322-25, 367
Monongahela, 131
Muscatatuck, 329, 334, 336, 344-45, 352-53, 362
Muskingum, 11, 46, 220, 264
New, 8
Niango, 322

Index

Ohio, 1, 2, 4, 6-11, 14, 17-20, 22-24, 26-30, 35, 49-52, 64-65, 79-80, 82, 89, 97, 111-13, 120-22, 125-26, 131, 136, 139, 143-44, 146, 148-49, 161, 164, 167-70, 174, 175-77, 182, 185, 201-02, 207, 212-15, 220-22, 227, 236, 238-39, 240-41, 247, 249, 256-59, 261, 263-65, 267, 270, 278-81, 286-88, 318, 325-27, 329, 333, 336, 338, 347, 354, 358, 365, 371
Portage, 358
Powell, 42, 69
Raisin, 355
Red, 43, 326
Savannah, 4
Scioto, 6, 9, 11, 15, 23, 46, 107, 113, 217, 219, 256, 314
St. Joseph's, 310, 336
St. Mary's, 194, 199, 227, 291-92, 310
Stillwater, 172, 189, 290
Tellico, 15, 60
Tennessee, 14, 60, 122
Thames, 357, 359, 361
Tippecanoe, 334
Upper Blue, 341, 344, 346, 352
Wabash, 23, 122, 214, 227, 230, 236, 238, 242-43, 246-47, 249, 257, 267, 271, 276, 290, 318, 325-26, 334-35, 340-41, 356
Watauga, 40, 41
White, 328, 331-32, 334, 344-45, 352-54
Whitewater, 313
Yadkin, 15, 40
Yellowstone, 367
Robertson, James, 29
Roche de Bout, 293-95, 297-98
Rocky Mountains, 322, 367
Royal Governor of New York, 17
Royal Governor of Virginia, 17
Royse, Frederick, 329
Ruddell, Isaac, 131
Ruddle, Stephen, 326
Ruddle's Station, 144-46, 177, 186
Russell, Henry, 19
Russell, William II, 18-19, 29, 36, 48, 356

Russell, William III, 19, 288, 352, 356
Saffenger, John, 231
Saint Asaph, 44
Salt Creek, 332
Salt Lick Trace, 80, 83, 87-89, 139
Sandwich (Ontario), 349-50, 359
Sargent, Winthrop, 237
Sauconk, 6
Saunders, Betty, 255
Saunders, John, 242, 255
Scholl, William, 314
Scippo Creek, 13, 34
Scott, Charles, 285, 289, 307, 312
Searcey, Bartlett, 213
Seventeen Fires, 340
Sevier, Valentine, 29
Shawnee / Shawanese Nation,
  Chalaakaatha, 2, 9, 13, 35, 50-51, 62, 69, 86, 89, 95, 101, 104, 126, 128, 133, 172, 201, 222, 259
  Kispoko, 2, 13, 18, 21, 35, 46, 54-55, 62, 69, 86, 101, 126, 128, 135, 143, 150, 252
  Makujay, 2, 4, 9-11, 13, 50, 52, 54, 62, 84-86, 95, 101, 104-105, 113, 126, 129, 158, 196, 199-200, 214, 221, 223, 237, 249-50, 259, 268, 333
  Piqua, 2, 4, 9, 13, 35, 50-51, 62, 69, 86, 101, 126, 129, 131, 158, 178
  Thawekila, 2, 126
Shawnee Peace Faction, 54
Shawnee War Faction, 55
Shawnee Expedition of 1756, 30
Shelby, Evan, 29, 138
Shelby, Isaac, 33, 285, 287, 351, 354, 357-358
Sherlock, James, 198-204, 212-13, 215
Silly Boys, 128
Simcoe, John Graves, 286-87, 312
Six Nations, 4, 6, 14, 50, 61, 143, 165-67, 198, 216, 218, 249, 264
Skagg's Trace, 44
Slaughter, George, 143, 148, 153, 186

Slover, John, 175
Smith, William Bailey, 111, 115
Soliday, Daniel, 344
Soliday, Jacob, 344
Sonnioto, 6
Sovereign, John, 189-90, 22-24, 233, 237
Spencer, Oliver M., 271
Spotsylvania County, 320
Springer, Uriah, 305
St. Clair, Arthur, 21, 263-64, 267-68, 270-72, 274-76, 285, 290
Standing Stone Village, 157-58, 171-72, 185-90, 193-94
Steele, William, 303, 305
Stewart, James, 33
Stewart, John, 15
Still, Murphy D., 366
Stoner Fork, 58, 80, 82, 88
Strode's Creek, 80, 88
Strode's Station, 146, 177, 179
Stuart, Henry, 55, 56
Sudduth, William, 288, 298, 303-304, 312
Sullivan's Station, 139
Swan Creek, 300, 309, 312
Sycamore Hollow, 43
Sycamore Shoals, 40-42
Symmes, Anna, 325
Symmes, John Cleves, 263, 265-66, 325
Sympson, James, 358
Tardineau, Bartholomew, 198
Tates Creek, 178
Taylor, Zachary, 352
Teque Creek, 367
Theyaendinega, 165
Thirteen Fires, 51, 228, 265
Thomas, Abraham, 148
Thompson, Moses, 339
Thompson, Robert, 331
Tippecanoe (Town of), 334
Tipton, John, 345, 355-56
Tipton's Island, 356
Todd, John, 65, 73, 75-76, 82, 180-181, 242, 246
Todd, Levi, 75, 131, 185, 242, 256
Todd, Robert, 288-289, 299, 308, 310
Tomlinson, Nicholas, 180
Towhead, 332, 334, 352
Trabue, Daniel, 118
Tracy, William, 103

Transylvania Company Ventures, 37, 40-42, 63, 64
Treaty at the Mouth of the Greater Miami River, 219, 229, 241, 249, 250, 259, 281
Treaty of Fort Harmar, 264
Treaty of Fort McIntosh, 219, 223, 281
Treaty of Fort Pitt, 51, 63, 226
Treaty of Fort Pitt, Second, 62
Treaty of Fort Stanwix, 14, 51, 264, 281
Treaty of Fort Wayne, 335-36
Treaty of Ghent, 361
Treaty of Greenville, 312, 314, 326, 363
Treaty of Grouseland, 327, 334
Treaty of Paris, 10, 215-16
Treaty of San Ildefonso, 320
Treaty of San Lorenzo, 316
Trent, Martha "Patty", 206
Trent, Obadiah H., 26, 34, 206
Trigg, Stephen, 180-81
Trudeau, Zénon, 316, 318-19
Tymochtee, 174
Union Camp, 24, 26
United Colonies, 51, 85, 122
Upper Canada, 286, 313, 347, 358
Upper Delaware Creek, 292
Upper Shawnee Town, 6, 11, 20, 28
Upper Shawneetown, 46
Vallonia, 336, 338, 344-45, 354-56

Vallonia Trace, 338
Van Bibber, Isaac, 318
Vincennes, 121-22, 124-26, 143, 239-40, 242-43, 245-47, 253, 262, 318, 325-26, 334-36, 340-41
Virginia Committee of Safety, 60
Virginia Convention, 63-64
Virginia General Assembly, 17, 75, 83, 111, 136, 138, 162, 164, 175
Virginia Land Commission, 136-137
von Dieskau, Jean Erdman, 9
von Steuben, Friedrich, 164
Wabapusito, 101, 178-79, 182-83
Wabash Campaign, 246
Wade, Dawson, 69
Wade, Richard, 57, 104, 213
Wakatomica, 20, 46
Wakitunikee, 219
Walls, George, 185-86, 188, 197-98, 200-06
Wapakoneta, 194, 313, 333-334, 347, 363, 365, 369
Wapatomica, 46, 48, 85, 136, 149, 157-58, 161-64, 170-71, 175-76, 181, 192-94, 198-200, 219, 221, 223, 240, 249, 252
War of 1812, 347, 349, 356, 361, 363
Warriors' Path, 6
Washington County, 361-62, 364

Washington, George, 8-9, 14, 17, 20, 164, 174, 184, 216, 220, 266-68, 270, 275, 285, 287, 313, 368
Washington, Lawrence, 8
Wayne Campaign, 332
Wayne, "Mad Anthony", 275-276, 278-280, 284-90, 292-95, 297-99, 301, 305-07, 309-10, 312-14, 325
Wells, Samuel, 171
Wells, William, 271, 274, 286, 290, 293-95, 351
West Augusta Committee of Safety, 54
West Fincastle Committee of Safety, 64
Westcott, Stukley, 150
Wetzel, Lewis, 109
Whitley, William, 131, 360
Wild Cat Creek, 227
Wilkinson, James, 301, 304-05
Williams, Jarett, 56
Williamson, David, 174
Wills Town, 193
Willstown, 48
Wilson, Henry, 187-88
Wood, James Jr., 49
Wright, Philbert, 331
Yellow Creek, 20-21
Young, Joseph, 346
Young, Samuel, 346
Zenor, Jacob, 345

About the Author

REX CALLAWAY WAS BORN IN ONARGA, ILLINOIS in 1950 and grew up in Illinois and Indiana. He received a B.A. in English Literature in 1973 from Indiana University -Bloomington, Ind. campus, and a J.D. in 1976 from the Indiana University School of Law–Bloomington. He has worked for the U.S. Environmental Protection Agency and the U.S. Department of Navy as a federal environmental attorney since 1977. Rex and his family currently live in Poway, California near the city of San Diego.

From the earliest days of his childhood, Rex was immersed in family oral history about Daniel Boone, the Callaway family, and the late eighteenth century Ohio River valley Indian wars. He set out upon a quest to research and validate the family oral history in 1997 and came to focus his effort upon reconstructing the life story of his great-great-great grandfather Micajah Callaway.

Books Published by American History Press
www.Americanhistorypress.com • (888) 521-1789

1609: A Country That Was Never Lost
Perfect bound paperback $18.95

A Great Conveniency: A Maritime History of the Passaic River...
Perfect bound paperback $18.95

A Spirited War: George Washington and the Ghosts of the Revolution in Central New Jersey
Perfect bound paperback $18.95

Children of the Cherokee East Volume One
Perfect bound paperback $12.95

Complete Delaware Roll of 1898
Perfect bound paperback $12.95

Exploring the Mason Dixon Line
Perfect bound paperback $17.95

From Georgia Tragedy to Oklahoma Frontier: A Biography of Creek Indian Chief Chilly McIntosh
Perfect bound paperback $18.95

Little Walkers Creek - A History of the Land and Its People
Perfect bound paperback $24.95

Now We Are Enemies: The Story of Bunker Hill
Thomas Fleming - special 50th anniversary edition hardback with decorated endpapers, a new Introduction by the author and a Foreword by Edwin S. Grosvenor, Editor in Chief of *American Heritage* magazine. $22.95

Scottish Colonial Schemes 1620-1686
Perfect bound paperback $22.95

Simon Girty Turncoat Hero
Casebound hardcover $28.95 ; Perfect bound paperback $19.95

South Carolina 1775: A Crucible Year
Casebound hardcover $26.95

Souvenirs of the Past Perfect
bound paperback $18.95

Taking the High Ground: How Boston Broke the British Grip
Perfect bound paperback $14.95

The Story of Tecumseh
Perfect bound paperback $18.95

The Women of the American Revolution - Volume III
Perfect bound paperback $22.95

The Women of the American Revolution -Volumes I and II
Perfect bound paperback $28.95

Come Walk With Me: Exploring Fairview Park - Rockport Cemetery, Cuyahoga County, Ohio
Perfect bound paperback, $24.95

Tomahawks and Treaties: Micajah Callaway and the Struggle for the Ohio River Valley
Perfect bound paperback